D1165523

3 .202 00575 5006

Atatürk

Other books by the author

TURKEY

DISCOVERING TURKEY

TURKEY: THE CHALLENGE OF A NEW ROLE

Atatürk

ANDREW MANGO

THE OVERLOOK PRESS
WOODSTOCK & NEW YORK

First published in the United States in 2000 by
The Overlook Press, Peter Mayer Publishers, Inc.
Lewis Hollow Road
Woodstock, New York 12498
www.overlookpress.com

Library of Congress Cataloging-in-Publication Data

Mango, Andrew.
Atatürk: the biography of the founder of modern Turkey / Andrew Mango.
p. cm.
1. Atatürk, Kemal, 1881-1938. 2. Presidents—Turkey—Biography. I. Title.
DR592.K4 M36   2000   956.1'024'092—dc21   [B]   99-086845

Manufactured in the United States of America
FIRST EDITION
1 3 5 7 9 8 6 4 2
ISBN 0-58567-011-1

To Mary

Daphne and Benedict

with love

Contents

———————————————✦———————————————

Illustrations

The author and publisher wish to thank the Turkish Ministry of Culture for permission to reproduce all the illustrations included here, except Nos. 9–12 and 16.

Preface

M USTAFA KEMAL ATATÜRK is one of the most important statesmen
of the twentieth century. He established and shaped the Turkish
republic, today the strongest state between the Adriatic and China in
the broad Eurasian land belt south of Russia and north of the Indian
subcontinent. He influenced the history of his country's neighbours.
For peoples ruled by foreigners, he showed a way to national independence in amity with the rest of the world.

Atatürk is usually known today as a radical modernizer and western-
izer. The description is true, but not sufficient. He imported Western
practices in order to bring his country into parity with the richest countries of the world, most of which were to be found in the West. But his
aim was not imitation but participation in a universal civilization, which,
like the thinkers of the European Enlightenment, he saw as the onward
march of humanity, regardless of religion and the divisions it caused. He
believed that the struggle for genuine independence should be waged by
each nation for itself in the name of an overarching secular ideal of
progress common to all, and therefore leaving no room for antagonism
towards the most advanced nations. He was an anti-imperialist only in
the sense that his ideal was a universal commonwealth of civilized people.
Above all, he was a builder, the greatest nation-builder of modern times.

Atatürk's vision was optimistic and humanist. His practice often fell
short of it. Moreover, particularly towards the end of his life, his thought
was contaminated by doctrines of ethnic and racial superiority current in
the contemporary West. Atatürk had, and still has, many opponents in
Turkey. Traditional Muslims saw in his ideal of secular progress an idol-
atrous juggernaut, and believed him to be an imitator of the infidels. For

others he was simply an unprincipled dictator. Nationalists in neighbouring countries have other bones to pick with Atatürk. He defeated the Greeks; his generals beat the Armenians; he wrote off the Arabs, while adding to his country a district which Syrian Arabs claim for their own. Kurdish nationalists hold him responsible for the policy of assimilating Kurds within the Turkish nation. All these anti-Turkish nationalists are to be found among Atatürk's detractors. Turkish and non-Turkish Marxists had their own critical reservations; but they no longer figure.

The controversy which surrounds Atatürk works to the advantage of the biographer and historian, as it throws up not only new arguments but also new sources of information. In Turkey, where the debate is particularly lively, new books on Atatürk proliferate. The first volume of Atatürk's collected writings and a new edition of his private letters appeared just as the manuscript of this book was nearing completion. So did a comprehensive refutation of criticism levelled at Atatürk by Islamist opponents. However, even before these latest works, enough fresh material had accumulated to justify a new biography. This material is almost entirely in Turkish. It consists of memoirs and diaries of Atatürk's contemporaries, extracts from his own notebooks and archive, histories of the republic, accounts of specific events, etc. The information these books contain is in the public domain, although many publications are out of print and others are hard to trace. This new biography is based largely on published Turkish sources, which until now have never been adequately checked, compared and collated.

I apologize to non-Turkish readers for the paucity of books in English and other European languages in my bibliography. The fact is that Mustafa Kemal was largely unknown in the West until 1919 when he assumed the leadership of the Turkish nationalist movement. Later, foreigners met him for official purposes, but none had privileged access to him. Western scholars who have written about him have relied, as I have done, on published Turkish sources: these I have usually cited direct.

My reliance on Turkish material, and the fact that Atatürk is a figure of Turkish history first and of world history second, have led me to adopt the modern Turkish phonetic spelling for proper nouns. One exception is Istanbul, where it would have been pedantic to dot the capital I, as Turkish spelling requires; nonetheless I have retained it for all other place names, such as İzmir (Smyrna), İzmit (Nicomedia), İznik (Nicaea), etc. Total consistency is impossible, first because modern Turkish spelling has not yet achieved it, and second because some of the Turks mentioned in this book spelled their names according to different conventions. On occasion I have modernized their spelling, changing, for example, Khalide Edib to Halide Edip. For some places which were once under

Ottoman rule I give the modern Turkish spelling, followed in brackets by their current name, e.g. Yanya (Ioannina, later Yanina in Greek Epirus). For others, I use the traditional English spelling: Salonica, Aleppo, Damascus, Baghdad, Mecca, etc. Surnames were introduced by law in Turkey in 1934. For the earlier period I give the forenames of Turks mentioned in the narrative and then in brackets the surname which they later adopted, e.g. Ali Fuat (Cebesoy), Falih Rıfkı (Atay), etc. With regard to Atatürk himself, I am not entirely consistent. In general, I call him Mustafa and then Mustafa Kemal before 1934, but occasionally the surname Atatürk slips in before he adopted it officially in 1934.

I have written this biography in London, drawing mainly on books diligently assembled for me by Ahmet Yüksel of Sanat Kitabevi, the prince of antiquarian booksellers in Ankara. I could not have done it without his help. As my work progressed, I discussed it with many friends on my frequent visits to Turkey. I am grateful to them all, particularly to Professor Sina Akşin, Dr Şahin Alpay (who alerted me to some interesting material in the American press), Şakir Eczacıbaşı (who sent me a photocopy of an article in the US magazine *The Caucasus*), Professor Selim İlkin (who has kept me supplied with Turkish press cuttings and other material on Atatürk), Altemur Kılıç (whose father was one of Atatürk's closest friends), Professor Emre Kongar (who gave me the photograph albums published by the Turkish Ministry of Culture, of which he was permanent under-secretary), Professor Baskın Oran, Ambassador Müfit Özdeş (whose grandfather was a personal friend of Atatürk), Professor Azmi Süslü (who heads the Atatürk research centre in Ankara) and Professor Mete Tuncay. I owe a double debt of gratitude to my friend Professor Metin And, for his hospitality during my visits to Turkey and his encouragement and advice throughout. I thank my friends Canan and Peter Reeves for reading and commenting on two draft chapters, and for their hospitality in Istanbul and Bodrum. I am grateful to the military history department (ATASE) of the Turkish General Staff for arranging for me an escorted tour of the Anatolian battlefields of the Turkish War of Independence.

In England I have received help and encouragement from my friends and colleagues Professor Clement Dodd and Dr William Hale. I am particularly grateful to Professor Geoffrey Lewis, who read the completed manuscript, made valuable suggestions and raised my spirit when I needed it most. I have received useful criticism from Dr George Harris of Washington. Caroline Knox of John Murray has been a longsuffering, helpful and enthusiastic editor. My style has benefited from the comments of my wife Mary, and my work from her patience. My faults are my own and I rely on my readers to point them out.

Note on Spelling and Pronunciation

Modern Turkish uses the Latin alphabet, modified to ensure that there is a separate letter for each main sound. The spelling thus aims at phonetic consistency. Consonants have more or less the same sound as in English, except that:

> *c* is pronounced as *j* in *j*oy
> *ç* is as *ch* in *ch*air
> *ğ* is silent, but lengthens the preceding vowel
> *j* is pronounced as in French, or as *s* in mea*s*ure
> *ş* is as *sh* in *sh*ip
> *h* and *y* are pronounced as consonants, as in *h*it and *y*ellow

Vowels have the following values:

> *a* as in f*a*ther
> *e* as in p*e*n
> *i* as in p*i*n (the capital also carries a dot, *İ*)
> *ı* is a back, close, unrounded vowel which does not exist in English, the nearest equivalent being the phantom vowel in the second syllable of rhy*thm* (in Turkish transliteration *ridım*)
> *o* as in p*o*t
> *ö* as in German, or in French *eu*
> *u* as in r*oo*m
> *ü* as in German, or in French *u* (in *u*ne)

The circumflex (ˆ) is sometimes used to indicate a long vowel, as in *siyasî* (si-ya-see, meaning political). Used after the consonants *k* and *l*, it indicates that the consonant is soft (palatalized), e.g. *kâr* (kⁱ-a-r, meaning profit, to distinguish from *kar* (k-a-r), meaning snow).

Maps

THE OTTOMAN EMPIRE

AUSTRIA-
HUNGARY

Vienna

Budapest

Austro-Hungarian
Occupation
1878-1908
1. BOSNIA
2. HERZEGOVINA
3. SANDJAK of YENİPAZAR
4. MONTENEGRO

BOSNIA

Buch

ROMA

Belgrade

SERBIA

Danu

Sarajevo

Sofia BU

(Yassal pri

Üskup

RU

KOSOV

İşkodra

Ohri

Pirlepe
Serez

MACE

RU

Manastır
Salonica

Yanya

THESSALY
(Annexed to
Greece 1881)

GREECE

Athens

ALGERIA

TUNISIA

MALTA

CRETE
(Autonomous 1897
thereafter Gre

Tripoli

Resülde
Derne

Benghazi

Ayn
Mansur

Tobru

TRIPOLITANIA

CYRENAICA

Ca

Calo

FEZZAN

MEDITERRANEAN

ITALY

ADRIATIC SEA

Ionian

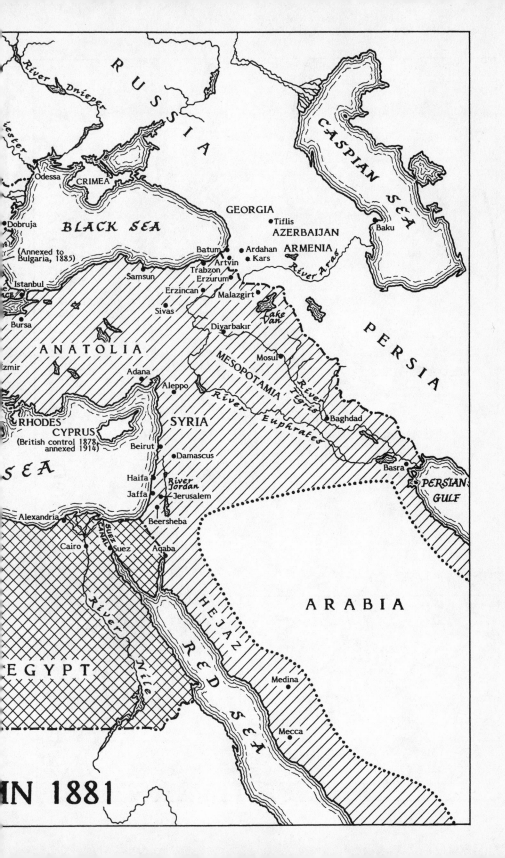

RUSSIA

River Dnieper

lester

River

Odessa

CRIMEA

Dobruja

BLACK SEA

(Annexed to
Bulgaria, 1885)

Istanbul

CE

Bursa

Samsun

ANATOLIA

zmir

RHODES

CYPRUS
(British control 1878
annexed 1914)

SEA

Alexandria

Cairo

EGYPT

River Nile

GEORGIA

•Tiflis

AZERBAIJAN

Batum

ARMENIA

Ardahan
Kars

Artvin

Trabzon

Erzurum

Erzincan

•Malazgirt

Sivas

Lake
Van

Diyarbakır

Adana

Aleppo

MESOPOTAMIA

Mosul

River Tigris

SYRIA

River Euphrates

Baghdad

Beirut

•Damascus

Haifa

River Jordan

Jaffa

•Jerusalem

Beersheba

SUEZ CANAL

Suez

Aqaba

HEJAZ

RED SEA

CASPIAN SEA

Baku

River Aras

PERSIA

Basra

PERSIAN
GULF

ARABIA

Medina

Mecca

IN 1881

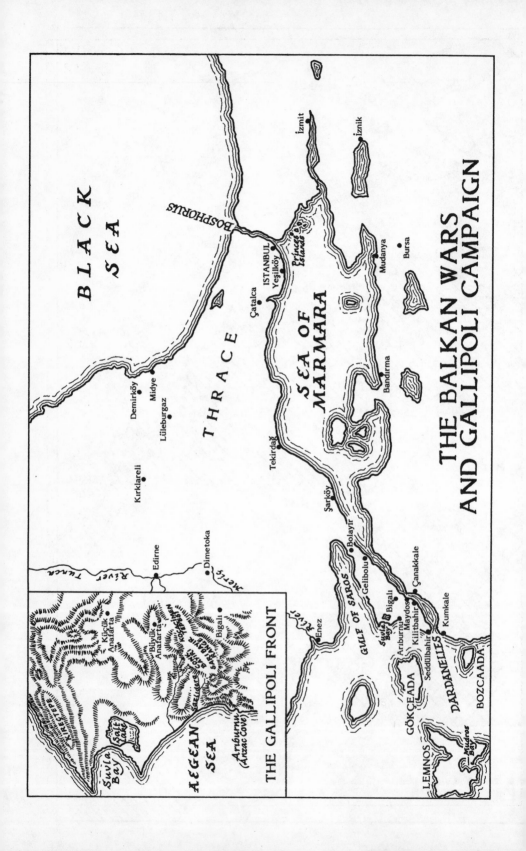

THE BALKAN WARS
AND GALLIPOLI CAMPAIGN

THE GALLIPOLI FRONT

BLACK SEA

BOSPHORUS

THRACE

SEA OF MARMARA

GULF OF SAROS

AEGEAN SEA

DARDANELLES

Demirköy
Midye
Lüleburgaz
Kırklareli
Edirne
Dimetoka
RIVER TUNCA
Meriç

İzmit
İznik
Mudanya
Bursa
Bandırma

İSTANBUL
Yeşilköy
Çatalca
Tekirdağ
Şarköy
Bolayır
Gelibolu
Bigalı
Enez
Maydos
Arıburnu
Kilitbahir
Çanakkale
Kumkale
Seddülbahir

Princes Islands

LEMNOS
GÖKÇEADA
BOZCAADA
Mudros Bay

Suvla Bay
Salt Lake
Küçük Anafarta
Büyük Anafarta
Bigalı
Arıburnu (Anzac Cove)

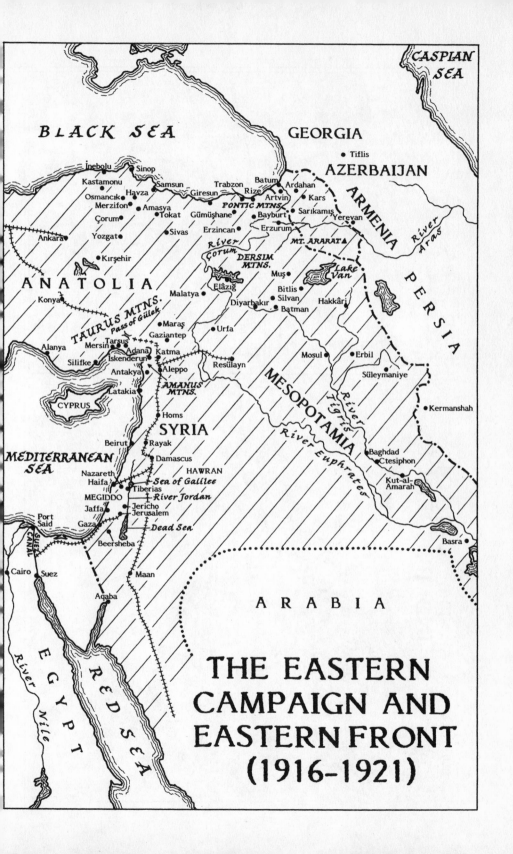

THE EASTERN
CAMPAIGN AND
EASTERN FRONT
(1916–1921)

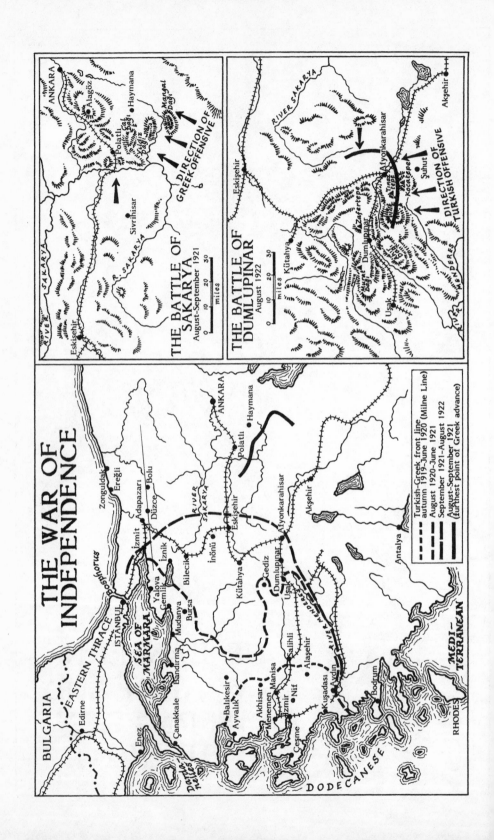

THE WAR OF INDEPENDENCE

Turkish-Greek front line
autumn 1919–June 1920 (Milne Line)
August 1920–June 1921
September 1921–August 1922
August-September 1921
(furthest point of Greek advance)

BULGARIA

EASTERN THRACE

Edirne
Enez

ISTANBUL
Bosphorus
SEA OF MARMARA

DARDANELLES
Çanakkale
Bandırma
Mudanya
Gemlik
Yalova

Zonguldak
Ereğli
Adapazarı
İzmit
İznik
Bilecik
Bursa

Düzce
Bolu

RIVER SAKARYA

İnönü
Kütahya

ANKARA

Haymana
Polatlı

Eskişehir

Afyonkarahisar
Dumlupınar
Gediz
Uşak

Akşehir

Ayvalık
Akhisar
Balıkesir
Menemen
Manisa
İzmir
Nif
Çeşme
Salihli
Alaşehir
Kuşadası
Aydın

RIVER MENDERES

Antalya

Bodrum

MEDI-TERRANEAN

RHODES

DODECANESE

THE BATTLE OF SAKARYA
August-September 1921

ANKARA
Alagöz
Polatlı
Çatı
Sivri
Dağı
Yıldız
Dağı
Mangal Dağı
Haymana

DIRECTION OF GREEK OFFENSIVE

R. SAKARYA

Sivrihisar

Eskişehir

RIVER SAKARYA

miles
0 10 20 30

THE BATTLE OF DUMLUPINAR
August 1922

RIVER SAKARYA

Afyonkarahisar
Zafertepe
Tınaztepe
Kocatepe
Çiğiltepe
Şuhut

DIRECTION OF TURKISH OFFENSIVE

Eskişehir

Aziziye
Dumlupınar
Kütahya
Uşak

RIVER MENDERES

Akşehir

miles
0 10 20 30

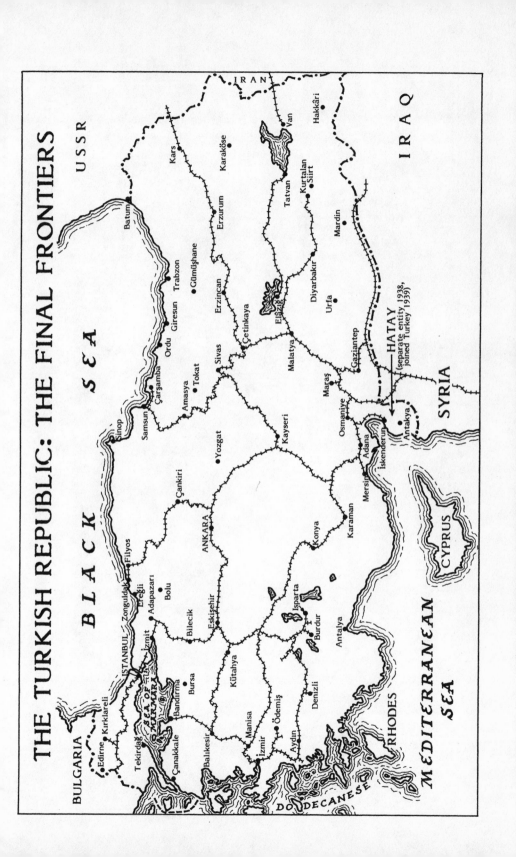

THE TURKISH REPUBLIC: THE FINAL FRONTIERS

Introduction

MUSTAFA KEMAL ATATÜRK was born during the *belle époque* of European civilization. In the last decades of the nineteenth century, Europe and its extensions across the oceans were at peace and could concentrate on advancing their power, knowledge and prosperity. France had recovered from the defeat in the war with Germany in 1870, the United States from the ravages of the Civil War. Germany was growing richer and stronger by the day. Austria-Hungary was a delicately constructed haven of peace. After its victory over the Ottoman empire in 1878, Russia was undergoing an economic transformation and expanding its power in Asia. Britain was spreading the benefits of peace, order and progress throughout its empire. Japan had opened its doors to the West, and was applying Western knowledge to lay the foundations of its industrial and military power. European civil servants, businessmen, engineers, scientists, doctors – and, increasingly, their American cousins – were organizing, developing, trading, building, teaching throughout the globe. Europe was mastering and transforming the world. It both gathered and scattered the fruits of its labour. But it also made victims.

It is misleading to describe the late nineteenth and early twentieth centuries as being uniquely the age of imperialism. Empires had existed throughout recorded history, and their founders and rulers had, quite naturally, believed that their power, their way of life, their values and their religion – their civilization, in short – benefited not only themselves, but also the peoples over which they held sway. The claim was often true.

What was new in the nineteenth century was the competitive co-existence of several empires, inspired by the same civilization. That civilization had developed within Christendom, but after the Enlightenment and the French Revolution, its organizing principle was not religion, but rationalism. In spite of its regional origin, rationalism could appeal to all men as creatures endowed with reason. However, while the application of reason to the mastery of the material world produced undeniable benefits, in the realm of human affairs its results were mixed. True, the exercise of reason could improve on traditional social and political arrangements. But the pursuit of rationalist policies, ideologies and theories created new differences and new tensions within and between existing communities.

At the same time, old divisions survived under new names. Where traditional Christian believers fought infidels, enlightened rationalists of Christian antecedents believed they were at grips with ignorant fanatics. Thus, Muslims had been infidels because they controverted Christianity. Now they were fanatics because they resisted rational enlightenment. Religious missionaries sought to convert infidels to the true faith. Similarly, enlightened European thinkers, teachers and rulers attempted to make fanatics see reason and mend their ways.

The observation that some communities fared worse than others, that some took to enlightenment while others resisted it, suggested to thinkers, who believed themselves to be rational, that humanity was divided into races with unequal capacities. By the end of the nineteenth century this inequality could be explained and justified by extending to human society the principles established by Charles Darwin in his study of the origin of species. Social Darwinists believed that races were to humans what species were to animals. Their views were widely spread and influential. Racial differences were seen not only between blacks and whites, Europeans and Asiatics, but also between Teutons, Latins and Slavs.

Rationalists reinforced another old division when they subdivided races into nations. The success of European peoples, united domestically and distinguished from their neighbours by language and historical antecedents, and consequently thinking of themselves as distinct nations, led to the belief that nations were the natural units of political organization.

It is not surprising that the authors of the French Revolution should have seen their people as *la grande nation*, since it was among them that Reason had triumphed and had produced a declaration of human rights of universal application. Nor is it surprising that their neighbours should have attempted to emulate them in ever-widening concentric circles. But while one can follow the concatenation of ideas which led from universal human rights, posited by reason, to the ideology of nationalism and the consequent belief that it was best for state and nation to coincide, it remains nevertheless true that nationalism and the brotherhood of man were not obviously compatible, even in theory. In practice, the ideology of nationalism, which flowed out of the French Revolution, split up existing states and communities. It produced much suffering and millions of victims, caused material losses and impoverished the lives even of winners in nationalist contests for territory and power. The fate of losers was much sadder.

Liberty, equality and fraternity were not logically incompatible with the existence of multinational empires, even if in practice they subverted the hierarchies on which these empires rested. But nationalism, which spread together with the ideals of the French Revolution, destroyed them. It added a new animus to old communal, religious, sectarian and tribal differences, endowing them with a rational explanation. Both ideology and observation found rational justification for aggression. National communities had mastered the new rational European civilization in unequal measure. Observably, this inequality was reflected in their performance, both domestically and in contest with other communities. This led to the conclusion that, like races, national communities were not only actually, but inherently, unequal in their aptitude for civilization and their propensity to unreasonable fanaticism. Nations, like individuals, could therefore be divided not only into advanced and backward, learned and ignorant, but into deserving and undeserving, rich and poor. It was not a dispensation with which the losers could agree. But they could only prove that they did not deserve their lot by gaining strength through the acquisition of the universal European civilization. Civilization was the prerequisite of success. Conversely, success in a national contest was proof of civilization.

Racial, regional, ethnic and national stereotypes have always been part of human discourse. They can be accepted as a convenient shorthand to denote differences in the way of life of specific communities. Rationalism did not reduce the use of racial or national stereotypes, but it explained them in new ways. Where medieval Arab geographers wrote that Slavs and other northerners were irascible, because red bile predominated in their temperament, rationalists dispensed with the theory of humours in favour of that of civilization. Vicomte de la Jonquière declared in 1881: 'The Ottoman people is not more recalcitrant to civilization than any other nation. It has native qualities for which one would look in vain in the other races of the empire: it is honest and decent. The ignorance in which it is plunged, the fanaticism of which it provides so much bloody evidence – all this should be attributed to those who are in charge of its destiny.'[1]

These were the dominant ideas in the dominant part of the world when Mustafa Kemal Atatürk was born in Salonica in 1880/1.

At the end of the nineteenth century the Ottoman state was more than six hundred years old, and it showed its age. The history of the state could be traced back to 1281 when Osman, a warlord (*bey*) of Turcoman (Türkmen) stock, inherited a principality in north-western Asia Minor and set about enlarging it at the expense of neighbouring Byzantine lands. To the east of Osman's original fief, the central plateau of Asia Minor had earlier been conquered by Seljuk (in modern Turkish spelling Selçuk) Turks, following their victory over the Byzantines at Malazgirt in 1071. The conquerors first called the land Rum (or Roman). The term Rumeli (Roman land, Rumelia in English) was later transferred to Ottoman conquests in Europe and was replaced in Asia Minor by Anadolu (Anatolia in English, from the Greek *Anatole*, meaning the East). Europeans found a simpler name. By the end of the twelfth century, they started referring to the lands conquered by the Turks as Turkey (first attested in the Italian form of *Turchia*).[2] This name travelled with Osman Bey's successors as they crossed into Europe at the beginning of the fourteenth century and spread their dominion further and further west. But the conquerors did not call their land Turkey or themselves Turks. They saw themselves as Muslims, ruling 'the land of Islam' (*darü'l-İslam*, literally the House of Islam), where they had established 'the state' (*devlet*, or in later bureaucratic usage *Devlet-i Aliyye*, the Sublime State, or again *Memalik-i Mahrusa*, the Divinely Guarded Dominions).

The Ottoman state was Muslim, dynastic and medieval in its organizing principles. Its government was based on Muslim religious law (*sharia*, in Turkish spelling *şeriat*), which was supplemented by royal ordinances (*kanun*) and customary law (*örf*), and stretched, sometimes beyond reason, to cover day-to-day requirements. In accordance with that law, non-Muslim monotheists who submitted to Muslim rule were given protected status and allowed to run their communal affairs. The three main non-Muslim confessional communities – Greek or Eastern Orthodox Christians, Armenian Gregorian (Monophysite) Christians and Jews – were known as *millet*, a term which later acquired the secular meaning of nation. Although its extent varied over time, the *millet* system of communal self-government gave the Ottoman state a multi-ethnic, multicultural character which was generally absent in Christian-ruled Europe. True, non-Muslims suffered disabilities in the Ottoman state, but they could survive and prosper, a prospect denied until modern times to Muslims in lands reconquered by Christian rulers, and enjoyed only fitfully by their Jewish subjects.

The non-Muslim *millets* were one element in a complex system of corporate government. Everybody had a master (*sahip*) who was personally responsible for the behaviour of his charges. Small pyramids made up the large pyramid of the Ottoman state, headed by the sultan or sovereign. He reigned absolute, but under the unchanging divine law, to 'enjoin the good and forbid evil', and to maintain justice (*adalet*), defined as perfect balance in the constituent elements of the state.

Throughout almost the entire history of the Ottoman state, its official ideology was religious. Its message was simple: follow the Prophet and his law, and all will be well. Although the practice of the state was more mundane, the official, religious ideology affected the cast of mind of the Muslim rulers of the state. Since they possessed revealed truth which had shown its worth during the expansion of Ottoman power, they were reluctant to turn to unbelievers for anything other than technical advice. When they did so, they had to disguise their purpose. In any case, the official ideology of the state was an obstacle to innovation.

Conservatism was not confined to the theory of government. Hippocratic medicine, Ptolemaic astronomy and geography, and other branches of medieval science survived in the Ottoman state long after they had been, first amended, then discarded in western Europe. Muslim apologists have always argued that Islam is not contrary to human reason. Moreover, particularly in modern times, they have insisted that Islam is the most reasonable of all religions. Nevertheless it remains true that official Ottoman Islam delayed the spread of the new learning based on the primacy of reason. But the new learning could not be stopped.

The Ottomans were prompt to use European military technology. But outside the military sphere, the penetration of European ideas and practices was slow. It was not until 1727 that a Hungarian from Transylvania, who had converted from Unitarianism to Islam, was able to set up in Istanbul a first printing press using Arabic characters. It was closed down after a few years, and printing had to be reintroduced later.

True, changes in production sometimes travelled quickly. The cultivation of new crops – potatoes, maize, tobacco – spread far and wide in Ottoman dominions. But social organization, including the organization of the armed forces, continued to follow pre-modern patterns until the nineteenth century. And the ruling mentality, often pragmatic in day-to-day affairs, remained medieval in its points of reference. As Turkish scholars are fond of saying today, Turkey has never had its Renaissance.

In 1529 and then again in 1683, Ottoman armies had laid siege to Vienna; in 1878, Russian troops were encamped outside the Ottoman capital, Istanbul. New learning had created the military, political and economic power of Russia which became the chief gravedigger of the Ottoman state. The organization and ordinance of the armies and navies of the Romanov tsars, and the wealth first of their agriculture and then of their manufacturing industry – achieved in every case by the use of western European techniques – outstripped the resources of the Ottoman state by an ever-widening margin from the eighteenth century onwards.

Early memoranda urging reforms were drawn up by Ottoman administrators in the eighteenth century. But little was done, as the Russians swept down to the Black Sea. Then in 1789, the year of the French Revolution, a reforming sultan, Selim III, mounted the throne in Istanbul and set about creating a model new army, as part of his new order (*nizam-ı cedit*). Selim III was influenced by the French example, largely out of fear for the safety of his dominions, a fear for which he was soon to find excellent grounds, as Napoleon invaded Egypt in the name of the French Republic in 1798.

The Ottomans' connection with the French was old. It went back to the alliance concluded in 1541 between Sultan Süleyman I (Suleiman the Magnificent) and Francis I of France against the Habsburg emperor Charles V. It was as part of that alliance that French merchants and other residents in the Ottoman state were given privileges, known as *capitulations*, which were later extended to other European states, and which had the effect of placing Europeans in the Ottoman state outside local jurisdiction. Freely given at first as a means of fostering trade, the capitulations were later resented by the Ottomans, while Europeans insisted on them as a defence of their nationals against the arbitrariness of a backward Asiatic state.

Selim III was deposed and then killed by a popular rising led by the Janissaries, the Sultan's slave troops which had turned into an unruly praetorian guard. Provincial notables tried to fill the void. But they were outmanoeuvred by Mahmut II, who disbanded and massacred the Janissaries in 1826, and set in train the process of westernizing reforms which continued under his successors. The reforms, known collectively as *Tanzimat* (the establishment of order), were crowned by the adoption of the Ottoman constitution in 1876 at the beginning of the reign of Abdülhamit II. Although within fifteen months the sultan had suspended indefinitely the sessions of parliament, the process of modernization in education, communications and administration went on throughout his despotic reign.

By the end of the nineteenth century, the Ottoman state had developed a military and civilian administrative machine fashioned on European models. Power was transferred from traditional groups – the Janissaries, feudal levies, the *ulema* (Muslim divines), guilds, provincial notables – to a European-style bureaucracy. Improvements in communications – the building of the first railways and the establishment of an effective telegraph network – allowed this bureaucracy to carry out the orders of the sultan and his ministers much more thoroughly than had ever been possible before. The Ottoman state had always traded with the world. By the end of the nineteenth century, it had become integrated in the world trading system through better communications, lower customs tariffs and foreign investments.

Thus the Ottoman state came to resemble, at least superficially, its neighbours to the west and north – the Austro-Hungarian and Russian empires. Like them, it was multi-ethnic. Like them, it was dynastic, while being ruled bureaucratically. Like them, it was threatened not so much by maladministration as by the interplay between foreign foes and separatist movements, which had won the allegiance of subject nationalities at home. But there was this difference: not just the rulers, but the national communities from which the rulers had come in Austria-Hungary and, to a lesser extent, in Russia had been trained in the new learning. In the Ottoman state, on the other hand, while the rulers had become enlightened, the mass of Muslims, who, in spite of the reforms, still constituted the ruling community, maintained in their illiteracy the habits of the pre-modern age. Contrary to the views of Muslim reformers, and to the claims of nationalist agitators among subject communities, it was not so much the Ottoman state as the Muslim community which was behind the times.

The Ottoman state kept its multi-ethnic character throughout its existence. Ottoman civilization was the common product of distinct religious communities speaking many different languages, coexisting within the same society while keeping their separate corporate identities. True, non-Muslim communities were not always content with their subordinate status. Particularly in the Balkans, agrarian discontent often had an ethnic component, since the major landowners were Muslims. Christian merchants and tradesmen had different grievances, in that they were denied a political status commensurate with their wealth. Often religious solidarity overrode Ottoman loyalty, as Ottoman Christians looked to the protection of the Christian powers of Europe and sometimes sided with them in war. But then Muslims –

Kurds, Arabs and local Ottoman governors wishing to consolidate their autonomy – were also open to subversion by the sultan's foes.

Muslims and non-Muslims were to be found in various proportions throughout the empire. But there were certain geographical and occupational patterns. Slav, Vlach (Romanian) and Albanian Christians made up a large part of the peasant population of the interior of the Balkan peninsula. Greeks were concentrated along the coasts, with the exception of the Turkish-speaking Greek Orthodox (known as Karamanlı) of central Anatolia, while Greek merchant communities were to be found in most towns.

The Armenians had begun to spill out of their original homeland on the eastern Anatolian plateau in late Byzantine times. Under the Ottomans they provided most of the artisans and tradesmen in Anatolia. Ottoman architecture, ceramics, textiles – areas of endeavour where the Ottoman state made a lasting contribution to world civilization – relied in large measure on Armenian craftsmen. Armenian merchants were busy in the overland trade with Asia and were generally dominant in Anatolia.

There were Jewish communities in most market towns in the Balkans and Anatolia. Istanbul, where the chief rabbi (*hahambaşı*) was deemed by the Ottoman government to be in charge of all the Jews in the empire, contrary to the tradition of Jewish communal self-government, was home to an important community; so were Salonica and İzmir (Smyrna). Most Jews, outside the Arab-speaking provinces, traced their descent to refugees from Spain and Portugal, who had been welcomed in the Ottoman empire after their expulsion by the Catholic Kings. The Jews prospered in the years of Ottoman greatness, then went into decline, as local Christians came to control trade with Christian Europe, and did not rise again in society until the second half of the nineteenth century, when their community was reinvigorated by the spread of new learning, mainly from France, and began replacing Christian competitors who laboured increasingly under the suspicion of disloyalty.

The degree to which the different religious communities mixed varied with time and place. They usually came together in work, while living in separate neighbourhoods and villages. The *şeriat* code allowed Muslim men to take Christian or Jewish wives, but did not allow non-Muslims to marry Muslim women. Converts to Islam were welcomed, but forced conversions were banned in theory, and rare in practice. However, thousands converted to Islam in the centuries of Ottoman expansion. In the main they came from communities which had been marginalized under Christian rule. In the Balkans, most Muslims were descendants of Slav and Albanian converts. Among Jews, there was an important wave of conversion to Islam after the failure of the Messianic movement led by Sabetai Sevi in the seventeenth century. His followers, and later converts from Judaism to Islam, retained until recent times a separate identity within the Muslim community, where they were known as *dönme* (converts) or *Selânikli* (people from Salonica).

Broadly speaking, the Muslims were employed by the state, which they served as soldiers or civilian officials; they were also landowners and peasants. The non-Muslims provided almost all the merchants, tradesmen and craftsmen, as well as making up a part of the peasant population. Because of their religious affinity with western Europe, Ottoman Christians took to new learning long before their Muslim neighbours.

Ottoman law and practice classified people by their religion. The Muslims were thus treated as a single community. But this community was divided in practice by language and way of life. In the Balkans, the main languages spoken by Muslims were Albanian, Serbo-Croat, Bulgarian, Greek and Turkish. In Anatolia, the Muslims spoke Turkish, Kurdish, Arabic and Caucasian languages. Ottoman Turkish – an amalgam of Turkish, Arabic and Persian – was the official, bureaucratic language of the state. Socially, there were important divisions between town and country, and between settled and nomadic populations. The state was based on towns. Thus urban Arabs were part of the state; nomadic Bedouins and Kurds were outside it.

Ethnic separatism did not become a threat to the cohesion of the Ottoman state until the beginning of the nineteenth century. Its roots were both at home and abroad. Discontent was home-grown; the ideology of nationalism came from Europe. Local risings, followed by European intervention – usually in the shape of wars launched by Russia – had led by 1878 to the creation of the independent states of Greece, Romania, Serbia and Montenegro. Bulgaria had become autonomous as a prelude to full independence; Bosnia and Herzegovina had come under the administration of Austria-Hungary, and Cyprus under that of Britain.

In Europe, the Ottoman state was reduced to Albania, Macedonia and Thrace – territories running in a broad strip from the Adriatic to the Turkish straits. In Asia, it ruled over Anatolia (with the exception of a north-eastern corner ceded to Russia in 1878) and the Arab lands. Egypt was theoretically under Ottoman suzerainty, but had in effect been lost to the sultans after the establishment of the Muhammad Ali dynasty at the beginning of the nineteenth century. However, the Ottomans still ruled Libya (Tripolitania and Cyrenaica), either directly or through local chieftains.

In 1893, an Ottoman census, which excluded Libya as well as territories no longer under the effective jurisdiction of the sultan, gave the total population of the state as 17 million.[3] It was certainly an underestimate, as many people avoided the registrars for fear of taxation and conscription, and, more importantly, as local customs did not allow many women to be counted. But it is the best indication we have of the population of the state, and the numbers of the religious communities within it, roughly at the time of Atatürk's birth. Of the 17 million, some 12.5 million were shown as Muslims. Of the rest, there were over 2 million Greeks, under a million Bulgarians, just over a million Gregorian, and another 150,000 Catholic and 37,000 Protestant Armenians, 180,000 Jews, and some 240,000 foreigners (most of whom were natives holding foreign passports).

In Ottoman possessions in Europe (excluding Istanbul, its suburbs and the Aegean islands), there were, according to the census, 1.4 million Muslims, out of a total population of 3.1 million. Most of the sultan's Muslim subjects lived in Asia. While official statistics made no mention of the mother tongue of residents, it was common knowledge that the greatest concentration of Turkish speakers was in Anatolia. Anatolia, the first Byzantine territory conquered by the Selçuk Turks, was still the Turkish heartland as the Ottoman centuries drew to a close.

At the end of the nineteenth century the ruling Muslim community of the Ottoman empire was gripped by anxiety. Their state had been in retreat for two centuries. Every time a province was lost, waves of Muslim refugees poured into the sultan's remaining possessions. In the Balkans, the first mass flight of Muslims followed the Greek rising of 1821 and the establishment of the Greek kingdom under European protection in 1830. This migration of Muslims was dwarfed by the influx of refugees during and after the Russian-Turkish war of 1877–8. Muslims flooded in from Bulgaria, which became independent in all but name. They came from Thessaly, which was ceded to Greece, a country not involved in the war, but deemed by the European great powers to deserve compensation for the gains achieved by countries which had been.

Even more Muslim refugees had come from the lands conquered by Russia in its advance to the south. Although most of these lands had been under Ottoman suzerainty only briefly, their inhabitants saw in the Ottoman state their protector and their refuge. First came hundreds of thousands of Turkic-speaking Tartars from the Crimea and the surrounding steppes, then the majority of Circassians and Abkhazians from the western Caucasus, and large numbers of Chechens from the northern slopes of the Caucasus, of Lezgis and other Daghistanis from its eastern slopes, of Muslim Georgians from Transcaucasia.

A younger contemporary of Mustafa Kemal Atatürk, the Turkish writer Şevket Süreyya Aydemir, born in a refugee settlement on the outskirts of Edirne (Adrianople), wrote in his autobiography:

> I was born during a war – the 1897 Turkish-Greek war. These were not tranquil years. They were pregnant with a bloody, perplexing century ... Ours was a refugee neighbourhood. The flotsam of torrents of refugees torn by wars and massacres from the Crimea, Dobruja, and the banks of the Danube, had been pushed back here step by step, as armies suffered defeat after defeat for one hundred and fifty, two hundred years, and as frontiers contracted ... In our neighbourhood of refugees, every family had come from a different place, and every one had a different story to tell about the places where they had stopped and whence they had fled. Day by day the number of people grew, as new refugees made their way through the frontier. When they abandoned their homes, their land, their birthplaces, these newcomers threw supplies of food, cooking utensils, blankets and bedding into oxcarts and took to the road. Women and children were perched on top of the loads. These miserable convoys were the returning remnants of the conquering armies that had settled in the Balkans, the banks of the Danube, and further afield, and had built towns, castles and villages ... [4]

Everywhere, Muslims were haunted by the thought that they were losing the state (*devlet elden gidiyor*, 'the state is slipping from our hands', or in the case of Turks who had adopted the terminology of the French Revolution, *vatan elden gidiyor*, 'the fatherland is slipping from our hands'). 'How can the state be saved?' was the question Muslims asked themselves. But when Ottoman reformers tried to save their dominions by adopting European ways, Muslim conservatives saw another threat, that of losing their traditional religion (*din elden gidiyor*, '[our] religion is slipping from our hands').

The feeling of Muslim insecurity was particularly strong in Macedonia. The province, except for its chief city of Salonica and the Chalcidice peninsula south of it, had been included in Greater Bulgaria, under the treaty of San Stefano (Ayastefanos, now Yeşilköy in Turkish), imposed by the victorious Russian army in 1878. When a few months later, as a result largely of British opposition to such a drastic extension of Russian influence, the treaty was revised at the Congress of Berlin, and Macedonia was reassigned to the Ottoman state, local Muslims could not but feel that the reprieve was temporary. The feeling found confirmation in the outbreak of guerrilla activity in Macedonia. This was spearheaded by the Internal Macedonian Revolutionary

Organization (IMRO), founded in 1893. IMRO drew its supporters from among Eastern Orthodox Slav-speaking Macedonians, whose grievances were partly ethnic and partly agrarian. Its slogan was 'Macedonia for the Macedonians', and its official aim was the creation of an autonomous Macedonia within a Balkan federation.

But, to the extent that it existed at all, the Macedonian identity was uncertain. The Slav language spoken in the province was barely distinguishable from Bulgarian, and Bulgarian nationalists refused to concede the existence of a separate Macedonian nationality. Even so, Bulgarian military intelligence cooperated with IMRO in the hope of making a reality of the Greater Bulgaria, promised at San Stefano only to be snatched away in Berlin. Seeing in IMRO an instrument of Bulgarian expansionism, Greek and Serbian intelligence services sought to counter it by setting up their own guerrilla bands to promote their claims to the province. But as everybody fought everybody else – the various Christian nationalists both each other and the Ottoman government, as everybody terrorized the local population, all actors kept an eye on the behaviour of the European great powers. It was the great powers which had imposed the treaty of Berlin, and which were now pressing, singly or in varying combinations, for reforms in the remaining Ottoman dominions. Particularly among Muslims, there was a feeling of dread in the face of the machinations and decisions of the great powers. Speaking of his schooldays in Edirne, Şevket Süreyya Aydemir wrote:

> Our conception of the great powers [the Ottoman Turkish term *düvel-i muaz-zama* can also be rendered as 'huge powers'] was vague. But what we understood and believed was that everything that the great powers wanted was harmful to our Ottoman state. After all, even in our own city of Edirne, the consuls of the great powers, driving through the streets in their carriages, and the consulate *kavases* [locally recruited guards, usually of Montenegrin origin], walking the streets in their gold-braided uniforms, looked down on us, as if from a great height.[5]

Muslims reacted to the threat by trying to strengthen their state and also by imitating the behaviour of their Christian neighbours. The same author remembered:

> Our most popular game was to play at bands [*çete*, guerrilla band; *çeteci*, bandit] and committees [*komite*, secret organization; *komiteci* or *komitacı*, member of such an organization, and, by extension, nationalist terrorist]. First, we chose *kaptans* [from Greek *kapetanios*, captain] and *voivodas* [a Slav word for military leader] ... from among the strongest and bravest of the children, who then split up into groups. Those who took part in the game would turn back the

edges of their fezes to make them look like the fur hats (*kalpak*) worn by Greek and Bulgarian bandits ... Instead of knives and guns, they stuck sticks and pieces of wood into their belts, and instead of bombs, they filled their pockets and sashes with stones.[6]

A culture of violence spread throughout the Ottoman state. It was the product of violent European strains – exemplified first by the Italian *carbonari* and then by the anarchists – grafted on to local habits of lawlessness. The gun, the knife, the grenade, assumed symbolic significance. They were used in secret initiation ceremonies in incongruous combinations with crosses, Bibles and Korans; they appeared in the emblems of secret nationalist organizations and the bannerheads of their literature. But there was this difference between Christian and Muslim communities: among the former, nationalism, although originally a secular movement, combined with religion, and clerics often encouraged or even took part in violent action; among the Muslims, nationalism developed in opposition to religion. The Muslim religious establishment stood for the whole Muslim community (*ümmet*), and not for the nations that were arising in its midst. On the other hand, the Greek, Serbian and Bulgarian Eastern Orthodox Churches, and the Armenian Gregorian Church, had become by the end of the nineteenth century bearers of their respective nationalist ideologies.

Hard-pressed by external and internal enemies, the Muslim community was also threatened by a decline in numbers. This was partly due to the effect of wars, as Muslims, outside Istanbul and certain other exempted areas, were subject to conscription, while non-Muslims did not, as a rule, serve in Ottoman armed forces. Another reason for the relative decline of the Muslim population was its backwardness in new European learning, and, in particular, medical knowledge. This made for higher rates of morbidity and mortality. Most doctors and pharmacists were non-Muslims, and the majority of Muslims still relied on traditional Hippocratic or folk medicine. Poverty, which came with backwardness, also depressed health standards.

Mustafa Kemal Atatürk was born during the reign of Abdülhamit II, the last Ottoman sultan to exercise autocratic power. Abdülhamit came to the throne in 1876, at the age of 34, in the middle of a domestic and an international crisis, which, not for the first time, threatened the survival of the state. In 1875, the Christian peasantry had risen in Bosnia-Herzegovina. In 1876, nationalist agitation led to a rising among the Bulgarians, which was suppressed with heavy loss of life. The massacre of Bulgarian villagers by bands of Muslim irregulars outraged public opinion in Russia, Britain and elsewhere. Statesmen who sought to preserve the Ottoman state were correspondingly weakened. The European great powers demanded immediate reforms. A constitutional party, which had arisen among the higher ranks of the Ottoman bureaucracy, tried to counter foreign-backed demands for local self-government by advocating voluntary reform throughout the empire. Liberal Ottoman bureaucrats convinced themselves that parliamentary government under a constitutional monarch would hold the state together and satisfy foreign critics. There was also strong Muslim religious agitation, directed against foreigners and against ineffective government at home. Abdülhamit II came to the throne as the candidate of the constitutional party.

The first Ottoman constitution was duly proclaimed on 23 December 1876, and parliament assembled on 19 March 1877. But instead of appeasing the Russians, parliament only served to hasten the tsar's declaration of war. On 14 February 1878, after the Ottoman armies had been defeated by the Russians, Abdülhamit dissolved parliament. While the constitution remained theoretically in force, the sultan thereafter ruled the country as an autocrat. His first task was the reconstruction of the Ottoman state which had lost territory both in Europe and in Asia.

Conditions were difficult: the country was flooded with refugees, the treasury was bankrupt, and the havoc caused by military operations had led to famine in some areas, notably in eastern Anatolia. Domestic peace was disrupted as nationalist agitation continued among Christians in Macedonia, and started among Armenians in Anatolia. Abdülhamit managed the crisis by exploiting the differences among his foreign and domestic foes. He used Russia against Britain, and Germany against both. He formed tribal regiments among the Kurds, on the lines of the Russian Cossacks. They were a means of co-opting and bribing unruly Kurdish tribes, and they helped keep Armenian nationalists at bay. But when attacks by Armenian nationalists led to violent and, usually, disproportionate retaliation by local Muslims, Abdülhamit's technique of discreet string-pulling was no substitute for firm orderly government. In any case, Abdülhamit was too apprehensive of powerful ministers to allow administrative continuity. Between the Congress of Berlin in 1878 and the reintroduction of the constitution in 1908, there were eighteen changes of government in Istanbul. Grand viziers were often allowed only a few months in office. They were then kept in reserve until the sultan decided to use their services once again.

The number of Armenian victims in the violence which swept Anatolia and broke out also in the capital in the 1890s is hotly disputed.

Turkish historians calculate that fewer than 20,000 Armenians and some 5,000 Muslims were killed. Armenian and pro-Armenian writers give much higher figures – 88,000 or more.[7] The fact that the Armenian population grew as a whole during and immediately after the reign of Abdülhamit, but that its growth was probably lower than that of Muslims and Greeks, argues for a lower, although still considerable number of casualties.[8] However that may be, it was the repression of the Armenians which damned Abdülhamit in the eyes of the Christian West. He was denounced as the Red or Bloody Sultan by politicians, publicists and cartoonists. Local black humour, which had the sultan complain: 'I said strike; I did not say kill', is probably nearer the truth. However, the importance of the Armenian troubles lay not so much in the number of victims which they caused, as in the animosity which they engendered between the Armenians and the Muslim majority among whom they lived. The more or less peaceful coexistence of Armenians and Muslims, which had lasted for over a thousand years, was ended in one generation.

Abdülhamit was suspicious, cunning and fearful. But he was not gratuitously cruel. Denunciations by police agents and informers flooded into the sultan's chancery in the palace of Yıldız, on the hillside above the seaside palace of Dolmabahçe. Dolmabahçe palace, built in 1853–5 by an Armenian architect for Sultan Abdülmecit on the European shore of the Bosphorus, appeared open to the world. Yıldız was a shelter from it.

The sultan and his functionaries knew, by and large, who the plotters and malcontents were. Some were imprisoned in provincial fortresses, some exiled, some lost their jobs; many were tempted into submission by offers of jobs and sinecures. The murder of the reforming statesman Mithat Paşa, known as the father of the 1876 constitution, was exceptional. Mithat Paşa's friend, the patriotic poet and publicist Namık Kemal, was imprisoned for a few months, then appointed district governor in one of the Aegean islands. Opponents who fled to Europe often returned home after striking bargains with the sultan's agents. Abdülhamit was a manipulator rather than a bloodthirsty tyrant.

The loss of Bulgaria, southern Serbia, Bosnia-Herzegovina and Cyprus, and the arrival of thousands of refugees, had increased the weight of Muslims in the remaining Ottoman territories. Abdülhamit based his policy on them. He tried to strengthen cohesion among Turks, Arabs, Kurds and Muslim Albanians round the Ottoman throne. He recruited Arab advisers and set up schools for the sons of Arab and Kurdish tribal leaders. He strengthened the bureaucratic Muslim clerical establishment and encouraged the building of mosques. He invested

heavily in education, which combined religious instruction with new
European learning. A network of secondary schools, divided into civil
and military, and leading to specialized institutions of higher education,
covered the empire. They were designed to train enlightened but pious
civil servants and soldiers. However, a diet of religious instruction and
translated foreign textbooks, studied in an atmosphere of unquestioning discipline, did not appeal to everyone, and the new schools became
nurseries of revolutionaries.

Abdülhamit made more use than had any of his predecessors of the
sultan's insubstantial title as caliph in order to enlist the support of
foreign Muslims. The caliph was theoretically the successor of the
Prophet Muhammad as leader of all Muslims. But not all Muslims
accepted the Ottoman sultan's right to the title, while the majority
who did, seldom let it affect their political behaviour. It was among
European powers which had numerous Muslim subjects, such as
Britain, Russia and France – or which, as in the case of Germany and
Italy, hoped to acquire them by extending their colonial possessions –
that the sultan's claims as caliph were given particular weight, and that
fears arose that he was pursuing a Pan-Islamic policy subversive of their
interests. True, Abdülhamit did try to mobilize Islamic sentiment both
to consolidate his own position and to put pressure on the European
great powers; but it was only one instrument of policy among many, and
his investment in Pan-Islamism was limited and ineffectual.

The construction of the Hejaz railway between 1900 and 1908, with
funds collected from Muslims at home and abroad, was probably the
greatest achievement and also the symbol of Abdülhamit's Islamic
policy. But in addition to the pious purpose of conveying Muslim pil-
grims quickly and safely to the holy cities of Mecca and Medina, the
railway was intended also to strengthen central control of the Arab
provinces. Its unpopularity with Bedouin tribes, which had lived off the
protection money paid by pilgrim caravans, demonstrated the practical
limits of Islamic solidarity.

Economic progress was at first slow, coinciding as it did with a cyc-
lical world crisis in the last years of the century. But the foreign credit
of the Ottoman state was gradually restored. Repayment of the accumulated foreign debt, which had stopped in 1876, started once again
in 1879, immediately after the Congress of Berlin. In 1881, an
Administration of the Public Debt was set up in Istanbul, which chan-
nelled into the pockets of foreign bondholders the proceeds of a
number of excise taxes, chief among them the tax on tobacco. To this
day, Turks think of the Ottoman Public Debt as a symbol of the colonial
control of their country's economy. But as foreign experts organized the

collection of taxes and dues, as they took over the marketing of the tobacco crop, they also raised state revenue and laid the foundations of a modern system of taxation.

For all his emphasis on Islam, Abdülhamit's reign was a golden age for foreigners and local non-Muslims. The Armenian troubles did not stop the employment of Armenians in public offices nor the growth in the prosperity of Armenian communities outside the areas directly affected. The short war which Abdülhamit fought successfully against Greece in 1897 did not affect the sultan's two million or so Greek subjects. The growth in their numbers, which had started earlier as Greeks emigrated from the newly independent but desperately poor Greek kingdom to make use of the economic opportunities offered in the Ottoman state by the Tanzimat reforms, continued under Abdülhamit. The sultan's Greek banker, Zarifis, symbolized the economic power of the community which used its wealth to build schools, clubs and philanthropic organizations and to extend its links with the outside world. Foreign missionaries also increased their educational activity. The Jewish community revived thanks to the schools set up by the Alliance Israélite Universelle. In 1893, Gabriel Arié, the director of the Alliance school in İzmir, who had earlier come from Bulgaria, wrote in a report:

> What strikes a Bulgarian when he enters Turkey is, before everything else, the air of freedom that one breathes. Under a theoretically despotic government, one definitely enjoys more freedom than in a constitutional state ... One almost does not feel that there is a government ... The absence of an irksome police, of crushing taxation, of very heavy civic duties here is what the non-Muslim subjects of the sultan should appreciate ...[9]

Communications improved. Harbour facilities, lighthouses and quarantine stations were built. While Muslim donations financed the Hejaz railway, foreign concessionaires built railways elsewhere in the empire. Salonica was connected to Vienna and the European railway network in 1889, Istanbul in 1890. Over one thousand miles of railway lines were built in Anatolia by British and German companies after 1878.[10] They facilitated the marketing and export of farm produce, particularly in the Aegean region. Production rose to meet increased demand.

Abdülhamit's main achievement was to give the Ottoman empire an interval of peace. The 1897 war with Greece was the only foreign war which he fought. True, there were nationalist risings and endemic banditry, but order and administrative efficiency improved. As a result, in the words of the American demographer Justin McCarthy, 'From 1878 to 1912, Ottoman Anatolia experienced a steady rate of population growth. The Muslim population increased by almost 50 per cent. The

Armenian population may have increased at a slightly slower rate, and the Greeks more quickly, but the Christian population as a whole increased like the Muslim population.'[11]

However, the progress achieved during the reign of Abdülhamit did not solve the main problems facing the Ottoman state. It even aggravated them, as progress was uneven and in any case lagged far behind that of the West. The main agents and beneficiaries of progress were foreigners and non-Muslim minorities. The latter tended to see the Ottoman state within which they prospered as a shackle on their energies, a shackle they became increasingly eager to throw off. Rising prosperity did not dampen the ardour of separatist nationalists. Rather, it provided them with funds and foreign connections for their activities.

Fragmentation along ethnic lines skewed both social and economic development. As trade and manufacturing were largely in non-Muslim hands, Muslims were poorly represented in the middle classes and also the manufacturing working class which emerged in the second half of the nineteenth century. They were less impressed by the improvement in their own lot than by the much greater prosperity achieved by their Christian neighbours, and the political claims which stemmed from it. As the Muslims acquired new European learning, so they came to share the perception of Christians and foreigners that they lived in a backward, ramshackle state.

Rıza Nur, a Turkish nationalist who was to have a chequered political career, relates how at the turn of the century, after graduating as an army doctor, he was posted to the Macedonian border. His job was to check whether flour imported from Bulgaria for the Ottoman army had been contaminated with poison and deadly plague germs, as had been claimed in a denunciation to the sultan. Reporting for duty to Nazif Paşa, the elderly commandant of the medical school, Rıza Nur asked to be supplied with a microscope and other scientific instruments. The commandant, dressed in an old-fashioned fez and a black frock-coat 'like a palace butler', would have none of it. 'It's not up to you to think. Go, you stupid man, and collect your salary. Anyway, you'll see the germs if you open your eyes wide enough.'[12]

In the eyes of the rising class of educated young Turks, the Hamidian regime stood for ignorance, backwardness, corruption and decline. They did not appreciate the sultan's skill at manipulation. The Ottoman term 'management for the public good' (*idare-yi maslahat*) caused derision. Irritated by censorship, the educated young were unimpressed by the growth in encyclopaedic publications, newspapers and books.

Military students and young officers were particularly critical of the sultan's defence policy. Manoeuvres were not held and the fleet was kept anchored in the capital, because, it was said, the sultan feared military plots. But he also wanted to avoid expense. Unlike his free-spending predecessors, Abdülhamit counted his pence. When the treasury was empty, salaries were paid late. This caused resentment in the Muslim middle class which relied almost exclusively on state employment. The army was commanded by old men, chosen for their loyalty and their prudence.

Yet Abdülhamit did try to improve military organization after the defeat of 1878. In 1880, he applied to the Kaiser for help with training. A German military mission entered Ottoman service in 1882, and between 1883 and 1895 the chief German military adviser, General Colmar von der Goltz (Goltz Paşa), improved the training of officers, and commissioned Turkish translations of German military manuals, extending to over 4,000 pages.[13] His efforts bore fruit in the Ottoman victory over the Greeks in Thessaly in 1897.[14]

Contemporary feeling among young, educated Turkish Muslims that the Hamidian regime was a tyranny which endangered the survival of the Ottoman state and, in particular, the existence of its Muslim ruling community, and that it presided over the terminal decline of Ottoman power, obscures to this day the fact that it was a good time for non-Muslims (except for a part of the Armenian community), and not a bad one for Muslims – whether Turks, Arabs, Albanians or Kurds. The multinational Ottoman empire into which Mustafa Kemal Atatürk was born, was creaking, but it was still functioning.

Western travellers were at one in describing the Ottoman empire as a colourful country. The adjective applied both to the mixture of peoples and religions to be found in it and to the physical aspect of the country. The majority of the people lived in villages. Traditional houses predominated. They were made of wood in the Balkans and the Black Sea coast, adobe in Anatolia, and stone in the uplands. Folk dress was still worn. Traditional methods of cultivation were prevalent in farming. But the impact of foreign markets produced an increasing emphasis on cash crops: tobacco in the Balkans, sultanas, figs and olives along the Aegean coast, and cotton in the newly drained Cilician plain round the town of Adana. Although cereals were extensively grown, poor inland communications and the persistence of subsistence farming forced cities to rely largely on imports of wheat, as well as of sugar, rice, tea, coffee and other necessities.[15]

Railways had opened up large tracts of the Balkans and western Anatolia. Further east, communications were difficult, as roads were poor throughout the country. Maritime traffic, which was extensive, was almost entirely in foreign hands. Officials posted to distant provinces usually started their journeys in foreign ships.

The cities were comparatively small in population, even where they had extensive suburbs, as in the case of Istanbul. According to the 1893 census the population of Istanbul with its suburbs stood at some 950,000. There were 210,000 people in the urban district of İzmir, 120,000 in Bursa, 105,000 in Salonica, 115,000 in Damascus.[16] The urban population was mixed in origin and religion. In Istanbul Muslims made up barely half of the population, in İzmir only 38 per cent, in Salonica 28 per cent.

Nevertheless, with their profusion of minarets and domes the cities were Islamic in aspect. The Ottomans had been great builders. Mosques, almshouses, dervish monasteries (*tekke*), shrines (*türbe*), Turkish baths (*hamam*) and fountains graced all the cities which they governed. In the nineteenth century, and particularly during the reign of Abdülhamit II, other public buildings were added: provincial and district government houses, barracks and secondary schools. These were solid stone buildings, many of which have survived to this day both in Turkey and in lost Ottoman provinces. The private houses in which Turks of substance lived were almost invariably wooden. The rich set their mansions (*konak*) or seaside residences (*yalı*) in gardens, with outhouses for stables, kitchens, staff quarters and laundries. The reliance on wood for domestic architecture made cities subject to frequent devastating fires.

The nineteenth century witnessed important changes in the urban landscape. Non-Muslims and foreign residents built extensively in stone and brick. About 100,000 foreigners came to the Ottoman capital between 1840 and 1900 as traders, skilled workers or investors.[17] They settled in the 'European' district of Pera (Beyoğlu in Turkish) and in the suburbs. In 1857, the neighbourhoods north of the Golden Horn, where native and foreign non-Muslims predominated, were given municipal self-government. Ottoman cities tended to be comparatively neat and tidy within various compounds (of religious buildings and private mansions), but filthy outside them. The nineteenth century saw efforts to clean up the cities and open up roads in the maze of wooden houses which made up the urban mass. Amenities in Istanbul, İzmir and Salonica improved considerably, although Europeans continued to complain of dirt and untidiness.

In the capital, where the well-to-do had summer houses along the Bosphorus or in the Princes Islands, and where Ottoman officials often lived in mansions outside the centre, communications became easier when the government formed a local steamship company (known as *Şirket-i Hayriye* or Beneficent Company), which ran British-made ferries and employed foreign engineers. An Istanbul Tramway Company was formed in 1869 and ran horse-drawn trams in the city centre and suburbs.

By the end of the nineteenth century, Istanbul, İzmir, Salonica and, to a lesser extent, Trabzon (Trebizond) began to resemble European cities. They had proper harbours and communications, attractive water-fronts, solid houses and shopping streets (in addition to their traditional oriental bazaars), adequate hotels, restaurants, *brasseries* (as well as traditional Greek taverns), schools and hospitals. There were smart villas, mansions and clubs. In Istanbul, blocks of flats began to be built in the Parisian style at the turn of the century. When foreign artists and musicians toured the capital, they found proper theatres for their performances.

True, the cities retained their 'oriental' neighbourhoods of wooden houses and narrow alleys. Whilst there were rich Muslims, mainly senior officials, some of whom moved to 'European' neighbourhoods, there were few rich Muslim neighbourhoods. But there were few slums, fewer than in comparable European cities. There were gypsy encampments outside the walls, but no shanty-towns such as those which today surround all Turkish towns.

Looked at closely, the main Ottoman cities left much to be desired. But the general aspect was pleasing, mainly because there was little pressure on space, and therefore room for trees and gardens. The urban mass was broken up by unwalled Muslim cemeteries, which Europeans found romantic. There was good architecture in mosques and churches, palaces and mansions. The main Ottoman cities had impressive old monuments as well as some modern amenities.

The trouble was that the amenities were provided and, to a large extent, enjoyed by non-Muslims and Europeans. Well-to-do Muslim families also used non-Muslim builders, plumbers, tailors, doctors and dentists; they went to non-Muslim shops; their menfolk amused themselves in foreign restaurants and cafés; stayed in hotels owned and run by non-Muslims. These divisions and disparities could not be sustained for ever.

The late Ottoman empire was a remarkably open country. Foreigners visited it, lived and travelled in it. They were protected by their consuls, subject to the jurisdiction of their consular courts, and could use their own post offices. Accounts left by foreign travellers and residents speak of an agreeable life, lived in villas in suburbs, such as Moda in Istanbul or Bornabat (now Bornova) in İzmir, with servants and parties, picnics and hunting trips. The expatriate life was a pleasant one. Many native Christians did as well or better.

The decline of the Ottoman empire into which Mustafa Kemal Atatürk was born was not visible to the naked eye. Today even Muslim Turks look nostalgically at pictures of their country a century ago. But their grandparents and great-grandparents had cause for concern. A nineteenth-century Ottoman reformer wrote that Istanbul might well become orderly and prosperous like Paris or London, but 'we would not be the ones who would profit from or taste these delights ... Rather, we would turn up from time to time as sellers of firewood and charcoal and gaze at it sadly.'[18] The question which haunted Muslim Turks was not whether the country would survive, but whether they would survive in it.

PART I

Early Years

I

A Home in Europe

———————◆———————

A TATÜRK WAS BORN in Salonica in 1880/1 into a family which was Muslim, Turkish-speaking and precariously middle-class. These basic facts require elaboration.

Muslims did not have surnames, except in the case of a few prominent families. Official identity was based on entries in population registers. These registers, which were kept more or less accurately in the second half of the nineteenth century, specified an individual's given name or names, the names of his or her parents, religion, place and year of birth.

It was customary to give a newborn baby a name when the umbilical cord was cut. This was known as the 'belly name' (*göbek ismi*), and was chosen from among the honorific titles applied to the Prophet Muhammad or other names having a pious connotation. Later the child might be given a second or even third name, by which he or she would become known. The use of two given names was a mark of social distinction. Atatürk started life as plain Mustafa ('the Chosen', one of the appellations of the Prophet).

Dates could be recorded in two different calendars. For religious purposes, Muslims used a lunar calendar dating back to the Prophet's flight from Mecca to Medina in AD 622. For administrative purposes, a solar calendar was introduced in 1839. Known as *Rumi* (Roman), this also dated back to AD 622, but the day and month were the same as in the (Christian) Julian calendar. The *Rumi* year started on 1 March, which corresponded to 13 March in the (international) Gregorian calendar in the nineteenth century, and to 14 March in the twentieth century. In 1917, thirteen days were added to the *Rumi* calendar. Thereafter, the day and month, but not the year, corresponded to the Gregorian calendar. In the official population register, Atatürk's birth was entered in the year 1296 in the *Rumi* calendar. That year extended from 13 March 1880 to 12 March 1881. There is no reason to doubt the accuracy of the entry.

The day and month of Atatürk's birth are uncertain. His mother was later to say that she had given birth to Mustafa during the 'forty [cold] days' of winter.[1] But Atatürk himself quoted his mother to suggest that his birth was in the spring,[2] adding 'It might well have been in May'. This justified his choice of 19 May, the date in 1919 on which he landed in Samsun to lead the Turkish armed resistance against the Allies, as his official birthday. His entourage questioned his mother's surviving women friends from Salonica and duly confirmed that their leader's birth occurred 'in the spring, probably in May'.

It was customary, particularly in families which boasted of Islamic learning, for the father to record the dates of birth of his children inside the cover of the family Koran. This was apparently done in Atatürk's family, but according to his mother, Zübeyde, there were two Korans in the house. The one in which the children's birth was recorded was lost.[3]

In the story of Atatürk's life fact and legend are hard to disentangle, and Atatürk was the main author of his own legend. What he said was repeated by his friends and relatives, and much of what the latter said was meant to please him. The biographer thus comes across a corpus of sayings and stories, echoing each other, and usually serving a political purpose. The purpose cannot be disregarded. The most likely date of Atatürk's birth is the winter of 1880/1.

Atatürk's father was Ali Rıza, a junior civil servant. He came from a local lower middle-class family. Ali Rıza's father Ahmet was known as Hafız Ahmet Efendi.[4] The title 'Hafız' indicated that he had learned the whole of the Koran by heart; the title 'Efendi', also applied to his son Ali Rıza, designated him as an educated man. Hafız Ahmet Efendi was apparently nicknamed 'the fugitive' (*kaçak*). The explanation offered is that he had taken to the hills following the murder of the French and German consuls in Salonica in May 1876. The consuls were killed by a mob of Muslims who were infuriated when local Christians enlisted foreign consular help to prevent the conversion to Islam of a Bulgarian girl. After the great powers had sent warships to Salonica, the local authorities hanged the ringleaders of the riot.[5]

There seems to have been a tradition of Islamic learning in the family, since Ali Rıza's brother Mehmet (Emin) was also a Hafız and taught in a Koranic primary school. Mehmet's son Salih appears to have carried on the tradition.[6] The Ottoman civil service was originally manned by clerics. When the administrative reforms of the nineteenth century produced a demand for secular civil servants, many of these came from clerical families. Ali Rıza exemplified this process at the lowest level of the administration. The son and brother of neighbourhood Koranic teachers, he became a junior civil servant.

Ali Rıza was first employed in the department of pious foundations (*evkaf*). This job took him to small provincial towns where he inspected the accounts of charities.[7] In 1876/7 he served as lieutenant in a volunteer battalion formed on the eve of the Russian-Turkish war.[8] At roughly the same time he married. He also changed his job, transferring to the customs service. The exact dates of these events in Ali Rıza's life are not known. They probably occurred at the end of the war in 1878.

The name of Ali Rıza's wife was Zübeyde, and she was twenty years his junior.[9] Her father, Sofuzade Feyzullah Ağa, earned a living from farming and trade in the small town of Langaza (now Langadha) to the east of Salonica. The title *Ağa* usually denoted landlords, but it does not seem that Feyzullah owned much or any land. He may have been a steward or bailiff on behalf of absentee landowners. This was certainly the case with his son Hüseyin Ağa who ran a farm near Langaza.

Feyzullah's family is said to have come from the country near Vodina (now Edhessa in western Greek Macedonia). The surname Sofuzade,[10] meaning 'son of a pious man', suggests that the ancestors of Zübeyde and Ali Rıza had a similar background. Cemil Bozok, the son of Salih (Bozok), who was a distant cousin of Atatürk and, later, his ADC, claims to have been related to both Ali Rıza's and Zübeyde's families. This would mean that the families of Atatürk's parents were interrelated. Cemil Bozok also notes that his paternal grandfather, Safer Efendi, was of Albanian origin.[11] This may have a bearing on the vexed question of Atatürk's ethnic origin.

Atatürk's parents and relatives all used Turkish as their mother tongue. This suggests that some at least of their ancestors had originally come from Turkey, since local Muslims of Albanian and Slav origin who had no ethnic connection with Turkey spoke Albanian, Serbo-Croat or Bulgarian, at least so long as they remained in their native land. But in looks, Atatürk resembled local Albanians and Slavs. Like his mother, he had blue eyes and fair hair. The nickname 'Red' applied to his paternal grandfather suggests that the latter was also fair. When he took up Turkish ethnic nationalism, Atatürk claimed that his ancestors had been Turkish nomads (*yörük*) settled in the Balkans after the Turkish conquest.[12] Nomads had certainly been sent by the sultans to newly conquered territories both to help defend them and to keep these unruly tribesmen out of harm's way. But there is no evidence that either Ali Rıza or Zübeyde was descended from such Turkish nomads. It has been said in support of Atatürk's claim to a Turkish ethnic origin that many Turkish nomads are blue-eyed and fair-haired. One of Atatürk's friends at the War College, and a future opponent, Arif, who came from a leading family of the Karakeçili tribe in inland Anatolia, resembled him to the extent of being taken for his brother.[13] However, blue eyes, fair hair, and European looks in general are more common among Balkan Slavs than they are among Turkish nomads in Anatolia. It is much more likely that Atatürk inherited his looks from Balkan ancestors, and his mother tongue from Turkish conquerors who had intermarried with locals for many generations. We do not know whether the Albanian Safer Efendi was a blood relative of Atatürk. But Albanians and Slavs are likely to have figured among his ancestors. Direct descent from Turkish nomads is not an essential ingredient of Turkish ethnicity.

Ali Rıza and Zübeyde lived first in the bridegroom's family house in the Muslim Yenikapı (New Gate) neighbourhood in Salonica. They had relatives elsewhere in the city. Atatürk's contemporary and distant relative Salih (Bozok) lived in a compound of houses which had all been bought by his wife's family in the neighbourhood of Kulekahveleri (coffee houses by the White Tower on the waterfront of Salonica).[14] Salih's cousin, Nuri (Conker), who was to become a loyal adjutant of Atatürk, lived next door. A third close companion of Atatürk, Fuat (Bulca), who was Salih's brother-in-law,[15] also grew up in Salonica.

It was in the family house in Yenikapı that Zübeyde gave birth to three children: a girl Fatma, and two boys, Ömer and Ahmet.[16] It is also likely that her fourth child, Mustafa (Atatürk), was born in the same house. Fatma died an infant. Soon after her death, Ali Rıza was appointed customs officer on the Greek frontier, at a place known as Çayağzı (Mouth of the River) or Papaz Köprüsü (Priest's Bridge).[17] His salary is said to have been 3 gold liras or 300 silver piastres a month. It was a reasonable amount – some twenty years later, Salih (Bozok) was paid 337.5 piastres as a young lieutenant. But officials rarely received their pay on time.

Ali Rıza's harsh life, surrounded by brigands in a remote frontier post, has become part of the Atatürk story.[18] It is said that Zübeyde joined her husband at Papaz Köprüsü and that her two surviving children, Ömer and Ahmet, died there, probably at the age of three. Ali Rıza is then said to have resigned from the customs service and to have become a timber merchant. However, the dates do not fit.

Biographies situate Papaz Köprüsü just below the southern slopes of Mount Olympus, on the new frontier between Greek Thessaly and Ottoman Macedonia.[19] But Thessaly was ceded to Greece on 24 May 1881[20] – at least two months after Atatürk's birth. Atatürk must therefore have been a few months old when Ali Rıza first went to the new frontier as a customs officer. But the pink house in which Atatürk is said to have been born in Salonica was built with the money Ali Rıza made as a timber merchant. His profits allowed him also to engage a maid and a wet-nurse for his baby son.

The most likely explanation is that Ali Rıza was a customs officer and a timber merchant at one and the same time.[21] Far from resigning from the civil service, he probably used his official appointment to engage in private trade. The main job of the customs and excise officer was to prevent the unauthorized export of timber from the Mount Olympus area to Greece. The forests belonged to the state, and the Ottoman forestry service was supposed to issue felling licences to villagers. In the circumstances, a customs officer would have been ideally placed to acquire timber from the local Christian villagers and to ship it to Salonica, a more prosperous city than any to the south of the frontier with Greece. Ali Rıza is said to have had a partner in Salonica, a timber merchant called Cafer,[22] who sold the logs. This theory would also explain how Ali Rıza got together the money to build himself a new house in Salonica.

According to Atatürk's younger sister, Makbule, who was a small child at the time of her father's death, Ali Rıza had to make repeated short trips to the frontier after his resignation in order to obtain timber, but he soon found that local Greek brigands demanded exorbitant bribes, failing which they set fire to the logs. It seems more likely that Ali Rıza did not spend much time at the frontier and did not take his family with him, that he made short trips officially as a customs officer, but in effect to obtain and ship timber, and that after some initial success he fell out with local villagers (or brigands, as the two terms designated largely the same people) who wanted the timber for themselves. He is then said to have complained to a senior Ottoman official in Salonica, by the name of Ali Paşa, who advised him to seek another occupation.[23] Thereupon he took up the trade in salt, which as a state monopoly offered openings to a man in the excise department. Ali Rıza is unlikely to have resigned from the civil service, where appointments were often sinecures. His family does not seem to have suffered any hardship until his death, and he may well have received his salary of 3 gold liras a month to the end of his days.

The house which Ali Rıza built in Salonica was situated in a neighbourhood called Ahmetsubaşı (or Kocakasım).[24] It is this solidly built, three-storey, pink-painted house on a slope leading down to the waterfront which has been designated as Atatürk's place of birth and preserved as a museum. Like all well-to-do Muslim houses, Ali Rıza's new family home was divided into two: one wing was used as private family quarters (*harem*), and another served as a reception area for male visitors (*selâmlık*).

After giving birth to Mustafa, Zübeyde bore two daughters of whom the first, Makbule, survived, and the second, Naciye, died. Thus of the six children of Zübeyde's first marriage, only two survived.

Ali Rıza died at the age of 47, when Mustafa was 7 or 8 years old. His widow attributed his death to the failure of his commercial schemes: 'The late lamented became very distressed when his business went badly in his last days. He let himself go. He resigned himself to his fate and faded away. His illness grew worse. There is no way he could have survived. When I became a widow, I was a 27-year-old young woman. I was given a monthly pension of two *mecidiye* [silver coins worth 20 piastres].'[25]

Ali Rıza's fatal illness has been attributed to 'consumption of the bowels', aggravated by drink. In any case, family tradition recorded him as a failure.

Salonica was no mean city during Atatürk's childhood. Its prosperity grew markedly in the long years of peace preserved by Sultan Abdülhamit II after the end of the Russian war in 1878. In 1889 the city was linked by rail to Europe via Serbia and Vienna.[26] Another line joined it to the capital, Istanbul, which also had direct communications with Europe via Bulgaria. In 1901, a modern harbour was built.[27] Electricity was installed in 1899 and an electric tram service started in 1907. Mills produced cotton and woollen cloth; tobacco was exported in considerable quantities under the auspices of the state monopoly (known by its French name, *Régie*), which was part of the foreign-controlled Public Debt Administration.

In the last forty years of the nineteenth century, the population of Salonica grew from about 70,000 to over 100,000. While the arrival of Muslim refugees from Thessaly and from exposed areas in the country-side increased the number of Muslims, Jews still formed the largest community and made up about half the population.[28] The Muslim neighbourhoods overlooked those inhabited by Jews and Greeks, most of whom lived along and immediately behind the waterfront. This spatial division was common in the Ottoman state. When towns were conquered, Muslims settled round the citadel, while Christians and Jews moved to the suburbs. Moreover, Turks seldom chose to live by the sea, which had a special attraction for Greeks.

In Salonica at the end of the nineteenth century, many of the neighbourhoods preserved their original character. Muslim districts had a central square overlooked by a mosque, with a Koranic school as an annex. They had communal baths, coffee houses where men met, small private gardens. European travellers found these Muslim neighbourhoods romantic and charming. Houses were huddled close together in poor Jewish districts, but more prosperous members of the community, like wealthy Greeks, were moving out to spacious villas on the waterfront. The worst Jewish slums were destroyed in the great fire of 1890. In its aftermath, streets were straightened and widened, a city plan was put in place and modernization began.[29] The Jews were prominent among the rising bourgeoisie, but also in the new working class. Most of the stevedores were Jews renowned for their toughness and militancy.

In addition to communal schools, Salonica had schools run by foreign missionaries, both Catholic and Protestant. In 1895 a modern Turkish daily newspaper appeared. Called *Asır* (The Century), it moved to İzmir in 1924 and survives to this day as *Yeni Asır* (The New Century). Jewish businessmen founded a local bank, the Banque de Salonique, which eventually moved to Istanbul. There were European-type cafés on the waterfront, usually run by Greeks, dancing schools and balls. An Englishwoman, Lucy Garnett, who lived in Salonica in the 1880s, was present at a charity fête in aid of a Jewish school:

> Dancing went on in the lower rooms, the apartments of the upper floor were reserved for cigarette-smoking, cards and conversation, while refreshments and supper were served under brightly illuminated trees and among the flower-beds of the garden attached to the school-house. The Governor-General, Dervish Pasha, and his son were present, and though they naturally did not condescend to join the dancers, moved about continually among them, and appeared to take a great interest in the proceedings. The Greek Archbishop made a distinguished figure in his tall cylindrical hat and black robes, seated side by side with the Jewish Khakham Bashi [*Hahambaşı*], or Chief Rabbi, in black and white turban. Ball dresses, however, were conspicuous by their absence; for, aware that the entertainment was to be partially *al fresco*, the European ladies had avoided low dresses, and many of the Salonica Jewesses, who had subscribed their *liras*, presented themselves in their brilliantly coloured native costumes, profusely adorned with seed pearls and gleaming with diamonds.[30]

The spread of European influences through trade, education and diplomacy led to tension within the communities between conservatives and modernizers. Masonic lodges were well established and some of the more prominent modernizers belonged to them. Among Muslims, new ideas were particularly widespread in the *dönme* community of descendants of converts from Judaism.

'The Dünméhs,' wrote Lucy Garnett, 'are, as a community, highly respectable, industrious, and prosperous. Poverty, indeed, is said to be non-existent among them, the wealthy helping those less successful in worldly affairs and supporting widows and orphans by an admirably organized system of charity.'[31] Unlike other Muslims, the *dönme* had no military tradition. In the army, they were to be found most commonly as military doctors. In civil life, they were active in business and the professions. They also took an active part in politics.

The network of new state schools provided the main conduit for European ideas to the Muslim community. These were organized in two parallel systems, civil (*mülkî*) and military (*askerî*), the first designed primarily to train civil servants, the second officers. In both streams, preparatory schools (*rüştiye*) led on to high schools or lycées (*idadî*) and then on to either the civil service college (*Mülkiye*) or to the War College (*Harbiye*) in Istanbul. Military high schools were usually set up in towns which served as headquarters for Ottoman armies. In European Turkey, the main military centres were Edirne, Salonica and Manastır (now Bitola in former Yugoslav Macedonia).

The struggle between conservative and progressive ideas, between traditional Islam and European free thought, marked Atatürk's life from the start. His mother was, not unusually, steeped in traditional attitudes, her piety earning her the nickname of *molla*.[32] His father, Ali Rıza, a junior civil servant with an eye to the main chance, believed in progress. Atatürk was to say later:

> My first memory of childhood concerns the problem of my schooling. This caused a bitter dispute between my parents. My mother wanted me to go to the neighbourhood [Koranic] school after initial prayers. My father, who was an official in the [customs and] excise department, was in favour of sending me to Şemsi Efendi's school, which had newly opened, and of having me educated in the new manner. In the end, my father found a clever way out. First, I started at the neighbourhood school with the usual ceremony. This satisfied my mother. A few days later, I left the neighbourhood school and was entered in Şemsi Efendi's school.[33]

The initial ceremony to which Atatürk referred was the procession headed by the Koranic teacher (*hoca*), who led the child from his home to the neighbourhood school. A portion (*cüz*) of the Koran, which the child was to memorize, and a lectern on which it would be placed, were carried aloft, and prayers were chanted. By having the ceremony performed for her son, Zübeyde not only satisfied her conscience, but also met the expectations of the neighbourhood, and showed that hers was a proper Muslim family. According to Lucy Garnett, Şemsi Efendi was a *dönme*, who opened his school primarily to educate girls in his community. The girls were taught the three Rs and needlework. 'With the younger pupils, however, the director looked for better success than with the "grown-up young ladies".'[34]

Zübeyde's son Mustafa was one of these younger pupils, but not for long. When he was 7 or 8 years old,[35] his father, Ali Rıza, died, and his mother, Zübeyde, took the family to the farm run by her half-brother Hüseyin Ağa at Rapla, near Langaza, in the plain stretching east of Salonica where Muslims were numerous.[36] Atatürk was fond of remembering this rural interlude, which he shared with his younger sister Makbule. The two children were given the job of chasing off crows from a field of broad beans;[37] they played together and, on one occasion, young Mustafa pushed his sister's face into a bowl of yoghurt.[38] There were, it seems, desultory attempts to have Mustafa taught, first at a Greek village school and then by an Albanian (or Armenian) farm clerk.[39] But soon Zübeyde decided to send her son back to Salonica to continue his education. He lodged with his paternal aunt,[40] and was enrolled in the state civil preparatory school (*mülkî rüştiye*).

The school did not prove a success. One day, Mustafa was beaten by a teacher known inappropriately as Kaymak ('[soft as] cream') Hafız for quarrelling in class with another boy. Thereupon his maternal grandmother, who was the senior member of the family in Salonica and who did not want him to go to a modern school at all, took him away.

In a newspaper interview in which he described his life, Atatürk said that on leaving the civil service preparatory school, he was determined to enter its military equivalent in Salonica, because he wanted to wear the smart Western-style uniform of military cadets.[41] The son of a neighbour (or perhaps lodger in the family house), one Major Kadri, was already enrolled in the military school, and young Mustafa was intensely jealous of him. Atatürk later told his companion Kılıç Ali that as a young boy he could not bear to be dressed in baggy oriental trousers, tied with a sash, which were worn by boys in Şemsi Bey's establishment. 'It was when I entered the military preparatory school and put on its uniform, that a feeling of strength came to me, as if I had become master of my own identity.' His mother Zübeyde told Kılıç Ali: 'My Mustafa was very particular about his clothes, even as a little boy. He behaved and spoke to others like a grown-up. He looked down on neighbourhood children playing in the street ... We all noticed how he spoke, head raised, hands in pockets.'

Zübeyde went on to describe her boy as gentle, shy and well-loved by the neighbours.[42] From an early age, Atatürk's pride was immediately noticeable; his shyness was seen only by those who worked with him.

His secretary Hasan Rıza Soyak was to say, 'according to his doctors, he was insomniac, constipated and shy.'[43] The first two afflictions developed in later life; the last was always there. It is also evident that from earliest childhood Atatürk hated the external signs of oriental life, and longed to look like a Western officer and gentleman.

Zübeyde, who had in the meantime returned to Salonica, was afraid of allowing her only son to join a dangerous profession, and did all she could to dissuade him. According to Atatürk's account, he sat the entrance examinations without telling his mother. She had no choice but to give her consent when he was accepted into the military preparatory school. Atatürk suggests in his interview that the initiative was totally his; but he was helped and perhaps even encouraged in his ambition by the neighbour, Major Kadri. Moreover Mustafa's choice was not unusual. Three members of his extended family, Salih (Bozok), Nuri (Conker) and Fuat (Bulca), all of whom became his trusted lieutenants, were to follow the same route. Salih Bozok, who appears to have been one year younger than Atatürk,[44] was beaten by the same teacher in the civil service preparatory school[45] before going on to the military school. It seems that the whole younger generation of Atatürk's extended family, as, no doubt, of other Turkish families in the empire's threatened provinces in Europe, decided at about the same time that their future lay in the profession of arms. Their choice did not depend on the heavy-handed Kaymak Hafız or on the lure of a smart uniform. Ambition, the feeling of self-preservation and patriotism all pointed in the same direction. In his childhood, as in his later career, Atatürk was not alone in his choices. But he was unique in his abilities.

2

The Making of an Ottoman Officer

ATATÜRK'S MILITARY EDUCATION lasted for thirteen years. In the
language of the time he became a 'school-trained' (*mektepli*) officer,
when that rising class challenged the continued existence of 'regiment-
trained' (*alaylı*) officers who had been promoted from the ranks without
the benefit of formal military education. The struggle between modernizers and conservatives affected the army along with the rest of society.

Military education reinforced in him an already masterful disposition. As the only surviving male in a fatherless household Atatürk was
the most important person at home. His sister Makbule was later to say
that he was too proud to play leapfrog, as he would not bend down to
allow other children to vault over him. Whatever the truth of this tale,
there is little doubt that young Mustafa did all he could to recreate in
school – and in later life – the pre-eminence which he enjoyed as of
right in his family. Apart from giving him an instinctive feeling of superiority, his childhood experience taught him the art of getting his own
way. Atatürk was later to declare:

There is one trait I have had since my childhood. In the house where I lived
I never liked to spend time with my sister or with a friend. Since my childhood I have always preferred to be alone and independent, and that is how I
have always lived. I have another trait: I have never had any patience with any
advice or admonition which my mother – my father died very early – my
sister or any of my closest relatives pressed on me according to their lights.
People who live in the midst of their families know well that they are never
short of innocent and sincere warnings from left and right. There are only
two ways of dealing with them. You either obey them or you ignore all these
warnings and admonitions. I believe that neither way is right. How could you

obey? To take heed of the warnings of a mother, twenty or twenty-five years my senior, wouldn't that have meant retreating into the past? But to rebel would have upset the heart and mind of a mother of whose virtue, good faith and superior womanly qualities I was convinced. That wasn't right either.

The dilemma resolved itself because, Atatürk went on to say, 'my mother and my sister believed in my revolutionary work and served me'.[1] As long as his womenfolk served him, he could be both firm and kind with them. In spite of his words to the contrary, Atatürk was never one to live a lonely life, at least not as this phrase is understood in the West. In a traditional society life is always lived in a crowd. Both in childhood and as an adult, he lived surrounded by friends, relatives and colleagues. However, he took his own counsel, and from an early age dominated his immediate circle. Atatürk was lonely only in the sense that leadership is a lonely business.

Atatürk was himself the author of two stories concerning his four years (1891–5) in the military preparatory school in Salonica.[2] Teaching in all schools in Turkey was – and, to a large extent, still is – by rote. To help the pupils learn the lesson by heart, teachers would appoint one of them to repeat it over and over again. This followed the French practice of employing *répétiteurs* (in Ottoman Turkish *müzakereci*). According to Atatürk, one day the mathematics teacher asked for volunteers to act as *répétiteurs*. 'At first I hesitated,' Atatürk declared in 1922. 'Seeing the kind of boys who stood up to volunteer, I preferred to remain seated. But having had to repeat the lesson after one such, I couldn't stand it a second time. I got up and said to the teacher "I can do better than that." The teacher then appointed me *répétiteur*, and my predecessor had to repeat the lessons after me.'

The second story which has become embedded in the Atatürk legend explains how he acquired a second name and became known as Mustafa Kemal. In the preparatory school, so Atatürk reported, he developed a special interest in mathematics. 'I soon equalled, and possibly even surpassed, our mathematics teacher in knowledge of the subject. I started working at problems well in advance of our lessons. I used to put questions in writing, to which my teacher would reply also in writing. The teacher's name was Mustafa. One day he turned to me and said: "My boy, your name is Mustafa and so is mine. This won't do. There must be some distinction. Fron now on you'll be called Mustafa Kemal." And that's how I've been known ever since.'[3]

The literal meaning of *Kemal* in Ottoman Turkish is 'perfection', and biographers have praised the mathematics teacher for his remarkable prescience. But a teacher content to remain plain Mustafa, while giving a flattering second name to his bright pupil, must have been not only prescient, but also remarkably self-effacing. Yet Atatürk adds that the mathematics teacher was 'a hard man', in other words authoritarian, at a time when teachers were not known for their softness. Atatürk's biographer, Şevket Süreyya Aydemir, heard another version of the story. According to this version, Atatürk acquired the second name of Kemal in order to distinguish him not from his teacher, but from a classmate, also called plain Mustafa.[4] That Atatürk became known by a high-sounding double-barrelled name when he was a student in the military preparatory school is not in doubt. But we have only his word for the somewhat self-serving origin of the story. It is much more likely that young Mustafa himself chose the second name Kemal, as a tribute to the patriotic poet Namık Kemal. Young as he was (he was 13 or 14 at the time), he would have heard of the poet who was to become, a few years later, the source of his youthful inspiration. Or perhaps an older person suggested the name to him.

Atatürk told both stories when he was an embattled commander-in-chief preparing for his final offensive. At that time even some of his supporters had doubts about the outcome. But Atatürk had no such doubts. Not only did he believe in his own greatness, he proclaimed it, and pointed to his schoolboy triumphs as portents. But whatever the origin of the second name, Atatürk was certainly a successful pupil at the preparatory school. He won his stripes as sergeant (*çavuş*), becoming leader of his class – a sign that he was trusted by the school authorities. He may have been proud, but he was not openly rebellious.

A third story relating to Atatürk's years in the preparatory school comes from the memoirs of his companion Kılıç Ali. One day in the early 1930s Atatürk invited to his table at Karpiç's restaurant in Ankara the journalist Ahmet Emin Yalman, who had fallen foul of the regime and had been forced to abandon his career. Ahmet Emin was by origin a *dönme* from Salonica. Turning to Kılıç Ali, Atatürk said:

Ahmet Emin's father, Osman Tevfik, was my teacher of Turkish calligraphy [in the Arabic script] in the preparatory school. At that time my handwriting was not at all good. It was no better than a scrawl. Not that it's any better today … In spite of this, Mr Tevfik used to give me full marks, as he knew that I would do well in other lessons. Isn't it strange that while the father gave me full marks, feeling that I'd be successful in other subjects, the son, who has seen the many services I've rendered the country, refuses to award me any marks at all?[5]

The opposition journalist protested that he had been misunderstood and promised to mend his ways forthwith. Soon afterwards, he appeared in print again. Throughout his life, Atatürk was convinced he was right. It was a conviction he was happy to share with those round him.

Sometime before Atatürk graduated from the preparatory school, his mother Zübeyde remarried. As a young widow with no means, she had little choice in the matter. The only alternative was to live off the charity of her relatives, none of whom was rich. Her second husband, Ragıp Efendi, was a widower with four children, two boys and two girls. He had emigrated from Thessaly when that province was ceded to Greece in 1881, and at the time of his second marriage was employed as a junior official in the tobacco monopoly.

Zübeyde's remarriage meant that Atatürk was no longer the senior male in the household. Refusing to accept the loss of status, he left the family house and lodged with a relative.[6] But although he was undoubtedly hurt by the remarriage, he discharged throughout his life the duties, which Turkish Muslim culture required of him, both towards his mother and his step-relatives. Ragıp Efendi stayed on in Salonica after the city was lost to the Greeks in 1912, and died there sometime later. Atatürk is said to have helped him financially towards the end of his life. Of Ragıp's two sons, the younger, Hasan, was employed in the tobacco monopoly, like his father. The elder, Süreyya, is said to have committed suicide while serving as a captain at Toyran (now Dhoirani, on the frontier between Greece and former Yugoslav Macedonia), the scene of much fighting in the First World War. Atatürk liked him, and remembered being given by him a flick knife to guard his virtue against immoral approaches. Falih Rıfkı, Atatürk's main publicist, explains: 'We all know that in those days when women were secluded, sexual morals were very low among the Turks.'[7] He does not add whether young Atatürk – by all accounts, a good-looking, blue-eyed, fair-haired youth – ever had to use the weapon.

There was one member of Ragıp Efendi's extended family who was to become tragically close to Atatürk in later years. This was the girl Fikriye, the daughter of Ragıp's brother, Colonel Hüsamettin. She was born in 1897, when Atatürk was 16. Her father was a modern-minded officer who gave her a proper education, including piano lessons.[8]

Atatürk's only surviving sister Makbule was later to regale journalists with romantic stories of her famous brother's childhood crushes. His first love was, it seems, a girl called Müjgân, the daughter of a family friend, Major Rüknettin. Next came Hatice, whose mother is said to have put an end to the friendship as she did not want to lose a daughter to a future officer who might be posted to distant parts. Then, Zübeyde arranged for her son to tutor Emine, the 15-year-old daughter of the military commandant of Salonica, and former neighbour, Şevki Paşa. Emine was later to say that she had fallen in love with Atatürk when she first saw him in the uniform of the preparatory school. She believed that her feelings were reciprocated, and claimed that when Atatürk left Salonica in 1899 to enter the War College, he sent her this note: 'I'm boarding the ship this very minute. This ill-starred moment will make us weep tears of blood. I swear inwardly that I shall not forget you, and I expect you to be equally faithful. Goodbye. Mustafa Kemal.' Emine added that Atatürk did, in fact, visit her on later trips to Salonica, but by then 'he was preoccupied entirely with the country's problems and the sufferings of the nation ... Great events intervened and stopped our marriage.'[9] This account which Emine gave to a Turkish journalist in 1965 contradicts the romantic story that she was later disfigured in an accident, that on learning the sad news, Atatürk immediately proposed to marry her, but that she died before the promise could be carried out.[10]

Zübeyde's account was shorter. While a student at the military preparatory school, Atatürk first tutored the son of a local Muslim notable (Evrenoszade Muhsin Bey, whose son-in-law, Mithat, later benefited from Atatürk's patronage and was made member of parliament for Bolu). Şevki Paşa's daughter came next. 'Fortunately they didn't carry on long,' Zübeyde said. 'He went to the high school at Manastır and the tutoring was interrupted.'[11]

One romantic story has it that, many years later at a party in the presidential palace of Çankaya, Atatürk was deeply touched by the song *'Eminem'* (My Emine!) and remarked cryptically, 'There is an Emine in every man's heart.'[12] On another occasion, he was quoted as saying that his first love was a Greek girl in Salonica, with whom he hoped to elope to Manastır, but was dissuaded by his maternal uncle Hüseyin Ağa.[13] In any case, Zübeyde was quickly relieved of her worries. Her son soon had other things on his mind.

In later life, Atatürk was to form romantic attachments with several women. Ritual flirtation, including the exchange of billets-doux, was part of the Western way of life, which he admired. But his work was all that mattered to him. He would act as romantic protector of women who served him, wished to be taught by him or formed part of an admiring audience. But he would not let them make any demands on him, beyond those which Turkish culture sanctioned. This emotional pattern seems to have been established early in childhood. An only son in a fatherless Turkish household is likely to develop a paternalistic character. In later life, Atatürk often addressed his closest personal associates, men and women, as 'Child!' (*Çocuk!*). It was when he was a

child himself that Atatürk learned to be kind to women but to go his
own way, allowing himself occasionally to pose as a lover, in the manner
of a French romantic hero.

Atatürk was the fourth best pupil in his class when he graduated from
the preparatory school in Salonica in 1898.[14] He could then have gone
on to the military high school (*idadi*) in his native city, but his mother's
remarriage made it more convenient for him to board in another city. It
is said that he would have liked to go to a school in Istanbul,[15] but that
an examiner, Hasan, advised him that the military high school in
Manastır would provide a better education.[16] In fact, he probably chose
Manastır because it was nearer home; it may also have been easier to
gain admittance to the school there as a free boarder.

Situated on an upland plain at the foot of the mountains, and lying on
the old Roman Via Egnatia, Manastır was an important commercial,
administrative and military centre. It was linked by rail to Salonica, and
was the chief town of a province, covering western Macedonia and
extending south to the Greek frontier. The city population of 37,000[17]
included an important Greek merchant community. The Muslims, who
could boast of sixty mosques,[18] were largely of Albanian and Slav
Macedonian origin. The provincial government and the army headquarters gave employment to Ottoman officials who faced the pressure of
Bulgarian, Macedonian, Serbian and Greek nationalists and of the
bands of irregulars who fought for them.

The military schools sought to inculcate loyalty to the sultan and to
the Ottoman state. Although there were many religious communities in
the state, the cadets were all Muslims, and the defence of the ruling
Muslim community was uppermost in their minds. In the ruling class,
the ideal of Ottoman patriotism, which the early reformers wished to
establish, tended under Abdülhamit II towards a narrower Muslim
Ottoman nationalism, before mutating into a still narrower Turkish
nationalism. In class, cadets acquired their first political ideas during
history lessons. Atatürk's history teacher, Major Mehmet Tevfik, was 'a
nationalist Turkish officer'. Atatürk was to say: 'I owe Tevfik a debt of
gratitude. He opened a new horizon before my eyes.' Atatürk discharged this debt in later years by making his former teacher member of
parliament for Diyarbakır (in the Kurdish south-east), and a member
of the Turkish Historical Society.[19] But it was not only in class that the
students formed an opinion of the world round them.

Atatürk acknowledged the influence of a fiery fellow-student, Ömer
Naci, who had fallen foul of the school authorities in Bursa and had

transferred to Manastır. Ömer Naci had a passion for Ottoman literature and particularly for poetry, and encouraged Atatürk to follow his lead in composing poems. However, the teacher of composition put an end to his literary pursuits, saying that they were incompatible with a military career. Nevertheless, Atatürk added, 'I retained an interest in fine writing.'[20] It was thus at the school in Manastır that Atatürk began acquiring his mastery of literary Ottoman, a euphonious and euphuistic idiom, where Arabic abstract nouns crowd together in alliterative groups of synonyms to raise the emotional tone rather than to clarify the meaning. Atatürk became an effective writer and speaker of this artificial tongue, which served him well in his public appearances. Unfortunately, it is now incomprehensible in its original form to Turkish readers, for whom translations into simple Turkish have to be provided.

Literature was intermixed with politics. It was almost certainly in conversations with Ömer Naci that Atatürk discussed the patriotic poems of Namık Kemal, 'the poet of liberty' whose writings were banned under Abdülhamit II. The excitement of liberal-nationalist rhetoric was to continue when Atatürk moved on to the War College in Istanbul. But with Atatürk dedication to a military career came first. Ömer Naci provided not only inspiration, but an example to be avoided. He joined the revolutionary Young Turks, fled abroad, returned for a political career after the Young Turkish coup of 1908, and died in 1915, from typhus contracted in Persia where he had been sent to stir up trouble against the Allies. He was one of the many romantic adventurers who hastened the end of the Ottoman state, and to whom Atatürk was temperamentally and then politically opposed.

With two other fellow-students Atatürk formed a lasting attachment. Ali Fethi (Okyar) was a year older. He came from a relatively well-off family at Pirlepe (Prilep), not far from Manastır. He knew French and is said to have introduced Atatürk to French political thought. The introduction was probably confined to talk on the dangerous subject of the French Revolution. French was taught at the school, but Atatürk found that he made little progress with the language. Mathematics remained as ever his best subject. But he was conscious of the importance of French as a key to European civilization, and during a summer holiday at home in Salonica, he followed a course run by the French Christian Brothers. Gradually he acquired a very serviceable knowledge of the French language, in which he came to read widely, and which he could also use in correspondence. His letters in French contain mistakes, but they show a wide knowledge of vocabulary. To the end of his life, Atatürk was apt to slip the odd French word into his conversation, having a particular liking for the word *déjà*. Of much more importance was the fact that the French model of culture, society and government was ever present in his mind. Again, he was far from unique: French influence was strong throughout the Ottoman ruling class. But Atatürk proved more consistently radical than most of his contemporaries in drawing on the French experience.

Another friend was a year younger. His name was Kâzım (Özalp) and he came from Köprülü (at that time in the province of Salonica, later [Titov] Veleš in former Yugoslav Macedonia). Kâzım was always a loyal subordinate, rising later to the rank of general in the Turkish army, before becoming President of the Grand National Assembly in the Turkish Republic. Kâzım reminisced:

> Mustafa Kemal who was known and liked by his classmates was also appreciated for his character by boys in our class. We did not work together, as we were in different classes, but we used to walk out together with other friends on days off. We used to go generally to coffee houses in the neighbourhoods of Kavaklaraltı [beneath the poplars] and Hanlarönü [in front of the caravanserais]. He used to chat, like the others, and sometimes play backgammon for a stake of 5 paras [the smallest coin, worth one eighth of a piastre]. One could see easily that Mustafa Kemal did not like losing. Nor did he like games of running and jumping. Rather than stroll and look around, he preferred to walk fast.[21]

Two years above Mustafa Kemal at the Manastır military high school was the man who was to become his main rival among revolutionary officers. His name was Enver, and he was to lead the Ottoman state to defeat in the First World War. Enver's family came from the old Ottoman fortress of Kili (now Kiliya in Ukrainian Bessarabia), near the mouth of the Danube. He had been born in Istanbul in November 1881 (1297 in the *Rumi* calendar) and was thus a few months younger than Mustafa Kemal. But the latter had lost a year in the civil preparatory school, while Enver seems to have been a year ahead of his age group in the military preparatory school and then the military high school in Manastır, the town where his father, an official in the public works department, had been posted. As a result, Enver was two years ahead of Mustafa Kemal right through his military education, which he completed when he passed out of the Staff College in Istanbul in November 1902.[22] Mustafa Kemal and Enver had friends in common, but they moved in different sets.

When Mustafa Kemal was in his second year in the military high school in Manastır a brief war broke out between the Ottoman state and Greece. It was caused by the despatch of armed bands from mainland

Greece to help Greek insurgents in Crete who were fighting for *enosis* –
the union of their island with Greece. The Ottoman government retaliated by declaring war on 19 April 1897. Within one month the Greek
army was defeated, Thessaly fell once again into Ottoman hands and
the road to Athens lay open. But the great powers intervened and
imposed an armistice. In return for a war indemnity and a minor frontier rectification in its favour, the Ottoman government agreed to make
peace with Greece. Crete remained within the Ottoman state, but as an
autonomous province, with Prince George of Greece acting as
Commissioner on behalf of the great powers. The way was thus opened
to the slow absorption of the island into the Greek kingdom. As in the
case of the Greek war of independence, and the war with Serbia in 1877,
the great powers did not allow the Ottomans to keep the fruits of their
victories.

The declaration of war produced an outburst of patriotic feeling
among Ottoman Muslims. Troops leaving military bases such as
Manastır were seen off by enthusiastic crowds, and were joined by volunteers. Mustafa Kemal was moved by the enthusiasm, but the story
that he tried to volunteer and went to Salonica on his way to the front,
only to be turned back by his mother, Zübeyde,[23] is apocryphal. His
friend Ali Fuat (Cebesoy) says more accurately: 'Mustafa Kemal was
chief among those who wanted to volunteer. Various reasons stopped
him. The war was very brief.'[24] Mustafa Kemal was clearly too intent on
his military career to run away from school, even for the best patriotic
reasons. But he must have shared the feelings of the young officer in
Manastır who could not keep back his tears when he heard that the
Ottomans had been forced to agree to an armistice.[25] The lesson that
the European great powers intervened when the Ottomans won, but
failed to intervene when they were defeated, was not lost on him.
Nevertheless, the swift victory won by the Ottoman commander
Ethem Paşa did raise the prestige of Sultan Abdülhamit and helped him
safeguard his dominions for another decade.

In November 1898, Mustafa Kemal passed out of the military high
school in Manastır. He was ranked second in his class.[26] Years of hard
work still awaited him in the War College in Istanbul, but his contemporaries in Manastır could now recommend him to a wider circle as a
successful and popular student.

On 13 March 1899, Mustafa Kemal entered the War College (*Mekteb-i
Harbiye* or simply *Harbiye*) in Istanbul at the age of 18.[27] The college
buildings, now used as a military museum, were set on a hill overlooking

the Bosphorus, in a new part of the city developed in the nineteenth
century. On the shore below stood the palaces and gardens of
Dolmabahçe and Çırağan, the latter the home of the deposed Sultan
Murat V. On the ridge to the south, at the edge of the European district
of Beyoğlu (Pera), the large barracks of Taşkışla (Stone Barracks)
housed part of the garrison of the capital. To the north, the slope rising
from the Bosphorus was covered by the walled compound of Yıldız
palace, the home of Sultan Abdülhamit II and the seat of power in the
state. In between stood the new smart district of Teşvikiye, favoured by
westernized Turks, while inland lay the neighbourhoods of Pangaltı and
Osmanbey, inhabited largely by Armenians. Istanbul was still a city of
open spaces and pleasing prospects, and cadets at the War College were
in no doubt that they were at the centre of an impressive imperial
capital. The contrast between the grandeur of the setting and the reality
of crumbling Ottoman power and of the growing encroachment of
native and foreign Christians was all the more poignant.

The cadets were treated roughly. They slept in dormitories; they were
shouted at and sometimes slapped by sergeants; they were fed on a
simple diet of stewed dry beans, mutton and rice. Atatürk loved the
rough food, and years later, when he was president of the republic, bean
stew remained his favourite dish. But, although kicked around by everyone in authority, the cadets were addressed as Efendi, and felt themselves to be gentlemen. Their society was democratic, the only group
set aside from the common mass being that of the imperial princes
(*zadegân*), who had separate quarters. But, contrary to the practice
current in many European countries, the princes were not destined for
effective military commands.

The student body was strictly controlled. Newspapers were not
allowed. Reading was limited to textbooks. Islamic worship – the five
daily canonical prayers, fasting during the lunar month of Ramazan
(Ramadan, the month of fasting) – was strictly enforced. So was the
prohibition of alcohol, but the bars, cafés and restaurants of Beyoğlu,
and of the harbour district of Galata below it, lay near at hand, and only
the most pious and strong-minded resisted their attractions or failed to
frequent the brothels, which were plentiful in the side-streets of the
Christian districts. Muslim gentlemen had an ambivalent attitude to
Beyoğlu and Galata. They were attracted by the entertainment the districts offered, but resented them as traps for the unwary. The ruination
of the careers and marriages of Muslim gentlemen in the low dives of
Beyoğlu was a favourite theme of Turkish novelists.

Like most of his comrades, Mustafa Kemal was drawn to the entertainment which the capital offered. As a boy, he had sat in the cafés of

Salonica, and neither he nor his friends took seriously the Islamic ban on alcohol. As in other Mediterranean countries, it was taken for granted that drinking and wenching were part of a young man's life, until the time came to settle down in marriage with a virgin bride chosen or at least approved by the family. While early marriages were common in traditional Muslim society, for men moulded by the new learning, education and the beginning of a career came first. Mustafa Kemal took care of both. But he also enjoyed his youth, undisturbed by religious scruples.

Mustafa Kemal had a pious mother. He had been subjected to years of religious instruction and practice, and he knew how to use the language of piety. Not only had he practised the rites of official, orthodox Islam, but during his home leave in Salonica he is said to have attended the ceremonies of whirling dervishes, and to have taken part himself, crying out 'Hu! Hu!' (an Arabic word meaning 'He' – God) as he whirled round.[28] But it was during the same home leave that Atatürk went to dancing lessons and learnt to waltz. If he did visit the dervishes, he seems to have set little store by the experience.

Mustafa Kemal's behaviour during his youth provides no evidence of religious conviction, while his adult life presents clear evidence of the contrary. Most Turkish officers and gentlemen accepted Islam as a general framework for their lives and the life of their society. Others, like Atatürk and many of his friends, seem to have been freethinkers from their earliest years. Islam had to be taken into account as a fact – sometimes an inconvenient fact – of other people's lives. In the eyes of many educated Muslims in Turkey, as in other Mediterranean countries, religion was the province of women; the sincerity of men who showed religious enthusiasm was suspect. Most of the cadets rejected the indoctrination to which they had been subjected. Their idealism was focused on a political objective – the defence of the ruling Muslim Turkish community into which they were born. In that aim they were utterly sincere. Members of Atatürk's generation nourished personal ambitions; some served their personal interests or those of their families and friends; some fell short of their ideals and even made deals with the enemies of their community. But none questioned the ideal of service to country and nation. There was backsliding, but no cynicism.

Within two months of entering the War College, Mustafa Kemal was appointed junior sergeant in charge of his class. Above his stripes, he wore a ribbon indicating his knowledge of a foreign language – French. It was a rare distinction among the 750 first-year students.[29] Nevertheless, it took Mustafa Kemal a year to find his feet. In the autobiographical interview which he gave in 1922, Atatürk said: 'During my

first year, I fell into naive youthful reveries. I neglected my lessons. The
year passed by in a flash. It was only when classes ended that I got stuck
into my textbooks.'[30]

Gradually, youthful reveries gave way to an intense power of concentration on the task in hand. But there was a price to pay. Years later,
when his secretary Hasan Rıza Soyak urged him to cut down his drinking, Atatürk replied:

> I've got to drink: my mind keeps on working hard and fast to the point of
> suffering. I have to slow it down and rest it at times. When I was at the War
> College and then at the Staff College, my mates in the dormitory usually had
> to wake me up in the morning. At night my mind would get fixed on a
> problem, and, as I thought about it, I was unable to sleep. I would spend the
> whole night tossing and turning in my bed, until finally I dozed off exhausted
> just before dawn. Then, naturally, I couldn't hear the sound of reveille. It's the
> same now. When I don't drink, I can't sleep, and the distress stupefies me.[31]

Hard work and hard thinking started in Mustafa Kemal's second year
in the War College; hard drinking developed gradually. Drinking was
convivial, it oiled conversation outside the walls of the college. Mustafa
Kemal's schoolmates from Manastır and fellow-countrymen from
Salonica provided him with a ready-made circle of friends. They
included Ali Fethi (Okyar), Kâzım (Özalp), and his closest friend and
distant relative Nuri (Conker), the last two being a year his junior. But
Mustafa Kemal also made new friends. The most important was a tall,
good-looking cadet, Ali Fuat (Cebesoy), who gave him an entry to the
highest ranks of the Ottoman military establishment.

Ali Fuat was the grandson of a famous soldier – Marshal Mehmet Ali
Paşa who was killed in action in command of the Danube army in the
war with Russia in 1877–8. Ali Fuat's father, İsmail Fazıl Paşa, was
employed in the general staff in Istanbul. When he first met Mustafa
Kemal, Ali Fuat declared proudly that all the men in his family were soldiers.[32] The family was prominent enough to be concerned in politics
and to be able to afford a measure of dissidence from official policies.
Sultan Abdülhamit preferred to conciliate and manipulate his potential
enemies, particularly when they were persons of rank. As a result of his
independent views, İsmail Fazıl's promotion had been delayed, and he
was given an uncomfortable posting in the eastern Anatolian town of
Erzincan as chief of staff of the 4th Army, which was guarding the
Caucasian frontier with Russia. But a brief unauthorized visit by his
wife to Paris, where she threatened to join Ottoman political refugees,
sufficed to secure İsmail Fazıl's promotion from Colonel to General,
and his transfer to the general staff in Istanbul.

Ali Fuat thus came from a privileged background. He had started his education not in a tough military school, but in the French Salesian college of St Joseph in Moda, at that time a charming suburb of European villas and gardens on the Asian shore, facing old Istanbul across the harbour. His family lived in a seaside mansion (*yalı*) first at Salacak and then at Kuzguncuk, suburbs situated also on the Asian shore of the Bosphorus, where Mustafa Kemal was soon invited, and where he heard affairs of state discussed in his presence by senior officers.

According to Ali Fuat, it was during an excursion with him to Büyükada (which Europeans knew as Prinkipo), the largest of the Princes Islands, where wealthy Istanbul residents had summer houses, that Mustafa Kemal had his first taste of *rakı*, the anis-flavoured spirit which Greeks produced to the delight of the Turks. Mustafa Kemal was then in his third and final year in the War College, and had already developed a fondness for beer. Having polished off a bottle of beer, Mustafa Kemal took a sip of *rakı*. 'What a lovely drink this is,' he said, turning to Ali Fuat, 'it makes one want to be a poet.'[33] *Rakı* is notorious for feeding the inspiration and ruining the livers of Turkish thinkers.

During holidays in Salonica, Mustafa Kemal went to cafés in the company of his contemporaries – his school friend Ömer Naci, his family companion Fuat (Bulca) and others. The young men discussed their hopes, eyed girls, and drank *rakı*. On one occasion when they pooled their resources to buy the smallest carafe of *rakı*, they only had 2 piastres left for solid food with which to line their stomachs. It was just enough to buy some chestnuts from a street stall. The budding poet, Ömer Naci, intoned, 'Life, life ... ' Mustafa Kemal completed the verse, 'is but a dry chestnut.'[34] The taste for *rakı* never left Mustafa Kemal, but in later life instead of dry chestnuts he used to pop into his mouth roasted chickpeas, known as *leblebi* in Turkish. Prudent drinkers go for more substantial *meze* (hors d'oeuvre).

Mustafa Kemal's determination to succeed, which became evident in his second year in the War College, drove him to acquire not only professional skill, but also social graces. He dazzled his friend Ali Fuat with his ability to waltz. Dancing, he declared, was an essential accomplishment for a staff officer. True, he was not one yet. Only the top graduates of the War College qualified for entry to the Staff College. But Mustafa Kemal, like Ali Fuat, was intent on doing so.

So too were two other cadets who were to play an important part in Atatürk's life. The first was Mehmet Arif. Arif stood at Mustafa Kemal's side until victory in the Turkish War of Independence. Then their paths parted with tragic consequences for the former. Another ambitious and

promising cadet was Kâzım Karabekir, who was a few months younger
than Mustafa Kemal, and studied in the class below. Kâzım was a family
friend of Ali Fuat and came from a similar background. He had been
born in Istanbul, the son of a general, Mehmet Emin Paşa, and had
passed out first from Kuleli, the top military high school in the capital.

Most of the leaders of the Turkish nationalist resistance movement
after the First World War were thus contemporaries at the Istanbul War
College at the turn of the century: Mustafa Kemal and Ali Fuat, Ali
Fethi in the class above, and Kâzım Karabekir in the class below. Cafer
Tayyar (Eğilmez) who was one year ahead of Mustafa Kemal, and Refet
(Bele) who was two years older, were also destined to become commanders of Turkish nationalist forces. Finally, two of Mustafa Kemal's
close lieutenants, Nuri (Conker) and Mehmet Arif, were also contem-
poraries. All these men were to fight together under the leadership of
Mustafa Kemal, but only one of them, the eternal subaltern Nuri
(Conker) was to stay at the leader's side after victory. A more important
supporter, who was to become Atatürk's successor, İsmet (İnönü) was
two years behind Mustafa Kemal. But he entered the Staff College by a
slightly different route, having passed out of the Artillery School
(*Mühendishane-yi Berrî-yi Hümayun*). It was thus in the classrooms of the
War College and of the Staff College that the war for Turkey's independence was won.

Patriotic talk about the dangers facing the country had been part of
the cadets' lives from their years in military high school. But, as Atatürk
remembered, their political ideas were at first vague:

> Political ideas came to be discussed during the years I spent in the War
> College. We did not at first have a clear perception of how things stood. It
> was the time of Sultan Abdülhamit. We used to read the books of Namık
> Kemal. We were closely followed. Generally, we could read only in the dormi-
> tories, after going to bed. The fact that readers of such patriotic works were
> persecuted, gave us the feeling that there was something rotten in the affairs
> of state. But we could not determine clearly what was wrong.[35]

Ali Fuat gives a more detailed description of the cadets' feelings:

> Sultan Abdülhamit II, in whose honour we had to shout 'Long live our
> Padishah' several times a day, gradually lost lustre in our eyes. We were indig-
> nant at the treatment of young enlightened supporters of freedom in the
> medical school who were sent into exile and whose careers were ruined. One
> day we might meet the same fate. As we heard that the government worked
> badly, that corruption was rife, that civil servants and officers did not receive
> their pay, while secret policemen and courtiers, covered in gold braid,

received not only their pay but purses full of gold, our confidence in the sultan, which was not strong at the best of times, was totally shaken. We saw that delivered into incompetent hands, the army was losing its effectiveness and prestige... But no one dared ask 'Where are we going? Where are you taking the country?' Afraid of the sultan and his secret policemen, people were plunged in abject oriental resignation ... There was no freedom in the country. As young students in the War College, we had read in secret and learnt the importance given to human rights and freedoms in the declarations of the French Revolution.[36]

The passage says it all. It shows the importance of the agitation in the Military Medical College where in 1889 students had formed a secret society which they called the Ottoman Union (*İttihad-ı Osmanî*). That society changed its name to Union and Progress in 1895, and went on to organize the successful coup of 1908. Ali Fuat makes clear also the influence of the French Revolution and its Declaration of Human Rights. For Atatürk, as his French biographer Alexandre Jevakhoff points out, it was to be 'the supreme point of reference' throughout his life.[37] But Ali Fuat's reminiscences show also how talk about freedom was linked in the cadets' minds with the perception that, fearful for his own safety, the sultan was deliberately weakening the armed forces. This sincere, albeit misplaced identification of freedom with military might was to destroy both within a few years of the Young Turks' coup.

In the meantime the example of France, where the revolution had given birth to victorious armies, inspired the revolutionary dreams of Ottoman cadets. Freedom-fighters aspired with a clear conscience to marshals' batons and Napoleonic glory. But while the example of France fired the cadets' imagination, that of Prussia also compelled admiration. Teaching in the War College and the Staff College bore the imprint of the reforms introduced by Baron von der Goltz. His Ottoman assistant, Colonel Esat (Bülkat), who had spent four years training in Germany, was at the time director of education at the War College. As General Esat Paşa, he was to win distinction in the defence of his native city of Yanya (Yanina, now in Greek Epirus) during the Balkan wars, and then as Mustafa Kemal's commanding officer in Gallipoli, where his role has been unjustly neglected. The staff of the War College may have been loyal to the sultan, but they were not prey to the 'abject oriental resignation' which the cadets perceived all round them, disregarding the changes taking place in the oriental world they despised.

Mustafa Kemal combined political agitation with concentration on his military studies. He was fashioning himself into a politically aware and politically ambitious professional soldier. In any case, he saw no contradiction between politics and soldiering. Both served the same purpose – the defence of the state. Mustafa Kemal was classed 27th among more than 700 cadets at the end of the first year. He moved up to 11th place at the end of the second year, and passed out 8th at the end of the final year, when he was commissioned Infantry Lieutenant No. 1474.[38] He was 21 years old and had achieved his immediate objective – admission to the Staff College which provided the essential preparation for a career in the high command.

But individual effort was not sufficient for success in the army and in affairs of state. Mustafa Kemal took care to keep in touch with those of his friends who did not make the Staff College and were posted to units, particularly those who were sent to serve in Macedonia. Macedonia, where European influence was strong, provided the best climate for political action. Mustafa Kemal visited his friends there during his holidays from the Staff College. Gradually, their talk turned to plotting.

Mustafa Kemal worked hard during his three years in the Staff College. At the same time, conspiratorial activity became more serious and more dangerous. Once again, Germany and France provided contradictory models. Some of the instructors had been trained in Germany. One such was Colonel Hasan Rıza who taught a course on the Franco-German war of 1870. 'Friends,' he used to say, 'the force that keeps the German army together is absolute discipline. When you begin your army service, always bear this in mind.'[39]

Another lesson, which Mustafa Kemal was to remember vividly, was given by Lieutenant-Colonel Nuri. It concerned guerrilla warfare, a subject made topical by risings in the Ottoman state. 'It is difficult to wage guerrilla war,' Nuri declared, 'but it is equally difficult to suppress it.' He set the students a task based on a rising on the outskirts of the capital, saying, 'In practical work one must aim at maximum verisimilitude. A rising can come from inside, as well as outside.' It was a daring suggestion, which drew from Mustafa Kemal the question: 'Can such guerrilla war come to pass?' 'It may,' replied Nuri; 'but enough said.'[40]

Ali Fuat who relates the story does not specify a date. But it was in 1903, during Mustafa Kemal's second year in the Staff College, that a rising took place in his native Macedonia. It was engineered by IMRO, and broke out on St Elijah's Day (*Ilinden* in Slav Macedonian), 2 August, subsequently chosen as the national day of the former Yugoslav republic of Macedonia. As previously in Bosnia, the revolt was the product both of nationalist agitation and of agrarian discontent. It led to intercommunal violence between Eastern Orthodox Slav Macedonians and

Muslim Albanians, and its suppression gave a fillip to Macedonian emigration to the United States and Canada. Nevertheless IMRO succeeded in its aim of provoking the intervention of the great powers. On 24 November 1903, Sultan Abdülhamit was forced to accept a programme agreed at Mürzsteg, outside Vienna, by Emperor Francis Joseph and Tsar Nicholas II. It provided for the appointment of an Italian to command the gendarmerie in Macedonia, with officers representing all the great powers to assist him, and with European civil agents to act as advisers to the Ottoman government in Salonica.[41]

While Sultan Abdülhamit II did his best to circumscribe European interference, his authority in Macedonia was weakened. This provided wider opportunities for Ottoman malcontents, while raising the fear of local Muslims that the province, like Bulgaria, Eastern Rumelia and Bosnia-Herzegovina was to be detached from direct Ottoman control, and that they themselves would come to be ruled by their Christian neighbours. Students at the Staff College did not have to be persuaded of the urgency of the task awaiting them.

Mustafa Kemal and his friends decided to produce a handwritten newspaper to explain the shortcomings which they had discovered in the administration and policy of the state. According to Ali Fuat, the first two or three issues of the paper were produced while they were still in the third year of the War College, but more effort was put into the project when they moved to the Staff College. Mustafa Kemal was leader of the group, which included Ömer Naci, his friend from Manastır, and another budding writer, İsmail Hakkı. Mustafa Kemal claims that most of the contents of the paper came from his pen. He goes on:

At the time İsmail Paşa [known as Zülüflü, i.e. the man with side-locks] was inspector of [military] schools. He got wind of our activity and approached the sultan. He put the blame on the director of the War College, Rıza Paşa, saying that the latter was either unaware of the existence of subversive students at the college or tolerated them. Rıza Paşa denied the charge in order to keep his position. One day we were busy on an article for the paper. We met in one of the classrooms where military vets were taught and closed the door, outside which we posted sentries. We were reported to Rıza Paşa who raided the classroom. Our writings were spread on the table right in front of him, but he pretended not to see. Nevertheless, he ordered our arrest for busying ourselves with matters outside our curriculum. As he left the room, he said, 'Loss of leave may be sufficient punishment.' He later decided that we need not be punished at all. It was partly an attempt to cover up the kind of incident for which he had been blamed, but his good will too was undeniable. We carried on our activity until we passed out of the Staff College.[42]

The bark of the sultan's officials was worse than their bite. The military revolutionaries, who profited from the relative mildness of the sultan's autocratic regime, behaved more sternly in later years when their own hold on power was disputed. Their feelings can be gauged from the outburst of Mustafa Kemal's friend Ali Fethi (Okyar) when he heard of the raid on the clandestine journalists in the veterinary science classroom. Fethi pointed in the direction of Abdülhamit's palace at Yıldız, exclaiming: 'That man out there is the author of all this. There will be no respite until the palace comes crashing round his ears. If I had a chance, I'd plant a bomb there.'[43] No bomb was ever planted in Yıldız palace. But on 21 July 1905, the Armenian revolutionary federation, Dashnaktsutiun, tried to kill the sultan with a time bomb, as he was returning from Friday prayers. Abdülhamit escaped, but twenty-six bystanders were killed. Death sentences passed on the plotters were commuted. As for Ali Fethi, he came round in time to a more generous assessment of Abdülhamit, when he acted as the sultan's gaoler in Salonica in 1909.

Mustafa Kemal, Ali Fuat and their friends did not spend their entire time studying and plotting. On days off they went to a German beerhouse, much frequented by foreigners, or to an establishment run by an Anglicized Armenian, known as John Paşa, which combined an English grocery store with a bar and restaurant. It was there that they had their first taste of whisky. On another occasion, when they were spending the evening in an open-air European café at Tepebaşı, which went under the French name of Petits-Champs, they asked the waiter to serve them whisky and soda in lemonade glasses. To their surprise, they were joined at the table by the War College director Ali Rıza Paşa, who introduced them to his companions, Fehim Paşa, known as chief spy of the palace, and another informer, Colonel Gani. The newcomers asked to be served with the same drinks that the young officers had in front of them. Fehim Paşa found the drink much to his taste, and pressing Mustafa Kemal and Ali Fuat to accompany him to a restaurant for dinner and a floor show, asked the waiter for 'more lemonade, only stronger'. Time was getting late, and Ali Rıza Paşa gave the young men a chit to see them safely past the sentries at the Staff College, where they arrived much the worse for drink. When challenged by the officer on duty, Mustafa Kemal and Ali Fuat explained with a straight face that they had spent the evening in the company of the sultan's chief spies. Ali Fuat notes in his account of the incident that Fehim Paşa, who had been promoted general at the age of 25 for his services as an informer, and who looked like a character out of a musical comedy, was lynched by the crowd in Bursa when the Young Turks forced Abdülhamit to reintroduce the constitution in 1908. The comedy of an accommodating and inefficient despotism was to end in tragedy.

Mustafa Kemal's outings took him to establishments run by foreigners, Armenians and, above all, by Greeks – places like Yonyo's by the harbour in Salonica, Stefan's near the Sublime Porte in old Istanbul, or Yani's near the railway station at Sirkeci.[44] In Istanbul, as in Salonica, he rubbed shoulders with non-Muslims in public places. Yet no non-Muslim figured among his friends in his youth or later, with the solitary exception of the Syrian Christian Salih Fansa, whom he met in Aleppo and in whose family house he lodged briefly in Istanbul at the end of the First World War.

Although Mustafa Kemal learnt French and could communicate in that language, he never picked up more than a few words of the non-Turkish languages spoken by Ottoman subjects. When he became president of the republic, he once goaded a Turkish academic of Cretan origin – the Muslims of Crete were Greek-speaking – to sing the jokey Greek song '*Ta koritsia ta kaïmena pou kimounde monacha*' ('Those poor girls who sleep alone').[45] Mustafa Kemal's knowledge of Greek does not seem to have extended much beyond the first line of this popular song. There was nothing unusual in this: the various ethnic communities led separate lives under the roof of the Ottoman state.

In later life Atatürk sought to revisit the scenes of his youthful adventures in Istanbul. But the old cafés and restaurants no longer existed, and the past could not be recaptured. The last disappointment came when Atatürk lay dying in Istanbul in 1938. Visited by his friend Ali Fuat, he remembered how as young cadets in their third year at War College they had ridden to the lodge built for Sultan Abdülaziz at Alemdağ in wooded open country in the hills to the east of the Asian shore of the Bosphorus. They had used the horses of Ali Fuat's father İsmail Fazıl Paşa and were accompanied by his Anatolian batman who served them a picnic lunch, eating most of it himself. Nature always had a strong appeal for Atatürk and the memory of this country idyll on the meadows outside the sultan's lodge survived in his mind as a moment of pure happiness.

Receiving Ali Fuat on his yacht *Savarona*, Atatürk made him promise to accompany him on an expedition to the same spot. Then as his illness progressed, and he saw Ali Fuat for the last time in Dolmabahçe palace, he said: 'Do you know what I've remembered? I mentioned it earlier on board the *Savarona*: the lodge at Alemdağ. I've told the doctors too, and they've agreed. Before returning to Ankara, I want to spend some time there. They're getting the place ready.' Ali Fuat comments: "He nursed a strange feeling. He was convinced that if only he could rest in the sultan's lodge at Alemdağ, he would get well."[46]

In December 1904 Mustafa Kemal completed his course at the Staff College. On the basis of his work over the three years, he was placed fifth among thirteen successful candidates in a class of forty-three. In his last year he was top of the class. Two years earlier, his future rival Enver had also been first in the third year, and second overall. While the thirteen won their cordons as Staff Captains, the remaining thirty had to content themselves with the title of Captain (Distinction). Mustafa Kemal's friend Arif was one of the latter, but he too passed the examination for staff officers a few years later.

On passing out, new staff officers were posted to the provinces for unit training (known by the French term *stage*). Some, including the initially unsuccessful Arif, were later sent for further training in Germany. Mustafa Kemal was counting on an initial posting to one of the two Ottoman armies in the Balkans: the 2nd Army, with headquarters in Edirne (Adrianople), or the 3rd Army, centred on Salonica. Not only would he then be nearer his home town, but, more importantly, he would find himself where the political action was. Enver had succeeded in winning a posting to the 3rd Army, despite having been briefly arrested and interrogated at Yıldız palace on suspicion of plotting with the sultan's cousin Abdülmecit (who was to be the last Ottoman caliph after the abolition of the sultanate).[47] Mustafa Kemal was not so lucky, and his failure to receive a posting in Macedonia or Thrace put him at an initial disadvantage among revolutionary officers. This had crucial, but mixed, consequences for his own career and the future of the Ottoman state. When the Young Turks' coup came in 1908, he was not among the leading group of military revolutionaries. But when that first group failed and destroyed itself and the Ottoman state, Mustafa Kemal and his friends had their chance to prove their worth, and took it.

As far as the authorities were concerned, Mustafa Kemal's case was more serious than Enver's. Mustafa Kemal later gave this account of the incident which changed the course of his life:

After we had passed out of the [Staff] College with the rank of Captain, we rented a flat in a friend's name in order to deal better with our [political] work during our time in Istanbul. We held our meetings there from time to time. But all our steps were watched and known. At this point an old friend called Fethi who had been dismissed from the army came to see us. He asked for our help, saying that he was penniless and had nowhere to sleep. We decided to help him and let him stay in our flat. We were to meet him two days later at his request. When I went to the meeting I saw an ADC from the sultan's chancery (*mabeyn*) at his side. A man called İsmail Hakkı [one of the contributors to the clandestine paper] was staying at the flat. They took him away immediately. A day later they arrested us. It transpired that Fethi was a secret agent for [Zülüflü] İsmail Paşa. For a time I was kept in solitary confinement. They then took me to the sultan's chancery and interrogated me. İsmail Paşa, the chief clerk and a bearded man [Mehmet Paşa] were there. We realized that we were accused of publishing a paper, running a [secret] organization, etc. Our comrades had already confessed. We were kept in prison for a few months and then freed. A few days later, all the [newly promoted] staff officers were called to the General Staff. We were to be sent in equal numbers to Edirne and Salonica, i.e. to the 2nd and 3rd Armies, as they then were. They told us that lots would be drawn, unless we agreed among ourselves where we wanted to go. I made a sign to my comrades; we talked for a bit, and we then sorted out those who were to go to the 2nd and 3rd Armies. But they interpreted our behaviour as proof of conspiracy. They exiled me to Syria for training with a cavalry unit.[48]

Ali Fuat, who was detained a day before Mustafa Kemal, provides a few more details. The arrested officers were kept in officers' cells in the War College and managed to communicate with each other. Ali Fuat was detained for twenty days; Mustafa Kemal, whom he calls the leader of the group, for a week or ten days longer. The commander of land forces (*Serasker*) Rıza Paşa did his best to secure for the young officers a posting in the Balkans, but the palace would not hear of it. Nevertheless, the young conspirators got off lightly. They were neither cashiered nor sent to dreaded exile in the oasis of Fezzan in southern Tripolitania, as they had feared. Moreover, Ali Fuat's father, İsmail Fazıl Paşa, promised to use his influence in the General Staff to secure their transfer from Syria to the Balkans as soon as possible. In the meantime, he knew the commander of the 5th Army in Damascus, Marshal Hakkı Paşa, as an honest and conscientious officer. Military revolutionaries could thus rely on the network of kinship, friendship and patronage in the armed forces. As for the palace, bluster and threats were followed by attempts at conciliation. The revolutionaries dramatized their clandestine work. But the palace knew what was going on, and hoped first to frighten and then to win over its opponents.

The authorities and the conspirators realized that the external environment was changing. The defeat of Russia by Japan in the war of 1904–5, which was applauded by educated Muslim Turks as a victory of Asia over their European enemy, was followed by the first Russian Revolution of 1905. That in turn encouraged ferment in Persia, where constitutional government was given a brief first try in 1906. Uncensored foreign newspapers were easy to obtain in Istanbul. Mustafa Kemal is said to have read the French newspapers *Le Matin* and

Le Petit Parisien.[49] In Turkey, then as now, foreign examples came readily to the minds of proponents of change.

Mustafa Kemal's and Ali Fuat's appointment to the 5th Army was promulgated on 11 January 1905. The two friends spent their last day in Istanbul together, drinking whisky in Ali Fuat's family mansion in Kuzguncuk on the Bosphorus. They then boarded an Austrian liner bound for Beirut.

3

Prelude to a Military Coup

———————◆———————

MUSTAFA KEMAL WENT to Syria in the company of Ali Fuat and Müfit (Özdeş), another newly promoted Staff Captain, who was to be one of his close companions in later life. The Austrian ship on which they were travelling called at İzmir on its way to Beirut. Beirut, like Salonica and, of course, Istanbul, was a lively, cosmopolitan city, with good hotels and entertainment, including a German beerhouse, which Ottoman officers frequented. It was the port for Damascus and for the 'privileged' – that is, autonomous – district of Mount Lebanon, which was ruled by a Christian governor appointed by the sultan, and policed by a force of gendarmes commanded largely by Christian officers. These arrangements under the *Règlement Organique* of 1861, imposed after French troops had landed to defend Christian Maronites (whose church was in communion with Rome) from the onslaught of Druze mountain tribesmen (whose religion was an idiosyncratic offshoot of Islam), worked so well that 'Mount Lebanon was widely recognized to be "the best governed, the most prosperous, peaceful and contented country in the Near East"'.[1] In 1905, the governor of Mount Lebanon was Muzaffer Paşa, a Catholic soldier of Polish origin. He was a well-meaning administrator, but unable to enforce his will in the face of local Christian opposition.[2]

'If you are posted here, you will not miss Istanbul,' Mustafa Kemal and his companions were told by an Ottoman officer who had preceded them to Beirut. But first they had to report to Marshal Hakkı Paşa, the commander of the 5th Army in Damascus, where they travelled by rail. Ali Fuat knew the Marshal's son Haydar (who trained in the princes' section of the War College) and was invited to stay in the commander's

mansiòn. For his cavalry training he was then given a privileged posting
to the mounted guard of Muzaffer Paşa, at the latter's picturesque residence at Beytüddin (Beyt Din) in the hills south of Beirut.

Mustafa Kemal was not so lucky. He was put up by young officers of
the 5th Army and was then posted to the 30th cavalry regiment, which
made sallies from its base in Damascus to chase Druze tribesmen in the
broken country of the Hawran to the south.[3] According to Atatürk's
adopted daughter Afet, the commander of the 30th regiment wanted to
prevent Mustafa Kemal from taking part in the punitive expedition
against the Druzes. His friend Müfit (Özdeş), who was attached to the
29th cavalry regiment, was also to have been left behind. The two
young staff captains then appealed to Marshal Hakkı Paşa for permission to go. When this was refused, they went nevertheless, and were
eventually admitted into the force after they had promised to keep quiet
about its behaviour. The reason for the secrecy was, apparently, that the
punitive expedition was preparing to enrich itself at the expense of villagers in the Hawran. Afet reports that, years later, Atatürk told Müfit
Özdeş:

> Do you remember, Müfit, when we decided to join the [expeditionary] force
> in Damascus, a lieutenant in the cavalry approached me and said, 'I have the
> greatest respect for you, sir. I advise you not to go on the expedition.' 'Why?'
> I asked him. 'Because your life may be in danger.' 'Why?' I asked him again.
> 'They'll kill you. You can't know or even imagine it, sir. Today the whole army
> in Syria shares a common interest. You look like someone likely to obstruct
> that interest. They won't put up with it. Your life is at stake.'[4]

Afet adds that when an attempt was made to share out the spoils of
the expedition among the officers, Mustafa Kemal sent Müfit to
Damascus with a full account of the takings. Earlier, when Müfit told
him that he had been offered some of the gold taken from the Druzes,
Mustafa Kemal asked him: 'Do you want to be today's man or tomorrow's?' 'Tomorrow's, of course,' replied Müfit. 'Then you can't take the
gold. I too haven't taken it, nor can I ever.' In a similar vein, Ali Fuat,
who was in Beirut at the time, quotes Mustafa Kemal as saying: 'The
idiots thought they could buy me, but they got nowhere.'[5]

The story portrays Mustafa Kemal as a knight in shining armour bat-
tling against the corrupt and ramshackle empire of Abdülhamit. Other
stories follow the same theme. Again according to Afet, Mustafa Kemal
showed kindness and understanding to local people and thus prevented
clashes with them. When the Ottoman cavalry were camped outside
Kuneytıra (today the ruined town of Kuneitra on the Syrian side of the
Golan heights), Circassians who had been settled in the district gath-

ered to raid the Ottoman headquarters. But, approached by Mustafa Kemal, they desisted, saying: 'We'll do whatever you say. But we shall not carry out the orders of officials who oppress us in the name of the state.' Later, when the cavalry moved into the Hawran, and faced Druze tribesmen, Mustafa Kemal is said to have saved the situation, telling his brother officers, 'I know them; they are honourable men, and they don't shoot at those who don't fire at them first.' When his advice was taken and the Druzes withdrew peacefully, Mustafa Kemal prevented the colonel who commanded the Ottoman gendarmerie in Damascus from reporting to the palace in Istanbul that the Druzes had been defeated. 'I'll have no part in a fraud,' Mustafa Kemal is reported to have said. 'No one has been defeated. If truth be told, they've won.' 'You're still ignorant,' the commander protested, 'you do not understand the sultan.' 'I may be ignorant,' replied Mustafa Kemal, 'but the sovereign must not be kept in ignorance, and must be made to understand what kind of people you are.'[6]

The facts behind the morality tale are more complicated. The pay of Ottoman officers was inadequate. It was also usually in arrears. The commander of the 30th regiment, Lütfi, was apparently so poor that when he took a walk with Mustafa Kemal in Damascus, he had to wear ordinary shoes, instead of boots, with his jodhpurs. He excused himself, saying, 'Sorry, I've no other trousers.' Lütfi and his comrades may well have been tempted to supplement their meagre official income with part of the proceeds of punitive expeditions and by other unorthodox means. But they did not grow fat at the expense of local people. The Druzes and, to a lesser extent, the Circassians were at loggerheads with their neighbours. Many Druze had migrated to the Hawran from the Lebanese mountains when they lost their grip on the Maronites, from whom they used to collect feudal dues. Afet says that the punitive expedition was mounted to retrieve 'usurped property'. That property belonged either to the local peasantry, who would then have petitioned the Ottoman authorities in Damascus for protection, or to the state itself, which was at the time building the Hejaz railway against considerable local opposition.

There was also the perennial problem of collecting taxes. Reporting fictitious successes to the government was a well-established practice which did not end with the dissolution of the empire. Local officials did not need the advice of a young staff captain to avoid clashes. Abdülhamit and his ministers always preferred peaceful accommodation. Revolutionary officers proved more brutal. When they took over in 1908, the new commander in Damascus, Sami Paşa, proclaimed martial law, and then summoned the Druze leaders to Damascus where he had many of them executed. Druze resistance continued nevertheless until 1911.[7] After the First World War, it revived, this time in the shape of a full-scale revolt against the French authorities which replaced the Ottomans in Syria.

Such corruption as existed in the Ottoman administration was well understood by local society, whose practices were even more corrupt. Nevertheless, revolutionary officers were sincere in their hatred of official corruption: what they wanted was power, not money. This was the spirit that animated Mustafa Kemal. Mustafa Kemal took his training seriously. But he was eager to resume political plotting. However, the local population was perfectly content with the regime, and although officers of the Ottoman 5th Army nursed grievances, they were primarily concerned with making ends meet. Damascus, like Beirut, enjoyed the fruits of peace and of the administrative improvements introduced by Sultan Abdülhamit. By the time Mustafa Kemal arrived, the Hejaz railway had been pushed some 400 miles south of Damascus, and a branch line had been built linking the Hawran with the port of Haifa (now in Israel).[8] Italian workmen were employed in railway construction, and, according to one story, young Mustafa Kemal, bored by the monotonous oriental life of Damascus, changed into workman's clothes and joined the Italians drinking at night to the sound of mandolins.[9]

More to the point, the newly constructed railways made it easier for Mustafa Kemal and other Ottoman officers and officials to move around Syria and Palestine. Abdülhamit employed Syrian notables in his court and Arab Syrian soldiers in his guard. As a result, 'local notables defended the policies emanating from Istanbul ... Even the autocracy and caprice of the sultan could be ignored' as long as their position was not threatened.[10] For all the efforts of Lebanese Christian intellectuals and a handful of disgruntled Muslim officials, Arab nationalism was in its infancy. Most Arabs in Syria and elsewhere in the Ottoman state were loyal to their Muslim sultan. However, Mustafa Kemal and his comrades did find a few kindred spirits. His regimental commander Lütfi was much given to remarking, 'Things can't go on like this.'

One day Lütfi took Mustafa Kemal and Müfit (Özdeş) to the souk in Damascus, to meet a political exile. The exile was a Turk called Mustafa (Cantekin, later a member of parliament under the republic). He had been caught plotting in the Istanbul Medical School, the birthplace of the Committee of Union and Progress. Expelled, briefly imprisoned, and then exiled to Damascus, Mustafa ended up as a shopkeeper. But he still tried to serve the cause by propagating the ideal of constitutional rule. For this purpose he may already have set up a clandestine society, called *Vatan* (The Fatherland), before Mustafa Kemal's visit.[11] But it made no impact until Mustafa Kemal arrived on the scene and took over plain Mustafa's embryonic group, which was renamed 'Fatherland and Freedom' (*Vatan ve Hürriyet*), two terms closely associated with the patriotic poetry of Namık Kemal, their main source of inspiration. The launch or relaunch of the organization occurred in the summer or autumn of 1905,[12] several months after Mustafa Kemal's arrival in Syria. A third founding member was a certain Dr Mahmut, no doubt a friend of the former medical student Mustafa. They enrolled a few Ottoman officers in Damascus, but not the grumbling Lütfi, who excused himself saying, 'I'm a married man with children. I share your opinions, but don't expect me to act.' Ali Fuat established a Beirut branch, but came to the conclusion that 'in that cosmopolitan environment it had almost no chance of success.'

Mustafa Kemal's own account of his first stay in Syria is brief:

> I was exiled to Syria. I was posted for training with a military unit in Damascus. There were at that time problems with Druzes, and troops were sent against them. I went with them and stayed there for four months. We formed a society called 'Freedom'. To extend it, I travelled to Beirut, Jaffa and Jerusalem under cover of training with different units. Organizations were established in these places. I stayed longest in Jaffa, and the organization was strongest there. But it looked impossible to organize in Syria the way we wanted. I was convinced that things would move more quickly in Macedonia and I tried to devise ways and means of getting there.[13]

New staff officers had to undergo unit training with three services: infantry, cavalry and artillery. Having completed his service with the cavalry in Damascus, Mustafa Kemal was posted to the marksmen's battalion (*nişancı taburu*, modelled after the French *corps de francs-tireurs*) in Jaffa for his infantry training. He stopped over in Beirut and spoke to Ali Fuat of his plans to visit Macedonia. The difficulty was that Mustafa Kemal's letter of appointment was marked 'To be posted where there are no facilities for travel to his home town'. The old boy network came to his aid.

A leave permit valid for travel to İzmir was procured with the help of Marshal Hakkı Paşa's son Haydar.[14] Mustafa Kemal had earlier written to Şükrü Paşa, inspector of artillery in Salonica, to inform him of his proposed trip to his home town, and to solicit his help. The Paşa, who was later to win fame as defender of Edirne in the Balkan war, was, as Ali Fuat warned Mustafa Kemal, 'a famous and patriotic soldier, but loyal to the sultan', and, as such, probably disinclined to aid enemies of the regime. However, Mustafa Kemal relied on the fact that there were family connections, probably through his classmate at the Staff College, Kemal from Ohri (now Ohrid in former Yugoslav Macedonia), who soon afterwards married Şükrü Paşa's daughter. We do not know how much Mustafa Kemal told Şükrü Paşa in his letter. But he claimed that the pasha let him know through intermediaries that he would do his best, probably to cover up the unauthorized leave. That was good enough.

Mustafa Kemal arranged for his comrades in Jaffa to inform him immediately if his absence were noticed. He then took ship to Alexandria and on to Piraeus. From there he sent a telegram to one of his friends in Salonica, Staff Captain Tevfik, who had passed out third, ahead of Mustafa Kemal, in the final examinations. A native of Salonica, Tevfik was to die there at the outset of his career. The telegram, couched in non-idiomatic French, consisted of the three words *Parti vapeur grec* ('Left by Greek steamship'). Tevfik understood and, meeting Mustafa Kemal at the harbour, got him past the customs and military police with the help of a comrade, Captain Cemil from Süleymaniye, who was serving as assistant to the central commandant of the city, and who thus had access to official correspondence. Cemil (Uybadın) was a faithful friend, and after the proclamation of the republic, Mustafa Kemal made him minister of the interior.

Although Mustafa Kemal says that he was travelling incognito, he went immediately to stay in his family house. Surprised at her son's unexpected arrival, Zübeyde asked him whether he had acted against the wishes of 'our Lord the Sultan'. Legend has it that Mustafa Kemal replied: 'Don't worry. I had to come here. As for our Lord the Sultan, I'll show you not now, but soon, what sort of man he is.'[15] Afet, who tells the story, reports also that Şükrü Paşa tried to avoid receiving Mustafa Kemal. When he finally saw him, he told the young plotter: 'There's nothing I can do. But I'll take a lenient view of your actions. Only, please, don't ruin me.'[16] It was the best that Mustafa Kemal could have expected, and he is unlikely to have felt the deep disappointment which his biographers attribute to him at the end of the interview.

Having assured himself of Şükrü Paşa's collusion, Mustafa Kemal put on his uniform and went to see Staff Colonel Hasan, who, as examiner at the military preparatory school, had advised him to pursue his studies at Manastır. After explaining his patriotic purpose, he assured Colonel Hasan that he would not compromise him. The colonel thereupon went to see his friend İskender Paşa, head of the army medical service in Salonica, and arranged a medical check-up for Mustafa Kemal at the military hospital. This allowed İskender Paşa to issue a medical certificate saying that Staff Captain Mustafa Kemal needed four months' change of air in Salonica. The form did not specify Mustafa

Kemal's post, thus concealing the fact that he was away without leave from his regiment.

With the medical certificate in his pocket, Mustafa Kemal set about recruiting members for the Salonica branch of his Fatherland and Freedom Society. According to Afet, the first recruits were his old school friend, the fiery orator Ömer Naci, the latter's friend, artillery officer Hüsrev Sami (Kızıldoğan), and three teachers in military schools: Hakkı Baha (Pars), teacher at the military preparatory school, and two of his friends, Tahir from Bursa, director of the same school, and *Hoca* (Teacher) Mahir, director of the military teacher-training school. The branch was formally founded at a meeting in Hakkı Baha's house. Hakkı Baha, Afet tells us, was newly married, and was wearing Japanese pyjamas when he let in the other conspirators. This, however, did not detract from the solemnity of the ceremony, where the conspirators took a revolutionary oath with their hand placed on Hüsrev Sami's pistol. According to Hüsrev Sami, Mustafa Kemal assured the assembled company that their only object was to save their 'ill-starred country'. He went on: 'Today they want to cut off Macedonia and all the Balkans from the community of the fatherland. Our country has partially and effectively come under foreign influence and rule. The sultan is a hateful figure, addicted to pleasure and autocracy, and capable of the lowest actions. The nation is being ruined by tyranny and despotism. Where there is no freedom, there is death and destruction,' etc.[17] Clearly, the threat to Ottoman rule in Macedonia was the main spur to action. The meeting took place in the first months of 1906. In December 1905, Sultan Abdülhamit had been forced by a naval demonstration of the great powers in the Aegean to agree to an international commission to supervise the finances of Macedonia.[18] At the end of the ceremony, Mustafa Kemal turned to the artilleryman Hüsrev, saying, 'Take your weapon. It is now holy. Guard it well. One day you'll give it to me.' Afet adds: 'This came to pass.'[19]

Inevitably, Mustafa Kemal's unauthorized presence came to the notice of the sultan's agents in Salonica, and enquiries were made both there and in Jaffa. If found in Salonica, he was to be arrested. Informed by Captain Cemil that the execution of the order could not be delayed by longer than a couple of days, Mustafa Kemal returned to Jaffa, having spent in Salonica the four months covered by his medical certificate.

The Salonica branch of the Fatherland and Freedom Society languished after Mustafa Kemal's departure, and when a few months later the Ottoman Freedom Society (which was to become the internal centre of the Union and Progress Society) was established in the same city under a different leadership, its members transferred to the new organization. Moreover, although it had a primacy of sorts in Salonica, Fatherland and Freedom was not the first Muslim clandestine group in the Ottoman state. A few years earlier, there was already a branch of the Paris-based Union and Progress Society in Şkodra (now Shkodër in northern Albania) and there were individual Unionists (*İttihatçı*, as they came to be called in Turkish) elsewhere.[20] But Mustafa Kemal showed that he was a leader with a personal following. True, he was soon over-shadowed by other military revolutionaries, and even in his native city his role in the revolution was not well known. A reader published in 1912 for a private school in Salonica does not even mention his name in this account of his first revolutionary initiative:

> A staff officer who transferred from the 5th Army [in Damascus] to the 3rd Army [in Salonica], had met in Damascus a man who had been expelled from the Medical School and was engaged in trade, and they decided to form a Freedom Society. They tried to set up a branch in Salonica. They conferred with young comrades of their class and with high-placed persons who now hold positions of honour, and they formed the [branch of their] society. However people doubted that the path chosen would lead to success. As a result, the society was unable to expand and remained in an embryonic state.[21]

There is no doubt that Mustafa Kemal's forced departure from Salonica delayed his political career. But it kept him in reserve for a more import-ant role.

When the enquiry concerning Mustafa Kemal's whereabouts reached the headquarters of the 5th Army in Damascus, Marshal Hakkı Paşa's son Haydar immediately informed Ali Fuat in Beirut. In his turn, Ali Fuat contacted Major Ahmet, the commander of the marksmen's batta-lion in Jaffa, who reported that Mustafa Kemal was on duty with units patrolling the Egyptian frontier from their base in Beersheba. Ottoman troops had been deployed in the area as tension had arisen with British authorities in Cairo, which were trying to prevent the building of a branch line of the Hejaz railway to the Ottoman fort at Aqaba (now Jordan's only port, squeezed between Israel and Saudi Arabia). The conflict was resolved in October 1906.[22] The construction of the line was stopped, thus easing British fears for the security of Egypt, and the frontier between Ottoman Palestine and Egyptian Sinai was marked out, leaving Aqaba in Ottoman hands. The line drawn in 1906 forms today the frontier between Israel and Egypt.

Mustafa Kemal did in fact go to the frontier after returning to Jaffa. A little later he visited his friend Ali Fuat in Beirut, where they appear in a group photograph dated 15 July 1906. It shows nine Ottoman officers, among them Mustafa Kemal sporting a Prussian military moustache. On 14 October 1906, Mustafa Kemal went for his artillery training to Damascus, where Marshal Hakkı Paşa reproved him gently, saying: 'My boy, you could have informed me in advance [of your clandestine trip to Salonica]. You put me in a spot.' On 20 June 1907, Mustafa Kemal completed his service with the artillery, and was promoted Adjutant-Major (*Kolağası*). His next posting, the final stage of his initial practical training, was to the staff of the 5th Army in Damascus. His better-connected friend Ali Fuat had in the meantime gone to Salonica for his training in artillery and then in staff work.

Mustafa Kemal secured a posting to the 3rd Army in Salonica on 16 September 1907. It seems that the move was helped by his former examiner Staff Colonel Hasan, who had asked for his protégé's transfer.[23] Mustafa Kemal's own account is, as usual, brief: 'I stayed in Syria two and a half or three years in all. During this time, everything [i.e. his previous plotting] was forgotten. I applied officially for transfer to Macedonia, and finally achieved my objective.'[24] Ali Fuat says that Marshal Hakkı Paşa helped Mustafa Kemal obtain the transfer. However that may be, the pasha was about to be dismissed (or may already have been dismissed) for his opposition to the policy of the palace in the Aqaba dispute.[25] This may help explain his relaxed treatment of radical officers: he was himself unhappy with the administration they were trying to undermine.

In Syria and Palestine, Mustafa Kemal found himself for the first time in a non-Turkish Muslim environment. Ottoman officers and officials who were not of Arab origin tended to keep to themselves. The difference in language and, to a large extent, in customs set them apart from the local population. Whether they were of Turkish, Albanian, Bosnian or Caucasian origin, they were seen and began to see themselves as Turks. They had been educated in Ottoman Turkish and used a simpler form of Turkish among themselves. Ali Fuat, who is the chief source of information on Mustafa Kemal's first service in Syria, claims that it was there that Atatürk showed the first signs of conversion to Turkish nationalism. Meeting Ali Fuat and other comrades in Beirut on his way to Damascus in 1906, so Ali Fuat reports, Mustafa Kemal was already maintaining that the problem that faced them was how to produce a Turkish state out of a crumbling empire.[26] On another occasion Mustafa Kemal told Ali Fuat that he had had a furious argument in Jaffa with an officer who was, like him, of Macedonian origin. This fellow-Macedonian had remonstrated with a Turkish sergeant for dealing harshly with Arab recruits who did not understand his commands. The Arabs, the officer said, were of a noble race, which had given birth to the Prophet, and the Turkish sergeant was not worthy of washing their feet. 'Shut up, Captain!' Mustafa Kemal shouted. 'The Arab race to which these privates belong may well be noble in many respects. But it is an undeniable truth that the race to which you, I, Müfit (Özdeş) here, and the sergeant belong, is also great and noble.' Mustafa Kemal would, of course, have stood up for Turks if anyone tried to run them down. But, like other revolutionary officers, he must have believed that the Arabs could be kept within the Ottoman state. Otherwise, he and his fellow-revolutionaries would not have volunteered for service in Tripolitania, when that Arabic-speaking Ottoman province was invaded by the Italians in 1911. The hope that the Arabs would remain in the Ottoman fold persisted in the minds of Turkish revolutionaries until defeat in the First World War finally laid it to rest.

Mustafa Kemal arrived in Salonica, this time on an official posting, at the end of September or the beginning of October 1907. He travelled by way of İzmir,[27] where he made friends with Dr Tevfik Rüştü (Aras), a native of Çanakkale, who had studied medicine in the French medical school in Beirut, and who was nurturing political ambitions. Tevfik Rüştü became an ally and Mustafa Kemal rewarded him many years later with the post of foreign minister in the Turkish republic.[28]

In Macedonia, revolution was in the air. Slav Macedonian, Bulgarian, Greek and Serbian nationalists had long been active in the area, disrupting the peace with their competing armed struggles. Now Ottoman Muslim revolutionaries joined in, copying the ruthless methods of their Christian neighbours. Freemasonry, with its questioning liberal spirit, its belief in progress and its secret rituals, was another source of inspiration. Mustafa Kemal appears to have joined the masons,[29] probably at this stage, although, according to one account, the initiation ceremony took place in Istanbul.[30] It would have been a sensible move by an ambitious military conspirator. During Mustafa Kemal's absence in Syria and Palestine, revolutionary officers had joined forces with civilian members of the Society of Union and Progress and established contact with its headquarters in Paris. The upper echelons of the Young Turks were thus all in place by the time Mustafa Kemal reached Salonica. He found himself excluded from the leadership of the conspiracy.

The 'internal centre' of the Society of Union and Progress (better known as the Committee, hence its English acronym CUP) was first established as the Ottoman Freedom Society (*Osmanlı Hürriyet Cemiyeti*) in September 1906.[31] Serving officers were involved from the start, and the revolutionary cause was promoted by subversion in the armed forces. But disaffected members of the civil service were equally prominent. Leadership of the Young Turks – as the CUP became known in the West (and later also in Turkey, where the term *Jöntürkler* from the French *Jeunes Turcs* is often used) – was collegiate and remained so to the end of their existence. But some leaders were more prominent than others.

The most powerful personality among the founders of the Ottoman Freedom Society in Salonica was a postal official, Talât. He was born in 1874 in Edirne into a family of junior civil servants. His father, an examining magistrate, came from a village in the mountainous south-eastern corner of present-day Bulgaria. Because of his peasant origin, his powerful build and his dark complexion, Talât was sometimes called a gypsy by his opponents. His manner was bluff, not to say brutal. He had to leave his civil preparatory school without a certificate after assaulting one of his teachers. He was then found a job as a postal clerk, and supplemented his salary by teaching Turkish in the Alliance Israélite school which served the large Jewish community of Edirne. At the age of 21, he was arrested along with two other radicals. Questioned about a letter in his handwriting which said, 'Things are going well. I'll soon reach my goal', Talât declared that he was referring to his love affair with the daughter of the Jewish headmaster. Although the girl supported his claim, Talât was imprisoned for two years, on a charge of tampering with official telegrams. After being pardoned, he was exiled to Salonica, where he was once again put on the payroll of the post office.[32]

Another prominent member was Mithat Şükrü (Bleda), a native of Salonica, who had been in touch with Young Turk émigrés after going to Switzerland to study mathematics. Mithat Şükrü had made use of the pardon granted by the sultan to repentant revolutionaries, and returned to his native city where he was sought out by Talât.[33] A third important member of the group was Rahmi (Evrenos), the son of a local landowning family. Probably the oldest member, who joined a little later, was a bearded 54-year-old lawyer, Manyasizade Refik. He had defended Mithat Paşa, the father of the Ottoman constitution, when the latter was accused of the murder of Sultan Abdülaziz. Refik's presence was both a link with the beginnings of the constitutional movement and a symbol of the revolutionaries' aim to force the sultan to reinstate the constitution. Once the Young Turks had succeeded in that aim in 1908, Manyasizade Refik became minister of justice. He died in the same year.[34]

The idea of forming the Ottoman Freedom Society was first agreed when Talât, Mithat Şükrü and Rahmi met at Yonyo's – the Greek café near the pier which Mustafa Kemal had earlier frequented. A second meeting followed in a beer garden, with Mustafa Kemal's own friends and nominal members of the Salonica branch of his Fatherland and Freedom Society taking part. Over glasses of the local 'Olympus' beer, the young revolutionaries worked out the rulebook of their clandestine society and the ritual of admission. This took place in Mithat Şükrü's house, where recruits were led blindfolded by the 'guide' who introduced them to the society. Apart from the guide, they were to know only two other members. Once in the house, the recruits would have their blindfold removed, and they would then take an oath of loyalty, with one hand resting on a Koran and another holding a pistol, which was to be used against them if they betrayed their oath.[35] According to another account, candidates for admission wore red cloaks, presumably to signify their readiness to shed their blood for the cause, while the rest of the company had their faces covered with a black veil.[36] Before the blindfolds were removed, a sepulchral voice gave vent to the high patriotic ideals of the society.[37] As the number of recruits increased, the procession of blindfolded men in strange cloaks arriving at night at Mithat Şükrü's house began to alarm the neighbours, not to mention his servant İbrahim, who asked Mithat Şükrü's newlywed wife: 'For God's sake, what kind of man is the master? What's going on here?'[38] The revolutionaries then moved to a quieter spot in the city.

This revolutionary pantomime came to the notice of the sultan's agents, but power was slipping from their hands, as the local authorities realized which way the wind was blowing. Talât had contacts in high places. According to Abdülhamit's usual practice, he was paid a stipend of 3 gold liras a month as an exile. Irked by his subsidized idleness, he applied to the governor of Salonica, Rıza Paşa, for active employment, and was appointed postal courier, in which capacity he maintained contact with revolutionaries outside the city. When the government in Istanbul decided to dismiss Talât from the postal service and exile him from Salonica, the latter was informed by a fellow-conspirator employed in the office of the grand vizier, Ferit Paşa, an Albanian whose family came from Avlonya (now Vlorë). Talât then went to the senior Ottoman administrator in Salonica, Hüseyin Hilmi Paşa, the Inspector-General for Macedonia, and said: 'I can't object to the dismissal, since the government has the right to employ or dismiss its servants. But if an attempt is made to exile me, the consequences will not be good for either of us.' The Ottoman chronicler, Mahmud Kemal İnal, who reports the conversation, adds: 'Hüseyin Hilmi Paşa was not totally ignorant of the existence of a secret force in Salonica. So he reassured Talât and promised to prevent his deportation. He was as good as his word.'[39]

The revolutionaries set little store by discretion. Mustafa Kemal's school friend Ömer Naci started a polemic, incongruously in a local chidren's paper (*Çocuk Bahçesi*, 'The Children's Garden'), where he declared, 'The glory and honour bequeathed by five centuries of history are now being buried for ever.' The artilleryman Hüsrev Sami lent his pen in support of the jeremiad. The articles caused great excitement in Salonica, and the palace sent cipher telegrams to the Inspector-General demanding that the two men be arrested. Talât was immediately informed, and persuaded them to go to Paris.[40] They left in March 1907, while Mustafa Kemal was still in Syria.

Apart from putting the two fiery revolutionaries out of harm's way, the trip had another purpose. The Ottoman Freedom Society in Salonica had no publication of its own. But publications were sent into the country by Ottoman political émigrés. The conspirators in Salonica had to decide whether to start their own publication or make common cause with the émigrés. The decision was complicated by the fact that the émigrés had split into two antagonistic groups at the Congress of Ottoman Liberals held in Paris in 1902.[41] The first was led by Ahmet Rıza, a former education official, who had adopted the philosophy of French positivists, and even used the positivist calendar in his paper *Meşveret* (published both in Turkish and in French under the title of *La Consultation*). Positivism, the philosophy elaborated by Auguste Comte (1798–1857), saw empirical science, including the new science of sociology, as the successor of revealed religion. Religion had its uses, but it had also had its day. The idea appealed to those members of the Ottoman élite who sought a place in the civilized world of the West. Ahmet Rıza was of their number. The positivists' slogan 'Order and Progress' was reflected in his organization's title 'Union and Progress', the word 'union' referring to the ideal of the fraternal coexistence of all the ethnic groups (known in French as *éléments*, a term of which the Ottoman Turkish *anasır* was the exact translation) in the Ottoman state. An earlier opposition organization had used the name of 'Ottoman Union' (*İttihad-ı Osmanî*), and the émigrés believed that the survival of the Ottoman state could be based on 'the union of [all ethnic] elements' (*ittihad-ı anasır*). Ahmet Rıza thought that this union could be brought about within a centralized, unitary state, enjoying parliamentary government under a constitutional monarch. His model was French, adapted to the wishes of Ottoman Muslim intellectuals.

The second group of Ottoman émigrés was formed by Prince Sabahattin, an exiled member of the Ottoman dynasty, who found his inspiration in British practice (as interpreted by the Frenchman Edmond Demolins in his book *À quoi tient la supériorité des Anglo-*

Saxons?). To propagate the virtues and emulate the achievements of the Anglo-Saxons, Prince Sabahattin founded a League for Private Initiative and Decentralization, which had obvious attractions for the non-Muslim minorities in the Ottoman empire.[42]

Ömer Naci and Hüsrev Sami found themselves in agreement with Ahmet Rıza's ideas and decided to join forces with him. Ahmet Rıza responded by sending his close collaborator Dr Nazım, an exile who was then working in a Paris hospital, to reconnoitre in Salonica. Both Ahmet Rıza and Dr Nazım had refused the sultan's pardon and had in consequence been sentenced to death *in absentia* for their revolutionary activities. Unable to travel openly, Dr Nazım had to be smuggled in by the conspirators of the Ottoman Freedom Society. According to Mithat Şükrü, they were in touch with Bulgarian, Serbian and Greek revolutionaries in Salonica. Their best contacts were with the Greeks, who met Dr Nazım in Athens and got him across the frontier into Ottoman Macedonia disguised as a bearded sheikh.

In spite of his disguise, Dr Nazım was recognized in Salonica by a childhood friend, a Jewish doctor called Dr Toledo. As usual, Talât was equal to the situation. He went straight to Dr Toledo's house, produced his pistol, and said: 'You're quite right. Nazım is in Salonica, as you've seen, and he is moving about incognito. No one apart from you has recognized him. If it becomes known that he is here and he comes to some harm, I'll blow your brains out with this pistol.' The argument was persuasive, and Dr Toledo denied on the spot that he had seen Dr Nazım.[43]

After discussions with Dr Nazım, the conspirators of the Ottoman Freedom Society in Salonica decided on 27 September 1907 to merge with Ahmet Rıza's group in Paris and adopt the latter's name of Union and Progress.[44] Their organization spread rapidly, particularly among officers of the 3rd Army in Macedonia and the 2nd Army in Thrace. To extend the network further, Dr Nazım went to İzmir, accompanied by İsmail Canbulat, a 26-year-old lieutenant who was among the founder members of the Ottoman Freedom Society. There they contacted a young landowner, Halil (Menteşe), who had mingled with the revolutionaries in Europe, before making use of the sultan's pardon to return home. Meeting first at Kramer's, the well-appointed European hotel in İzmir, the three conspirators targeted officers serving in the area and made sure that their units could not be used successfully against any military rising in Macedonia.[45]

The Salonica revolutionaries tried also to set up an organization in Istanbul, but there they were less successful. Talât and Manyasizade Refik went secretly to the capital where they met the novelist and journalist Hüseyin Cahit (Yalçın), who was at the same time headmaster of a high school. Hüseyin Cahit refused to become a member, saying that it was impossible to keep a secret in Istanbul. However, if the Salonica organization came out into the open and wanted support in the capital, he promised to organize a demonstration by his students.[46] Muslims in Istanbul did not feel themselves threatened like their kinsmen in Salonica. They also had a bigger share of the benefits of the sultan's government. There were, of course, many palace spies in the capital, but there was also little revolutionary enthusiasm. Unable to make headway among senior officials in the capital, Talât obtained an entry into the circle of Muslim tradesmen in the old city of Istanbul. This class, to which he was close in social origin, was resentful of the dominance of domestic and foreign non-Muslim businessmen and thus open to patriotic rhetoric. Talât's agent here was *Kara* (Black) Kemal, a former colleague in the postal service, who proved to be an adroit popular organizer.

One recruit who had joined the Ottoman Freedom Society in Salonica before its name was changed to Union and Progress was Adjutant-Major Enver. Enver had been posted to Macedonia on graduating from the Staff College in 1902.[47] His decision to join the Ottoman Freedom Society in October 1906 had been prompted by the example of Balkan guerrilla bands. As he said himself,

> I went to Salonica in September 1322 [1906]. There I spoke to my uncle Captain Halil. We had earlier discussed the possibility of forming bands in Anatolia, on the lines of the Bulgarian bands, in order to alert the people and thus, at least, save Anatolia from the fate which threatened Rumelia [the Ottoman possessions in the Balkans]. Halil asked me whether I still held the same views. Finally, he told me that there was a secret society in Salonica, formed to act in the manner we had been thinking of for the sake of the whole country. After swearing me to secrecy, he told me that he had become a member of that society.[48]

Enver joined the Ottoman Freedom Society and was put in charge of its branch in Manastır, the headquarters of the 3rd Army (part of whose command was situated in Salonica). In September 1907 he won accelerated promotion to the rank of Major.[49] Three months later, he was assigned at his own request to anti-bandit operations (*eşkiya takib heyeti*), conducted from Manastır.[50] While his fellow-conspirators in Salonica were collaborating with Greek revolutionaries, Enver fought and destroyed a Greek armed band, which had assassinated sixteen Bulgarian villagers.[51] On other occasions, he came to grips with Bulgarian and even Albanian guerrillas.

Another important early recruit was Staff Major (Ahmet) Cemal (the future triumvir, known in the West as Jemal Pasha). Cemal served on the Marshal's personal staff in Salonica and was at the same time military inspector of the railway network in Rumelia, a post which allowed him to keep in touch with members of the society throughout the Ottoman possessions in the Balkans.

Thus by October 1908, when Mustafa Kemal arrived in Istanbul, the leadership of the Young Turkish movement had come together: Talât, Enver, (Ahmet) Cemal, Mithat Şükrü (Bleda), Rahmi (Evrenos), Dr Nazım, İsmail Canbulat, Halil (Menteşe), *Kara* Kemal had all preceded him in the Society of Union and Progress. So had Mustafa Kemal's own band of personal followers, including Ali Fuat (Cebesoy), although his friends carried little weight in the conspiracy. Mustafa Kemal had no choice but to follow their example. He joined the Society of Union and Progress not later than February 1908.[52]

Mustafa Kemal's transfer was originally to the headquarters staff in Manastır. But even before his arrival from Syria, his friends changed his posting, this time to the personal staff of Marshal Hayri Paşa, commander of the 3rd Army in Salonica. Ali Fuat reports that Mustafa Kemal had asked him by letter to find him an appointment in Salonica, and that he had arranged the change of posting with the help of Rahmi (Evrenos), whose family were close to the Marshal. Ali Fuat had just been transferred from Salonica to Karaferye (now Verroia), two hours by rail to the west, where he was to command operations against a guerrilla band. This created a vacancy on the Salonica staff, which Mustafa Kemal filled.[53]

Mustafa Kemal's duties do not seem to have been onerous. Occasionally he acted as referee in small-scale manoeuvres held by units stationed around Salonica.[54] But his time was largely taken up with revolutionary politics. The grip of the CUP on the officer corps of the 3rd Army became stronger when, after the death of Hayri Paşa, the command passed to Esat Paşa, formerly director of studies at the War College in Istanbul. The new Marshal's younger brother Vehip was himself a leading member of the CUP branch in Manastır. Marshal Esat Paşa's personal chief of staff in Salonica was Topçu (Gunner) Ali Rıza Paşa, who was assisted by three young officers, Major (Ahmet) Cemal, Major (Ali) Fethi (Okyar) and Adjutant-Major Mustafa Kemal. All three were members of the CUP, as Atatürk was to say later.[55]

Politics began to take a violent turn. Some supporters of the palace were intimidated. Mithat Şükrü warned the governor of Manastır, Hıfzı Paşa, who happened to be married to his aunt, not to report the activities of the conspirators to Istanbul. Enver approved an assassination attempt aimed at his brother-in-law, Lieutenant-Colonel Nazım, the central commandant of Salonica, who worked for the palace as local security chief. In the event Nazım was wounded together with CUP member İsmail Canbulat, who had engaged him in conversation in front of an open window of his house, while the killer was waiting outside.[56] Then the *müftü* of Manastır (in this case, it seems, an army chaplain) was shot in Salonica, as he was preparing to go to Istanbul with reports of the conspiracy.[57]

Mustafa Kemal was himself involved in a cover-up, when he replaced the injured Nazım, who had in the meantime fled to Istanbul, as investigator of an incident at Serez (now Serrai in Greek Macedonia), where an officer had been denounced for subversive talk. Arriving from Salonica, Mustafa Kemal comforted the local commander, Marshal İbrahim Paşa, with the words: 'Your Excellency! It is beyond belief that any individual in the area of your exalted command could entertain feelings against the sovereign. The investigation on site will easily bring out the discipline established by your exalted person and the feelings of loyalty inspired by you. If you wish, I shall submit to Your Excellency a copy of the report of my investigation.' This was precisely what İbrahim Paşa wished to hear. Mustafa Kemal's report naturally exonerated the accused officer and recommended that the person who had denounced him should be punished for libel.[58]

The incident had an important consequence. Alarmed by reports of sedition in the 3rd Army, the palace recalled to Istanbul Marshal Esat Paşa, his personal chief of staff Ali Rıza Paşa, and two other officers, including Enver. Enver went into hiding. On the Marshal's personal staff, Major Cemal removed himself discreetly from Salonica, while Major Fethi (Okyar) had left earlier to become commandant of the gendarmerie college. Only Mustafa Kemal was left to receive the new 3rd Army commander, who was none other than Marshal İbrahim Paşa from Serez. When İbrahim Paşa attempted to establish discipline in the army, Cemal and other members of the CUP approached his son, Colonel Nurettin (who also acted as his father's ADC),[59] with a warning to the Marshal to keep off their patch. Thereafter, İbrahim Paşa heard and saw no evil.[60]

On 22 June 1908, on the eve of the Young Turk revolution, Mustafa Kemal was given the additional job of inspector of the railway line from Salonica to Üsküp (Skopje, now the capital of former Yugoslav Macedonia).[61] Using this post, he became chief liaison officer ('general guide') between the CUP headquarters in Salonica and the society's branch in Üsküp, while Ali Fuat fulfilled the same function between Salonica and Manastır.[62] In a letter to Atatürk's biographer, Şevket

Süreyya Aydemir, Ali Fuat was to say later: 'Appointment as "guide"
meant in those days that one was out of favour [with the leadership]. In
our case the reason was that we both believed that the revolutionary
policy of the society was inadequate. We used to say this and express
criticism in secret meetings.'[63]

Mustafa Kemal voiced his criticism not only in clandestine meetings,
but in impassioned discussions over drinks in cafés and beerhouses in
the centre of Salonica – at Yonyo's, Crystal, Theoklis's or the Olympus
Palace. After he had become president of the republic, Atatürk
described the scene at Yonyo's:

> Revolutionaries were sitting at one table as I drew near. I noticed that they
> were drinking *rakı* and beer. Their talk was most patriotic. They spoke of
> making a revolution. The revolution, they said, needed great men. Everyone
> wanted to be a great man. But how and like whom was one to behave to
> achieve greatness? One of the company shouted: 'I want to be like Cemal.'
> All the others followed suit, saying, 'Bravo! Yes, like Cemal! Then, all these
> gentlemen, none of whom I knew closely, turned to me. I looked at them
> with a fixed gaze. They did not notice that I was holding back, and expected
> me to confirm their opinion of Cemal, with whom I was in touch day and
> night, and whom I knew better than any of them. I can't explain why, but I
> made no move to satisfy the company.[64]

An opportunity to explain occurred one day when Mustafa Kemal
and Cemal were making their way by tram from their office to the
Olympus Palace. Cemal had written an unsigned article in a Salonica
newspaper. He asked Mustafa Kemal what he thought of it, and was
rewarded with the frank reply that it was nothing out of the ordinary.
Mustafa Kemal went on: 'Don't fall into the temptation of trying to
please pea-brains ... If you condescend to gain strength from the favour
of this or that man, you may get by at present, but you'll have a rotten
future.' Remembering the scene in 1926, and thinking clearly of himself,
Mustafa Kemal claims that he gave this advice to Cemal:

> Greatness means that you won't try and please anyone, that you won't deceive
> anyone, that you will discern the true ideal for the country, that you will strive
> for it, that everyone will turn against you and will try to make you change your
> course. You will have no means to resist. They will pile up endless obstacles
> in your path and you will surmount them, knowing all the time that you are
> not great, but little, weak, resourceless, a mere nothing, and that no one will
> come to your aid. And if after that they call you great, you'll laugh at them.[65]

Cemal became known as 'the Great Cemal Paşa' in subsequent years,
and the stories which Mustafa Kemal told of their early encounters

were meant to show that from the start he had seen that the future triumvir of the CUP had feet of clay. Nevertheless he continued to look
on Cemal as a potential ally and patron until the last year of the Great
War. But while Mustafa Kemal was almost certainly less outspoken with
Cemal than he later claimed, he was not content to be in the outer circle
of the revolutionaries, and made no secret of his resentment, particularly when he was in his cups. There were certainly good grounds for
criticism. The CUP had neither a clear leadership structure, nor a clear
policy beyond the restoration of the constitution. Ali Fuat claims that
he had himself been disappointed when he first took part at a central
meeting of the conspirators: 'I asked, "All right, let's assume that we've
forced Sultan Hamit to restore constitutional rule. What then?" "The
rest will be easy," I was told.'[66] Was 27-year-old Mustafa Kemal more
realistic? Ali Fuat claims that he was, repeating that even before the
Young Turk revolution, Mustafa Kemal was thinking of the need to
establish a Turkish national state. According to Ali Fuat, the subject
came up again when Mustafa Kemal visited him at Karaferye, shortly
after his arrival in Salonica. Mustafa Kemal argued that

In the Balkans, we should keep both eastern and western Thrace, and the
frontier to the north of Edirne should be rectified at the expense of Bulgaria.
A conference should be held under Ottoman chairmanship in Istanbul with
representatives from Albania, Austria-Hungary, Serbia, Bulgaria and Greece.
Ottoman possessions in the Balkans, outside Thrace, should be ceded to
these countries on the basis of national majorities. Albania should become
independent. Bosnia-Herzegovina should be shared fairly between Serbia
and Austria-Hungary. The [Aegean] islands near the coast of Anatolia should
remain within the Turkish state, and the rest should go to Greece. Our southern borders should take in the provinces of Hatay, Aleppo and Mosul, and
the rest should be ceded to the Arabs. There should be no change in the east
and north-east of Anatolia. Any Greek, Bulgarian and Serb minorities left in
Turkey should be exchanged against Turks left outside [the new frontiers].[67]

The reference to Hatay, which Turkey annexed on the eve of the
Second World War, makes one wonder how accurate Ali Fuat's memory
was when he published his reminiscences in 1966. Moreover, Atatürk's
close companion and future ADC, Salih Bozok, did not except Mustafa
Kemal from his judgement when he wrote: 'Our generation cannot be
absolved of responsibility [for the loss of Ottoman possessions in the
Balkans]. Ignorance and negligence are no excuse. Where we went
wrong was in believing that the constitution was the goal. We thought
that once the goal was reached, there would be nothing more to do.'[68]
However, the idea of nationally homogeneous states replacing

empires was certainly around in the first decade of the twentieth century. Even earlier, there had been talk of exchanging the Muslim population in northern Bulgaria, north of the Balkan mountains, against the Christian population in southern Bulgaria (or Eastern Rumelia, as it became known after 1878). In the event, the Ottoman state was to lose both parts of Bulgaria. In later life, Atatürk showed that he knew when his country had to cut its losses. The seeds of his realism must have been present in his youth. Even so, it is difficult to believe that he was ready to surrender his home town of Salonica as early as 1907.

Mustafa Kemal's ambition and his hard-drinking habits certainly made an impression on his companions, even if his prescience did not. He made no secret of the first two aspects of his character. He was always ready to hold the floor. He was a boon companion, particularly when he was allowed to dominate the scene. Many years later, another close friend, Nuri (Conker), told the story how at a drinking session in Salonica, Mustafa Kemal promised to make him prime minister. 'And what will you be?' Nuri asked. 'The man who appoints prime ministers,' Mustafa Kemal replied.[69] Mustafa Kemal was open about his ideas, his ambitions and his habits. He was also meticulous both in his staff work and in his dress. But the early years of revolutionary plotting revealed another side to his character. When he was not on top, he was critical of those who were. He alone deserved to be leader.

The Young Turk revolution was a messy affair. It was a process of spontaneous combustion, rather than a carefully planned operation. The CUP had subverted the armed forces in the Balkans and round İzmir. The civil authorities in Macedonia feared the revolutionaries and were forced into collusion with them. Even the central government in Istanbul was less than loyal to Abdülhamit, whose suspicions, fed by a self-interested palace camarilla, made a misery of the lives of senior officials. Reproved on one occasion for arriving at Yıldız palace in a motor car, a vehicle which Abdülhamit feared in case it were used in a sudden raid, then ordered to remove its tyres, the grand vizier Ferit Paşa remarked that he envied the lot of stevedores in the port of Istanbul.[70]

The main external stimulus to the military rising was the publication of an Anglo-Russian project of reforms in Macedonia, agreed at the meeting between Edward VII and Tsar Nicholas II at Reval (now Tallinn, the capital of Estonia) at the end of May 1908. The project, which provided that the governor of Macedonia, though an Ottoman subject, should be appointed with the agreement of the great powers, and that he should be assisted by European officers paid for from the revenues of the province, was endorsed by France, but opposed by Austria-Hungary and Germany.[71] Its chances of success were therefore slight. The danger which the Reval meeting presented to the Ottoman state lay elsewhere. Its survival had been helped by the rivalry, first, between Britain and France and then between Britain and Russia. Now all three were coming together to confront Germany and Austria-Hungary. An international game with two players held fewer opportunities for Ottoman statesmen than one involving five players. Worried that Macedonia was about to go the way of Egypt, Bosnia-Herzegovina and, most recently, Crete, which were lost to the Ottoman state in all but name, the CUP sent a manifesto to the consuls of the great powers in Salonica. It claimed that it alone could bring peace to Macedonia, and that Europe should therefore abandon its futile schemes of reform.[72]

While the Salonica revolutionaries discussed high politics, its military members in the field were faced with a critical choice. Their identities were, by and large, known to agents of the palace. If they did not act, they would be neutralized. The first to act was Adjutant-Major Niyazi, an ethnic Albanian, stationed at Resne (Resen, between Manastır/Bitola and Ohri/Ohrid). On 3 July 1908 he took to the hills at the head of 200 soldiers and a number of civilian supporters, issuing a manifesto which demanded the restoration of constitutional government. The palace responded by asking a divisional commander, General Şemsi Paşa, also an ethnic Albanian, to crush the rebels with a force which included his own irregular retainers. On 7 July, Şemsi Paşa was assassinated by one Lieutenant Atıf, a member of the CUP in Manastır. Further north, a gathering by Albanians at Firzovik in the province of Kosova (Kosovo) was manipulated by the CUP to produce a declaration in favour of constitutional rule.[73] In the meantime, Major Enver, who had fled from Salonica on 25/26 June to evade arrest, was joined by other revolutionaries as he made his way to Köprülü (Veleš).

Apparently after Enver had left Salonica, the CUP headquarters in that city awarded him the title of 'Inspector-General of the internal organization for Rumelia and of the executive force of the Ottoman Society of Progress and Union'.[74] The title implies that Enver was to coordinate risings throughout the area, and that the CUP headquarters wanted to assert control over the wild men at Manastır. On 22 July, the CUP in Manastır warned the sultan that if he did not restore the constitution, they would act against him. The following day, Niyazi and another CUP officer, Adjutant-Major Eyüp Sabri, entered Manastır, surrounded the mansion of the governor Hıfzı Paşa, and kidnapped the army commander Osman Paşa. On the same day, 23 July 1908, Enver proclaimed the constitution at Köprülü. Similar scenes followed throughout Macedonia, with revolutionary officers in the lead. The revolution of the Young Turks was essentially a military coup led by officers in their twenties, and supported by some civilians, mainly junior civil servants, who came from a similar educational background.

The grand vizier Ferit Paşa, who had personal knowledge of the feelings of Albanians, assessed the situation with fair accuracy when he said in a telegram to the governor of Manastır: 'It is unlikely that local people should have thought up these political demands. It is obvious that the demands are based on instructions and incitement.'[75] But even Ferit Paşa's loyalties were divided. When told that his compatriots were agitating at Firzovik, he is said to have exclaimed in his native Albanian: 'Well done, boys!'[76] Perhaps it was an expression of amused cynicism on the part of an experienced politician.

Nevertheless, the palace did make some last-minute efforts to stop the rising. Reserve troops were sent from Anatolia in the week before the proclamation of the constitution. But the conspirators in İzmir had undermined their loyalty. Another military commission was despatched from Istanbul. But the civil authorities in Macedonia, headed by the Inspector-General Hüseyin Hilmi Paşa in Salonica and Hıfzı Paşa in Manastır, at the centre of the rebellion, advised that resistance was hopeless. The grand vizier Ferit Paşa, who had opposed the despatch of troops from İzmir and dismissed the findings of the military investigation commission sent to Salonica, was removed from office on 22 July. He was replaced by the 70-year-old *Küçük* (Little) Sait Paşa, who had served six previous terms as grand vizier under Abdülhamit. The new cabinet immediately recommended that the constitution of 1876, whose operation Abdülhamit had suspended, but which appeared in official yearbooks throughout his reign, should be implemented. On 24 July the sultan issued a decree restoring constitutional rule and ordering parliamentary elections. Nine days later, a more detailed imperial decree was published. After detailing the liberal principles of the new administration, it added: 'Since my imperial military forces are the greatest source of the power of the state, I consider it essential that progress be made in military matters and that weapons and other equipment should be improved, and I have issued special orders to this effect to the war ministry.'[77] The military revolutionaries had their reward.

Throughout the crisis Mustafa Kemal continued to work in Salonica on the staff of the 3rd Army commander İbrahim Paşa. Şevket Süreyya Aydemir, the author of biographies in Turkish of both Atatürk and Enver Paşa, claims that it was Mustafa Kemal who handed to Enver, at a railway station south of Köprülü, the authorization of the CUP to act as its 'Inspector-General for Rumelia'.[78] The account which Atatürk gave in 1927 is more cryptic: 'I went to Üsküp [Skopje], where, it was believed, there had been [undue] haste in arranging demonstrations to proclaim the constitution, in order to coordinate action with arrangements being made in Salonica and elsewhere.'[79] We know that Mustafa Kemal acted as CUP courier along this portion of the line, of which he was theoretically military inspector. It is highly likely that Talât, Cemal and other revolutionary leaders in Salonica sent him to urge their comrades in the field to synchronize their activities. Mustafa Kemal may have met Enver as he fulfilled his mission, but we know that he did not accompany Enver when the latter returned in triumph to Salonica. In any case, before and after the proclamation of the constitution on 24 July 1908, Mustafa Kemal was primarily a staff officer in Salonica, who, like many of his comrades, was a rank-and-file member of the CUP. Both his military and his political career had barely begun. But his party had won power and Salonica was the arena where the struggle for leadership was joined.

4

An Impatient Young Turk

SULTAN ABDÜLHAMIT'S DECREE restoring constitutional rule was published on 24 July 1908 (11 July 1324 in the *Rumi* calendar). On the same day, Major Enver, who had already proclaimed the constitution in Köprülü (Veleš) and Tikveş (both in former Yugoslav Macedonia), arrived by train in Salonica, where he was met by a large crowd and greeted as 'the champion of freedom' (*hürriyet kahramanı*). The reception party was headed by Talât and Major Cemal, who declared, 'Enver, you are now Napoleon!'[1] True, there were two other prominent 'champions of freedom', Majors Niyazi and Eyüp Sabri (Akgöl), but they were at Manastır, and the action had moved to Salonica, which the revolutionaries now called 'the Mecca of freedom' (*Kâbe-yi hürriyet*).[2]

A wave of festive excitement swept over Salonica. Muslim *hocas*, rabbis and Greek priests embraced in the streets, where they were joined by bearded Bulgarian revolutionaries who had emerged from their hideouts in the hills. Mithat Şükrü (Bleda), a prominent member of the CUP, was to say in his memoirs, 'People who did not know what freedom was or what the constitution meant took part in the general rejoicing.' But there was a dark side to the change. Some of the sultan's agents had been shot, and the crowd rushed to spit at their corpses.[3]

On 25 July the CUP leadership visited Hüseyin Hilmi Paşa, the Inspector-General for Macedonia and the senior civil official in the area. Having covered up the revolutionaries' activities before the restoration of the constitution, the pasha immediately put himself at their disposal.[4] The CUP found a building for its headquarters, using it as a base for extending its control over the whole Ottoman state. A delegation which included Talât, Major Cemal and Rahmi (Evrenos) went to

Istanbul to discuss immediate measures, including the holding of elections, with the grand vizier Sait Paşa. A few days later, Sait Paşa resigned when the CUP objected to his decision to allow the sultan to nominate the ministers of war and of the navy, and he was replaced by his long-standing rival, 76-year-old Kâmil Paşa. Born in Cyprus, Kâmil Paşa was considered an Anglophile, and *ipso facto* a liberal. He succeeded in working with the CUP for six months, during which elections were held, before he too was forced from office in a dispute about the nomination of the army and navy ministers. Political power depended on control of the armed forces, which the CUP had no intention of yielding to its rivals. Kâmil was replaced by the CUP's faithful friend, Hüseyin Hilmi Paşa, the former Inspector-General for Macedonia, who had earlier entered the government as minister of the interior. The headquarters of the CUP, which Kâmil Paşa described as 'the hidden hand' (*ricalü-l'gayb*), remained in Salonica until the newly elected chamber of deputies met in Istanbul in December 1908. In the eyes of the revolutionaries, the capital, Istanbul, was 'a Byzantine whore' (*Kahpe Bizans*), whose feelings for their cause were fickle.[5] Distrust of the sophistication of Istanbul, where ideological simplicities came up against entrenched and well-connected interests, was a trait which Atatürk came to share with his fellow-revolutionaries.

The blueprint of the CUP was simple. The Ottoman state was to be run from the centre by a parliamentary government applying a uniform set of laws, allowing no exceptions and no foreign interference. Freedom, justice and brotherhood would prevail since all the sultan's subjects, irrespective of religion or mother tongue, would be equal before the law. Backward oriental habits, such as nepotism, corruption and the proliferation of sinecures, were to be rooted out. Money thus saved would be used to strengthen the armed forces and the civil administration. Appropriate educational qualifications would be required of all officers and civil servants.

At no point did this simple but grand design fit an easygoing state made up of largely self-governing religious communities, tribes and provinces, held together by a manipulative sovereign, where authority was exercised by traditional leaders of society, where exceptions to rules were well understood, where foreign interference was part of the general and constantly adjusted equilibrium. The revolutionaries were themselves products of this traditional society, and, for all their training in the ideology of the Enlightenment and their initial insistence on anonymous equality, they split into cliques based less on abstract ideas than on kinship, friendship, religion and geographical origin. The leaders of the CUP were young, and their ambitions were matched by their inexperience. They had no choice but to work through elder statesmen and the officials of the *ancien régime*. But the revolutionaries interfered in the work of their nominees and destroyed their authority.

When Mustafa Kemal returned to Salonica from his short train trip to the north and found that the constitution had been proclaimed, Marshal İbrahim Paşa, on whose personal staff he was serving, called him in and asked, 'Will you keep me in command of the [3rd] Army or won't you? If you don't, let me go back to Istanbul immediately and avoid attacks and insults against my person.' Pointing to the inkstand on his desk, he added: 'This inkstand is all I have here. I'll take it and go.' Speaking in 1927, Atatürk recalled that he discussed the matter with 'other comrades who had authority in the name of the Society', and informed his commander that he could stay. But a few days later, a lieutenant who had escaped to the hills sent an insulting telegram to İbrahim Paşa, who again called Mustafa Kemal and remonstrated with him saying, 'You've advised me that you would keep me here. So, why this insult?' Mustafa Kemal explained that the Society had not had time to communicate with all its members in the field. But a little later there was another incident when İbrahim Paşa objected to the unauthorized trip to Manastır, made at the invitation of the local CUP committee, by Muhlis Paşa, the commander of the troops guarding the frontier with Greece. The Manastır committee responded by describing İbrahim Paşa as a rare specimen of servility to Sultan Abdülhamit. It declared itself surprised that he should dare issue orders to freedom-fighters and demanded that he should resign his command. 'After this,' Atatürk recalled, 'İbrahim Paşa could not stay on in Salonica. He took his inkstand, as he said, and went away.'[6]

He was replaced by Mahmut Şevket Paşa, the governor of the largely Albanian province of Kosova (Kosovo), where he had won the respect of revolutionary officers. A bearded 52-year-old German-trained officer of Chechen descent, Mahmut Şevket Paşa had such a fierce aspect that four years later, when the CUP made him grand vizier in the middle of the Balkan war, the sultan, Mehmet V, trembled whenever he heard the sound of his boots crunching on the palace floor.[7]

Supporters of the CUP – young officers, civil servants, Muslims (and some Jews) inspired by the ideas of the Enlightenment, and, of course, time-servers and people who had fallen out with the *ancien régime* for personal reasons – began forming Union and Progress clubs throughout the Ottoman state. The CUP headquarters in Salonica sent trustees (*mutemet*) to direct these clubs. But it found that 'some of those who worked in the name of the Society behaved contrary to its aims and interests and even compromised its honour.' The CUP then decided to appoint Responsible Secretaries (*Kâtib-i Mesul*) from among 'trust-worthy, honourable and capable young people' to run its provincial branches. One such young person was (Mahmut) Celal (Bayar), a clerk in the Deutsche Bank branch office in Bursa, where his father was also employed as cashier. (Mahmut) Celal was sent as Responsible Secretary to the CUP Club in İzmir.[8] After the First World War he organized Turkish nationalist resistance in the area, and later became minister of national economy and then prime minister at the end of Atatürk's life.

The rise to power of self-styled freedom-lovers was accompanied by demotions and sackings of civil and military officials, accused of irregularities. 'Reorganization commissions' (*tensikat komisyonları*), set up to eliminate sinecures and inefficiency, were often used to settle personal scores. The losers began to make trouble for the CUP, which attributed its problems partly to individual mistakes, but largely to a misrepresentation of its noble aims.

One of the provinces where there was immediate trouble was Tripolitania (Libya, which was at the time divided administratively into the province of Trablusgarp/Tripoli and the special district of Bingazi/Benghazi). It had been used by Sultan Abdülhamit as a dumping ground for dissidents. Tripolitania was loosely governed by the elderly and kindly Recep Paşa, who had made a name for himself by allowing political exiles to escape to Europe. After the proclamation of the constitution, Recep Paşa was appointed war minister in Kâmil Paşa's government.[9] He returned to a hero's welcome in Istanbul, and soon afterwards died of a heart attack, brought on, it was said, by the excitement of the occasion. In his absence, a revolt broke out and CUP supporters were chased out of the province. The CUP in Salonica decided to send out an emissary to pacify the population. The emissary was young Adjutant-Major Mustafa Kemal.

Atatürk later told Afet that the decision to send him was taken in his absence by the CUP central committee in Salonica in order to get rid of him.[10] He became aware of it only when he saw his name written on a blackboard in the committee room. He then asked for details from Hacı Âdil (Arda), a prominent Unionist who had chaired the committee. Hacı Adil explained that the mission was a sign of the trust in which he was held by the CUP, and gave Mustafa Kemal one thousand gold liras 'for his expenses', which, in view of the size of the sum, were clearly intended to include bribes to local Arabs.

There is no reason to read sinister motives into this decision to send to a distant province a young and ambitious member on the fringes of the leadership of the CUP. Other emissaries were sent out at the time, and Mustafa Kemal may have been chosen because of his experience of

Ottoman-Arab relations in Syria. However, he was suspicious of his comrades who had beaten him to the leadership of the CUP. He was to recall in 1922:

> After the proclamation of the constitution everybody came out into the open. Until then our work had been pure and disinterested. [At least] I saw everybody in that light. So when people began to push themselves forward I found the sight unbecoming. I took a critical view of the behaviour of some comrades, and I did not avoid open criticism. The first measure that came to my mind to combat the evil was to apply the principle that the army should withdraw from politics. But other comrades were not in favour.[11]

In fact the leading military members of the CUP did remove themselves from the domestic political arena. On 13 January 1909, Major Enver was appointed military attaché in Berlin. Major Fethi (Okyar) was posted to Paris, Major Ali Fuat (Cebesoy) to Rome, and Major Hafız Ismail Hakkı to Vienna.[12] The behaviour of Major Niyazi, who was the first to raise the standard of revolt, was even purer and more disinterested. He wrote his account of the rising, and had it officially confirmed by the CUP committee in Manastır. After publishing it, he resigned his commission and returned to his home town of Resne to build a primary school.[13]

Mustafa Kemal's trip to Tripoli was brief and successful. He set out by ship in September 1908.[14] He met the local notables: Hasune (Hassuna) Paşa, the mayor of Tripoli (who was to surrender the city to the Italians in 1911), Şeyh Mansur in Bingazi and other sheikhs, and made peace between them and the Ottoman administration. He visited the British honorary consul J. Alvarez, whom he impressed with his 'energetic character and resolute temper'. In private, Alvarez reported, Mustafa Kemal was 'very silent and of a reserved disposition'. But at a public meeting in Tripoli he was 'an eloquent and fluent speaker', expounding 'the principles and objects pursued by his party with remarkable lucidity'.[15]

Afet's account stresses Mustafa Kemal's courage in confronting rebellious Arab tribesmen and re-establishing the authority and morale of Ottoman officials and military officers. In fact, he gave early proof of his realism. He left local notables in place, assuring them that constitutional Ottoman government would defend their interests. His conduct showed that he was learning how to work with the means available to him. He distinguished between immediate needs and distant goals.

Back in Salonica, Mustafa Kemal was appointed chief of staff of the 17th reserve division in January 1909.[16] He concentrated his attention on the urgent task of improving military training.[17] Along with other revolutionary officers, Mustafa Kemal believed that Abdülhamit's fear of military manoeuvres and his refusal to allow the use of live ammunition in training exercises had left the Ottoman armed forces unprepared for modern war. When the ban on the use of live ammunition was lifted during Mustafa Kemal's service in Syria, he is said to have compiled a firing manual from such Turkish-language sources as he could find.[18]

The CUP had seen the restoration of constitutional government primarily as a means to defend the territorial integrity of the Ottoman state. Its hopes were quickly disappointed. In October 1908, while elections to the Ottoman chamber of deputies were still in progress, Austria-Hungary formally annexed Bosnia-Herzegovina, which it had been administering since the Congress of Berlin in 1878; Bulgaria, enlarged since that Congress through its union with Eastern Rumelia (Southern Bulgaria) in 1885, but still formally an Ottoman vassal state, declared its independence; and Crete, which had become autonomous in 1897, proclaimed its union with Greece. Ottoman authority had been nominal in all three places, but their formal loss was a blow to the new regime. Great power mediation sorted out the problems with Austria-Hungary and Bulgaria, where the Ottoman government was forced to accept the *fait accompli*. The dispute with Greece dragged on, as crowds of Muslim demonstrators chanted 'Crete is our life. Our blood is its price!' (*Girit bizim canımız. / Feda olsun kanımız*). European encroachment was one thing; encroachment by Greeks cut Muslim Turks to the quick.

The chamber of deputies, elected by indirect suffrage (with electoral colleges chosen in the first round), was opened on 17 December 1908. The speech from the throne was read by the sultan's secretary in the presence of Abdülhamit who was wildly cheered as he drove through the streets of Istanbul. Of the deputies 142 were Turks, 60 Arabs, 25 Albanians, 23 Greeks, 12 Armenians, 5 Jews, 4 Bulgarians, 3 Serbs and one Vlach (Romanian).[19] Some serving officers were elected, but the leading military revolutionaries, like Enver and Cemal, did not stand. Neither, of course, did Mustafa Kemal, who was, in any case, still an inconspicuous junior officer. Leading civilian members of the CUP, like Talât and Halil (Menteşe), became members of parliament, and the CUP central committee began to meet in Istanbul.

The chamber fractured largely on ethnic lines. The national minorities wanted both equality and the preservation, and if possible the extension, of their existing rights and privileges. The CUP believed that equality was sufficient. Theoretically, the CUP had an absolute majority of 160 deputies, but party discipline was weak. The opposition Liberal Party (*Ahrar Fırkası*), grouped round Prince Sabahattin, had a nominal strength of 10 deputies, but could make common cause with ethnic parties. The ideologue of the CUP, Ahmet Rıza, who had returned from Paris along with other political exiles, was elected speaker of the chamber. His subsequent role in Turkish politics was slight, as the initiative lay with domestic revolutionaries.

Opposition to the CUP gradually mounted. In the army, the CUP threatened the careers of officers who had not been trained in military colleges, but had been promoted from the ranks. Discontent was also fed by the attempt to transfer from the capital units held by the new regime to be unreliable and to replace them with troops from the Balkans, which were assumed to be loyal to the constitution. Students in religious schools were up in arms against the decision to end their exemption from military service unless they passed examinations appropriate to their clerical calling.[20] Pious Muslims were genuinely frightened by the agnosticism, not to say atheism, of leading CUP members, such as Ahmet Rıza, and the threat that this posed to the clerical establishment. The demand for the integral application of the *şeriat* arose as a reaction to the behaviour and presumed intentions of 'infidel Unionists' (*İttihatçı gâvurlar*). The Islamist campaign was led by the Muhammadan Union (*İttihad-ı Muhammedî*), founded on 5 April 1909.[21] Its name mimicked Union and Progress (*İttihat ve Terakki*), the title of the revolutionary party.

Discontent, expressed both in Islamic and in liberal terms, was voiced loudly by the press, which was no longer subject to censorship. People who had become accustomed to seeing foreign conspiracies everywhere assumed that after the fall of Kâmil Paşa, British support, which had in any case been largely platonic, was lost to the new regime. On 6/7 April 1909, an opposition journalist, Hasan Fehmi, whose newspaper *Serbesti* (Freedom) had published a document implicating the CUP in blackmail to extract money from officials of the old regime, was murdered as he was crossing Galata bridge on the Golden Horn in Istanbul. The assassin could not be found. As escape from such a constricted spot would have been difficult without help from high places, people assumed that the assassin came from the CUP.[22] Hasan Fehmi's funeral turned into a large-scale demonstration against the CUP. University students handed protests to the government and the speaker of parliament.

Finally, on 12/13 April 1909,[23] a mutiny broke out among precisely those troops which had been sent to the capital to guard the constitution. As mutineers, accompanied by teachers and students of religious schools, marched to parliament, the grand vizier Hüseyin Hilmi Paşa resigned. Sultan Abdülhamit replaced him with an elder statesman, Tevfik Paşa (who was destined to be the last grand vizier of the empire in 1922). The number of victims was initially small. They included the justice minister, Mustafa Nazım Paşa, whom the mutineers mistook for the 'infidel' parliamentary speaker, Ahmet Rıza; Âdil Arslan Bey, the Druze amir who had been elected deputy for Lâzkiye (Latakia), and who had the misfortune of resembling the CUP publicist, Hüseyin Cahit; and a naval officer Ali Kâbuli, who was preparing to bombard Yıldız palace, the residence of Sultan Abdülhamit.[24] The immediate effect of the revolt was to destroy the power of the CUP in the capital, as leading members of the Society were forced into flight or hiding.

Once again, Salonica became the centre of the CUP, whose supporters in the 2nd and 3rd Armies decided to crush 'the reaction' in Istanbul, before their enemies had time to consolidate. Officers who were members of the CUP quickly put together a force and despatched it by train to the vicinity of the capital. Mustafa Kemal took an active part in the operation. According to his own account, he went with the troops to Istanbul as their chief of staff, under Hüseyin Hüsnü Paşa, the original commander of the force. It was also he who named the force 'Operational Army' (*Hareket Ordusu*). According to Atatürk, the name 'Freedom Army' was originally proposed, when the CUP drew up a declaration of its aims for the benefit of foreign ambassadors in Istanbul. But since 'the entire army was dedicated to freedom', and only a part of it was to take part in the operation, he used the term 'Operational Army'.[25]

In fact Mustafa Kemal's role was limited and brief and the suppression of the revolt in Istanbul did not propel him to the front rank of military revolutionaries. The first detachments set out from Salonica on 15 April. On 19 April, a company of gendarmes from Salonica occupied the railway station at Yeşilköy (at that time St Stefano, in Turkish, Ayastefanos), just outside the capital. Troops also arrived from the 2nd Army in Edirne. Adjutant-Major İsmet (İnönü), who headed the CUP committee in Edirne, served as their chief of staff. On 20 April, the reserve division stationed in Salonica joined the force outside Istanbul under its commander Hüseyin Hüsnü Paşa, with Adjutant-Major Mustafa Kemal as his chief of staff. But Hüseyin Hüsnü Paşa was senior commander of the troops from Salonica for only two days, since on 22 April, Mahmut Şevket Paşa, the commander of the 3rd Army, arrived to take charge of the operation,[26] with his own chief of staff. The 'Operational Army' was reorganized in two divisions: the first made up of troops from Salonica (under Colonel Hasan İzzet), the second from units of the 2nd Army in Edirne.[27] Worse still for Mustafa Kemal's political prospects, Enver arrived post-haste from Berlin, as did the other 'champions of liberty', such as Niyazi who led a detachment of volunteers from his native Resne. In addition to regular units, the Operational Army included a motley collection of freedom-fighters, even Bulgarian revolutionaries.

At first, Mahmut Şevket Paşa pretended that the aim of his forces was to free Sultan Abdülhamit from the grip of mutineers.[28] But the CUP had other plans. Brushing aside possibilities of conciliation, the Operational Army entered Istanbul, storming the buildings held by the mutineers. Enver led in person the attack on Taşkışla barracks, not far from the War College.[29] Mustafa Kemal's friend Kâzım Karabekir was chief of staff of the 2nd division of the Operational Army, which occupied Yıldız palace.[30]

Deputies and senators emerged from hiding and met at Yeşilköy as a General National Assembly (*Meclis-i Umumî-yi Millî*). The name, modelled on the French Assemblée Nationale, showed the potent inspiration of the French Revolution. Earlier, the speaker of the chamber had addressed the demonstrators in Istanbul as 'Citizens!', before hiding from their wrath.[31] After the occupation of Istanbul, the parliamentarians moved to their proper premises in the capital. The speaker of the joint session was the former grand vizier Sait Paşa, but the driving force was Talât. As deputy speaker of the chamber of deputies, he forced the Şeyhülislâm (Sheikh al-Islam, the head of the Muslim clergy) to endorse the decision of the assembly to depose Abdülhamit in favour of his brother Mehmet Reşat. The new sultan was proclaimed as Mehmet V.

The decision was communicated to Abdülhamit by a parliamentary delegation which included an Armenian and a Jewish deputy. In Muslim eyes this was an act of impiety, since the sultan was also theoretically caliph of all Muslims and his deposition had been sanctioned by the *fetva* (*fatwa*, canon law ruling) issued by the Şeyhülislâm. A few hours later, Abdülhamit was packed off by train to Salonica, accompanied by two of his wives, his youngest son and a few servants. Mustafa Kemal's friend Fethi (Okyar) acted as his military escort, and then assumed command of the soldiers who guarded the former sultan in his new residence, the mansion of the Jewish industrialist Allatini, on the Salonica waterfront. Abdülhamit had had no part in organizing the mutiny of 13 April, but the mutineers had spontaneously turned to him as their sovereign, and the CUP feared that, if left on the throne, his strong personality would become the focus of opposition to the new regime. His successor Mehmet V, who had been kept in seclusion by Abdülhamit, was both weak-willed and ignorant of the realities of power. He was the perfect constitutional monarch, prepared to do the bidding of politicians who governed through him. After retaining briefly the services of Tevfik Paşa as grand vizier, the sultan duly reinstated Hüseyin Hilmi Paşa, the friend of the CUP.

Mahmut Şevket Paşa became Inspector-General of all three Ottoman armies in Europe – the 1st Army in the capital, the 2nd in Edirne and the 3rd in Salonica. When Hüseyin Hilmi Paşa resigned at the end of 1909 after a disagreement with the CUP,[32] and was replaced by the Ottoman ambassador in Rome, İbrahim Hakkı Paşa, Mahmut Şevket Paşa was appointed war minister. Some considered him a military dictator. He served rather as a prop to the CUP, whose leading civilian member, Talât, became minister of the interior.

The justice of the revolutionaries produced more victims than had the mutiny in Istanbul. Nearly eighty 'counter-revolutionaries' were sentenced to death and hanged. Apart from mutinous soldiers, they included Derviş Vahdeti, the leader of the Muhammadan Union, and editor of its inflammatory sheet *Volkan* (The Volcano), such supporters of the *ancien régime* as 'Kabasakal' (rough-bearded) Mehmet Paşa (who had interrogated Mustafa Kemal and Ali Fuat when they were arrested in 1905), and even Sultan Abdülhamit's tobacco blender. Units which had taken part in the mutiny were sent off to build roads in Rumelia.[33]

Hikmet Bayur, author of a Turkish biography of Mustafa Kemal, is probably right in crediting him with the authorship of the telegram which his commander Hüseyin Hüsnü Paşa sent to the general staff in Istanbul on 19 April. This declared that the mutiny had stained the honour of the Ottoman army, threatened dire punishment on those who had violated the constitution 'which fulfils the requirements of the *şeriat*', and promised that soldiers and sailors who submitted to the orders of the Operational Army would be spared. On the same day Mustafa Kemal drafted a proclamation in similar terms which Hüseyin Hüsnü Paşa addressed to the people of Istanbul.[34] A photograph shows Mustafa Kemal rushing with a briefcase at the suburban railway station of Bakırköy (known at the time as Makriköy) outside Istanbul. It was in the telegraph office of Bakırköy, where Mustafa Kemal was writing down the orders of Mahmut Şevket Paşa, that he first met Hüseyin Rauf, a nationalist naval officer, with whom he was to work closely in the Turkish War of Independence.[35] The two were introduced by Major Cemal, the 'great man' in the making, whose pretensions Mustafa Kemal claims to have criticized in Salonica.

Cemal did not stay long in Istanbul. On 14 April, the day after the

mutiny in the capital, serious intercommunal troubles erupted between
Muslim Turks and Armenians in Adana, the chief city of Çukurova
(Cilicia). As elsewhere in the Ottoman state, order there had been
undermined after the fall of the old regime. Muslim apprehensions were
fed by a firebrand Armenian prelate, Archbishop Moushegh, who had
urged his people to buy arms. Bloody anti-Armenian pogroms swept
Adana and near-by towns and villages. Up to 20,000 Armenians and
some 2,000 Muslims were killed, and a large part of the city was burned
down. Cemal was despatched to Adana as governor to restore order.
He did this with a firm hand. Forty-seven Muslims, including a *müftü*
and one Armenian, were hanged, and relations between the CUP and
Armenian nationalists were salvaged, at least for a time. Cemal set with
a will to reconstruct the province, where he is still remembered as one
of the best governors it has ever had.[36] It was a foretaste of the role
which he was to play as Ottoman governor of Syria during the First
World War.

Mustafa Kemal returned to Salonica after the reconquest of Istanbul by
the CUP and its allies. Back on the staff of the 3rd Army, he threw
himself into the task of improving the readiness of Ottoman troops in
Macedonia. In February 1909, before his service with the Operational
Army, Mustafa Kemal had published in Salonica a short brochure on
infantry combat training, based on a German manual. In it he pointed
out sensibly that the introduction of a new drill was bound to cause
confusion, which had to be remedied before it threatened the combat
effectiveness of the army.[37] Mustafa Kemal was passionately interested
in the art of war.[38] As he was to say in 1912, he believed that 'the safety
of the fatherland and the happiness of the nation require above all that
the world should be shown that our army is still the army that had
planted its lance in the walls of Vienna.'[39]

Immediately after the revolution of 1908, the new regime had asked
the German government to send back to Turkey Baron von der Goltz
(Paşa), whom Sultan Abdülhamit had first employed in 1883 to modernize his army. The German Chancellor, Prince Bernhard von Bülow,
agreed, but only after the problem posed by Bulgaria's declaration of
independence had been settled. Von der Goltz arrived in Salonica in
August 1909 to put the local Ottoman garrison through its paces.
Mustafa Kemal was later to say that rather than wait for the visiting
Prussian general to decide the form which military exercises should
take, he decided to produce his own plan. 'It is certainly important,' he
argued, 'to benefit from the great sage and thinker Goltz, the author of

"The Nation in Arms" [*Das Volk in Waffen*, translated into Turkish in 1884]. But it is even more important that the Turkish staff and commanders should be able to show how their country should be defended.'

According to Atatürk's Turkish biographers, von der Goltz approved Mustafa Kemal's plan for the exercise, which was held in the valley of the Vardar (Axios) near Salonica. What is certain is that Mustafa Kemal was on the staff of the 3rd Army at the camp at Cumalı from which the exercise was directed in the last two weeks of August 1909. It involved the trooping of a cavalry brigade commanded by Suphi Paşa, a German-trained general who was head of the cavalry department in the war ministry in Istanbul. In a letter to Ali Fuat (Cebesoy), who had originally introduced him to Suphi Paşa, Mustafa Kemal wrote:

> I could not bear the obvious mistakes made during the manoeuvre, and afterwards I criticized the pasha bitterly in the presence of all his officers, even though in doing so I exceeded my authority and my rank. The pasha looked hurt, but did not bear me malice ... My behaviour may have been contrary to discipline. But if a person trained in Germany does not work at the art of command, what can we expect of those who have not had this advantage? Perhaps when they see that they are criticized by their juniors, our commanders will learn to do better.[40]

Suphi Paşa was later to serve as a commander in the Caliphate Army which the Istanbul government raised against Mustafa Kemal during the War of Independence. Meeting him in the railway station in Ankara after the nationalist victory, Mustafa Kemal asked him why he had accepted a command in the caliph's motley troop. 'In order to be defeated by you, Pasha,' Suphi replied.[41] Flattery was a passport to safety.

Mustafa Kemal published his account of the exercise soon after it was completed.[42] But his frankest thoughts were reserved for the ears of his friends, as they met in the bars and restaurants of Salonica. According to Afet, after a lecture in the officers' club in Salonica, Mustafa Kemal declared:

> The revolution must be completed. We can do this. I will do this ... As far as I'm concerned, the senior commanders of the Ottoman empire are useless. For me, the command structure of the army stops at majors. Tomorrow's great commanders will come from their ranks. I'll keep officers up to the rank of major on the army roll. The rest I'll get rid of.[43]

Mustafa Kemal's contempt for his senior commanders is illustrated by this story told by his friend Behiç (Erkin):

After the revolution, the general staff used to set military problems for staff officers, whose marks were then entered in their personal records. One day, at a gathering in the White Tower café [in Salonica], I asked Atatürk, 'Have you worked out your solution to the problem sent by the general staff?' 'No,' he replied, 'I haven't and I shan't. I think it would have been more useful if I had set them a problem.'[44]

The rejuvenation of the armed forces was an aim which most military revolutionaries shared. But they were divided by political ambition. The divisions came out at the CUP congress which opened on 22 September 1909 in Salonica, where the headquarters of the Society had returned after the troubles in Istanbul.[45] Mustafa Kemal took part as delegate of the CUP branch in Tripoli, which he had visited a few months earlier. His friend Dr Tevfik Rüştü (Aras) was general secretary of the congress. This was an influential position since there was no permanent president, a chairman being elected at the beginning of each session. Mustafa Kemal was to say later that he too took his turn in the chair.[46]

Mustafa Kemal drew attention to himself by arguing that the continued involvement of serving officers in the CUP was bad for the army and bad for the Society.[47] 'The 3rd Army,' he argued, 'very many of whose officers are members of the Society, cannot be considered an army in the modern sense. And the Society, which relies on the army, is unable to grow roots among the people.' He therefore proposed that officers whose services were needed by the Society or who wished to remain in it, should resign from the armed forces, and that a law should be passed banning the military from membership of any political organization. This proposal was opposed by delegates who argued that the mutiny in Istanbul had shown the need for close links between the army and the Society. By trying to sever these links, they said, Mustafa Kemal was behaving like a reactionary. It was decided to send a military member, Refet (Bele, later a nationalist commander in the War of Independence), to Edirne to sound out the officers of the 2nd Army. The two most prominent CUP men in the 2nd Army, İsmet (İnönü) and Kâzım Karabekir, supported Mustafa Kemal's proposal,[48] which was then approved by the congress. A law banning military involvement in politics was finally passed some two years later. Mustafa Kemal referred to it in a letter which he sent to Behiç (Erkin) from Cyrenaica on 29 July 1912, saying: 'When I told a congress, where I happened to be present, "let go of the soldiers", I was called a reactionary and condemned to death. Time and events bring out the truth, but they also deal a mortal blow.'[49]

The mortal blow was the fall from power of the CUP in 1912, while the 'death sentence' to which Atatürk referred was later described as an attempt on his life, made by a military member of the CUP one night as he was returning home from the congress. Atatürk apparently recognized the assassin, and dissuaded him from his deed. According to one of Atatürk's Turkish biographers, the journalist Falih Rıfkı Atay, the assailant was Enver's uncle Halil.[50] The story is almost certainly apocryphal. What probably happened was that feelings ran high and threats were made, which Mustafa Kemal took seriously.

The decision of the congress made little practical difference. It was interpreted formally as meaning that serving officers should not hold political office, but the CUP continued to rely on its military members. Enver and Cemal remained in the army. Both, it is true, left the capital – Enver going back to Berlin as military attaché, while Cemal was sent to restore peace in Adana. But their influence in the CUP was unimpaired. Nor did Mustafa Kemal resign from the CUP. But, as he was to observe in 1922, after the Salonica congress 'the disagreement between us and certain personalities in Union and Progress intensified to breaking point, and has continued to this day'.[51]

Having made his point at the CUP congress, Mustafa Kemal returned to his staff duties in Salonica. An opportunity to extend his military knowledge presented itself in the summer of 1910 when he was invited along with other Ottoman officers to observe the French army manoeuvres in Picardy. The group was led by (Gunner) Ali Rıza Paşa, on whose staff Mustafa Kemal was serving in Salonica. In Paris they were met by Mustafa Kemal's friend Major Fethi (Okyar), who had returned as military attaché after the suppression of the rising in Istanbul. Mustafa Kemal travelled by train from Salonica in the company of another officer from the 3rd Army, Major Salâhattin, an ethnic Albanian. Atatürk was to say later that, as soon as they had crossed the Serbian frontier, he removed the fez, which was part of his military uniform, and replaced it with a peaked cap, bought earlier in Istanbul. Salâhattin objected. 'We are travelling first class by grace of the sultan,' he said, 'and are representing the state. People should see that we are Ottomans and Muslims.' But a little later when the train stopped in Serbia and a boy shouted 'A Turk, dammit!' at the sight of Salâhattin, the latter also produced a peaked cap from his bag.[52] A photograph taken in September 1910, during a visit by the Turkish observers at the manoeuvres to the Schneider armaments factory, shows them all smartly dressed in civilian clothes and wearing bowler hats. The visit was important, as the Ottoman state was re-equipping its army, and the French hoped to divert from Germany orders for quick-firing guns.

The CUP persisted in its efforts to cure the ills of the Ottoman state by trying to force all its inhabitants into a uniform mould. Before long, the opposition which had been routed when the Operational Army occupied Istanbul began to re-form. But as the capital was under martial law, open resistance to the CUP erupted in the provinces. At the end of March 1910, the district governor of İpek (now Peć), in the largely Albanian province of Kosova (Kosovo), was gunned down as he was walking in the local market in the company of a leading military supporter of the CUP.[53] It was the beginning of three consecutive revolts among the Albanians, hitherto the defenders of the western marches of the state. On 9 June, an opposition journalist, Ahmet Samim, himself of Albanian origin, was assassinated in Istanbul. The CUP was once again held responsible. The government reacted by passing a number of draconian laws, restricting the right to demonstrate and the freedom of the press, and banning all ethnic associations. In the words of the American historian Stanford Shaw, 'Ottoman society thus was far more restricted in the name of public order after the constitution had been restored than under Abdülhamit.'[54] In the provinces, the army resumed its old occupation of chasing bandits. But it was more brutal now that it was in power and was guided by a superior ideology.

The war minister Mahmut Şevket Paşa decided to take personal charge of operations against Albanian rebels. Mustafa Kemal was to say later that the minister 'took him along as chief of staff'.[55] But as he was not even a full Major at the time, the version given by his friend Kâzım (Özalp) is more likely. According to Kâzım, Mahmut Şevket Paşa arrived in Salonica in September 1910 and assembled a staff which included Mustafa Kemal along with other officers.[56] One of them was Mustafa Kemal's close friend, Nuri (Conker), another Kâzım (Özalp) himself; all appear to have been active members of the CUP. Mustafa Kemal, who was appointed to the staff of the 5th Army Corps in Salonica in January 1911, soon after his return from France, appears to have joined Mahmut Şevket Paşa in Albania in March of that year.[57]

The Albanian revolt was suppressed with a firm hand, and a population which was used to carrying arms was ordered to give them up. As the sultan's head of chancery, Lütfi (Simavi), noted, 'Unnecessary violence by a government, which did not know what it was doing, led to a catastrophe.'[58] The Catholic Malësia tribesmen in northern Albania joined the revolt. They too were suppressed. As Albanian nationalism, originally encouraged by Abdülhamit as a counterweight to the Slavs, spread, involving Muslim as well as Catholic and Eastern Orthodox Albanians, the Ottoman government decided to organize a royal visit by Mehmet V to mobilize Muslim loyalty. In June 1911, on the anniversary of the defeat of the Serbs at the battle of Kosova (Kosovopolje) in 1389, the sultan led the prayers of a vast congregation of Muslims on the historic battlefield. The effect was spoiled by the inability of a local Ottoman cleric, specially chosen for the purpose, to translate the sultan's address into Albanian. Albanian nationalists demanded the creation of an autonomous region covering the western part of Rumelia (the provinces of Manastır, Kosova, İşkodra and Yanya). The government responded by promising limited reforms, including tuition in Albanian. It was not enough. Egged on by the opposition in Istanbul, in which ethnic Albanians were strongly represented, a third revolt broke out in 1912.

Mustafa Kemal does not appear to have given much thought to the political problems posed by the Albanian revolt. He was concentrating on military matters, including intelligence, since it was an open secret that the Albanians were procuring arms from neighbouring countries. According to one report, he crossed secretly into Bosnia, with the help of an Ottoman officer serving on the frontier with Austria-Hungary. The officer was Major Fevzi, who, as Marshal Fevzi Çakmak, was to become his chief of the general staff under the republic.[59] But while politics were not discussed, hats were. According to Kâzım (Özalp), when the army headquarters was established in the Albanian countryside, Mahmut Şevket Paşa was struck by the untidy headgear of his officers, some of whom were wearing squashed fezes, others local mountaineers' caps with tassels. 'A solution must be found to this problem of headgear,' declared the pasha. 'What do you suggest?' 'Hats,' Mustafa Kemal is said to have replied. The hat was a symbol of westernization. But it was a step too far, and the general opinion was that officers should wear Cossack-type fur hats (*kalpak*) and men cloth caps without peaks.[60]

After his return to Salonica, Mustafa Kemal was present at an exercise by the 15th artillery regiment, which was commanded by a German officer in the Ottoman service. Congratulated by the German on the success of the operation against the Albanians, Mustafa Kemal replied, 'The Turkish army will have done its duty when it defends the country from foreign aggression and frees the nation from fanaticism and intellectual slavery.' He added: 'The Turkish nation has fallen far behind the West. The main aim should be to lead it to modern civilization.'[61]

Occasionally, Mustafa Kemal listened, and to no one more carefully than to Ziya (Gökalp), an intellectual born in Diyarbakır, in the Kurdish area, and trained in the military veterinary school, from which he was expelled, and then briefly imprisoned for revolutionary activities. Like many of his contemporaries, Gökalp was strongly influenced by French writers, in his case particularly by the sociologist Émile Durkheim (1858–1917), from whom he derived his notion of religion as social cement. Religion, Gökalp believed, inspired culture, which was specific to individual national societies, while civilization, meaning primarily science and technology, was universal. Like other members of the CUP, Gökalp started by defending the concept of a common Ottoman patriotism.[62] But, before long, he became the chief ideologist of a Western-oriented Turkish nationalism, based not on ethnic origin, but on common culture and language. Gökalp was invited to Salonica in 1909 and became a member of the CUP central committee.[63] He held court in the Crystal café, where according to Atatürk's biographer Enver Behnan Şapolyo, Mustafa Kemal learnt from him 'the ideals of nationalism and of populism, which were to inform the republic of Turkey . . .'[64]

The last years of prosperous, multinational Ottoman Salonica were a period of intellectual ferment. The ideology of Turkish nationalism, which was gradually gaining strength in Istanbul under the twin influence of Western orientalists, who wrote about the role of the Turks in Muslim history, and of Turkic exiles from the Russian empire, who were copying the ideas of Pan-Slavism, was sharpened in Salonica by contact with the nationalism of Balkan peoples. An influential literary review, *Genç Kalemler* (Young Pens),[65] campaigned for a simpler Turkish language, relying more on its own vocabulary than on borrowings from Arabic and Persian. It was in *Genç Kalemler* that Ziya Gökalp published his celebrated poetic manifesto of Pan-Turanianism, the romantic ideology which sought the union of all Turkic-speaking peoples:

> The country of the Turks is not Turkey, nor yet Turkistan,
> Their country is a vast and eternal land: Turan![66]

Turkish ethnic nationalism did not displace the traditional feeling of Islamic solidarity or the desire of Turks educated in the new learning to become part of Western civilization. Ziya Gökalp gradually evolved a synthesis of all three tendencies. The trouble was that the young revolutionaries knew the West largely from books, and the Islamic countries, including Turkic-speaking lands outside the Ottoman state, not at all. The swirl of new ideas often produced among them a spirit of ignorant romanticism, to which the example of Balkan revolutionaries and of Prussian militarists added an edge of violence. Within a few years that spirit came to be embodied in Enver, the aspiring Napoleon of the

Young Turk revolution. By 1914 he was a fully-fledged and dauntless adventurer, who had the measure of the domestic scene but not at all of international power politics.

Enver was drunk on half-digested ideas. The fondness for *rakı*, which Mustafa Kemal openly displayed as he enjoyed the amenities of his lively home town, was a safer form of indulgence. *Rakı* notwithstanding, Mustafa Kemal was sober in his approach to his career. He was to say later:

> I was working on military training. In the course of my work I often had to express criticism orally and in writing. This criticism was particularly hurtful to old commanders. It was claimed that my behaviour showed that I was better at theory than at practice, and, as a penalty of sorts, I was made commander of the 38th infantry regiment. But their anger turned into a blessing. When I became commander, all the units of the Salonica garrison began to take part voluntarily in my regimental exercises. Other officers were seen at the lectures I gave. This activity aroused suspicion in Salonica, and Mahmut Şevket Paşa was prevailed upon to summon me to Istanbul, where I was given a job on the General Staff.[67]

According to Ali Fuat (Cebesoy), the criticism which led to Mustafa Kemal's transfer was contained in a report he submitted on 30 June 1911 to the 5th Army Corps commander Hasan Tahsin Paşa (who was to surrender Salonica to the Greeks the following year).[68] What happened in fact was that the military press in Salonica published a report by Mustafa Kemal on manoeuvres commanded by Hasan Tahsin Paşa, which, according to the author, revealed that unit commanders lacked practical experience.[69] This public airing of the critical views of an officer who was not yet a full major was interpreted as a breach of discipline.

On 13 September 1911, Mustafa Kemal was posted to the 1st section of the General Staff in Istanbul.[70] But, as he complained in a letter to Salih (Bozok) in Salonica, 'no one has addressed a single question to me ... People are all afraid of each other, just as at the time of Abdülhamit. Self-sacrificing efforts are needed to save the army and the country ... [But] Istanbul is corrupt. People think only of their personal interest.'[71] After a few days in Istanbul, Mustafa Kemal was ordered on to Tripoli in Libya. In a letter to his friend Fuat (Bulca) on 17 October, he complained that 'Ever since the Tripoli problem first came up [in 1908], there have been constant attempts to send me there.'[72] He embarked on the steamship *Şam* ('Damascus') bound for Libya. Three days later, as Italy declared war on the Ottoman state, the ship was ordered back to Istanbul,[73] where Mustafa Kemal returned to twiddle his thumbs on the general staff, but not for long. This time he himself volunteered for service in Libya against the Italians. He left on 15 October, still furious with Mahmut Şevket Paşa. A letter which he wrote on 29 July 1912 from Derne (Darna) in Cyrenaica includes this diatribe against Mahmut Şevket Paşa, who had by then resigned as war minister:

> Instead of agreeing only ten months ago to silence and condemn to inactivity an insignificant Adjutant-Major like myself, and of being content to spend his time nodding in the direction of fools who surrounded him on all sides for their own hidden purposes, instead of behaving like a stupid puppet in the hands of intriguers, it would have been much better if he had surrendered his office there and then to more capable hands.[74]

Mustafa Kemal never saw Salonica again. Within little more than a year, the city had fallen to the Greeks. All the Turks who had the means to go, left. Minarets were pulled down one by one. In 1917, much of Salonica was destroyed by the most disastrous of all the fires which swept it periodically. After 1923, the remaining Muslims were forcibly exchanged against Greeks expelled from Turkey. The Jewish community, to which Salonica owed its vitality, was reduced in numbers and in wealth, but survived in the main until it was wiped out by the Nazis in the Second World War. There are still traces of more than five centuries of Ottoman rule in the new homogeneously Greek city of concrete apartment blocks, but those traces are few and far between. One of them is the pink wooden house in which Atatürk lived with his mother. In February 1937, the town council of Salonica donated the house to the Turkish government,[75] which has since kept it up as a museum. A plaque outside commemorates Atatürk as the founder of the Turkish republic and 'architect' of the (short-lived) Balkan Pact. In September 1955, when the Cyprus dispute entered its violent stage, an untrue report that Atatürk's house in Salonica had been bombed was one of the causes (or excuses) of a pogrom which led to the emigration of practically the entire Greek community in Istanbul. The pink house has been well guarded since then.

Atatürk himself never looked back on Salonica. He was a practical man who concentrated on the work in hand. In any case, he had mixed feelings about his years in Salonica. He had spent his youth there at a time when Ottoman rule in the west was under permanent threat. He had all the more reason to transfer his energies to an area where he and his community could feel safe.

PART II

The Long War

5

Adventure in the Desert

————————◆————————

ON 29 SEPTEMBER 1911 Italy went to war with the Ottoman state in order to wrest from it its last possession in North Africa, the province of Tripoli and Cyrenaica. It was the beginning of Turkey's Great War, which, except for a break of one year (September 1913 to November 1914), was to last until the conclusion of the treaty of Lausanne in July 1923. These twelve years from 1911 to 1923 saw the rise of Mustafa Kemal from an obscure Adjutant-Major to a victorious Marshal, recognized internationally as the leader of the new Turkish national state.

As soon as the war with Italy broke out, the grand vizier İbrahim Hakkı Paşa resigned. He was succeeded in office but hardly in power by the elderly Sait Paşa. Mahmut Şevket Paşa, who stayed on as war minister, admitted frankly at a meeting of officers in the War College in Istanbul that Tripoli could not be defended: the army was too weak and the navy almost non-existent.[1] In fact, he had himself earlier sanctioned the transfer of a division of Ottoman troops from Tripoli to fight insurgents in Yemen.[2] The chief of the general staff, Ahmet İzzet Paşa, was already in Yemen (where he was to remain until after the outbreak of the Balkan war two years later), having quarrelled with the war minister and his chief German adviser, von der Goltz Paşa, over the reorganization of the Ottoman armed forces.[3] However, the CUP decided to defend the indefensible.

As soon as news of the war reached him, Major Enver left his post of military attaché in Berlin, and persuaded the CUP central committee in Salonica to launch a guerrilla war against the Italians by mobilizing Arab tribes in the Libyan desert.[4] Enver's star was rising. After the suppression

of the mutiny in Istanbul in April 1909, he had become formally engaged
to the sultan's niece Naciye, a young girl born in 1898.[5] He was no longer
just an ambitious revolutionary officer, but a member of the family of
the caliph, a title likely to impress the Bedouin.

As both Britain, which controlled Egypt, and France, which held the
protectorate over Tunis, had declared their neutrality, and as direct sea
communications with Tripoli had been severed by the Italians, Enver
travelled incognito to Alexandria, where he arrived on 19 October
1911.[6] He was not alone: all the leading revolutionary officers in the
CUP rushed to Libya by such means as they could come by.

The decision of the CUP to organize Arab resistance against the
Italians was inspired by its experience in Macedonia, where the
Ottoman authorities had found themselves confronting local armed
bands led by officers infiltrated from the Bulgarian, Greek and Serbian
armies. Until 1911, the Ottoman government had desisted from such
unorthodox operations. Even after the Italian invasion, the grand vizier
Sait Paşa and the war minister Mahmut Şevket Paşa hesitated to provide
official cover for the 'self-sacrificing [i.e. volunteer] officers' (*Fedaî
Zabıtan*) who travelled to Libya. If they were intercepted by British or
French authorities, they were to be described as 'adventurers acting
against the wishes of the Ottoman government'.[7] The adventure had
serious consequences. It was from among the volunteers who went to
Libya that there arose the clandestine Special Organization (*Teşkilât-ı
Mahsusa*), which was to promote CUP objectives among Muslims
outside the Ottoman state, and repress CUP enemies within it.
Answerable directly to Enver, the Special Organization gave rise to rival
efforts by German, British and other military intelligence officers
during the First World War and thereafter.

Empires run a risk when they encourage guerrilla wars and subversion. Old-fashioned Ottoman statesmen saw the danger. The grand
vizier Damat Ferit Paşa, who tried to stop Mustafa Kemal from organizing popular resistance against the Allies at the end of the First World
War, was to say later: 'The decision to prolong the war in Tripoli by
organizing armed bands led to the Balkan war and to the advance to the
gates of Istanbul of small nations, which had earlier been subject to us;
this in turn prepared the ground for the Great War with its calamitous
consequences for humanity and for the Ottoman state.'[8] Damat Ferit
Paşa exaggerated the untoward consequences of the involvement of
Ottoman officers in Libya, just as he was proved wrong in his assessment of Turkish popular resistance in Anatolia in 1919. He failed to see
the difference between romantic expectations of popular resistance, and
the realistic assessment at which Mustafa Kemal had arrived after the

Ottoman defeat in the First World War. But with the wisdom of hind-sight, Damat Ferit could see that in 1911 Ottoman officers were needed more urgently in the Balkans than in Libya. By setting out to defend every inch of Ottoman territory, and by trying to impose uniform government on all the far-flung provinces of the empire, the CUP dispersed its energies and weakened it at vital points. As its leading officers rushed off to the periphery, it lost power in the capital on the eve of the Balkan war.

On 11 December 1911, the newly formed opposition party, Concord and Freedom (*İtilâf ve Hürriyet*, usually referred to in the West as *Entente Libérale* or Liberal Union), won a by-election by a single vote in Istanbul. Fearing that public opinion was turning against it, the CUP procured the dissolution of parliament and cheated its way back to power in fraudulent elections (known in Turkish history as *sopalı seçim*, or 'big stick elections') in January and February 1912. The grand vizier Sait Paşa was now supported theoretically by 264 deputies out of 270. Squeezed out of parliament, the opposition showed itself in the army, where a group calling itself Saviour Officers (*Halâskâr Zabitan*) challenged the supremacy of the CUP. On 9 July 1912 Sait Paşa was forced to sacrifice the war minister Mahmut Şevket Paşa. A week later, Sait Paşa resigned, one day after the parliament had expressed its confidence in him by 194 votes to 4. He explained: 'They [the deputies] have expressed their confidence in me, but I have no confidence in them.'[9]

On 22 July 1912, a cabinet of elder statesmen, including three former grand viziers, was formed by the elderly general Gazi Ahmet Muhtar Paşa, who had defended Kars and Erzurum in the war with Russia in 1878. The war ministry was given to Nazım Paşa, a bluff soldier who disliked military politicians. The newly elected parliament, packed with CUP supporters, was dissolved on 5 August, and an attempt was made to round up the leaders of the CUP: some fled abroad, others hid in the capital.[10] In Macedonia, Unionist officers were removed from their commands; in Albania, where anarchy reigned, some Unionist officers were murdered.[11]

Mustafa Kemal volunteered for service in Libya while the CUP was still in power and Mahmut Şevket Paşa was still minister of war. He left Istanbul on 15 October 1911,[12] on board a Russian ship. He travelled disguised as a journalist, under the name of Şerif, and was accompanied by the CUP 'national orator' Ömer Naci, and two CUP desperadoes, Sapancalı Hakkı and Yakup Cemil. The nationalist naval officer Rauf (Orbay), who met Mustafa Kemal in Egypt, and knew his dislike of military adventurers, was surprised by the company he kept. Mustafa Kemal excused himself, saying: 'I have been friends with Ömer Naci for years. I enjoy his conversation. But I do not share the ideas of any of them. What can you do? We are travelling companions, by force of circumstance.'[13] In any case, Mustafa Kemal's eyes were fixed not on the rank-and-file adventurers round him, but on the leading adventurer, Enver. Before leaving Istanbul, Mustafa Kemal and his party had asked the CUP central committee for money to cover their travelling expenses. They were told to join Enver, but given no money for the journey. Mustafa Kemal had to raise £200 sterling on his own promissory note.[14]

Enver was senior in rank, having been promoted full Major in 1907; he was senior in the councils of the CUP; as a future member of the Ottoman dynasty, he was senior in social standing. He also beat Mustafa Kemal in the race to Cyrenaica. Mustafa Kemal arrived in Alexandria on 29 October 1911, and set out for Cyrenaica three days later.[15] Like other Ottoman officers, he was helped by Egyptian sympathizers to find his way to the frontier.[16] But he was injured soon after setting out, and had to return to spend a fortnight in hospital in Alexandria, where he was joined by his childhood friends Nuri (Conker) and Fuat (Bulca).[17] The party finally left Alexandria by train on 1 December 1911. Six hours later they got off at the last station in the Western Desert, and transferred to horses, while their luggage was loaded on to camels. After a journey of eight days, they arrived at the frontier, which the British authorities had moved westwards, annexing to Egypt the small port of Sallum. As Mustafa Kemal and his friends tried to cross the frontier, they were detained, but were able to proceed after leaving 'others' behind.[18] On 9 December 1911, Nuri (Conker) wrote to Salih (Bozok):

> Today we have crossed the frontier from Egypt into Bingazi [Cyrenaica]. The danger [of interception] is past. Our next objective is [the promontory of] Resüldefne [Ra's al-Dafna], at a distance of two days' journey. Our health is good. We journey by day and sometimes by night. There's no sign of habitation along our path, except for isolated Bedouin tents. As we travelled secretly through Egypt, a foreign country, we had to keep away from inhabited areas. We have been spending the nights under canvas, and are cooking our own food. You should see Mustafa Kemal sorting out dry beans. Fuat (Bulca) is our chef.[19]

In a postscript Fuat (Bulca) added: 'Desert life isn't easy … I dream of the sparkling waters of Rumelia. The water here is the colour of fermented millet.' The party arrived at Resüldefne on 12 December, and put up at the only house in the place, which was like 'a large storehouse.

Considerable amounts of supplies arrive here. [Resül] Defne is the first staging post for volunteers [*mücahit*, literally warriors for Islam, entering Ottoman Libya].'[20]

On 30 November, on the eve of Mustafa Kemal's departure from Alexandria, the general staff in Istanbul informed Enver that Mustafa Kemal was promoted from Adjutant-Major to full Major.[21] A few days earlier, on 12 November 1911, Enver had been promoted Staff Lieutenant-Colonel and appointed commander for the whole of Cyrenaica. In a telegram to the war ministry, which he signed as governor and overall commander of Cyrenaica, Enver reported that 'Staff Major Mustafa Kemal joined the army at his own request on 18 December 1911.' This was probably the date on which Mustafa Kemal made contact with Ottoman regular troops and reported for duty in Cyrenaica.

In the account which he gave in a letter to a friend, Mustafa Kemal said that he fought his first engagement with the Italians outside Tobruk on 22 December 1911. Tobruk had been occupied by the Italians on 4 October, but, as elsewhere along the coast, Ottoman troops and Arab tribesmen camped opposite the Italian lines, stopping any advance into the interior. The commander of the Ottoman forces outside Tobruk was, unusually, a general, Ethem Paşa. Although Ethem Paşa asked that Mustafa Kemal and Nuri should be assigned to his command,[22] the party decided to move further west to the encampment outside the port of Derne on the coast, which served as headquarters for Cyrenaica. Mustafa Kemal wrote that he was given the command of the eastern column, with Fuat (Bulca) as his chief of staff, while Enver, who had preceded him, commanded the western column, with Nuri (Conker) as his chief of staff. Later, he added, as operations increased in scope, Enver became commander for the whole of Cyrenaica, while he was put in charge of the Derne sector.

In fact, Enver had already been appointed to overall command in Cyrenaica by the time Mustafa Kemal arrived. He treated the province as his personal fief, and even printed money bearing his own signature.[23] Inevitably, friction developed between Enver and Mustafa Kemal. News of it must have spread to Istanbul, for a year or so later (on 19 February 1913) Mahmut Şevket Paşa, who had by that time become grand vizier, noted in his diary that he had heard that Mustafa Kemal had not got on with Enver during the Libyan campaign.[24] Before leaving for the front, Mustafa Kemal told Rauf (Orbay), 'If Enver obstructs my work, rather than take measures against him and cause discord, I'll return to Istanbul.'[25] But he stayed on, and the Ottoman officers who commanded Arab tribesmen split into factions. One of these officers was a thick set, round-headed desperado called Ali (Çetinkaya), who gave his allegiance to Enver. It was a decision for which he apologized to Mustafa Kemal many years later, when he became his chief agent of repression in the early years of the Turkish republic.

For the Ottoman officers, including Mustafa Kemal, the war in Libya was both a patriotic duty and a political necessity. The CUP had to show itself more capable of defending the integrity of the state than had been Sultan Abdülhamit. The Arabs had to be shown that the regenerated Ottoman state was capable of defending them, whilst the officers themselves hoped that their endeavours in Libya would enhance their careers. Asked by his biographer Hikmet Bayur why he had taken part in the hopeless task of defending Libya, Mustafa Kemal replied: 'At the time, I myself saw that it was hopeless. But I had to do it to keep my material and moral position in the army and among the officers who were my contemporaries. In any case they hadn't given me any work to do in Istanbul.'[26]

We need not doubt that Mustafa Kemal believed that his career required his presence in Libya. But would he have gone if he had known not only that the mission was useless, but that, during his absence, the Greeks were to capture his native town, where his mother still had her home? In the letter he sent to Salih (Bozok) from Cyrenaica on 8/9 May 1912, Mustafa Kemal said optimistically that the task which he and his comrades had set themselves was to retrieve 'these warm and friendly borderlands of the fatherland'.[27] But on 21 December of the same year, after disaster had struck in the Balkans, he admitted that his decision to fight the Italians in Cyrenaica had been 'precipitate and pointless'.[28] Wisdom came with experience.

Mustafa Kemal spent most of his time in Libya in the camp at Ayn Mansur (Ain Mansur), outside Italian-held Derne. The camp had been set up by Enver, who had established in it a workshop to produce cartridges, a newspaper (called *al-Jihad*, 'The Holy War'), a military training camp and a school for the sons of tribal sheikhs.[29] Ill health put a brake on Mustafa Kemal's activity. After taking part in an engagement outside Derne on 17 January, he developed an eye infection, and temporarily lost the sight of his left eye. He was treated for a month in the camp hospital, but after fighting another engagement on 4 March, he suffered a recurrence of the eye inflammation and had to take to his bed for a fortnight. In his letter of 22 May, Mustafa Kemal said that he was still unable to see with his left eye, that doctors had suggested that he should go to Egypt for treatment, but that he had refused to go. He added sadly: 'When this war ends and I bid farewell to military life, I wonder how I shall be able to find a restful retreat.'[30]

Ottoman officers in Cyrenaica relied on the Sanusi brotherhood for the bulk of their forces. The brotherhood was a strictly orthodox order of Sufis, or Muslim mystics, founded by an Algerian, Muhammad ibn Ali al-Sanusi (known in the West as the Grand Sanusi), who established his first centre (*zaviye*, in Arabic *zawiyyah*) in Cyrenaica in 1843. By the end of the nineteenth century, the Arab tribes in Cyrenaica were in effect ruled by the Sanusis on behalf of the Ottoman state.[31] The Grand Sanusi was buried in the oasis of Cağbub (Jaghbub, Giarabub in Western literature), deep in the Western Desert, just west of the Egyptian frontier. In 1911 this was the main headquarters of his second successor Seyit Ahmet Şerif (Sayyid Ahmad al-Sharif, the title *sayyid* denoting the Sanusis' claim to descent from the Prophet Muhammad). Ahmet Şerif was a loyal subject of the Ottoman caliph. In any case, the Italian invasion threatened not only Muslim rule, but the autonomy of the tribes, their land and livelihood. What Enver and Pan-Islamists failed to realize was that Muslim solidarity was effective when it complemented self-interest and the instinct of self-defence. In Cyrenaica, the CUP aim of preserving the integrity of the Ottoman state coincided with the desire of the Arab tribes to remain in control of their lives. Not only Enver but many Western strategists drew from the Libyan war the conclusion that Muslim solidarity was a powerful force everywhere, at least potentially. Events in the course of the First World War were to prove them wrong.

When he took over the whole of the Derne sector on 6 March 1912,[32] Mustafa Kemal had under his command eight Ottoman officers, some 160 Ottoman regular soldiers and volunteers, an artillery company, two machine-guns captured from the Italians, and 8,000 Arab tribesmen. The tribesmen were supplied by the Sanusi *zaviyes* and led by their sheikhs, who were in turn answerable to Ottoman officers attached to each formation. For almost a year (October 1911 to end of September 1912), these Arab irregulars under Ottoman command pinned down inside Derne some 15,000 regular Italian troops with strong artillery support.[33] Italian attempts to move into the interior were beaten back in more than half a dozen engagements fought in the hills and ravines round Derne. One difficulty which Ottoman officers faced was that the Arab tribesmen came and went as the spirit moved them. Ottoman officers tried to keep regular records, which were needed as the tribesmen were paid 2 piastres (one fiftieth of a Turkish gold lira) a day,[34] in addition to their rations. Mustafa Kemal had to warn the sheikhs that pay and food would be forfeited if their men slunk away. In a report dated 25 January 1912, in which he explained the reasons for the failure of an attack on Italian positions, Mustafa Kemal pointed out that the main concern of the sheikhs was to extract as much money as possible from the Ottomans. They had an interest, therefore, in avoiding battle and prolonging the war.[35]

Throughout the campaign Mustafa Kemal behaved like a meticulous young staff officer. He organized regular reconnaissance missions, insisted on proper duty rosters, demanded discipline in guard duties, tried to make sure that the troops' water flasks were filled at the start of missions. He saw to the provision of rations, and worried even about the cleanliness of spoons and napkins and the proper comportment of waiters in the officers' mess. Throughout his life, Mustafa Kemal was obsessive about order, personal cleanliness and good clothes. They were symbols of the civilization which he had chosen. In the camp outside Derne he also organized lectures and training sessions, made sure that Ottoman newspapers were obtained and read, and asked that proper records of engagements should be kept for historical purposes. Saying that these records were to include an account of the troops' morale, Mustafa Kemal added in brackets, 'a true account'.[36]

Meticulousness was combined with unselfconscious patriotism. In a letter he sent from Ayn Mansur on 8 May 1912 to his friend Salih (Bozok) in Salonica, Mustafa Kemal wrote:

> Tonight there was a party for all the commanders and officers of our forces in Derne ... In the sincere glances of these good-natured heroic comrades, of these low-rank but great commanders, who make the enemy tremble, I read the desire to die for the fatherland. This brought back the memory of all my comrades in Macedonia, of all the heroic members of our army. A feeling of great joy and pride welled up in my heart, and I told my comrades: the fatherland will surely be safe; the nation will surely find happiness, because the fatherland has many children willing to sacrifice their safety and happiness for those of the country and the nation.[37]

Mustafa Kemal's romantic, patriotic optimism, characteristic of his generation of officers throughout Europe, was to suffer a rude shock before the year was out. But while he was soon to shed many of his illusions, and develop a more astringent outlook, his belief in his people – and in himself – never wavered.

While Mustafa Kemal concentrated on military matters, Enver plunged into the politics of the conflict – the relationship with the Sanusis and the encouragement of Islamic solidarity. The war minister Mahmut Şevket Paşa was misinformed when he reported on 16 November 1911 that Mustafa Kemal had gone to the oasis of Calo (Jalo, Gialo in Western literature) in order to mobilize the Sanusis.[38] But Mustafa Kemal's friend Nuri (Conker) did go as Enver's emissary to

Cağbub in April 1912 to meet Seyyit Ahmet Şerif. In a letter which he sent from this isolated oasis to Salih (Bozok) in Salonica, Nuri wrote:

> In this blessed spot even three-year-old girls are not allowed out. Females live and die where they are born. Such is the local custom. Although in military camps there are both men and women, we have not been able to see a woman's face for the last three months, as they are all hidden behind heavy veils. We lead ascetic lives like the monks of Mount Athos. If we go on from here, our next stop will surely be paradise.[39]

The letter is characteristic of the attitude of most CUP officers. They posed in Arab headdresses and robes and saw themselves as romantic desert warriors. But they could not help looking down on Arab tribesmen, whose manners, poverty and general backwardness shocked them. These Arabs were fellow-Ottomans and brothers in religion, but they were also a joke, at least among friends.

Unable to break out of their coastal enclaves, the Italians sought to force the Ottoman government to the negotiating table by naval attacks in the eastern Mediterranean and the Red Sea. In March 1912 the Italian fleet bombed Beirut; the following month, forts guarding the entrance to the Dardanelles were bombarded; in May the Italians occupied Rhodes and the other islands of the Dodecanese in the Aegean sea; in July Italian torpedo-boats succeeded in entering the Dardanelles straits. Worried that the whole edifice of Near Eastern peace erected after the Congress of Berlin was about to crumble, and that their economic interests would suffer in the collapse, Russia, France and Britain attempted to mediate, largely by trying to persuade the Ottoman government to make concessions to the Italians. But the CUP would not allow the government to accept the Italian annexation of Libya in exchange for sweeteners, such as the recognition of the sultan's religious leadership of Libyan Muslims. Even Gazi Ahmet Muhtar Paşa, who had originally advocated a peaceful settlement with Italy, was unable to agree to the cession of Libya when he became grand vizier.

The deadlock was broken when Montenegro broke off diplomatic relations with the Ottoman state on 8 October, thus setting off the process which led to the Balkan war. Throughout the summer reports had been appearing that the Balkan states – Serbia, Montenegro, Bulgaria and Greece – had sunk their differences and were getting ready to mount a combined attack on the Ottomans' remaining possessions in Europe. Italy had a dynastic connection with Montenegro through the marriage of King Victor Emmanuel III to Elena, daughter of Nicholas I of Montenegro. This allowed it to play the Balkan card in order to put pressure on an obdurate Ottoman government. The

Balkan threat provided Gazi Ahmet Muhtar Paşa with the justification
to take the step which he had advocated all along and give way to Italy.
On 18 October 1912 peace was concluded at Ouchy, near Lausanne in
Switzerland. The Ottomans accepted the Italian annexation of Libya,
while the Italians agreed to evacuate the Dodecanese after the withdrawal of Ottoman forces from their new possession.

Enver was aghast. In a telegram to the war ministry in Istanbul on 27
October 1912, he argued that it was dangerous to tell Arab tribesmen
that peace had been concluded, and impossible to stage a mass withdrawal of Ottoman forces. He refused to send back his weapons and
supplies, and argued that a self-sustaining administration could be
established in Cyrenaica. He himself was determined to stay put, presumably at the head of an Arab government. Mustafa Kemal would
have nothing to do with such fancies, and in the same telegram Enver
reported that Staff Major Mustafa Kemal and Captain Fuat (Bulca) had
been sent back.[40] Enver himself had to change his mind before long
when he realized the extent of the Ottoman disaster in the Balkans. He
returned to Istanbul on 20 December 1912.[41] But before leaving, he
made arrangements for the continuation of the guerrilla war. This gave
the Italians an excuse to stay put in the Dodecanese, which remained in
their possession until the closing stages of the Second World War, to the
lasting benefit of these islands.

On 10 November 1912, the Ottoman High Commissioner (ambassador) in Egypt, Rauf Paşa, reported that Mustafa Kemal had arrived in
Egypt on his way to Istanbul and asked for funds to cover his expenses
and those of another hundred Ottoman officers and officials who were
to follow him from Derne. He had no money for this, he said, and it
would create a bad impression if the returning officers were left to their
devices in Egypt.[42] Mustafa Kemal travelled to Istanbul via Vienna,
Hungary and Romania. He chose this roundabout route in order to
have his eyes treated in the Austrian capital.

In the year which he spent in Cyrenaica, Mustafa Kemal proved
himself a courageous, resourceful and meticulous staff officer. He drove
himself hard, without ever losing a sense of reality. He succeeded in
working with local people, but did not build wild schemes on the basis
of their cooperation. As ever, he kept his own counsel. He gained field
experience, but failed to advance his ambition. On 17 May 1912,
Mustafa Kemal's name was not included in the list of Ottoman officers
to whom the Ottoman parliament expressed its gratitude. Enver headed
the list.[43] On 28 July 1912, when the grand vizier Sait Paşa reported to
the Ottoman parliament on the defence of Cyrenaica, he praised the
services of Enver, but made no mention of Mustafa Kemal. Pressed to

name other volunteers, the grand vizier replied: 'The reason why I have mentioned only Enver by name was that he has been of great help to me since my assumption of office.'[44]

The desert war of 1911–12 did not pass unnoticed in the outside world. There were German officers in Enver's camp; foreign correspondents came and went. But although other Ottoman officers were occasionally mentioned, it was Enver who attracted most attention. He had first expressed his Napoleonic ambitions when the CUP seized power in Salonica in 1908. In Cyrenaica he thought of himself as prince of the Arabs, loved by the tribesmen and feared by the Italians. Then, just as Napoleon had abandoned his troops in Egypt in 1799 to seize power in France, so Enver cut short his adventure in Cyrenaica in 1912 in order to dominate the destiny of the Ottoman state. As for Mustafa Kemal, he was to tell the English journalist Grace Ellison in 1923: 'I don't like Napoleon at all. He intruded his person into everything. He fought not for a cause, but for himself. That's why he came to a bad end. It's inevitable for such people.'[45] Clearly, 'such people' by then included Enver.

6

Fighting Disaster

B Y THE TIME Mustafa Kemal arrived in Istanbul in November 1912, Ottoman possessions in Europe had been reduced to the capital and its immediate environs to the west, the Gallipoli peninsula, and three besieged fortress towns – İşkodra (Scutari, Shkodër) in northern Albania, Yanya (Ioannina, Yanina, now in Greek Epirus) and Edirne (Adrianople), the chief town of eastern Thrace. Macedonia, for whose sake the CUP had seized power in 1908, was lost quickly and irretrievably.

During the summer of 1912, the Balkan states – Montenegro, Serbia, Greece and Bulgaria – had concluded a series of interlocking alliances and understandings. In September they mobilized under the pretext of holding military exercises. On 8 October, Montenegro declared war on the Ottomans. On 13 October, Bulgaria and Serbia delivered an ultimatum to the Ottoman government, demanding autonomy for ethnic communities in the Ottoman state.[1]

In Istanbul, policy was made in the streets. After coming to power, the Gazi Ahmet Muhtar Paşa government tried to meet unrest in the army in the Balkans – and at the same time to conciliate Balkan neighbours – by demobilizing 120 battalions of trained regular troops. The CUP, now in opposition, came out in favour of war as the only means of keeping the Ottoman possessions in Europe, and incited students to stage bellicose demonstrations outside the Sublime Porte, the office of the grand vizier. Cowed by the demonstrators, but reluctant to face war, the government deliberated for three days before rejecting the ultimatum of the Balkan states. Finally on 17 October, Balkan ambassadors in Istanbul were handed their passports, and war was declared. On the following day, the Greek king George I, acting as the mouthpiece of his irredentist prime minister Eleftherios Venizelos, published a proclamation summoning his people to fight for the liberation of oppressed Christians.[2]

The Ottoman government now responded to the mobilization of its Balkan neighbours by ordering its own troops to mobilize. An attempt was made to turn back troops which were earlier allowed to go home. A new command structure was improvised: with the chief of staff Ahmet İzzet Paşa away in the Yemen, the war minister Nazım Paşa became deputy commander-in-chief (deputizing theoretically for the sultan), while forces in the Balkans were divided into an Eastern Army in Thrace, under Abdullah Paşa, a Western Army under Ali Rıza Paşa, an Army of the Vardar in northern Macedonia under Zeki Paşa, and the Alasonya (Elasson in Thessaly) Army on the Greek frontier. Mahmut Şevket Paşa, the friend of the CUP, was offered this last command, but refused, explaining later: 'The appointment was offered to me in order to tarnish my reputation and my military honour. How could I sacrifice my reputation?'[3]

As students continued to demonstrate outside Yıldız palace, apprehension reigned within. True, the commander-in-chief, Nazım Paşa, remained debonair. Asked whether there were plans for military operations, he replied, 'It seems some plans were made when Mahmut Şevket Paşa was war minister. I'll ask for them.'[4] Others were more realistic. The governor of Istanbul, Cemil Paşa, begged the sultan's private secretary Ali Fuat (Türkgeldi) to convince the sovereign of the need to stop the war, saying: 'We're in no state to fight. I saw the troops at last year's manoeuvres ... We can't make war with these soldiers.'

Ottoman territory in Europe, where a narrow band of land in western Thrace linked Istanbul and eastern Thrace with Macedonia and Albania, was difficult to defend against a simultaneous attack from all quarters. Moreover, according to official Turkish sources, Ottoman troops were outnumbered. No more than 580,000 soldiers could be mustered against a combined strength of 912,000 troops of the Balkan allies.[5] However, this disparity does not explain the sudden collapse of Ottoman armies on all fronts, particularly since they had adequate military material and, arguably, food supplies, although usually in the wrong places.

The day before war was declared, the war minister Nazım Paşa gave an assurance that military preparations were complete in Thrace, where, according to the Eastern Army commander Abdullah Paşa, there were 116,000 Ottoman troops. Nazım Paşa even issued instructions for the Ottomans to attack at once,[6] although existing plans were based on a defensive strategy. But the Bulgarians struck first. On 22 October they pushed four columns towards the Ottoman positions at Kırklareli (known at that time as Kırkkilise, or Forty Churches), east of Edirne. On 25 October, they outflanked them on the east, whereupon the Ottoman defenders turned and fled. Advancing south, the Bulgarians then caught the main Ottoman force at Lüleburgaz, and routed it between 29 October and 2 November. The remnants of the army struggled to the Çatalca lines, the last barrier before Istanbul. Edirne was surrounded and the Gallipoli peninsula cut off, as the Bulgarians pushed through to the sea of Marmara at Tekirdağ (Rodosto in Western literature).

In the meantime, another Bulgarian column advanced south along the Mesta (Nestos) valley and severed communications between Ottoman Thrace and Macedonia. The fate of Macedonia was decided by a single battle. It was fought at Komanova (Kumanovo), just south of the Serbian frontier. The Ottoman army resisted for a day, then fled before the advancing Serbs, as rumour spread that enemy cavalry had appeared in the rear. The Western Army commander, Ali Rıza Paşa, tried to organize resistance in Manastır, but it took the Serbs only four days to capture the city.[7] The Greeks advanced north against feeble resistance and entered Salonica on 9 November, a few hours ahead of the Bulgarians.[8] Albania, cut off and partly penetrated by advancing Serbs, Montenegrins and Greeks, declared its independence, which Austria-Hungary subsequently ensured. At sea, the Greek navy quickly won mastery in the Aegean, occupying all the islands, outside the Italian-held Dodecanese, while Crete was officially annexed to the Greek kingdom. The honour of the Ottoman navy was saved by the cruiser *Hamidiye*, commanded by Hüseyin Rauf (Orbay), which bombarded the Bulgarians in the Black Sea, the Greeks in the Aegean and the Serbs and Montenegrins in the Adriatic, and eluding its pursuers, returned to a hero's welcome in Istanbul on 7 September 1913.

Not only Ottoman soldiers, but hundreds of thousands of Muslim civilians fled before the armies of the Balkan allies. They had good reason to take to the road. When Prizren in Kosovo was captured by the Serbs soon after the outbreak of the war, some 12,000 local Muslims were massacred, according to contemporary press reports; the oldest mosque was turned into a church, and another totally destroyed.[9] Similar scenes took place all over European Turkey, with the Bulgarian army acquiring particular notoriety for its harsh treatment of Muslims and their property.[10] Western Thrace became a staging place for fleeing Muslims. Tens of thousands of refugees crowded into Istanbul, from where most were sent on for resettlement in Anatolia. As the dream of a Greater Albania was shattered, Albanian nationalists turned on their kinsmen who remained loyal to the Ottomans. Niyazi, the ethnic Albanian 'hero of freedom' in 1908, was shot dead by an Albanian nationalist.[11]

The sultan asked the cabinet and elder statesmen to consider peace overtures, but as no decision could be reached, Gazi Ahmet Muhtar Paşa was, with some difficulty, persuaded to resign on 29 October.[12] Even so, he tried to delay surrendering his seal of office, saying that he could not find its box. But the sultan's chief secretary insisted that the seal was needed immediately for the new grand vizier; the box could wait.[13] The new grand vizier was the elderly Kâmil Paşa, who was by then the declared enemy of the CUP. A year earlier, he had written a long memorandum to the sultan, in which he had predicted accurately the course of events, asked that CUP should stop interfering in the government, and advocated an alliance with Britain.[14] But he was no longer able to put his advice into practice. His hold on power in a country shocked by defeat was precarious. Nevertheless he started exploring the possibilities of making peace, while retaining the services of Nazım Paşa as war minister. The failure of a Bulgarian attempt to break through the Çatalca lines on 3 November gave him a respite. The chief of staff, Ahmet İzzet Paşa, returned from the Yemen and, having assumed the command of Ottoman forces in the field, organized the despatch of reinforcements from Anatolia.[15] On 3 December, the Ottomans signed an armistice with the Bulgarians and the Serbs,[16] the latter having sent a contingent to aid the Bulgarians besieging Edirne.

Mustafa Kemal returned to Istanbul just after the Bulgarian advance had run out of steam at the Çatalca lines. Meeting his friend Salih (Bozok) in a reading room near the Sublime Porte, inappropriately named *Meserret* (Joy), which prominent members of the CUP used to frequent, Mustafa Kemal burst out, 'How could you leave Salonica, that beautiful home town of ours? Why did you hand it to the enemy and come here?'[17] The decision of Hasan Tahsin Paşa, whose career had begun in the gendarmerie and who had been appointed to the command of the Alasonya (Thessaly) Army when Mahmut Şevket Paşa refused the post, to surrender Salonica with all its stores to the Greeks without firing a shot, was considered particularly shameful. Yet that unfortunate general saw his forces cut off on all sides, and did come to advantageous terms with the Greeks, who, in order to steal a march on the advancing Bulgarians, agreed to transfer back to Turkey the weapons of the Salonica garrison after the conclusion of peace. The promise was not kept.[18]

As at the beginning of the war with Italy, the leading revolutionary officers in the CUP hastened to join the fighting. On 21 November, Mustafa Kemal was appointed director of operations on the staff of the Straits Composite Force (*Bahr-i Sefit Boğazı Kuva-yı Mürettebesi*), which had been assembled at Bolayır, at the neck of the Gallipoli peninsula. The force commander was Fahri Paşa, and his chief of staff Mustafa Kemal's old friend Fethi (Okyar), to whom Mustafa Kemal probably owed his appointment. After returning from Tripolitania, Fethi had been entrusted with the delicate task of escorting the deposed Sultan Abdülhamit to Istanbul before the Greeks entered Salonica.[19] Fearful as ever of an assassination plot, Abdülhamit refused at first to move, and it was with difficulty that Fethi coaxed him on board the *Lorelei*, the German *stationnaire* (naval vessel permanently stationed off Istanbul), which had been sent to rescue him. Salih (Bozok) travelled with the former sultan to Istanbul, and then served in the guard posted at Abdülhamit's new, and last, residence, the Beylerbeyi palace on the Asian shore of the Bosphorus.[20]

At Gallipoli, where the Bolayır force had its headquarters, Mustafa Kemal found himself not far from another friend and ally, Dr Tevfik Rüştü (Aras), who was in charge of the Red Crescent hospital in his native town of Çanakkale.[21] Tevfik Rüştü was an active member of the CUP, which was increasingly restive in opposition. After the conclusion of the armistice, the Ottoman government pinned its hopes on negotiations in London where the great powers were trying to mediate a peace settlement. By the middle of January 1913, it became clear that the Balkan allies would make peace only if the Ottomans relinquished all their territory in Europe to the west of a line running diagonally across Thrace from Enez at the mouth of the Meriç (Maritza) river to Midye (now Kıyıköy) on the Black Sea, leaving Edirne to the Bulgarians. On 17 January, the great powers recommended that the Ottoman government should accept these terms.[22] As the grand vizier Kâmil Paşa was steeling himself to make peace, Talât, who had emerged as the strongest civilian personality in the CUP, began preparations for a coup.[23]

He summoned the leading military and civilian members of the CUP to a meeting in Istanbul, which took place on 21 January. Fethi (Okyar) travelled to it from his headquarters in Gallipoli. Enver could not make it. After his return from Cyrenaica, he was appointed chief of staff of the 10th army corps, consisting of reserves rushed from Anatolia. By the middle of January 1913, this force was gathering for embarkation at İzmit and Bandırma on the Asian shore of the sea of Marmara. Speaking in Enver's absence, Fethi argued that the war was lost, that it was better that an anti-CUP government should incur the unpopularity of signing peace, and that a coup should be staged only if free elections were not permitted thereafter.[24] He then left, believing, it seems, that his view had prevailed. But the meeting reconvened the following day when Enver finally arrived. On that day, 22 January, Kâmil Paşa had summoned a Grand Council to discuss peace terms. He had brushed aside the sultan's advice that the CUP should also be invited, saying: 'They were a revolutionary party centred on Salonica. Salonica is gone. Now it's their turn to go.'[25] Empowered by the Council to pursue peace initiatives, Kâmil Paşa submitted to the sultan's approval a proposal that Edirne should become a demilitarized free city, whose Muslim heritage would be protected.[26] Talât and Enver had other ideas.

Enver put a simple question to the revolutionaries: 'Do you trust the government?' 'No,' they replied. 'In that case, let's overthrow it tomorrow.'[27] There had already been some preparations for the coup. First, the CUP had turned to the war minister Nazım Paşa, believing him to be sympathetic to a resumption of hostilities.[28] When he refused to commit himself, Mahmut Şevket Paşa, the former war minister who had worked with the CUP in the past, had been approached and, after some hesitation, had agreed to become grand vizier after the overthrow of Kâmil Paşa.[29] Feeling in the army was, in any case, favourable to a patriotic stand. Officers serving on the Çatalca lines had approached the palace and demanded to know what the government intended to do.[30]

On 23 January 1913, Enver led a small band of his supporters to the Sublime Porte. They forced their way into the building. One of the CUP 'volunteers', a desperado named Mustafa Necip, was killed by the bodyguard of the war minister, Nazım Paşa. Another desperado, Yakup Cemil, then shot dead the war minister. According to one account, Nazım Paşa had provoked the intruders when he shouted, 'Bastards. You've let me down. This is not what you had promised.' Talât was to confirm later that the CUP had offered to make Nazım Paşa grand vizier.[31]

The conspirators then forced Kâmil Paşa to submit his resignation to the sultan. The elderly grand vizier started his brief note with the words, 'At the suggestion of the military ...' Enver forced him to add, 'and of the people'.[32] Sultan Mehmet Reşat V raised no difficulty when Enver arrived at the palace, and duly appointed Mahmut Şevket Paşa grand vizier. The following day as the new grand vizier assumed his office, a crowd chanted, 'Paşa, save Edirne!' The task was not easy.

News of the coup, which immediately became known as 'the raid on the Sublime Porte', came as an unpleasant surprise to Fethi, Mustafa Kemal and others at the Gallipoli headquarters. It seems that Talât had to go himself to Gallipoli to justify the coup.[33] But only military action

could provide sufficient justification. On 30 January, the Mahmut
Şevket Paşa government rejected the peace terms transmitted by the
great powers.[34] On 3 February, the armistice expired and the Bulgarians
resumed their bombardment of Edirne. It was clear that the starving
city could not hold out much longer. Something had to be done quickly.

Enver had the answer. He persuaded Mahmut Şevket Paşa to
approve a combined operation to strike at the right flank of the
Bulgarians in front of the Çatalca lines.[35] His 10th corps would land at
Şarköy on the northern shore of the sea of Marmara, and meet the
Composite Force which would attack the Bulgarians from the west. The
success of the plan required accurate timing and coordination. Neither
could be achieved.

Fethi (Okyar) admitted later that he had originally informed headquarters that his Composite Force could deal with the Bulgarians facing
it. It seems that he was in favour of an attack to dislodge the enemy
from high ground overlooking his lines. But the combined operation
was delayed until 6 February, and by that time the Bulgarians had
brought up reinforcements. The Composite Force attacked without
waiting for confirmation that the 10th corps had sailed across the sea of
Marmara. It was beaten back and lost half its men. When the 10th corps
finally arrived in the evening of 6 February, it found the Bulgarians
masters of the coast. Headquarters ordered it to re-embark and sail on
to Gallipoli. After remonstrating, Enver agreed.[36] Leaving his men
behind, he went to Istanbul to await their arrival in the capital.[37]

The failure of the combined operation at Şarköy was followed by
furious recriminations between, on the one hand, the 10th corps commander Hürşit Paşa and his chief of staff Enver, and on the other, the
Composite Force commander Fahri Paşa, his chief of staff Fethi and
director of operations Mustafa Kemal. Mahmut Şevket Paşa intervened
personally, deciding in favour of Hürşit Paşa, who was put in command
of both forces. The decision was not surprising since the new grand
vizier owed his position to Enver.

Fethi and Mustafa Kemal fought their corner. From their forward
positions in Bolayır, they sent on 17/18 February a memorandum to
Mahmut Şevket Paşa, arguing that the coup which had brought him to
power could only be justified if Ottoman troops mounted an immediate
offensive to relieve Edirne. The memorandum, which was drafted by
Mustafa Kemal, suggested that the troops waiting in naval transports
off Gallipoli should be transferred to the Çatalca lines. They would then
take part in the push to Edirne, which would be supported by the rest
of the troops round Gallipoli, and by further landings along the coast.
A copy of the telegram was sent to the deputy commander-in-chief

Ahmet İzzet Paşa.[38] Soon afterwards, when they were told that Hürşit Paşa had been put in overall command, Fahri Paşa, Fethi and Mustafa Kemal resigned their posts. Ahmet İzzet Paşa, who received first the memorandum and then the resignations on 22 February, sent off a furious telegram to the grand vizier complaining that Fethi's real purpose was to score points off the authors of the coup at the cost of endangering the whole Ottoman army. He knew perfectly well that the operation which he proposed was impossible to execute. Ahmet İzzet Paşa concluded:

> Seriously, no army in the world has ever been run by youths devoid of official responsibility, nor has victory ever been won by an army harbouring this degree of anarchy, discord and mischief. If the government is incapable of taking legal action to subject these irresponsible gentlemen to military discipline, it could at least ask their friends to use their influence and invite them to make some personal concessions and have some pity on this poor country – in short, persuade them to obey rules and regulations ... [39]

The grand vizier Mahmut Şevket Paşa had to intervene personally. He went to Bolayır, accompanied by Hürşit Paşa and Enver, and patched up a reconciliation with the commanders of the Composite Force.[40] Nevertheless, Fethi left Bolayır, while Mustafa Kemal became chief of staff of the Bolayır corps, which was now detached from the straits command.[41] Both Mahmut Şevket Paşa and Ahmet İzzet Paşa were reluctant to risk a major offensive, but they allowed Enver, who was on the Çatalca lines now that the 10th corps had crossed over from Asia, to stage a minor attack. One division moved forward and won back some territory near Büyük Çekmece (not far from the present Atatürk International Airport in Istanbul). 'This satisfied the offensive spirit of young officers,' Mahmut Şevket Paşa noted.[42] It did not, however, help the Ottoman defenders of Edirne, who finally surrendered on 24 March 1913.[43] The city's fortifications had been designed to withstand a siege of forty days to two months and thus allow time for the mobilization of the Ottoman army.[44] In fact, Edirne held out for nearly six months under the brave command of Şükrü Paşa. The remnants of the Ottoman garrison were imprisoned in Sarayiçi, a small island separated from the city of Edirne by the river Tunca. There, among the ruins of an old Ottoman palace, some 20,000 prisoners of war are said to have perished from disease and starvation.[45]

Fighting continued along the Çatalca lines until 30 March, when a last Bulgarian offensive was beaten back.[46] Enver took part in the engagement at the head of volunteers from among revolutionary officers, who were to form his Special Organization, and of cadets from the Istanbul

War College. As the war had reached a stalemate, and as Yanya had already fallen to the Greeks on 19 March, the Mahmut Şevket Paşa government bowed to the inevitable, and agreed to cede Edirne and all territory west of the Enez–Midye line in Thrace. A peace agreement and an armistice were signed on this basis in London on 30 May 1913.[47]

It was a few days after the fall of Edirne that Mustafa Kemal showed his mettle once again. On 7 April 1913, Ahmet İzzet Paşa informed the Composite Force in Gallipoli that Muslim clergy were to be sent to raise the morale of the troops. Mustafa Kemal sent a curt reply the following day, saying that his brother officers and the regimental chaplain were giving the troops all the advice that was necessary and that the despatch of extra preachers would only serve to propagate the view that the soldiers were demoralized, and that the authorities were reduced to prayerful supplications.[48] As a revolutionary officer and a member of the CUP, Mustafa Kemal did not have to mince his words.

Once the fall of Edirne had exposed the futility of the 'raid on the Sublime Porte', Mahmut Şevket Paşa's grip on power weakened and political intrigue intensified. The ousted grand vizier Kâmil Paşa returned to Istanbul from his exile in Egypt in order to marshal forces against the government. He was placed under house arrest and expelled after three days on 31 May.[49] Then on 11 June 1913, Mahmut Şevket Paşa was assassinated on his way to the Sublime Porte.[50] Cemal, who had been appointed military governor (*Muhafız*) of the capital after the coup of 23 January, acted quickly and resolutely. The assassins and their alleged political patrons were rounded up. On 24 June, twelve real or alleged plotters, including the sultan's nephew-in-law, Damat Salih Paşa, were hanged in Istanbul. Sait Halim Paşa, a pliant and polite member of the Egyptian royal family, was chosen by the CUP to be the new grand vizier. Talât became interior minister. He and Cemal ensured that the CUP acquired a monopoly of power, which was to last until October 1918. But if the opposition to the CUP was now suppressed, faction continued within it.

The new CUP administration was lucky. The Balkan alliance had begun to crumble. Greece and Serbia had decided to make common cause against Bulgaria, which was also faced with territorial demands by Romania. Proud of their newly won fame as the 'Prussians of the Balkans', the Bulgarians struck first. On the night of 29/30 June, eighteen days after the assassination of Mahmut Şevket Paşa in Istanbul, they attacked the Serbian army in Macedonia. The Serbs defeated them, while the Greeks pushed east out of Salonica and occupied all of southern

Macedonia. To meet the new danger, the Bulgarians pulled back the bulk of their forces facing the Ottoman army. The CUP seized the opportunity to recapture lost ground. At the insistence of the new interior minister, Talât, an initially hesitant cabinet disregarded the warnings of the great powers, and secured the sultan's approval for an order to the Ottoman army to advance to Edirne.[51] Three days later, on 21 July 1913, the fifth anniversary of the Young Turks' revolution, Ottoman troops entered Edirne, having met practically no resistance from the Bulgarians.

According to Turkish biographers of Atatürk, the first unit to enter Edirne was a brigade of his Bolayır corps.[52] However that may be, the commander of the advancing troops was Hürşit Paşa, who was in charge of the 10th corps. His chief of staff, Enver, rode at the head of the troops and was acclaimed as the second conqueror of Edirne (the first being Sultan Murat who captured the city in 1361 and made it the capital of the Ottoman state). Enver had thrust himself to the front of the stage once again. The Bolayır corps commander Fahri Paşa and his staff took offence at being assigned a secondary role. Their forces moved south of Edirne, crossed the Meriç (Maritza) and occupied Dimetoka (now Dhidhimotikhon, in Greek western Thrace). A prominent member of the CUP, Haci Âdil, who had been installed as governor of Edirne, had to go to Dimetoka and patch up the quarrel between the rival commanders. Falih Rıfkı (Atay), then a young reporter of the CUP newspaper *Tanin*, and later Atatürk's chief publicist, was present at the meeting. It was the first time that he had set eyes on Mustafa Kemal. Mustafa Kemal, he noted, did not look like the guerrillas (*komitaci*) employed by the CUP, who wore peasant felt caps, were covered in bandoliers and carried rifles slung over their shoulders. In Falih Rıfkı's description, Mustafa Kemal appears as a fair-haired young officer in a smart uniform, with proud, piercing eyes. He said little, but was clearly accorded greater importance than his rank warranted.[53] This account, which Falih Rıfkı no doubt embellished when he published it in 1952, agrees nevertheless with what we know of Mustafa Kemal's habits.

Enver's guerrillas, who, a little later, were formally incorporated into the Special Organization, pushed west and set up a Provisional Government of Western Thrace for the overwhelmingly Muslim local population. It was a repetition of the arrangements which Enver had made when he left Cyrenaica, and a precursor of similar attempts to hang on to territories inhabited by Turks, in defiance of the great powers.

Mustafa Kemal did not take part in Enver's project in western Thrace. He went back to Istanbul, where the leadership of the CUP, and, with it, the fate of the Ottoman state were about to be decided.

The great powers, whose role was reduced to easing rather than preventing changes brought about by war, did nothing to help Bulgaria. On 29 September 1913, Bulgarian representatives signed a peace treaty in Istanbul, under which the Ottomans kept eastern Thrace, including Edirne and Dimetoka.

The peace treaty provided for an exchange of populations on either side of the frontier. In Turkish eastern Thrace only Bulgarians were officially affected. But, unofficially, the CUP coerced also as many Greeks as it could to leave the area. According to the leading CUP member, Halil (Menteşe), 100,000 Greeks were pushed out. A little later, similar tactics were used to force 200,000 Greeks to leave their homes on the Aegean coast of Anatolia.[54] Muslim refugees from the Balkans took their places. As the peace treaties signed with the Balkan states gave their new Muslim subjects the option of settling in Ottoman territory, the flow of refugees continued after the end of the war. It was a step leading to the creation of homogeneous nation states.

The families of Mustafa Kemal, Salih (Bozok) and other prominent Turkish-speaking Muslims, including *dönme* families of Jewish origin, made haste to establish themselves in Istanbul and İzmir. Mustafa Kemal found for his mother Zübeyde a government-owned terraced house – in effect a grace-and-favour dwelling – in Akaretler, the street leading down to the palace of Dolmabahçe. Fikriye, the 16-year-old niece of his stepfather Ragıp, moved to a more traditional house in the old city, near the mosque of Sultan Ahmet (the Blue Mosque). But she was a frequent visitor at Akaretler,[55] and from that time on was available to serve and please Mustafa Kemal.

But he had also other feminine company, which was intellectually more stimulating. This was provided by two sisters, Corinne and Edith, the daughters of Ferdinand (Ferdi) Paşa, a doctor of Italian origin employed in the Ottoman army medical corps.[56] Corinne had married a friend of Mustafa Kemal, a young Turkish officer called Ömer Lütfü, and set up house near the War College in Istanbul. Ömer Lütfü was killed during the Balkan war, leaving his young widow to make her way in westernized Turkish society. Mustafa Kemal frequented her salon, cultivating an *amitié amoureuse* with her, and when he left Istanbul at the end of 1913, he began exchanging with her playful sentimental letters in French. Occasional visits to Istanbul allowed him to keep the friendship alive until after the end of the First World War. Then he left Istanbul for Anatolia, while Corinne settled in Italy. She returned to Istanbul in 1941, three years after Atatürk's death, and died in 1946. Edith's daughter,

Melda Özverim, who married a Turk, denied later that Atatürk ever had an affair with either sister.[57] We may well believe her. But in educating Mustafa Kemal in the ways of polite European society, the two Italian women played a significant part in his life.

Eastern Thrace was devastated by the Balkan wars, and ethnic cleansing dislocated life there and along the Aegean coast of Turkey. But the capital, Istanbul, and commercial cities in Asia, such as İzmir, Aleppo and Damascus, still preserved the multi-ethnic, cosmopolitan life which had enjoyed a golden age in the reign of Abdülhamit II. True, refugees from the Balkans filled the poorer quarters of the capital and thronged its quays, but the European district of Beyoğlu and the smart suburbs along the Bosphorus and in the Princes Islands were untouched. They provided a comfortable setting for political intrigue. At the conclusion of the Balkan wars the main struggle was fought within the CUP, and it was won by adventurous, hard men. Enver, whose exploits were extolled by CUP newspapers, began to appear as the champion of youth against middle age, of daring against caution, of Muslim patriotism against cosmopolitanism. But first he had to oust his more cautious comrades.

When the Balkan wars ended, Mustafa Kemal put up in the Istanbul house of his friend and patron Fethi (Okyar).[58] Fethi had resigned his commission as Lieutenant-Colonel in order to devote himself to politics. His decision may have been affected by the recriminations which had followed the failure of the Şarköy operation. It was also consistent with the principle, which everyone voiced but few respected, that revolutionary officers should choose between the army and politics. Whether as an inducement to leave the army, or in recognition of his popularity among the rank and file, Fethi was appointed secretary-general of the CUP on the eve of the party conference held in Istanbul in September 1913. It is said that his first action was to cut off the funds of the armed volunteers, or desperadoes (*fedai*), who served as Enver's striking force.[59] This invited the hostility of the party executive (or General Centre, *Merkez-i Umumî*), dominated by Enver and his allies. Fethi says in his memoirs that when he had accepted the post of secretary-general, he had, in any case, demanded that the dominant position of the executive should be clarified.[60] However, his proposal that party policy should be determined by the CUP parliamentary group, and that the executive should confine its activity to internal party organization, was set aside.[61]

Immediately afterwards, Talât, who as minister of the interior had become the leader of the civilian wing of the CUP, suggested to Fethi that he should accept the post of Ottoman ambassador in Sofia. Fethi consulted Cemal, the military governor of Istanbul, but still only a Lieutenant-Colonel, who advised him to accept, in view of the importance of the post. The importance lay in the fact that the CUP was working for a reversal of alliances, and had decided to court Bulgaria as a counterweight to Greece, from which it was still hoping to recover the Aegean islands. Fethi, who believed Cemal to be his friend, agreed and suggested that Mustafa Kemal should accompany him as military attaché. Mustafa Kemal, in the words of his biographer Falih Rıfkı, knew how to bide his time. Unable to make his way against Enver, he left his rival in command of the field in Istanbul. On 27 October 1913, Mustafa Kemal was appointed military attaché to Sofia. In theory he held the same post simultaneously in three other Balkan capitals – Bucharest, Belgrade and Cetinje – but his work was in effect limited to Bulgaria.[62]

The departure of Fethi and of Mustafa Kemal prevented disagreement among the military members of the CUP. The swift collapse of the army in the Balkan wars had stunned the officer corps. A committee of enquiry was set up. It was dominated by CUP officers, who believed that the generals inherited from the reign of Abdülhamit were largely responsible. But one member of the committee, Major İsmet (İnönü), saw that the governments which held power after 1908 shared responsibility for the defeat. İsmet had served under Ahmet İzzet Paşa in the Yemen. As he was to say in his memoirs, the thirty-five battalions employed in the pointless campaign there could have been used much more profitably in the Balkans.[63] But, while politics were clearly involved, defeat brought to light the disorganization of the Ottoman armed forces. The leaders of the army, young and old, were convinced that only German help could remedy it. German advisers had been employed since the reign of Abdülhamit, and many Ottoman officers, including Ahmet İzzet Paşa, had been sent to Germany for training. But more was needed than instruction and the submission of reports. The commanders of the Ottoman armed forces agreed with the German military attaché in Istanbul, that German officers had to be put in positions of command in order to carry out the reforms which they deemed necessary.[64]

The German ambassador in Istanbul, Baron von Wangenheim, was first approached by Mahmut Şevket Paşa on 23 January 1913. The agreement of the German emperor was communicated to his successor, Sait Halim Paşa, on 17 July 1913, and a contract defining the functions of the German mission was signed on 27 October, the day on which Mustafa

Kemal was appointed to Sofia.[65] A Prussian officer, Otto Liman von Sanders, was appointed head of the German 'military reform mission', which consisted of forty-two officers, most of them with the rank of major or captain.[66] They were all promoted one rank in the Ottoman service, Brigadier Liman von Sanders becoming an Ottoman Major-General when he arrived in Istanbul on 14 November. The contract provided that he should become commander of the 1st army corps in Istanbul, an appointment which he deemed essential in order to give practical effect to the reforms. But Russia, horrified at the prospect of a German in command of the Ottoman capital, objected immediately, and was supported both by Britain and France. Liman von Sanders argued that his appointment did not set a precedent, since the Ottoman navy was commanded by the British admiral Arthur Limpus, while the gendarmerie had a French commander. Hectic diplomatic exchanges produced a compromise which in effect strengthened Liman von Sanders' position. On 14 January 1914, he was promoted General in the German army and, consequently, Marshal in the Ottoman service, a rank too high for the command of an army corps. He was given a new post as Inspector-General of the Ottoman army. He also had a new Turkish interlocutor.

In October 1913, immediately after the CUP conference, Enver launched his campaign to substitute himself for Ahmet İzzet, Paşa as Ottoman war minister. The campaign was fought round the issue of the rejuvenation of the officer corps. On 2 January 1914, Talât visited Ahmet İzzet Paşa and asked him to approve a list of compulsory retirements from the army. When he refused, Talât demanded and obtained his resignation. On the following day, the sultan learned from the press that Enver had been appointed war minister.[67] 'It's impossible, he's far too young,' exclaimed the aged sovereign. Nevertheless, the following day he duly issued a decree, appointing Enver minister of war and chief of the general staff. Simultaneously, he was promoted Brigadier, only nineteen days after becoming full Colonel.[68]

Enver's first action was to abolish the army council, and to retire a large number of officers, variously estimated at between 800 and 2,000, including two marshals, 33 generals and 95 brigadiers.[69] In the cabinet reshuffle, Enver's ally, Cemal, was appointed navy minister and given the rank of General. The sultan's chief secretary, Ali Fuat (Türkgeldi) commented: 'When Enver and Cemal took over the land and sea forces, they used the pretext of rejuvenation to retire those officers who had been commissioned before them, young and old, good and bad. Thereafter the reins of government passed from the Sublime Porte into Enver's hands.'[70]

Ali Fuat oversimplified. Although Enver was supreme in military matters, the CUP government remained collegiate right up to 1918. At the top, power was divided between Talât, Cemal and Enver. But other prominent members of the CUP, like Halil (Menteşe), minister of foreign affairs and then of justice, or Rahmi (Evrenos), the quasi-autonomous governor of İzmir, enjoyed considerable power. They all had their following; they sometimes disagreed, but they hung together to the end. Nor did the victorious faction deal harshly with its critics within the CUP. Fethi, who was relatively liberal in his views, his protégé Mustafa Kemal, and friends like Tevfik Rüştü (Aras), retained their personal links with individual leaders and enjoyed considerable freedom of action in pursuing their ambitions.

When he heard of Enver's appointment as war minister, Mustafa Kemal wrote from Sofia to Tevfik Rüştü (Aras): 'Enver is energetic and will want to do something. But he doesn't stop to reflect. He is thinking of giving the job of chief of the general staff to İsmail Hakkı, who will not be able to do a thing. If I am appointed, we could get somewhere.'[71] İsmail Hakkı, an active member of the CUP, who was known as *Topal* (Lame, on account of an injury he had sustained), did not become Enver's chief of staff. He served as the army's director of supplies until the end of the Great War and attracted the hatred of the civilian population by his requisitions.[72] But he did deputize for Enver when the latter commanded the ill-fated expedition in the Caucasus. Enver chose as his assistant in the general staff another CUP militant, Hafız Hakkı, a bright contemporary from the War College. Hafız Hakkı, who like Enver had married into the Ottoman royal family, died of typhus a year later on the Caucasian front. There was, of course, never any question of Enver appointing a man as independent-minded as Mustafa Kemal to the general staff. The two men, both ambitious to pass into history as saviours of their country, were temperamentally incapable of working together.

The Liman von Sanders mission set to work in earnest in the opening months of 1914. German officers took charge of the Ottoman general staff and war ministry. When Enver's friend Hafız Hakkı was subordinated to the German von Bronsart Paşa (Bronsart von Schellendorf), he made the best of the situation, saying: 'We lack knowledge. We have to learn. We have no right to invoke the principle of state sovereignty at the cost of harming the country by our ignorance.'[73]

Liman von Sanders was shocked to see that the families of Ottoman officers fed at military canteens, as they could not afford to buy their own food, that soldiers were dressed in rags and sometimes went barefoot, that officers neglected their men, that horses were mangy and military hospitals filthy. Anxious not to lose face, Ottoman officers tried to conceal the extent of the disorganization of the army from their German advisers.[74] Liman von Sanders was no fool. Before long, he saw much more clearly than the German embassy in Istanbul the gap between Enver's ambitions and the means at his disposal. But policy was not made by the German military mission. It did its best to help create the new Ottoman army which Enver wanted to see. Patriotic Ottoman officers swallowed their pride and cooperated with their German mentors. Inevitably there was friction, but impressive results were achieved in a short time.

Nevertheless the relationship was flawed from the start. As İsmet (İnönü) was to note later: 'There must be a limit to the infringement of the responsibility and sovereignty of a state. In the reforms undertaken at the end of the Balkan war that limit was overlooked.'[75] It was a feeling which was fully shared by Mustafa Kemal. He was to say later: 'Our comrades reduced the Turkish nation and army to an unnatural state. It was unnatural because the army was handed over to a foreign military mission. I do not wish to criticize the Germans and their military mission. It is our head of state and our statesmen who deserve criticism.'[76]

7

A Diplomatic Interlude

M USTAFA KEMAL ARRIVED in Sofia on 20 November 1913.[1] He left
his luggage at the Ottoman embassy, where he thought that the
ambassador, his friend Fethi (Okyar), who was single at the time, would
put him up. But when Fethi asked him what he was to do with the
luggage, Mustafa Kemal took the hint, and went to a hotel. Fethi,
Mustafa Kemal's biographer Falih Rıfkı Atay notes, was careful with his
money,[2] unlike Mustafa Kemal who found it difficult to make his salary
stretch for more than a fortnight.[3] After a few days at the Grand Hôtel
Bulgarie, Mustafa Kemal moved to the Splendide Palace. It was, he
wrote, 'newly built and really comfortable. It has bathrooms, room
service, anything you like. The entertainment it provides is reason
enough to stay in this hotel.'[4]

But the hotel must have been beyond his means, for some time later
he became a lodger with a German family, Gustav and Hildegard
(Hilda) Christianus and their 7-year-old daughter. Frau Hilda was to say:
'At first we used to speak French. Then I began to teach him German
... He used to come over frequently to our part of the house for a chat.
He knew that I loved red roses and used to bring me one every time he
came.'[5] He also made the family a gift of a Turkish red carpet. Mustafa
Kemal liked to behave like an *homme galant*. When he saw off the
Christianus family on a trip out of Sofia, he declared in his newly learnt
German, '*von Herz zu Herz geht ein Weg*' (there is a path that leads from
heart to heart).

As Mustafa Kemal found his feet in Sofia society, he spread his attentions to other ladies. A local Turk introduced him to the salon of Mme
Dourzi, who was known as a Parisian lady. Writing to Corinne, Mustafa

Kemal protested that it was impossible to see a single pretty woman in Sofia, adding for good measure, 'Allow me to tell you that I did not find the Parisian lady at all beautiful.' He said that he had been taken to a *café concert* called 'New America', where, he assured Corinne, he did not respond to the charms of two Hungarian ladies who joined him in a box.[6] Flirtations with members of Bulgarian society were another matter. Mustafa Kemal got to know Dimitrina (Mara), the daughter of the Bulgarian war minister, General Kovachev; Elena, the daughter of a Bulgarian member of parliament, Dino Achkov; Nicolina, the daughter of the Bulgarian prime minister, Radoslavov.[7] The fact that their two countries had just fought a cruel war, which had left a legacy of human suffering, did not prevent easy social relations between middle-class Turks and Bulgarians. Bulgarian attitudes to the Turks were complex: there was ethnic hatred manifesting itself in atrocities on both sides. But there were seventeen Turkish members of the Bulgarian parliament, and rich members of the Turkish community enjoyed a comfortable life.

The high point of Mustafa Kemal's social life in Sofia came on 11 May 1914 when he was invited to a fancy dress ball at the military club in the presence of King Ferdinand. Mustafa Kemal turned up dressed in the authentic uniform of a Janissary, specially sent to him from the military museum in Istanbul by permission of the war minister Enver Paşa. Returning the uniform, Mustafa Kemal wrote to his friend Kâzım (Özalp), who had arranged the loan, that he had been the centre of attention at the ball, and that questions about his dress gave him the opportunity to speak at length of the military prowess and past victories of the Turks.[8]

One of Atatürk's Turkish biographers, Şevket Süreyya Aydemir, says that although much has been written about Mustafa Kemal's stay in Sofia, most of the stories have been fabricated.[9] This is almost certainly true of the story that he had proposed to Mara, but that her father General Kovachev forbade the marriage. That Mustafa Kemal was not contemplating marriage can be inferred from a letter which he sent to Salih (Bozok) on 7 November 1914, on the eve of his return to Turkey. After mentioning the marriage of their joint companion Fuat (Bulca), Mustafa Kemal wrote: 'Let's see what my lot will be. Naturally, there can be no question of it [my marrying] so long as I'm here.' A week earlier, Mustafa Kemal had sent rather a stiff letter of congratulation to Fuat. 'Life is short,' he wrote, 'and most men see in marriage the most reasonable means of crowning it with happiness. Those who do not observe this rule are few and exceptional. These exceptions do not disprove the general rule. These unfortunates are rather the victims of circumstances which do not permit the observance of this pleasant rule, perhaps because they are afraid of marriage.'[10] Mustafa Kemal was referring to himself: courageous, decisive and intensely ambitious in the world of men, he was excessively courteous, but essentially shy with women of his new social rank, whose company he enjoyed. When he finally married, briefly and unsuccessfully, it was his young bride who had made the running.

Nevertheless, the company of educated women – Bulgarian, local Turkish or western European – added to Mustafa Kemal's enjoyment of life in Sofia. The town had been transformed in the thirty-five years which had elapsed since it had been chosen as the capital of the new Bulgarian state. It had acquired impressive public buildings, a theatre, an opera house, and comfortable villas set in gardens. But the old main mosque was still standing, not far from the newly built cathedral commemorating the country's liberation, or perhaps creation, by the tsar's armies in 1878. Sofia showed how a small, provincial Ottoman town of wooden houses and narrow streets could become an agreeable European city with wide tree-lined avenues. The Ottoman ambassador Fethi (Okyar) found the experience painful: 'This country, where I went as an ambassador, was but fifty years ago a province within our borders.' Speaking of 'the millions of our fellow-citizens we have abandoned to their fate', Fethi wrote, 'for us, who remembered not the remote past, but things as they were five years ago, what had happened was heart-rending.'[11] Fethi, who had already served as military attaché in Paris, was unlikely to have been impressed by Sofia. But for Mustafa Kemal, the year he spent in Sofia was the longest he had ever lived in European surroundings. And Sofia inspired in him not sadness, but the will to emulate. According to one story, one evening when he went to the opera, Mustafa Kemal asked whether all the singers and musicians were Bulgarians. Told that they were, he exclaimed: 'Now I understand why the Bulgarians won the Balkan war.'[12]

The transformation of the Bulgarians had amazed the Turks. The Bulgarians had been generally regarded as among the most backward of the sultan's subjects. The American missionary Cyrus Hamlin, the founder of Robert College (whose premises now house the University of the Bosphorus) in Istanbul, remembered that in the middle years of the nineteenth century, 'Every spring, there was an advent of Bulgarian shepherds and ostlers in the streets of the capital – strong, rude men in sheepskin clothing, with their shrieking bagpipes and rude country dances, dashing their sheepskin caps upon the pavement to every passer-by for *bakshish*. They seemed but little above savage life.'[13] The Bulgarians attributed their progress to the work of 'popular enlighteners'

– nationalist teachers who imparted new learning as they went out to the people in the spirit of the Russian *narodniks* (populists). Their example was not lost on Mustafa Kemal, who was later to adopt populism (*halkçılık*) as one of the six basic principles of the Turkish republic.

Foreign travel always had a serious purpose for the revolutionary officers in the CUP: there was much to learn for future use in their own country. At the same time that Mustafa Kemal was absorbing the lessons of Bulgaria's progress, his future prime minister İsmet (İnönü) and his companion-in-arms in the Turkish War of Independence, Kâzım Karabekir, both military members of the CUP, were dutifully going round the museums and other public buildings of Vienna, Munich, Berlin and Paris. İsmet was particularly impressed by the active role played by women in the social life of western European countries.[14]

On 1 March 1914, Mustafa Kemal was promoted Lieutenant-Colonel.[15] This promotion did not affect his official duties in Sofia, which were fairly light. A military attaché normally deals with intelligence. But Mustafa Kemal appears to have done little more than pass on such items of information as came his way. In any case, his resources were limited. On 16 February 1914, he had asked that 500 liras should be sent to him to enable him to do his job.[16] The information he provided was sometimes unwelcome. Soon after his arrival, he reported that the chief of the Bulgarian general staff, General Fichev, had told him that during the Balkan war German officers, and in particular Goltz Paşa, had passed on to the Bulgarians information on the movements of Ottoman troops.[17] Kâzım Karabekir, who had been appointed to the 2nd (intelligence) department of the Ottoman general staff in January 1914,[18] warned Mustafa Kemal that his reports had angered the German officer who was head of the department. In reply, Mustafa Kemal said that he had himself been surprised at the information passed on to him, and that a letter he had just received (from Istanbul) had explained matters and cleared up the misunderstanding. His only motive had been to serve his country, and the angry reaction of the German officer was therefore unjustified.[19]

Mustafa Kemal was suspicious of the Bulgarians. In a long commentary he wrote in Sofia on a series of lectures given by his friend Nuri (Conker) on the qualities required of military commanders, Mustafa Kemal warned that the Bulgarians still hoped to regain Edirne.[20] He argued that the Ottomans should respond by giving their officers better training, and by instilling in them a spirit of initiative and the desire to take the offensive. This was indeed the aim of the reforms initiated by Enver with the help of the German military mission. In spite of his distrust of the Germans and his feelings of rivalry, Mustafa Kemal tried to keep on good terms with Enver, at least formally. He wrote to Enver to congratulate him on his efforts to rejuvenate the Ottoman officer corps. According to Kâzım Özalp, Enver was delighted to receive the letter from a regular critic, and asked his uncle Halil (Kut), who was at that time commander of the Istanbul garrison, to show it to CUP comrades.[21] This did not alter the fact that Mustafa Kemal and Fethi were in virtual exile in Sofia. The CUP leaders in Istanbul left Ottoman embassies largely in the dark when they took decisions on foreign policy.

The CUP leadership believed that the Ottoman state had lost territory in North Africa and the Balkans because it had been left out of the European system of alliances. Their adversary Kâmil Paşa had advocated joining Britain and France. But the Entente had been extended to include Russia. On 30 June 1913, before the Balkan war had been formally concluded, Russia proposed to foreign ambassadors in Istanbul that, in order to meet the grievances of the Armenians, most of eastern Turkey should be governed as a single province under a Christian governor-general and that local Muslims and Christians should have an equal share in the administration and local security forces, even though Muslims outnumbered Christians in the area. Germany believed that the plan would facilitate Russian expansion into Anatolia, where it was financing the construction of the Baghdad railway. With German support, the government of Sait Halim Paşa succeeded in watering down the Russian proposals. On 8 February 1914 it reached an agreement with Russia, under which, instead of a governor-general, two European inspectors-general were to be appointed in eastern Anatolia to oversee reforms. Even so, the agreement was bound to cause dismay among Muslims who had seen similar arrangements form the prelude to the loss of Ottoman Macedonia. The CUP-dominated government decided therefore to withhold news of it from the public.[22]

In spite of the invitation it had extended to the German military mission and the wide powers with which it had endowed it, the CUP leadership had not yet ruled out other options. The Ottoman government had three immediate aims: to secure a binding guarantee of the territorial integrity of the Ottoman state, to win back the Aegean islands occupied by Greece during the Balkan war, and to abolish foreign privileges in Ottoman territory under the system of capitulations. No formal negotiations took place with either Britain or France, although the navy minister Cemal held discussions at the Quai d'Orsay when he was invited to France to attend manoeuvres in June 1914. The discussions took place after the assassination of the Austro-Hungarian heir apparent, Archduke Franz Ferdinand, by a Serbian terrorist on 28 June 1914. As events led inexorably to the outbreak of the First World War, the French showed little interest in Cemal's proposals, and when he returned to Istanbul he gave way to Enver's insistence on an alliance with Germany.[23]

Enver is usually described as pro-German. In fact, like the other CUP members, he was first and foremost an Ottoman patriot. But he was convinced of the superiority of the German army over those of the Entente. His experience in Libya had also led him to believe that Muslims everywhere would rise in response to a call made in the name of the Ottoman sultan caliph. He had in mind Egypt, which was under British control, Persia, which Russia and Britain had divided into zones of influence, the precariously independent emirate of Afghanistan, and the Muslim subjects of Russia in central Asia and Transcaucasia, of Britain in India and of France in North Africa. Based on almost total ignorance of Muslims outside the Ottoman state, Enver's hopes of effective Muslim and Turkic solidarity under Ottoman leadership were shared by Kaiser Wilhelm, whose thinking was influenced by German orientalists, many of them excellent scholars but poor political advisers.

The fact that Enver's grandiose designs could only be realized at the expense of Russia, Britain and France, helped draw him into the orbit of Germany. On 22 July, only a few days before the outbreak of the World War, Enver told the German ambassador von Wangenheim that the Ottoman government wished to conclude an alliance with his country, and that a German refusal would strengthen the hand of Ottoman ministers who favoured the Entente. A similar proposal was made by the grand vizier Sait Halim Paşa to the Austro-Hungarian ambassador, Marquess Pallavicini. Both ambassadors had considerable reservations, fearing that the proposed alliance would add to their countries' burdens.[24] But they were overruled by the Kaiser.

In Istanbul, the grand vizier Sait Halim Paşa summoned the sultan's secretary Ali Fuat (Türkgeldi) asking him to obtain the sovereign's authorization for the conclusion of a secret defensive alliance with Germany, which, he said, would safeguard the future of the Ottoman state.[25] The sultan did as he was told, and the secret alliance was signed in Istanbul on 2 August 1914. It was a curious document specifying that if Russia intervened militarily in the dispute between Austria-Hungary and Serbia, thus activating the alliance between Germany and Austria-Hungary, then the Ottoman state would join in on the side of Germany. Yet the previous day Germany had already declared war on Russia. Far from being defensive, the alliance thus involved the Ottomans retrospectively in an offensive war. Under another provision, the

Ottomans undertook to allow the German military mission an effective say in the command of Ottoman armed forces. This toned down, but did not alter much, the previous German insistence that command over the Ottoman armies should be in the hands of German officers.

On the day the alliance with Germany was signed, the Ottoman government ordered a general mobilization and stopped payment of its foreign debt. It also prorogued parliament until November, thus preventing any discussion of its policy. On 7 August censorship was imposed on the press and on telegraphic communications. The Great War had started: the great powers – Germany and Austria-Hungary on one side, Russia, France and Britain on the other – fell on each other. Keeping silent about its alliance with Germany, the Ottoman government declared armed neutrality, and kept up contacts with the embassies of the Entente countries. A member of the German military mission, Kress von Kressenstein, was to write later:

> In spite of the insistence of the German high command that Turkey should enter the war immediately, the Turkish government, influenced in particular by the navy minister Cemal Paşa, decided at first to remain neutral, and to act only after it had completed its mobilization. The ability of Turkish statesmen to maintain neutrality until 2 November 1914, when Turkey entered the war, and their success in concealing their true aims from the Allied representatives in Istanbul, were a masterpiece of oriental diplomacy.[26]

However, the First Lord of the Admiralty, Winston Churchill, was not deceived, and he ordered the sequestration of two Ottoman warships, *Sultan Osman* and *Reşadiye*, which were ready for delivery in British yards. The Ottoman navy minister, Cemal Paşa, describes the profound shock which he felt at the news, which, he says, was announced on '1 or 2 August'.[27] The British decision to seize the two warships, whose cost had been covered by public subscription, is often described as a mistake. But Enver, Talât and the speaker of parliament Halil (Menteşe) were already committed to an alliance with Germany, and since Enver and Talât were clearly in control, the hesitation of Cemal and the opposition of some CUP members, notably the finance minister Cavit, were not to be relied upon. Churchill could not afford the risk of adding to the armament of a potential enemy.

Enver tried to mislead the Russians by informing their military attaché General Leontyev on 5 and 9 August that Turkish troops could be withdrawn from the Russian border and be directed instead against Austria-Hungary, if Russia agreed to an alliance with Turkey in exchange for an extension of Ottoman territory in Thrace and the return of the Aegean islands to the Ottoman state.[28] The fact that the offer was not meant seriously was demonstrated a day later, on 10 August, when Enver allowed the German cruisers *Goeben* and *Breslau* to enter the Dardanelles and thus escape British warships in the Mediterranean. When the Allies insisted that under the rules of neutrality, the Ottomans had a duty either to expel the two German ships or to disarm and intern their crews, a fictitious sale was quickly arranged. The two warships were renamed *Yavuz* and *Midilli*, but their German crews continued to man them under their commander Admiral Souchon.

As the Allies hesitated to call the bluff of the Ottoman government, the latter continued to put its plan into operation. On 9 September, Admiral Souchon was given the command of the Ottoman navy,[29] following the departure of the British mission under Admiral Limpus. On the same day, the Ottoman government informed foreign envoys that it was unilaterally abolishing the capitulations as from 1 October.[30] This disturbed even the German ambassador. On 27 September, the German commander of the Dardanelles, Weber Paşa, ordered the mining of the entrance to the straits. On 20 October the decisive step to war was taken when the Ottoman government signed an agreement for a German loan of 5 million gold liras, most of which was to be disbursed after the Ottoman state entered the war. The finance minister Cavit was not present at the meeting of the cabinet, at which Enver and Talât's plans for the beginning of hostilities were almost certainly agreed in principle. On 22 October, Enver handed Admiral Souchon a secret order, reading: 'The Turkish fleet will secure naval mastery in the Black Sea. Seek the Russian navy and attack it without prior declaration of war.'[31]

The sultan, the Ottoman high command, and ministers opposed to immediate entry into the war, including the grand vizier Sait Halim Paşa, were kept in the dark. They were all taken by surprise when on 29 October, the eve of the Muslim holiday (*Şeker Bayramı*) which marks the end of Ramazan, the Ottoman navy under the command of the German admiral Souchon, and including both German and Turkish-manned units, attacked Russian ports in the Black Sea and sank a number of Russian warships. Sait Halim Paşa was dissuaded with difficulty from submitting his resignation. But four ministers, including Cavit and the minister of posts Oskan Efendi, an ethnic Armenian, resigned. The war was a tragedy for the Armenians, who lived on both sides of the Ottoman-Russian frontier: many sympathized with the Russians, most wanted to be left in peace. But whatever their actions and their feelings, they perished in their hundreds of thousands within a year of the outbreak of hostilities.

Even after its initial act of aggression, the Ottoman government tried to prevaricate. Claiming that the clash had been caused by Russian war-ships interfering with Ottoman naval manoeuvres, it offered an enquiry into the circumstances. But the Allies had had enough. Russia declared war on 2 November, Britain and France on 5 November. The Ottoman government responded with its own declaration of war on 11 November.[32] Two days later, at a ceremony attended by Sultan Mehmet V in the hall of the old palace of Topkapı, where the relics of the Prophet Muhammad were kept, a *fetva* was read allowing the proclamation of a *cihat* (*jihad* or Holy War). Its propriety was doubtful, since the Muslim Ottoman state was joining an alliance of Christian states in their war against other Christian states. Nevertheless, on 23 November Mehmet V decreed as caliph that the proclamation of the *jihad* should be published throughout the world of Islam. Eşref Kuşçubaşı, a leading member and later the leader of Enver's Special Organization, noted that in Istanbul the proclamation was received coolly, adding that elsewhere there must have been even less enthusiasm.[33]

Mustafa Kemal was kicking his heels in Sofia as the small clique headed by Enver and Talât plunged the Ottoman state into war, with little con-sultation and less forethought. On 15 August, Talât and Halil (Menteşe) went first to Sofia and then to Bucharest in order to persuade the Bulgarians to enter the war on the side of the central powers and of the Ottomans, the Romanians to stay neutral, and the Greeks to settle the dispute over the Aegean islands. The mission achieved nothing, as, unlike the CUP government in Istanbul, the three Balkan states were weighing up offers from all sides before making up their minds. Mustafa Kemal predicted correctly that the Bulgarians were not ready to commit themselves, and that the war would last for a long time. Writing to his friend Tevfik Rüştü (Aras) on 17 September, he said that hasty decisions should be avoided. There was no need to fear that the Ottoman state would forfeit advantages by delaying entry into the war. The French army was capable of recovering from its initial reverses. 'Our comrades will accuse me of pessimism,' Mustafa Kemal went on, 'if the Germans are in Paris by the time you receive this letter. But I don't care.'[34]

At about the same time, Mustafa Kemal wrote also to his friend Salih (Bozok) who had asked for his opinion on the developing crisis. 'We have declared mobilization without fixing our objective,' replied Mustafa Kemal.

This is very dangerous. It is not clear which way we shall head. It is very difficult to keep a large army idle for any length of time. Looking at

Germany's position from a military point of view, I am by no means certain that it will win this war. True, the Germans have overrun strong fortifications at lightning speed and are advancing towards Paris. But the Russians are pushing to the Carpathians and are pressing hard the Germans' Austrian allies. The Germans will thus have to set aside a part of their forces to aid the Austrians. Seeing this, the French will counter-attack and put pressure on the Germans. The Germans will then have to recall their troops from the Austrian front. It is because an army which zigzags to and fro must come to a sad end that I do not feel certain about the outcome of this war.

Mustafa Kemal then informed Salih that he had asked Enver for a transfer to active service, saying that he had no intention of staying on as military attaché simply in order to obtain the odd item of information at a time when his country was getting ready for a great struggle. He wanted to be given a field command. 'If for any reason they do not want to allow me to return, let them say so clearly and I shall then decide my course of action.'[35]

Mustafa Kemal's fears were amply justified when the French stopped the German advance on Paris in the first battle of the Marne in September. Nevertheless, he used much more diplomatic language when he addressed a friendly letter to Cemal Paşa, the member of the CUP ruling triumvirate with whom he had the closest relations. Writing on 9 November, after the resignation of the four ministers who had disapproved of the war, he recommended that Cemal should summon Fethi (Okyar) from Sofia to assist him in government. 'Our nation is totally tied to the future of Germany and Austria, which are about to demonstrate their strength,' he wrote. 'Vital problems affecting us will be decided between now and the happy outcome [of the war].'[36]

It is impossible to say whether Mustafa Kemal was opposed to the war in principle. The views which he expressed later were coloured by the imperatives of the moment. When he led the Turkish national resistance between 1917 and 1923, he was concerned to avoid a general imputation of war guilt, and wished, in particular, to exonerate the mass of CUP members who had rallied to his call. This explains his statement in an interview in 1921 that 'When a general war broke out in the world, the constraints of [our] geographical position, of past events and of the balance of power made it impossible [for us] to stay neutral, and for this reason we joined the German side ...' In the same interview, he recalled that he had explained to Allied representatives in Istanbul in 1918/19 that they themselves had left no room for Ottoman neutrality, since 'tsarist Russia was on your side'.[37] Mustafa Kemal was more guarded in his replies to Turkish journalists in 1923, after his troops had won the War of Independence. Asked about responsibility for the world war, he said:

I must admit that I never understood the aims of the Ottoman state in entering the war ... So I have to leave the political question undecided. Was it possible to avoid the war altogether? Or could we have delayed our entry? It is
worth reflecting on these questions. But after we entered the war, many mistakes were made in its conduct. The strength of a nation should be expended
to defend its own existence. It is totally wrong to forget that and to use one's
forces for the purposes of foreigners. Those who led the war, forgot our own
existence and became prisoners of the Germans ... There have thus been
innumerable mistakes in the conduct of the war. Responsibility for them falls
on Enver Paşa alone. If one has to widen responsibility, then the nation itself
is responsible. Enver Paşa is dead. It is wrong to pin responsibility on commanders who carried out his orders. Those who carried political responsibility have also died one by one ... This is all I want to say on the subject.[38]

Later still, Atatürk said to his prime minister İsmet İnönü:

The leaders of the CUP who took over the government were our close comrades. At first we were all together. We opposed them after the revolution [of
1908], when we said that as military men we should not meddle in politics. We
could not agree and parted company. We left politics and fought in the war.
We were not directly involved in government. After going through successive
experiences, we made our careers and came to our present position. But our
erstwhile comrades took over the country right at the beginning of their
careers. Today, we are not the men that we were at that time. But they tried to
ward off dangers without the benefit of the experience which we have since
acquired. How could they have done it? They lacked not only experience but
ability beyond a certain point. What they did was what they were capable of.[39]

Hasan Rıza Soyak, who served as Atatürk's secretary for many years,
provides probably the most accurate assessment when he says:

Atatürk was not in favour of entering the First World War so long as it was
not clear how the situation would develop. He was in favour of avoiding hasty
decisions, of waiting, of seizing favourable opportunities, of choosing the
most suitable time and side, depending on military developments, if a decision was to be made to enter the war, and, in any case, of ensuring beforehand the best conditions for our existence and interests.[40]

As a military attaché in Sofia, who was not consulted on crucial decisions, Mustafa Kemal could, of course, enjoy the luxury of criticizing in
private those who had pushed him aside. At the same time he continued
to press the war ministry in Istanbul for a front-line appointment.
Enver refused, arguing that the job of military attaché was more important.[41] Mustafa Kemal told his biographer Hikmet Bayur that he had
also approached Enver through Süleyman Askeri, a comrade of the

Cyrenaica campaign, who had become the first head of Enver's Special Organization. When Askeri passed through Sofia after trying to organize popular resistance against Serb rule in Macedonia,[42] Mustafa Kemal asked him to persuade Enver to appoint him to a command in Mesopotamia (Iraq).[43] In fact it was Askeri himself who was appointed governor and commander in Basra. The city had been captured by the British Indian army in November, immediately after the outbreak of the war with Turkey, and in an attempt to recapture it in April 1915, with a force of Turkish regular troops supported by Arab tribesmen, Süleyman Askeri was defeated at the hard-fought battle at Shuaiba, outside Basra, on 14 April 1915, when the Arabs hung back, intent on looting the losing side.[44] Desperate at this failure of the *jihad*, Süleyman Askeri shot himself.[45]

Mustafa Kemal finally got his way when Enver left the headquarters in Istanbul to lead in person an offensive against the Russian army in the Caucasus. A telegram arrived in Sofia signed by Enver's deputy, İsmail Hakkı, ordering Mustafa Kemal to leave immediately to assume command of the 19th division. He was ready to go, and left Sofia on 20 January 1915.[46]

8

A Move to the Front

⟡

THE FIRST WORLD WAR started in the Near East with a series of bungled operations. As on the Western Front, the generals learnt as they went along, at terrible human cost. The Ottoman armies rushed in first and suffered two defeats. Then the British attacked and were also twice defeated. The Ottomans paid a heavy price for their haste, the British (and French) for their procrastination.

On 21 October, before the outbreak of hostilities, Enver sent to the German high command a war plan which he had prepared with the help of his German chief of staff, Bronsart von Schellendorf. In addition to the naval attack in the Black Sea, it provided for an engagement with the Russian army in the Caucasus, an attack on the British in Egypt, and the proclamation of the *jihad*. The previous month, Enver had informed the Ottoman military attaché in Berlin that he had sent agents to organize risings in the Caucasus, Egypt, Algeria, Afghanistan and India.[1] The mission to Afghanistan was entrusted to Mustafa Kemal's friend, the naval officer Hüseyin Rauf (Orbay). 'All I know about Afghanistan is its name,' objected Hüseyin Rauf. 'How does one get there? May I go by way of America?'[2] Nevertheless, he agreed to go and to cooperate with the German agents Wilhelm Wassmuss and Oskar von Niedermayer, sent to stir up the Persians and Afghans against the British.

When the war started, Hüseyin Rauf crossed the frontier into Persia. Given by Enver the empty title of 'Commander-in-chief, Southern Persia', he kicked his heels outside Kermanshah, before returning to Istanbul to carry out his proper job as naval chief of staff. The German agents stayed on in Persia and Afghanistan, spending large sums of gold to little effect. The head of the German military mission, Liman von Sanders, who had doubts about the effectiveness of the *jihad*, was to note in his memoirs that not a single one of the German secret missions achieved worthwhile results.[3] Fortunately, the cost of these adventures in human lives was small. In comparison, initial military operations were a disaster.

In November, a Russian advance in the direction of Erzurum was checked by the Ottoman 3rd Army under Hasan İzzet Paşa, at Köprüköy, just inside Ottoman territory. Then, as the opposing armies were consolidating their positions, Enver Paşa arrived in Erzurum on 6 December, accompanied by Bronsart von Schellendorf. Enver was at one and the same time commander-in-chief (formally deputy commander-in-chief standing in for the aged Sultan Mehmet V), war minister and chief of the general staff. Not content with these tasks, he took over in person the command of the 3rd Army and led an enveloping operation against the Russians.

On 18 December, in the middle of a snowstorm blowing across the desolate highlands, 80,000 Ottoman troops launched their offensive. They were ordered to surround the Russian positions at the small frontier town of Sarıkamış. To do so they had to cross a mountain range, rising to a height of 10,000 feet, in temperatures of $-26°$ C. The range has the evocative name of Allahuekber, 'God is Great', the traditional battle cry of Muslim warriors. The courage of the troops could not prevent a disaster. Thousands of ill-prepared and inadequately clothed and fed Ottoman soldiers froze to death. The remnants were routed by the Russians outside Sarıkamış. Of the 80,000 only some 10,000 managed to struggle back to Ottoman territory, where they were decimated by a typhus epidemic. On 8 January, Enver Paşa decided to return to Istanbul, leaving the command of an army which had practically ceased to exist to his friend Hafız Hakkı Paşa. A little later, when Hafız Hakkı died of typhus, Enver offered the command to Liman von Sanders, who at the outbreak of war had taken charge of the 1st Army in Istanbul. Liman von Sanders refused.[4]

A second Ottoman failure followed, this time on the Egyptian frontier. The operation was directed by the navy minister Cemal Paşa. Leaving Enver theoretically in charge of the navy, which was in fact commanded by the German admiral Souchon, Cemal went to Damascus as commander of the 4th Army and governor-general of Cilicia, Syria and Arabia. As soon as he arrived, he proceeded to carry out Enver's promises to the Germans. Accompanied by his German chief of staff, Kress von Kressenstein, and by members of Enver's Special Organization, Cemal led a force of 18,000 troops across the

Sinai desert to the Suez canal. On 2/3 February 1915 the Turks reached
the canal and succeeded in getting 600 men across. They were over-
whelmed by British forces. The people of Egypt did not rise against
British rule, as Enver and Cemal had hoped, and the Turkish expeditionary force returned to Palestine having suffered some 3,000 casualties and achieved nothing.[5] Cemal, who, according to some reports, had
abandoned his initial objections to the war in the hope of becoming the
Khedive, or quasi-independent ruler, of Egypt, was to launch a second
expedition against the Suez canal in July 1916. It failed like the first.[6]

When Mustafa Kemal arrived in Istanbul from Sofia at the end of
January 1915, he found Enver back in the war ministry. His reminiscences of the encounter were published in the Istanbul newspaper
Milliyet in 1926, the year in which he damned the leadership of the CUP
and all its works. Mustafa Kemal had never been impressed by Enver.
According to his biographer Hikmet Bayur, who had heard him speak
on the subject, he believed that Enver

> did not work things out. How his designs and decisions were to be carried out
> was for him a matter of detail. He was generally ignorant in military matters,
> as he had not progressed step by step from the command of a battalion to
> that of a regiment, and so on. Having taken part in fighting with bandits and
> tribes in Macedonia and Cyrenaica, he had used political backing to rise to the
> top. His march on Edirne in 1913 could not be counted an active command
> since it had been undertaken against a Bulgarian army which had ceased to
> exist after its defeat by the Serbs, Greeks and Romanians. As a result, when-
> ever he issued orders to a division or an army corps, he never considered
> what was needed to carry out and follow up the operation, and behaved
> almost as if he were ordering a sergeant to move forty or fifty soldiers to seize
> a hill. The disaster at Sarıkamış was the consequence of this attitude.[7]

Atatürk's account of his meeting with Enver at the beginning of the
Great War illustrates his opinion of his commander-in-chief:

> Enver was a little thinner and his complexion was pale. I spoke first:
> – You're a little tired, I said.
> – No, not that much, he replied.
> – What's happened?
> – We fought – that's about it …
> – What's the position now?
> – Very good, he replied.
> I didn't want to upset Enver Paşa further, and turned to the subject of my
> appointment.

– Thank you, I said, you have kindly appointed me commander of the 19th division. Where is it? And which corps and army is it part of?

– That's right, he said. If you enquire with the general staff you'll get precise information.

Enver looked preoccupied and tired and I didn't prolong the conversation … I applied to the general staff of the commander-in-chief, introducing myself as Lieutenant-Colonel Mustafa Kemal, commander of the 19th division. But they looked at me blankly wondering who I might be. There was no one in the general staff who knew of the existence of my division. That put me in an embarrassing position … almost as if I were playing a confidence trick on them.[8]

The account which Mustafa Kemal submitted to the Ottoman war history department in January 1917 is briefer:

While I was military attaché in Sofia, I was summoned to commmand the 19th division, which was being formed at Tekirdağ [on the northern shore of the sea of Marmara]. The Allied threat to the Dardanelles allowed no time to bring the division up to strength, and I was ordered on 25 February to proceed to Maydos at the head of only the 57th regiment.[9]

Maydos (now Eceabat) is a small harbour in the southern part of the Gallipoli peninsula. Across the strait, which narrows at this point, lies the provincial centre of Çanakkale (Chanak in English sources). A little south of Maydos, the fort of Kilitbahir (Key of the Sea) guarded the narrows.

The decision to launch an operation 'to bombard and take the Gallipoli peninsula with Constantinople as its objective' was taken by the British War Council on 8 January 1915, in response to an appeal made by the Russians on 2 January for action to divert the Turks from the front in the Caucasus.[10] On 19 and 25 February a joint British and French fleet bombarded the forts on either side of the entrance to the Dardanelles. Landing parties were put ashore to add to the damage caused by naval guns. At Seddülbahir (literally, Sea Barrier), the fort at the southern tip of the Gallipoli peninsula, a Turkish sergeant, Mehmet, achieved national fame by rushing at a British sailor with a rock, when his rifle jammed. Mustafa Kemal helped publicize this incident,[11] which gave birth to the term *Mehmetçik* (Little Mehmet), used to this day as a nickname for Turkish soldiers.

There followed a pause in Allied activity, which afforded the Turks time to ship in reinforcements. Two more regiments (the 72nd and 77th) arrived to bring up to strength Mustafa Kemal's 19th division. But they were not the troops which he expected. 'The regiments assigned to me,' he complained to the chief of staff of his corps commander, 'are made up of Arabs. Some ... are opposed to the war. Their training is inadequate. Please take them back and give me my two other regiments from the Tekirdağ depot. These are real Turkish lads and they are now better trained.'[12] Corps headquarters refused.

At the time of the first Allied bombardment, Turkish forces in the Dardanelles area came under two separate commands. The defence of the Gallipoli peninsula was entrusted to the 3rd corps, under Esat Paşa, a general of Albanian origin who had become famous as the defender of Yanya (Yanina) in the Balkan wars. But the forts at the entrance to the straits and the land defence of the waterway were the responsibility of the Çanakkale Fortified Area, commanded by Cevat Paşa (Çobanlı). As commander of the Maydos area, Mustafa Kemal was responsible simultaneously to the 3rd corps and to the command of the Fortified Area for the defence of the eastern shore of the peninsula.[13]

On 18 March 1915, a joint British-French fleet attempted to force its way through the straits. The attempt failed in front of the Kilitbahir narrows. Three battleships (the French *Bouvet*, the British *Irresistible* and *Ocean*) were sunk, and several other ships damaged. Mustafa Kemal noted in his report: 'It was a naval operation entirely. Shore defence was under the command of Cevat Paşa (Çobanlı). My connection with the fighting was through him ... During the naval battle ... in which the enemy was defeated, I was responsible for protecting the land area [i.e. the eastern shore of the Gallipoli peninsula].'[14] The disposition and command structure of Ottoman forces changed a few days later.

The first bombardments in February caused considerable apprehension in Istanbul. While Liman von Sanders made ready to defend the capital, preparations were put in hand to transfer the government to Anatolia. However, after the failure of the Allied fleet to force the Dardanelles, Enver decided that every effort should be made to hold the straits against a landing, which was now seen as imminent. On 26 March Liman von Sanders was offered and accepted the command of a new 5th Army, which was to include all the forces in the Dardanelles area.[15]

Arriving in Gallipoli, Liman von Sanders produced a new battle plan. He knew from agents in the eastern Mediterranean that a large Allied army was assembling for an assault, but he did not know at what precise point the landings would take place. He decided that Turkish forces were spread out too thinly along the threatened shores on either side of the mouth of the straits. Instead, he concentrated them in three areas: at the Bolayır isthmus, the northern neck of the peninsula between the sea of Marmara and the gulf of Saros in the Aegean; at the southern tip of the peninsula, and on the Asian shore, at the entrance to the straits. He thought that the relatively low-lying Bolayır isthmus was the most likely place for an Allied landing. But, while the terrain here was easier than the tangle of hills further south, it was also nearer Thrace, where the 2nd Ottoman Army was concentrated, and Istanbul, which the 1st Army was guarding against a possible Russian attack from across the Black Sea. Mustafa Kemal claimed after the event that, having served in the area at the close of the Balkan wars, he had always expected the Allies to land in the southern part of the peninsula.[16]

On 31 March 1915, Mustafa Kemal's newly appointed chief of staff, Major İzzettin (Çalışlar), noted in his diary:

Today, Liman von Sanders came to Maydos accompanied by the corps commander, Esat Paşa, and inspected shore defences. Liman Paşa is the commander of the 5th Army, Cevat Paşa of the [Straits] Fortified Area; [the German admiral, von] Usedom Paşa, is Coastal Inspector, Esat Paşa commands the 3rd corps and [the German] Weber Paşa is the commander of the Composite Corps on the Asian shore. It appears that the Germans want to keep the straits defence command entirely in their own hands.[17]

Major İzzettin was right. Liman von Sanders preferred to have Germans in as many key positions as possible. It was a recipe for friction with Turkish officers. Mustafa Kemal was to say later that when he was first introduced to Liman von Sanders, in Maydos, the latter asked him why the Bulgarians had not sprung into action. 'I replied, "Because they are not convinced that Germany will win." "And what do you think?" asked the German Marshal. "I agree with the Bulgarians," I said.'[18] One need not doubt that Mustafa Kemal's recollections reflected his feelings at the time of his first meeting with Liman von Sanders, even if the words he used were different.

Liman von Sanders worked feverishly in the four weeks following his appointment to strengthen defences and train his troops. He made maximum use of the delay caused by the change of the Allies' plan from a purely naval to a combined operation, a delay which was to lead to the failure of Winston Churchill's Dardanelles enterprise.

The Allies landed on 25 April 1915. In spite of fierce Turkish opposition, they established beachheads at three points. From north to south, these were around Arıburnu point (Anzac Cove), then at the southern tip of the peninsula around the ruins of Seddülbahir fort (Cape Helles), and, finally, across the strait in Asia, around the fort of Kumkale (literally Sandcastle). The French troops which occupied this last beachhead were soon afterwards withdrawn, and the rest of the campaign was dominated by the attempts of the British and French troops at Cape Helles to break through to the north, and of the British and Anzacs in the Anzac Cove area to advance to the east across the peninsula. Both lines of advance were barred by scrub-covered hills, divided by deep ravines.

On the morning of 25 April, Mustafa Kemal's 19th division was being held in reserve at Bigalı village, near Maydos, some five miles away from Anzac Cove on the other side of the peninsula. It was the 9th Turkish division under Colonel Halil Sami which took the brunt of the first wave of Allied landings from Seddülbahir to Arıburnu. Liman von Sanders was far to the north, on the Bolayır isthmus, keeping an eye on Allied ships carrying out diversionary manoeuvres in the gulf of Saros. Halil Sami asked Mustafa Kemal to send a battalion immediately to help hold the hills east of Arıburnu point. Mustafa Kemal responded by leading his 57th regiment, a cavalry company and a mountain battery across the peninsula. In his account of the engagement, he said that, after riding ahead, he had stopped at the crest of a hill and was waiting for his troops to catch up when he met a group of retreating Turkish soldiers from the 9th division. His account goes on:

> – Why are you running away? I asked.
> – The enemy, sir … they said.
> – Where?
> – Over there, they said pointing to hill altitude 261 metres. [This hill led to a higher peak known as Conk Bayırı, Chunuk Bair in British sources.] Sure enough, an enemy line was advancing towards the hill … and was already nearer me than were my own troops. I don't know whether reason or intuition impelled me to turn to the retreating soldiers and say,
> – You mustn't run away from the enemy.
> – We've no more ammunition left, they replied.
> – If you've got no ammunition, you have your bayonets.
> I ordered them to fix their bayonets and lie down.[19] As they did so, the enemy too lay down. We had won time.

Mustafa Kemal goes on to say that when his 57th regiment reached him he ordered it to turn the enemy's northern flank, saying: 'I don't order you to attack. I order you to die. By the time we are dead, other units and commanders will have come up to take our place.'[20] Mustafa Kemal's recollections may have been influenced by the fact that in this and subsequent engagements his 57th regiment was almost entirely wiped out.[21] His order to the troops was somewhat different. This order, which was found on the body of a dead Turkish soldier, read: 'I do not expect that any of us would not rather die than repeat the shameful story of the Balkan war. But if there are such men among us, we should at once lay hands upon them and set them up in line to be shot!'[22]

In the fighting on 25 April, Mustafa Kemal succeeded in holding the important hill of Conk Bayırı. The following night, the 77th regiment, made up of Arab conscripts, fled in panic,[23] and Mustafa Kemal's position remained critical for another twenty-four hours. But with the arrival of reinforcements, the Turkish lines round Anzac Cove were stabilized. On 30 April, the 5th division joined in a counter-offensive, which was beaten back with heavy loss of life.[24] The previous day, Mustafa Kemal had been awarded the Ottoman order of *İmtiyaz* (Distinguished Service) for his part in the defence of Arıburnu. Mustafa Kemal's divisional headquarters overlooked a gully. The place had no name, until Esat Paşa's chief of staff, Lieutenant-Colonel Fahrettin (Altay), called it Kemalyeri (Kemal's Place).[25] Liman von Sanders tried to keep an eye on this part of the front by appointing the German Major Reimond as Mustafa Kemal's chief of staff. But Mustafa Kemal was perfectly satisfied with Major İzzettin, and sent Reimond away on 15 May.[26]

Pinned down round Anzac Cove, the Allies were similarly unable to break out of their southern beachhead around Seddülbahir (Cape Helles). Believing that the danger there was greater than at Arıburnu, Liman von Sanders put a German officer in charge, forcing the Ottoman Colonel Halil Sami into retirement. When the French evacuated their beachhead on the Asian shore, Ottoman troops opposing them were moved to help contain the Allies' southern beachhead, while troops which had been held in readiness round Bolayır reinforced the northern front at Arıburnu. Gradually, reinforcements arrived from as far afield as Syria.

As trench warfare took a heavy toll of the defenders, who were exposed to constant naval bombardment, intrigues and recriminations developed in the Ottoman command. As early as 3 May, Mustafa Kemal went over the head of his immediate commander, Esat Paşa, and sent this letter to the commander-in-chief Enver Paşa:

I had earlier explained to you the special importance of this sector as compared with all other sectors. The measures which I had taken as Maydos area commander might have stopped the enemy coming ashore. But Liman von Sanders Paşa did not know either our army or our country, and did not have the time to study the situation properly. As a result, his dispositions left the landing sites totally unguarded and facilitated the enemy landings. When the enemy landed four brigades round Arıburnu, I was informed by the sector commander Colonel [Halil] Sami. I attacked the enemy's left flank and threw all of it back into the sea. But the enemy then landed the same number of troops in the same place and counter-attacked. I repelled them, having no choice but to attack superior enemy forces with the reinforcements at my disposal. The enemy's forces were once again destroyed ... But the terrain and the lack of skill of the commanders round me make it impossible to achieve a definite result ... I urge you strongly not to rely on the mental ability of the Germans, headed by von Sanders, whose hearts and souls are not engaged, as ours are, in the defence of our country. I believe that you should come here in person and take over the command as the situation requires.[27]

Whether or not in response to this appeal, Enver did visit the Gallipoli front on 11 May and spent an hour with Mustafa Kemal at his Kemalyeri headquarters.[28] He must have decided that his ambitious subordinate needed closer supervision, for on 17 May Esat Paşa announced that he was assuming direct control, and transferred his headquarters to Kemalyeri. Declaring that the first stage of the battle had come to a successful end, as the enemy had been pinned down on the beaches, Esat Paşa expressed his gratitude to all the troops involved and 'particularly to Mustafa Kemal, the commander of the 19th division, who was at the head of the troops'.

The front, defended by the northern group, was now divided into three sectors. Mustafa Kemal was assigned the northern sector on the right wing of the group.[29] Liman von Sanders remained in overall command. On 19 May the Ottoman army launched an attack against the Allied beachhead at Anzac Cove. It was beaten back with heavy losses on both sides. On 23 May, Mustafa Kemal was awarded the Iron Cross. If it was an attempt to make him better disposed towards the Germans, it did not have much effect. The following day, a truce was arranged for one day to bury the dead. Mustafa Kemal's chief of staff, Major İzzettin (Çalışlar), noted in his diary: 'We saw thousands of our dead on the battlefield – a token of our heroism. The British delegates were dignified and cool. Their behaviour was correct.'[30]

On 29 and 30 May Mustafa Kemal led another major attack at Sazlıdere, a dry torrent bed leading down from Conk Bayırı. Fighting went on until the early hours of the morning. Major İzzettin noted: 'Our repeated attacks have not been successful. Our casualties have been heavy. This has increased the sense of security of the English. But they lack daring. If only they attacked, we could then counter-attack and enter their positions. Thank God, our fighting spirit is strong. But waiting is oppressive.'[31] The Anzacs did attack on 5 June. They were beaten back, but, contrary to Major İzzettin's expectations, the bloody stalemate continued.

On 1 June Mustafa Kemal was promoted full Colonel. Five days later he wrote a proud letter to Hilda Christianus, his German landlady in Sofia:

> To win friends one has got to work and make sacrifices to an extraordinary extent. For example, when you had asked me when I would be promoted Colonel, I replied, 'That's earned on the battlefield.' 'Prove it,' you said. Well, to satisfy your wish I became a Colonel five days ago. On top of it, His Majesty the Sultan has honoured me with both silver and gold battle medals, and the Bulgarian King Ferdinand has raised me to the rank of Commander of the Order of St Alexander. Kaiser Wilhelm (the greatest commander of our times) has honoured me with the Iron Cross – I value it greatly. All these achievements I owe to your noble inspiration.[32]

Earlier, on 17 May, he had written an equally self-confident letter to Corinne Lütfü in Istanbul:

> So far I have been successful throughout, and, if I stay where I am, I believe strongly that I shall always be successful. Don't be surprised that my name has not become known. I have preferred to honour Sergeant Mehmet as the hero of this important battle. But have no doubt, it was your friend who directed the battle and it was he again who found Sergeant Mehmet in the fighting ranks.[33]

Corinne was in touch with important people in the capital, and Mustafa Kemal sought her views on the relative standing of the political and military leaders. To advance his fortunes he needed to know the broader picture.

The costly failure of attempts to dislodge the Allies led to changes in the disposition of Ottoman forces. The 5th division which held the central sector was withdrawn, and on 2 June Mustafa Kemal's 19th division was reinforced and assigned a wider front. When Mustafa Kemal objected that his forces were not adequate for the task, the northern-most sector was detached from his command and handed over to the German Lieutenant-Colonel Wilmer. This time, Mustafa Kemal complained that the bed of the torrent Sazlıdere, which had been chosen as the dividing line between his command and Wilmer's, could not be adequately defended if responsibility for it was shared.[34] The language used by Mustafa Kemal upset Esat Paşa, and Major İzzettin had to present himself at group headquarters to offer assurances of his divisional commander's respect for his superior officer.[35]

On 5 June, a CUP delegation under Talât Paşa turned up at Mustafa Kemal's headquarters.[36] But this sign of official favour was followed by a reversal of fortune. On 29 June, Enver Paşa arrived at Kemalyeri with a suite which included Lieutenant-Colonel İsmet (İnönü), Atatürk's future prime minister.[37] In the night of 29/30 June, Mustafa Kemal ordered his 19th division to advance, misinterpreting Allied fire as a preparation for a major attack. The advance was held and Mustafa Kemal's troops suffered nearly a thousand casualties. This drew a rebuke from Enver Paşa, which Liman von Sanders sent down the line through Esat Paşa. Mustafa Kemal argued that his attack had been authorized and blamed his officers for failing to consolidate initial gains.[38] This excuse did not satisfy Enver who cancelled Mustafa Kemal's appointment as acting corps commander.[39]

Mustafa Kemal's behaviour at the front had caused controversy and a question mark hung over his future. On 19 July, when the heir apparent, Yusuf İzzettin, visited Mustafa Kemal's headquarters, a surprising proposal was made. The army personnel department wanted to know whether Mustafa Kemal was willing to go to Tripoli, with the rank of Brigadier and the authority of an army commander.[40] Tripoli, or rather Cyrenaica, was the site of one of Enver's sideshows, and Enver's younger brother Nuri had been sent there to lead Sanusi tribesmen against the British in Egypt. Mustafa Kemal replied that he would consider the offer and discuss it later in Istanbul.

On 20 July, during a lull in the fighting, Mustafa Kemal sent another letter to Corinne Lütfü.

> Our life here [he wrote] is truly hellish. Fortunately, my soldiers are very brave and tougher than the enemy. What is more, their private beliefs make it easier to carry out orders which send them to their death. They see only two supernatural outcomes: victory for the faith or martyrdom. Do you know what the second means? It is to go straight to heaven. There, the houris, God's most beautiful women, will meet them and will satisfy their desires for all eternity. What great happiness![41]

Mustafa Kemal did not associate himself with his men's beliefs.

Meanwhile in Gallipoli, Liman von Sanders was receiving reports that the Allies were preparing further landings to break the stalemate. As he prepared to meet them, he had to fight off not only the resentment of Turkish officers, but, more seriously, intrigues centred on the German embassy in Istanbul. On 26 July he was surprised to hear that the chief of the German general staff, von Falkenhayn, had decided to summon him to general headquarters on the Western Front, and proposed that the elderly von der Goltz Paşa, who was without a proper job in Istanbul, should stand in for him, with the German military attaché, Colonel Lossow, as his chief of staff. Furious at this attempt to send him away on the eve of a decisive battle, Liman von Sanders threatened to resign. Von Falkenhayn relented, although he still insisted that Colonel Lossow should join the Gallipoli headquarters. He arrived on 13 August, but had to leave soon afterwards as Liman von Sanders refused to give him any work to do.[42] Even if Enver had no hand in the affair, reports of friction between Ottoman and Turkish officers, which were circulating in Istanbul, had obviously raised questions about the ability of Liman von Sanders to command Turkish troops. However, he survived in senior command posts until the end of the war, while von Falkenhayn's subsequent service in Turkey was brief and unsuccessful.

The second stage of the Gallipoli campaign opened on 6 August when British, Anzac and Indian forces started landing in Suvla bay, just north of the Arıburnu sector defended by Mustafa Kemal. Mustafa Kemal claimed later to have predicted accurately where the attack would come,[43] while Liman von Sanders again fixed his attention on the Bolayır isthmus and on the Asian shore near Kumkale.[44] Mustafa Kemal would certainly have stressed the importance of his immediate vicinity, while Liman von Sanders had to consider the danger to his positions all along the peninsula. The landings were supported by a push north from Anzac Cove. Conk Bayırı was again threatened, and Mustafa Kemal sent his childhood friend Nuri to defend it at the head of his 24th regiment.[45] Nuri could not prevent the temporary loss of Conk Bayırı, but his role in the fighting was remembered later when Atatürk chose for him the surname Conker (Man of Conk).

As Allied forces succeeded in fanning out from the beaches of Suvla bay, Liman von Sanders ordered two Ottoman divisions which were guarding the Bolayır isthmus to march south and counter-attack the British on the ridges overlooking the bay. However, when the Ottoman reinforcements arrived, their commander, Colonel Feyzi, asked for more time. His troops had to cover on foot a distance of twenty-five miles; they were tired, and not all had reached their new positions. Furious that his order had not been carried out, Liman von Sanders dismissed Feyzi and chose Mustafa Kemal to replace him.[46] In the memoirs which he published immediately after the war, Liman von Sanders accorded this brief mention to Mustafa Kemal:

> Mustafa Kemal, who had achieved his first military successes in Tripolitania, was a commander willing to take on duties and responsibilities. On 25 April he used his own initiative to join the battle with his 19th division and pushed the enemy back to the beaches. Then for three months he put up an indomitable resistance against constant violent attacks. I was thus able to place total trust in his energy and determination.

When the offer of the new command was communicated to Mustafa Kemal through Esat Paşa's headquarters, he demanded that all the forces along the new front, north of Arıburnu, should be put under his orders. Asked by the 5th Army chief of staff, Lieutenant-Colonel Kâzım (İnanç), whether this would not be excessive, Mustafa Kemal replied, 'On the contrary, it's not enough.'[47] After some hesitation, Liman von Sanders agreed,[48] and Mustafa Kemal was given charge of six divisions, which defended the sector stretching from Kireçtepe ridge (Limestone Hill) on the northern edge of Suvla bay to Conk Bayırı, overlooking it from the south.[49] Two small villages, Great and Little Anafarta, lay in the middle of the sector, and Mustafa Kemal's forces were named after them the 'Anafartalar [Turkish plural of Anafarta] [Army] Group'.

On 9 August, when Mustafa Kemal took over the command, the Ottoman defenders were hard pressed. But he felt elated. He was to say later: 'For four months, I had lived three hundred metres away from the firing line, breathing the fetid smell of corpses. Having left in dungeon-like darkness, at eleven o'clock that night, I was able to breathe clean air for the first time.'[50] Mustafa Kemal's chief of staff, Major İzzettin, described the fighting at the southern end of the Anafartalar front: 'After a sleepless night, our right flank [the right flank of the 19th division] started the battle for Conk Bayırı. The situation round the hilltop is critical ... The divisional adjutant sustained a grave wound as he went to find out what was happening. His assistant Hakkı has been taken to hospital at Lapseki suffering from dysentery ... There is no one left and work has stopped in the headquarters [of the 19th division].' The position was saved on 10 August. Major İzzettin noted:

> Good weather. At dawn we started attacking Conk Bayırı and pushed back the enemy. The crisis has been overcome. [Mustafa] Kemal's energy and effectiveness have borne fruit. We have all breathed a deep sigh of relief. The enemy is subjecting Conk Bayırı to intense shelling from ships and shore mortars and field guns. At least 15,000 shells have been fired. Our soldiers have fought heroically under this infernal fire ... Still tired and disoriented. I hope I'll be able to snatch some sleep ... tonight. Today the Italians have declared war. We are expecting them to land troops.[51]

Mustafa Kemal had led in person the counter-attack on Conk Bayırı. He was to say later: 'All men, all creatures suffer from tiredness. But men have a mental force which allows them to go on without resting.' He also remembered telling his men that he would signal the attack by raising his riding whip. When he gave the signal, Turkish soldiers rushed up the hill with fixed bayonets. In subsequent fighting a piece of shrapnel struck Mustafa Kemal in the chest and shattered his watch, which prevented injury to his body. He later gave the watch as a memento to Liman von Sanders in exchange for one which bore the German Marshal's family coat of arms.[52]

On 10 August, Mustafa Kemal won control of the ridges at the southern end of his front. On 16 August his forces frustrated an Allied attack at the northern end against Kireçtepe. A further major Allied attempt to break out of the beachhead was defeated on 21 August. Attacks in the last days of August were also unsuccessful. All the while, reinforcements were reaching the Turkish defenders. Mustafa Kemal was to claim later that he eventually commanded no fewer than eleven divisions and a cavalry brigade on the Anafartalar (Suvla bay) front.[53] However, on 19 August the Anafartalar Group was split into two army corps. Mustafa Kemal was given the command of one of these – the 16th corps. But he still exercised overall command of the Anafartalar Group.[54]

As trench warfare set in round Suvla bay at the beginning of September, tempers began to fray once again. Liman von Sanders turned up regularly, sometimes every day, at Mustafa Kemal's headquarters. The Germans' grip on the command structure was tightened when Major Eggert replaced Fahrettin (Altay) as Esat Paşa's chief of staff. Some Ottoman units in Mustafa Kemal's sector were also commanded by German officers.[55] On 20 September, Mustafa Kemal fell ill,[56] presumably with malaria. His temper worsened with ill health. The failure of Enver Paşa to come to his headquarters, when he visited the peninsula on 24 September and inspected the trenches on Conk Bayırı, was the last straw. Mustafa Kemal gave vent to his accumulated frustration by submitting his resignation on 27 September. Liman von Sanders sent Turkish officers to dissuade him, but Mustafa Kemal refused to change his mind.[57] The difficulty of his position in Gallipoli was not the only consideration. Mustafa Kemal saw other, more promising, openings ahead of him.

Unable to extract from the Allies promises for the cession of all the territory which he coveted in Macedonia and Thrace, King Ferdinand of Bulgaria finally decided to throw in his lot with the Germans. Russian defeats leading up to the capture of Warsaw by the Germans in August 1915 helped him make up his mind,[58] whilst the failure of the Allies to force the Dardanelles removed the fear of immediate retaliation. On 3 September, the Ottomans ceded Demoteka (Dhidhimotikhon) in western Thrace to the Bulgarians in exchange for a military alliance. A new theatre of operations was opening up in the Balkans. Mustafa Kemal hoped that he would be given the command of the army which was being hastily put together to help the Bulgarians.

In the meantime, Liman von Sanders tried to repair the breach between Mustafa Kemal and Enver. In a letter to Enver on 30

September,[59] he praised Mustafa Kemal's services in the defence of the Gallipoli peninsula, and asked that his resignation should not be accepted. Enver obliged by sending a conciliatory telegram to Mustafa Kemal: 'I was sorry to hear of your illness. During my last visit to Çanakkale [i.e. the Gallipoli] peninsula, I did not have the time to visit you, as I wanted to see various other positions. I hope that you will soon recover and that you will continue to command your troops with the success which you have achieved until now.'

Mustafa Kemal had other plans. He wired back on 4 October: 'I send you my special thanks for your kind words concerning my illness. I am sure that you will honour me also by allowing me to render greater services to you at the head of the force brought together with an eye to events likely soon to take place.'[60]

However, instead of the appointment in Macedonia, Mustafa Kemal was offered the following day the command in Mesopotamia (Iraq), where British troops under General Townshend had captured Kut al-Amarah and were preparing to press on to Baghdad. Mustafa Kemal accepted, provided that he was appointed military commander and governor-general of the whole of Iraq, and was allowed to choose his own staff.[61] It seems that he was expecting either this or a similar senior command, since on 11 October he wrote to his friend Salih (Bozok) in Istanbul:

> The enemy facing us is now exhausted. Let's hope he will soon be thrown out altogether. In any case, the country is safe on this side. It is surprising that what ... our friends have told you hasn't yet come about. Yet, it [presumably, Mustafa Kemal's new appointment] has definitely been earned ... You know that all I want is to serve the country in a big way. The hopes expressed by ... our friends refer to the material basis for the service which I wish to render. When the time comes for this – if that's my destiny, then it'll happen. I was depressed for some time. I thought of retiring and cutting myself off. But it was not to be ...[62]

Mustafa Kemal's hopes were disappointed. In the middle of October, the command in Mesopotamia was given to the elderly German Marshal von der Goltz Paşa. In Thrace, the German Colonel Back was put in charge of the 2nd Ottoman Army, which, against the advice of Liman von Sanders, was strengthened with troops withdrawn from the Gallipoli peninsula and replaced with unsatisfactory Arab recruits.[63]

In Gallipoli, relations between Mustafa Kemal and Liman von Sanders deteriorated, particularly after the departure of Esat Paşa, who was appointed commander of the 1st Army in Istanbul. A visit by Enver to Mustafa Kemal's headquarters on 31 October only served to make matters worse. Liman von Sanders had proposed that the 2nd Army should advance from Thrace to Salonica, where the Allies had landed on 3 October, following Bulgaria's entry into the war. Mustafa Kemal did not commend the plan to Enver. Worse, he had complained to headquarters in Istanbul that there were far too many German officers around, and he had actually sent away a German who had been appointed to the 11th division. Liman von Sanders retaliated by declaring that henceforth he would not send a single German officer to the Anafartalar Group. In one case, where an Ottoman officer had disobeyed a German, Mustafa Kemal refused to hand him over to Liman von Sanders for a court martial. He also rejected Liman von Sanders's criticism of the way in which his troops had reconnoitred British positions. Major İzzettin noted on 30 November: 'These incidents created misunderstanding and coolness between the two commanders and led to the departure of Mustafa Kemal to Istanbul under cover of a medical report.'[64]

As cold weather set in, Mustafa Kemal built for himself a log cabin near the front line. When a Turkish officer complained to Liman von Sanders that the defenders lacked adequate roads, the latter replied, 'Kemal should have built roads, and not a villa for himself.' 'The Marshal has once again shown his pettiness,' noted Major İzzettin in his diary. On 5 December Liman von Sanders handed Mustafa Kemal the report granting him leave on medical grounds. The Marshal was 'inwardly angry, outwardly embarrassed'. Finally, Mustafa Kemal left for Istanbul on 10 December in the company of his CUP friends Fethi (Okyar) and Tevfik Rüştü (Aras), and another prominent CUP member, Dr Bahattin Şakir. He handed over command of the Anafartalar Group to Brigadier Fevzi (Çakmak), his future chief of staff in the War of Independence and later under the republic.[65] It was, theoretically, a temporary arrangement, but then the Anafartalar Group was also a temporary command structure.

Mustafa Kemal was with his friend Salih (Bozok) at Beylerbeyi palace in Istanbul, where the deposed Sultan Abdülhamit was kept under guard, when news came that the Allies had evacuated the Arıburnu–Anafartalar beachhead on 19/20 December. As he rushed to the war ministry to obtain further details, Mustafa Kemal told his friend: 'I had realized that the enemy was about to withdraw, and so I had proposed an offensive. But they turned it down. This upset me. As I was also very tired, I came to Istanbul. If the enemy had withdrawn, as successfully as he has done now, while I was still there, I would have been even more upset. Lucky that I'm here.'[66]

Even if one discounts this claim to prescience, Mustafa Kemal's achievement in Gallipoli was solid enough. True, there were other commanders, Turkish and German, who played an important part in the defeat of the Allied enterprise. Although his hunches were often wrong, the army commander, Liman von Sanders, did manage to get troops where they were needed. Given the scale of Ottoman casualties – 55,000 killed in action, 21,000 dead from disease, 100,000 injured, 64,000 invalided out during the fighting and 10,000 missing[67] – the despatch and disposition of reinforcements was of vital importance. In this the 5th Army headquarters commanded by Liman von Sanders was successful. Under him, Esat Paşa in the north and Cevat Paşa (and, briefly, Vehip Paşa) in the south both performed well with the help of German officers. Mustafa Kemal was the outstanding front-line commander in the northern sector. At Arıburnu he worked under Esat Paşa, who must share the credit for the defence of the sector. At Anafartalar, Liman von Sanders, who considered himself the author of the successful defence of the peninsula, was always close at hand. Mustafa Kemal was not alone the saviour of Istanbul, but he made a notable contribution to the defence of the capital. He displayed personal courage and inspired his men who were fighting in appalling conditions. Although his ambition and self-righteousness made him a difficult man to work with, and though he made no secret of his resentment of German involvement and interference, his ability was not in doubt.

Gallipoli was the foundation of Mustafa Kemal's career. At first, however, his fame did not extend much further than the ranks of the Turkish military. Attempts at wider publicity inside Turkey were unsuccessful; Enver had no wish to see potential rivals build up a popular following. As for the Allies, the tribute in the British official war history appeared after the war, when Mustafa Kemal was already courted as president of the Turkish republic. In 1919, Andrew Ryan, the British embassy dragoman (or chief local expert) in Istanbul, who should have been well informed about such personalities, knew nothing of Mustafa Kemal.

9

Fighting on All Fronts

———————◆———————

MUSTAFA KEMAL SET to work to consolidate his reputation as soon as he arrived in Istanbul on sick leave in December 1915. He sent news to his chief of staff İzzettin in Gallipoli that he had been given a respectful welcome by all classes of the population in the capital.[1] But official recognition was not forthcoming. Mustafa Kemal extended his sick leave by a month,[2] and used the extra time to bring his achievements to the notice of his country's leaders. In his reminiscences published in 1926, the year in which he crushed opposition to his rule, Mustafa Kemal said that he had been only human in expecting that people would be pleased with his 'modest services', given that he had 'saved the capital'. So he made the rounds of 'important Ottoman personalities'; he wanted to share with them, he said, important thoughts on the country's vital problems in such matters as education, science and, of course, current events.

One of the men he decided to visit was the foreign minister.[3] Mustafa Kemal does not name him, but the holder of the post was the CUP grandee, Halil (Menteşe).[4] Halil had spent two months in Berlin persuading the Germans to launch an offensive in the Balkans in order to open a land route for supplies to the Ottoman army. He then negotiated the alliance with the Bulgarians which secured the rear of the defenders of Gallipoli.[5] It was this alliance which robbed the Allied operations in Gallipoli of any remaining chance of success. We do not know whether Mustafa Kemal had hoped that Halil would obtain for him a senior command in the new Macedonian theatre of operations. Whatever his hopes, the account which Mustafa Kemal gave ten years later shows that the meeting went badly. Mustafa Kemal argued that the military

situation was precarious. Faced with either an implicit or an explicit criticism of the Ottoman high command, the foreign minister advised
Mustafa Kemal to put his arguments directly to the military. Mustafa
Kemal says that he replied: 'Are you aware, sir, that this country no
longer has a national general staff, but a German general staff, whose
first action with regard to the Turkish army has been to sack a rebel
soldier like myself? Are these the people to whom you wish to send
me?'[6]

The background to this conversation can be gathered from a letter
which Mustafa Kemal sent to Major İzzettin, and which the latter
received in Gallipoli on 7 January 1916. In this, Mustafa Kemal reported
that he had been well received in Istanbul, but that everyone advised
him to obey orders. İzzettin noted in his diary that Mustafa Kemal 'will
return to his corps. He has decided to agree to anything: even if all they
give him is a division, it seems that he will accept. So, the position is
weak.'[7] Mustafa Kemal was without a command: the Anafartalar Group
was disbanded on 26 December, and the 16th corps had been taken
over by the German Colonel Kannengiesser. Unable to advance his
career through the CUP in Istanbul, Mustafa Kemal went off to Sofia,
apparently to wind up his affairs there. It was in Sofia that he finally
heard that he had been reappointed commander of the 16th corps.

The Allies evacuated their southern beachhead round Cape Helles
on 8/9 January 1916. The barren Gallipoli peninsula in which the two
sides had crammed some three quarters of a million men[8] was now
quiet. Troops which had taken part in the fighting were redeployed. The
Ottoman 16th corps was transferred to Edirne on the Bulgarian border.
On 27 January Colonel Kannengiesser relinquished command, and
Mustafa Kemal arrived by train in Edirne to take over. The following
day was a Friday. Mustafa Kemal and his staff drove through crowded
streets to the great mosque of Sultan Selim for Friday prayers.
Triumphal arches were put up, and placards proclaimed 'Long live
Mustafa Kemal, the hero of Arıburnu and Anafartalar'. The hero's
reception had been prepared by Major İzzettin. Earlier, when the governor of Edirne was told of Mustafa Kemal's impending arrival, he was
uneasy and sent off a telegram to Liman von Sanders, asking how he
should behave.[9] Clearly, Mustafa Kemal's reputation for controversy
had preceded him.

In Istanbul it was another story. A ceremony was held at which the
sultan – and he alone – was proclaimed Gazi (*Ghazi*, victorious warrior
for the faith). The standards of regiments which had fought in Gallipoli
were paraded, while Enver read the royal speech. Behind him stood
Mustafa Kemal's erstwhile commanding officer, Esat Paşa, side by side

with Ahmet İzzet Paşa, the most senior Ottoman general who was about to be recalled from semi-retirement. Mustafa Kemal's name was not mentioned.[10] Nor was there any mention of him, when the 57th regiment which he commanded at Arıburnu, and the 27th regiment (in Halil Sami's 9th division) to whose rescue he had come when the British first landed, were commended in imperial decrees on 30 November 1915, and had their banners decorated in the presence of Enver Paşa.[11] Mustafa Kemal's name appeared only once in the magazine *Harp Mecmuası* (War Magazine), which was sponsored by the Ottoman war ministry. The December 1915 issue[12] carried on an inside page, down column, a photograph captioned 'Colonel Mustafa Kemal, Commander Anafartalar Group': it showed Mustafa Kemal, looking drawn and tired, standing under some trees in Gallipoli.[13] An article in the same issue describes the death of six young officers spurred on to action by a resolute commander in the Arıburnu sector, but does not name the commander. The magazine appears to have had a policy of naming only the CUP leaders and the most senior generals.

But while the charge of deliberate discrimination against Mustafa Kemal cannot be proved,[14] there is no doubt that he was angry at the lack of publicity and did his best to remedy it. However, it was only in March 1918, when the Turkish nationalist magazine *Yeni Mecmua* (The New Review) published a commemorative issue on the third anniversary of the naval battle in the Dardanelles, that Mustafa Kemal was able to bring his exploits to the notice of the public. He did so in an interview with Ruşen Eşref (Ünaydın), a journalist who became a personal friend,[15] and was the first in a line of publicists whom Mustafa Kemal employed during and after his rise to power. It was his first break, even though the interview appeared only on page 130 of the commemorative issue. Until then, as Atatürk's Turkish biographer Enver Behnan Şapolyo admits, Mustafa Kemal's name was not known in the country.[16] It is this interview, published nearly three years after the event, which is the source of the popular perception of Mustafa Kemal as the victor of Gallipoli and the saviour of Istanbul.

The 16th corps was still subject to the orders of Liman von Sanders who wanted to lead his army against the Allies in Macedonia.[17] The German high command did not support his proposal. The Ottoman high command too had different priorities. The western approaches were safe. In the south, Townshend's advance had been held at the battle of Ctesiphon (Salman Pak in Turkish) on 25 November 1915, and his retreating forces were surrounded at Kut al-Amarah by Ottoman troops commanded by von der Goltz Paşa. Goltz died of typhus on 19 April 1916. Ten days later, Townshend surrendered in Kut to the new

Turkish commander, Enver's uncle, Halil (Kut) Paşa. In Palestine, Cemal Paşa's 4th Army was still holding the Sinai front.

In the east, however, the Russians had defeated the Ottoman 3rd Army. Erzurum fell on 16 February 1916. To stop the Russian advance, Enver decided on a pincer movement: while the 3rd Army would counter-attack from the west, the 2nd Army was to be transferred from Thrace and attack the Russian left flank, south of lake Van, from the south. Esat Paşa's brother Vehip Paşa was appointed commander of the 3rd Army. When Vehip Paşa had been briefly in charge of the southern (Cape Helles) sector in Gallipoli, while Esat Paşa was Northern Group commander, Liman von Sanders had noted that by having two brothers in neighbouring commands he had avoided the feelings of mutual animosity which frequently developed between Turkish generals.[18] This feeling was not slow to manifest itself on the Caucasus front in 1916. Overall responsibility was given to Ahmet İzzet Paşa, who was appointed commander of the 2nd Army. His army consisted of three corps, one of which, the 16th, under Mustafa Kemal's command, was assigned to the right flank, south-west of lake Van. But as Vehip Paşa relied on his close links with the CUP and rejected Ahmet İzzet Paşa's authority, joint action by the 2nd and 3rd Armies could not be achieved.[19]

It took at least forty days to transfer troops from western to eastern Turkey. The Baghdad railway, which stretched at the time only as far as Ceylanpınar (known then as Resülayn) in upper Mesopotamia, still had two gaps in the Taurus and Amanus ranges. The tunnels through the mountains were not completed until the last months of the war. Troops had to cover up to 600 kilometres on foot, as the motor transport units set up by Germans and Austrians could not cope with the needs of four Ottoman armies on the eastern and southern fronts. The transfer of the 2nd Army started in April. It was not completed until August.

After six comparatively restful weeks, Mustafa Kemal left Edirne on 11 March. On 19 March he arrived by train in Aleppo. A long car journey followed over bad roads. When cars broke down, horses had to be used. Finally, on 27 March, Mustafa Kemal and his staff reached Diyarbakır (spelled Diyarbekir at the time), where his corps, which consisted of two divisions, was assembling. On 1 April 1916, he was promoted Brigadier-General.[20] He would henceforth be addressed as *Paşa* and not *Bey*. It was his last promotion in the World War, and he achieved it on merit at the age of 35. Some Turkish biographers believe that Enver had deliberately delayed Mustafa Kemal's promotion, and that, when he finally agreed, he said: 'You can be sure that when he is made *Paşa*, he will want to become Sultan, and that if he became Sultan, he would want to be God.'[21] Enver was obviously aware of Mustafa Kemal's ambitiousness, but the record shows that the latter's career followed the normal pattern.[22]

On 16 April, Mustafa Kemal established his corps headquarters in the small town of Silvan, north-east of Diyarbakır.[23] Eastern Anatolia is inhospitable at the best of times. In 1916 its social fabric had been torn apart by the deportation of the Armenians. The decision to deport the Armenians had been taken by the CUP government in Istanbul in April 1915, when Mustafa Kemal was busy defending the Gallipoli peninsula. The Armenians were drawn to the Russians as fellow-Christians and likely protectors. Armenians from Russian Transcaucasia fought in the Russian army, where they were joined by volunteers from among their kinsmen in Turkey. There were also Armenian risings behind Ottoman lines. The CUP leadership, shaken by the defeat at Sarıkamış and fearing disaster in the Dardanelles, exaggerated the extent of Armenian subversion. In any case, Armenians were deported not only from the war zone, but also from the rest of Anatolia and even Thrace, with the exception of the communities in Istanbul and İzmir. It was a brutal act of ethnic cleansing, for which CUP leaders gave the simple justification, 'It was them or us.'[24] The deportations strained Ottoman communications and deprived Anatolia of almost all its craftsmen.

Soon after the Armenian clearances, hundreds of thousands of Muslim refugees, many of them Kurds, came flooding in from the areas occupied by the Russians. In Trabzon (Trebizond), the Russian commandant, General Schwartz, took strong measures to stop intercommunal bloodshed.[25] But elsewhere, the Armenians were able to exact revenge on Muslims. The Russian division which moved south of lake Van and occupied Bitlis was commanded by an Armenian, General Nazarbekov (Nazarbekian), and supported by Armenian volunteer detachments.[26] Not surprisingly, Muslims fled from the area. When Mustafa Kemal arrived in Diyarbakır, hungry Kurds were roaming round towns whose social fabric had been destroyed.

Enver's plan provided for a joint operation by two Ottoman armies. But before the 2nd Army had assembled in the south, the Russians attacked and routed the 3rd Army in the north. On 18 April 1916, they captured Trabzon on the Black Sea coast. In July they occupied a large area to the south, including the towns of Gümüşhane, Bayburt and Erzincan. Further south still, the Russians advanced from lake Van and pushed the 2nd Army back towards Diyarbakır. The Turks counter-attacked on 3 August. On 6 August, Mustafa Kemal's 16th corps recaptured Muş. The following day, his troops entered Bitlis and pushed on to the south shore of lake Van. It was an important success which earned Mustafa Kemal the golden sword of the order of *İmtiyaz*. But the gains were short-lived. The Russians attacked again at the end of August, and Mustafa Kemal withdrew his troops to the south and moved his headquarters back to Silvan. The Russians returned to Muş, but Bitlis remained in Ottoman hands.

The fierce Anatolian winter set in early in this land of mountains, stopping further important engagements, but adding to the misery of Ottoman troops, badly supplied and inadequately clothed as ever. Diseases were rampant in filthy military hospitals, defeating the efforts of Turkish and German medical staff.[27] In the circumstances, Ottoman commanders did well to establish a front which held until the Russian Revolution led to the collapse of the tsar's armies a year later. True, this defensive achievement fell well short of Enver's hopes: the Russians had realized their main objective of protecting the Caucasus, and had kept a large slice of Turkish territory. But, battered as they were, the Ottoman armies did not disintegrate, and, in the end, the morale of the Russians broke before that of the Turks.

On 25 November 1916, Mustafa Kemal became deputy commander of the 2nd Army, when the commander, Ahmet İzzet Paşa, went on leave to the capital. His promotion had important consequences. The fighting in the east had brought together most of the officers who were to lead the Turkish nationalist forces in the War of Independence. On the Caucasus front in 1916, they found themselves under Mustafa Kemal's command and learned to accept him as their leader. These officers included Mustafa Kemal's War College friend Ali Fuat (Cebesoy), Cafer Tayyar (Eğilmez) and, most importantly, İsmet (İnönü). But relations with the leader were not always easy. On 13 January 1917, Major İzzettin noted in his diary, 'İsmet and Mustafa Kemal Paşa cannot work together',[28] while Mustafa Kemal was to say to his biographer Falih Rıfkı (Atay):

> I did not like İsmet at the time, because he was Enver's man. [At the beginning of the war, İsmet was director of operations on the staff of the commander-in-chief.] I told him to prepare the order to withdraw. He left, but did not come back. I sent my ADC Cevat [Abbas Gürler] to find out what was happening. He reported that İsmet was at his desk, thinking. We were to abandon land and towns. There was no other way to save the army. But it was a difficult decision to take. I said to Cevat, 'Go and tell him that if he can't write out the order himself, I'll dictate it.' A little later İsmet came with the order for a withdrawal. It was a model of its kind, beautifully thought out and drafted.

Falih Rıfkı comments: 'To the end, İsmet İnönü served Atatürk as a brilliant staff officer and Number Two.'[29]

Relations with superiors and equals were more difficult. Ahmet İzzet Paşa criticized Mustafa Kemal's first tactical withdrawal on 21 August 1916,[30] and dismissed some of his officers.[31] Before his appointment as deputy army commander, Mustafa Kemal was offended when the command of a neighbouring corps was given to his junior Cafer Tayyar (Eğilmez), the future Turkish nationalist commander in Thrace during the War of Independence. Major İzzettin noted in his diary: 'Strength of intellect and character don't always prevail. Important services which the country expects are sometimes withheld because of emotion and ambition. People who determine our destiny should be able to manage men, whatever their level or morals.'[32]

Mustafa Kemal did not spare his closest lieutenants. His childhood friend Nuri (Conker), who had fought at his side in Gallipoli, was dismissed when he failed to carry out an order.[33] Mustafa Kemal had referred earlier to Nuri's impetuous courage. In a letter to Corinne on 30 September he joked again about the belief that paradise was the reward of Muslim soldiers who died on the battlefield. 'Fortunately,' he wrote, 'Nuri has listened to my advice to be patient until the mansion which is being built for him in paradise is quite ready.'[34] Mustafa Kemal loved Nuri 'like a true brother',[35] and he soon took him back into his favour.

Ali Fuat (Cebesoy) was more circumspect. When his troops were rescued by Mustafa Kemal on a mountain ridge, he saluted smartly, and was rewarded with a brotherly embrace. As fighting died down with the onset of winter, Mustafa Kemal found time to keep a diary. His observations are remarkably detached:

7 November. Immediately after crossing Batman bridge, we saw a man lying on the road. He appeared dead from hunger. Another two, between the bridge and our bivouac. It seems they are refugees … After the bridge, two horses that have just died (men and horses are dying of hunger).

9 November. Saw many refugees on the road, going back to Bitlis. They are all hungry and wretched. A child, aged four or five years, abandoned by its parents and left to die, was dragging its feet 100 metres behind a man and a woman. I reproached them for not taking the child with them. 'It's not ours,' they said.

16 November. I inspected the hospitals in Bitlis and found them clean. I spoke to the Şeyh [local religious leader], who had an arm amputated. The chief doctor reports that when the houses allocated to the hospital were cleaned, they found the heads of some ten or fifteen Muslim women. I went on and visited the mosque called Şerefiye. It's full of dead animals and rubbish. A ruin. I came across an orphan called Ömer and took him along. When they saw this, they brought me another three orphans. This time I contented myself with giving them money.

21 November. Up at 5 a.m. Made my toilet, ready for departure. Packed up. Told the ADC that Bitlis reminded me of the ruins of Pompeii. Went on to talk of the ruins of Nineveh, and so of history ...

Mustafa Kemal notes the books he read. They are a catholic selection, starting with Alphonse Daudet's *Sappho – Moeurs Parisiennes* (whose plot did not impress him), and going on to a Turkish treatise entitled *Can one deny the existence of God?* This prompted the comment, 'Religious thinkers have done their best to twist science and philosophy to back up their law.' Military science is also mentioned:

Commanders must get to know their troops from the inside. They'll then be able to issue orders with greater confidence. Superior officers must talk to their subordinates and accustom them to expressing themselves freely. It is useful to know what a subordinate thinks ... I want to write a book on military matters, entitled *Military Morale, Training and Manners*. I know a work in French which would help me.

Mustafa Kemal's thoughts turned also to the social scene:

22 November. For eight or nine hours, until after 9 p.m., I chatted with my chief of staff on abolishing the veiling of women and improving our social life. 1. Educating capable mothers, knowledgeable about life. 2. Giving freedom to women. 3. Leading a common life with women will have a good effect on men's morals, thoughts and feelings. There is an inborn tendency towards the attraction of mutual affection.[36]

On 17 October 1916, Mustafa Kemal heard that he had been appointed commander of the Ottoman troops fighting alongside the Bulgarians in Macedonia. His chief of staff Major İzzettin noted in his diary: 'It would be wonderful if the headquarters staff went with him. We would then get out of these wretched surroundings and still be able to perform a useful service.'[37] But while one division was sent to the Balkans, the army commander Ahmet İzzet Paşa refused to let Mustafa Kemal go.[38] As the front remained quiet, Mustafa Kemal spent some of his free time writing a record of his actions in the Gallipoli campaign on the basis of notes prepared by Major İzzettin.[39] In the meantime, Enver had become preoccupied with a new danger.

Sharif Husayn, the hereditary *emir* (*amir*, prince) of Mecca, had long been negotiating with the British in Cairo. In October 1916, he raised the standard of revolt and proclaimed himself king of the Arabs.

General Fahrettin (Türkkan), the Ottoman commander in the Hejaz, had no difficulty in defending his headquarters in Medina. But the forces at his disposal were too weak to seek out and subdue Husayn's Bedouins, who were supplied by the British. Enver decided that Mustafa Kemal, who had dealt successfully with the Arabs in Cyrenaica in 1911–12, was the right man to win back control of the Hejaz. On 18 February 1917 Mustafa Kemal received news that he had been appointed commander of the Hejaz expeditionary force, with the authority of an army commander.[40]

Ottoman forces in the Hejaz were subject to Cemal Paşa, the commander of the 4th Army and governor-general of Syria, and on 26 February Mustafa Kemal presented himself at Cemal's headquarters in Damascus for discussions which were to be chaired by Enver. These discussions led to a change of plan. The three generals came to the conclusion that rather than reinforce Fahrettin in his strategically useless outpost, it would be better to withdraw his troops in order to reinforce the Palestine front. Mustafa Kemal then pointed out that Fahrettin was better placed than any newcomer to evacuate his own troops. Enver agreed and appointed Mustafa Kemal substantive commander of the 2nd Army, under Ahmet İzzet Paşa, who was to become overall commander of the eastern front against the Russians.[41] But the sensible decision to withdraw from the Hejaz was vetoed by Talât Paşa, who had become grand vizier on 3 February, after the resignation of Sait Halim Paşa. In the view of the government, the prestige of the sultan as caliph required the continued presence of his troops in the Muslim holy places.

The amicable nature of Mustafa Kemal's meeting with Enver in Damascus[42] contradicts stories that he had been plotting against the commander-in-chief. It has been alleged in various memoirs that on his return from Gallipoli, Mustafa Kemal had proposed to Cemal to stage a coup against Enver;[43] that, after being appointed to the east, he had sent a circular telegram to army commanders proposing joint action against the commander-in-chief,[44] or that, alternatively, after the first Russian Revolution in February/March 1917, Mustafa Kemal and Vehip Paşa proposed that their 2nd and 3rd Armies should march on Istanbul and overthrow the government.[45] Similar intentions attributed to Cemal Paşa were taken seriously by the Allies.[46]

In fact the only plot of which there is evidence was hatched by the CUP desperado Yakup Cemil, who had achieved notoriety by shooting the war minister Nazım Paşa in 1913, and who was apparently deeply offended by Enver's refusal to give him a field command. Yakup Cemil was court-martialled and shot on 11 September 1916. During his interrogation, he is said to have declared that the country could be saved

only if Mustafa Kemal replaced Enver as commander-in-chief and minister of war. Referring to the story, Mustafa Kemal said later: 'I would
have accepted the two posts, but I would have had Yakup Cemil hanged
first. I am not one to come to power with the backing of such people.'[47]
But while there is no evidence that Mustafa Kemal engaged in plots
against Enver, he was clearly unhappy at the conduct of the war. On 30
July 1916, Major İzzettin noted in his diary that Ahmet İzzet Paşa who
had visited Mustafa Kemal's headquarters had complained that the
Germans were running the army in their own interest. His diary entry
continues: 'Thereupon our Paşa [Mustafa Kemal] set out his own
thoughts and certain ideas were discussed. It may be that by his show of
concern İzzet Paşa is trying to play up to Kemal Paşa.'[48] Ahmet İzzet
Paşa was an upright old-fashioned soldier. Whatever the nature of the
ideas which he discussed with Mustafa Kemal, they were unlikely to
have amounted to a conspiracy.

In Damascus, Enver does not appear to have given much thought to the
offensive launched by the new British commander in Mesopotamia,
General Maude. But before February was out, Turkish front-line
troops, commanded by Colonel Kâzım Karabekir, who had earlier
fought successfully on the southern sector in Gallipoli, had been
defeated and Kut al-Amarah was reoccupied by the British. On 11
March, British forces entered Baghdad. The loss of this historic city
caused consternation in Istanbul and moved Enver to devise yet
another grandiose plan, in which the city was to be recaptured by
Turkish troops sent across the desert from Syria. To command the
operation, the Ottoman government obtained the services of General
(Marshal in Turkey) Erich von Falkenhayn, who had been removed
from the office of chief of the German general staff after his failure to
capture the French fortress of Verdun. Following his arrival in Istanbul
on 7 May 1917 with a staff of German officers, a German Asia Corps of
brigade strength was created for service in Syria alongside Ottoman
troops. This force was to include the 6th Army in Mesopotamia, the 4th
Army in Syria, and a new 7th Army which was to assemble in Aleppo.
The three armies were named the Lightning Group (*Yıldırım Grubu* in
Turkish, *Group F* in German records).

On 24 June 1917, Mustafa Kemal and his commander, Ahmet İzzet
Paşa, who had in the meantime returned from leave in Istanbul, went to
Aleppo to attend a meeting chaired by Enver. On the way, Ahmet İzzet
told Mustafa Kemal that he would probably be offered the command of
the new 7th Army; but no formal offer was made at the meeting,[49]

which discussed the proposed Baghdad operation. As Mustafa Kemal returned to fret in Diyarbakır, the command of the 7th Army was offered to the 3rd Army commander Vehip Paşa, who turned it down.[50] On 4 July, Mustafa Kemal finally heard that he would be appointed commander of the 7th Army, provided his chief of staff were German or a Turkish officer who spoke German.[51] Mustafa Kemal accepted the appointment. His ADC Salih (Bozok) says in his memoirs that when he congratulated him on his new command, Mustafa Kemal replied: 'I shall accept, not, as you think, in order to work under Falkenhayn, but, on the contrary, to stop him in his tracks, as I know why he has taken charge of the Lightning Group.'[52] Whether or not these words were spoken, there is no doubt that, like many other Turkish officers, Mustafa Kemal believed that the Germans were serving their own interests first and the Ottoman state second.

Nevertheless, Mustafa Kemal applied himself energetically to his new job. Arriving in Istanbul in the middle of August, he appropriated forcibly a building in the old city to serve as his headquarters. There he met his new commander Marshal Falkenhayn,[53] while his troops assembled from the European fronts. In 1916, Enver had sent three army corps (seven divisions in all) to fight in Macedonia, Romania and Galicia.[54] Over the next two years, these troops, which were better equipped than their comrades in Ottoman territory, were drawn upon to reinforce operations in Asia. One by one, units assigned to the 7th Army were sent by train to Aleppo, where Falkenhayn's headquarters was set up. Mustafa Kemal himself left Istanbul for Aleppo on 8 August. At a station north of the Taurus mountains, he conferred with Cemal Paşa, until then the unquestioned master of Ottoman possessions south of the Taurus and west of the Syrian desert.[55] Cemal was on his way to Istanbul.

While German troops and their equipment, which was more voluminous than that of the Turks, were being laboriously moved south, and Turkish reinforcements were arriving both from Europe and from the Caucasian front, German transport officers reconnoitred the Syrian desert and advised that the crossing was more difficult than Enver had suggested. Falkenhayn went to Germany to discuss the situation, conferring on his return with Enver and Cemal in Istanbul. It was decided that it was too dangerous to attack Baghdad before the Sinai front was secured. For this purpose, an offensive would first be launched against the British in the south. Once the British had been thrown back across the Suez canal, the Lightning Group would turn round and march on Baghdad. Cemal says in his memoirs that, knowing the weakness of Ottoman armies, he was opposed to any offensive – either in Sinai or

across the Syrian desert.[56] However that may be, he withdrew from the
argument, and accepted a German invitation to visit the Western Front
in Europe.

In the meantime, Mustafa Kemal's opposition to the Germans was
brought forcibly into the open. The first disagreement arose over
relations with local Arabs. Mustafa Kemal heard that Kress von
Kressenstein, the German commander on the Gaza front, had reached
an understanding with the sheikh of a local Arab tribe. This, Mustafa
Kemal argued, was a mistake, since an exclusive agreement with one
tribe always antagonized other tribes, and created difficulties for the
Ottoman administration. On 24 August he sent a message to
Falkenhayn, copy to Enver, saying that he did not consider himself
bound by the agreement and asking that he should be told who had the
authority to conduct relations with the tribes.[57]

On 14 September 1916, while Cemal was still away, the headquarters
of his 4th Army in Damascus was told by Enver that, in accordance
with Falkenhayn's orders, Mustafa Kemal's 7th Army was being moved
to the Sinai front.[58] This confirmed the decision to postpone the march
on Baghdad and to strike south first. But in order to accommodate the
new strategy the command structure had to be adjusted. Now that
Falkenhayn was going to stay in Syria rather than march on Baghdad,
was Cemal to surrender his authority to him? Moreover, how would
Mustafa Kemal's 7th Army fit into the command of the Sinai front,
which had until then been successfully discharged by Kress von
Kressenstein, nominally under Cemal's orders?

On 20 September Mustafa Kemal made his views clear to his commander-in-chief, Enver Paşa, in a report of which he sent a copy to the
grand vizier and interior minister, Talât Paşa.[59] İsmet (İnönü), who had
been appointed corps commander in the 7th Army, says that he had
drafted the document,[60] but the frank and forcible views which it
expressed were undoubtedly Mustafa Kemal's, who signed it as commander of the 7th Army. After painting a dark picture of maladministration, demoralization and disorganization in the rear and of weakness
in the army, Mustafa Kemal proposed that the Ottomans should pursue
a purely defensive strategy, recalling every single soldier sent abroad,
and concentrating on the Sinai front. Warning that the Germans were
intent on taking over the Arab provinces for themselves, Mustafa
Kemal insisted that civil and military control should remain in Ottoman
Muslim hands. The report makes it clear that he was not yet thinking in
terms of a Turkish national state. Speaking of British ambitions in
Palestine, he argued that Turkey would suffer an irreparable vital blow if
it were to lose its remaining religious influence in the Muslim world and

some of its most prosperous possessions. However, the report fore-shadows his future strategy in urging administrative reform in order to secure a solid territorial base. Otherwise, 'if, God forbid, continued warfare led to further losses and calamities', Turkey would be left with territory and people too weak to resist.

Turning to immediate arrangements, Mustafa Kemal insisted that if units of his 7th Army were to participate in fighting on the Sinai front alongside the 4th Army units commanded by Kress von Kressenstein, he should be in overall command. He developed this point in a supple-mentary report which he sent to Enver on 24 September. After claim-ing that both in Gallipoli and on the Caucasus front he had acquired great experience in conducting operations with forces which had not been fully assembled, and which arrived gradually as the fighting went on, Mustafa Kemal put two alternatives. Either he should be given responsibility for the defence of the Sinai front, as commander of the 7th Army, under Falkenhayn's overall command, or he should be allowed to go.

Enver refused to make a choice. First, he asked Mustafa Kemal to await Cemal's return to Aleppo. Mustafa Kemal agreed. Then, on 2 October, Enver told Mustafa Kemal that the Sinai front was long enough to accommodate two independent army commands and that he had full confidence in 'Marshal Falkenhayn Paşa' as overall commander. Mustafa Kemal replied that Falkenhayn had already undermined his authority as commander of the 7th Army. Enver promised to find out how Falkenhayn intended to use the armies on the Sinai front, and asked Mustafa Kemal to stay on in the meantime.[61] While the telegrams were being exchanged, Enver worked out a compromise which was communicated to Ottoman authorities in the field at the beginning of October. Falkenhayn would have full authority in military operations on the Sinai front, but would keep Cemal Paşa informed. Cemal was given a new title of commander-in-chief, Syria and Western Arabia. This did not disguise the fact that his 4th Army had been whittled down, and replaced by the 7th Army under Mustafa Kemal and an 8th Army under Kress von Kressenstein, both answerable to Falkenhayn. The two armies were assigned to the Sinai front. Control over Palestine was taken away from Cemal and given to Kress von Kressenstein. Cemal was compensated by being given nominal authority over Ottoman troops isolated in the south-western corner of Arabia.[62] It was a messy arrangement with two armies manning the same front, while in the rear there was no clear demarcation of authority between Falkenhayn and Cemal.

Cemal notes in his memoirs that he had agreed to the new structure with a heavy heart, on the understanding that the transfer of troops on the Sinai front from his authority to that of Falkenhayn was temporary, and that he would retain full powers behind the front line, as well as control over military units keeping the Bedouins at bay east of the Jordan.[63] Nevertheless, when he returned to Aleppo, he agreed with Mustafa Kemal that Falkenhayn 'had been created by Allah for our tribulation'. Mustafa Kemal told Cemal that he could not possibly work under Falkenhayn and was therefore resigning. Cemal promised to follow suit after he had seen Enver who was about to visit his command.

Mustafa Kemal resigned his command on 4 October after an angry exchange of letters with Falkenhayn, whom he refused to meet face to face to discuss their differences.[64] Fevzi (Çakmak), who had stood in for Mustafa Kemal in Gallipoli, now replaced him as commander of the 7th Army. Mustafa Kemal was to say in 1926[65] that, before leaving Aleppo, he returned to Falkenhayn a sum in gold which he had been given in Istanbul when he had assumed command of the 7th Army. According to Mustafa Kemal's account, the gold was intended as a bribe, but he insisted on giving a receipt for it, and demanded the receipt back before he left Aleppo. However, this did not leave him enough money to buy his ticket back to Istanbul. Cemal Paşa came to his rescue by buying from him his private stable of horses for 2,000 gold liras. Later, Cemal Paşa said that he had sold the horses for 5,000 liras, and insisted on paying the difference to Mustafa Kemal. This small capital helped Mustafa Kemal make ends meet over the next two years. However, Cemal Paşa makes no mention of this story in his memoirs.[66] Neither does Salih (Bozok), the ADC who handed Mustafa Kemal's letter of resignation to Falkenhayn, and who is supposed to have retrieved the receipt for the gold.[67] Like other Ottoman commanders, Mustafa Kemal had no personal wealth. Cemal Paşa helped him with funds. Later, when their paths diverged, Mustafa Kemal found it necessary to justify the transaction and insist that the money did not come from German sources. In fact, the gold which the Ottoman state needed to finance the war – and to bribe Arab tribesmen – was, in the first place, supplied by the Germans.

When Mustafa Kemal returned to Istanbul, some time towards the end of October 1917, he found that Enver Paşa had tried to regularize his position by reappointing him commander of the 2nd Army.[68] Mustafa Kemal refused the post, and Enver avoided an open breach by granting him one month's leave of absence.[69] Mustafa Kemal installed himself in the best hotel in the capital, the Pera Palace. He was by now an avowed critic of the conduct of the war by a government which stood low in popular esteem.

Almost immediately after his arrival in the capital, on 31 October, the new British commander in Egypt, General Allenby, attacked on the Sinai front, and broke through the Ottoman lines in the eastern sector round Beersheba. On 9 December Allenby entered Jerusalem. Cemal Paşa was convinced that its Ottoman defender, Mustafa Kemal's friend Ali Fuat (Cebesoy), was ordered to withdraw because the Germans wished to safeguard the Christian holy places.[70] Ottoman forces managed to establish a new defence line north of Jaffa and Jericho, but the loss of Jerusalem was a heavy blow to the reputation of their commanders. On 12 December Cemal Paşa left Damascus and returned to Istanbul to resume his nominal duties as navy minister. He was in tears at the loss of his satrapy. Kress von Kressenstein was relieved of his command by Falkenhayn, who himself was replaced on 25 February 1918 by Liman von Sanders.[71]

In Istanbul, Mustafa Kemal did not keep his criticism to himself. According to one story, he visited Enver in the war ministry, where the argument became so heated that both men drew their guns.[72] Atatürk's ADC Salih (Bozok) provides a different version, according to which the director of supplies, *Topal* (Lame) İsmail Hakkı Paşa, suggested to Mustafa Kemal that a coup should be staged to remove Talât and install a military cabinet. A report of the conversation reached the grand vizier,[73] who informed Enver. Thinking that Mustafa Kemal was the author of the plot, Enver summoned him to the war ministry. Mustafa Kemal emerged shaken from the interview, fearing that he would be court-martialled. However, Enver took no further action.[74] The story that Enver demanded that Mustafa Kemal should choose between politics and the army, whereupon he promised not to engage in politics,[75] refers probably to a meeting between the two at this time. Atatürk's friend Hüseyin Rauf (Orbay), who was chief of naval staff, reports that when Cemal Paşa returned to Istanbul from Damascus, Mustafa Kemal's criticism of his failure to keep his promise and resign simultaneously with him stung him so much that he suggested to Enver that Mustafa Kemal should be court-martialled.[76] Rauf claims that he then managed to mend relations between Mustafa Kemal, Cemal and Enver.

None of these stories is convincing. It is a fact that Mustafa Kemal had disagreements with the CUP triumvirate of Enver, Talât and Cemal. They were all aware of the weakness of the Ottoman state and of the irresistible spread of war weariness. But none of them was in favour of a separate peace; Mustafa Kemal made this clear in the report which he had sent to Enver from Aleppo, in which he said: 'There is no escaping the fact that we will have to stay with the Germans to the end in order to get out of the difficulties in which we are bogged down today.'[77] The disagreement was about immediate tactics. Mustafa Kemal wanted the Ottoman state to adopt a defensive policy, husband its forces, and regain its freedom of action. Enver, on the other hand, had not lost his gambling habit. The Bolshevik revolution had broken out in Russia, and on 3 December 1917, Ottoman headquarters informed all units that the Russians had asked for an armistice.[78]

The armistice on the eastern front allowed the Germans to transfer troops to the west for one last push. For Enver, it opened also the prospect of realizing the dream of Islamic union which the *jihad* had signally failed to achieve. The rest of the CUP did not know which way to turn. Cavit, who had returned to the ministry of finance, was a critic of the war. Hüseyin Rauf (Orbay) says that he warned Talât that America's entry into the war spelled defeat for Germany.[79] The search for a way out had begun. But it is unlikely that handguns were brandished and conspiracies hatched. Tension showed itself in a more mundane way: Mustafa Kemal was accused of retaining the services of a staff officer and bringing back two official cars from Aleppo. He replied to Enver that he was entitled to keep his personal ADC, and that he was giving up the wrecked car which he had brought to Istanbul for repairs.[80]

The reminiscences which Mustafa Kemal published in 1926 appear to give the main facts, so far as he was concerned:

> I had settled in a suite in the Pera Palace hotel in Istanbul. I was plunged in the sad thoughts that come to a man who believes that all is lost. But I also consoled myself like a man believing that all could also be regained. I was in this frame of mind when an approach was made to me on behalf of Enver Paşa, as the sultan's deputy. Later he spoke to me personally, saying: 'The German emperor has invited our sultan to his general headquarters. We decided that our sultan is unable to undertake the journey, and suggested that the heir apparent should go in his place. Would you agree to accompany him?' Believing that a journey in the company of such a person would serve me well, I accepted.[81]

The heir apparent was Mehmet Vahdettin, the 56-year-old younger brother of the ailing Sultan Mehmet V. He had moved up in the succession after the suicide of Prince Yusuf İzzettin in 1916, and was known as a critic of the CUP leadership. Unlike his brother, who was content to serve as a figurehead for the CUP, Vahdettin was swayed by the advice of his brother-in-law Damat Ferit Paşa, a founder member of Freedom and Concord (*Hürriyet ve İtilâf*), the party opposed to the CUP.

Mustafa Kemal's account of his journey with Prince Vahdettin should be read in the light of subsequent events. Nevertheless there is a piquant immediacy in his description of their first meeting in the palace:

As we stood around, the throng of frock-coated gentlemen, all looking unconcerned, was joined by another frock-coated figure. Neither I nor my friend [Colonel Naci (Eldeniz), one of Mustafa Kemal's teachers in the War College who was to join the suite] could make out who or what the new arrival was or what we should be doing. He came in, bowed slightly in our direction, and sat on the right side of the sofa. He shut his eyes and appeared lost in deep thought. For some reason, he then opened his eyes and showed his benevolence by saying to us, 'I am honoured by your company, and happy too.' He then shut his eyes again. I wondered whether a reply was called for, feeling I was in the presence of someone who was in a trance ... He then opened his eyes again and said: 'We are going on a trip, are we not?' 'Yes, we are going on a trip,' I said. I must admit that I felt right away that I was up against a madman, but I could not help saying in a matter-of-fact way, 'Highness, we shall travel together. We shall leave in two days' time. You have to be at the station on Saturday ...' We took our leave and got into a luxurious palace carriage. I then spoke to Naci roughly in these terms:
– Poor, wretched, pitiful man. What can one do with them?
– You've said it.
– This poor man will be sultan tomorrow. What can one expect of him?
– Nothing.
– We have minds to reason. We understand the country's fate, its past and future. What can we do?
– It's tough, Naci replied.[82]

Mustafa Kemal's first impression was confirmed when Vahdettin arrived at Sirkeci station in Istanbul. The heir apparent had taken offence at his demotion from full General to Major-General, and showed his displeasure by refusing to wear a military uniform. He greeted the guard of honour 'in an abnormal and senseless way' by raising his two hands in the air.[83] But once they were together on the train, Vahdettin became more approachable, addressing Mustafa Kemal, so the latter reports, as 'the commander who saved Istanbul'. Be that as it may, subsequent events confirm Mustafa Kemal's statement that he had begun to have hopes of influencing Vahdettin. Before the trip was over, he was urging the heir apparent to take over the command of the 5th Army, which had its headquarters in Istanbul, and appoint him his chief of staff. To this suggestion, so Mustafa Kemal says, Vahdettin replied that he would think the matter over when he returned to Istanbul. 'This,' Mustafa Kemal related in 1926, 'made me lose hope in him.'[84] But his eyes were still fixed on the 5th Army.

The Turkish party was received by Kaiser Wilhelm in his headquarters in Bad Kreuznach. On being presented to the emperor, so Mustafa Kemal says, the Kaiser asked him, 'Are you the Mustafa Kemal who commanded the 16th corps and fought at Anafartalar?' 'Yes, Excellency,' Mustafa Kemal replied in French, repeating the mistake which he had made when he addressed the Bulgarian King Ferdinand as 'Excellency' rather than 'Your Majesty'.[85] According to Mustafa Kemal, the German commander Ludendorff was in a melancholy mood; yet the latter was to launch his final great offensive on the Western Front only three months later. There is no reason, however, to doubt Mustafa Kemal's statement that he tried to convince Vahdettin of the folly of relying on a German victory.

Another story which rings true concerns an angry exchange with the German military governor of Alsace, who criticized the Ottomans' treatment of the Armenians. 'We are here to find out the true position of the German army, not to discuss the Armenians,' Mustafa Kemal replied, 'and we are returning to our country having understood that position.'[86] Mustafa Kemal visited the front line in Alsace, where, he says, his German hosts were so surprised by his military knowledge that he had to explain to them that he was 'a comrade, who has commanded a division, an army corps and then whole armies'.[87] After visiting the Krupp factories, the Turkish party spent ten days in Berlin, where Vahdettin told a German journalist that women had begun to work in public in Turkey, and that although progress was slow, 'we are making the effort to give equal rights to our women'.[88] Mustafa Kemal was not alone in favouring women's emancipation in the Ottoman state.

When the heir apparent and his suite returned to Istanbul on 4 January 1918, Mustafa Kemal fell ill with an infection in his left kidney. Doctors saw him in his apartment in the Pera Palace hotel, but he continued to suffer from painful spasms. He says in his reminiscences that he spent a whole month in bed, improved somewhat and then had a relapse; this did not prevent him from continuing to put himself forward. In a letter to Ali Fuat (Cebesoy) on 23 January, he reports that he had been offered the command of either the 1st or the 5th Army, within a new group to be commanded by Liman von Sanders, and that he had chosen the 5th.[89] Whether or not such an offer was indeed made, Liman von Sanders was soon afterwards appointed to succeed Falkenhayn on the Syrian front, and there was no job for Mustafa Kemal in Istanbul. On 19 February he attended a ceremony at the German embassy, where he was decorated with the *Cordon de Prusse*.[90]

The fact that the journalist Ruşen Eşref (Ünaydın) published his long interview in March suggests that Mustafa Kemal was intent on appealing to a wider public. The interview took place in the house occupied by Mustafa Kemal's mother in Akaretler, where Ruşen Eşref was received by Mustafa Kemal in a room full of war mementoes and photographs. The superlatives do not sound accidental:

> In this broad, shady room, covered up to the windows and the ceiling in carpets, prayer rugs and kilims, which lay even on sofas and armchairs, Mustafa Kemal Paşa's face seemed to come out of a Rembrandt portrait. I cannot remember ever having seen such deep meaning in a young face. Among the waves of light and shade, the attractive face of this fair-haired man combined opposites – determination and calm, modesty and dignity, softness and hardness, simplicity and intelligence.[91]

The interview appeared in three consecutive issues of *Yeni Mecmua* (The New Review), the organ of the association of Turkish nationalist clubs (*Türk Ocakları*, Turkish Hearths), supported by the CUP,[92] which is indicative of the company which Mustafa Kemal kept at the time. Mustafa Kemal's main political ally was also in the capital. Fethi (Okyar), whom Mustafa Kemal saw in Sofia on his way to Germany,[93] returned to Istanbul on 21 December 1917. Having resumed his political career as member of parliament for Istanbul, Fethi was in close touch with the CUP leadership, and was invited to take part in the Ottoman delegation, led by the grand vizier Talât Paşa, which signed the peace treaty of Brest Litovsk with Bolshevik Russia on 3 March.[94] Believing that possession is nine points of the law, the Ottoman command had denounced its armistice with the Russians on 5 February, and troops of Vehip Paşa's 3rd Army began to reoccupy lost territory.[95]

The Ottomans had another reason to march east: nationalist Armenians were filling the vacuum left by the Russians, who had earlier tried to prevent revenge killings and the ethnic cleansing of Muslims.[96] The tsarist general Nazarbekov was now commander of an Armenian corps, and Muslims both west and east of the 1914 frontiers of the Ottoman state stood in peril of their lives. The treaty of Brest Litovsk provided that the population of the three provinces (Kars, Ardahan and Batum) ceded to Russia in 1878 should be allowed to determine its fate in a plebiscite; the advance of the Ottoman army ensured that they would choose to rejoin the Ottoman state.[97] It was also during Mustafa Kemal's long illness in Istanbul that the deposed Sultan Abdülhamit died, on 10 February 1918. Mustafa Kemal shed no tears at the passing of the ruler against whom he had plotted in his youth.

Despairing of a cure in his own country, Mustafa Kemal applied to

Enver for leave and money to seek treatment in Vienna. Both were granted, and he left Istanbul by train on 25 May, accompanied by his batman Şevki. His luggage was lost on the journey and he had to acquire a new wardrobe in the Austrian capital. A Viennese specialist, Professor Zuckerandl,[98] sent Mustafa Kemal to the Cottage Sanatorium in Vienna, followed by spa treatment in Karlsbad (now Karlovy Vary in the Czech Republic). When Mustafa Kemal complained about the room reserved for him in a local *pension*, the Austrian doctor who supervised the treatment retorted: 'Have you come here for serious treatment or for a rest in a luxury hotel? The regime which I shall prescribe for you will leave you no time for entertainment.'[99]

There were many Turkish visitors in Karlsbad, among them Cemal Paşa's wife and brother, the finance minister Cavit, and the CUP journalist Hüseyin Cahit (Yalçın), who had seen Mustafa Kemal in action in Gallipoli.[100] Their main complaint was that they could not find enough bread, which was rationed. However, they did not go hungry. Mustafa Kemal dined with his compatriots, went for walks and carriage rides, read French novels (and also a critique of Marx's *Le Capital*, in French translation), took German and French lessons, and kept a diary. A passage addressed in French to a Miss Brandner defends the record of the Turkish army.[101] Elsewhere he set out his views on reform:

> If I ever acquire great authority and power, I think that I would introduce at a single stroke the transformation needed in our social life. I do not accept and my spirit revolts at the idea entertained in some quarters that this can be done [only] gradually by getting the common people and the *ulema* to think at my level. After spending so many years acquiring higher education, enquiring into civilized social life and getting a taste for freedom, why should I descend to the level of common people? Rather, I should raise them to my level. They should become like me, not I like them. Nevertheless, there are some points here which should be gone into. It would be wrong to make a start before deciding them.[102]

Once again he reflected on the position of women in Turkey. On 6 July he noted in his diary: 'Let's be courageous in the matter of women. Let's forget fear. Let's adorn their minds with serious knowledge and science. Let's teach chastity in a healthy, scientific way. Let's give top priority to giving women honour and dignity.' The following day, he noted in his diary that he had no intention of getting married.[103]

Mustafa Kemal's rest in Karlsbad was cut short by the news that the elderly Sultan Mehmet V had died on 3 July and that Vahdettin had succeeded to the throne under the name of Mehmet VI. A French-speaking wag in Istanbul remarked, '*Les Mehmets se suivent mais ne se ressemblent pas*' (One Mehmet follows another, but they are not alike).[104] Vahdettin was known to be more likely than had been his brother to assert himself against the CUP leadership, which, however, still had the capital in its grip.

The news reached Mustafa Kemal on 5 July. He was to say later that while the fate of sultans left him unconcerned, the thought of being absent from the capital at a time of change troubled him.[105] Even so, he took his time, as he considered the balance of power in his country. On 8 July he entered in his diary the questions which preoccupied him:

1. What is Cemal Paşa's position, and how does he finance his way of life?
2. Why is Talât Paşa cool towards Cemal Paşa?
3. What line is Enver Paşa taking towards me? And what can I do about it?
4. What attitude is the new sultan likely to adopt?

On 19 July Mustafa Kemal sent a telegram to Lütfi Simavi, who had accompanied him on the trip to the Kaiser's headquarters and who had just been appointed head of the sultan's chancery. Asking Lütfi to convey his loyal greetings to the sovereign, Mustafa Kemal said that the succession had filled him with hope, adding: 'While I am sad at the eternal loss of the late sultan, my regrets are tempered by the fact that the country, the nation and the army will no longer be a toy in incapable hands.'[106] But the new sultan hesitated to make a break with the past, and reappointed Talât as grand vizier.

A few days after Vahdettin's succession Mustafa Kemal received a telegram from his ADC Cevat Abbas (Gürler) informing him that his presence was required in the capital. He replied that he was not yet cured. But on receiving a second telegram demanding his immediate return, Mustafa Kemal left Karlsbad on 27 July. However, he was delayed by an attack of Spanish flu in Vienna and did not reach Istanbul until 4 August.[107] On arrival, he learnt that he had been summoned from Karlsbad by Ahmet İzzet Paşa, his commander on the Caucasus front, who had been appointed chief ADC to Vahdettin.

In the account which he gave in 1926, Mustafa Kemal reports that he was received three times by the new sultan. In the first audience, he says that he suggested to Vahdettin that the sovereign should become substantive commander-in-chief and that the chief of the general staff should act as his deputy. In fact, six days after Mustafa Kemal's return, on 10 August 1918, Vahdettin did issue a decree stating that the title of deputy commander-in-chief had been changed to chief of staff of the commander-in-chief, and that the office would be discharged as before by 'my royal relative and personal adjutant, the war minister, Senior Divisional General [*Birinci Ferik*] Enver Paşa',[108] but it is doubtful that Mustafa Kemal had prompted the change.

In the second interview, so Mustafa Kemal says, he once again urged the sovereign to take over the army; Vahdettin replied that he had already discussed the matter with Talât and Enver, and that his first concern was to make sure that there was enough food for the people of Istanbul. Recalling events in 1926, Mustafa Kemal said that he had been shocked by the response, since Vahdettin had earlier made clear his dislike of the two CUP leaders. Their third meeting took place at a public audience, after Friday prayers on 16 August, when, in the presence of two German generals, Vahdettin told Mustafa Kemal that he had appointed him commander of the 7th Army in Palestine. Mustafa Kemal attributed this public announcement of an appointment to a command which he had relinquished the previous year to a ruse by Enver. In the account which he gave in 1926, Mustafa Kemal says that he had told Enver that the three weak armies which defended the Palestine front should be amalgamated and that he should be appointed commander of all the forces there. 'My suggestions were received ironically,' Mustafa Kemal recalled.[109]

However, Mustafa Kemal's official record of service shows that his reappointment to the 7th Army took effect on 7 August 1918.[110] He must therefore have known about it before he attended the sultan's public audience. Moreover, Mustafa Kemal must have known that the Ottoman government could not replace Liman von Sanders as commander of the Lightning Group, particularly in view of the presence within it of the German Asia Corps. He had earlier agreed to serve under Liman von Sanders in Istanbul. By accepting to do so on the Syrian front he would please the new sultan and consolidate the influence he had begun to establish during the trip to Germany. Mustafa Kemal's return to the 7th Army looks therefore like a career move. Nevertheless, it was a risky decision.

Liman von Sanders had warned that the Ottoman state was no longer capable of fighting on more than one front.[111] Yet Enver had opened a new front in the Caucasus, where an army of Islam under the command of his younger brother Nuri Paşa was pushing towards the important oil centre of Baku. In order to deny the oil wells to the Germans (and Turks) a detachment of British troops had been sent to Baku and was trying to weld local Russians and Armenians into a proper fighting force. But the defenders could not act together, and Baku fell to the Turks on 15 September 1918.[112] However, the diversion of men and supplies to the Caucasus inevitably weakened the Ottoman front in Palestine. Enver promised to transfer troops to Palestine, but few arrived, and some deserted on arrival.[113]

Mustafa Kemal arrived in Aleppo on 26 August 1918, then continued his journey south to take over his headquarters in Nablus in Palestine. Liman von Sanders, whose group headquarters were in Nazareth, to the north of Nablus, wrote in his memoirs: 'This capable general, whom I knew well from the Gallipoli campaign, saw that his army had been reduced in numbers and that his units were exhausted, and realized that he had been deceived, as Enver had given him far too favourable a picture on the basis of inaccurate figures.'[114] Mustafa Kemal described his impressions more graphically in a letter which he sent on 11 September to his doctor in Istanbul, Rasim Ferit (Talay):

> I have studied Syria thoroughly once again and visited the front line ... My conclusion is that Syria is in a pitiable state. There is no [overall Ottoman] civil governor or commander. Instead, there is an abundance of English propaganda. English secret agents are everywhere. The people hate the government and look forward to the arrival of the English as soon as possible. The enemy is stronger than we are in men and equipment. We are like a cotton thread drawn across his path.[115]

The thread was irreparably torn eight days later. Mustafa Kemal's 7th Army was holding the central sector, some twenty-five miles long. His forces consisted of two corps – the 3rd under Colonel İsmet (İnönü) and the 20th under Brigadier Ali Fuat (Cebesoy). Together they numbered only some 7,000 front-line troops. On its right flank, General Cevat (Çobanlı) had 10,000 men in his 8th Army; on his left, the 4th Army, commanded by General Cemal (Mersinli), had 12,000 front-line troops and held another 5,000 in reserve.[116] Liman von Sanders had strengthened his left flank, east of the Jordan, where he had earlier beaten back two British attacks, and where Allenby made diversionary moves on 16–17 September. However, Allenby reversed the successful tactic, which had culminated in the capture of Jerusalem, when he feinted in the west and delivered the main blow in the east. This time, he directed his main attack on 18–19 September against the Ottoman 8th Army holding the western, coastal sector. Outnumbered ten to one, the 8th Army fell apart in the battle of Megiddo. British troops then swung against Mustafa Kemal's 7th Army, which retreated east towards the Jordan. Ali Fuat's corps was badly mauled, but İsmet managed to lead his 3rd corps to the Jordan, which he crossed on 25 September.

Messages from general headquarters in Istanbul were comic in their irrelevance. On 20 September, the day after the British breakthrough, Enver congratulated Mustafa Kemal on his appointment as honorary ADC to the sultan.[117] At roughly the same time, Liman von Sanders received a telegram asking whether he wished to contribute to the prizes awarded in a sack-race in Istanbul.[118] He had more pressing concerns. On 20 September British cavalry raided his headquarters in Nazareth. The German Marshal managed to escape to Tiberias, where he planned a new defence line stretching from the sea of Galilee to the north-east, along the Yarmuk river valley. But, for the first time in the war, Ottoman troops had lost the will to fight.

There were, it was estimated, some 300,000 deserters.[119] In addition, while the front line was thinly manned, large numbers of officers and men managed to stay in the rear. Troops were badly fed, and just as they had no proper winter clothing in the Caucasus, so they had no light tropical clothes for the summer heat of the Jordan valley. Finally, Turkish troops saw that they were fighting in a foreign land. The Arab Revolt had had no appreciable military impact until Allenby's final offensive. But once the Ottoman armies were defeated, the Bedouins descended on them like vultures, while the Arabs in the towns, who had given little trouble to the Ottoman government, hastened to change sides. Earlier, Arab troops in the Ottoman armies were considered unreliable but not disloyal by their Turkish commanders. Now, as Ottoman soldiers decided to go home, an ethnic split occurred. While Liman von Sanders tried to hang on to as much territory as possible, the best Turkish commanders concentrated on saving their troops for the defence of their homeland.

Unable to establish a front in northern Palestine and Jordan, Liman von Sanders realized quickly that he could not hold Damascus either. When Mustafa Kemal arrived in that city he found that Liman von Sanders had moved his headquarters north to Baalbek (in the Bekaa valley in present-day Lebanon). Before leaving, Liman von Sanders had changed the command structure. The 8th Army headquarters under General Cevat (Çobanlı) was ordered back to Istanbul, as that army had practically ceased to exist. Such Ottoman forces as remained on the left flank east of the river Jordan, including units of Mustafa Kemal's 7th Army, were subordinated to General Cemal (Mersinli), commander of the 4th Army, who was the most senior Ottoman officer in Syria.[120] On 29 September Mustafa Kemal was appointed commander of the remnants of his 7th Army and of the 8th Army, which were still to be found west of the Jordan, and were retreating in confusion on the right flank.[121] He was to proceed to Rayak (Riaq), a railway station south of

Baalbek, to reorganize these troops. On 1 October 1918, Australian cavalry entered Damascus. An Arab administration was installed and immediately proved its unfitness to govern as riots convulsed the city.[122]

On the same day, Liman von Sanders held a conference at the temporary headquarters of the German Asia Corps near Rayak. He had managed to extricate most of the Germans by paying protection money to the Druzes to ensure safe passage through the mountains. Now he met his two Turkish commanders, Mustafa Kemal and Cemal (Mersinli). Mustafa Kemal says in his reminiscences that he himself took the 'mad' decision to retreat to Aleppo.[123] Liman von Sanders claims that he gave the order to withdraw to Homs (in Syria), where all Ottoman troops were to assemble.[124] In any case, with Turkish troops in full flight, the decision to withdraw was a formality.

For a time, contact with British forces was lost. The retreat north from Damascus proved comparatively easy, as local Arabs were still quiescent.[125] Mustafa Kemal arrived in Aleppo with his headquarters on 5 October. On 7 October he sent off a furious telegram to Istanbul. 'The withdrawal,' he wrote, 'could have been carried out in some order if a fool like Enver Paşa had not been director-general of operations, if we did not have here a commander – Cevat Paşa – at the head of a military force of five to ten thousand men, who fled at the first sound of gunfire, abandoning his army, and wandered round like a bewildered chicken, and a commander of the 4th Army, Cemal Paşa, ever incapable of appreciating a military situation, and if above them we did not have a group headquarters [under Liman von Sanders], which lost all control from the first day of battle. Now there is nothing left to do but to make peace.'[126] It was an ungenerous and unwise outburst. Mustafa Kemal had no need by now to manage Enver Paşa or Liman von Sanders, but the other two generals still had a future in the Ottoman army. Nevertheless, he could not resist the temptation to clear himself at the expense of his companions in arms.

While Colonel İsmet led his corps to the north, Mustafa Kemal managed to form two divisions of 5,500 men each and position them on hills south of Aleppo.[127] On 25 October his troops stood their ground in the first serious engagement fought since the battle of Megiddo. But the situation in Aleppo was becoming untenable. Bedouins had entered the town, as townspeople rose and occupied public buildings. After street fighting, in which he was personally involved, Mustafa Kemal succeeded in regaining control, largely by distributing money to the Bedouins.[128] But he had already begun to move his troops out of the city, and on 26 October he established his headquarters at Katma, north of Aleppo. As he did so, he checked a probing attack by advancing British forces. It was the last engagement of the war.

On 30 October 1918, an armistice between the Allies and the Ottoman state was signed on board HMS *Agamemnon*, anchored in Mudros harbour on the island of Lemnos, outside the Turkish straits. On the same day, Liman von Sanders, who had earlier moved his head-quarters to Adana in southern Turkey, was instructed by the Ottoman government to transfer to Mustafa Kemal the command of the Lightning Group of Armies. The change took effect on 31 October. Mustafa Kemal's policy of keeping in with Sultan Vahdettin and with his chief ADC Ahmet İzzet Paşa had paid off. Stealing a march on his senior fellow-commander Cemal (Mersinli), Mustafa Kemal was now in charge of the whole southern front from a point south of İskenderun on the Mediterranean, through Iraq, where the Turks still held Mosul, to Persia. The armies manning this long line were weak and hungry, but they were in regular formation. They had been defeated, but had been saved from total collapse. Mustafa Kemal now bent his energies on preserving what was still in Turkish hands – territory, people and the military strength to guard them.

Mustafa Kemal's third, and last, stretch of active service in the World War had lasted barely two months – from the end of August to the end of October 1918. His one achievement was to re-establish, however precariously, a front on the southern edges of Anatolia. He could do little to save the bulk of his forces in Palestine,[129] but he reorganized the remnant led home by İsmet and others. As the war ended, the Turkish heartland was still in Turkish hands. Mustafa Kemal had strengthened his position by returning to the Palestine front in the last days of the war. Although largely unnoticed by the Allies, and still not well known in his own country, Mustafa Kemal had come out of the war in charge of the longest front held by the Ottoman armed forces. He was only 37, and still a Brigadier. But his professional reputation was high among Turkish commanders. True, they knew him as a difficult man to work with. He was ambitious and wilful. He had strong political views, and played politics to get his way. He was convinced he knew best. But then he usually did, for he had good sense, a rare quality in a world that had torn itself to pieces.

PART III

The Will of the Nation

10

Figures in a Ruined Landscape

—————————◆—————————

THE DECISON OF the Ottoman government to seek an immediate end to hostilities with the Allies was precipitated by the collapse of Bulgaria in the middle of September 1918. For nearly three years the Bulgarians had held off the Allied expeditionary force centred on Salonica. But their front was finally broken by French, British, Serbian and Greek troops commanded by the French general Franchet d'Esperey. The Bulgarians sued for an armistice, leaving Istanbul exposed to an Allied advance.

The grand vizier Talât Paşa was the first to admit defeat. He had gone to Germany on 3 September to sort out disagreements in the Caucasus.[1] Passing through Sofia on his way back, he was told by the Bulgarians that they were abandoning the fight. 'We've had it' ('*Boku yedik*', literally 'We've eaten shit'), Talât Paşa told his Turkish companions as he boarded the train to Istanbul, where he arrived late on 27 September.[2] Enver remained hopeful a little longer. On the day of Talât's return, he sent a telegram to Zeki Paşa, the Ottoman representative at the German supreme headquarters, asking him to urge the despatch of German and Austrian troops to stiffen the Bulgarians. But the Bulgarians signed an armistice, amounting to a capitulation, on 29 September, and on 2 October Enver too was forced to admit in a telegram to his brother Nuri Paşa in the Caucasus that the game was up.[3]

On 7 October, Talât informed the CUP parliamentary group that he intended to resign,[4] as a new government would be better able to negotiate with the Allies. However, when Sultan Vahdettin asked the 74-year-old Tevfik Paşa to form the new administration, Talât insisted that the CUP, which was still in control of the capital, should be strongly represented in the cabinet. Tevfik Paşa refused. So Talât stayed on for a few days as caretaker prime minister, and read the royal speech in the presence of Sultan Vahdettin, when the latter opened the new session of parliament on 10 October. The speech announced that while Bulgaria was seeking a separate peace, the Ottoman state, together with its other allies, had approached the American President Woodrow Wilson for help in making peace.[5] The presence of German troops in and around Istanbul, as well as considerations of military honour, demanded a careful approach to peacemaking. But, at the same time, the Ottoman leadership knew that, as the bulk of their remaining troops was concentrated in the Caucasus and the Syrian front, the capital was defenceless against an attack from the west. Time was needed to recall troops from the Caucasus. As a stopgap measure, the Germans were persuaded to ship a division from the Crimean peninsula to Turkish eastern Thrace in order to reinforce the seven or eight thousand Turkish troops available for the defence of Istanbul.[6]

These measures did not affect the accelerating collapse of the CUP regime. On 9 October, Ahmet İzzet Paşa, Mustafa Kemal's commanding officer in south-eastern Turkey in 1915–16, formed a new government, which included members of the CUP opposed to the war party. Cavit, who had extracted every penny he could from the Germans when he rejoined the government in 1917, remained minister of finance. But the two most important appointments were those of Fethi (Okyar) as interior minister and of another friend of Mustafa Kemal, Colonel (i.e. naval Captain) Rauf (Orbay), former chief of the naval staff, as navy minister.

This was, more or less, the cabinet which Mustafa Kemal wanted to see in power, except for one important particular. A few days earlier he had sent a confidential telegram from Adana to his doctor, and agent, in Istanbul, Rasim Ferit (Talay), for transmission to the sultan's ADC, Naci (Eldeniz). He wrote:

I learn that Talât Paşa's cabinet is paralysed and that Tevfik Paşa is encountering difficulties in forming a stable government. The army is incapable of fighting, and existing forces cannot defend themselves. With every passing day the enemy's position is becoming more favourable and overwhelming. Peace must be made immediately, either jointly or separately, and there is not a moment to lose. Otherwise, it is by no means unlikely that the whole country will be lost and that our state will suffer irreparable damage. In full loyalty to our respected sovereign, I suggest that if Tevfik Paşa has indeed come up against difficulties, then for the sake of the country's safety, the post of grand vizier should be given to İzzet Paşa and that the latter should form a cabinet based on Fethi, Tahsin [Özer, whom Mustafa Kemal knew as governor of Damascus], Rauf, (İsmail) Canbulat [a leading member of the CUP, who had become an opponent of Enver], Azmi [a former governor of Beirut], the Şeyhülislâm Hayri [Ürgüplü, a CUP supporter], and your humble servant. I am convinced that such a cabinet would be able to control the situation…[7]

Although Mustafa Kemal did not specify it, he saw himself as war minister in the new administration. However, by the time his telegram reached the palace, Ahmet İzzet Paşa had already formed his government, in which he retained the war ministry for himself. Disappointed at the news, Mustafa Kemal sent a second telegram to Dr Rasim Ferit on 16 October asking him to find out from Rauf and Fethi the true reason why he had not been made war minister and chief of the general staff. İzzet Paşa sent a conciliatory reply saying that Mustafa Kemal was needed as commander in the south, but that 'after the conclusion of peace, we hope that Divine Providence will grant that we work together.' Mustafa Kemal declared in 1926 that he replied: 'Peace will be slow in coming. We shall have to pass through many crises till then. I had asked for the war ministry believing that I could serve the country in the [intervening] period. After peace has come, many others would be better fitted than I to discharge the peacetime duties of a war minister. That is why I do not believe that it is essential or even useful that we work together in peacetime.'[8] By 1926, Mustafa Kemal had become president of the republic, while Ahmet İzzet Paşa was a retired old gentleman on a meagre pension.[9] In October 1918, their relative position was different. Told about Mustafa Kemal's telegram from Adana, Ahmet İzzet Paşa turned to his ADC and said: 'Things have come to a pretty pass when Mustafa Kemal recommends to the sovereign to make me grand vizier.'[10]

Enver, who lost his job as war minister and chief of the general staff when the new government took office, is said to have been more generous in his views. Dr Adnan (Adıvar), a prominent Turkish nationalist who was to serve under Mustafa Kemal in Anatolia before breaking with him in the aftermath of the War of Independence, reported that Enver remarked: 'İzzet Paşa will not do as war minister. Mustafa Kemal alone is up to the job.'[11] While Mustafa Kemal was left in Adana, one of his corps commanders, Colonel İsmet (İnönü), was given the job of under-secretary in the war ministry in Istanbul.

The Ottoman government had made peace overtures to the Allies even before Ahmet İzzet Paşa had taken office. But there were no immediate results. A better channel of communication offered itself when the British general Sir Charles Townshend, who had surrendered in Kut in 1916, and was now kept in comfortable captivity in a villa on the island of Büyükada, offered his mediation. His offer was accepted and Townshend made his way to Mudros bay, on the island of Lemnos, off the entrance to the Dardanelles, where Admiral Calthorpe, commander-in-chief of the British Mediterranean fleet, had his headquarters. On 22 October, Calthorpe informed Ahmet İzzet Paşa that he had been authorized to sign an armistice and asked him to send delegates for the purpose.

The choice of delegates proved difficult. The sultan wished the delegation to be headed by his brother-in-law Damat Ferit Paşa, whose most important previous government job had been as embassy secretary in London, and who had dabbled in politics as leader of the CUP's opponents, the Party of Freedom and Concord. 'The man is mad,' Ahmet İzzet Paşa claimed to have replied. But the sultan insisted, and arranged for Ferit Paşa to meet the grand vizier in the senate. According to Ahmet İzzet Paşa, his view of the sultan's brother-in-law was quickly confirmed when the latter addressed him in the following terms: 'As soon as I see the admiral [Calthorpe], I shall propose that an armistice be concluded on the basis of the full territorial integrity of the [Ottoman] state. If the admiral refuses, I shall ask him for a cruiser to take me to London, where I shall request the king to receive me as an old friend of his father. This is how I shall save the state from the whirlpool into which it has been pushed by the Unionists [the CUP].'[12]

After consulting his cabinet colleagues, Ahmet İzzet Paşa refused point-blank to appoint Ferit Paşa, and chose instead the navy minister Rauf, who, like Mustafa Kemal, had quarrelled with the Germans during the course of the war, and who was moreover influenced by the Anglophile tradition of the Ottoman navy and had struck up a friendship with General Townshend. The sultan accepted the appointment with bad grace, but insisted that the instructions to the delegation should specify that the rights of the caliphate, the sultanate and the Ottoman dynasty should be fully safeguarded, and that if autonomy were to be granted to any Ottoman province, this should be administrative only and not political; otherwise independence would be preferable.[13]

The first condition, which the sultan dictated personally, showed his apprehension that the dynasty and the institutions which it embodied might perish in the turmoil of defeat. It was also a sign that Vahdettin put his throne before anything else. As for the second condition, if Vahdettin believed that political autonomy would place the Arab provinces under the tutelage of non-Muslim powers, whereas independence would preserve Muslim rule, he was, for once, prescient. In any case,

Ahmet İzzet Paşa cut the discussion short by pointing out that, while he was personally determined to defend the rights of the dynasty, the sultan's instructions referred to peace terms and were not relevant to the conclusion of an armistice.

Rauf and his companions left the capital on 24 October, and negotiations with Admiral Calthorpe started on 27 October on board the battleship *Agamemnon* in Mudros bay. The Turkish delegates asked for a standstill on all battle-fronts and offered to demobilize and to open the straits to the Allies. As the war had left the Ottoman state penniless and its people starving, they also requested financial help and food supplies.[14] The Ottoman leadership believed these were reasonable terms. True, their army had been defeated in Palestine and Mesopotamia, although not elsewhere. But it was still holding all the battle-fronts. There had been massive desertions, leading to banditry in the interior of the country, but no mutinies, let alone a revolution. The Ottoman state was in control of its core territory from the Bulgarian frontier to the Caucasus in the east and Syria in the south.

The Ottoman leaders knew, of course, that after they had entered the war, the Allies had drawn up plans to partition their country. Although the original partition scheme, which the Bolsheviks had published, had become invalid after the Russian Revolution, the Ottomans suspected that the plans had been adjusted. But the British prime minister Lloyd George had declared in January 1918 that he had no intention of depriving Turkey of Thrace and Asia Minor, provided that the straits were internationalized and that Arabia, Armenia, Mesopotamia, Syria and Palestine did not revert to Ottoman sovereignty. More importantly, Wilson's Fourteen Points, which provided the basis for all negotiations to end the war, specified (in point 12) that the Turkish portion of the Ottoman state should enjoy full sovereignty, on condition that subject nationalities had the right to free development.[15] With the Arab provinces already under British occupation, the Ottoman leaders' main concern was to keep what they still held. To achieve it, they were ready to exchange Allied for German protection. But Rauf was instructed to insist that no Allied military forces should land at any point in the country.[16] This he failed to achieve.

The original Allied terms for an armistice with Turkey provided for the occupation by Allied troops of important strategic points. But on 22 October, Admiral Calthorpe was told not to insist on this, provided he succeeded in the main aim of detaching Turkey from Germany and opening the straits. Germany and Austria-Hungary were still fighting, and the British government wanted an armistice with Turkey as soon as possible in order to concentrate on the main enemy. But the Ottomans' desire for a quick end to hostilities was even stronger. Fearing an imminent collapse, they decided to purchase British good will with concessions which they regretted soon afterwards. Calthorpe sensed this, and after three days of hard, but polite, bargaining, he secured Ottoman agreement to an armistice which departed little from the harsh terms initially demanded by the Allies. Abandoning his opposition to Allied landings, Rauf conceded the Allied occupation of Dardanelles and Bosphorus forts, the occupation of railway tunnels constructed by the Germans in the Taurus mountains, the occupation of 'any strategic points in the event of a situation arising which threatens the security of the Allies' (article 7), the surrender of Turkish troops in the Arab provinces (including Mesopotamia) and their withdrawal from Cilicia and Transcaucasia (articles 16 and 17).[17]

The armistice embodying these terms was signed on 30 October. All that Rauf could achieve was a promise by Calthorpe in a non-binding confidential letter that only British and French troops would be sent to occupy the straits. Calthorpe added that he would recommend to his government that a small Turkish force should remain there. This promise was indeed kept. But Calthorpe's assurance that he would inform the British government of Turkish opposition to any landing of Greek troops in Istanbul and İzmir and to the occupation of Istanbul, so long as the Ottoman government safeguarded order and Allied interests in the capital, did not affect future Allied decisions.[18]

Nevertheless, Rauf was euphoric when he returned to Istanbul. 'I have discovered,' he told a reporter, 'that the British are not aiming at the destruction of the Turkish nation ... I saw that our country, contrary to what was expected, will not be occupied. I assure you that not a single enemy soldier will disembark in our Istanbul ... Yes, the armistice we have concluded is better than we had hoped for.'[19] The grand vizier Ahmet İzzet Paşa was equally satisfied. In a telegram to Admiral Calthorpe, he expressed his gratitude for the friendly reception of the delegates, adding, 'I pray that no future event will again disturb the friendly relations and accord between our two countries.'[20] But Ahmet İzzet's peace of mind was soon shattered. The day after the armistice was signed, he fell ill with Spanish flu. The following night, 1/2 November 1918, seven leaders of the CUP, headed by Enver, Talât and Cemal, fled from Istanbul on board a German ship, which took them to the Crimea.[21] From there they made their way to Berlin.

Opposition newspapers in Istanbul launched a campaign against the government for failing to prevent the escape of the CUP leaders. In the eyes of the Freedom and Concord Party, Ahmet Paşa's administration was, in any case, the rearguard of the CUP, since it included three former members of the latter. Using the opposition campaign as justification, Vahdettin, who had not received the armistice delegation on its return to the capital, asked the speaker of the senate, Ahmet Rıza, to impress on the grand vizier the need to get rid of the former Unionists, particularly in view of the impending arrival of British officers in the capital. Ahmet İzzet Paşa tried to procrastinate, but after being harried by the palace, he consulted his ministers and decided to resign.

On 7 November four British officers arrived in Istanbul on board the Ottoman torpedo-boat *Basra*. The following day, the cabinet submitted its resignation, stating angrily that the attempt to impose conditions on the prime minister was incompatible with the constitution.[22] Ahmet İzzet Paşa had managed to stay in power for just twenty-five days.[23] He was succeeded by Tevfik Paşa, whom the sultan had wanted to appoint grand vizier in the first place. The new government, which was announced on 11 November 1918,[24] just as all hostilities ended in the west, appeared to justify Talât Paşa's earlier warning that there was no one of any use outside the ranks of the CUP.[25] Abdullah Paşa, the disastrous army commander in the Balkan war, became war minister. As far as Turkish nationalists were concerned, the one redeeming feature was the appointment of Cevat (Çobanlı) Paşa, the successful defender of the southern sector in Gallipoli, as chief of the general staff.

Ottoman hopes that the armistice would signal a halt in the advance of Allied armies were quickly disappointed. On 1 November, the British commander in Mesopotamia, General Marshall, ordered his troops to occupy Mosul. The commander of the Ottoman 6th Army, Ali İhsan (Sabis), protested that there were no grounds for invoking article 7 of the armistice, since the security of the Allies had not been threatened, and that Mosul was not part of Mesopotamia where, under article 16, Turkish garrisons had to surrender. However, the grand vizier Ahmet İzzet Paşa ordered him to comply, saying: 'The British government could, if it so wished, occupy our whole country, since we have no forces to stop them. But I fail to understand how the British can use the sophistry of one of their officers to break the word they gave two days ago.' Mosul was occupied on 8 November. But Ali İhsan Paşa took care to send into the interior of eastern Anatolia such arms and supplies as he could secrete away, and encouraged the organization of local Turkish militias.[26]

Mustafa Kemal was faced with the same problem on 5 November, when the British commander in Syria notified him that he intended to occupy İskenderun, on the grounds that he needed to use its harbour in order to supply British troops in Aleppo. Two days earlier, Mustafa Kemal had sent a telegram to Ahmet İzzet Paşa asking for a clarification of the armistice terms. In particular, what were the borders of Cilicia – an antique geographical term which did not correspond to any administrative unit – from which Ottoman troops were to be withdrawn under article 16 of the armistice? Until the position became clear, Mustafa Kemal proposed to form a new division from young recruits under his command, to strengthen the gendarmerie, and to move military stores north of the Taurus range. These were clearly preparations for continued resistance to the Allies.

Mustafa Kemal followed this up on 6 November with a warning to the grand vizier that he had issued orders to his troops to open fire if the British tried to land in İskenderun, and that, at the same time, he was moving his 7th Army from northern Syria into Cilicia. He ended his telegram with a clear challenge to the government. 'My innate disposition,' he wrote, 'does not allow me to apply faithfully orders which justify the deceptive practices of the British, more eloquently than the latter do themselves ... I therefore request you to appoint speedily a successor to whom I could immediately hand over my command.' On the following day, 7 November, Ahmet İzzet Paşa replied that the order to open fire at British troops landing in İskenderun was contrary to the policy and the interests of the state and should be immediately rescinded. The grand vizier informed Mustafa Kemal that the Lightning Group of Armies had been abolished, and that only the headquarters of the 7th Army remained in existence.

Mustafa Kemal now adopted a softer tone. He cabled back immediately that he had countermanded his order to resist a British landing by force. He explained that he wanted to hold İskenderun to avoid his troops in northern Syria being cut off. Now their withdrawal had been completed. Mustafa Kemal assured the grand vizier that he would justify the trust placed in him by carrying out his new duties for the good of the country. But could not the historic name of the Lightning Group be kept instead of the ephemeral name of the 7th Army?

It could not, and there were to be no new duties for Mustafa Kemal. Following the publication of the imperial decree on 7 November abolishing the Lightning Group of Armies, Mustafa Kemal was placed at the disposal of the war ministry and recalled to Istanbul.[27] Before this order was communicated to him, Ahmet İzzet Paşa sent a last telegram addressed to Mustafa Kemal as commander of the 7th Army. He warned that it was folly to endanger the armistice for the sake of İskenderun. 'We must bear in mind that we are powerless, and we must speak and act accordingly,' concluded Ahmet İzzet Paşa. This was too much for Mustafa Kemal. In a last telegram, which he signed with his name without any title, he let loose his indignation. 'If we ourselves were to help the British achieve results which they might otherwise obtain only if we fought on to the end at the side of Germany and were then totally defeated, we would be writing a black page in the history of the Ottoman state to the discredit of the present government.' Nevertheless, Mustafa Kemal ended his telegram on a conciliatory note. He was not arguing with his superiors, he said; but he was unable to desist from expressing views he had formed for the good of the country.[28]

Mustafa Kemal was to say in March 1923 that it was in Adana in November 1918 that he had first tried to halt the nation's drift to disaster. But he had no chance of success at the time.[29] He is also reported to have urged Ali Cenani, a notable from the near-by town of Antep (later Gaziantep) to set up a resistance organization, to which he promised to supply arms.[30] Ali Cenani reported: 'The weapons which were then given out at the orders of the Gazi [Mustafa Kemal] formed the basis of our defence organization.' However, the weapons sent to the rear or distributed to local Muslims by Mustafa Kemal, like similar measures taken by Ali İhsan Paşa further east, could not stop the Allied occupation of Cilicia and Upper Mesopotamia. Unlike Mustafa Kemal, the Muslim population was not yet ready to resist. As Zamir (later Damar) Arıkoğlu, a leading Turkish nationalist in Adana, explained in his memoirs: 'Unfortunately, the mentality prevailing at the time and war exhaustion had left the people listless and inactive. Four years of wartime suffering and sadness had laid the country low … It was not easy to move a mass of people, whose hearts were full of material and moral suffering and whose life had become a burden to them. In spite of the advice of [Mustafa Kemal] Paşa, there were no signs of resistance.'[31]

On 25 November 1918, a French officer, Colonel Raymond, arrived in Adana and told the Ottoman governor that French troops would occupy the city, that Ottoman troops should be immediately withdrawn and that leading CUP members should leave. Adana was occupied on 21 December.[32] What caused particular distress to local Muslims was that the French were accompanied by detachments of armed Armenian volunteers, and that many Armenian civilians, deported to Syria in 1915, returned, repossessed their old property, and tried to avenge themselves on their Turkish neighbours. Intercommunal violence was the inevitable result. It was not European military occupation, but the prospect of losing the country to local Christian minorities, which, after the first shock had worn off, called forth Turkish popular resistance. By that time regular Ottoman troops had been withdrawn north of the Taurus. The 7th Army was disbanded immediately after Mustafa Kemal's recall. All that was left was the weak 2nd Army, commanded by Mustafa Kemal's former subordinate Nihat Paşa (Anılmış). Before he was removed at Allenby's demand on 22 January 1919, Nihat moved into the interior such military supplies as he could, but had to leave behind 126 truckloads.[33]

The commander of the Ottoman 9th Army on the Caucasian front, Yakup Şevki Paşa (who had replaced Vehip Paşa after the latter had fallen foul of the Germans[34] in June 1918), was luckier as he too sought to obstruct Allied demands. He delayed until 25 January 1919 the full withdrawal of his army behind the pre-war Ottoman-Russian frontier, and saved the bulk of his equipment and supplies. As he left former tsarist territory, he handed over power to the Kars National Muslim Council (*Şura*, a word also used as the translation of the word 'Soviet'), which changed its name on 18 January 1919 to National Provisional Government of South-West Caucasus. This body was dissolved by British troops on 19 April 1919 and its members exiled to Malta. The following month Armenians occupied Kars.[35]

Further east, Brigadier Kâzım Karabekir withdrew his 1st Caucasian Corps from north-western Persia. Returning through Batum, which was still under Ottoman occupation, he found Japanese field guns and ammunition in military stores and had them shipped to Trabzon.[36]

Everywhere, Ottoman military commanders were trying to conserve such resources as they could. The war ministry in Istanbul, which they and their friends controlled, was sympathetic to their efforts. Mustafa Kemal believed that, were he war minister and chief of the general staff, he could have obstructed the Allies more successfully. But Cevat (Çobanlı), Fevzi (Çakmak) and their staff did what they could to safeguard the nucleus of Turkish military power.

It was an uphill task. The army was demobilized, not only because the Allies had insisted on it, but because Turkish troops wanted to go home. When the Ottoman state mobilized in 1914, the strength of the army rose from 400,000 to 640,000, including 24,000 officers.[37] Total Ottoman war casualties are estimated at 325,000 dead, 350,000 wounded and 250,000 prisoners. But as more men were called up, the strength of the army was maintained: there were more than 700,000 men under arms at the end of 1916, and, at least theoretically, 560,000 when the armistice was signed in 1918.[38] By May 1919, 338,000 men were demobilized, while many others faded away.

The war ministry did its best to reorganize its remaining forces. A scheme which it submitted to the government on 2 January 1919 provided for an army of 61,000 men, armed with 41,000 rifles, 720 machine-guns and 256 field guns. However, it proved impossible to bring together this force, as the number of conscripts dwindled to 43,000. Nevertheless, the war ministry laid the ground for future expansion by keeping in existence a large number of units – no less than twenty divisions, organized in nine army corps. The divisions, whose initial complement was set at only 2,000 men, could be brought up to strength as the need arose.[39]

The main problem concerned armament. Under article 20 of the armistice, the Allies took over all the arms and equipment of demobilized Turkish troops. In Anatolia, some of the equipment could be hidden. But the main military stores were in and around the capital, and Allied sentries were posted to guard them.[40] Although nationalist Turkish officers quickly learnt how to smuggle supplies from these stores, inadequate armament hampered the organization of effective resistance to Allied plans. Nevertheless the idea of resistance arose the moment Allied soldiers set foot on Turkish soil. The Ottoman high command had sought an armistice, but it had not capitulated. Mustafa Kemal was not the only Ottoman commander to lay plans for resistance as soon as he learnt the terms of the armistice. But he was to prove the most effective.

Mustafa Kemal arrived at Haydarpaşa station in Istanbul on 13 November 1918. Built by German architects in 1908 as the starting point of the Baghdad railway, this turreted baronial building affords a panoramic view of Istanbul harbour from the Asian shore. After 1927, Atatürk was regularly photographed on the steps of the station as he was met by throngs of officials on his annual summer visit to the old capital. The scene was different in 1918. The station had been badly damaged by an explosion of munitions the previous year. As Mustafa Kemal, accompanied by his ADC, got off the Adana train, there was only one man to welcome him – his doctor Rasim Ferit (Talay).[41] When he reached the wide steps of the station, the first sight to meet his eyes was that of fifty-five Allied warships steaming into the harbour and preparing to cast anchor in front of Dolmabahçe palace on the European shore. Passengers for the European shore had to wait until the warships had cleared the harbour.

Depressed at the sight of enemy occupation, Mustafa Kemal is said to have told Dr Rasim Ferit: 'I've made a mistake. I shouldn't have come. Come what may, I must find a way of getting back to Anatolia.'[42] According to another report, he said, as he looked at the Allied fleet: 'Just as they have come, so too they will go.'[43] Neither story is convincing. Far from regretting his return to the capital, Mustafa Kemal was impatient to start canvassing for a government with enough mettle to safeguard the territory still in Ottoman hands, a government which he hoped to dominate. As for his reported remark about the fleet, this should be seen in the light of a debate which developed after victory had been won in the War of Independence. Mustafa Kemal's comrade-in-arms and later political opponent Kâzım Karabekir, who returned to Istanbul from Persia on 28 November 1918, was to claim that he had always foreseen that the Turks would have to fight only Armenians and Greeks, as the Allies were too tired to pursue a war in Anatolia. The Allied fleet in Istanbul was no more than a scarecrow, he said.[44] Mustafa Kemal's reported remark about the inevitable departure of the Allied grand fleet invested him with similar prescience.

On arrival, Mustafa Kemal put up, as usual, at the Pera Palace hotel rather than at his mother's house in Akaretler street in Beşiktaş, inland from the palace of Dolmabahçe. But whether because the hotel was uncomfortably full of Allied officers, or, more likely, because it was too expensive for a peacetime brigadier, he soon moved to a house in the European neighbourhood of Beyoğlu (Pera), belonging to Salih Fansa, a Christian Arab from Syria whom he had come to know in Aleppo. Madame Selma Fansa then helped him find a narrow, three-storey town house, which he rented from its Armenian owner, in Osmanbey (in the district of Şişli), near the War College. He moved there on 21 December 1918.[45] The house which he rented was not far from his mother's home in Akaretler. His friend, Mme Corinne Lütfü, lived near by in Beyoğlu. As for Fikriye, who provided female company when he needed it, she could be relied upon to commute from her family home in the old city. But more important than these personal considerations was the fact that the modern part of the city, north of the Golden Horn, was the centre of political activity. The Allied commanding officers and high commissioners were there; so were the sultan and his officials; parliament and the politicians.

The Allied fleet landed 3,500 men, mainly British, who joined a French brigade sent by train from the Macedonian front, after the French had taken control of the railway in European Turkey.[46] Having been squeezed out of the armistice negotiations in Mudros bay, the French were determined not to yield sole control of the Ottoman capital to the

British. Friction between the two main Allies was complicated by the appearance of Italians on the scene. The job of maintaining order in the city was then divided among the three Allied contingents. But as they jostled for power and influence, they trampled not only on the pride, but also on the property of Muslim Turks, whose houses they requisitioned.

Of the three, the Italians emerged from the start as the most accom-modating, courting the Turks, whom the British and the French had no hesitation in antagonizing. Under the secret treaty of London, concluded in 1915, Italy had been promised a 'just share in the Mediterranean region adjacent to the province of Adalia [Antalya]', in the event of the partition of Turkey in Asia, as part of the price for the Italian entry into the war on the side of the Allies. A year later, the Italian zone was extended to include İzmir and even Konya in central Anatolia.[47] The Italians had learnt in Libya that it was difficult to occupy Ottoman territory by force. A zone of influence could be achieved more easily, if they posed as protectors of Muslim Turks against the out-right territorial claims which Greece was known to entertain. Greece had entered the war only in July 1917, after the Allies had removed the pro-German King Constantine and brought to power in Athens the liberal politician Eleftherios Venizelos. Venizelos relied on Britain and France for the realization of his ideal – the creation of a homogeneous Greek state encompassing all the coastlands of the Aegean sea. The French had reservations; the British government under Lloyd George succumbed to the blandishments of Venizelos.

The Allies were divided from the start; they had more pressing con-cerns in Europe; they were war-weary and they had demobilized rapidly. Gradually, Turkish leaders began to see the picture, although they differed in their evaluation of it. All sensed that Allied disagreements could be exploited; most believed that they should present themselves as reliable partners in a stable peace. All wanted to keep control of the territory which they still held when the armistice was signed. The Ottoman experience suggested that this could best be achieved with the help of a foreign protector. The main Allied powers all had their Turkish admirers: America was attractive, idealistic, rich and, fortu-nately, remote; Britain appeared strong and had served Ottoman inter-ests well against Russia in the past; France was an old partner too, and its culture had moulded the thinking of educated Ottoman officials. The CUP had chosen Germany in its bid for independence, and its mistake was for all to see.

But the ideal of independence had taken root. What, however, was the best way of achieving independence and maximum territorial extent? By cooperating with the Allies, singly or severally, by resisting one or more of them, or by a combination of the two methods? The question, which had no easy answer, moved to the centre of Turkish politics as soon as the armistice was signed. Calculations of both national and personal interest affected the attitude of individual Turks. So of course did individual temperament. Atatürk was to say later, 'Freedom and independence define my character.'[48] His record proved it.

The Tevfik Paşa government tried diplomatic means to limit Allied encroachment. On 19 November 1919, the Ottoman foreign minister Reşit Paşa protested that the occupation of Istanbul, outside the straits forts, was contrary to the armistice terms.[49] The protest was rejected. But what worried the Turks more was the presence of four Greek warships in the Allied fleet, and the landing of Greek sailors, who patrolled sections of the city, and of a Greek-Cretan regiment, which guarded the Greek patriarchate.[50]

Pride was not the only reason for the Ottomans' objection to the Greek military presence. Istanbul was a divided city. Precise figures cannot be given, since the population of the capital had been swollen by large numbers of refugees. But of a total of approximately one million inhabitants, Muslims accounted for little more than half. Among non-Muslims, Greeks, who numbered more than 300,000,[51] predominated. The presence of Greek troops was bound to inflame separatist, nationalist aspirations among them. Together with most other non-Muslims (except for the Jews who, by and large, remained loyal to the Ottoman state), they made their feelings clear by welcoming the Allies with transports of joy, as liberators.

In Istanbul Mustafa Kemal thus found himself surrounded by non-Muslims – Greeks, Armenians, Levantines, Europeans – who were opposed to all he stood for. 'The dark days of the armistice', as the Turks remember the Allied occupation, were for most non-Muslims the happiest days of their lives – and also the most prosperous, as commerce, which they largely controlled, revived. It was against this background of non-Muslim gaiety, of Turkish depression, and of pervasive intrigue both within the ethnic communities and between them and the Allies, that Mustafa Kemal set to work as a soldier with a political cause. The cause was the independence of the Turkish-speaking Muslim nation and of its fatherland. As ever, he was convinced that he alone was capable of achieving it.

His first call was on his friend Rauf, the outgoing navy minister. Together they went to see Ahmet İzzet Paşa in the grand vizier's office, which the latter was about to vacate. They appear to have persuaded him to withdraw his resignation and form a new government, which would include Mustafa Kemal.[52] However, before this could happen, parliament would have to reject the nomination of Tevfik Paşa as Ahmet İzzet's successor. Two allies were to help them achieve this: Fethi (Okyar) and İsmail Canbulat. Like Mustafa Kemal and Rauf, they were former CUP dissidents. After the flight of its wartime leaders, the CUP dissolved itself, transferring its assets to a new Renovation Party (*Teceddüt Fırkası*), which comprised most of its former adherents, including İsmail Canbulat and Mustafa Kemal's friend Dr Tevfik Rüştü (Aras).[53] However, Fethi preferred to form his own Party of Freedom-loving Ottoman Common People (*Osmanlı Hürriyetperveran Avam Fırkası*), which attracted the support of some thirty members of parliament. To propagate his views, he published the newspaper *Minber* (The Pulpit), which Mustafa Kemal helped finance. Mustafa Kemal knew the value of publicity, of which Enver had starved him during the Great War. He now had *Minber* to bring his achievements and his views to the attention of the public.[54]

While trying to influence parliament against Tevfik Paşa, Mustafa Kemal sought also an interview with Sultan Vahdettin, who received him on 15 November. This was the first of four interviews which Mustafa Kemal was granted by the sovereign during the six months he spent in the capital.[55] Mustafa Kemal needed to convince the sultan of his loyalty. He succeded in this, although his hope of achieving power with Vahdettin's help was disappointed. The sultan feared the army, which had overthrown Abdülhamit, and hoped that Mustafa Kemal, known as an opponent of Enver Paşa, and also, more generally, of military involvement in politics, would keep it loyal to the throne. Events were to prove him wrong. But while the sultan wanted to use Mustafa Kemal, he had no intention of bringing him to power. He preferred to work through men who had married into the dynasty – Damat Ferit and Tevfik Paşa.

However, the immediate obstacle to the designs of Mustafa Kemal and of his allies was the fear felt by supporters of the former CUP, inside and outside the chamber, that a refusal to endorse Tevfik Paşa would hasten the dissolution of parliament. The dissolution of the chamber of deputies, which the CUP dominated, was favoured by the Allies and advocated by all domestic opponents of the CUP. The sultan was certainly one of the latter, but he was too careful to make the first move. On 18 November parliament met to discuss the programme of Tevfik Paşa's government. The vote was inconclusive, for although only twenty-seven deputies – all, it seems, supporters of Fethi's party – voted against the government, there was no absolute majority in favour.

Mustafa Kemal continued his efforts to unseat Tevfik Paşa. He claimed in 1926 that many deputies assured him of their support, but that when the vote was taken again on 19 November, they reneged on their promise. The fact is that the leader of the Renovation Party, Sabri (Toprak), spoke in favour of Tevfik Paşa. This raised the number of votes cast for the new government. Even so, an absolute majority could not be achieved, but as a simple majority was sufficient on the second vote, Tevfik Paşa was confirmed in office.[56]

Unable to unseat Tevfik Paşa and to achieve prominence in a successor government, Mustafa Kemal sought another interview with the sultan, who received him on 29 November, as *Minber* pursued its campaign for a new, strong government.[57] According to Mustafa Kemal's reminiscences, published in 1926, when questioned closely by the sultan on the loyalty of the army, Mustafa Kemal replied that he had no reason to doubt it. The sultan, so he claimed in 1926, later falsified the tenor of the interview, saying that Mustafa Kemal had spoken in favour of the dissolution of parliament and had promised that he and his military comrades would support this step which the sovereign was contemplating.

Squeezed between a pro-CUP parliament, on one side, and the Allies, the palace, and domestic opponents of the CUP, on the other, Tevfik Paşa tottered. On 2 December he introduced press censorship. On 11 December, the war minister Abdullah Paşa resigned.[58] This unfortunate general, who had come up against the opposition of a 'league' of senior officers,[59] was replaced by his chief of staff Cevat (Çobanlı), while another officer with a good war record, Fevzi (Çakmak), became chief of the general staff. A third commander who had fought both in Gallipoli and in Syria, Brigadier Kâzım (İnanç), was already assistant chief of the general staff. The war ministry under-secretary, İsmet (İnönü), was put in charge of a committee set up to study the military aspects of the peace setttlement.[60] As politicians squabbled, patriotic Turkish officers sought to bring the remaining Ottoman armed forces under their control. As a result of their efforts, the general staff became the main centre of resistance to Allied plans.

Mustafa Kemal was the most politically active member of this group. While Tevfik Paşa was trying to fight off the parliamentary opposition, Mustafa Kemal contacted other former prominent CUP moderates – the outgoing finance minister Cavit, and the senate speaker Ahmet Rıza – to explore the possibility of forming a nationalist government under Ahmet Rıza. But the leaders of the Renovation Party were wary of Mustafa Kemal; they were determined to refuse him the war ministry, and the discussions petered out. As Mustafa Kemal's contacts with former members of the CUP became known, a report was published on 29 December that he was about to join the Renovation Party. He immediately issued a denial, saying that he was retaining his rank and position in the army.[61] In theory, this ruled out political activity; in practice Mustafa Kemal had embarked on the full-time political career which he was to pursue to the end of his life.

The majority in parliament continued to attack Tevfik Paşa, against whom it tabled a vote of no-confidence. On 21 December, Tevfik went to the palace and asked the sultan to dissolve the chamber immediately, before he was defeated in parliament. Vahdettin did so readily, asking Tevfik to remain in office. To remove fears that this inaugurated an indefinite return to personal rule by the sultan, a government announcement was published on 2 January 1919, promising fresh elections four months after the conclusion of peace.[62]

Mustafa Kemal was not a novice in domestic politics. But his dealings with foreigners had been confined largely to military matters. Now foreigners were in control of the capital, and he needed to sound them out. Could the Allies be dissuaded from supporting the cause of Greek and Armenian separatists? If they could not, how far would their support extend for the ethnic adversaries of Muslim Turks? The British, whom Mustafa Kemal had fought in Syria, were the strongest single power and therefore the main actors in the Near East. Rauf, who had relied on British good will, was quickly disappointed. This did not put off Mustafa Kemal. On 17 November, four days after his return to Istanbul, he gave an interview to three Turkish nationalist newspapers. 'I do not wish to doubt the good will of the states which have concluded the armistice with us, and that of the British government which has drawn up the armistice terms on behalf of these states,' he declared. 'If misunderstandings arise in the implementation of the terms, their cause should be immediately determined and an agreement should be sought with the other parties.'[63] The interview published in *Minber* added the words: 'There can be no friends more benevolent than the British.'[64]

The interview took place in the Pera Palace hotel. The correspondent of the *Daily Mail*, G. Ward Price, was also invited to the hotel, where, according to his memoirs, Mustafa Kemal was flanked by his friend Colonel Refet (Bele), a courageous officer, short, wiry, and strong-willed. Ward Price says that Mustafa Kemal offered his services to the British, arguing that the French should be kept out of the country, and that if the British assumed responsibility for Anatolia, they would need the cooperation of experienced Turkish governors. Ward Price reported the conversation to British military intelligence, which dismissed it as unimportant.[65] Allowance should, of course, be made for lapses of memory and the vagaries of interpretation, but it is not improbable that Mustafa Kemal should have wished to play off the British against the French, who were at the time about to occupy Adana, or that he should have thought of the possibility of returning to Anatolia as a military governor with British support in order to prevent the cession of territory to Armenians and Greeks. That, for most Turks, was the immediate danger.

There is an echo of this meeting in Mustafa Kemal's account of a subsequent episode. On 7 February 1919, Field Marshal Allenby arrived from Egypt to present the Ottoman government with a list of demands, chief among them the immediate recall of Ali İhsan Paşa, and the demobilization of his 6th Army, which continued to obstruct the British in Mesopotamia. The demands were accepted. Atatürk was to claim later that Allenby wanted him to be appointed commander of the 6th Army, and that when he refused, he lost his ADC, his official car and his allowance as army commander.[66] This makes no sense, as the 6th Army was soon after disbanded on 2 March 1919,[67] in accordance with British demands. Mustafa Kemal's loss of his privileges as army commander was inevitable once he became an unemployed brigadier, particularly in conditions of acute financial stringency. In fact, the proposal that he should take over the 6th Army had come from the Ottoman war minister, Ömer Yaver Paşa. Mustafa Kemal refused, saying that the job was insubstantial, and that the offer looked like an attempt to get rid of him.

One British subject who sought to cultivate relations with prominent Turks was the Scottish Presbyterian minister Dr Robert Frew, who could put to political use his ability to dispense relief aid.[68] Mustafa Kemal met Dr Frew twice under the auspices of a certain Monsieur Martin.[69] According to the Kemalist journalist Falih Rıfkı Atay, Mustafa Kemal rejected Frew's suggestion that, in order to gain credit with the Allies, the Turks should dissociate themselves from the crimes committed by the CUP.[70] In the speech which he delivered in 1927, Mustafa Kemal described Dr Frew as a British adventurer.[71] Turks were, and remain, convinced that Frew was a high-level British intelligence agent. He is more likely to have been a freelance go-between, who believed that he could make friends for Britain. In any case, neither he nor any responsible British official succeeded in spotting Mustafa Kemal as the future leader of Turkish national resistance.

The suggestion attributed to Dr Frew reflected a major British preoccupation. Just as de-Nazification became a guiding principle of Allied policy in Germany after the Second World War, cleansing Turkey of the CUP and punishment for Unionist crimes weighed heavily on British – and Allied – thinking after the conclusion of the armistice at Mudros.[72] The chief crimes attributed to the CUP were the massacre of the Armenians, deportations of Greeks from the Aegean coast and the mal-treatment of British POWs, particularly the 13,000 British and Indian troops captured in Kut in Mesopotamia in April 1916.[73] The British thought it best that the Ottoman authorities should themselves arrest the culprits.[74]

On 14 December 1918, the Tevfik Paşa government decided that persons accused of crimes during the deportations should be tried by court martial. A court martial, consisting of enemies of the CUP, was duly formed two days later. In January 1919, the sultan informed the British High Commissioner through an intermediary that he was ready to arrest all those the British wished to see punished, but that he feared that drastic action might provoke a rebellion.[75] Most Turks, including Mustafa Kemal, argued, on the other hand, that crimes had been com-mitted against the Turks, as well as by them. This argument was put to the Allied high commissioners by the grand vizier Tevfik Paşa on 12 February 1919.[76]

As the hunt for war criminals and profiteers was enthusiastically taken up by domestic opponents of the CUP, all former members of that party, including opponents of Enver, Talât and Cemal, felt threat-ened. One man who had every reason to fear for his safety was Kara Kemal (Black Kemal), a Unionist who had organized Muslim guilds of tradesmen in the capital and had formed 'national' – that is, Turkish Muslim – companies to squeeze out Christian business. Kara Kemal had been appointed minister of supply under Talât Paşa, and just before the latter fled the capital, he became a founding member of a secret society called *Karakol* (The Sentry),[77] which in effect took over from Enver's *Teşkilât-ı Mahsusa* (Special Organization). According to Rauf, Kara Kemal discussed with Mustafa Kemal the possibility of kidnap-ping the grand vizier Tevfik Paşa – an idea which was abandoned when another leading Unionist, İsmail Canbulat, came out against it. Canbulat is also said by Rauf to have dissuaded Mustafa Kemal from plotting the overthrow of the sultan, as he was opposed to the participation of Kara Kemal in the venture.[78]

There is no reason to doubt that Mustafa Kemal was in touch with the CUP underground in Istanbul or that wild schemes were discussed by men well used to revolutionary plots, and now fighting for their sur-vival. But, as his record shows, Mustafa Kemal was averse to adven-tures. He had been received by the sultan for a third time on 20

December, on the eve of the dissolution of parliament.[79] *Minber* ceased publication on or soon after 21 December.[80] Mustafa Kemal's attempts to enter government with the help of members of parliament who had once belonged to the CUP, had failed. But he could still bank on his presumed loyalty to the sultan. Tevfik Paşa's position was, in any case, precarious. Mustafa Kemal had not yet exhausted the possibility of achieving his aim by political means in the intrigue-ridden capital.

A first group of some thirty former members of the CUP was arrested on 29/30 January 1919,[81] and taken first to police headquarters and then to Bekirağa Bölüğü, the military detention centre in the old city.[82] Kara Kemal and İsmail Canbulat were among them. So was Mustafa Kemal's old political ally, Dr Tevfik Rüştü (Aras). Why was Mustafa Kemal left out, and why was he not arrested later when a second batch of former CUP members was consigned to the military detention centre? The most likely reason was that Vahdettin and his government both needed and feared the army, which remained under the control of young commanders risen to prominence in the Great War. The British could detain and exile to Malta Ottoman commanders who, they believed, were obstructing the implementation of the armistice terms; the Ottoman government dared not do so. The resignation of Abdullah Paşa had shown that older generals, who had been purged by the CUP, could not control the army. There was, it is true, a small number of younger officers who had fallen foul of the CUP, and who had formed an association under the name of *Nigehban* (The Guardian) at the beginning of 1919. But they were losers with little support in the officer corps. The war minister, Cevat (Çobanlı), immediately declared that serving officers could not form a political association, adding, 'I'm the only guardian of the army'; and Mustafa Kemal, claiming also to advocate the political neutrality of the armed forces, demanded from the war ministry that the society should be suppressed. Nevertheless, it continued its shadowy existence as a minor thorn in the side of nationalist officers.[83]

Mustafa Kemal's freedom would have been threatened only if the British had decided to act against him. The Italian High Commissioner, Count Carlo Sforza, claims in his memoirs that at the beginning of 1919, 'British agents' in Istanbul were preparing to arrest Mustafa Kemal and exile him to Malta.[84] Sforza adds that Mustafa Kemal got to know of it and, 'questioned as to whether he could count on my support, I answered that an apartment was at his disposal at the Italian embassy. That also became known, and sufficed to stop the British intelligence service from taking steps that might have entailed diplomatic complications.'[85] Sforza, who claims, probably incorrectly, to have met Mustafa Kemal in 1908,[86] does not say that he met him face to face in 1919, but rather that he was in touch with 'Mustafa Kemal and his friends'.[87] At the time, Sforza was trying to prevent the Greek occupation of İzmir, which the Italians wanted to see within their zone of influence. He was also seeking an assurance from Turkish nationalists that they would not obstruct his efforts to win over Sayyid Ahmad, the Sanusi leader who had fled from Cyrenaica to Turkey at the end of the war. According to Sforza, 'Mustafa Kemal and his friends' responded by sending this message: 'The maintenance of Turkish domination over the Arabs has been one of the causes of our decline. Let them settle matters with you as they please, and as you please.'[88]

Mustafa Kemal was to put a different construction on his contacts with the Italians. He told his biographer Falih Rıfkı Atay that an Italian intermediary suggested that he might take the lead in organizing resistance against the Greeks in Izmir, that he thereupon visited Count Sforza and was shocked to find that the latter confined his remarks to the willingness of the Italian embassy to ensure his personal safety – an offer which Mustafa Kemal refused.[89] However, another story suggests that the initiative came from Mustafa Kemal. According to this version, an Italian detachment tried to search Mustafa Kemal's house in Şişli. This was avoided only when Mustafa Kemal threatened to complain personally to Count Sforza.[90] Falih Rıfkı gives yet another version, or perhaps an account of a different incident. Italian soldiers, he says, tried to enter the house of Mustafa Kemal's mother in Akaretler. When Mustafa Kemal complained to their commander, he was given a card stating that no one was authorized to enter the house forcibly. Nevertheless, another Allied detachment (presumably British) did enter and search his mother's house.[91]

These stories suggest that Mustafa Kemal sought Italian help against a possible British move to arrest him. He may well have used Corinne Lütfü as an intermediary. She was of Italian origin and was to move permanently to Italy a little later. A document stating that his house was under Italian protection might well have been procured. But the precaution was unnecessary, as the British did not have Mustafa Kemal in their sights. There were many Turkish specialists on the staff or in the pay of British authorities in Istanbul. But, as Count Sforza remarked acidly, 'the greatest field of action for the blunders of those specialists – the blunders of experts are always the grossest – was with the Turks'.[92]

Contacts with the French had to wait until after Mustafa Kemal had left Istanbul. In the capital, even those Turks who had been influenced by French culture – and Mustafa Kemal was one of them – were shocked by the behaviour of General Franchet d'Esperey, the French commander, whose official designation as Allied Commander in the Near East was not taken seriously by the British. Franchet d'Esperey had paid a flying visit to Istanbul on 23 November 1918, but he made his official entry on 8 February – the day after Allenby's visit – when he rode into the city on a white horse, and was wildly cheered by local Greeks, Armenians and Europeans.[93] A Turkish writer compared him variously with Napoleon, with a Roman emperor staging a triumphal entry into the forum, or with a French conqueror seeking to impress the natives of Timbuktoo.[94] In fact, he was probably trying to impress the British as much as the local populace. But while educated Turks pointed to the contrast between Franchet d'Esperey's antics and the ideals of the French Revolution, the French High Commission in Istanbul had already warned Paris that 'the Turks who had been flattened are beginning to raise their heads ... If it came to a real punch-up, we would be thrown into the sea in twenty-four hours.'[95]

There was to be no punch-up in Istanbul, only a succession of government crises. On 12 January 1919, Tevfik Paşa formed a new government. An elderly general, Ömer Yaver Paşa, who had been purged by the CUP, became war minister,[96] while the nationalist general Fevzi (Çakmak) retained control of the army as chief of the general staff. On 25 January 1919, Tevfik Paşa's government was shaken by the flight from prison of Dr Mehmet Reşit, former governor of Diyarbakır, who had been accused of war crimes against the Armenians.[97] Dr Reşit committed suicide when he was about to be recaptured.[98] As Damat Ferit's Freedom and Concord (Liberal Union) Party intensified its campaign against Tevfik Paşa, the latter formed a new government on 24 February, in which the war ministry was given to yet another retired general, Ferit Paşa.[99] However, Fevzi (Çakmak) continued as chief of the general staff. The following day, Franchet d'Esperey presented to the government a list of thirty-six alleged war criminals and demanded that they should be put on trial. In response, Tevfik Paşa submitted for the sultan's signature a decree, which suspended constitutional safeguards in order to allow the trial to go ahead. Pretending to be a loyal guardian of the constitution, the sultan refused to sign, whereupon Tevfik Paşa resigned and opened the way to a government under Damat Ferit Paşa, whom the sultan had come to prefer.[100]

Damat Ferit Paşa assumed office on 4 March at the head of the first government from which all CUP sympathizers were excluded. But nationalists remained in control of the army, with Fevzi (Çakmak) about to be replaced by Cevat (Çobanlı) as chief of the general staff, under the new war minister Şakir Paşa. Damat Ferit's main concern was to win the trust of the Allies by repressing the remnants of the CUP and conciliating the minorities. Like Vahdettin, he aligned himself totally on British policy. This antagonized the French, as well as the Italians. On 8 March, the government issued a decree establishing a new court martial to try war criminals. Although the text was more extreme than that proposed by Tevfik Paşa, the sultan signed it, and on 9 March the authorities arrested all leading former members of the CUP, including the wartime grand vizier Sait Halim Paşa and Mustafa Kemal's close friend and ally Fethi (Okyar). On 10 April, the first execution took place: a provincial district governor, Kemal, who had been found guilty of war crimes against the Armenians, was hanged in Istanbul.

The sultan had been careful to confirm the death sentence only after he had obtained a *fetva* (canonical decision) from the Şeyhülislâm (the head of the Islamic establishment) that it was in accordance with canon law.[101] This did not prevent Kemal's funeral from turning into a protest demonstration by thousands of Turkish nationalists. Damat Ferit and the Allies were alarmed: both the Renovation Party and Fethi's Party of Freedom-loving Ottoman Common People were closed down on 5 May. But what really worried Turkish nationalist commanders was the decision on 14 March to recall the governor of İzmir, the nationalist general Nurettin Paşa, who had fallen foul of the local Greek archbishop Chrysostom, and the despatch to that city of a weak retired general, Ali Nadir Paşa, as military commander.[102]

Nationalist officers, of whom he was about to become the leader, formed Mustafa Kemal's intimate circle in Istanbul. Rauf claims to have met him almost every day.[103] But he was a naval officer, and, as the Ottoman navy had ceased to exist, the responsibility for thwarting the Allies would have to fall on the army. Commanders who were ready to discharge this responsibility met frequently in Mustafa Kemal's house in Şişli. His closest companion was Ali Fuat, his friend from War College days and his subordinate as commander of the 20th army corps on the Syrian front. After the armistice, Ali Fuat had moved his troops to Ereğli, in the province of Konya, north of the Taurus;[104] Konya was the headquarters of the 12th army corps under the command of another nationalist officer, Colonel Fahrettin (Altay).[105] In December, Ali Fuat had gone to Istanbul to be treated for malaria, and there met Mustafa Kemal repeatedly. According to his memoirs, at their last meeting in February 1919, Mustafa Kemal told him that if he were not despatched to Anatolia on an official mission, he would join the commander in Anatolia whom he trusted most. Ali Fuat says that he replied, 'My army corps is at your disposal.'[106] A little later, Ali Fuat was ordered to move his troops north to Ankara, the last station on the northern spur of the Anatolian railway.

Ali Fuat says in his memoirs that he had agreed a plan of action with Mustafa Kemal in Istanbul. Their immediate objective was to stop the demobilization of Ottoman troops, retain arms and equipment, and ensure the appointment or retention of like-minded comrades in important commands and of sympathetic officials in the civil administration. To back this plan, which relied primarily on the military and the civil service, they would try to eliminate party political conflicts among the Muslims and strengthen the morale of the Muslim population.[107] Whether or not these objectives were elaborated as precisely as Ali Fuat claims, they did represent the thinking of Mustafa Kemal and his friends in Istanbul and they were broadly shared by the officers in control of the general staff. The importance of Anatolia as the bastion of the Turkish nation was taken for granted. The idea had to be entertained seriously by the CUP when Istanbul was threatened by the Allied landings in Gallipoli in 1915; it was then to guide the actions of Ottoman commanders in 1918, as they tried to move their men and supplies inland out of reach of the victorious Allies. But one point remained controversial. What were patriotic commanders and officials to do if the Ottoman government opposed them? The revolutionary concept of the national will could be invoked. But who was to interpret it? As ever, Mustafa Kemal was convinced that he could and would. But it was too early to spell it out.

Another close confederate in Istanbul was Colonel Refet (Bele), who had become commander of the gendarmerie in October 1918. This was an important post. As the army was scaled down in accordance with armistice terms, nationalist Turkish officers tried to use the gendarmerie as an alternative force to hold the country together. Like Mustafa Kemal, Refet was born in Salonica in 1881. Mustafa Kemal trusted his loyalty.

Of the officers who conferred with Mustafa Kemal in Istanbul, Kâzım Karabekir was best placed to advance the nationalist cause. In December 1918, he was appointed commander of the depleted 14th army corps in Thrace. After transferring his troops across the sea of Marmara to Anatolia, he secured the command of the strongest remaining Ottoman force, the 15th army corps with headquarters in Erzurum, in the east. This corps had 12,500 men and 22 guns, and together with the 3rd army corps of 4,700 men and 24 guns, stationed further west in Sivas, made up the 9th Ottoman Army.[108]

Kâzım Karabekir says in his memoirs that on 11 April 1919, the day before leaving Istanbul to take up his appointment in Erzurum, he called on Mustafa Kemal and explained to him that he proposed to lay the foundations of a Turkish national government in eastern Anatolia, which could later extend its authority throughout the country. 'It's an idea,' Mustafa Kemal replied, according to Karabekir, who adds that he pressed Mustafa Kemal to cut short his stay in Istanbul and move to Anatolia. 'Events justify your arguments,' Mustafa Kemal is said to have replied, 'I'll try to come, when I get better'[109] – Mustafa Kemal was at the time ill with an ear infection. While Kâzım Karabekir's evidence should be read in the light of his subsequent break with Mustafa Kemal, it is a fact that both Karabekir and Ali Fuat preceded him in Anatolia. But both were officially posted there. Mustafa Kemal, although senior in service, was still without a posting; nor had he yet made full use of his links with Vahdettin. Not a man to act on impulse, he was awaiting authority to organize the army for the nationalist cause. To secure it, he stayed on in Istanbul.

Mustafa Kemal, Rauf, Ali Fuat, Karabekir and Refet (Bele) were the original military planners of the Turkish War of Independence. They had the support of like-minded officers in positions of influence. These included two Major-Generals: Cevat (Çobanlı) and Fevzi (Çakmak), who succeeded each other in the posts of chief of the general staff and war minister. Both were in good standing with the government. One highly intelligent, but careful, military supporter was Colonel İsmet (İnönü), Mustafa Kemal's former subordinate on the eastern and southern fronts. İsmet was a frequent visitor at the house in Şişli. One day, as they were looking at a map of Anatolia, Mustafa Kemal asked, 'What's the best way to get there?' İsmet says that he replied: 'From any direction. There are as many roads as measures one can take. The problem is to decide how to proceed in our work.'[110] Karabekir, who calls İsmet 'my closest dear friend', but with whom he was to quarrel later, says that İsmet believed in 1919 that resistance was impossible, and was thinking of resigning his commission and taking up farming.[111]

The nationalist officers had a shared background. They knew each other well; they had served together in the Great War; two of them – Ali Fuat and Karabekir – were related. But the observation of Liman von Sanders that Turkish generals tended to quarrel and be jealous of each other, held true for this band of brothers. İsmet (İnönü) was to say in his memoirs that Karabekir was afraid of Mustafa Kemal, and that the two disliked each other. According to İnönü, when Karabekir left Istanbul to take up his command in Erzurum, he told him: 'I'm afraid you too will make common cause with Mustafa Kemal.'[112]

Karabekir's immediate objective was to hold the pre-war Ottoman frontier against Armenian and Georgian encroachment. Both opponents were fully occupied trying to control the territory evacuated by the Turks further east, and did not present a military threat to Karabekir as long as he could resist British attempts to reduce and disarm his troops. But the Greek threat in the west was serious, for the Greeks had more men and better equipment than had the Turks. Venizelos had made his ambitions clear in a pamphlet in December 1918: he wanted both Thrace and western Anatolia. He was prepared to let the British devise their own arrangements for Istanbul, and he proposed that the province of Trabzon, on Turkey's eastern Black Sea coast, where there was an important Greek community, should be incorporated in Armenia. The Greek ownership of territory taken from Turkey would be made irreversible by a gradual exchange of populations. Clearly many more Turks would have to be uprooted than Greeks, of whom there would be comparatively few left outside the frontiers claimed by Venizelos.

On 3/4 February 1919, Venizelos submitted the Greek claim to the Allied Council of Ten, which passed it on to a committee for study.[113] The Greeks of Istanbul went even further than Venizelos. On 16 March, the Greek community in Turkey, represented by the patriarchate in Istanbul, severed relations with the Ottoman government and renounced its civic responsibilities as Ottoman citizens. The Greeks of Istanbul, which Venizelos did not claim, opted for union with Greece.[114] Inevitably, intercommunal relations deteriorated throughout the country.

As the Allies deliberated, the Italians struck to pre-empt the Greeks. On 28 March 1919 they landed in Antalya on Turkey's Mediterranean coast. Within four weeks they pushed their detachments as far as Bodrum in the south-west and Konya in the centre. On 29 April an Italian warship entered İzmir harbour.[115] Under the terms of the armistice, the only grounds for occupation was the emergence of a situation which threatened the security of the Allies (article 7). In fact, Allied security was not threatened directly anywhere in Turkey. But in the aftermath of the war, internal security had broken down in many places. There had always been brigands; now there were hundreds of thousands of deserters and displaced persons of all communities. Intercommunal fighting began in disputed areas, as Christian and Muslim armed bands clashed. It was in these areas – from west to east: in Thrace, western Anatolia, the central and eastern Black Sea coast, eastern and southern Anatolia – that Muslims began to organize in defence of the preservation of their rule, their homes and, ultimately, their lives.

Appealing to President Wilson's endorsement of the right of nations to self-determination, these Muslim organizations generally called themselves Societies for the Defence of National Rights. Two such societies had been founded in Edirne and İzmir on 1 December 1918. The first claimed the whole of Thrace – eastern and western – for its Muslim inhabitants, the second sought to prevent a Greek occupation of Aegean Turkey. Three days later a Society for the Defence of National Rights in the Eastern Provinces was formed in Erzurum.[116] A similar organization was set up in Trabzon on 12 February 1919.[117] A Society of Cilicians was founded in Istanbul to speak for the provinces under French occupation south of the Taurus. Provincial leaders of the CUP played an active, if not predominant, part in setting up these organizations. They were joined by notables and other traditional leaders of the community – landowners, merchants, professional people (mainly lawyers) and *müftüs* (salaried clerical officials). The societies thus had both a modernist and a conservative wing. Their official purpose was to agitate for the interests of the Muslims, but they also tried to organize armed resistance. The Society for Thrace decided to set up armed units in January 1919. The Erzurum society resolved to establish contact with the army, and when Kâzım Karabekir arrived in the city on 3 May 1919, he became its patron.[118]

All these societies had their agents and sympathizers in Istanbul. Mustafa Kemal and other nationalist commanders took notice as they made their own plans in which the army was to play the main role. The grand vizier, Damat Ferit, had other ideas. He thought that order could be restored, administratively, by disarming the population while strengthening the gendarmerie, and, politically, by re-establishing good intercommunal relations. Undeterred by the decision of the Greek patriarchate to opt out of the Ottoman state, he decided to despatch to troubled areas Commissions of Admonition (*Heyât-ı Nasiha*), headed by imperial princes. Greeks and Armenian members were sought, but leading members of the two communities stood aloof, as their patriarchs refused to name representatives.

One commission, led by Prince Abdürrahim, crossed the sea of Marmara and made its way to İzmir, where it was received enthusiastically by the Muslims who took this opportunity to declare their determination to remain within the Ottoman realm. The commission then deliberated whether to go on to Antalya, where Italian troops had newly landed. It decided to proceed on the sensible grounds that 'Italian policy aims at winning the support of Muslim people.' This proved to be true both in Antalya and in Konya, where the Italian commander asked that his troops be allowed to greet the prince. It was while the commission was in Konya that news came of the Greek landing in İzmir. Damat Ferit Paşa's government ordered the commission back to

Istanbul. As he took leave of the local Ottoman corps commander, Colonel Fahrettin (Altay), Prince Abdürrahim said: 'Our hope rests in you.'[119]

The commission sent to Thrace was headed by Prince Cemalettin, who was flanked by two leading nationalist generals, Cevat (Çobanlı) and Fevzi (Çakmak). They were boycotted by local Christians almost everywhere.

The despatch of royal commissions bearing the sovereign's greetings to his subjects of all religions could not hold the country together, although it did bring momentary comfort to the Muslims, and demonstrated their support for the throne. Nor did it put an end to Allied complaints that Christians were being maltreated in the provinces. In a desperate attempt to stop the Greek landings, Damat Ferit suggested that British troops should be sent to help Ottoman security forces maintain order in western Anatolia. The offer was turned down.[120] But there was another area where intercommunal fighting had begun. This was the long stretch of Turkey's Black Sea coast, east of Sinop, which the Greeks knew as Pontus.[121] As elsewhere in Anatolia, the local social fabric had been torn apart by the expulsion of the Armenians. Now, tension was fed by the arrival of thousands of Greek refugees, some of local origin, who had migrated to tsarist Russia and were fleeing from the Bolshevik revolution.

Venizelos had proposed an Armenian umbrella for Black Sea Greeks. However, the latter – through their spokesman the archbishop of Trabzon, Chrysanthos Philippidis, who joined the patriarchal delegation to the Paris peace conference in March 1919[122] – preferred an independent republic of the Pontus, which they expected to dominate. Local Muslims were determined to prevent this. Known generally as Laz, although the Laz tongue, which is akin to Georgian, survived only in small pockets in the eastern part of the littoral, they were famous for their fierce attachment to their religion. The Laz had become Muslims in the fifteenth–sixteenth centuries after the destruction by the Ottomans of the Byzantine kingdom of Trabzon (Trebizond), and they had the fervour both of frontiersmen and of late converts. Their number had been swollen by the arrival of Circassian and other Muslim refugees from the Caucasus. These people who had fled infidel Russian rule were not prepared to bow to the Russians' Armenian and Greek former protégés.

Intercommunal tension was particularly high in and around the coastal towns of Giresun and Samsun, where there were sizeable Greek communities. The Giresun branch of the Trabzon Society for the Defence of National Rights secured the local district governor's permission to employ against the Greeks a notorious local bandit, Topal (Lame) Osman, whose name was a byword for brutality. Topal Osman had worked for the authorities before. He had been lamed by an injury in the Balkan war in which he had served as a volunteer; he had led a band of volunteers against the Russians in the Great War; and he had been used to round up deserters, some of whom he enlisted in his band. Topal Osman terrorized the people of Giresun: Greeks, in the first place, and Armenians, but also any Turks who sought to oppose him. He is said to have kept a local Ottoman administrator in a hole in the ground for three days, until the governor of Trabzon requested the French to send a naval vessel to Giresun and save the wretched man.[123] Topal Osman was the most notorious of the leaders of the Muslim bands (*çete*), which swung into action in all disputed areas, and were soon to be dignified with the collective name of 'national forces' (*kuva-yı milliye*).

On 9 March 1919, 200 British soldiers landed in Samsun to help establish order. On 21 April, the British High Commissioner Admiral Calthorpe complained to the grand vizier that 'councils' (or 'soviets', *şura*) had been set up by the Ottoman army in inland areas of eastern Anatolia, from Sivas to Erzurum, and asked that immediate measures should be taken to disband them.[124] To the Ottoman government this sounded like a prelude to an extension of the Allied occupation. In fact the Allies had neither the men nor the will to reinforce their presence in the Black Sea area, let alone venture into the interior of Anatolia. In March 1919, just after the small British detachment had landed in Samsun, the British government decided to withdraw from the Caucasus.[125] A British military intervention in eastern Anatolia was now out of the question. The Ottoman army had the area to itself. True, British officers continued their efforts to disarm Ottoman troops. But they had no force to back them.

The sultan and Damat Ferit did not see the whole picture in Istanbul where they were overawed by the British military presence. According to Ali Fuat (Cebesoy), Damat Ferit discussed Admiral Calthorpe's warning about disorder in eastern Anatolia with his interior minister Mehmet Ali.[126] The latter suggested that Mustafa Kemal be sent to the area. Mehmet Ali had met Mustafa Kemal through Ali Fuat, to whom he was related by marriage; the meeting had taken place in the house of Ali Fuat's father and Mustafa Kemal's first patron, İsmail Fazıl Paşa. Mehmet Ali appears to have been impressed, and soon afterwards visited Mustafa Kemal in his house in Şişli, bringing with him the navy minister Avni Paşa, who was related by marriage to the war minister

Şakir Paşa. The war ministry was at the time in the process of setting up three inspectorates to reorganize the army, a plan which the grand vizier had explained to Andrew Ryan, the dragoman at the British High Commission. Fevzi (Çakmak) was to be inspector of the 1st Army, based in the capital, and Cemal (Mersinli) of the 2nd Army in Konya. It was in this context that the Ottoman government proposed to make Mustafa Kemal inspector of the 9th Army in Erzurum.

After calling on Mustafa Kemal in Şişli, Mehmet Ali asked him and the navy minister to lunch at the Cercle d'Orient, the club in Beyoğlu which was frequented by senior Ottoman officials as well as by local Europeans and foreigners. On another occasion, Avni Paşa sent his car to collect Mustafa Kemal for lunch at the navy ministry. Finally, Mustafa Kemal was summoned by the war minister Şakir Paşa, who handed him a file on the situation in eastern Anatolia and explained that his task as inspector would be to resolve Greek complaints of harassment. With the minister's permission Mustafa Kemal then went to discuss his terms of reference with the chief of the general staff. As Fevzi (Çakmak) was absent in Thrace, the terms were agreed with his deputy, Brigadier Kâzım (İnanç). Mustafa Kemal's appointment as inspector of the 9th Army was promulgated on 30 April. The instructions issued to him were approved by the cabinet a little later.

The terms of reference were wide. True, the purpose of the mission was defined in terms acceptable to the Allies. Mustafa Kemal was to re-establish order, see to the collection and safe storage of weapons, investigate reports that the army had colluded in the establishment of 'councils' (or 'soviets') and, if true, put an end to the practice. This part of the document was probably dictated by the war minister himself.[127] However, Mustafa Kemal's hand can be seen in what followed. Not only was the 9th Army and the civil administration in eastern and central Anatolia subordinated to him, but commanders and civil administrators in surrounding areas, further west and south, were instructed to take heed of his communications. Although Mustafa Kemal was responsible to the war ministry, he was also allowed to communicate directly with other departments of state. In effect he was being named the government's commissioner for the whole of Anatolia from Ankara eastwards. There is no reason to disbelieve Mustafa Kemal's claim that the war minister was too worried to sign the instructions over his official seal.[128] The inspector of the 2nd Army, Cemal (Mersinli), complained from Konya that he saw no reason why Mustafa Kemal should be given such exceptional powers. The grand vizier replied that the sultan had taken the decision to test the ability of Mustafa Kemal with whom he had a special relationship of trust.[129]

Armed with his terms of reference, Mustafa Kemal chose his own staff of fifteen officers and two cipher clerks. His friend Colonel Refet (Bele), who was appointed commander of the 3rd army corps in Sivas, was to travel with him. The staff included two army doctors, İbrahim Tali (Öngören), who had treated Mustafa Kemal in Tripolitania in 1911, and Refik (Saydam), who was to become his personal physician during the War of Independence, and then minister of health, and finally prime minister, under the republic. In Mustafa Kemal's life, periods of intense activity were interspersed with bouts of illness. Service life was unhealthy; malaria was rampant in large tracts of Ottoman territory. Mustafa Kemal's fondness for drink and late nights – what his opponents called debauchery – did not help. Sensibly, he liked to have a personal doctor near him.

Mustafa Kemal's chief of staff was Colonel Kâzım (Dirik), a contemporary born in Macedonia, whose career had followed Mustafa Kemal's pattern: membership of the CUP, war service in Gallipoli and on the Syrian front. His assistant was Lieutenant-Colonel Arif, Mustafa Kemal's friend in the War College.[130] Mustafa Kemal always insisted on choosing his own staff, from whom he expected total loyalty. Though ready to listen to objections, once he had made up his mind, he did not brook opposition, which he construed as disloyalty.

The job of inspector of the 9th Army was the best that Mustafa Kemal could secure after five months of politicking in Istanbul, and he accepted it readily. In spite of his links with the palace and his contacts with Damat Ferit's Freedom and Concord Party, his position in the capital was becoming risky. On 14 March an Istanbul newspaper carried an unfounded report that he had been arrested; a few days later he had become embroiled in a lawsuit with another newspaper which had described Ottoman commanders in the war as brigands. Mustafa Kemal took it upon himself to reply, accusing the writer of seeking the ruin of the country. As the newspaper then sued him, Mustafa Kemal tried to postpone the hearing of the case:[131] he could not afford to have his true colours and intentions exposed prematurely. His friend Rauf had already resigned his commission; although the grand vizier tried to dissuade him, Rauf had insisted on his decision, telling Damat Ferit that government policy was bound to give rise to a rebellion, and that he wished to assume his responsibilities as a civilian.[132] Mustafa Kemal did not want to become a civilian prematurely.

On 13 May Mustafa Kemal was invited to dinner in the grand vizier's house.[133] Cevat (Çobanlı), who was about to take over from Fevzi (Çakmak) as head of the general staff, was also there. Mustafa Kemal was to say later that they used the opportunity to dispel the suspicions which Damat Ferit was beginning to feel about his mission. The account adds that as they left the mansion Cevat (Çobanlı) asked Mustafa Kemal, 'Are you about to do something?', to which the latter replied, 'Yes, Pasha, I'll do *something*.'[134] The following day Mustafa Kemal visited his friend Fethi (Okyar) who had been detained in the second wave of arrests of CUP personalities and was kept in the Bekirağa Bölüğü military prison, and told him about his mission in eastern Anatolia.[135] Mustafa Kemal wore military uniform, which made for easier access, but was bound to invite the suspicion of the authorities. However, this did not matter unduly as he was about to leave the capital.

On 15 May Mustafa Kemal paid a farewell visit to the general staff. Fevzi (Çakmak), who was about to relinquish the post of chief of the general staff to become inspector of the 1st Army, and his successor Cevat (Çobanlı) were there. Fevzi claimed later that the two had agreed that arms and equipment were not to be surrendered to the Allies, that a national administration was to be set up in Anatolia, that it should rely on 'national forces' of guerrillas, and that military action should not be confined to defence.[136] According to Fevzi, Mustafa Kemal agreed readily, saying that it was precisely with these ends in view that he was going to Anatolia. Cevat (Çobanlı) then gave him a personal cipher, while Fevzi organized the despatch of officers and of smuggled arms and equipment to Anatolia. It is, however, unlikely that the two generals had already decided to break with the sultan's government, and unbelievable that they had chosen to rely on bands of irregulars. Nevertheless, they were broadly in agreement with Mustafa Kemal's designs and were prepared to collude in the smuggling of men and arms from the capital to the interior of Anatolia.

It was probably on the same day that Mustafa Kemal was received by the sultan in a private audience, at the end of which he was presented with a gold watch bearing the sovereign's monogram. Mustafa Kemal claimed later that Vahdettin told him: 'Pasha, you have already rendered many services to the state. They are now part of history. Forget about them, for the service you are about to render will be more important still. You can save the state.'[137] These words, which the sultan may or may not have uttered, have been used by Vahdettin's apologists as evidence that he had sent Mustafa Kemal to Anatolia specifically to organize Turkish national resistance. They claim also that the sultan gave him a considerable sum in gold for the purpose. Vahdettin's subsequent actions belie this interpretation; nor did Vahdettin himself claim any such intention in the long justification which he published in the Hejaz after his flight from Istanbul in 1922, and in which he criticized the actions of Rauf, Fethi and Mustafa Kemal.[138] It is, however, true that the interior minister, Mehmet Ali, who had chosen Mustafa Kemal for the Anatolian mission in the first place, did give him a small sum from the ministry's secret funds.[139] This did not stop Mustafa Kemal from being perennially short of money during his travels in Anatolia.

It was during the last days of Mustafa Kemal's stay in Istanbul that the Allies decided to let Greek troops occupy İzmir. The decision was taken by Lloyd George, President Woodrow Wilson and Clemenceau in Paris on 6 May. Their purpose was to prevent the Italians from making good their claims to western and south-western Anatolia. Lloyd George, whose knowledge of the Near East was, at best, sketchy, was the prime mover, overriding objections which had earlier been expressed by British officials. Venizelos, who aimed to annex İzmir all along, agreed immediately, saying that he had troops available for the purpose.[140] On 14 May, Allied detachments occupied the İzmir forts and informed the Turkish governor that the Greeks were about to land.[141] As news of the decision spread, local Greeks began to celebrate, while Turks held a public meeting at which they founded an Anti-Annexation Society (*Redd-i İlhak Cemiyeti*) to combat the threat of the permanent loss of the area. The organizers of the meeting freed Turkish convicts from prison, broke into the armoury of the barracks, and started distributing arms among Muslims.[142]

The landing of the Greek troops on 15 May went disastrously, but predictably, wrong. As Greek troops advanced to the barracks, where the Ottoman commander Ali Nadir Paşa had been ordered to offer no resistance, a Turk in the crowd fired a shot, killing the Greek standard-bearer.[143] Greek troops panicked and started firing both at the barracks and the government house. Turkish officers and officials were beaten up and humiliated, Turkish property was looted. During the first day, 300 to 400 Turks were killed or wounded, against 100 Greeks, two of whom were soldiers.[144] Disorder then spread into the interior. The Allies sent a commission of enquiry. The Greeks imposed martial law and sent a tough High Commissioner, Aristeidis Stergiadis, who sought to restrain the large local Greek community and kept the Ottoman civil governor in place. But the damage done to the cohabitation of Christian Greeks and Muslim Turks was irreparable, and Turkish nationalist sentiment was aroused throughout the country.

Mustafa Kemal was to say in 1924, 'If the enemy had not stupidly come here, the whole country might have slept on heedlessly.'[145] In the same address to the people of İzmir, Mustafa Kemal recalled his first brief visit to the city on his way to Syria in 1905. 'At that time,' he said,

'I saw this beautiful quayside full of members of a race which was our sworn enemy, and I concluded that İzmir had slipped away from the hands of its true and noble Turkish inhabitants. But there was no way I could divulge this truth in those days.' Mustafa Kemal may or may not have foreseen the ethnic war which was destined to destroy 'infidel İzmir' (*gâvur İzmir*), as the city's prosperous Christian neighbourhoods were known to the Turks. But he was prepared for it when it came.

When Mustafa Kemal made his farewell call on the office of the grand vizier in the morning of 15 May, he found the ministers stunned by the news that Greek troops were landing in İzmir. The grand vizier Damat Ferit had been informed of the Allied decision only the previous evening, and the sultan had sent his chief secretary to the Porte to find out whether it was indeed the Greeks who had landed. According to the chief secretary's memoirs, the grand vizier broke into French, as Ottoman officials tended to do in moments of tension, and said in a despairing voice, '*Situation une des plus critiques!*' But he still hoped that the occupation would be effected by Italian troops.[146]

According to Mustafa Kemal, ministers interrupted their meeting when he arrived at the cabinet office, and asked him what they should do. 'Be firm,' he replied. 'Where, here?' they asked. 'Do what you can here, and then carry on by joining me,' Mustafa Kemal claims to have told them.[147] Once again, the conversation does not ring true. Mustafa Kemal was as yet in no position to push himself forward as the leader of Turkish national resistance in Anatolia. A few days later, in the first telegram which he sent to the grand vizier from Samsun on 20 May, he declared diplomatically that the indignation of the public and of the army at the occupation of İzmir was tempered by the certainty that Damat Ferit's government would act decisively to defend national interests.[148]

The following day, 16 May, Mustafa Kemal attended the sultan's general audience for the last time, and then boarded the *Bandırma*, an old and barely seaworthy tramp steamer which was to take him and his staff to Samsun.[149] As on previous occasions, he arranged for his friend and confidant Dr Rasim Ferit (Talay) to act as his personal agent in the capital. Rauf (Orbay) is said to have warned Mustafa Kemal that the British were plotting to sink the *Bandırma* in the Black Sea.[150] Istanbul was full of rumours, and Mustafa Kemal may well have feared that the British would nip his mission in the bud. In fact, John G. Bennett, the British liaison officer at the Ottoman war ministry, hesitated before issuing a travel permit for Mustafa Kemal and his suite, but was told by his superiors that Mustafa Kemal enjoyed the sultan's full confidence.[151] The *Bandırma* was checked for contraband goods by Allied control officers before it left the harbour. 'The fools,' Mustafa Kemal is said to have exclaimed during the inspection, 'we are not taking contraband or arms, but faith and determination. But they cannot appreciate a nation's love of independence and will to fight. All they rely on is material force.'[152] It is an inspiring tale.

Mustafa Kemal left Istanbul with a better posting than either Ali Fuat or Kâzım Karabekir had secured, let alone Rauf who was to follow him to Anatolia as a civilian. Yet he was to claim later that the real reason why he was sent to Anatolia was to remove him from Istanbul, and that his mission was in effect an exile.[153] It is hard to accept this, for if the motive of the Ottoman authorities was to get rid of Mustafa Kemal, they could have asked the British to deport him. He was, however, undoubtedly right when he said in his 1927 speech that the Ottoman government did not realize his purpose; he had hoodwinked both the sultan and Damat Ferit. But Mustafa Kemal's reference to his exile reflects the bitterness which he felt at the failure of his original plan: he had sought power in the capital; he had tried to influence his country's leaders – the sultan, politicians of all parties, intellectuals, journalists. But he failed: Istanbul rejected him. Leaving the city was a wrench. Not only was it still the centre of decision-making, but it was civilized, comfortable. An electric tram ran in front of his house in Şişli, there were clubs and restaurants, mansions and receptions. The comforts of Istanbul cooled the ardour of many Turkish nationalists. Mustafa Kemal too was fond of comfort. But his burning ambition, in which his fortune was inextricably linked to that of his country, made him opt for the rigours of Anatolia. He had little sympathy for those who made a softer choice and justified it on grounds of national interest.

İsmet (İnönü), whom Mustafa Kemal visited on the eve of his departure, describes the latter's six-month stay in Istanbul as a morally exhausting period of struggle.[154] It was also a pause for thought. Mustafa Kemal was too good a tactician to plot his future course of action in detail, but his vision of the future was clear. In his first interview in November 1918, he said: 'A nation must be strong in spirit, knowledge, science and morals. Military strength comes last ... Today it is not enough to have arms in hand in order to take one's place in the world as a human being.'[155] Always present in Mustafa Kemal's mind was the ultimate objective of securing Turkey's place in the community of civilized nations.

I I

Meeting the People

THE *BANDIRMA* SAILED slowly, hugging Turkey's Black Sea coast. The weather was stormy and most members of Mustafa Kemal's party were sea-sick.[1] After rounding the northernmost point of the coast, the ship stopped briefly in the open roadstead of Sinop. The district governor invited Mustafa Kemal ashore, but the latter excused himself, saying that he was feeling unwell.[2] Mustafa Kemal was still recovering from his ear infection; he had also not fully shaken off the effects of the kidney inflammation which had incapacitated him the previous year. On 19 May, three days after leaving Istanbul, the *Bandırma* cast anchor off a wooden jetty in Samsun. This Black Sea town had a mixed population of Greeks and Turks: the former more numerous inside the town, the latter in the countryside. Samsun had developed in the years before the Great War as an outlet for the export of tobacco; this crop had become the mainstay of the local economy, thanks to the efforts of the *Régie*.

Mustafa Kemal and his party disembarked and took up residence in a hotel, the *Mıntıka Palas*, or Regional Palace,[3] whose grand name belied a modest reality. The hotel had stood empty for some time, and the local authorities furnished it at the last moment with beds from a military hospital and bedding from neighbouring houses.[4] Mustafa Kemal set to work immediately.

The 19th of May has been celebrated as a national holiday in Turkey since 1935.[5] In Turkish popular thinking it marks the beginning of the War of Independence. In fact, resistance to foreign encroachment had started sporadically as soon as the armistice was concluded on 30 October 1918. But it was on 19 May 1919 in Samsun that Mustafa

Kemal initiated his campaign to unite under his leadership the disparate elements of Turkish resistance.

It was also on 19 May that British authorities in Istanbul, which had authorized Mustafa Kemal's departure, had second thoughts. In a letter to the Ottoman war minister, General Sir George Milne, commander of the British Army of the Black Sea, pointed out that the Ottoman 9th Army was being disbanded. Why then was a 'chief of staff', accompanied by a large suite, sent to Sivas? The description of Mustafa Kemal as 'chief of staff' and the mention of Sivas suggest that the information supplied by the grand vizier Damat Ferit in April to the British mission dragoman Andrew Ryan on the establishment of the army inspectorates had not been properly assimilated.[6]

The Ottoman war ministry replied on 24 May that Mustafa Kemal's inspectorate took in two army corps (the 3rd and 15th), and that his task was to make sure that units obeyed war ministry orders, that breech blocks were removed from guns, and that public disorder was prevented. Mustafa Kemal would not establish his headquarters in Sivas or anywhere else, but would cover the whole area.[7] In fact, the purpose of Mustafa Kemal, and of the two corps commanders, Kâzım Karabekir in Erzurum and Refet (Bele) in Sivas, was to make sure that breech blocks and other military equipment were not handed over to the British. The Ottoman general staff, which was at the time doing its best to preserve its forces and equipment against the Greek advance on the Aegean coast, shared this purpose.[8]

Mustafa Kemal proceeded carefully and methodically. His aim was to encourage, organize and lead the Muslim inhabitants of Turkey, whom he and his companions saw as the Turkish nation. The army was to be the backbone of resistance, but it needed the cooperation of civil officials; popular support was also essential. Difficulties were involved in mobilizing all three components.

The army had a cadre of patriotic officers ready to defend the country. But although they were united by a common ideal, they were divided by personal and professional jealousies. The forces at their disposal were woefully weak and ill-equipped. What is more, officers were conditioned to obey orders, ultimately from headquarters in Istanbul. Fortunately, the general staff was sympathetic to the national cause. Fortunately also, the best officers had developed a spirit of initiative, first in the revolutionary struggle against Abdülhamit and then in foreign wars. The civil service too did not lack patriotic officials, but initiative had been sapped out of them. To survive, they had to lie low and do as they were told.

Among the people, obedience to authority was instinctive. True, the instinct was tempered by mute, passive resistance when survival required it, and, more rarely, by individual rebellion. Peasants, who accounted for the majority of the Muslim population, would do their best to avoid conscription, but fought well when forced into the army. Officers sometimes volunteered for service, men hardly ever. Moreover, the country had been exhausted by incessant warfare. Harsh physical conditions and maladministration had developed effective strategies of survival among the Muslim people of Anatolia. Mustafa Kemal and his companions had to take them into account. Civilian support could be elicited most easily where there was an immediate threat, not just of foreign occupation, which could be seen as transient, but of permanent dispossession at the hands of ethnic rivals. This was the case in eastern Anatolia, which the Europeans called Armenia, while the Ottomans used the euphemism 'the six provinces' (*vilâyat-ı sitte*). They were mentioned specifically in the armistice terms, under which the Allies reserved the right to occupy them 'in case of disorder' (article 24), while elsewhere occupation could be justified, theoretically, only if Allied security were threatened (article 7).

Survival strategies dominated also the behaviour of the Kurdish tribes. In the east, which was claimed by Armenian nationalists, they lent a ready ear to the argument of Turkish nationalists, such as Kâzım Karabekir, that they could avert the Armenian threat only by making common cause with the Turks. But in what Mustafa Kemal called 'quiet' areas, which included the central Kurdish provinces around Diyarbakır, local leaders preferred to wait and see.[9]

Throughout the country, ethnic conflict, which had been heightened by the displacement of a large number of Christians in Anatolia and of Muslims who had fled before the Russians during the Great War, was intensified by attempts at repatriation. Armenians were returning not only to the areas in Cilicia and upper Mesopotamia under British and then French occupation, but also to central Anatolia, reclaiming houses taken over by Muslims and raising fears among the latter that they would be called to account for their part in wartime deportations. The problem was particularly acute in Aegean Turkey, where 113,000 Muslims, most of whom had fled from Greece in the aftermath of the Balkan wars, had been settled in Greek houses and were now facing eviction.[10]

Mustafa Kemal saw agitation as his first task. The Greek occupation of İzmir and its extension along the Aegean coast and inland made the task easier. Protest meetings were held throughout western Turkey on 15 May, when Greek troops landed. On 18 May there were meetings in Bursa, in Havza (near Samsun) and in Erzurum. On 23 May, a mammoth protest meeting outside the great mosque of Sultan Ahmet (the Blue Mosque) in Istanbul heard the impassioned oratory of the nationalist woman writer Halide Edip (Adıvar), an early feminist trained in an American school. A second meeting held in the same square on 30 May led to a demand by the British High Commissioner Admiral Calthorpe that further meetings should be banned in the capital.[11]

Immediately after the occupation, Damat Ferit resigned, forming a new government on 19 May. Şevket Turgut Paşa, who was sympathetic to the nationalists, became minister of war. But a sworn enemy of the CUP and a leading advocate of accommodation with the Allies, the journalist Ali Kemal, was given the key post of interior minister.[12] On 24 May representatives of various Muslim organizations took part in a Crown Council which discussed the consequences of the Greek occupation of İzmir. Halide Edip was excluded as a woman.[13] Seeking to conciliate the nationalists, the government released some forty political prisoners. This alarmed the British authorities which deported sixty-seven nationalists held in the Bekirağa military prison.[14] However, there was also a move to reassure the Turks. On the initiative of the French, the peace conference in Paris agreed to hear the views of an Ottoman delegation led by the grand vizier Damat Ferit.

In Samsun, where a large Greek community relied on the presence of a detachment of British troops, Muslims were ill placed to agitate. Instead, Mustafa Kemal sought to strengthen the Ottoman administration, proposing to the government that it call up new recruits and allocate some of them to the gendarmerie; he also suggested that gendarmes should be given bonuses for hunting down bandits. The government replied that, as the pay of the gendarmerie had been improved, Mustafa Kemal should encourage voluntary recruitment;[15] mobilization, even on a local scale, was bound to alarm the Allies.

On 21 May Mustafa Kemal met the British relief officer, Captain L.H. Hurst, and two of his colleagues to discuss the security situation. The British officers did not mince their words. The Ottoman government, they said, was incapable of ruling Turkey and needed foreign intervention and protection for at least a few years. Mustafa Kemal contested this firmly, but politely. The troubles in the province of Samsun, he replied, would end the moment the Greeks gave up their political – in other words, separatist – aims. Greeks had no rights to sovereignty anywhere in Ottoman lands. Turks would not put up with foreign rule, although 'experts from the most civilized nations, like the English, would be welcome as advisers'. Mustafa Kemal's report of the conversation to the grand vizier combined the usual expressions of loyalty with an implicit warning: the nation, he said, was united and, having chosen the principle of sovereignty and of Turkish sentiment, was firm in its attachment and obedience to the present government.[16] Three days after his arrival in Anatolia, Mustafa Kemal thus spelled out the principle of Turkish national sovereignty; he also took it upon himself to speak for the nation.

Mustafa Kemal told the British officers on 21 May that he was proceeding to the interior on a tour of inspection.[17] On the same day he sent a telegram to Kâzım Karabekir in Erzurum saying that he wished to join him as soon as possible, but that law and order problems would detain him in the Samsun area for a few days. Karabekir replied that he would be happy to meet him, and that there was no difficulty in travelling by car from Trabzon to Erzurum, while the road to Sivas was bad and there was no petrol to be found on the way.[18] However, Mustafa Kemal was in no hurry to join Karabekir before consolidating his own position. He sent a telegram to his friend Ali Fuat, now at the head of the 20th army corps in Ankara, saying that he wanted to establish contact with him, and asking for news of the situation around İzmir. Then, instead of going to Trabzon, Mustafa Kemal accepted the invitation of the district officer (*kaymakam*) of Havza to take the waters in the local hot springs, which were believed to bring relief to sufferers from kidney disease. Havza was a small, predominantly Muslim town, fifty miles inland from Samsun, from which it is separated by low ranges of hills.

On 25 May, Mustafa Kemal left Samsun, having asked Colonel Refet (Bele) to act as governor of the province until a substantive appointment was made from Istanbul.[19] He travelled in an open Benz car, which was found in the military depot.[20] The car kept breaking down, and as the party proceeded on foot, Mustafa Kemal is said to have taught them a marching song, adapted from a Swedish original. The lyrics were appealing in their simplicity: 'The mountain-tops are swathed in smoky mist, the sparkling stream flows and doesn't stop, the sun is raising its head above the horizon. Let's march, friends. Let earth, sky and water hear our voice. Let the ground groan under our firm steps.' This became the theme song of the young officers who fought in the Turkish War of Independence.[21] Soldiers had their own folk songs.

The district officer had let it be known locally that Mustafa Kemal was to spend three or four weeks resting in Havza.[22] This suggests that Mustafa Kemal needed time to contact his friends. Havza was a salubrious place for the preliminary groundwork. Its Muslim inhabitants, who had already held a meeting to protest against the Greek occupation of İzmir, gave Mustafa Kemal a friendly reception. He urged them to found a branch of the Society for the Defence of National Rights. He attended Friday prayers in the main local mosque on 30 May. This was followed by a public meeting at which a Muslim notable – an official of the *Régie* – asked the participants to be ready to sacrifice themselves for the recovery of İzmir. Local Greeks expressed their alarm to their Metropolitan (Archbishop) Germanos in Samsun, who reported matters to Captain Hurst.

Hurst set out from Samsun on 1 June to see for himself. The next morning he met Mustafa Kemal, who received him 'correctly', and said that he intended to go to Amasya and then on to Trabzon and Erzurum, as part of his mission to establish order. Nevertheless, Hurst left Havza 'with the feeling that mischief was afoot'.[23] On 6 June he reported to the British High Commissioner in Istanbul that Mustafa Kemal was 'organizing a movement which is only too likely to find an outlet for its energies in massacres'.[24] Any attempt by the Turks to defend their interests tended to be seen by Allied officials as preparation for a massacre; the Christian minorities which wished to shake off Turkish rule did their best to foster this interpretation. The fate of Muslim Turks did not figure in Allied concerns.

On 8 June, the High Commissioner, Admiral Calthorpe, sent a remarkably realistic despatch to the Foreign Office: 'It has come to my certain knowledge that various army officers have left Constantinople (Istanbul) with a view to organizing opposition to the Greeks. The movement is so natural, and I feel it is so universal, that it seems to me hopeless to endeavour to stop it.'[25] Nevertheless, British authorities urged both the acting grand vizier (Damat Ferit was on his way to Paris) and the Ottoman war ministry to relieve Mustafa Kemal of his command.

On the same day, 8 June, the acting grand vizier informed the British that the Ottoman cabinet had decided, despite considerable misgivings, to recall Mustafa Kemal.[26] The war minister, Şevket Turgut Paşa, showed more mettle and reminded the British that they themselves had authorized Mustafa Kemal's mission. Having said that, he too asked Mustafa Kemal politely to 'do him the honour of coming to Istanbul'. On 11 June, Mustafa Kemal tried to gain time by enquiring why he was being recalled. The war minister feigned ignorance, but the chief of the general staff, Cevat (Çobanlı), told him confidentially that the demand had come from the British.[27] From Samsun, Hurst kept up the pressure. On 12 June he reported that Mustafa Kemal

has been carrying on a large telegraphic correspondence with the surrounding towns and beyond, so much so as to have practically monopolized the telegraph, and his officers have been seen in several or most of the towns and villages of the neighbourhood, where his influence has certainly not made for conciliation. I am of the opinion that a definite movement against the Greeks is being organized and will be let loose as soon as it is obvious that Smyrna [İzmir] is irrecoverable.[28]

Captain Hurst was well informed. Mustafa Kemal made constant use of the telegraph lines, which covered the whole of Turkey, providing easy communication in areas where travel was difficult. He established contact with all important army commands, while continuing to give the war ministry in Istanbul the benefit of his views. His message to his fellow-commanders was clear. On 29 May he told headquarters in Erzurum, Sivas and Ankara that 'determined and honest hands' had to lead the nation along the shortest road to independence 'in our lands'. This duty fell to 'the patriotic charge of us soldiers, because of our special knowledge'.[29] When the war office informed him of British fears for the safety of Armenian refugees returning to Sivas, he replied that the Christians had nothing to fear so long as the aggression to which Muslims had been subjected in and around İzmir was not repeated.[30] On the same day, 3 June, Mustafa Kemal sent a circular telegram to all commanders, asking them to make sure that Societies for the Defence of National Rights and other local assemblies demanded from the government that the Ottoman delegation to the Paris peace conference insisted on the country's full independence and the principle that nowhere should the Muslim majority be subordinated to Christian minorities.[31] Since this was tantamount to direct interference with government policy, members of Damat Ferit's administration, who still pinned their hopes on conciliating the Allies, were only too happy to support British efforts to have Mustafa Kemal recalled.

However, a counterweight to Britain was beginning to be felt in the Black Sea area. On 7 June, Mustafa Kemal's officer for intelligence and political affairs, Major Hüsrev (Gerede), sent a letter to Kâzım Karabekir in Erzurum in which he discussed the possibility of a tactical alliance with the Bolsheviks. There is nothing in the letter to suggest that Mustafa Kemal met Bolsheviks in Havza, but he may have made contact with Turkish Communists who were travelling in the area at the time.[32] Hüsrev's despondent letter speaks of the Bolsheviks as a last resort, just as other nationalist Turks were thinking of America as a possible protector. The letter throws a light also on the influence of Mustafa Kemal's strong personality. Kemal Paşa was not drinking, because of his state of health, reported Hüsrev, who said he was happy to serve him, seeing his moral courage, his attachment to the country and his intelligent grasp of affairs. These qualities, Hüsrev added, inspired in him the hope that Mustafa Kemal would serve the nation well in its time of trial.[33]

It was while Mustafa Kemal was in Havza that armed resistance began against the Greeks in western Anatolia. On 28 May, when Greek troops landed in Ayvalık, a coastal town with a Greek population, north of İzmir, they met with fire from a regular Ottoman unit commanded by Lieutenant-Colonel Ali (Çetinkaya).[34] Ali (known as *Bald* Ali), with whom Mustafa Kemal had worked in Cyrenaica, had been an active member of Enver's Special Organization. Towards the end of the war he commanded a special unit set up to prevent a coup against Enver.[35] The resistance put up by Ali's regiment was reported to Mustafa Kemal by Colonel Bekir Sami (Günsav), acting commander of the 17th corps, which had moved up the coast from İzmir.[36] Elsewhere, in western Anatolia, commanders cooperated with local bands of outlaws (known as *zeybek* or *efe*) in an effort to halt, or at least harass, advancing Greek troops. Guerrilla warfare was starting. Mustafa Kemal did not ignore the value of irregulars, and established contact with the band of Lame Osman in Giresun.[37]

Rauf (Orbay), who had discussed plans for resistance in Anatolia with Mustafa Kemal and Ali Fuat (Cebesoy) in Istanbul, left the capital on 23 May.[38] Rauf was of Circassian origin. Crossing the sea of Marmara to Bandırma, he made contact with fellow-Circassians who had been settled in large numbers in north-western Anatolia after they had been expelled from their ancestral lands in the Caucasus by the Russians in the previous century. Bekir Sami (Günsav), the military commander, who kept in touch with Mustafa Kemal, was a Circassian known to Rauf.[39] The Circassians were a fighting people, none more so than three brothers, Reşit, Tevfik and Ethem, who had all worked in Enver's Special Organization. Rauf, who had Ethem under his command in Persia in 1915, renewed his acquaintance with them and encouraged them to join the embryonic national resistance organization. He then travelled south, meeting resistance leaders in areas threatened by advancing Greek troops.

Having seen the position on the ground in western Anatolia, Rauf joined Ali Fuat in Ankara on 6 June.[40] Two days later, Ali Fuat informed Mustafa Kemal in Havza that 'a gentleman you know has come here with some friends' and suggested a meeting half-way at Osmancık. Mustafa Kemal replied that he did not have enough petrol for the journey and asked the pair to meet him at Havza. Ali Fuat agreed. But as he and Rauf neared the end of their journey, they learned that Mustafa Kemal had suddenly left Havza and had gone to Amasya, some twenty miles to the south. In his six-day speech Mustafa Kemal said cryptically that he had to leave Havza 'for pressing reasons'.[41] Rauf (Orbay) explained later that after receiving the telegram from the war ministry on 8 June summoning him to Istanbul, Mustafa Kemal became worried that a British detachment might be sent to stop him travelling further inland.[42] To avoid the danger, Mustafa Kemal left Havza on 13 June,[43] without giving anybody notice of his move, and made for Amasya, an important Muslim centre, nestling picturesquely in the deep valley of the Yeşilırmak river. Mustafa Kemal could feel safe there, as the 5th Caucasian division, a part of Refet's 3rd corps, was quartered in the town.[44] He was still, precariously, the senior commander in the area, but under the slightly different title of Inspector of the 3rd Army (the 9th Army having been given that number on 15 June,[45] as part of the reorganization of Ottoman armed forces under three inspectorates). Ali Fuat and Rauf finally joined him on 19 June. Refet arrived the following day.[46]

Mustafa Kemal worked out his strategy as he waited for his friends. Tension in the country was rising. In the Aegean area Greek troops were forced back at several places. But they returned with reinforcements to wreak vengeance on the Muslim population. Many were killed; there was wholesale destruction of Muslim property; thousands fled. The Allied decision to allow Greek troops to land in İzmir was leading to the devastation of Aegean Turkey and the pauperization or expulsion of the Muslim majority of its inhabitants. This suited the design of Venizelos to create a homogeneous area of Greek settlement and annex it to Greece. But it was folly to expect that local Muslims would not fight for their lives and their homes. The Anti-annexation Societies which had sprung up all over the area deluged the government in Istanbul and Allied authorities with protests and calls for resistance.

Fearing that agitation would compromise the position of the Ottoman delegation in Paris, the interior minister Ali Kemal sent out instructions on 16 June that post offices throughout the country should refuse protest telegrams.[47] It became increasingly clear to Turkish nationalists and to endangered Muslims throughout the country that the government of Damat Ferit, having failed to prevent the loss of territory to ethnic adversaries, was now hampering efforts to reverse or even limit the losses. Mustafa Kemal had a powerful argument: if the Ottoman government in Istanbul would not or could not defend the Muslims of Turkey, then an alternative authority would have to shoulder the task. From Havza he had made enquiries about the existence of

Societies for the Defence of National Rights in the area of his inspectorate. He had also encouraged their formation. Now in Amasya, he
decided that these societies should provide legitimate cover for an alternative authority. In Russia, Lenin had used a similar tactic in taking over
the workers' and soldiers' soviets, which had sprung up independently
of him. Just as Lenin had no intention of handing power to the soviets
and wanted the Bolsheviks to act in their name, so Mustafa Kemal saw
the Defence of Rights Societies primarily as instruments of popular
mobilization and a source of legitimate authority for the actions of
Turkish nationalist officers, led by himself. Lenin drew on the preaching
of Karl Marx, Mustafa Kemal on the basic principle of the French
Revolution that the nation was the sole source of political sovereignty.

On 18 June – on the eve of the arrival of Ali Fuat and Rauf in Amasya
– Mustafa Kemal made his position clear in a telegram to Colonel Cafer
Tayyar, the commander of the 1st corps, isolated in Edirne in Turkish
Thrace. He argued that while the government in Istanbul was powerless, the entire population of Anatolia had united in the defence of
national independence, that all army commanders, without exception,
were similarly determined, and that 'almost all' civil administrators had
also been enrolled in the cause. British propaganda in favour of an independent Kurdistan had failed, and 'Kurds and Turks had come
together'. It had been agreed that Societies for the Defence of National
Rights and Anti-annexation Societies should provide an 'inclusive title'
for the prosecution of the cause. It had further been agreed that all such
societies in Thrace and Anatolia should come together and form a powerful central committee. To escape foreign influence and control by the
Istanbul government, this committee should have its seat in central
Anatolia, Sivas being the most convenient place. Mustafa Kemal therefore asked Cafer Tayyar to send 'one or two' delegates from the Society
in Thrace to Sivas. Claiming that he had exchanged views with members
of the Society for Thrace while he was in Istanbul, Mustafa Kemal
requested Cafer Tayyar to send him a power of attorney to act in its
name until the arrival of its own delegates.[48] The telegram described the
situation as Mustafa Kemal wished to see it. The reality was somewhat
different.

Mustafa Kemal had a habit of deliberating before taking decisions,
but he did not wait on others. In this case, his tactic was clear. Although
he signed the telegram 'Brigadier Mustafa Kemal, Inspector of the 3rd
Army and Honorary ADC of His Majesty', Mustafa Kemal knew that
he was about to lose the title conferred on him by Sultan Vahdettin. The
power of attorney for which he asked would allow him to take part in
a meeting of the Societies for the Defence of National Rights, and

eventually act in their name. He would then derive his authority from the nation rather than from the sultan.

Mustafa Kemal discussed his draft declaration with Ali Fuat and Rauf on 19 and 20 June. In the evening of the 20th, they were joined by Refet. They sought and obtained agreement by telegram from Cemal (Mersinli), 2nd Army inspector in Konya, and Kâzım Karabekir, commander of the 15th corps – the strongest in the army – in Erzurum.[49] The same day, Mustafa Kemal isssued on his own authority a circular to post offices threatening with court martial any official who obeyed the interior minister's ban on the transmission of telegrams from resistance organizations. In another circular, he asked civil governors to call on National Rights Societies to occupy telegraph offices and impede official communications with the capital until the ban was revoked. At the same time he asked the grand vizier's office and the war ministry to lift the ban. Three days later, the government compromised, allowing the transmission of telegrams, provided they were approved by local authorities. But the authority of determined local army commanders prevailed. Mustafa Kemal was to say that he had won the War of Independence by his use of telegraph wires.[50]

The final text of the Amasya Circular (*Amasya Tamimi*), as it came to be known, was approved and signed on the night of 21/22 June. It followed closely the arguments which Mustafa Kemal had put to Cafer Tayyar, but it was more precise. Explaining the need for a 'national body', free from outside control and influence, the circular gave notice of the decision to hold 'a national congress' in Sivas, which, however, would be preceded by a congress of the eastern provinces, already fixed for 10 July in Erzurum. Three delegates were invited from every administrative district (*liva*), and they were to travel to Sivas in secret. The congress in Erzurum would send its own delegates to the meeting in Sivas.[51]

Congresses were popular after the Great War as a means of influencing state policy. As early as 7 December 1918, a 'National Congress' published a proclamation in Istanbul calling for the union of 'national forces'.[52] However, the latter term had not yet come to mean guerrilla forces, but designated political parties, educational, literary, press and women's organizations. The moving spirit was a military eye-surgeon, Esat Paşa (Işık), who had been close to the CUP. He was to be deported to Malta in 1920. Esat Paşa's congress failed to make an impression in Istanbul. This did not discourage Turkish nationalists from organizing congresses in areas threatened with occupation. The first was held in Balıkesir on 28 June 1919; it was followed by further congresses in Balıkesir and in other towns of western Anatolia. Although their purpose was to provide a civilian base for armed resistance, these regional assemblies did not challenge the Istanbul government directly.[53] However, the national congress summoned from Amasya did present such a challenge, as the authors of the circular realized. According to Rauf, when Refet saw the text he said: 'I understand that, if necessary, a national government will be set up. Is that so?' He then signed the text without hesitation.[54] In the six-day speech, which he delivered in 1927 after his break with his original companions in the War of Independence, Mustafa Kemal pointed out that the Amasya Circular was signed by him and members of his staff. 'There were also,' he added, 'other signatures. But their presence was the result of a fortunate accident, of a coincidence.' He then went on to claim that Refet did not wish to sign the circular, and, when pressed to do so by Ali Fuat, contented himself with a 'special sign' on the document.[55] However, the subsequent actions of the signatories show that none of them was half-hearted.

Action envisaged in the circular was to be carried out by named military commanders and civil administrators with nationalist credentials. Again according to Rauf, one of them, Cemal (Mersinli), wired from his headquarters in Konya that he was buying arms from the Italians, and that he thought it possible to stage an armed rising.[56] However, a few days later Cemal sought leave to go to Istanbul; he did not return to Anatolia. Holding the rank of Major-General, he was the most senior officer contacted by Mustafa Kemal and his friends: he did not wish to play second fiddle to them.

As the Amasya Circular was being issued, Mustafa Kemal wrote to a number of political personalities in Istanbul who sympathized with the nationalist cause. They included the former grand vizier Ahmet İzzet Paşa, and the original ideologue of the CUP, Ahmet Rıza, who had lost the chairmanship of the senate after Damat Ferit had come to power.[57] Mustafa Kemal warned them that meetings and demonstrations were not enough, one had to rely on the strength of the nation. The nationalist opposition in Istanbul should therefore be guided by the nationalist sentiment expressed in Anatolia, rather than the other way round. As for himself, he was determined to stay in Anatolia as 'an individual member of the nation', relying on all his 'responsible and valuable friends' who were in charge there.[58] He thus claimed the primacy of Anatolia in the opposition campaign, and not yet in the government of the country, and presented a picture of collegiate resistance by military and civil officials.

Mustafa Kemal had strengthened his position in Amasya, but he had not yet won the leadership of Anatolian resistance. True, he had only one potential rival, Kâzım Karabekir, a brigadier like him, but one year younger in age and two years junior in promotion. Karabekir was loyal, but opinionated. When the war minister, Şevket Turgut Paşa, asked him on 21 June to stand in for Mustafa Kemal Paşa, Karabekir declined, saying that there was no one to whom he could hand over his command, and that it would be harmful to remove Mustafa Kemal.[59] Nevertheless, Kâzım Karabekir thought that Mustafa Kemal's reaction to the ban on nationalist protest telegrams had been too harsh.[60] More seriously, he was worried that Mustafa Kemal might accept excessive commitments to secure the help of the Bolsheviks. Mustafa Kemal reassured him on 23 June, saying that he agreed with Karabekir that Turkey should be neutral in the conflict between the Bolsheviks and the Allies, while using the former in order to fend off the latter. However, contact should be established with the Bolsheviks right away to find out whether they could supply arms, ammunition, equipment, money and 'if necessary, men'. Bolsheviks need not enter the country in any numbers; discussions with their delegates could be held at the frontier.[61] Mustafa Kemal's grasp of political realities extended beyond the country's frontiers.

The Ottoman government's response to Mustafa Kemal's tactics was confused. Only the interior minister Ali Kemal was determined to get rid of him. On 23 June he sent a circular to provincial authorities saying that although he was a great soldier, Mustafa Kemal did not understand politics. His telegrams on behalf of 'insubordinate, disrespectful and illegal organizations whose sole activity was to extort money from the people' had ended up by increasing the sufferings of Muslims in the Aegean region. It was up to the war ministry to ensure Mustafa Kemal's return to Istanbul, but as interior minister he was ordering provincial authorities to have nothing to do with him.[62]

When Mustafa Kemal left Amasya on 26 June,[63] in the company of Rauf, he was unaware of the interior minister's telegram. But it had already reached Reşit Paşa, the governor of Sivas, the city lying on Mustafa Kemal's route to Erzurum. Since Mustafa Kemal planned to stop there in order to make preparations for the congress which he and his friends had decided to convene, the governor asked for instructions as to how he was to receive Mustafa Kemal. Istanbul spoke with two voices. The interior minister Ali Kemal's attempt to halt resistance in Anatolia embroiled him in a violent argument with the war minister Şevket Turgut and on 26 June they both resigned. The new interior minister (Reşit Âkif Paşa) wired to the governor of Sivas that Mustafa Kemal should be treated like any dismissed general.

The situation was complicated by the fact that a supporter of the Istanbul government, Colonel Ali Galip, who had been appointed governor of Mamuretülaziz (now Elâzığ), in the Kurdish area, was in Sivas at the time. According to the account Mustafa Kemal gave in his 1927 speech, long after Ali Galip had been exiled from Turkey as a traitor, the latter insisted that Reşit Paşa should arrest Mustafa Kemal, and stuck notices on the walls proclaiming Mustafa Kemal a rebel. But Reşit Paşa decided to interpret his instructions loosely and went out by car to meet Mustafa Kemal who had stopped for a rest in the state model farm outside the city. Mustafa Paşa insisted on sitting next to the governor in the latter's car as they drove to the headquarters of Refet's 3rd corps in Sivas. According to Mustafa Kemal's account, Ali Galip called on him there and managed to convince him that his real purpose was to help him.[64] Whatever the truth of the matter, Mustafa Kemal's position in Sivas was delicate. He did not tarry, and, after a sleepless night, left for Erzurum the following morning, 28 June.

The distance between Sivas and Erzurum is about 350 miles. But roads were little better than rough tracks and it took Mustafa Kemal, Rauf and his party (Refet stayed on in his headquarters in Sivas) a week to reach their destination. Both Sivas and Erzurum lie on the treeless plateau of eastern Anatolia, which rises from west to east, from an altitude of 4,000 feet at Sivas to 6,000 feet at Erzurum. To the south of the road, the Dersim (now Tunceli) massif, 10,000 feet at its highest point, was home to unruly Kurdish tribes, professing their own form of Shiite Islam and speaking a Kurdish language (Zaza) unintelligible to the majority of Ottoman Kurds. The Dersim tribes augmented their meagre livelihood from their herds of sheep and goats by extracting subsidies for good behaviour indifferently from the Ottoman author-ities and from their domestic and foreign enemies. The alternative to subsidies was brigandage. In the Great War, the tribes had provided ser-vices to the Ottomans, the Russians and to fleeing Armenians. Now they were hungry, and travellers in the area feared their attacks.

However, nothing untoward happened to Mustafa Kemal and his party. The road took them to Erzincan, once the headquarters of the Ottoman army in the east, now largely a ruin, the town having been devastated and its Muslim inhabitants slaughtered by the Armenians during their retreat in 1918.[65] On 2 July in Erzincan Mustafa Kemal received a telegram from the palace. The sovereign realized, it said, that Mustafa Kemal's initiatives had been inspired by patriotic feeling, but the situation was not as bad as it looked in the provinces, which could be secured from the capital. There was no need for Mustafa Kemal to return to Istanbul, where foreign authorities might treat him harshly; nor did the sultan wish to dismiss him. The best course would be for him to take two months' leave of absence and spend it in the town of his choice.[66] The sultan's cunning was transparent, but the telegram suggested weakness in the Ottoman government.

The following day, 2 July 1919, Kâzım Karabekir met Mustafa Kemal ten miles outside Erzurum. Karabekir had come with his staff, a detachment of troops and his 'children's army' – abandoned Muslim children he had rescued and organized in a boys' brigade.[67] Leading citizens had also turned up to welcome two national heroes – Mustafa Kemal and Rauf – who had taken the trouble to lend their weight to the defence of this outpost of Ottoman Islam. There was a second ceremony at the city's Istanbul gate, where military and civil officials welcomed the party, to the accompaniment of a military band. The guests were escorted to the headquarters of the Erzurum fortress. The following day was the anniversary of Sultan Vahdettin's accession to the throne and Mustafa Kemal sent a telegram of loyal greetings to his sovereign.[68] But the impression that he represented the sultan's authority could not be sustained.

As soon as Mustafa Kemal arrived he was handed a cipher telegram from Refet in Sivas. Refet was pressing him to resign from the army immediately and stay on in the safety of Erzurum; he was prepared to send on Mustafa Kemal's papers, but wanted to keep 500 liras for any emergency.[69] Mustafa Kemal was shaken. He had arrived in Erzurum wearing his general's uniform, with the cordon of an imperial ADC, and the medal of the Ottoman Order of Merit. The people, he believed, respected authority, particularly military authority, and he wanted to use his title as long as possible.

In Istanbul, the British were determined to deprive him of this possibility. The High Commissioner Admiral Calthorpe reported to the Foreign Office on 23 June that Mustafa Kemal Paşa, who had made a 'considerable reputation for himself during the Gallipoli fighting', had become 'a centre for national and anti-foreign feeling'. The despatch was minuted by George Kidston, of the Eastern Department, 'I know nothing of Mustafa Kemal ...'[70] On 5 July, Lieutenant J.S. Perring who had succeeded Captain Hurst as British relief officer in Samsun reported to Calthorpe that Mustafa Kemal had been dismissed, but that he had issued an appeal to the Turkish people telling them to obey his orders only, as the government was incapable and was selling the country to foreigners. However, 'the whole movement appears to have had little success and for the most part not much interest is taken; the worst feature is the organization of brigand bands.'[71]

Perring was quickly disabused. The following day, as the British company in Samsun was replaced by a Gurkha unit, Refet informed the

British control officer that the rotation had not been authorized by the Ottoman government, and that he would oppose by force any move by the Gurkhas into the interior. He himself would withdraw Ottoman troops (the depleted 15th division) from Samsun.[72] The new war minister, Ferit Paşa, immediately ordered Refet to desist, and asked him to try and persuade Mustafa Kemal to return to Istanbul, where the British had promised not to take any action against him. The war minister had conveyed the same promise to Mustafa Kemal on 5 July. He replied that he was now serving 'the forces of the nation', which had manifested themselves in response to calamity; if Ferit Paşa was unable to prevent the extension to eastern Anatolia of the fate which had overtaken İzmir, Mustafa Kemal advised him to resign. The game, as he called it, was coming to an end.

On 7 July Mustafa Kemal issued his last order as inspector of the 3rd Army. It was a circular to all commanders demanding that military and 'national' organizations should on no account be disbanded, that commands should not be surrendered, except where newly appointed officers were capable of cooperating (in the national cause), that, likewise, arms and ammunition should not be handed over, and that there should be a united military response to any further movement of 'enemy' troops. There should be no interference with 'national forces' – the nationalist irregulars who had taken the field. The army should become the agent of the national will, which alone could guarantee the safety of the caliphate.[73] This order, which was prompted by the news that the Inspector of the 2nd Army, Cemal (Mersinli), whose recall had also been demanded by the British, had decided to return to Istanbul, was a clear invitation to military revolt and a challenge to the validity of the armistice.

The following day, Calthorpe demanded that both Mustafa Kemal and Refet should be recalled immediately.[74] On the night of 8/9 July Mustafa Kemal spent several hours in telegraphic communication with the war minister, Ferit Paşa, who was sitting in the telegraph office in the sultan's palace. In the Erzurum telegraph office, Karabekir, Rauf and Mustafa Kemal's chief of staff, Colonel Kâzım (Dirik), were following the exchanges. First Mustafa Kemal and Ferit bandied compliments. Arguments followed. Seeing that the exchange was leading ineluctably to his dismissal, Mustafa Kemal submitted his resignation from the army. Ferit Paşa responded by saying that the sultan had cashiered him.[75] The fact that the break was the inevitable result of Mustafa Kemal's determined stand, did not diminish the danger which it posed to him. His fate was now in the hands of his host, Kâzım Karabekir, who was appointed acting Inspector of the 3rd Army on 21 July.

Karabekir says that he accepted the appointment this time, with the agreement of both Mustafa Kemal and Rauf.[76]

Karabekir stood by Mustafa Kemal. In his 1927 speech, Mustafa Kemal said that soon after arriving in Erzurum he called a meeting to discuss the situation. It was attended by Karabekir, Rauf, members of Mustafa Kemal's staff, and three civil administrators – the governor of Erzurum, Münir, and the governor of Bitlis, Mazhar Müfit (Kansu), both newly dismissed from their posts, and a former district officer, Süreyya. Mustafa Kemal argued that the national struggle should be waged by people fully prepared to take the consequences; a leader was needed, but it did not have to be himself. He then adjourned the meeting. When the group reassembled, Mustafa Kemal went on, all present promised to support him; only the ex-governor Münir asked for the time being to be excused from active participation. Mustafa Kemal thereupon explained that the success of the enterprise required that, in spite of his resignation, he should continue to be regarded as the senior commander and that his orders should be obeyed. 'This was agreed and confirmed in full.' Mustafa Kemal claimed that he had reached similar agreements with Generals Cevat (Çobanlı) and Fevzi (Çakmak), who succeeded each other as CGS, and with Colonel İsmet in Istanbul.[77]

Mazhar Müfit, who became an unquestioning follower of Atatürk, confirms this account. He adds that it was agreed, nevertheless, that all decisions at the Sivas congress, which was to follow the Erzurum congress, would be taken in the name of a Representative Committee (*Heyet-i Temsiliye*) – a committee representing the full congress as a permanent executive.[78] Rauf, who later fell out with Mustafa Kemal, tells a different story in the letter which he sent to Karabekir in 1941. According to his account, the two of them – presumably as a consequence of Mustafa Kemal's departure from the army – moved from an army building to the civil governor's house. There on 10 July, twenty-four hours after his resignation, Mustafa Kemal went through official papers with his chief of staff Colonel Kâzım (Dirik). When the work was finished, Colonel Kâzım said: 'Pasha, you've resigned from the army. I can't therefore stay on [as your chief of staff]. Allow me to apply to General Karabekir for a military appointment. To whom am I to hand over the documents?' Mustafa Kemal was shaken. 'Is that so? All right, then give the documents to Hüsrev (Gerede),' he said to Colonel Kâzım. Then, when the latter left the room, he turned to Rauf with the words: 'Wasn't I right? Don't you see now the value of official titles and of the support they give? Doesn't this behaviour on the part of a man who only yesterday served me wholeheartedly prove the truth of my view?' Rauf goes on to say that he had never seen Mustafa Kemal in such a despairing mood, and that when he tried to console him, saying that he could rely on Karabekir, Mustafa Kemal replied: 'Let's hope you're right. Would that the Americans, God curse them, accepted a mandate [over Turkey] and got the country and the nation out of trouble.'

At that moment Mustafa Kemal's ADC announced that Karabekir had arrived and was waiting to be received. Believing the worst, Mustafa Kemal looked at Rauf and said bitterly: 'You see. Am I not right?' But when Karabekir entered, he turned to Mustafa Kemal as to a superior officer and said: 'I've come to pay my respects on behalf of all the officers and men under my command. You remain our respected commander, just as you've been until now. I've brought a car and an escort of cavalry as befits a corps commander. Pasha, we're all at your service.'[79]

This is one of three incidents (the second relating to the rising in Yozgat in 1920, and the third to the Sakarya battle in 1921), in which Mustafa Kemal's future opponents tried to use the occasion as evidence that his will could falter. It does not detract from the fact that the leadership of Mustafa Kemal was accepted by Karabekir in Erzurum. The acceptance was helped by the presence of Rauf, respected as a hero by all Turkish nationalists, and by Mustafa Kemal's preliminary work in mobilizing the support of nationalist commanders and civil governors. But it was Mustafa Kemal's character which tipped the balance. His vision was grander than that of Karabekir, who believed that it was enough to hang on in eastern Anatolia for the time being.[80] Karabekir was, as the British control officer Colonel Rawlinson remarked, a 'first-class officer' and a 'thoroughly competent commander';[81] he was not afraid to criticize Mustafa Kemal, but in the end always yielded to the latter's superior determination. Mustafa Kemal had slight seniority, a more impressive war record, and a much clearer grasp of politics. But the decisive factor was his self-confidence. Moments of despair were fleeting. Karabekir wanted the leadership of national resistance to be collegiate; Mustafa Kemal saw himself as the supreme leader. As he was to say in 1927, 'History has proved incontrovertibly that success in great enterprises requires the presence of a leader of unshakeable capacity and power.'[82]

The leader kept his ultimate aims to himself. Mustafa Kemal said in 1927 that it was immediately clear to him that the monarchy would be the relentless enemy of the national will. But to spell out the consequence, in other words the inevitability of a republic, would frighten people who found the prospect contrary to their traditions, their mental capacity and their mentality. In order to preserve unity in the struggle for independence, Mustafa Kemal was obliged to keep to himself as 'a national secret the great capacity for development which I discerned in the nation's conscience and future'.[83] One of Mustafa Kemal's companions in Erzurum, the former provincial governor Mazhar Müfit (Kansu), claims in his memoirs that he was allowed to share the leader's secret designs. In a conversation which occupied the night of 7/8 July, Mustafa Kemal is said to have allowed Mazhar Müfit to note down five long-term objectives: the proclamation of a republic, 'appropriate treatment' of the dynasty, abolition of Islamic dress for women and a ban on the wearing of the fez by men, and the introduction of the Latin alphabet.[84] There is little doubt that Mustafa Kemal did indeed harbour these designs, although he was probably not as explicit as Mazhar Müfit claims.

Lieutenant-Colonel Rawlinson, the British control officer, who was in Erzurum at the time, saw which way the wind was blowing, and informed London of the possibility of Turkish nationalists setting up 'a great future Moslem Republic'.[85] Rawlinson met Mustafa Kemal, and in the account which he published in 1923, after Mustafa Kemal had become famous, he paid tribute to his striking personality, his strength of character, patriotism, competence and wide-ranging knowledge.[86] There may be an element of hindsight in this encomium, but Rawlinson had clearly been impressed by the 'great Turk' who was 'European rather than Asiatic in type, with fair hair and blue eyes ... more Teutonic than Turkish in appearance'.

But what counted in Erzurum in July 1919 was not Teutonic looks, but determined, clever politics. As delegates from Defence of National Rights Societies were slow in arriving, it was decided to postpone the opening of the congress to 23 July, the anniversary of the reintroduction of constitutional government in 1908. This emphasized the democratic character of the coming meeting. But democrats had to be guided to the right choice of leader. Kâzım Karabekir arranged for two delegates of the Erzurum Defence of National Rights Society to resign and to cede their places to Mustafa Kemal and Rauf, who thus gained the right to attend the congress as full members. Mustafa Kemal was then selected as chairman of the preparatory committee (*heyet-i faale*).[87] It was a first step to the chairmanship of the congress itself.

At this point signs of opposition emerged. The meeting was to be a joint one of the Trabzon Society for the Maintenance of National Rights and the Eastern Provinces' Society for the Defence of National Rights, which had its seat in Erzurum; but one of the Trabzon delegates, Ömer Fevzi, objected to the election of a military commander to the chair on the grounds that this would create an unfavourable impression abroad. Karabekir responded by persuading other delegates from Trabzon to accept Mustafa Kemal as chairman, with two vice-chairmen, one from Erzurum the other from Trabzon.[88]

The Erzurum congress opened at 11 a.m. on 23 July 1919 in a single-storey building which had originally housed an Armenian school. Mustafa Kemal arrived with Kâzım Karabekir. Although he had left the army, Mustafa Kemal was still dressed in his military uniform, with the cordon of imperial ADC. Both Mustafa Kemal and Karabekir were present when sheep were sacrificed and opening prayers recited in Arabic by a mufti, who was one of the Trabzon delegates. Kâzım Karabekir and other serving officers then departed, leaving the fifty-six delegates, Mustafa Kemal and Rauf among them, to begin their deliberations.

It was Mustafa Kemal's first experience of democratic politics. The delegates had come from genuine grass-roots nationalist organizations and were determined to have their say. As soon as the meeting opened, Ömer Fevzi proposed that the election of the chairman should be postponed to the following day. He was outvoted, and Mustafa Kemal was elected to the chair in a secret vote by a large majority.[89] Thanking the delegates, Mustafa Kemal used all the resources of Ottoman eloquence to describe the progress of the country's partition, the impotence of the government in Istanbul and the machinations of the Allies and their dupes. Only in Anatolia, he declared, could a national administration gain control over the country's fate, free from outside interference. This clear call for the formation of an alternative national government ended with a prayer for the safety of the nation and of the exalted institution of the sultanate and caliphate.[90] A telegram of loyal greetings was then sent to the sultan.

The following day, as Mustafa Kemal took the chair, yet another delegate from Trabzon objected that the chairman should not be in military uniform. It could be interpreted, he argued, as an attempt to dominate a civilian meeting. Mustafa Kemal excused himself on the grounds that he did not have civilian clothes. But he did not repeat the mistake; by the time the congress reconvened he had procured morning-dress from the wardrobe of the governor of Erzurum.[91] A more serious objection had been raised by the government in Istanbul as soon as the congress opened. The congress, it argued, violated the constitution by substituting itself for parliament. It should therefore be wound up and Mustafa Kemal and his comrades should be arrested and returned to Istanbul.

At Mustafa Kemal's suggestion, the congress responded with a circular to the sovereign, the government and all civil and military authorities, refuting the charges, declaring its loyalty to the sultan and demanding that a new parliament should be elected in accordance with the constitution.[92] It then proceeded to debate the terms of a declaration and the articles of association of the movement. The declaration had been drafted by the preparatory committee under Mustafa Kemal: it was now subjected to careful scrutiny by the delegates. Conservatives objected to a clause which pledged respect for 'modern and humane ideals' on the grounds that modernity was an irreligious fad. The objection was countered by young delegates,[93] and modernity survived in the final declaration and in subsequent statements based on it.

It was the purpose of the congress to unite the nationalist organizations of the Black Sea coast and of eastern Anatolia. But drafting the articles of association of the new body – the Eastern Anatolia Society for the Defence of National Rights – did not prove easy. First, Rauf's proposal for branches to be chaired by local governors was rejected. More important was the disagreement over the formation of a permanent executive, the Representative Committee, which would act on behalf of the Society. Delegates from Trabzon did not wish to entrust decisions to a small body: this objection however was outvoted.[94] The membership of the executive then came up for discussion. Mustafa Kemal saw this body as the nucleus of a future government and was determined to lead it; but even his closest companions had doubts. On 5 August he called a meeting of five companions and asked them to write down on a piece of paper whether they thought he should be a member of the Representative Committee: two were in favour, three against. Having read the slips, Mustafa Kemal pocketed them and announced his decision to enter the committee, and gave the names of eight other members whom he wanted to see elected. There were no objections.[95]

On 7 August, the congress met in final session. The membership of the Representative Committee was approved, as decided by Mustafa Kemal. Delegates were told that a national congress would meet in Sivas a fortnight later. They agreed that their executive should be represented there by three members, and that if the Erzurum congress decisions were endorsed, they would have the right to merge the Eastern Anatolia organization in a countrywide Society for the Defence of National Rights in Anatolia and Rumelia. They were not to make any other changes.[96]

On the same day, the congress published its declaration. Proclaiming the indivisible integrity of the eastern provinces as part of the Ottoman state, it went on to defend the same principle for all the lands under Ottoman control when the armistice was signed on 30 October 1918. It was a national rather than a regional charter, which set out the principle that national forces should be allowed to operate freely and the national will should prevail for the defence of the realm. It demanded that parliament should be summoned immediately; it welcomed the technical

and economic help of any country which did not covet Ottoman territory, and it declared that the Eastern Anatolia Society for the Defence
of Rights was a non-party organization and that all Muslims were
members *ipso facto*.[97]

This was the first version of Turkey's declaration of independence
and it bears the imprint of Mustafa Kemal's hand. It was subsequently
amended twice, but its principles remained unchanged. It also showed
the way to the realization of these principles. Describing realistically any
Allied act of occupation and intervention as support for Greek and
Armenian separatism, it declared that this would be met with the united
resistance of all Muslims. Moreover, should the Ottoman government
'abandon or neglect' the eastern provinces, a provisional administration
would be formed to defend the area and govern it in accordance with
existing Ottoman laws. If congress was not sitting at the time, the
Representative Committee would discharge the duties of a provisional
government.[98]

On 24 August, Mustafa Kemal registered the articles of association
of the Eastern Anatolia Society for the Defence of National Rights, and
the membership of its executive (the Representative Committee) with
the office of the governor of Erzurum, in accordance with the law on
associations.[99] In fact, three of the nine members of the committee,
including the two representatives from Trabzon, took no further part in
its proceedings.[100] Five members of the committee, headed by Mustafa
Kemal, informed Kâzım Karabekir on 9 August that they had coopted
him as a member,[101] Mustafa Kemal signing this communication simply
as 'member'. One must assume that at some stage he must have been
formally elected chairman of the committee in accordance with the
rulebook. However, he did not use the title in official correspondence,
which he signed simply 'on behalf of the Representative Committee'.[102]
In his 1927 speech, Mustafa Kemal said that nothing could be expected
from a committee which included such 'wretched people' as the leader
of the Kurdish Mutki tribe and a sheikh of the dervish Nakşibendi
order in Erzincan.[103] In fact, Mustafa Kemal saw the Representative
Committee, like the Society which it represented, as his personal instrument. However, two members had their own minds, Rauf and a former
governor of Beirut, Bekir Sami (Kunduh). The latter had been elected
to the membership although he was not present at the congress. They
were both of Caucasian origin.

Just as the Erzurum congress ended, military units in Anatolia
received circulars from the *Karakol* secret society set up by the CUP in
Istanbul. The move disturbed Mustafa Kemal. Certainly, Kara Vasıf, the
leader of *Karakol*, was known to him as a staunch Turkish nationalist;

but Mustafa Kemal's strategy was based on the creation of an open national resistance movement under his own leadership. Although many, if not most, Turkish nationalists had been associated with CUP, that party, which had led the Ottoman state to defeat in the Great War, was unpopular in the country. In the upper ranks of Ottoman society, many supported the Freedom and Concord Party, which had a long-standing feud with the CUP. The nationalist movement could succeed only if it united the majority of Muslims in Turkey. CUP members were welcome as individuals, provided they took their orders from Mustafa Kemal; but he would not allow them to act as an organized caucus. Mustafa Kemal was a rebel from within the ranks of the Ottoman establishment, not a popular revolutionary. He wanted to bring order out of chaos. Freelance conspirators complicated this task and risked frightening off the commanders on whom he had to rely.[104] *Karakol* was stopped in its tracks in Anatolia.[105] But it continued its activity as the main underground nationalist organization in the capital.

In Istanbul, in the meantime, the position of Damat Ferit and of his patron, the sultan, had weakened. Damat Ferit had returned from Paris empty-handed on 15 July. He had submitted a memorandum to the peace conference, claiming lands even beyond the armistice lines, including south-eastern Bulgaria, the islands in the eastern Aegean, and northern Mesopotamia and Syria, and suggesting autonomy for the Arab provinces under Ottoman sovereignty. These demands were met with derision and Damat Ferit was informed that there was no point in his staying on in Paris. The following day, the heir apparent, Prince Abdülmecit, sent a petition to the sultan urging the formation of a government of national unity, which would pay attention to demands voiced in Anatolia. The sultan, already shaken by a fire in Yıldız palace on 8 June, which rumour attributed to sabotage, was alarmed. But he stuck by Damat Ferit, who formed yet another government on 21 July. This included two generals sympathetic to the nationalists, Salih Paşa and Ali Rıza Paşa. A third, Mustafa Kemal's old commanding officer, Ahmet İzzet Paşa, was also included, but resigned after a week, in protest at the order to arrest the leaders of the Erzurum congress.[106]

On 30 July, when the Erzurum congress was still sitting, the Ottoman government decided in principle to hold fresh parliamentary elections.[107] But Damat Ferit tried to drag out the preparations as long as possible in the hope of neutralizing the nationalist officers active in Anatolia. The military situation on the ground had in the meantime stabilized, with the settling by the Allied Supreme Council on 18 July of the limits of Greek (and Italian) occupation:[108] Greek troops were to keep within a line (known as the Milne line), surrounding İzmir and its hinterland from Ayvalık in the north to the Menderes (Meander) river in the south. However, guerrilla activity continued.

Mustafa Kemal stayed on in Erzurum for another three weeks after the conclusion of the congress; the meeting in Sivas was proving difficult to organize. Refet (Bele) had followed Mustafa Kemal's example and had resigned from the army on 13 July.[109] He was replaced as commander of the 3rd corps by Colonel Salâhattin, who asked Karabekir on 10 August whether there was any point in proceeding with a congress in Sivas now that the Ottoman government had promised to hold elections. Karabekir, who had in the meantime lost his title as 3rd Army inspector, but retained command of the 15th corps in Erzurum, replied that a meeting in Sivas was necessary in order to extend to the whole country the decisions reached in Erzurum. However, care would be taken not to alarm the Istanbul government.[110]

Then on 20 August the governor of Sivas, Reşit Paşa, informed Mustafa Kemal of his fear that the French might occupy Sivas and arrest the delegates if a congress were held. Mustafa Kemal replied that the fear was groundless.[111] He guessed correctly that the French had neither the troops nor the will to march on Sivas. But the argument he used, that the Allies would appreciate an expression of Turkish patriotism in Sivas, as they had already done in Erzurum, was patently false. While these exchanges were proceeding, Mustafa Kemal was exercised by the mundane problem of finding the money necessary to cover the expenses of his journey to Sivas. There were only 80 lira left of the 1,500 lira collected for the needs of the Erzurum congress. A retired major, settled in Erzurum, came to the rescue and donated his savings of 900 lira.[112] It was enough for the purpose.

Before leaving Erzurum, Mustafa Kemal wrote to his mother for the first time since he had left Istanbul. There was no need to worry, he assured her. 'The whole people of Anatolia, the entire nation have showed me great affection and confidence, saying: We shan't let you go,' he wrote. So he had had no choice but to leave the army and become the leader of the people, and as soon as he did so, the English had tried to win him over. The Ottoman government, Mustafa Kemal went on, would never be strong enough to get the better of him. As for his immediate plans, he would have to stay on in Anatolia for some time until everything was solved, but soon parliament would meet and a legitimate government would come to power, making it possible for him to return to Istanbul. In the meantime he was going to Sivas for the congress and would then return to Erzurum. Could his mother send him some clothes with the trusted man who delivered the letter? He sent his greetings to his Christian Syrian friends, the Fansas. 'Madame Fansa had a dream about me. It looks as if it'll come true. _Inshallah_, we shall soon meet in total joy.'[113]

Mustafa Kemal was pleased at the prospect of parliamentary elections. But even before they were held, he was convinced that the people had already chosen him as their leader. The decision of the Erzurum Society for the Defence of National Rights to grant him the freedom of the city[114] was a start.

On 29 August Mustafa Kemal left Erzurum in a convoy of three cars protected by a machine-gun detachment. Apart from his own party, which now included the retired governor Mazhar Müfit (Kansu), he was accompanied by Rauf and, rather unwillingly, by the cleric Raif Efendi, the chairman of the Erzurum Society for the Defence of National Rights. The convoy stopped in Erzincan to collect the local Nakşibendi sheikh Fevzi Efendi, a sleeping member of the Representative Committee. Once again, there were fears that the party would be attacked by Dersim Kurds: Ali Galip, the governor loyal to the Istanbul government, was active in the area. Mustafa Kemal had a machine-gun mounted on the front car and insisted that the journey should continue. There was no attack, and the party reached Sivas on 2 September without mishap.[115]

Preparations for the meeting had been made by the local branch of the Society for the Defence of National Rights with the help of the governor Reşit Paşa and the corps commander Selâhattin. The local high school, one of the many built during the reign of Abdülhamit, was chosen as the venue of the congress. Mustafa Kemal was given a bedroom on the first floor; Rauf too had his own room. The building was not overcrowded: only thirty-eight delegates had turned up, including Mustafa Kemal and his party from Erzurum.[116] The resistance organizations of the Aegean provinces had held their own congress in Alaşehir between 16 and 25 August and agreed on an unwritten truce so long as the Greeks did not advance beyond the Milne line. They did not send any delegates to Sivas.[117]

Unlike the Erzurum congress, which was genuinely representative of resistance organizations in the Black Sea area and eastern Anatolia, the meeting in Sivas brought together nationalist militants who were largely self-appointed. One of them was Ali Fuat's father, the elderly general İsmail Fazıl Paşa, an unelected delegate from Istanbul. Another was the leader of the _Karakol_ secret society, Kara Vasıf, who called himself delegate of Antep (later Gaziantep), a Turkish town north of Aleppo. There was also the former Ottoman ambassador in Washington, Alfred

Rüstem, a converted Pole whose family name was Bilinski. 'Pasha,' he said, turning to Mustafa Kemal, 'do not forget that we are not a body formed in accordance with the law on associations. Our true identity is that of a revolutionary committee.'[118] But Mustafa Kemal would have none of it; he wanted to produce the appearance of a countrywide legal association of patriotic organizations to serve as a cover for his assumption of the leadership of the Turkish national struggle.

Although it was sparsely attended, the Sivas congress held lively debates. The first, as usual, concerned the chairmanship which Mustafa Kemal had assumed provisionally at the start of the proceedings on 4 September. İsmail Fazıl Paşa suggested that it would be more democratic to have a separate chairman for each session. He was outvoted, and Mustafa Kemal was confirmed in the chair. The following day, the delegates swore an oath that they would not try to revive the CUP or serve the interests of any political party.[119]

It was a crucial decision. Most delegates, like the bulk of Turkish nationalists, had been associated with the CUP. This link, which was stressed by their political opponents, risked dividing the ranks of the national resistance movement. It also stood in the way of the attempts of Turkish nationalists to avoid a clash with the major Allies, who abhorred the CUP, while resisting the claims of their Greek and Armenian protégés. It was a difficult and delicate task. The Turkish resistance movement, which was taking shape under Mustafa Kemal's leadership, was the successor of the CUP, which had brought the Ottoman state into the war against the Allies. Yet there had been a change, which the British in particular failed to see. In November 1919, two months after the Sivas congress had distanced itself from the CUP, Sir Eyre Crowe, the permanent under-secretary at the Foreign Office, wrote to the Foreign Secretary Lord Curzon: 'In my personal opinion Mustafa Kemal's movement is essentially CUP and imperialist in the sense of aiming at a Turkey free from all foreign control, and as far as possible in continued possession of those parts of the empire which are largely inhabited by other nationalities.'[120] Crowe was wrong. Independence was not an imperialist aim. And Turkish nationalists, unlike some Ottoman friends of the Allies in Istanbul, had written off the Arab provinces. The territory they strove to keep had an overall Muslim – Turkish and Kurdish – majority. The declaration published in Erzurum had already defined that territory as lying within the 1918 armistice lines. The Sivas meeting was to reaffirm it.

However, before it did so, the concept of complete independence had to be upheld. On 28 April 1919, the Paris conference had accepted the charter of the League of Nations, which made provision for the establishment of mandates, under the supervision of the League, for territories which were not ready to exercise independence through self-determination. On 20 May, a Society of Friends of Britain (*İngiliz Muhipleri Cemiyeti*, literally English-lovers' society) was formed in Istanbul, with a cleric, Sait Molla, as chairman;[121] the Reverend Robert Frew acted as its recruiting agent. But Lloyd George's decision to support the Greek landing in İzmir cut the ground from under its feet. The French had similarly put themselves out of court by moving into the territory south of the Taurus mountains where they championed the Armenians. This left the United States as a possible protector. A Wilson Society had been formed in Istanbul in December 1918, basing itself on the American president's ideal of national self-determination and, in particular, on his readiness to see it applied to areas inhabited by a Turkish majority.

The idea of an American mandate appealed to the liberal wing of the CUP and to those Ottoman patriots and Turkish nationalists who had been, or had become, critical of the CUP subservience to the Germans, but who believed that Turkey could not survive without the support of a great power. They did not think only of the weakness of the country after its defeat in the Great War. There was also the backwardness of its people by the standards of 'modern civilization'. A convinced Turkish nationalist, Rıza Nur, was to write after his break with Mustafa Kemal:

> If America were to accept the mandate and behave in a just and honest manner, it could within twenty years bring us a degree of development which Turks, left to themselves, would not be able to achieve in a century. It would make Turkey prosperous, rich and happy and turn Turks into a strong and civilized nation. Look at Egypt under the British. Its population has grown by some ten million in thirty years. The country is totally prosperous and orderly, the nation rich. Such a nation can gain independence in a trice. At least that's one way of thinking at a time of such justified despair. True, slavery is bad even in paradise. But the nation risked losing everything. The thinking may have been wrong, but to accuse people of treachery is unfair.[122]

Lloyd George encouraged Wilson to accept a mandate for Anatolia, and particularly for the provinces claimed by the Armenians. Wilson responded by sending two commissions – one, led by the academic Henry King and the sanitary equipment magnate Charles Crane, to Syria, and another to Anatolia under General James Harbord.[123] The King–Crane commission arrived in Istanbul on 7 June, returning to the Ottoman capital on 21 July after visiting Syria. Its report, recommending that Ottoman territory within the armistice lines should be divided into three entities – Istanbul and its environs, Armenia, and the rest of

Anatolia – and that all three should be placed under US mandate, was not known to the delegates in Sivas.[124] But there was in town an American journalist, Louis Edgar Browne of the *Chicago Daily News*, who acted as a freelance go-between.[125]

On 4 September, the day the congress opened in Sivas, an Ottoman staff officer arrived in Erzurum with a memorandum from Ahmet İzzet Paşa suggesting that a US mandate should be sought. There was also a letter from Ahmet İzzet's protégé, Colonel İsmet (İnönü), coming to the same conclusion. Karabekir, who received the documents in his Erzurum headquarters, decided to withhold them from the delegates in Sivas in order to avoid weakening the cause of Turkish independence.[126] However, Mustafa Kemal had been informed even before he had left Erzurum that an influential group of patriots in Istanbul, including the feminist writer and nationalist orator Halide Edip (Adıvar) and the *Karakol* leader Kara Vasıf, had come out in favour of a US mandate. Responding to the information, he cabled to Ali Fuat in Ankara on 19 August that only a government supported by parliament and embodying the national will had the right to make deals with America or any other foreign state.

The matter came up for discussion in Sivas on 8 September. The former governor Bekir Sami (Kunduh), whom Mustafa Kemal had chosen for the Erzurum Representative Committee, presented a memorandum bearing twenty-five signatures, arguing that the USA should be accepted as a mandatory power. From the chair, Mustafa Kemal warned delegates that the American, Louis Edgar Browne, was present in no official capacity in Sivas, though he had spoken to him, and had been told that the US might well reject the request to assume a mandate in Turkey.[127] This salutary warning did not prevent the elderly İsmail Fazıl Paşa, the *Karakol* leader Kara Vasıf and others from supporting a US mandate, while young men who represented Istanbul medical students denounced the idea in fiery terms and were joined by some provincial delegates. The following day, Rauf drew attention to the passage in the Erzurum declaration which welcomed aid from any foreign power which respected the country's independence and integrity. There was no harm, he said, in saying clearly that the delegates had America in mind. Thereupon, congress agreed that Mustafa Kemal together with the vice-presidents of the congress should invite the US Senate to send a commission of enquiry to Turkey before allowing the signature of a peace treaty with a non-representative Ottoman government.[128] A letter to this effect was given to Browne on 9 September for transmission to Washington.[129]

The discussion had no practical effect. Harbord and his mission arrived in Sivas on 20 September. They were told by Mustafa Kemal that Turkey realized that it needed the aid of an impartial foreign country. 'After all our experience we are sure that America is the only country able to help us,' Mustafa Kemal acknowledged in a statement on 15 October.[130] But this did not amount to a request for a US mandate. Harbord recommended that a single US mandate should cover both Armenia and much of Turkey; 'there is no wisdom,' the mission report argued, 'in now incorporating Turkish territory in a separate Armenia, no matter what the aspirations of the Armenians.'[131] But President Wilson gave his support to Armenian claims the following year, and in any case the proposal for a mandate over Ottoman lands was never put to the US Congress.

The failure of the Senate on 19 November to ratify US membership of the League of Nations showed the unreality of the debate held two months earlier in Sivas. Nevertheless, support for a US mandate and, by extension, any call for US aid – aid which Mustafa Kemal did not oppose under the right conditions – have been interpreted as proof of treachery in Turkish domestic politics to this day. Mustafa Kemal used this weapon as early as 1927 against Rauf, when he presented himself, correctly, as a staunch supporter of full independence, adding disingenuously that he could not remember whether the invitation to the US Senate had actually been sent.[132]

With the idea of the mandate out of the way, congress adopted the rules of association of the unified Society for the Defence of National Rights in Anatolia and Rumelia, in which the Eastern Anatolia Society was now merged. The number of members of the Representative Committee was increased to sixteen. Again most of them were sleeping members; apart from Mustafa Kemal, only Rauf, Refet (who was coopted), Bekir Sami and Kara Vasıf (who returned to Istanbul) carried any weight. They all accepted Mustafa Kemal as leader, and he had no difficulty in obtaining counter-signatures whenever he issued instructions in the name of the committee. Leadership of the committee opened the way to leadership of the country, for the Representative Committee was once again empowered to act as a provisional administration if the Ottoman government abandoned or neglected 'these [unspecified] parts [of the country]'.[133]

On 11 September 1919, the Sivas congress published a declaration which repeated the principles established in Erzurum: the independence and integrity of the Ottoman lands within the armistice lines, fair treatment but no special privileges for minorities, resistance to Greek and Armenian territorial claims, acceptance of disinterested foreign aid, and the immediate election of parliament. It proclaimed that the country's independence and integrity and the 'exalted office of the caliph and sultan' could be safeguarded only if national forces were allowed full play and the national will reigned supreme.[134] The proclamation was compatible with a constitutional monarchy, if Sultan Vahdettin was prepared to act as a constitutional monarch. But he had other ideas.

The work of the congress took place under the shadow of a physical threat to Mustafa Kemal and his companions in Sivas. On 3 September, the Ottoman interior minister Âdil and a new and virulently anti-nationalist war minister, Süleyman Şefik, ordered Ali Galip, the governor of Mamuretülaziz,[135] to recruit a troop of 100 to 150 Kurdish horsemen and lead them to Sivas to arrest Mustafa Kemal and disperse the congress.[136] On 5 September, Ali Galip arrived in Malatya where he met Captain Edward Noel, a British Indian army officer, who had espoused the Kurdish cause. Having first come across the Kurds during his war service in Persia,[137] Noel made contact at the end of hostilities with Ottoman Kurdish tribal leaders who were trying to promote the cause of Kurdish self-rule. The most active were Şerif Paşa of the Baban dynasty of Süleymaniye (now in Iraq), the Bedirhan family, which had been paramount in the Diyarbakır area, and Abdülkadir, leader of a dynasty of sheikhs from Şemdinli (now in the extreme south-eastern corner of Turkey). As a result of his contacts, Noel convinced himself of the existence of Kurdish nationalism and became an insistent advocate of the creation of a British-supported independent Kurdish state. The Ottoman government in Istanbul was disturbed by the prospect and closed down Kurdish nationalist clubs at the beginning of 1919. However, as military commanders in Anatolia rallied to the cause of a defiant Turkish nationalism, the government of Damat Ferit in Istanbul tried to use the Kurds against them. Mustafa Kemal, having foreseen the danger, had done his best, as soon as he arrived in Anatolia, to enlist the cooperation of Kurdish tribal leaders, some of whom he had met during the campaign in 1915–16.

Noel had arrived in Malatya accompanied by members of the Bedirhan family. Another member of the family was the local district officer. News of their arrival was communicated to Kâzım Karabekir in Erzurum, who informed Mustafa Kemal in Sivas. On 7 September a small detachment of Ottoman cavalry was ordered to proceed from Elâziz to Malatya and arrest the Bedirhans. Mustafa Kemal also despatched by car to Malatya a trusted young officer, Lieutenant Recep Zühtü, of the 3rd corps in Sivas, who had already accompanied him to Erzurum, and whom he was to use on special missions in subsequent years. In view of Karabekir's claim that he had earlier dissuaded Mustafa Kemal from sending assassins to get rid of Ali Galip, Recep Zühtü may well have been sent for the same purpose.[138] However, by the time he arrived, the threat of a Kurdish rising had evaporated. Ali Galip had decided that it was too risky to send the Kurds on a raid to Sivas,[139] and had fled to Syria with Noel and the Bedirhans, at the approach of the small force of Ottoman cavalry. In any case, while Ali Galip was loyal to the Istanbul government and was willing to act against Mustafa Kemal, he shared the dislike for Kurdish nationalism felt by most Ottoman officials. His opposition to Kurdish nationalism led later to his acquittal by a Turkish court martial which tried him for his connection with the projected raid on Sivas.[140] He was nevertheless exiled in 1924 and died in Romania.[141]

Ottoman officers on the spot made light of the Ali Galip affair. The commander of the 5th Caucasian division who was sent to the area reported:

> Ali Galip is mad, and I informed corps headquarters right from the start that his crazy venture would fail. It is impossible to bring together Kurds in Malatya and march them to Sivas. Move the Kurds, and within two days they return home with their plunder. If they don't, two or three platoons and a machine-gun are enough to rout hundreds of them. If, on top of this, they hear gunfire, that's the end of the matter. Here … it's the army which is in charge and is trusted by the people and the tribes. Civil officials, with their unsound practices, have no influence over the tribes. Without the army, the civil administration can do nothing.[142]

This judgement was vindicated when the army foiled another attempt to arrest Mustafa Kemal. The Istanbul government had ordered the Ankara governor Muhittin Paşa to proceed to Sivas and assume control of the city. But he was seized by nationalists on the way, at the orders of Ali Fuat, who had earlier been dismissed by the Istanbul government, but was named by the Sivas congress 'commander-in-chief of all national forces in western Anatolia'.[143]

Mustafa Kemal made full use of the Ali Galip affair in his propaganda. What better proof could there be of the government's treachery than this attempt to sow dissension among Muslims by raising Kurdish tribes against Turkish patriots? As he was to say in 1927, it was perfectly clear to him that Sultan Vahdettin and the grand vizier Damat Ferit were both privy to the Ali Galip plot. Yet for tactical reasons he pretended that Damat Ferit was keeping the sovereign in the dark.[144] On 10/11 September he cabled to the interior minister Âdil: 'You are preventing the nation from petitioning the sovereign. Wretches, murderers, traitors! You are plotting with the enemy against the nation ... When you learn the fate of your emissaries, remember that it is the harbinger of your own end.'[145] The following day, Mustafa Kemal informed all commanders and civil governors on behalf of the congress that they were to sever relations with the Istanbul government, as the latter had lost its legitimacy by stopping petitions from reaching the palace and engaging in treacherous activities. Then, without waiting for the response, he declared the congress closed.[146]

It was too much for Kâzım Karabekir in Erzurum. He had not been consulted. The powers conferred by the Erzurum congress had been exceeded. The formal break with Istanbul should have been avoided. The congress should not have been prorogued. Moreover, Mustafa Kemal should not have signed the insulting telegram to interior minister Âdil with his own name, as it had been agreed that all communications should be made on behalf of the Representative Committee. Karabekir sent telegram after telegram of complaint to Mustafa Kemal in Sivas, but once again yielded to Mustafa Kemal's stronger will. On 20 September he cabled to him: 'It is a truth not worth discussing or doubting that the Sivas congress represented the whole nation and that all of its decisions should be obeyed. Our numerous communications related to the shape of the organization ...'[147]

Karabekir was to claim in his memoirs that he had done his best to protect Mustafa Kemal against a growing feeling among the people and army officers that he was creating pretexts for establishing his personal dictatorship:[148] that was probably his own feeling. But Karabekir was content to be the 'Saviour of the East' and was unwilling to challenge Mustafa Kemal for the national leadership. As for Mustafa Kemal, as long as he had his way, he was prepared to mollify Karabekir. 'In view of the immorality prevailing in our country, it is impossible to avoid the gossip of people with evil consciences,' he cabled on 19 September. 'The only response is to march unhesitatingly in unshakeable and outspoken solidarity towards our glorious aim. You are fraternally aware that I prefer to act in full unity with my honourable companions rather than on the strength of my personal convictions alone. However, I am always open to your fraternal views ...'[149]

The pretence that the monarch was not to blame for the government's misdeeds was maintained even after the sultan had issued a proclamation on 20 September stating that he was well aware of the situation in Anatolia and calling on all his subjects to obey the government in the run-up to the elections.[150] That call had no effect. The failure of Ali Galip and Muhittin Paşa allowed nationalist commanders to gain control of the civil administration throughout most of unoccupied

Anatolia. On 24 September, the nationalists arrested the governor of
Trabzon. Two days later, the governor of Konya, Cemal, who was loyal
to the Istanbul government, was forced to flee at the approach of Refet
who had been sent from Sivas to gain the city.[151] On 27 September, as
the Istanbul government was losing the last vestiges of authority in
Anatolia, Mustafa Kemal held a night-long telegraphic conversation
with Abdülkerim Paşa, whom the government had recruited as a go-
between. Abdülkerim was an old friend of Mustafa Kemal from
Salonica. He was an honest soldier who spoke like a dervish. He had
developed a private language with Mustafa Kemal, using, part seriously,
part jocularly, the vocabulary of mystic piety. Mustafa Kemal addressed
him as 'the great presence' (*büyük hazret*); he reciprocated, calling
Mustafa Kemal 'the pole star of guidance' (*kutbü'l-aktap*). His mediation
proved fruitless, however: Mustafa Kemal insisted that Damat Ferit had
to resign immediately.

Only the Allies could now save Damat Ferit, and they failed to do so,
as they wanted to avoid open warfare with Turkish nationalists.
Between 20 and 25 September, British forces were withdrawn from
Merzifon and Samsun in the Black Sea area and from Kütahya in
western Anatolia.[152] The British commander in the important railway
centre of Eskişehir, between Istanbul and Ankara, was instructed that
his sole task was to control the railway and that he was to withdraw if
armed conflict threatened. On 28 September Damat Ferit asked the
Allies permission to send 2,000 troops to Eskişehir. This was refused on
the grounds that such a force could not control the situation and that if
more troops were sent a civil war would follow.[153] Two days later Damat
Ferit resigned. The sultan asked Tevfik Paşa to form the new government. When he refused, the sultan turned to Ali Rıza Paşa, one of
Abdülhamit's generals, who had served unsuccessfully as commander
of the Ottoman western army in the Balkan war, but who, as a soldier,
at least shared a common language with the nationalist commanders in
Anatolia.

Thus, in little more than four months, Mustafa Kemal was able to
procure the fall of a prime minister who had despatched him to
Anatolia. The new government now looked to him as 'commander of
the national forces'.[154] Mustafa Kemal's political tactics had proved successful. But the job of achieving Turkey's independence still remained
to be done.

12

The Birth of Kemalism

———————◆———————

T HE APPOINTMENT OF Ali Rıza Paşa as grand vizier and the decision
to go ahead with parliamentary elections was an important success
for Turkish nationalists. In the capital, Turkish police started pulling
down Greek flags flying over buildings owned by Greeks who were
Ottoman subjects.[1] More seriously, as Turkish nationalists were now in
control of unoccupied Anatolia and represented the main hope of the
Muslims in occupied parts of the country, elections promised to bring
them a majority in parliament. Local Greeks boycotted the elections, as
they had decided to renounce their allegiance to the sultan.

However, Mustafa Kemal saw that the new situation, which he
had helped create, held a danger for the cause of Turkish nationalism
and for his leading position within it. Turkish military commanders
in the provinces had forced a change of government in Istanbul, as
the Young Turks had done in 1908. But the capital was under Allied
occupation, and the freedom of action of the new government was
limited. Moreover, although the inclination of the Ali Rıza cabinet
was broadly nationalist, the tendency to conciliate the Allies had not
been banished. In particular, the new government believed that the
integrity of the Ottoman state could be defended more easily if it
denounced loud and clear the CUP, which had plunged the country into
the Great War, acknowledged war guilt and prosecuted alleged war
criminals. Mustafa Kemal, on the other hand, was opposed to anything
that might split the nationalists, most of whom had supported the CUP.

The first task was to unite them under the umbrella of the newly
created Society for the Defence of National Rights in Anatolia and
Rumelia, and of its Representative Committee, the government-in-

waiting which he controlled. It was not easy. Andrew Ryan, the British dragoman in Istanbul, may have been misled by Mustafa Kemal's propaganda into believing that the congress in Sivas had been 'more numerously attended' than had its predecessor in Erzurum,[2] when in fact it had been a smaller and less representative gathering. But the nationalist resistance in western Anatolia knew better. Mustafa Kemal had promised them a 'general congress', to which they had begun to elect delegates. But he no longer needed it after obtaining the authority of the Sivas congress.

The chairman of the Western Anatolia National Movement Antiannexation Society (*Hareket-i Milliye Redd-i İlhak Cemiyeti*), Hâcim Muhittin, gave way, but with a heavy heart, noting in his diary on 11 October 1919 that 'Mustafa Kemal Paşa's domineering character had been obvious all along.'[3] Nor was it enough to weld the nationalists together. The control exercised by nationalist officers in the provinces was patchy. They had enemies even among Muslims. Muslim society had been used to authoritarian rule; when it weakened, local rivalries surfaced. Politicians in Istanbul, whose career had been shaped by their opposition to the CUP and who now relied on the Allies, could appeal to similarly disposed local leaders.

Both society at large and specific groups within it were split. Some Circassians sided with the nationalists, others were at the beck and call of the sultan's palace. Kurdish tribes were, as usual, hopelessly divided. While religious conservatives feared the return to power of 'infidel Unionists', whom they saw actively engaged in the nationalist cause, many clerics realized that the defence of the faithful could not be left to the mercy of a caliph surrounded by foreign troops. Outside the religious establishment, some dervishes sensed infidelity in the nationalist cause, while others, such as the members of the heterodox Bektaşi fraternity, espoused it as a counterweight to oppression by the sultan's clerics. In small communities, where one family network threw in its lot with the nationalists, its local enemies took the other side.

If resistance to Allied encroachment was to be effective, Mustafa Kemal had to impose some order on a chaotic situation. Yet he had no forces under his direct command. In many places, he had to rely on outlaws. The consequences can be seen from the reminiscences of a young nationalist doctor (Ali Naci Duyduk), who took part in the Erzurum congress as delegate of Giresun. When he returned to his native city, he found that Lame Osman had become master of it.

He was looking for an excuse to pick a quarrel with us. He threatened and insulted me on many occasions. I was the chairman of the Giresun Youth Association. He summoned our members and told them to get rid of me.

When they refused, he closed down the association and destroyed its building ... Educated people among our friends were terrified ... [Lame Osman]
ordered me to move to Erzurum. I had to give way. When a close friend
warned me that I would be murdered on the way, I sought refuge in a French
ship in the harbour and sailed to Istanbul.[4]

Mustafa Kemal stayed on in Sivas, exchanging telegrams with the
new government in Istanbul, with military commanders and with sympathizers. His policy was clear-cut. The 'national forces' under his leadership would support the government if it adopted the programme for
national independence, drawn up at the congresses in Erzurum and
Sivas, if it avoided any decisions on the fate of the country pending the
election of parliament, and if it chose delegates to the peace conference
among people enjoying the nation's confidence, in other words, among
Turkish nationalists.[5] It took a week to reach a qualified agreement on
these points, and on 7 October 1919, Mustafa Kemal lifted the ban
which he had imposed on direct communications with the capital, on
condition that the Representative Committee was allowed to send telegrams to branches of the Society for the Defence of National Rights
throughout the country.[6] On the same day Mustafa Kemal sent yet
another loyal telegram to the sultan, thanking him for dismissing Damat
Ferit and appointing a cabinet which would act in accordance with the
demands of the nation.[7]

But mistrust between Sivas and Istanbul persisted. True, Mustafa
Kemal accepted the new war minister, Cemal Paşa (Mersinli), as an
advisory member of the Representative Committee, and, as such, its
delegate in Istanbul.[8] But while demands for government action were
addressed to Cemal Paşa, requests for confidential information went to
two members of the *Karakol* secret society, Kara Vasıf and Colonel
(Galatalı) Şevket, who, as military commander of the straits, had an
office in the war ministry. Cemal Paşa was too close to the grand vizier,
Ali Rıza, a general loyal to the sultan and, as such, a feeble obstacle to
the policy of accommodation with the Allies, which the palace
favoured. Mustafa Kemal was to say in 1927 that Ali Rıza rightly suspected him of wanting to establish a republic.[9] But the immediate
problem was caused by Mustafa Kemal's determination to keep out
government officials he considered untrustworthy.

As friction continued, the Istanbul government offered to send to
Anatolia the navy minister, Salih Paşa, a general who had not seen active
service in the Great War, for direct negotiations with the Representative
Committee. Mustafa Kemal agreed to meet the minister in Amasya. On

16 October he left Sivas in the company of only two other members of
the Representative Committee, Rauf and Bekir Sami. Three days of
negotiations with Salih Paşa, from 20 to 22 October, ended in a fragile
agreement. Mustafa Kemal insisted that it should be embodied in a
protocol and signed, as the government would then be seen to have
recognized the Representative Committee.

This was done. Mustafa Kemal agreed that every effort should be
made to avoid the election of any candidate implicated in the misdeeds
of the CUP. Otherwise, the elections would be free. In the meantime,
care would be taken to avoid embarrassing the government by interfering with appointments. Salih Paşa agreed in his personal capacity that
the newly elected parliament should meet in Anatolia, as the French
assembly had met in Bordeaux when the Germans occupied Paris in
1870, and as the German assembly had just done in Weimar. When the
newly elected parliament would be seen to function freely, the Society
for the Defence of National Rights would dissolve itself. Two secret
protocols spelled out measures to step up national resistance and fixed
the composition of the Ottoman delegation to the conference where
peace with Turkey would be concluded.[10] Mustafa Kemal had succeeded in establishing himself as an official interlocutor and the
unofficial supervisor of the Istanbul government.

It was a remarkable achievement, given the weakness of his position.
As soon as he left Sivas, a local religious dignitary, Şeyh Recep, claiming
to speak for over 160 Sivas notables, succeeded in sending to the capital
a telegram accusing Mustafa Kemal of acting on behalf of a small group
intent on covering up 'evil deeds', in other words the record of the CUP.
Mustafa Kemal demanded immediate punitive action and was reassured
when the governor of Sivas informed him that the senders of the telegram had been arrested.[11] There was trouble elsewhere in the country.
An armed group tried to take over the town of Adapazarı, east of
Istanbul, saying, 'We do not want Mustafa Kemal on the sultan's
throne.'[12] Agitation against the nationalists had started among
Circassians on the Asian shore of the sea of Marmara. There was also a
rising in Bozkır, south of Konya.

A common complaint was that 'national forces' were exacting forced
contributions from the civil population. This was true, but inevitable, as
nationalist resistance required both money and supplies. But the line
between contributions to the cause and banditry was a fine one, and
it was drawn only when the nationalists established their own organs
of authority in Anatolia. In the capital, the *Nigehban* (Guardian) society
of officers opposed to the CUP had, according to Mustafa Kemal,
joined forces with the Freedom and Concord Party and the Anglophile

Society of Sait Molla to form a common front against the nationalists.[13]

Mustafa Kemal blamed the government for failing to prevent or repress anti-nationalist activity. But while the government was hesitant, local military and civil officials, often prompted by Mustafa Kemal, took action, and opposition to the nationalists was suppressed. Where there were not enough soldiers or gendarmes, help was provided by resistance detachments, some of which were supplied by Circassian or Turkoman tribesmen sympathetic to the nationalists. Mustafa Kemal was beginning to win the civil war within Ottoman society, a war which he had to fight before engaging the foreign enemy. The more dynamic elements in society were on his side. Opposition came from losers, confirming once again Talât Paşa's boast that there were no effective personalities outside the CUP. What is more, in the person of Mustafa Kemal, former members of the CUP now had a clear-sighted leader, who combined prudence with determination.

As soon as he returned to Sivas from Amasya, Mustafa Kemal summoned military commanders to a meeting to discuss policy during and after the elections. His insistence that the newly elected parliament should meet in Anatolia found practically no support. That a sultan fearful for his throne would oppose it was to have been expected. However, not only the government but Mustafa Kemal's closest allies, both in the capital and in the provinces, argued that it would be better to test the Allies' professed respect for democratic institutions by keeping the parliament in Istanbul. Salih Paşa quickly forgot that he had agreed to transfer the session to Anatolia, and remained in the government.

As news of disorder in the country multiplied and as the nationalists' opponents expressed concern about the safe conduct of the elections, the Istanbul government despatched two fact-finding commissions to the provinces. Heading the commission sent to eastern Anatolia was (Mustafa) Fevzi (Çakmak),[14] the patriotic general who had replaced Mustafa Kemal in Gallipoli in 1915, and who had become, first, chief of the general staff and then 1st Army inspector after the Great War. Fevzi arrived in Sivas on 25 November 1919, during the meeting of nationalist commanders and members of the Representative Committee.

Kâzım Karabekir, who had come earlier from Erzurum, claims in his memoirs that, in the course of a two-hour discussion, Fevzi tried to persuade him to abandon Mustafa Kemal. According to Karabekir, Fevzi argued that Mustafa Kemal was a man of dissolute character, whose quest for dictatorial power would cost the country dear, and who was already scheming to get his aides elected to the new parliament. Karabekir replied that he had himself offered the leadership to Mustafa Kemal in Istanbul, as he had found none better, and that he would continue to support him for the sake of national unity as long as the latter did not pursue personal policies. Were Mustafa Kemal to do so, his comrades could easily stop him.[15] Karabekir wrote his memoirs when he was an embittered opponent of Atatürk; he may well have exaggerated both Fevzi's criticism and his own role in making peace between Mustafa Kemal, Fevzi and other critical generals. Moreover Fevzi was the friend and protector of İsmet (İnönü) with whom he later made common cause against Mustafa Kemal's opponents. Karabekir's description of Fevzi should be seen in the light of what was to come. 'I was convinced he was an honourable and zealous man,' he wrote. 'His weakness was that he feared [superior] strength and was too pessimistic. In the conditions of the day I knew that he would do his best to carry out his orders, as he believed that power lay in Istanbul.'[16] Fevzi continued to serve the Istanbul government until the Allied occupation of the capital some four months later. A strict disciplinarian in the Prussian tradition, he then served Mustafa Kemal (and later İnönü) faithfully as chief of the general staff for a record twenty-three years.

The Sivas meeting brought together fourteen nationalist leaders. They deliberated for a fortnight, from 16 to 29 October, and agreed finally that parliament should meet in Istanbul, but that newly elected deputies should be interviewed on their way to the capital and instructed in the aims of the Representative Committee. Commanders would do their best to strengthen the Society for the Defence of National Rights throughout the country and ensure the cooperation of civil authorities. The Representative Committee would move to a locality near Eskişehir on the railway line from Istanbul to Ankara and determine the tactics of its supporters in parliament. If the government and parliament accepted any 'negative' decisions at the peace conference, the Representative Committee would shoulder the task of implementing its own programme – in other words, lead the struggle for the country's independence and integrity.[17] Mustafa Kemal had secured a fall-back position. If, as he expected, parliament failed to bring to victory the nationalist cause in Istanbul, he would be ready to lead it from Anatolia.

The defence of the national territory could not wait on the deliberations of the peace conference. Between 23 October and 1 November, French troops took over from the British the occupation of Maraş, Antep and Urfa in south-eastern Turkey, as they had earlier done in Adana and the rest of Cilicia. They brought with them Armenian detachments and proceeded with the resettlement of Armenians expelled in the Great

War. Intercommunal fighting followed. Mustafa Kemal decided to undertake the organization of Turkish fighters opposed to French and Armenian occupation, but this had to be done discreetly to avoid a direct confrontation between the Turkish nationalist leadership and France. Ali Fuat had brought with him to Sivas a nationalist officer, Emrullahzade Asaf, who had served in the Great War as adjutant to Enver and then to his brother Nuri in the Caucasus. Mustafa Kemal was suspicious of close associates of Enver, but after a while he saw in Asaf the ruthlessness needed in a leader of irregulars, and despatched him to coordinate the resistance bands round Maraş and Antep. He was given the *nom de guerre* of Kılıç Ali (Ali the Sword) and became an unquestioning supporter and confidant of Mustafa Kemal until the end of his life.[18] Two other regular officers were despatched to lead guerrillas against the French in Cilicia.[19]

The French, whose primary concern in the Levant was to establish themselves in Syria, began to have second thoughts about the wisdom of taking on Turkish and Arab nationalists at the same time. The British were making enemies of the Turks, while trying to win over the Arabs by foisting on the French the Hashemite prince Faysal as king in Damascus. As the French struggled to get rid of Faysal, they needed to secure the northern frontier of Syria, and avoid an alliance between Faysal and Turkish nationalists. The Taurus mountains formed Syria's natural northern bulwark, but the land immediately to the south of them was predominantly Turkish, and Turkish nationalists were determined to retain it. Could some accommodation be reached?

Georges Picot, the joint author of the wartime Sykes–Picot agreement on the partition of Ottoman lands in the Near East, met the nationalist commander Refet (Bele) in Konya on 29 September 1919. Picot was at the time French High Commissioner in Syria and Armenia, and was about to hand over in Beirut to his successor General Gouraud, whose area of responsibility was redefined as Syria and Cilicia. In France, the results of the elections held on 16 November presaged the end of the ascendancy of Georges Clemenceau, who had gone along, albeit with misgivings, with Lloyd George's Greek policy. On his way back to Paris, Picot stopped in Sivas and held discussions with Mustafa Kemal between 5 and 7 December.[20] If one discounts the story of Mustafa Kemal's meeting with Count Sforza in Istanbul, it was his first personal contact with an important Allied representative.

Picot referred to the coming government change in France, and said that he had ordered the withdrawal of Armenian units from occupied Turkish territory. France recognized Turkish independence and, in his personal opinion, would be ready to withdraw its troops if its economic interests in Cilicia were secured. In the meantime, he asked that the Turkish nationalists should stop attacking French troops. Mustafa Kemal agreed on condition that the French and Armenians did not attack either, and issued orders to resistance detachments to that effect, while continuing to strengthen their organization. 'Our impression from the discussions,' Mustafa Kemal cabled to Karabekir, 'is that the French see that it is in their interest to favour Turkey in the East.'[21] The truce did not last long, and the French had to be prodded step by step into an agreement with Turkish nationalists, but the wedge between the two principal Allies, Britain and France, was now ready to be driven in.

Mustafa Kemal spent three busy months in Sivas. He was now a civilian, and photographs show him in stiff collar and tie and a morning coat at official meetings, his head covered with a fez, as was the custom of civil officials, or on informal occasions wearing a *kalpak*, the Caucasian or Cossack fur hat, and a thick belted jacket, like a gentleman on a hunting trip. The *kalpak*, which provided protection to riders in the harsh Anatolian weather, gradually became the symbol of the nationalist resistance – it was Asian, Turkish and dashing. Mustafa Kemal took care to look well-dressed. But money was short. The company living in the school which served as the nationalist headquarters joked whether they could afford sugar with their tea.[22] When Kâzım Karabekir arrived from Erzurum, Mustafa Kemal gave him his room on the first floor and moved to the coffee-maker's cubbyhole on the ground floor.[23] Politics was the main subject, but talk easily turned to fancy.

One day as Mustafa Kemal had driven out to the state farm outside Sivas and was waiting for the government's commissioner Fevzi Paşa, he questioned the manager about the economics of farming. If he were to invest one thousand liras in cattle, what would his profit be after a year. 'Fifty liras,' said the manager, 'if we make allowance for depreciation.' 'Not worth it,' replied Mustafa Kemal, 'but what about sheep?' 'That's more profitable, but more risky, as sheep are subject to disease.' Kâzım Karabekir, who was in the party, intervened. 'The Russians have left behind a lot of electrical equipment in Erzurum,' he said. 'Now that you've become a freeman of Erzurum you could take up electrical contracting.' 'There are better openings here in growing sugar beet,' said the farm manager; 'if we had a sugar mill we would have enough feed for milk cows.' 'Let's first finish the work in hand,' said Mustafa Kemal, putting an end to the conversation.[24] But the dream survived. When he became president of the republic, Mustafa Kemal built his farm in the steppe outside Ankara. But, unlike Cincinnatus, he did not retire from public office to devote himself it.

*

Elections went ahead in two rounds, according to Ottoman law. As electoral colleges emerged from the first round, it was clear that nationalist candidates would dominate parliament. But they still had to be organized into an effective party. This could not be done from Sivas, particularly as most members of the Representative Committee had stood as candidates and would be expected in the capital as soon as their election was confirmed. Kâzım Karabekir, who had returned to Erzurum, advocated a Fortress East policy and argued that the Representative Committee should stay put, but he gave way when the Committee decided to move to Eskişehir. Mustafa Kemal was determined to be nearer the capital in order to exert pressure on the government and the politicians in Istanbul from close quarters. Not only opponents but supporters had to be watched, as they were apt to change tack when out of Mustafa Kemal's range. At a last meeting of the Representative Committee in Sivas, Rauf reported that the Allies were stopping traffic on the railway line between Eskişehir and Ankara. It was therefore decided to transfer the headquarters to Ankara,[25] making use of the railway line whenever possible, without relying on it.

There were three cars available for Mustafa Kemal's party. Spare tyres and petrol were obtained from 'Miss', the unnamed headmistress of an American school for Armenian girls. The former governor, Mazhar Müfit, laid siege to the manager of the Sivas branch of the Ottoman Bank, Oskar Schmidt, who stayed away from his office saying he was ill, but was eventually persuaded to lend enough money to cover the party's travel expenses.[26] On 18 December, Mustafa Kemal and his friends set out across the snow-covered Anatolian plateau. It took them two days to cover the 120 miles to Kayseri, where they were received in style by a procession of lantern-carriers. During the two nights he spent in Kayseri, Mustafa Kemal met religious dignitaries and made arrangements to spread the message of the Society for the Defence of National Rights. There was then a detour to visit the tomb of Hacı Bektaş, the founder of the Bektaşi dervish order and the main shrine of Alevis (heterodox Shiites) in Anatolia. The Bektaşis were known for their relaxed interpretation of Islam, and when Mustafa Kemal dined with the head (*Çelebi*) of the order, Cemalettin, *rakı* was drunk freely as the two men reached agreement on the need to defend the country. *Çelebi* Cemalettin announced that he was joining the national resistance movement and promised to order his followers to support it.[27]

The party's next stop was Kırşehir, where Mustafa Kemal made the first of his many speeches to young people. These were students, teachers and other young officials who had formed a local youth association. 'Youth', meaning young people educated in Western learning and having at least high school diplomas, was – and to some extent still remains – a caste in Turkey. It was this caste which Mustafa Kemal, himself a young man of 38, sought to enlist in the cause of national independence and (Western) civilization. His message was that 'enlightened people' had to take the initiative in organizing the nation. The national organization was as yet an empty framework, which educated people had to fill. Mustafa Kemal's message was clear: 'In order to make sure that civilized opportunities open up for us, we must speak as masters of the country.' But first the country had to be made secure. 'We have traced the borders. We shall not surrender them to foreigners. We are totally confident.'[28]

After dinner in the house of the district governor, who was also a founder of the Ankara Society for the Defence of National Rights, Mustafa Kemal addressed a crowd which had assembled outside in the bitterly cold weather. Excited by the welcome, he quoted the well-known couplet of the Ottoman patriotic poet, Namık Kemal, the source of his youthful inspiration:

> The enemy has pressed his dagger to the breast of the motherland.
> Will no one arise to save his mother from her black fate?

He went on, 'Another Kemal has now sprung from the nation's breast', and added:

> Even if the enemy presses his dagger to the breast of the motherland,
> A man will be found to save the mother from her black fate.[29]

Mustafa Kemal was to repeat the verse and his antiphonal response at a meeting of the Grand National Assembly in Ankara. But it was in the poor steppe town of Kırşehir, in the heart of Turkish central Anatolia, where the heterodox beliefs of Turkoman tribesmen had shaped Turkish popular culture, that Kemalism can be said to have been born on 24 December 1919.

Mustafa Kemal arrived in Ankara on 27 December 1919 after a difficult journey. Time after time, the three open cars which carried his party had to be extricated from snow drifts or dragged out of the deep mud into which the road from Kırşehir had dissolved.[30] Having survived the journeys, which had started in Samsun, these German vehicles were to become a familiar sight on the rough roads of the future capital of Turkey, where horses and oxen provided the only means of transport.[31]

News had been sent in advance that the Representative Committee of the Anatolia and Rumelia Society for the Defence of National Rights was on its way to take up residence in Ankara. But of the Committee's nominal membership of sixteen, only four, including Mustafa Kemal, were in the party. In effect, the Committee was Mustafa Kemal and Rauf (Orbay). Soon it was Mustafa Kemal alone.

The convoy stopped on the heights of Dikmen, today an inner suburb of the sprawling town, but in 1919 a wind-swept hilltop from which the walled old town could be seen across a stretch of marshy ground. It was a typical central Anatolian crisp winter day, with the sun shining on snow-capped mountains. A welcoming party was waiting, led by Brigadier Ali Fuat (Cebesoy), still in effective command of the 20th army corps from which he had been dismissed by the Istanbul government, and by the acting governor Yahya Galip (Gargı), representing the civil authority in the absence of the governor, as the nationalists in Ankara had kept out of their town the two officials appointed one after the other by the Istanbul government to fill the post. Ali Fuat's deputy, Lieutenant-Colonel Mahmut, commander of the 24th division, was there too at the head of a detachment of cavalry. The welcoming party included a group of local notables, led by the chief cleric, the *müftü* of Ankara, Rıfat (Börekçi), a staunch nationalist who headed the provincial Committee for the Defence of National Rights.[32]

Ali Fuat and Yahya Galip joined Mustafa Kemal in the front car as the party drove down to the town's outskirts. They passed in front of the unfinished building, designed as a CUP club, where a company of French troops was quartered, and drove on to the main Muslim shrine outside the walls. This was the mosque of Hacı Bayram, the fifteenth-century founder of a dervish order close to the Bektaşis, venerated both by Sunni and Alevi (Shiite) Turks. Prayers were recited at the shrine, which abuts on the ruins of the temple of emperor Augustus. Riders in national costume, dervishes, townspeople, schoolchildren, acclaimed the leaders of the national resistance movement. There were no dissenting voices, as in Sivas: Ankara was solid in supporting the cause championed by Mustafa Kemal. There had been a thriving Armenian community in the town; local Muslims, who had taken over the Armenians' property, did not want to see them back.

Protocol required that there should be a formal welcome in government house. Following this, Mustafa Kemal was driven to the lodgings which had been prepared for him in the farm school, standing on a low hill in open country, on the way to the present-day airport. Ankara had no more than half a dozen modern buildings outside the walls. Inside, the old city, which had once been wealthy on the proceeds of the trade in mohair – the wool of the Angora goat – had sunk into poverty as the expulsion of the Armenians had been followed by a disastrous fire. Amenities were limited to basic lodging houses, coffee and teahouses, and a few badly stocked shops, some of them run by a small community of Sephardic Jews. Narrow, roughly paved streets, lined with dilapidated houses with overhanging eaves, led up to the medieval citadel. The citadel dominated low-lying marshy ground, where malarial mosquitoes bred in profusion. Beyond it, the hillsides were dotted with orchards and summer houses, most of them built originally by Armenian and Greek merchants. Mustafa Kemal, who detested the dirt of tightly packed oriental towns, kept for the rest of his life to the more salubrious open outskirts of Ankara.

On the day after his arrival, Mustafa Kemal addressed a delegation of local notables in the assembly hall of the farm school. It was a long speech. He accused the Allies of breaking the terms of the armistice by occupying the country, defended the historical record of his people, and set out his aim of securing a fully independent state within the 1918 armistice lines which 'encompass the portions of our fatherland inhabited by Turks and Kurds. To the south live our Arabic-speaking co-religionists. But the portions within the lines are an indivisible part of the Ottoman community.' However, independence was not enough. 'I believe that an important patriotic and national duty lies beyond it. We have to reform our domestic condition and prove by our actions that we are capable of becoming an active member of the community of civilized nations.' The precise political arrangements would be determined by national aspirations. In the meantime, the nation would have to exercise control over the government in Istanbul.[33] This he proceeded to do himself, acting as usual on behalf of the nation.

The elections held in the autumn of 1919 had resulted in a triumph of Turkish (and Muslim) nationalists, almost all of whose leaders figured in the list of 168 successful candidates. There had, of course, been pressures on the electors, but these were local, and the elections demonstrated that advocates of Turkish (and Muslim) resistance had the upper hand almost everywhere. Mustafa Kemal was elected member of parliament from Erzurum. But he was determined to stay in Ankara, where, as the Representative Committee had decided, elected deputies were to call on their way to Istanbul in order to concert their tactics. But the government of Ali Rıza Paşa objected that this would give the impression that parliament was manipulated from outside. In any case, most successful candidates preferred to hasten to the capital, and few stopped in Ankara to listen to Mustafa Kemal's advice. He had two immediate aims: to persuade nationalist deputies to form a coherent party under the name of the Group for the Defence of National Rights, and to secure his own election as president of the chamber of deputies. This would give him legal authority to act on behalf of the elected representatives of the people, should the chamber be unable to function freely in the capital.

The Ali Rıza government shared the fear that the Allies might prevent a meeting of the newly elected government in Istanbul. Nationalist guerrillas were active throughout the provinces, and it was an open secret that they were helped by officers of the Ottoman army and armed with weapons which had been kept back from the Allies, contrary to the terms of the armistice. In response to Allied pressure, the new defence minister Cemal Paşa (Mersinli) tried to persuade Mustafa Kemal to agree to the replacement of two commanders active in the resistance movement: Ali Fuat (Cebesoy), whom the Representative Committee had appointed commander of (irregular) national forces, and Colonel Fahrettin (Altay), commander of the 12th corps in Konya, who was supplying arms to the weak Turkish forces facing the Greeks south-east of İzmir.[34] Mustafa Paşa refused, even though another staunch nationalist, Nurettin Paşa, had been nominated to replace Colonel Fahrettin.

On 29 December, the Istanbul government revoked the order cashiering Mustafa Kemal, and returned his decorations, while declaring that he had resigned from the armed forces.[35] Mustafa Kemal was not impressed. Rumours had reached him that Greece was preparing to annex the İzmir area, and on 9 January 1920 he informed Colonel Fahrettin that he was planning to take the field at the head of all Turkish forces in western Anatolia to fight the Greeks.[36]

In fact, it was too early for serious military operations. Mustafa Kemal had established contact with guerrilla bands throughout Anatolia and had persuaded regular units to help them. But the army was still a skeleton – a nucleus of less than 50,000 officers and men which had to be expanded before it could resist an enemy advance. It was at this point that Colonel İsmet (İnönü), who was kicking his heels in Istanbul, decided to see for himself how things stood in Ankara. He left the capital on 8 January, and arriving in Ankara a few days later, was immediately invited by Mustafa Kemal to begin military planning at the farm school.[37]

The first question was whether Turkish national interests could be secured by a revolutionary guerrilla war alone. İsmet was against it. He believed that war with Greece was inevitable and that the Greek army could only be stopped by a regular Turkish army. The immediate task was, therefore, to build up the strength of Turkish regular army units. Mustafa Kemal agreed.[38] On 1 December 1919, when Colonel (Galatalı) Şevket, a member of the *Karakol* secret nationalist society in Istanbul, informed him that Turks in Bulgarian Thrace (in the district of Kardzhali/Kırcaali) were planning a rising, he replied, 'One cannot achieve stable results through a revolution.'[39]

Guerrilla activities caused problems not only with the Istanbul government, but also with the *Karakol* society in Istanbul, which Mustafa Kemal sought to subordinate to his Representative Committee. Turkish and Greek bands were operating on the Asian outskirts of Istanbul, between the capital and İzmit. Both the Istanbul government and *Karakol* decided that one of the Turkish guerrilla leaders, Yahya Kaptan, a former member of Enver's Special Organization, was a dangerous bandit who was harming the national cause. Troops were sent by sea to capture him: he surrendered and was killed. Mustafa Kemal was outraged; Yahya Kaptan had placed himself under his orders. He alone, acting of course in the name of the Representative Committee, could withdraw the licence of guerrillas.[40] Guerrilla activity was a necessary temporary expedient, which had to be exercised under his authority.

In the first week of January 1919, Rauf (Orbay), the second most senior nationalist leader in Ankara, left for Istanbul to take his seat in parliament.[41] The session of what was to prove the last Ottoman parliament was opened on 12 January in the presence of only seventy-two deputies. The speech from the throne, read by the interior minister Damat Şerif Paşa, a member of the dynasty by marriage, deplored the Greek occupation of İzmir and made a plea for national unity in the search for a just peace.[42] Parliament then recessed for ten days.

The following day, 13 January, the last great popular demonstration in occupied Istanbul took place in the square in front of Sultan Ahmet (the Blue Mosque). Three Turkish nationalist speakers addressed a crowd of 150,000 people and demanded that the country, including western Thrace (which the Ottoman state had given up in 1914) and southern and eastern Anatolia, should remain Ottoman and Turkish.[43] The fact that fourteen months after the end of the war, the Allies had not made up their minds on the fate of Turkey, gave rise to unrealistic expectations. The hope that Turkish popular clamour, accompanied on the one hand by guerrilla activity, and on the other by a policy of courting the Allies, would ensure the independence and integrity of Turkish lands, stood in the way of Mustafa Kemal's plans. He was convinced that the Allies would be impressed only by Turkish firmness, backed up by force. Concessions were worse than futile: they were dangerous.

The determination of the new Ottoman government was tested even before parliament had a chance to vote it in. The Allies were unhappy with the choice of Cemal Paşa (Mersinli) as war minister and of Cevat Paşa (Çobanlı) as chief of the general staff, suspecting rightly that both were promoting cooperation between the Ottoman war ministry and nationalist commanders in Anatolia. On 20 January they demanded that the two generals should be replaced within forty-eight hours.[44] The following day, Cemal Paşa informed Mustafa Kemal that, while the cabinet had decided to reject the ultimatum, he and Cevat Paşa had agreed to resign. Mustafa Kemal was incensed. In successive telegrams to Cemal Paşa, to the grand vizier Ali Rıza Paşa and to nationalist parliamentarians, he argued that to accept the ultimatum would be tantamount to conceding sovereignty to foreigners. It would be preferable to force the British to remove the Ottoman government as a whole.[45]

Nevertheless, the two generals submitted their resignations in the evening of 21 January. On the following day, probably before he had learnt the news, Mustafa Kemal asked commanders in Erzurum, Konya and Sivas to get ready to arrest British control officers in their areas, should the British in Istanbul arrest Ottoman ministers and deputies, and particularly Rauf (Orbay).[46] But the game between the British and Turkish nationalists in Istanbul had not yet been played out, and on 25 January Mustafa Kemal informed corps commanders in Anatolia that the resignation of the two generals would be taken up by elected parliamentarians, and that the Representative Committee would not intervene in the matter.[47]

However, events did not wait on the deliberations of the Ottoman parliament. Turks were under pressure from Greeks in the west, and from Armenians, protected by French troops, in the south. On 21 January, the Turks in Maraş, in eastern Cilicia, rose against the French and their Armenian protégés, who were cut off by guerrillas operating in the countryside. Mustafa Kemal decided that guerrilla warfare should be stepped up. The French were the first target, perhaps because earlier contacts had suggested that military pressure could persuade them to come to an acceptable accommodation with Turkish nationalists. An attempt was made – probably more for propaganda purposes than in any hope of effective action – to concert operations with Arabs resisting the French in Syria.[48] More seriously, regular troops were ordered to help guerrillas both in Maraş and in Urfa, further south. Near the capital, a group of guerrillas crossed the sea of Marmara in the night of 26/27 January, and emptied the arms depot at Akbaş, on the Gallipoli peninsula, after overpowering French sentries.[49] Mustafa Kemal attributed the initiative for this daring raid to his friend from Macedonia,

Colonel Kâzım (Özalp), commander of the 61st division at Balıkesir, south of the sea of Marmara.[50] On 8 February, Turkish nationalist forces, led by the local gendarmerie commander, entered the town of Urfa, which had been occupied by the French.

Relations between the Allies and Turkish nationalists in Istanbul were nearing breaking point. But Mustafa Kemal was not in control of the nationalists in the capital. His hope of being elected president of the chamber was disappointed on 31 January when another candidate, Reşat Hikmet (who had won fame by being briefly detained by the French), was chosen. When Reşat Hikmet died shortly afterwards, the presidency went to Celalettin Arif, a nationalist, but not a member of Mustafa Kemal's circle. On 3 February, Fevzi Paşa (Çakmak), a nationalist general senior to Mustafa Kemal, was appointed war minister. Other ministerial changes followed, and the reshuffled cabinet was overwhelmingly endorsed by parliament on 9 February. A few days earlier, the nationalist majority in parliament finally organized itself as a party. But instead of adopting the name of the Society for the Defence of National Rights, which Mustafa Kemal was fashioning as his political vehicle, the parliamentarians called themselves 'Alliance for the Well-being of the Fatherland' (*Felâh-ı Vatan İttifakı*)', taking their name from a phrase used in the speech from the throne. Mustafa Kemal was to make fun of the name, calling the parliamentarians 'the fellahs of the fatherland'.[51]

As leading nationalists gathered in Istanbul, Mustafa Kemal was in danger of becoming isolated in Ankara. When Fevzi Paşa became war minister, he summoned Colonel İsmet back to the capital. İsmet complied. He travelled in the company of Mazhar Müfit (Kansu), the comptroller of Mustafa Kemal's headquarters, who had been asked by Rauf to take up his seat as member of parliament for Hakkâri, a mountainous region inhabited by Kurds. Of the nationalist leaders, only Ali Fuat (Cebesoy) remained in Ankara. The departure of intellectual and social equals was accompanied by the growth of a personal staff of young officers ready to do Mustafa Kemal's bidding. Recep Zühtü (Soyak), whom Mustafa Kemal had used on special missions in the east, was put in charge of a new paper, *Hakimiyet-i Milliye* (National Sovereignty), launched on 10 January, as the organ of the Society for the Defence of National Rights.[52] Another young officer, Major Recep (Peker), newly graduated from the Staff College in Istanbul, made his way to Ankara in February,[53] and soon impressed Mustafa Kemal with his organizing ability. Short and bullet-headed, Recep relished his role as Mustafa Kemal's enforcer. A childhood friend, Salih (Bozok), was summoned from Istanbul and put to work in the headquarters at the farm school.[54]

Mazhar Müfit was replaced as comptroller by another friend from the War College, Lieutenant-Colonel Arif,[55] a brave and headstrong officer whom Mustafa Kemal used as a troubleshooter. Arif had a will of his own. The others did as they were told.

As Ankara waited, the government in Istanbul continued its attempts to square the circle, and please both the Allies and the nationalists. On 14 February it asked provincial authorities to punish any interference in the administration. The threat was clearly directed against local Societies for the Defence of National Rights. Mustafa Kemal countered it with a circular on 17 February saying that the Society was more necessary than ever and that it should step up its activities everywhere.[56] On the same day parliament adopted unanimously a National Pact (*misak-ı millî*), which added to the demands included in the text approved by the congress in Sivas.

The Pact demanded that the inhabitants of the Arab countries, of the districts lost to Russia in eastern Anatolia in 1878 and of western Thrace should be allowed to determine their own future. Where the Sivas text claimed only the lands within the 1918 armistice lines, the parliamentarians in Istanbul added the words 'and outside'. The Sivas document welcomed the help of well-disposed foreign states. In Istanbul, the matter was put negatively: the country would not tolerate any infringement of its independence.[57] As had happened before and would happen again in Turkish history, a more or less free parliament opened the way to competition in nationalist rhetoric. While Mustafa Kemal concentrated on practical objectives and knew where to cut his country's losses, parliamentarians repeated Damat Ferit's mistake at the Paris peace conference and succeeded only in exasperating the Allies. But the Istanbul text did include one significant, although inconspicuous, novelty: the word 'Turkey' occurs for the first time in the phrase 'the peace treaty with Turkey' (article 3). Foreigners had long called the country 'Turkey'; Turks were beginning to follow suit.

The Allies had an opportunity to reverse their policy. In October they received the report of the commission, chaired by the US representative in Istanbul, Admiral Bristol, set up to enquire into the bloodshed which followed the Greek occupation of İzmir. The commission reported that Greeks should not be left alone in occupation of the area, unless it was proposed to annex it to Greece, but that such an annexation would be contrary to the principle of 'respect for nationalities'. Moreover, Turkish national sentiment 'will never accept this annexation. It will submit only to force, that is to say, before a military expedition which

Greece alone could not carry out with any chance of success.'[58] The British commander, General Milne, backed this conclusion, reporting that guerrilla activity would continue as long as Greek troops remained, and that any further Greek advance would only add to the difficulties.[59] On both sides, soldiers were consistently more realistic than politicians.

The Allies did not change course. They bickered, adjusted their plans, but plunged deeper into the mess. At a meeting which started in London on 12 February they decided to leave Istanbul to the Turks, but to assign the İzmir zone to the Greeks under nominal Ottoman sovereignty. The new French prime minister, the radical-socialist Alexandre Millerand, who had replaced Clemenceau, spoke in favour of Greek withdrawal from İzmir, but he was overruled by Lloyd George,[60] spellbound as ever by Venizelos. Anti-Turkish feeling intensified when the conference heard that the French had been forced out of Maraş (on 11–12 February) and that most of the Armenians who had returned to the area had perished.[61] This prompted the British government to advocate a fatal step. If the Allies could not control Anatolia, they could at least extend their control in Istanbul, and force the Ottoman government to do their bidding. Once Istanbul was firmly under control it would be easier to impose a harsh peace settlement. However, it was not easy to achieve Allied agreement on the occupation of Istanbul. Discussions went on for almost a month. In the meantime, Anatolia was threatened with a breakdown of authority, as nationalists in Ankara and in Istanbul, the government, the palace and the Allies all pulled in different directions.

On 16 February an anti-nationalist Circassian officer, Anzavur Ahmet, whose band had earlier been routed by the nationalist Circassian, Ethem, went into action again – this time against the nationalists who had carried off the arms and ammunition stored at Akbaş. The leader of the Akbaş raid was killed and the arms destroyed. On 3 March, the grand vizier Ali Rıza Paşa resigned. The Allies had demanded that he should ensure the withdrawal to a distance of three kilometres of Turkish nationalist forces facing the Greeks round İzmir. Ali Rıza was unable to deliver this: resignation was an admission of impotence. Nationalists feared that this would open the way to the return to power of their enemy Damat Ferit Paşa. As a result of Mustafa Kemal's efforts, the palace was bombarded with telegrams from all over the country warning against the formation of a government ready to sacrifice national interests. To avoid a confrontation, the sultan appointed as grand vizier Salih Paşa, who had reached an accord with Mustafa Kemal in Amasya the previous year. Fevzi Paşa, whose patriotic credentials were not in doubt, was retained as war minister. It was a shrewd move which kept the nationalists divided. However, British policy came to Mustafa Kemal's rescue.

On 10 March the British secured Allied approval for the plan to take action against Turkish nationalists in Istanbul. The following day the Italians leaked the news to Rauf (Orbay) in Istanbul, advising him and other leading nationalists to leave the capital. Rauf informed Mustafa Kemal, saying that the leak might be a plot to get rid of the nationalists and bring in Damat Ferit. He therefore intended to stay on in Istanbul and work for the defeat of the 'colourless' cabinet of Salih Paşa.[62]

Mustafa Kemal was already aware that the British would strike in Istanbul: the commander of the French detachment in Ankara had told him that the British contingent occupying the railway station was preparing to leave and that train traffic to Ankara would then be stopped. He agreed with Rauf that parliament should remain in session in order to protest at the British action, but he advised Rauf and his closest collaborators to join him in Ankara. They would be needed if a government were to be formed there.[63] Rauf refused, arguing that flight might anger remaining members of parliament and make it difficult for the session to be transferred to Ankara.[64] In his six-day speech, delivered after his break with Rauf, Mustafa Kemal suggested – using the time-honoured formula 'far be it from me to suggest' – that Rauf and his companions might have preferred imprisonment at the hands of the British in Malta to the dangers of resistance in Anatolia.[65] This was unfair. Rauf was a brave and honourable man. But he was not ready to break with the inchoate nationalist majority in parliament, which was as yet unwilling to abandon the capital and, with it, all hope in the sultan. However, the speaker of parliament, Celalettin Arif, did escape on 15 March and made his way to Ankara.

In the night of 15/16 March British troops began to occupy key buildings and arrest Turkish nationalists. It was a messy operation. There was a clash in a building in the old city used jointly as headquarters of the Ottoman 10th Caucasian division and by the military music school: five Turkish soldiers were killed when troops of the British Indian army stormed the building. But the commander of the division, Lieutenant-Colonel Kemalettin Sami, escaped and made his way to Anatolia where he served with distinction in the nationalist forces.[66] Rauf (Orbay) reacted with characteristic constitutional propriety: he went to the palace. He claims to have urged the sultan not to sign any international agreement without first obtaining the approval of parliament. Vahdettin is said to have replied: 'The nation are a flock of sheep. I am the shepherd.'

Rauf then went on to the chamber. The building was on the shore of
the Bosphorus, and it was easy to escape from it by boat. But Rauf
refused to do so; both he and Kara Vasıf, the leader of the *Karakol*
society, surrendered when a British detachment arrived to arrest them.
In all, eighteen Turkish nationalists were arrested and deported to Malta
– among them the former war minister Cemal Paşa (Mersinli), his chief
of staff Cevat Paşa (Çobanlı), and a group of journalists[67] (one of the
latter, the American-trained Ahmet Emin (Yalman), was to become
Turkey's leading liberal editor). In Ankara, Mustafa Kemal was kept
informed of the progress of the operation by a patriotic telegraphist,
Hamdi from Manastır in Macedonia. He too was to make his way to
Ankara to serve in the nationalist headquarters.

Mustafa Kemal was ready for the British move. First he sent a telegram to all military units and nationalist organizations, urging that the
safety of non-Muslims – who could easily have become the target of
Turkish indignation – should be assured; a second telegram asked that
misleading declarations from the capital should be disregarded. He sent
protests to foreign powers and asked his supporters to organize protest
rallies throughout the country. Most important of all was a proclamation to the nation in which he declared that the forcible occupation of
Istanbul had put an end to the 700-year-old Ottoman state. 'Today the
Turkish nation is called to defend its capacity for civilization, its right to
life and independence – its entire future.'[68]

By discrediting the Ottoman government and putting out of action a
rival nationalist organization in the capital, the British had removed the
main obstacle to Mustafa Kemal's designs. They had also given hos-
tages: in retaliation for the arrest of Turkish nationalists in Istanbul,
Mustafa Kemal ordered the detention of British officers in Anatolia.
The chief hostage was Major (later Colonel) Rawlinson in Erzurum.
British troops guarding the railway lines removed themselves in time, as
Turkish nationalists proceeded to destroy key bridges and tunnels.[69]

On 18 March, the chamber met for the last time in Istanbul. It sent a
protest to the parliaments of the Allied countries, deploring the violation of the immunity of its members, five of whom had been arrested.
It then decided unanimously to adjourn indefinitely.[70] The following
day, Mustafa Kemal sent a circular to all civil governors and military
commanders, asking them to proceed with the election of 'an assembly
endowed with extraordinary powers to manage and control the affairs
of the nation'. Every district was to elect five representatives. Deputies
who managed to make their way from Istanbul would join the assembly.[71] In the end, eighty-four members of the last Ottoman chamber
were to take their seat in the assembly in Ankara.[72]

Nationalists who were not immediately rounded up decided that the time had come to flee the capital. One of the fugitives was the woman writer and fiery nationalist orator Halide Edip (Adıvar); another was Colonel İsmet (İnönü), who left Istanbul secretly on 20 March in response to a summons by Mustafa Kemal. They all made their way by land through bandit-infested country, where a civil war was in progress between the supporters of the sultan and those of Mustafa Kemal. A group of nationalists, including Mustafa Kemal's early supporter Mazhar Müfit (Kansu), left more comfortably by sea. They were given false French passports by French agents and taken to General Gouraud, the French High Commissioner in Syria. Gouraud discussed with them terms for an agreement with Turkish nationalists and sent them to Ankara to report to Mustafa Kemal, who was not blind to the advantages offered by Allied disunity.[73]

However, one obstacle remained to the consolidation of Turkish nationalist resistance under the leadership of Mustafa Kemal. Salih Paşa, who had burst into tears when asked to become grand vizier,[74] was still in office, and his war minister Fevzi Paşa (Çakmak) was still attempting to persuade commanders in Anatolia to remain loyal to the sultan's government. The attitude of Colonel Fahrettin, commander of the 12th corps in Konya, was critical, and for the present he seemed to be siding with Istanbul. Mustafa Kemal sent Refet (Bele) to persuade him to change his mind, if he could, or arrest him, if he could not. On 3 April, Fahrettin arrived at the railway station of Sarayönü, north of Konya, where he was put on board the train to Ankara 'with every sign of respect, but in fact under guard'.[75] By the time he arrived, the situation in Istanbul had changed.

Faced with an Allied demand to disavow the nationalists, Salih Paşa resigned on 2 April. The sultan decided to replace him with Damat Ferit, the arch-enemy of the nationalists. When the deputy speaker of parliament objected that it was a disastrous choice, Vahdettin replied: 'If I wanted, I could give the office of grand vizier to the Greek or the Armenian Patriarch, or to the Chief Rabbi.' 'You could indeed,' responded the deputy speaker, 'but it would serve no useful purpose.'[76] On 5 April Damat Ferit formed his fourth cabinet: Fevzi Paşa lost the war ministry. On the same day, Colonel Fahrettin returned to Konya and called on his officers to place themselves under Mustafa Kemal's orders.[77] He was then confirmed in the command of his army corps. The dividing line had finally become clear. Mustafa Kemal had no longer any serious rivals in the leadership of the Turkish nationalist resistance.

13

An Embattled Leader

MUSTAFA KEMAL HAD a quality rare among his compatriots. He was
a superb organizer, with a clear grasp of priorities. The nationalists who flocked to Ankara in March and April 1920 found a leader who
knew his way through the chaos let loose by Allied occupation and
intervention. There were two immediate requirements: the first was
military – to keep control of as much territory as possible; the second
political – to create a centre of effective, legitimate authority. Mustafa
Kemal saw to both needs. His headquarters in the farm school had what
amounted to a military and a political office. Through his military secretary, Hayatî, he kept in touch with local commanders of nationalist
forces – both regular units and guerrillas. A political secretary, Recep
(Peker), pushed forward preparations for the election of a National
Assembly.

Theoretically a civilian, Mustafa Kemal wore the costume of a
country gentleman on a hunting trip – breeches and a hacking jacket.
He worked far into the night, taking decisions, dictating telegrams,
receiving visitors.[1] The atmosphere was free and easy. Important fugitives from Istanbul, who had been assigned beds in the dormitory of
the Ankara teacher training college, dropped in for news or chats with
the leader and his companions. Simple set meals were served in the
refectory of the farm school. In between, Mustafa Kemal drank endless
cups of Turkish coffee and chain-smoked. Writing in embittered exile in
France, Rıza Nur, one of the nationalist deputies who joined Mustafa
Kemal in Ankara, accused him of drinking to excess.[2] He could not
have done so and worked as effectively as he did. His military doctor,
Refik (Saydam), was in constant attendance, as Mustafa Kemal was

subject to recurrent attacks of fever, almost certainly a symptom of malaria, which was endemic in the country.

As ever, Mustafa Kemal knew the value of publicity. On 6 April, a room in the farm school became the first office of the Anatolian Agency, the press agency of Turkish nationalists, which trumpeted the successes of the resistance and the failures of its enemies, and combed the foreign press for encouraging reports. Mustafa Kemal's chief publicists were two refugees from Istanbul – Halide Edip and Yunus Nadi, the latter a journalist who became editor of the nationalist newspaper *Yenigün* (The New Day). Typically, Mustafa Kemal began by checking the output of his press agency to ensure that it served his policy. Once he was satisfied, he let his journalists get on with the job.[3] Again, unlike most of his compatriots, he knew how to delegate.

In Istanbul, the sultan and his grand vizier, Damat Ferit Paşa, hastened to disavow the nationalists, as the Allies had demanded. On 11 April, the Ottoman chamber of deputies, which had already adjourned its session, was officially dissolved by the sultan. On the same day, the Şeyhülislâm, as chief cleric of the Ottoman state, published a decree of outlawry in the form of a canonical decision (*fetva*), declaring that the nationalist forces were infidels, and that it was incumbent on believers to kill them. Five days later, this was answered by a contrary *fetva*, drawn up by the nationalist *müftü* of Ankara, Rıfat (Börekçi), and signed by 250 of his colleagues throughout Anatolia.[4] It declared that the caliph was the prisoner of infidels, that it was the duty of the faithful to save him and his dominions, and that *fetvas* issued at the behest of enemy states lacked validity.[5]

Damat Ferit's *fetva* was followed by risings among Circassians and Abkhazes in north-western Anatolia. Anzavur, Mustafa Kemal's chief enemy among the Circassians, swung north from his home territory south of the sea of Marmara. His band and like-minded local people chased out nationalist officials from towns as far east as Bolu, half-way between Istanbul and Ankara, and Beypazarı, lying even nearer Ankara, further south. On 18 April, the Istanbul government issued a decree establishing Disciplinary Forces (*Kuva-yı İnzıbatiye*) to fight the nationalists. On 22 April, Colonel Mahmut, commander of the 24th division and Ali Fuat's deputy in the 20th corps, was ambushed and killed by Circassians west of Bolu. But the rebels, as Ankara called the Circassians loyal to the palace, were too disorganized to build on their successes, particularly since Ankara could rely on its own Circassian supporters, led by Ethem and his brothers. Their cavalry column, which was given the name of Mobile Forces (*Kuva-yı Seyyare*), soon became the most formidable of all the units of irregulars serving Mustafa Kemal.

While rebel Circassians were kept at bay in the west, nationalist organizations throughout the country designated their delegates to the assembly which Mustafa Kemal had summoned in Ankara. Over 300 delegates were elected, Mustafa Kemal emerging this time as deputy for Ankara. However, not all of them could or even wanted to travel to Ankara in time for the opening on 23 April, and only 120 answered the roll call on 24 April.[6] They included deputies originally elected to the last Ottoman parliament in Istanbul. Mustafa Kemal's insistence on the formation of a national assembly was inspired by the example of the French Revolution, an inspiration he shared with many Ottoman modernizers. But other considerations played a part. He needed a better title than that of spokesman of a shadowy executive of the Society for the Defence of National Rights, which had been registered as a private association. More importantly, he had to mobilize the Muslim people of Anatolia in defence of their territory. Leaders of local society – whether government officials, professionals, landowners or clerics – were the best people to do it.

In his first speech in Ankara, he said that while one had to work from the roots upwards to build a solid organization, at the start one had no choice but to work from the top downwards, since until individuals had learnt to think for themselves, masses could be manipulated.[7] The social composition of the assembly reflected this need. Nearly half the deputies were civil or military officials, one fifth professionals (mainly lawyers), another fifth self-employed (merchants and landowners), and one in six, clerics.[8] Culturally, the members were divided between modernizers (mainly officials and professionals) and conservatives (clerics and local notables). Socially, they were, by the standards of Turkish society, predominantly middle class. The Grand National Assembly – a name chosen to emphasize its comprehensive character – had its Jacobins, but it was not a radical body.

The sultan and Damat Ferit tried to mobilize Islamic feeling against the nationalists, by presenting them as Bolsheviks or at least 'Godless Unionists' – the residue of the 'masonic' CUP. Anzavur called his band 'Muhammad's forces' (*Kuva-yı Ahmediye* and then *Muhammediye*); Damat Ferit's Disciplinary Forces were also known as the Army of the Caliphate (*Hilâfet Ordusu*). Mustafa Kemal decided to trump the religious card. A circular which he sent on 21 April described the religious ceremonies which would precede the opening of the assembly: the Koran and portions of the compendium of the Prophet's tradition would be recited, sheep would be sacrificed, a hair from the Prophet's beard and his reputed standard would be borne in procession, prayers would be offered for the safety of the sultan and caliph, his realm and people. Mustafa Kemal demanded that similar ceremonies should be organized throughout the country, with special prayers and sermons explaining the patriotic duties of the new assembly.[9]

The opening ceremony took place as planned on 23 April, a Friday, chosen specially as the day of Muslim congregational worship. Mustafa Kemal and such deputies as could make it in time assembled at the Hacı Bayram mosque. After prayers, a procession was formed, led by a cleric carrying a Koran on a lectern, while another man held above his head what purported to be a hair from the Prophet's beard.[10] As a crowd of onlookers shouted '*Allahuekber*' (God is great), the deputies and accompanying officials walked to the CUP club building, which the French had vacated and which was chosen as the meeting place of the assembly. The building had been made ready in great haste. To complete the roof, tiles were taken from a primary school under construction;[11] to seat the deputies, desks were borrowed from the local high school. The procession stopped in front of the building, where more prayers were recited and sheep sacrificed. The deputies then moved inside for the formal opening. Real business began the following day.

Mustafa Kemal made a long speech recapitulating events since the conclusion of the armistice in 1918. The struggle against foreign domination had been led by the Representative Committee of the Society for the Defence of National Rights. The time had now come to transfer the leadership to the National Assembly. The latter could not content itself with being a legislature; it had to act as the executive as well. Mustafa Kemal proposed that the assembly should designate those of its own members whom it wished to exercise executive functions. It was, he said, a basic Islamic principle to grant the greatest authority to the united mass of believers.[12] The term for the latter was *cumhur*, from which Ottoman lexicographers had coined the word *cumhuriyet* to designate the republic established in France after the revolution. Mustafa Kemal was to say later that the form of government which he proposed to the assembly was in fact a republic, although he could not say so at the time.[13]

But the principle of an assembly, exercising both legislative and executive powers, had also found a contemporary expression in Russian *soviets*. And the term which he proposed to designate ministers, *vekil*, whose literal meaning was deputy or representative, was translated into French as *commissaire*, commissioner or commissar.[14] The title of the government of the Grand National Assembly (Committee of Executive

Commissioners: *İcra Vekilleri Heyeti* or *Heyet-i Vekile*) bore an unmistakable similarity to the Committee of Executive Commissars (*Ispolkom* for short), as the Soviet government called itself. But more important than the nomenclature, was the proposal that the president of the assembly should also head the executive, in other words that he should be speaker of parliament and executive president at the same time. Mustafa Kemal's loyal lieutenant, Recep (Peker), was made administrative secretary of the assembly. A tough disciplinarian, he served his master well.

On the same day, 24 April 1920, Mustafa Kemal was elected president of the assembly. There was opposition. Celalettin Arif claimed the presidency as the speaker of the last Ottoman chamber of deputies. But, as Mustafa Kemal was to say later, opposition was overcome when he explained that objections to his person were used as a weapon by the Istanbul government and the country's enemies.[15] In Ankara, where he was the host, he grasped the prize which had been denied to him in Istanbul. His brief acceptance speech ended with the prayer that 'our master the sultan ... should reign for ever, free from foreign bonds'.[16] Mustafa Kemal hastened to announce his election in a cable to Kâzım Karabekir in Erzurum, the most powerful nationalist commander in Anatolia. He had begged the assembly not to give him any office, he wrote, lest propaganda attacks against his person harm the national cause. But he could not refuse when 110 votes out of 120 were cast for him. Karabekir responded with a two-line message of congratulations.[17]

The following day, Mustafa Kemal issued his first proclamation to the nation as president of the Grand National Assembly. 'We, your deputies, swear in the name of God and the Prophet,' he declared, 'that the claim that we are rebels against the sultan and caliph is a lie. All we want is to save our country from sharing the fate of India and Egypt.'[18]

A day later, Mustafa Kemal sent a businesslike telegram to the government in Moscow. It opened with these words: 'We agree to cooperate with Russian Bolsheviks in their efforts to save the oppressed from imperialist governments.' If the Bolsheviks moved against Georgia to incorporate it into their state and remove British forces from it, Turkey would undertake to take action against 'the imperialist Armenian government' and to ensure that Azerbaijan became a member of the Bolshevik 'group of states'. In the meantime, Mustafa Kemal requested that the Bolsheviks should send 'a first instalment of five million gold [roubles]' as well as ammunition, equipment and sanitary supplies.[19] It was the beginning of a long process of bargaining.

On 27 April it was the sultan's turn to receive a telegram from Mustafa Kemal. He pledged the assembly's loyalty, as its president. 'We are gathered round your throne, to which we are attached more than ever,' he assured the sovereign.[20] The addressee was Sultan Vahdettin, but the intended audience were the conservative Muslim people of Anatolia. In the memoirs which she wrote in exile, Halide Edip was to describe Mustafa Kemal as an amoral cynic;[21] it would be more accurate to say that he believed that all was fair in war. Moreover, as leader of a people who lived in a different cultural universe, he could not but experience a sense of detachment.

It took the assembly a week to form a government on the lines proposed by Mustafa Kemal. Before it did so he found another staunch supporter. Fevzi Paşa (Çakmak) who, as minister of war in the Salih Paşa government, had tried to win over the nationalist commanders in Anatolia for the sultan's cause, fled from the capital when Damat Ferit came to power. On 25/26 April Mustafa Kemal was informed that Fevzi had suddenly turned up at Ali Fuat Paşa's headquarters in Osmaneli (then known as Lefke), east of İznik (Nicaea). Ali Fuat (Cebesoy) claims in his memoirs that Mustafa Kemal cabled back, 'Send him where he's come from', but that he was then persuaded to turn a cold rejection into a warm welcome.[22] The story is suspect. It is true that Mustafa Kemal owed no favours to Fevzi, but the latter was known as a capable patriotic commander who enjoyed the respect of the officer corps. Mustafa Kemal did not need Ali Fuat's prompting to make the most of Fevzi's ability and prestige. As for Ali Fuat, by the time he wrote his memoirs he had good reason to be jealous of Fevzi, a latecomer whom Mustafa Kemal pushed to the front at the expense of his original companions.

Fevzi was enthusiastically received in Ankara on 27 April. At Mustafa Kemal's suggestion, the deputies suspended their deliberations and went to the railway station to welcome the newcomer. Again at Mustafa Kemal's suggestion, Fevzi was given the credentials of a deputy and was immediately elected to the provisional executive, which preceded the formation of the government. His first service was to assure the assembly that he had been received by the sultan before Damat Ferit's accession to power, and that the sovereign had implored him to establish contact with the nationalists in Anatolia.[23] It was a confirmation of the convenient myth that the assembly was the true interpreter of the sultan's wishes. But the myth could not stop the spread of civil strife.

On 29 April the Grand National Assembly voted a draconian law of high treason, prescribing the death penalty for anyone who challenged its legitimacy.[24] On 1 May, the Istanbul government responded by sentencing to death Mustafa Kemal and a number of his supporters, including Ali Fuat, Halide Edip and her husband Adnan (Adıvar).[25]

This did not stop the assembly in Ankara from approving the form of government proposed by Mustafa Kemal. The executive was elected on 3–4 May and consisted of ten ministers or commissioners under the chairmanship of Mustafa Kemal. All were deputies. Fevzi Paşa (Çakmak) became war minister, while Colonel İsmet (İnönü) was elected chief of the general staff with a seat in the cabinet.[26] Mustafa Kemal's original companions, Kâzım Karabekir, Ali Fuat (Cebesoy) and Refet (Bele), retained their field commands but were subordinated to the two newcomers: Fevzi and İsmet. They did not relish the change. Nevertheless, they did their best to advance the nationalist cause. The first task was to win the civil war, which had broken out spontaneously when central authority disintegrated, but whose flames Damat Ferit was now fanning.

The new Ankara government first turned its attention to the threat which faced it in north-western Anatolia. Regular army detachments under the command of Ali Fuat (Cebesoy) and Refet (Bele), guerrillas led by Mustafa Kemal's companion Lieutenant-Colonel Arif, including men of his own Karakeçili tribe, and, above all, the column of the pro-nationalist Circassian Ethem, went into action against Anzavur's Circassians and Abkhazes. During the expedition, Arif was presented by villagers with a bear cub from the forests of Bolu. It became his inseparable companion and earned him the nickname Arif the Bear-keeper (*ayıcı*). By 21 May Anzavur had had enough. In the last clash on that day, he fell from his horse and injured his leg. He thereupon decided to return to Istanbul, complaining to Damat Ferit that he had not received sufficient support from the sultan's government.

The sultan's Disciplinary Forces of some 4,000 men were the next target. Having massed near İzmit, which was held by a British battalion, they ventured east in support of Anzavur's forces, but fell back when these were defeated. On 14 June 1920 the nationalists attacked. Part of the Disciplinary Forces changed sides and joined the nationalists. The rest withdrew behind British lines, while their commanders looked on from the Ottoman warship *Yavuz*, anchored in the gulf of İzmit. The remnants of the Disciplinary Forces were then shipped back to Istanbul, where they were officially disbanded on 25 June. The nationalists dealt harshly with their enemies. Seven regular army officers serving with the Disciplinary Forces, as well as a number of local notables who had taken sides against the nationalists, were hanged when the forces of the Ankara government regained control of the town of Düzce, east of Bolu.[27] Trouble in north-western Anatolia rumbled on, but the back of the resistance there to the Ankara government was broken. Within three months of Damat Ferit's accession to power, one fact had emerged clearly: the Istanbul government could not put together an effective military force against the nationalists.

The clash outside İzmit, when the nationalists defeated the Disciplinary Forces, had serious consequences. British forces opened fire on the nationalists and bombed them from the air to force them back from the vicinity of the capital.[28] Nevertheless, there was panic in Istanbul. The British commander, General Milne, asked for reinforcements. He was told that only Greek troops were available.[29] This gave Venizelos the opportunity for which he had been looking.

Before making up their minds on the Turkish peace settlement, the Allies had asked Marshal Foch to determine the military strength needed to impose a treaty on the Turks. On 30 March, Foch reported that at least twenty-seven divisions would be required, and that these were not available. Venizelos was ready to oblige. He was warned by the British government that he could not expect help in a war between Greece and Turkey, but he disregarded the warning, hoping to involve Britain in hostilities. Allied representatives in Istanbul advised their governments against a resumption of warfare in Turkey; their warnings too were not heeded.[30]

Between 19 and 26 April, the Allies held a conference in San Remo, on the Italian Riviera. A plan to partition Turkey was agreed. Lloyd George went along with Venizelos, and the French, who needed British support to hold down the Germans, and who were promised Lebanon, Syria and a slice of Turkish territory further north, went along with Lloyd George, against their better judgement. The Italians, who were far from satisfied with the promise of a zone of influence in southern Anatolia, could not stop the plan, although they were resolved to sabotage it. Venizelos now wanted to create facts on the ground in preparation for a peace conference. For over a year Greek troops had not been allowed to cross the Milne line, which had been drawn round İzmir. On 20 June, in exchange for the despatch of one Greek division to the İzmit peninsula, Lloyd George and Millerand authorized a 'concerted action' in the İzmir area.[31] Given an inch, Venizelos took an ell. On 22 June, Greek troops crossed the Milne line, and moved east and north.

Mustafa Kemal saw the Greek threat coming. On 21 June he went by train to Eskişehir to confer with Ali Fuat (Cebesoy), who was appointed commander of the western front three days later.[32] But the forces at his disposal were too weak to resist the Greek army. It took the Greeks less than a month to occupy the Aegean coast of Turkey, north of İzmir, and the southern shores of the sea of Marmara. Bursa, the first capital of the

Ottoman state, fell on 8 July. The Greeks' eastward advance took them
as far as Uşak, on the edge of the Anatolian plateau, some 200 miles east
of İzmir. Simultaneously, the Greeks cleared eastern Thrace of the weak
Ottoman detachments which garrisoned it. Edirne, the second capital
of the Ottomans, was occupied on 25 July, and the senior Ottoman
commander, Colonel Cafer Tayyar, who was in charge of the nationalist
forces in Thrace, surrendered on 27 July. Except for guerrilla bands
operating behind the Greek lines, Turkish nationalists were now
confined to the Anatolian plateau and the Black Sea coast.

In Ankara, a storm of indignation broke out in the Grand National
Assembly, where the platform was draped in black as a sign of mourning at the loss of Bursa. Deputies clamoured for the heads of nationalist commanders who had failed to stop the enemy. They wanted to
know why the Turkish front had collapsed. Parliamentary critics took
the floor as soon as the Greek advance began. At a secret session on 3
July Mustafa Kemal provided them with a ready answer. The reverses
had been caused by the Istanbul government which had weakened the
army and instigated risings against the authority of the assembly. Damat
Ferit and his friends were a worse enemy than the British. The first task
was to re-establish national unity.[33] In a proclamation to the nation the
previous day, Mustafa Kemal appealed to the Turkish people's religious
sentiment: 'We call on the whole nation to come together in unity and
rise against the Greeks in total determination. The *jihad*, once it is properly preached, will, with God's help, result quickly in the rout of the
Greeks.'[34]

Mustafa Kemal had good cause to blame domestic troublemakers.
One reason for the rapid advance of the Greeks was that Turkish troops
had been busy elsewhere putting down risings. When the Greeks
crossed the Milne line, the column of the Circassian Ethem was east of
Ankara fighting rebels in the province of Yozgat. The rising started on
13 June, just as the troubles in the north-west were ending. It was led by
an important feudal clan, the Çapanoğulları, which had fallen foul of
the CUP before the Great War, and which saw Mustafa Kemal's nationalists as the successors of the CUP. When local army units proved incapable of controlling the rising, Mustafa Kemal summoned Kılıç Ali and
his guerrillas who had been fighting the French in eastern Cilicia. When
they too failed, Ethem was called in from the west. Mustafa Kemal and
all the senior nationalist commanders met him when he arrived by rail
in Ankara. Ethem was given a room in the farm school, where Mustafa
Kemal, Fevzi and İsmet explained to him the gravity of the situation.[35]
Yozgat lay within the province of Ankara, and the rebellion threatened
the nationalist headquarters and its communications with Kâzım

Karabekir's forces in the east. Mustafa Kemal was deeply worried: his opponents were to say later than he was on the point of losing his nerve.[36] The fact remains that he dealt effectively with the threat.

Ethem was given a hero's welcome in the National Assembly, of which his brother Reşit was a member, and where he arrived wearing Circassian national dress, with a dagger stuck in his belt. He left Ankara with extraordinary powers to suppress the rebellion, and with ideas well above his station. Ethem's force of 2,000 men and five guns crushed the rebels. Yozgat was recaptured on 23 June, and the remnants of the supporters of the Çapanoğulları were put to flight a few days later.[37] The repression was bloody, and the town of Yozgat was looted by Ethem's men.[38] Flushed with victory, Ethem blamed the nationalist leadership – both civil and military – for the spread of the rebellion, and demanded that the governor of Ankara, Yahya Galip, should be despatched to the court martial he had established, to answer charges of negligence.

Mustafa Kemal had no intention of sacrificing his officials. He congratulated Ethem on his victory, and declared that Yahya Galip had been dismissed and that arrangements were being made to send him to Yozgat, while at the same time arranging for the interior ministry to advise Ethem that the governor was too sick to travel. Ethem was furious. He decided that Mustafa Kemal was responsible for the governor's negligence, and therefore for the outbreak of the rebellion. His anger increased when he learnt that Yahya Galip's illness was diplomatic and, as tale-bearers hastened to report to Mustafa Kemal, he threatened to hang 'the president in front of his own assembly'. But the rift was papered over. Ethem was persuaded to leave Yahya Galip in peace, and was met with open arms when he returned to Ankara. Mustafa Kemal was at hand to congratulate Ethem's victorious guerrillas. As the welcoming party left the station, İsmet (İnönü) said to Mustafa Kemal: 'They are armed to the teeth, each one of them. They look down on everyone else in their confident pride. Who controls the country today? Them or us?' 'We do,' replied Mustafa Kemal, 'because we have the brains.'[39] Ethem did not stay long in Ankara. He was despatched against the Greeks, whose positions he raided near Demirci, east of Izmir, forcing a Greek division to withdraw from the town. It was the first Greek reverse since the start of their offensive.[40]

There were other risings. In October, supporters of the sultan captured government offices in the conservative city of Konya in central Anatolia. Troops holding the front against the Greeks had to be moved to the area, where the authority of the Grand National Assembly was re-established by 15 November.[41] The weakness of the Ankara government was exploited by some Kurdish tribes, which raised the standard of revolt in the south-east. But, as usual, the Kurds were divided, and other tribes helped the troops of the Ankara government suppress the rebels.[42]

Soon Mustafa Kemal acquired his own bodyguard of cut-throats. On 29 October 1920, the notorious guerrilla leader Lame Osman and his band disembarked in İnebolu, the supply port of Ankara on the central Black Sea coast. They preyed on local people until Mustafa Kemal summoned them to Ankara, where these black-clad warriors were employed to guard his residence.[43] In the summer of 1920 Mustafa Kemal moved to the stationmaster's house by the tracks of Ankara station, where he could be in closer contact with front-line units. But his general staff stayed behind in the farm school.[44]

Sultan Vahdettin and the government of Damat Ferit had convinced themselves that resistance to the Allies was worse than futile. It would only result in the loss of Istanbul, and would save neither eastern Thrace nor the İzmir area which had been allocated to Greece at San Remo. The decisions reached there were communicated to the Ottoman government on 11 May. Damat Ferit tried to persuade the Allies to soften their terms, but to no avail. As the Greeks continued their advance, the Allies met in Spa in Belgium, and demanded that the Ottoman government should decide by 27 July whether it was prepared to accept the draft peace treaty which they had drawn up. On 20 July Damat Ferit advised acceptance. The sultan thought it prudent to put the question to a crown council, which met in Yıldız palace on 22 July. All but one of the sultan's councillors – the retired artillery general Ali Rıza Paşa – agreed that there was no choice but to accept the Allied terms.

The Allies had organized a signature ceremony at Sèvres, the Paris suburb which is home to the renowned French porcelain works. It was there, on 10 August 1920, that three Ottoman plenipotentiaries – a little-known former education minister, the ambassador to Switzerland and a distinguished poet, Rıza Tevfik, known as 'the philosopher' – signed the treaty which put an end to the Ottoman empire in all but name. The fact that the loss of Ottoman territory was to be gradual fooled no one: the İzmir area would vote on incorporation in Greece within five years; President Wilson would determine the frontiers of Armenia; the League of Nations would decide whether the Kurds were capable of independence, should they wish it.[45] The sultan retained Istanbul, but under Allied control, and the rest of Anatolia, apart from large zones of influence granted under a separate document to France in the south-east, and to Italy in the south. Foreigners would retain the privileged status which they had enjoyed under the capitulations. No patriotic Turk could be expected to accept such a dispensation.

However, signature did not exhaust the legal process of peacemaking. The treaty of Sèvres had to be ratified by parliament under the Ottoman constitution, and parliament had been dissolved by the sultan. Elections could not be held without the cooperation of Turkish nationalists. Following the mad logic of their position, the Allies asked for the formation of a government in Istanbul capable of reaching an understanding with the nationalists. Damat Ferit rendered his last service to the Allies by submitting his resignation on 'grounds of health'. He then left the capital to take his ease in Karlsbad: he had ceased to matter.

On 21 October Damat Ferit was succeeded by the elderly Tevfik Paşa, the eternal conciliator, who sought immediately to contact the Ankara government. The atmosphere in Ottoman Istanbul had changed. The treaty of Sèvres had demonstrated that Mustafa Kemal had been right all along in urging resistance to the Allies. Legal action against nationalists was stopped, as the Ottoman war minister signed a document declaring that there was no doubt that the 'national forces' had sought to defend the fatherland, and that they should therefore be praised rather than arraigned in court.[46] Sultan Vahdettin later tried to take credit for the fact that he had brought to power Tevfik Paşa's cabinet which allowed the Kemalists to establish their influence in Istanbul, although it was clear that 'they bore ill will towards my person and my authority'.[47]

Ankara was in no mood to compromise. On 19 May, the Grand National Assembly had voted to deprive Damat Ferit and his colleagues of their Ottoman citizenship. On 18 July it swore to accept nothing short of the terms laid out in the National Pact – full independence within the 1918 armistice lines, with territorial additions where possible. On 19 August it decreed that members of the crown council who had recommended the acceptance of the Sèvres treaty and the plenipotentiaries who signed it should be treated as traitors.[48]

The Greeks occupied the most productive areas of western Anatolia, and risings against the nationalists were still taking place in the interior. But Mustafa Kemal was conscious of two great advantages: his fellow-countrymen had had proof that his was the patriotic cause, and the Western Allies had shown that they were unwilling to commit military forces to impose the treaty of Sèvres. Mustafa Kemal's task now was to beat the Greeks and pre-empt the Armenians. But although the task had become simpler, it was not easy, for he still lacked an adequate army. He needed time to establish the authority of the Grand National

Assembly in the free areas of Anatolia, and to build up and supply a regular army. The Greek army was well equipped and had access to European arms factories. Turkish nationalists had only the caches of arms which they had preserved from the hands of Allied control officers; there was little or no money to buy fresh supplies. The only way out was to divide the enemies and acquire foreign friends. Mustafa Kemal put all his skills to this task. He had to act as a politician and diplomat first, and as a soldier second. He had to be patient and cunning enough to avoid dangerous commitments. Few of his companions understood the need or Mustafa Kemal's skill in meeting it.

The patriotism of the nationalists gathered in Ankara was not in doubt. But they were swayed by emotion – above all, by xenophobia, as understandable in the circumstances as it was blinding in its effects – and divided by ambition and personal jealousies. With the exception of a few surviving feudal dynasties with local following, Turkish society lacks a hereditary aristocracy. Its ethos is egalitarian. Education has always been the passport to its ruling élite. Since the number of people trained in the new, Western knowledge was small, they had to be jacks of all trades. As a result, many believed themselves to be omniscient. The country had more than its share of military politicians. There were also lawyers, doctors, dentists and vets who fancied themselves experts in politics and foreign diplomacy. It was this know-all, fractious, stubborn, egalitarian crew that Mustafa Kemal had to lead. He had to find among them people who were not only competent, but amenable to his leadership. It is not surprising that many fell by the wayside.

14

A Fighting Diplomat

FROM THE MOMENT he set foot on Anatolian soil in May 1919, Mustafa Kemal was intent on establishing relations with the Russian Bolsheviks. The Greeks had sent two divisions to Odessa in January 1919 to help the French, who had intervened in the Russian civil war on the side of the White Russian commander, General Denikin. The expedition was withdrawn a few months later,[1] but it placed the government of Venizelos in the camp of the enemies of the Bolshevik revolution. In Mustafa Kemal's eyes, the Bolsheviks were, diplomatically, a useful counterweight to Britain, France and their protégé, Greece. Militarily they were even more necessary, as the only major outside source of money and supplies.

However, at the beginning of 1920, communications between Ankara and Bolshevik Russia were difficult. The independent Transcaucasian republics of Georgia, Armenia and Azerbaijan lay across the direct land route. Mustafa Kemal was worried that Britain might use these republics to complete the encirclement of Anatolia. In a circular telegram to corps commanders on 5 February 1920, he argued that Turkey should employ all the means at its disposal and take every risk to foil the construction of a Caucasian barrier which threatened it with the definitive loss of independence.[2] Kâzım Karabekir, who had a clearer view of Transcaucasia from his base in Erzurum, was more relaxed. He saw no immediate danger of a hostile Caucasian barrier. In any case, he told Mustafa Kemal, it would be disastrous for Turkish troops to take action before the Bolsheviks had crossed the Caucasian range.[3] Events proved him right.

Denikin's White Russians were defeated by the Bolsheviks and were evacuated to the Crimea in March 1920. In April, the 11th Red Army massed north of the Azerbaijan frontier. On 26 April it crossed the border. A day later, local Bolsheviks demanded that the nationalist government of Azerbaijan should cede power to them. The Azeri president, Mämmäd Ämin Räsulzadä (Mehmet Emin Resulzade), implored parliament in Baku not to give way. Even if the Red Army had come in order to help Turkey, 'the saviour of Azerbaijan', it was an invasion force which would re-establish Russian rule. Parliament disregarded his plea, and on 28 April power passed to the Azerbaijan Provisional Revolutionary Committee, whose chairman awaited the arrival of the Red Army before he turned up in Baku.[4]

However, Armenia, ruled by the nationalist Dashnak party, still barred Turkey's access to the Bolsheviks. In May, Armenian Bolsheviks attempted to seize power before the arrival of their Russian comrades. They were defeated; the 11th Red Army paused at the Armenian frontier. However, the situation of the Dashnaks was precarious. Their republic had been formed within the frontiers of tsarist Russia, which included the province of Kars, lost by the Ottomans in 1878, regained in 1918, but evacuated the following year under the armistice of Mudros. Turkish nationalists claimed that the inhabitants of the lands lost to Russia in 1878 had voted to rejoin Turkey in 1918. The Armenians, most of them refugees from Anatolia, tried to pre-empt Turkish claims by driving out local Muslims, who had formed armed resistance bands, often under the command of Turkish officers. Turkish nationalists now had an opportunity to make good their claims and rescue their kinsmen.

However, the 15th corps under Kâzım Karabekir's command, numbering only 12,000 men and 40 guns,[5] did not have a clear numerical superiority over the newly created Armenian army, whose officers had served in the tsar's forces.[6] To make up the deficiency, Kâzım Karabekir ordered a partial mobilization in the eastern provinces on 8 June, a measure which appeared to receive the backing of Ankara when, a week later, his title was changed to Commander of the Eastern Front. The Armenians tried to complete their occupation of Kars province by entering the district of Oltu with its overwhelmingly Muslim population: the Turks accused them of atrocities and threatened counter-measures. The scene was set for a reckoning. On 9 July, the last British and French troops in Transcaucasia left the port of Batum, ceding the city to the nationalist government of Georgia.[7] The fate of the area was thus left to the interplay of local forces.

This time, Mustafa Kemal chose caution, while Kâzım Karabekir pressed for action. The hope of regaining lost Ottoman territory, which lay within the 1918 armistice lines, had to be balanced against the need to secure Soviet Russian aid. On 11 May, the Grand National Assembly sent its foreign minister Bekir Sami (Kunduh) at the head of a delegation to Moscow. He did not arrive until 19 July.[8] Bekir Sami was not alone in purporting to speak in Soviet Russia in the name of Turkish nationalists. Before the occupation of Istanbul, the *Karakol* secret society had sent one of its members, Baha Sait, to the Caucasus in order to enlist Bolshevik help. On 11 January 1920, Baha Sait signed an agreement with the Bolsheviks promising to carry out anti-British agitation across western Asia, from the Black Sea to India, in exchange for Bolshevik assistance. The agreement was disowned by Mustafa Kemal with the backing of Kâzım Karabekir,[9] whose main contact in Transcaucasia was Enver's uncle Halil Paşa (Kut). Halil Paşa, who had served with Karabekir in the Mesopotamian campaign, claimed that he had been instructed by Mustafa Kemal to advance the Turkish nationalist cause among the Bolsheviks. He spent some time in Azerbaijan and then moved to Moscow where he introduced himself as the representative of Turkish national forces. He organized the repatriation of Turkish POWs, who had formed a unit ready for service in the ranks of Turkish nationalists, and the despatch of a first instalment of weapons by sea to Trabzon and of Russian gold by land from Azerbaijan.[10]

The question of Turkey's representation in Moscow was further complicated by the arrival of Enver Paşa on 7 August. Undeterred by the collapse of his policies in the Great War, Enver fancied himself the leader of a vast Islamic revolutionary organization. He thought that he could impress the Bolsheviks with his anti-British projects and render valuable services to the Turkish national cause. Enver outlined his plans to Mustafa Kemal in a letter from Moscow. Mustafa Kemal sent a polite reply on 4 October in which he warned Enver that Pan-Islamic agitation might alarm the Russians.[11] Mustafa Kemal did his best to keep the defeated leaders of the CUP at arm's length. He replied to the letters of Talât and Cemal, as well as Enver, thanking them for their offers of services, but insisting that there was now a properly constituted government in Ankara, and that they should support its policies from abroad. In the meantime, Enver had gone on to Baku to take part in the Congress of the Peoples of the East, which the Bolsheviks had organized. In this chaotic gathering, which opened on 1 September 1920, Enver's presence proved controversial. Although he had travelled to Baku in the company of leaders of the Communist International, the members of the Turkish Communist Party, headed by Mustafa Suphi, would not let him speak, saying that his proper place was in the dock of a people's tribunal.[12] Having heard his speech read on his behalf, Enver returned to intrigue in Berlin.

Negotiations with the Bolsheviks proved difficult. On 24 August a treaty of cooperation was initialled, but three days later the Soviet commissar for foreign affairs, Georgi Chicherin, asked that Turkey should cede to the Armenians a part of the provinces of Van and Bitlis, in addition to the territories which lay within the Russian empire in 1914 (with the exception perhaps of the frontier town of Sarıkamış).[13] Bekir Sami could not communicate direct with Ankara and sent a member of his mission, Yusuf Kemal (Tengirşenk), to Trabzon with a request for instructions. Mustafa Kemal finally replied on 16 October. Turkey, he told Bekir Sami, would not cede an inch of territory. Bekir Sami was to sign the draft friendship treaty only if the Russians agreed.[14] But by then Mustafa Kemal had decided that new facts could be created on the ground. On 20 September he acted on the hint that the Bolsheviks might be prepared to let the Turks have Sarıkamış, and allowed Kâzım Karabekir to occupy the western approaches to Kars. On 24 September, Karabekir ordered his troops to move forward, saying that the Russians had become convinced of the need for the operation. Sarıkamış was occupied against feeble Armenian resistance on 29 September.[15]

Having secured his new front, Karabekir returned to Erzurum, where political intrigues were straining his relations with Mustafa Kemal. The intrigue centred round Celalettin Arif, who had hoped to become president of the Grand National Assembly, but had to content himself with the positions of vice-president and justice minister. Local mobilization and the provisioning of Karabekir's troops had caused hardship among the inhabitants of Erzurum, a town devastated in the Great War. Not unusually, a small group of local notables put the blame on the nationalist leadership, accusing it of misappropriation. Celalettin Arif, who had been elected member for Erzurum, arrived in the town and assumed the functions of acting governor. Mustafa Kemal was quick to react. On 5 September, the assembly decided that its members could not hold civil service posts, except for embassies, and on 23 September Mustafa Kemal ordered Celalettin Arif to return to Ankara immediately.[16]

A surprising feature of the affair was that Karabekir, the virtual master of Erzurum, and, as such, the implicit target of local discontent, appeared for a time to favour Celalettin Arif's appointment as governor-general of the eastern provinces. Two nationalist critics of Mustafa Kemal were also involved: Hüseyin Avni (Ulaş), like Arif a member of the assembly for Erzurum, and Colonel (later Brigadier) Halit (known as 'the Madman', a former member of Enver's Special Organization).[17] It seems likely that Celalettin Arif tried to set up in Erzurum a national-ist centre in opposition to Mustafa Kemal. He failed when Karabekir, a good soldier but a poor politician, realized that he was threatened alongside Mustafa Kemal.

Mustafa Kemal was aware that internal disorganization and subver-sion posed an immediate threat to his position. The Bolsheviks, in par-ticular, were dangerous friends. True, there was no mass popular support for Bolshevism in Turkey – or anywhere else, for that matter. But the attempt to obtain Moscow gold and weapons had encouraged the emergence of Communist sympathizers in the disorganized ranks of Turkish nationalists. Damar (Zamir) Arıkoğlu, a nationalist leader from Adana, recalled in his memoirs:

> There was no lack of Communist propaganda in Ankara. Some of my friends among the deputies regretted that Communism had not been adopted officially. 'What are we waiting for?' they asked. 'Why don't we proclaim Communism and thus inspire our people with a new spirit and a new enthu-siasm? We've no property or riches left. So what's holding us back?' ... The colour red, the symbol of Communism, became fashionable ... Many pinned pieces of red cloth to their fur hats. Not a few wore red ties.[18]

Sympathy for Communism was strongest among CUP militants. They had started as revolutionary nationalists. Now some of them, par-ticularly the intellectuals of the party, had begun to toy with revolution-ary internationalism. Lenin's promise to emancipate the subject nationalities of the tsarist empire had also made an impression on the Circassians settled in Turkey. The Circassian guerrilla leader Ethem was, as he said in his memoirs, 'an enthusiastic and sincere partisan of Soviet friendship, until the day when the sublime and attractive principles con-cerning the freedom of nationalities, which Lenin proclaimed, were vio-lated by the Soviets themselves'. Ethem fancied that 'among the leaders of the Turkish revolution, it was I whom the Moscow comrades trusted most.'[19] In May 1920, a semi-clandestine organization called the Green Army (*Yeşil Ordu*) emerged in Ankara,[20] its programme combining Islamic militancy with scraps of socialist ideology:[21] it attracted several of Mustafa Kemal's comrades.

A similar approach was advocated by a number of deputies who called themselves the People's Group. On 4 September, members of the group secured the election to the ministry of the interior of a leading member of the Green Army, Nazım Bey, in preference to Mustafa Kemal's candidate Colonel Refet (Bele). The Circassian, Ethem, who was in Ankara at the time, claims in his memoirs that Mustafa Kemal

asked him to persuade Nazım to resign.[22] Nazım did resign on 6
September and was replaced by Mustafa Kemal's candidate, Refet.[23]
However, Ethem lent his support to the Green Army in the sector of
the western front where his forces were concentrated. He even had a
Bolshevik battalion, which carried the green and red pennant of the
Green Army. On 14 September, the commander of the western front,
Ali Fuat (Cebesoy), warned Mustafa Kemal that a Bolshevik newspaper,
called *Yeni Dünya* (The New World),[24] had started publication in
Eskişehir and was claiming that Mustafa Kemal was the leader of the
People's Group.[25]

Mustafa Kemal's reply on 16 September[26] gives the fullest account of
his skilful balancing act. Any help that the Bolsheviks gave would be
accepted, but their agreement would not be sought for an attack on the
Armenians, which would open the road to Azerbaijan. The Bolsheviks
were poor and would seek an accommodation with the West; their professions of friendship for Turkey were a device to impress the British
and the Islamic world until such an accommodation was achieved. At
the same time, they were trying to subvert Turkish society in order to tie
the country to Russia. The Bolsheviks and the British were both trying
to conquer Turkey from within. But just as he would not allow any
public denunciation of Communism, so too he would try to keep up
discreet contacts with the British, who were interested in arranging an
exchange of prisoners. Once subversion from both the east and the
west was blocked, it would be sufficient to stop the Greeks at any line of
defence for victory to be achieved. In the meantime, social reforms had
to be avoided. It was a remarkably clear and prescient programme. But
it could not be spelled out to the fractious assembly.

The Turkish nationalist writer, Yakup Kadri Karaosmanoğlu, who
visited Ankara in 1921, remarked that Mustafa Kemal was not universally popular in the assembly. The most common complaint was that he
devoted his entire time to politics, instead of leading the army.[27] But
politics had to come first. In order to pre-empt the People's Group,
Mustafa Kemal presented his own populist programme to the assembly
on 18 September 1920; it stated, 'The People's Government of Turkey
is exercised by the Grand National Assembly.' A right-wing Unionist,
Ali Şükrü, described it as 'mock-Bolshevism'.[28] Ali Şükrü represented
Trabzon, a frontier town like Erzurum, where Turkish nationalist
feeling was combined with fear of the Russians, whether Red or White.
It was a stronghold of the CUP, where loyalty to Enver was still potent.

The assembly expressed its Islamic feelings on 14 September when it
passed a law prohibiting alcohol. This did not stop Mustafa Kemal from
obtaining his regular supply of *rakı*. On 17 September, the assembly

formally rejected Soviet terms contrary to the National Pact.[29] Mustafa Kemal then came up with a remarkable stratagem. On 18 October the interior ministry registered an official Turkish Communist Party consisting of the nationalist military leadership (İsmet, Fevzi, Ali Fuat, Refet) and Mustafa Kemal's closest civilian collaborators. Ali Fuat was informed by a telegram starting with the words: 'To the Commander of the Western Front: Dear Comrade!' The essential message was that the Green Army had been subsumed inside the new party and that no one would be allowed to engage in activity on behalf of Communism or Bolshevism without a written authorization and a membership card, bearing a photograph, issued by the official party. The Turkish Communist Party, the telegram claimed, was directly linked with the Third International.[30]

The same claim was repeated in a letter which Mustafa Kemal sent to Ethem telling him that both of them, as well as Refet, had become members of the Turkish Communist Party. Mustafa Kemal went on to ask Ethem to transfer to Ankara the printing press of *Yeni Dünya*, which would become the organ of the new party. Ethem, who had donated the press, reputedly the most modern in Anatolia, says that he allowed the transfer.[31] The paper survived in Ankara for a couple of months, at the end of which its editor was tried and sent into exile.[32] Its presses were taken over by Yunus Nadi's *Yenigün*. The Third International never accepted the membership of the Turkish Communist Party invented in Ankara.

Efforts to contain Bolshevism inside the country were accompanied by a clear demonstration that Mustafa Kemal was capable of acting independently in Transcaucasia. On 24 October, Karabekir was given authority to wrest Kars from the Armenians. There was no time to lose. On 11 October, a Soviet plenipotentiary, Boris Legran, had arrived in Erivan (Yerevan) to negotiate an agreement with the Armenian government. On 28 October he signed a draft treaty which recognized the province of Kars as part of Armenia.[33] On the same day Karabekir launched his offensive. The Turkish 9th division, under the command of 'Mad' Halit, was ordered to march fifty miles and cut off Kars from the east. Halit executed the manoeuvre, but two Armenian armoured trains foiled his attempt to cut the railway from Kars to Gümrü (Alexandropol). In the meantime, Kars railway station fell to units of the Turkish 12th division.

Intent on securing the honour of capturing Kars castle, Halit ordered his troops into the town. Kars castle, where the Turks had withstood long sieges in their wars with the Russians, fell on 30 October.[34] The fortress was so large that the Armenian generals and ministers had to wait for nearly two hours before the Turkish troops could find them and accept their surrender.[35] More than 2,000 Armenian troops, including three generals, were taken prisoner; 676 guns, most of them old, were captured. Turkish losses were 9 dead and 47 wounded.[36] Clearly, the Armenian army had not had time to become a serious fighting force. But Halit's insistence on snatching from the 12th division the glory of the conquest of Kars allowed the bulk of Armenian troops to escape towards Gümrü in the north-east.

Their respite was brief. On 6 November, Karabekir's troops reached the Arpaçay river, the eastern border of the district of Kars. Two days earlier the Armenians had asked for an armistice. On 7 November they accepted Karabekir's terms under which they were to evacuate all the territory west of the Arpaçay river, and withdraw their forces ten miles to the east of it, leaving the town of Gümrü undefended. However, two days later Karabekir communicated even harsher terms demanded from Ankara. The Armenians were to surrender the bulk of their weapons and withdraw even further to the east. The Armenian government in Erivan refused, and the Turkish army resumed its advance, gaining the fertile district of Iğdır, north of Ağrıdağ (Mount Ararat). The mountain continued to figure on the coat of arms of the Armenian republic, but its ownership passed to Turkey. Finally, on 18 November, the Armenians accepted the Turkish demands in full. On 2 December the armistice was confirmed by the treaty of Gümrü which fixed the present frontier between Turkey and Armenia.[37] It was the first treaty signed by the government of the Grand National Assembly and it marked a Turkish victory.

By a tragicomic coincidence, on 22 November, four days after the Armenian capitulation, President Woodrow Wilson finally delivered his decision on the western boundaries of Armenia, which the treaty of Sèvres had reserved for his arbitration. Armenia, Wilson decided, should be given a stretch of Turkey's Black Sea coastline, including the port of Trabzon, as well as Erzurum, Van and Bitlis in the interior. Sir Eyre Crowe, the permanent under-secretary at the Foreign Office, called it Wilson's 'castle in the air'. To avoid embarrassment, the award of the President of the United States was left unpublished.[38] Mustafa Kemal was to comment in 1926: 'Poor Wilson did not understand that a frontier which is not defended with bayonets, force and honour cannot be secured by any other principle.'[39]

Nationalist Armenians never ratified the treaty of Gümrü. On the day it was signed, Armenia was proclaimed a Soviet socialist republic. The Soviets had refused to sign the treaty negotiated earlier by their emissary Legran with the nationalist government of Armenia. Now, the

Red Army moved from Azerbaijan into what was left of Armenia. It arrived in Erivan on 6 December.[40] The Kemalists thus gained direct land access to the Russian Bolsheviks.

Karabekir had won a famous victory, and he could now call himself the Conqueror of the East. He was promoted Major-General on 31 October 1920, while Mustafa Kemal was still technically a retired Brigadier. He was the only nationalist commander whose prestige could rival Mustafa Kemal's, but he was slow to put it to political use. He remained Commander of the Eastern Front until the post was abolished in October 1923. Some of his troops were gradually transferred to the west. 'Mad' Halit was given command of the İzmit front, facing the Allies in Istanbul, and promoted Brigadier in 1922. Karabekir did not ask for a transfer, nor did Mustafa Kemal insist on one. He had served his purpose.

After Karabekir had secured the east, the situation in the south also improved. Turkish irregulars fighting the French in Cilicia and upper Mesopotamia were under the command of regular army officers and obeyed the instructions of Mustafa Kemal. He knew that the French were prepared to withdraw from most of Cilicia if they were left in undisputed possession of Syria. But pressure against them had to be kept up to bring them to the conference table and to secure a favourable territorial settlement. The French had withdrawn from Maraş and Urfa, but were hanging on to Cilicia. The first task of the Turkish nationalists was to force them out of the Taurus mountains, which form the northern rampart of the Cilician plain (Çukurova in Turkish). In May 1920, a French unit holding the railway station of Pozantı was cut off. The small town of Pozantı lies north of the Cilician gates (the pass of Gülek in Turkish) – the route taken by conquerors from Alexander of Macedon to Emperor Frederic I Barbarossa, who was drowned near by during the Third Crusade. When two French attempts to relieve Pozantı failed, the garrison of some 500 men abandoned the town and tried to force their way south through the mountains. On 28 May, the column was ambushed by some forty Turkish irregulars. The French commander, Major Mesnil, surrendered. He had been told by his superiors that 15,000 Turkish irregulars were operating in the area. In fact, he was faced with a small group of villagers, armed with rifles and shotguns.[41]

The capture of over 500 French soldiers with two mountain guns, 13 machine-guns and more than 800 rifles was followed by a twenty-day truce under which the French agreed to give up Pozantı and other outlying areas. The conclusion of the truce was criticized in the assembly.

It also worried both the Russians and the Hashemite King Faysal who was trying to hold out against the French in Syria.[42] There had been some cooperation between Turkish nationalists and Arab tribes along the Turkish-Arab linguistic frontier. Mustafa Kemal had now shown that he was prepared to strike a separate deal with the French. Arab nationalists, who had a long history of dealing separately with the British, could look after themselves.

The truce served Mustafa Kemal's aim to establish his government as a valid interlocutor with the Allies. But the French were not yet ready for a deal acceptable to Turkish nationalists, and Mustafa Kemal denounced the truce when French troops landed to guard French-owned collieries at Ereğli on the Black Sea coast, and occupied the coal port of Zonguldak.[43] On 5 August, Mustafa Kemal travelled to Pozantı in the company of Fevzi Paşa to coordinate guerrilla operations. Action now shifted to eastern Cilicia, which the treaty of Sèvres had placed under French mandate. On 15–16 October, Turkish irregulars stormed the Armenian stronghold of Haçin (Hadjin, now Saimbeyli) in the Taurus mountains. The French were more successful further south. On 9 February 1921, the Turkish defenders of Antep, who had withstood a ten-month siege, surrendered to a force of 15,000 French troops. The assembly awarded the town the honorific prefix *Gazi*, 'Warrior for the Faith', and the town thus acquired its present name of Gaziantep.[44] The battle for Antep was the last major engagement on the southern front. The French now awaited developments on Turkey's western front. The terms of their settlement with Turkish nationalists would depend on the ability of the latter to withstand the Greeks.

The Greeks were much more formidable than the Armenians, and, unlike the French, they were ready to fight the Turks for territory. The main difficulty facing Mustafa Kemal was that the Turkish divisions on the western front were under strength and had to rely on irregulars, who were less disposed than were their comrades in the south to obey the orders of the general staff. True, the Ankara government had decreed on 16 May 1920 that 'generally' all militias should be merged in regular forces and should be provisioned at the expense of the defence budget:[45] as a result, three detachments of irregulars were turned into regular units. But the forces of the Circassian Ethem and of the guerrilla leader Demirci Efe remained a law to themselves.

The nationalist government was still too unsure of itself to order a general mobilization. Even those recruits who were under arms tended to slip back to their villages, saying that the sultan had abolished compulsory military service. Treatment of deserters varied. If they were tried under the law of high treason, passed by the assembly, they had the right to appeal. On the other hand, commanders impatient of legal delays executed them along with other enemies of the nationalist cause. To regularize matters, on 11 September 1920 the assembly passed a law which introduced an ominous innovation – the establishment of three-member Independence Tribunals, which the assembly elected from among its own ranks. No appeal was allowed against the verdicts of these political tribunals. The Independence Tribunals were modelled on the revolutionary tribunals set up in France in 1793,[46] although others saw a parallel with the Extraordinary Commissions (known by the Russian acronym *Che-Ka*), which the Bolsheviks used to eliminate their enemies.[47] However, local custom and the vigilance of the assembly prevented the establishment of revolutionary terror. The most common punishment inflicted on deserters was the bastinado, at the rate of ten strokes on the soles of the feet for every act of desertion. It was only when deserters turned into bandits that they were liable to be hanged; death sentences were often commuted if the culprits agreed to serve on the front.[48]

The demise of the surviving irregular militias was hastened by a botched operation which they undertook with units of the regular army under the command of Ali Fuat (Cebesoy). The Circassian Ethem decided that a Greek division holding the small town of Gediz, south-west of Kütahya, in the central section of the western front, was vulnerable to attack. Ali Fuat agreed and asked permission of the general staff in Ankara to mount a combined operation with Ethem's irregulars. İsmet (İnönü) objected that there was trouble again in Konya, and that in any case it was too early to mount an offensive. Mustafa Kemal's strategy was based on building up the army to hold a defensive line; irregulars were useful for hit-and-run raids, but regular units had to be conserved. A training course for officers had been established in Ankara, but it was not until 1 November 1920 that it produced its first graduates.

Nevertheless, the attack on Gediz went ahead on 24 October. The Greeks were taken by surprise and the town was captured the following day. But there was no coordination between Ethem's irregulars, who tried to cut off the Greeks, and regular units fighting ten miles away. The Greeks returned to Gediz; the Turks retook the town on 12 November, but the Greeks slipped out of encirclement. To draw away the Turks, the Greek forces in Bursa moved east towards the Anatolian escarpment and captured another slice of Turkish territory. Ethem, who lost 200 killed and 500 wounded in the operation, blamed the regular army for its failure.⁴⁹ Relations between guerrilla leaders and army officers deteriorated.

Mustafa Kemal decided that the disorder on the western front had to end: Ali Fuat had got on too well with Ethem at the cost of his own authority. On 8 November he was recalled to Ankara, where he arrived dressed as a guerrilla.⁵⁰ On 21 November he was appointed ambassador to Moscow. Mustafa Kemal was to make a habit of appointing to foreign embassies people who had become an embarrassment at home. The following year, Celalettin Arif was sent to represent the Ankara government in Rome – he never returned to Turkey. In the case of Ali Fuat, appointment to Moscow made sense, given that he was a friend of Ethem, who considered himself to be the Bolsheviks' friend. But any sympathy that Ali Fuat may have felt for the Bolsheviks did not survive his stay in Moscow.

After Ali Fuat's removal, the command of the western front was split in two. Colonel İsmet, the chief of the general staff, was given the northern sector; Colonel Refet (Bele), the interior minister, was put in charge of the south. The defence minister, Fevzi Paşa (Çakmak), was made acting chief of the general staff. All three were law-and-order men. Refet once again put down the rising in Konya and then turned his attention to the guerrilla leader, Demirci Efe. When Demirci Efe refused to integrate his band in the regular army, Refet moved against him and captured him on 30 December. He was kept under guard until the end of the war, when he was allowed to settle to a quiet life in the countryside.

Ethem, with whom Demirci Efe was in contact, was a more formidable leader. He had supporters in the assembly, where his brother Reşit was a deputy. Mustafa Kemal had told Ali Fuat that he could, if he wished, take Ethem and his brothers with him to Moscow. In response, Mustafa Kemal received a telegram from Ethem's headquarters saying that his proposal to remove the Circassian brothers had created the impression that he was preparing to proclaim himself dictator;⁵¹ the brothers would neither go away nor submit. Ethem, who suffered from a stomach complaint, came to Ankara for medical treatment, but also to rally support in the assembly through his brother Reşit. He left a third brother, Tevfik, as acting commander of the Mobile Forces in Kütahya. Tevfik refused to take orders from the front commander, Colonel İsmet (İnönü), expelled the civil governor appointed by the latter, and threatened to execute him if he returned. Mustafa Kemal ordered Colonels İsmet and Refet to move their troops in readiness for action against the Mobile Forces. But he did not show his hand right away.

The decision to discipline the irregulars affected the nature of the

1. Atatürk's mother, Zübeyde

2. Photograph reputedly of Atatürk's father Ali Rıza in officer's uniform at the time of the 1877–8 war with Russia. 'That's not my father,' Atatürk is reported to have said when shown the picture (Atay, *Çankaya*, 17)

3. The pink house in Salonica where Atatürk spent his childhood

4. Graduation photograph: Atatürk in the uniform of a Staff Captain (1905)

5. Ottoman officers in Beirut, 1906: Atatürk is seated first from left; Ali Fuat (Cebesoy), first from right

6. With a group of Ottoman officers in Cyrenaica in 1912,
during the war with Italy (seated on the right, next to his friend Fuat Bulca)

7. During the Balkan war in 1912/13
with Rauf (Orbay)

8. In Janissary costume at a fancy dress
ball in Sofia, 1914

9. Enver Paşa, Ottoman (deputy) commander-in-chief in the Great War

10. Talât Paşa, interior minister at the start of the Great War, in the uniform of a cavalry Second Lieutenant

11. Ottoman army commanders at the beginning of the Great War: (*left to right*) Liman von Sanders, Cemal Paşa and von der Goltz

12. Colonel Mustafa Kemal, commander of the Anafartalar Group in Gallipoli, 1915

13. Ottoman and German officers in Gallipoli: (*left to right, standing, first row*) Fahrettin (Altay), Mustafa Kemal and his commanding officer Esat Paşa

14. On the eve of the Erzurum congress: Mustafa Kemal, still wearing the cordon of imperial ADC, with the governor of Erzurum, Münir (Akkaya) (*left*) and Rauf (Orbay) (*right*). Members of Mustafa Kemal's suite in the back row: (*left to right*) Dr Refik (Saydam), Hüsrev (Gerede) and Kâzım (Dirik)

15. Prominent nationalists at the Sivas congress: (*left to right*) Muzaffer Kılıç (ADC), Rauf (Orbay), Bekir Sami (Kunduh), Mustafa Kemal, the journalist Ruşen Eşref (Ünaydın), Lieutenant-Colonel Cemil Cahit (Toydemir) and Cevat Abbas (Gürer) (ADC)

16. Mustafa Kemal's companion Fikriye in Istanbul on the eve of his departure for Anatolia in 1919

17. The villa on Çankaya hill, as it was in 1921 when Mustafa Kemal chose it for his permanent home

18. (*below*) Mustafa Kemal's wife Lâtife in 1924

19. Mustafa Kemal chatting to İsmet in Çankaya after the
second victory at İnönü in 1921

20. Nationalist commanders in the War of Independence:
(*first row, left to right*) Ali Fuat (Cebesoy), Refet (Bele), Marshal Fevzi (Çakmak),
Kâzım Karabekir and Fahrettin (Altay)

21. Mustafa Kemal with Refet (Bele), war minister in 1921

22. İzmir after the fire, September 1922

23. Crowd outside the assembly in Ankara on 23 April 1921,
the first anniversary of its inauguration

24. Victory monument in Ankara, 1929

25. Visiting the port of Mersin in Lâtife's company, 1923

26. Mustafa Kemal addresses the citizens of Bursa in September 1924, the second anniversary of their liberation

27. Inspecting the first crop on his farm outside Ankara

28. Introducing the hat in Kastamonu, in 1925, with his companions
Fuat (Bulca) (*left*) and Nuri (Conker) (*right*)

29. A boat trip on the Bosphorus in 1927: assembly speaker Kâzım (Özalp)
is seated next to Mustafa Kemal. Three of 'the usual gentlemen', Kılıç Ali, Salih
(Bozok) and Recep Zühtü, are standing behind them

30. Dancing with the
bride in 1929, at the
wedding of his adopted
daughter Nebile and Raşit,
a secretary at the Turkish
embassy in Vienna

31. With his adopted daughter Afet İnan and İsmet İnönü in Istanbul in 1935

32. On a trip to the Kurdish area in 1937, with his new prime minister Celal Bayar and his adopted daughter, the military pilot Sabiha Gökçen

33. In conversation with the visiting Shah of Iran (Reza Shah Pahlavi) in 1934. On the left, foreign minister Tevfik Rüştü Aras

34. With King Edward VIII and Mrs Wallis Simpson in 1936, watching a regatta in Istanbul

35. At Florya beach in Istanbul in 1935, as his summer house
was being completed

36. Holding by the hand his youngest adopted daughter Ülkü at Haydarpaşa station
in Istanbul, in May 1938, less than six months before his death

regime in Ankara. Whatever their services to the national cause, the *çetes*, as the bands of irregulars were known, were an element of disorder, and disorder was the breeding ground of Bolshevism. Mustafa Kemal stood for order. On the eve of the fall of the Damat Ferit government, the elderly Marshal Ahmet İzzet Paşa, known for his sympathy with the nationalist cause, was visited by British officers who asked him whether 'the gentlemen in Anatolia' were totally committed to Bolshevism. He replied: 'Most of them are military commanders, country notables and landowners, and educated people. It is inconceivable that such a group should incline to the theory of Communism. But if Western countries persist in applying unjust pressure, they may well throw themselves into Russia's arms.'[52]

As soon as he had succeeded Damat Ferit, the grand vizier Tevfik Paşa sought to establish contact with Anatolia through Ahmet İzzet Paşa, who had become interior minister in his administration. On 25 November, Mustafa Kemal agreed to meet a delegation headed by Ahmet İzzet at Bilecik, on the railway line from Istanbul to Ankara. Mustafa Kemal made use of the meeting to remove the brothers Ethem and Reşit from Ankara. He insisted that they should be part of a delegation from the Grand National Assembly which would meet the Ottoman ministers. However, when the train from Ankara stopped in Eskişehir, Ethem took fright. Hearing that army units were moving in, he fled to Kütahya. Reşit, who stayed behind, had an angry exchange with Mustafa Kemal. In his six-day speech, Mustafa Kemal said that when Reşit insisted on his brothers' freedom of action, he replied: 'Until now I have dealt with you in all sincerity as an old friend and have striven for a solution in your favour ... From now on you are faced with the president of the Turkish Grand National Assembly and of its government. As head of state, I am ordering the commander of the Western Front to take all necessary action.'[53]

The following day, Reşit was allowed to join his brother in Kütahya, while Mustafa Kemal went on to Bilecik to meet Ahmet İzzet Paşa. He had earlier suggested that the trip should be undertaken discreetly.[54] Ahmet İzzet Paşa, who expected a private encounter with 'an old comrade-in-arms', was taken aback when faced with a parliamentary delegation from Ankara.[55] Mustafa Kemal was not interested in an exchange of views on policy. His purpose was to make use of Ahmet İzzet and his suite, which included the navy minister and former grand vizier Salih Paşa, in order to bolster the prestige of the Ankara government. Mustafa Kemal was to say later that he greeted the Ottoman delegation with the words: 'I am the president of the Turkish Grand National Assembly and of its government. Whom do I have the honour of meeting?' Surprised, the Ottoman ministers reeled off their titles, whereupon Mustafa Kemal said that, as he did not recognize the government in Istanbul, he would not hold any discussions so long as the gentlemen from the capital insisted on calling themselves ministers.[56] In his memoirs, Ahmet İzzet Paşa says simply that, surprised at the presence of a parliamentary delegation, he did badly in the discussions: 'but it would not have mattered if I had done well'.[57] After this brief encounter on 5 November, the Ottoman ministers were taken by train to Ankara, where, they were told, the talks would continue.

In effect, they were kidnapped: unbeknown to them, the Anatolian Agency was instructed by Mustafa Kemal to announce that Ahmet İzzet Paşa and his companions had decided to remove themselves from foreign pressure and join the nationalists in Anatolia.[58] Mustafa Kemal was to say later that he was prepared to offer appropriate positions to both Ahmet İzzet and to Salih Paşa, provided they accepted the nationalists' principles. 'But they were not so disposed. Not once did they enter the building of the Grand National Assembly.'[59] There could be no meeting of minds, as Ahmet İzzet and Salih Paşas were unwilling to compromise the continued existence of the sultan's government in Istanbul. In March 1921, they were finally allowed to return, thanks to Colonel İsmet (İnönü)'s mediation, but only after they had promised to resign.[60] When they subsequently accepted ministerial office again, Ahmet İzzet Paşa becoming the last Ottoman foreign minister, Mustafa Kemal claimed that they had breached an oral understanding, while Ahmet İzzet argued that he had not promised he would never accept office again after his resignation.[61]

After the pashas had been taken to Ankara against their will, Ethem sent a telegram to the Grand National Assembly demanding that they should be allowed to return to Istanbul. Members of the assembly, he declared, were concerned only with their personal interests. They were no better than the members of the old Ottoman parliament who had contributed to the defeat in the Great War by neglecting their duties.[62] Nevertheless, the assembly tried to conciliate the Circassians, and sent a peace delegation to Kütahya. As the delegates contented themselves with transmitting Ethem's demands, which included the dismissal of Refet and his cavalry commander Fahrettin (Altay), the Ankara government recalled them on 27 December. Three days later, a force of 15,000 troops under the command of Colonel İsmet in the north and of Colonel Refet in the south moved against the Circassians. Ethem put up no resistance as the regular army occupied his stronghold in Kütahya. On 2 January 1921, the Ankara government made a last offer: Ethem and his brothers would be pardoned if they gave up their commands.

The Circassians, however, preferred to parley with the Greeks, who profited from the weakening in the Turkish lines by moving forward on 6 January. The following day, Ethem signed a protocol allowing him to take refuge behind Greek lines. By 17 January his Mobile Forces had ceased to exist: 725 Circassians, headed by Ethem, Reşit and Tevfik, crossed over to the Greeks; others scattered, some joining Turkish regular units. Mustafa Kemal's decision to impose his government's authority on the irregulars, even after the start of a Greek offensive, had been risky, and he faced criticism in the assembly. But this was stilled by Ethem's flight to the enemy. He was proclaimed a traitor, and the Independence Tribunal condemned him and his fellow-fugitives to death. The era of the militias was over, to the chagrin of romantics who wanted to see Mustafa Kemal as the leader of a people's war. It was an unrealistic expectation. Mustafa Kemal, denied the Ottoman war ministry in November 1918, had now become the leader of the Ottoman army which was reconstituting itself as the Turkish national army under the best of its Prussian-trained officers.

The formation of an orderly new state on the foundations and, largely, with the personnel of its Ottoman predecessor was signalled on 20 January 1921, when the assembly passed the Law of Fundamental Organization (*Teşkilât-ı Esasiye Kanunu*).[63] It read like a revolutionary constitution. Sovereignty, it declared, belonged unconditionally to the nation, and administration would be based on popular self-rule. The country was for the first time named officially as the State of Turkey, ruled by the Government of the Turkish Grand National Assembly. The Assembly enjoyed full legislative and executive powers. It could also declare war, make peace and conclude treaties – decisions which required a royal decree under the Ottoman constitution. Provinces were to enjoy autonomy under elected councils. However, the central government would name provincial governors and regional inspectors-general to maintain its authority throughout the country.

At Mustafa Kemal's insistence, the sultan was not mentioned. In the debate in the assembly, Mustafa Kemal declared that the sultanate and the caliphate were accepted in principle, but it was better not to define the remaining prerogatives of these institutions. Mustafa Kemal assured Kâzım Karabekir that a republic was nowhere implied in the text;[64] his immediate concern was to obtain the legal authority to lead the country. The law introduced an innovation: the council of ministers, each one of whom was to be elected separately by the assembly, would itself elect a chairman, in other words a prime minister. But as president of the

assembly, Mustafa Kemal was to be *ex officio* head of the government
also. Mustafa Kemal then ensured the choice of his faithful supporter
Fevzi Paşa (Çakmak) as prime minister. It was another instance of his
ability to preserve the leadership, while delegating day-to-day administration to loyal lieutenants.

Mustafa Kemal took every opportunity to stress the populist character of the regime in Ankara, but romantics could not fail to see its rigid
hierarchical structure. One such romantic was the 19-year-old poet
Nazım Hikmet, who came from a well-connected family of Ottoman
officials. On 3 January 1920, he and three other young writers arrived at
the small port of İnebolu on the Black Sea, which served as an entry
point for travellers to Ankara. As Mustafa Kemal had informed the
assembly, nationalist authorities along the Black Sea coast were vigilant
– 'there is not a bird that flies by without our knowledge'.[65] The district
governor of İnebolu asked Ankara whether the writers, who were sporting red scarves and making no secret of their Communist sympathies,
were to be admitted. Permission was granted.

Nazım Hikmet made his way to Ankara where he was befriended by
left-wing Unionists, including the journalist Muhittin (Birgen), who was
the nationalists' press director. Nazım Hikmet was taken to the assembly and introduced to Mustafa Kemal. 'Some young poets,' Mustafa
Kemal said to him, 'have taken to writing poems without a subject. My
advice to you is to write committed poetry.'[66] Nazım Hikmet took the
advice, but not in the sense meant by Mustafa Kemal. Turkey's best
modern poet was to put his talent at the service of the Bolsheviks. Even
in the long years of Stalin's tyranny, he never deviated openly from the
Moscow line. By the time Nazım Hikmet had arrived in Ankara, the
Circassian Ethem's defeat had led to a persecution of all 'unofficial'
Communists. Disappointed, Nazım Hikmet obtained a job as a village
schoolmaster. A few months later, he made his way to Soviet Russia.

Turkish Communists in Russia disregarded the signals from Ankara.
Their leader was Mustafa Suphi, the Paris-trained son of a Turkish provincial governor. On his return from France, he had quarrelled with
the CUP, fled to Russia, was interned there during the Great War, joined
the Bolsheviks after the revolution, and became founding leader of the
Turkish Communist Party in Baku in September 1920. Mustafa Kemal
warned him immediately that social changes in Turkey had to be left to
the discretion of his government.[67] Mustafa Suphi was not deterred.
Accompanied by his wife and seventeen comrades, he joined a group of
Soviet officials who were being sent to set up an embassy in Ankara.
They arrived in Kars on 28 December 1920 and met the Eastern Front
commander, Kâzım Karabekir, and Ali Fuat Paşa who was travelling in

the opposite direction to take up his post as Turkish ambassador in Moscow.

Mustafa Suphi was worried that his party might be attacked by Turkish nationalists if they proceeded to Erzurum. But he turned down Karabekir's suggestion that he return to Baku.[68] 'We are trying to understand Mustafa Kemal's principles,' Mustafa Suphi told Ali Fuat. The latter warned Mustafa Kemal that Mustafa Suphi was a cunning operator who would try to make the 'official' Turkish Communist Party subservient to Moscow.[69] Leaving the Soviet embassy party in Kars, Mustafa Suphi and his friends travelled to Erzurum. The local governor did not allow them into the town, and sent them by road to Trabzon, intending, as he told Mustafa Kemal, to ship them back to Russia under guard. Mustafa Kemal's only response was to ask the governor how many companions Mustafa Suphi had and whether they were all travelling together.

The Communists arrived in Trabzon on 28 January 1920, after a difficult journey marked by hostile demonstrations. Sympathizers in Trabzon had prepared a welcoming ceremony, in which the Soviet Russian consul was to take part. But as the welcoming party waited, Mustafa Suphi and his companions were taken to the harbour by a different route. They were met by a Unionist mobster, Yahya, master (*kâhya*) of the guild of boatmen, who controlled access to ships using the open roadstead. Yahya put Mustafa Suphi and twelve companions (the others seem to have fallen off on the way) on board a motor launch, which was accompanied by a second launch full of his armed men. Mustafa Suphi thought that they were being taken to İnebolu on their way to Ankara. There was an angry argument when he realized that they were travelling east, back to Russia. Whether in the heat of the argument or, more likely, by pre-arranged design, Yahya's armed men in the second boat fell on Mustafa Suphi and his friends, and flung them into the sea. Whether they shot them first is not clear. Yahya's men returned to Trabzon the following morning, 29 January. The boat on which the Communists were travelling disappeared.

The murder of the Turkish Communists was organized and carried out by right-wing Unionists, many of whom had served in Enver's Special Organization. Later, after Mustafa Kemal had stopped Enver's bid to re-enter Turkey through Trabzon, these men were removed from the scene. Yahya was shot in front of the Trabzon barracks on 3 July 1922.[70] There is little doubt that the killing had been ordered by the military authorities, determined to put an end to Yahya's strong-arm 'harbour government', which terrorized Trabzon, just as Lame Osman had terrorized Giresun, down the coast. With Yahya silenced, there was no way of determining whether he had received instructions from Ankara to liquidate Mustafa Suphi and his companions. Clearly, Mustafa Kemal wanted them out of the country, just as he had wanted Ethem and his brothers removed from their commands.

Mustafa Kemal's record shows that he did his best to get rid of his opponents without bloodshed. But if they refused to submit, there were always people willing to act in line with his presumed wishes. Yahya needed little encouragement to kill the Communists. A wink was enough, and it probably came from local nationalist authorities. Mustafa Kemal could have intervened to stop the crime, but did not do so. In 1923, he told Turkish journalists that his government had stopped the Russians setting up a Communist organization in the country. 'We arrested some people. In other words, we applied fairly strong measures. This did not please the Russians.'[71] However, the murder of Mustafa Suphi and of his companions did not affect the course of relations between the Bolsheviks and Kemalist nationalists. Both parties were realists. It fell to the lot of the romantic poet Nazım Hikmet to mourn the death of the Communists in one of the most moving poems in modern Turkish literature.

The press chief of the Ankara government, Muhittin (Birgen), followed Nazım Hikmet to Bolshevik Russia. In a letter to Kâzım Karabekir, he described the nationalist capital as 'a hell designed to rot one's nerves and one's morals'. He went on:

> I am convinced that the success of the struggle in Anatolia demands that military operations should be accompanied by social action. We came to Ankara to defend this view. After a year, we saw that the Istanbul government has been recreated in Ankara under another name ... The Government of the People and the Nation exists in name only. In fact, the people of Anatolia have not backed the struggle and have persistently risen against it.[72]

There was much truth in Muhittin's complaint. But the people of Anatolia would not have responded to the Communist message; they were used to firm leadership, which Mustafa Kemal provided, and, in spite of occasional backsliding, they settled down under him, as they had earlier settled down under the sultans and their governors.

Muhittin was worried that the Ankara government might come to an agreement with the West, even though he did not believe that Mustafa Kemal favoured this course. In fact, this was precisely what Mustafa Kemal had in mind, but on his own terms. He knew how to pick his way through the political intrigues that so disgusted romantic intellectuals. And if the latter found no room for their idealism, there were other idealists who were fired by Mustafa Kemal's message. They were the young officers who joined his army, and young teachers and civil servants who wanted to bring civilized order to the country. Less sophisticated than metropolitan intellectuals, they were not put off by the intrigues of their elders. But it was easy to lose sight of them in the babel of nationalist politics.

Mustafa Kemal was the master politician in Ankara. Except for a few brief train journeys, undertaken to sort out domestic political problems, he stayed in town, trying to mould the assembly to his wishes, conferring with his ministers, and sending out a stream of telegrams to commanders in the field, local administrators and others. His power base was still weak and this forced him to work discreetly by persuasion and manipulation. He avoided public speeches outside the assembly, which often met in closed session. He did most of his work in private meetings, which continued far into the night, when discussions were lubricated by *rakı*.

Some order was introduced into his domestic arrangements, when Fikriye decided to join him. On 11 November 1920, she arrived by boat unexpectedly at Ereğli on the Black Sea, saying that she could no longer stay in Istanbul, as her brother had left to join the nationalists and her sister had died.[73] The district governor asked Mustafa Kemal for instructions. Mustafa Kemal's ADC, Salih (Bozok), replied that arrangements should be made to allow Fikriye to proceed to Ankara in the company of a friend from Salonica, Mithat, who had earlier arrived in Ereğli. The pair travelled to Ankara, where Fikriye became Mustafa Kemal's housekeeper, private secretary and companion in the stationmaster's house (known locally as 'the villa'), which served as both his lodgings and his office.

A slender, pretty, 23-year-old, dressed in ladylike European clothes, Fikriye was totally devoted to Mustafa Kemal. She could play the piano and create a corner of cosy domesticity in a wild frontier setting. She could ride, in spite of her weak state of health – she was tubercular and, like Mustafa Kemal, contracted malaria. As a sign of their intimacy, she wore a necklace made of his amber worry beads. She made no demands on him, and got on well with the wives of his companions – his ADC Salih, the writer Ruşen Eşref – and his Levantine lady friend, Madame Fansa, in whose house he had stayed in Istanbul in November 1918. Fikriye seemed the ideal, discreet companion. But Mustafa Kemal knew that his mother, Zübeyde, thought that Fikriye was unsuitable as a wife, and that his sister Makbule did not get on with her. Neither lady would have easily yielded up Mustafa Kemal to another woman. Mustafa Kemal was a dutiful son. In any case, he was happy to remain unattached, provided his needs were met. Marriage could wait.

15

Stopping the Greeks

A T THE END of 1920, the international position of Turkish nationalists was strengthened by the sudden fall from power of their main
foreign enemy. On 14 November – three months after the signature of
the treaty of Sèvres – one of its chief beneficiaries, the Greek prime
minister Eleftherios Venizelos was defeated in general elections. The
elections were held in the aftermath of the sudden death of young King
Alexander of Greece, bitten by a monkey in the gardens of his palace on
the outskirts of Athens. Venizelos went off to France to bide his time.
In a plebiscite on 5 December, there was a majority for the return of
Alexander's father, Constantine, the brother-in-law of Kaiser Wilhelm.
    Constantine had tried to keep his country neutral in the Great War,
and was, in consequence, deposed by the Allies in 1917. The latter now
had an excuse to change their policy towards Turkey. The French and
the Italians, who had been dragged unwillingly in the wake of Lloyd
George's Philhellene schemes, seized the opportunity with both hands.
Even the British government associated itself with a formal notification
that no further financial assistance would be given to Greece following
Constantine's return.[1] But Lloyd George had convinced himself that
a Greater Greece would safeguard Britain's interests in the eastern
Mediterranean, and was determined to salvage the essence of the treaty
of Sèvres. With this end in mind, he called a conference in London in
February 1921 to bring together representatives of the Allies, Greece
and Turkey. The Allied High Commissioners in Istanbul asked that
Mustafa Kemal or his representatives should be included in the
Ottoman delegation.[2]
    Constantine's return led to a purge of Venizelist commanders in the

Greek army, who were replaced by officers dismissed between 1917 and 1920. Immediately after the fall of Venizelos, one of his military opponents, Anastasios Papoulas, was released from imprisonment in Crete, promoted Lieutenant-General and appointed commander-in-chief of the Greek army in Anatolia. Constantine and his prime minister Dimitrios Rallis were eager to score a military success on the eve of the London conference. Papoulas was ready to oblige. Encouraged by news of the revolt of Ethem's Circassians, he ordered his troops on the northern sector of the front to advance from Bursa and attack Colonel İsmet's headquarters in Eskişehir.

The Greeks were more numerous and better armed than their Turkish opponents.[3] On 9 January 1921, the Turks, entrenched on the Anatolian escarpment near the railway station of İnönü, came under attack. The following day, they had to fall back. The general staff in Ankara gave İsmet permission to abandon Eskişehir, while at the same time sending reinforcements to help hold a new line further east. But on 11 January, İsmet was surprised to learn that the Greeks had turned back, believing that they were not strong enough to face Turkish reinforcements.[4] Papoulas described the operation as a reconnaissance in force. Mustafa Kemal claimed it as a great victory. Turkish losses were light – 95 killed and 183 wounded[5] – reflecting the limited scope of the engagement, which is known in Turkish history as the first battle of İnönü. A few days later, the troops of the Grand National Assembly dispersed the last of Ethem's irregulars further south, while the Greeks looked on. On 1 March, İsmet was promoted Brigadier-General. He would henceforth be called Pasha.

Mustafa Kemal made skilful use of the invitation to send representatives to the London conference. The invitation had been indirect and had reached him through the Istanbul government. In order to ensure a direct approach and thus secure Allied recognition of his government, he made it his aim to persuade the Ottoman government to step aside. On 28 January 1921 he asked the grand vizier Tevfik Paşa to persuade Sultan Vahdettin to issue a decree recognizing the Ankara government; the cabinet in Istanbul would then be dissolved. The sultan could stay on in his palace, his expenses borne by the Grand National Assembly which would send a delegation to exercise authority in Istanbul. Mustafa Kemal warned that if the sultan refused, his position would be shaken.[6] It was a polite way of threatening Vahdettin with deposition.

Tevfik Paşa tried to sidestep Mustafa Kemal's demands by insisting that participation in the conference was essential at a time when the Greeks were preparing a major offensive, and that the Allied insistence that Ankara should be represented in the Ottoman delegation was a concession with which Mustafa Kemal should content himself.[7] The fact was that the Ankara government had yet to prove itself on the field of battle; until that happened it could not expect to be treated as the Allies' main interlocutor in Turkey.

Having staked out his position, Mustafa Kemal obtained the authority of the assembly to send a separate delegation to London. It was headed by the nationalists' foreign minister, Bekir Sami (Kunduh), and it made use of the facilities which the Italians were always ready to provide. The nationalist delegates boarded an Italian warship in Antalya. From Rome, Bekir Sami cabled to Mustafa Kemal that he had received a direct invitation to the conference, and that he was therefore proceeding to London.[8] 'The direct invitation' appears to have been a face-saving device produced by the Italians, as the British government baulked at the idea of extending official recognition to the Ankara government. In London, Tevfik Paşa played his part skilfully. He was old and sick, and had his legs wrapped in a blanket at the conference table at St James's palace. But he had his wits about him. Without resigning his own authority, as Mustafa Kemal had demanded, Tevfik Paşa invited the Ankara delegates to explain the Turkish position. This was done in eloquent French by the adviser of the Ankara party, Nihat Reşat (Belger), an eminent Turkish doctor who was at the time living in Paris, where he divided his time between medicine and the advocacy of the Turkish cause in a review called *Écho de l'Orient*.

The conference at St James's spent its time exploring dead ends: minor modifications of the treaty of Sèvres, which Ankara had rejected in its entirety; a commission of enquiry into the ethnic composition of the territory occupied by the Greeks; arrangements for an autonomous administration for the İzmir region. The talks were doomed to failure since the Turks insisted that Greece should withdraw its troops from western Anatolia and eastern Thrace, while the Greeks had convinced themselves that they could make good their territorial ambitions by force of arms.

Lloyd George was happy to see the Greeks make the attempt, although he could not promise them any material support. The imminent failure of his policy of supporting Greek expansion stared him in the face. The French and the Italians were ready to make terms with Turkish nationalists; even British military authorities in Istanbul were establishing discreet contacts with the Kemalists through their representative in Istanbul, Hamit, the vice-president of the Turkish Red Crescent Society. Lloyd George consoled himself with scandal-mongering. Bekir Sami, he told King George V, was 'a ruffian' who had been 'traced to a sodomy house in the East End. He was the representative of Mustapha Kemal, a man who I understand has grown tired of affairs with women, and has lately taken up unnatural sexual intercourse.'[9] Of Bekir Sami's sexual orientation we know nothing, but all the evidence shows that Mustafa Kemal was far from tired of affairs with women.[10] Lloyd George was not particular about the methods he used: the king, he knew, was easily shocked, while his own nonconformist conscience was infinitely flexible. Lloyd George's denunciations did not stop one of his officials, Robert Vansittart of the Foreign Office, from negotiating with Bekir Sami an agreement on the exchange of Turkish detainees in Malta against British officers imprisoned by the Kemalists in Anatolia. The agreement was rejected by Ankara because it excluded Turks accused of war crimes.[11]

The same fate awaited two other, and more important documents signed by Bekir Sami in London. On 9 March he reached an agreement with the French: it provided for the cessation of hostilities, and the evacuation by the French of the territory in southern Turkey, lying within the 1918 armistice lines, with the exception of the district of İskenderun (Alexandretta) which was to enjoy a special status to safeguard its Turkish culture. In exchange, the French were to be allowed a privileged role in the economic development of southern and eastern Turkey.[12] Under another agreement signed on 12 March, the Italians promised to work for Turkish rights in Thrace and İzmir and withdraw their troops, in exchange for economic privileges in central and western Turkey.[13] Although the agreement was never ratified, the Italians quietly withdrew their troops from southern Turkey, between April and July 1921.[14]

Bekir Sami believed that he had struck a good bargain: the Allies could have their economic zones of influence, on which they had agreed after concluding the treaty of Sèvres, provided they amended the territorial settlement and left the Turks in control of the land lying within the 1918 armistice lines. Mustafa Kemal decided that it would not be politic to put the argument to the assembly.[15] It was better to procrastinate, and see whether an improvement in the military situation would make it possible to negotiate better terms. In the meantime, the three unratified agreements could initiate the process of peacemaking with the three Western Allies and serve to distance them from Greek and Armenian claims.

Mustafa Kemal's ability to influence the course of the conference was limited. But, although the conference broke up without agreement, it had served his purpose. It provided an opportunity to publicize the National Pact and to exploit differences between the Allies. It was a step towards the recognition of the Ankara government. Most importantly, it led to a declaration by the Allies that they would be neutral in the war

between Greece and Turkey.[16] This was what Turkish nationalists had
sought all along. They had picked off the Armenians. Now they had
neutralized the great powers. Only the Greeks remained to be dealt
with. Mustafa Kemal relied on subordinates to fight his diplomatic
battles, subordinates who could be disowned when they made mistakes,
or if conditions allowed a better settlement. Just as he avoided taking
the field at the head of the army, unless absolutely necessary, so he
never took the lead in diplomatic negotiations.

While the Allies were manoeuvring behind each other's back in
London, Turkish nationalists rounded off their territory at the expense
of Georgia. On 12 February 1921, the Red Army launched an attack on
the nationalist government of Georgia. On 25 February it occupied the
Georgian capital, Tiflis (Tbilisi).[17] The Turks had to act quickly if they
were to regain the rest of the territory which they had lost to the
Russians in 1878. On 22 February, the Georgian ambassador in Ankara
was informed that Turkish troops would occupy the districts of
Ardahan and Artvin: they entered Ardahan the following day. Georgian
nationalists invited them to advance further in order to keep out the
Red Army. On 11 March, Turks occupied the important port of Batum
(Batumi), only to cede it five days later to (Soviet) Georgia under an
agreement which Ali Fuat Paşa had finally succeeded in negotiating in
Moscow.[18]

Attached to the agreement was a letter in which the Soviet foreign
commissar Chicherin promised to remit to Turkey 10 million gold
roubles 'for economic development';[19] deliveries of arms were also
speeded up. In all, the Bolsheviks supplied the Kemalists with more
than 45,000 rifles, 300 machine-guns, and nearly a hundred field guns,
with appropriate ammunition:[20] they came from stocks left behind by
foreign armies on Russian soil, as well as from Russian supplies, and
they played an important part in keeping nationalist armies in the field
against well-equipped Greek forces. The Moscow treaty fixed Turkey's
eastern frontiers, but these were not confirmed until the nominally
independent Soviet Socialist Republics of Georgia, Armenia and
Azerbaijan signed an agreement with Turkey in Kars on 13 October
1921.[21] Like the French, the Bolsheviks did not commit themselves
finally until the Kemalists had shown their worth in battle.

The war with the Greeks now entered its decisive phase. General
Papoulas brought in fresh troops and launched a second assault on
İsmet's positions on 26 March. The Turks had also brought in rein-
forcements and the two armies were roughly equal in numbers: 37,000

men of the Greek 3rd corps facing 35,000 Turkish troops on the İnönü sector. But the Greeks were better equipped, particularly with machine-guns and motor transport. Once again, the Greeks fought well and made initial gains, capturing the commanding height of Metristepe on 27 March. The Turks counter-attacked at night but failed to recapture the peak. The situation worried Mustafa Kemal and his prime minister (and acting chief of the general staff) Fevzi, in Ankara. The battalion guarding the Grand National Assembly and a regiment of the Caucasian division, quartered in Sivas, were despatched to the front.

On 31 March, İsmet counter-attacked again: this time, the Greeks were forced to retreat. On 1 April İsmet sent a telegram to Mustafa Kemal from the newly recaptured peak of Metristepe. 'The enemy,' he announced, 'has abandoned the battlefield to our arms, leaving thousands of dead behind.'[22] Mustafa Kemal replied in style:

> Few commanders in the whole history of the world have faced a task as difficult as that which you undertook in the pitched battles of İnönü. The independent life of our nation was entrusted to the heart-felt care of your commanders and comrades-in-arms, who have honourably discharged their duty under your brilliant direction. It was not only the enemy you have defeated, but fate itself – the ill-starred fate of our nation ...[23]

İsmet's generalship was certainly better than that of Refet, who commanded the southern sector of the western front. The general staff in Ankara had guessed correctly that the Greeks would once again direct their main thrust towards the Turkish positions at İnönü, and detached some of Refet's forces to reinforce them. Mortified, Refet submitted his resignation. He was persuaded to stay on. After the Greeks had withdrawn from İnönü, some Turkish units were moved south where the Greeks had captured the important town of Afyonkarahisar. Refet counter-attacked, forcing the Greeks to evacuate Afyonkarahisar on 7 April. On 11 April, Refet informed Ankara that his army had won 'the honour of delivering the final blow against the enemy.'

Mustafa Kemal expressed his pleasure in orotund terms: 'Our army has reappeared on the stage of history in thunderous majesty.'[24] But the celebration was premature. Refet's ambitious outflanking move failed, and the Greeks straightened their line round a strong position at Dumlupınar, west of Afyonkarahisar. Their troops retreated in good order both from İnönü and, over a much shorter distance, from Afyonkarahisar. Turkish losses were over 5,000 dead in İnönü, and 400 dead in the southern sector. Tactical mistakes by Turkish commanders were compounded by the poor morale of their men: 2,000 of İsmet's troops and 4,000 of Refet's weaker forces deserted during the battle.[25]

Mustafa Kemal's rhetoric concealed the wavering mood of the Anatolian peasants, who did not always trust the determined but ill-trained young officers leading them into battle.

Still, the Greeks had been momentarily stopped, and Mustafa Kemal put the fact to good use. The military command structure was reorganized, and the northern and southern sectors of the western front were unified under İsmet's command. The Turkish success at İnönü encouraged Mustafa Kemal to improve on the terms negotiated by Bekir Sami in London. On 8 June, the French politician Henry Franklin-Bouillon, former chairman of the foreign affairs committee of the French National Assembly, came to Ankara, theoretically in a private capacity, but in fact as the representative of the French foreign minister Aristide Briand.[26] On 13 June, Major Douglas Henry, representing General Sir Charles ('Tim') Harington, the Allied commander-in-chief in Istanbul, arrived in İnebolu, where he met Refet, newly released from his military duties on the western front. The ostensible subject for discussion was the exchange of detainees, but the real purpose was to explore the possibility of an understanding between London and Ankara. Bekir Sami who had laid the ground for the negotiations had conveniently left the scene: on 16 May he resigned the foreign ministry, after having faced strong criticism in the assembly.[27]

In Ankara, Franklin-Bouillon was treated to a lecture on the National Pact and its insistence on Turkey's full independence. There was more French than British capital invested in Turkey, and France relied on the system of capitulations to safeguard its economic interests. Like all Turkish nationalists, Mustafa Kemal demanded that the capitulations should be abolished. France was not yet ready for this. After some tough bargaining, Franklin-Bouillon left for Paris, saying that more time was needed for an agreement.[28] But as a sign of good will, the French withdrew from the coal port of Zonguldak on the Black Sea on 21 June.[29]

The contacts with the British were more tortuous. After a preliminary discussion, Major Henry returned to İnebolu with a letter in which Harington said that he had understood that Mustafa Kemal wished to meet him, and suggested that the meeting should take place on board the British battleship *Ajax*. He would listen to what Mustafa Kemal had to say, but would not be empowered to negotiate. Mustafa Kemal replied that Major Henry had left a signed copy of a letter which made it clear that it was General Harington who had asked for a meeting. If Harington was ready to hold discussions on the basis of Turkey's known demands for full independence and the withdrawal of all enemy troops, then he would be welcome in İnebolu. If, however, he was interested only in exchanging views, Mustafa Kemal could send a subordinate for the purpose.[30] There was no reply, but Major Henry returned and sought information on British detainees and on the intentions of the Turkish military concerning Istanbul.[31]

Whether Major Henry misinterpreted Refet (or vice-versa) is immaterial: Harington had used Henry and Mustafa Kemal had used Refet to establish contact. Both could be disowned. But Mustafa Kemal got the clear impression that Harington wanted to parley, while Harington began to see that, under the right conditions, an agreement with Mustafa Kemal was perfectly possible. However, distrust of British intentions remained strong in Ankara. On 24 May, an Indian Muslim, Mustafa Saghir, arrived in Ankara as the representative of the Khilafat (caliphate) movement, at that time the main pressure group of Indian Muslims. The nationalist authorities accused him of being a British agent and of planning to assassinate Mustafa Kemal. He was tried by the Independence Tribunal, was found guilty and was hanged. According to Kılıç Ali, the expert in covert operations who had become the most feared member of the tribunal, Mustafa Saghir admitted that he had worked for British Intelligence for many years. Frank Rattigan, the British Acting High Commissioner in Istanbul, tried unsuccessfully to save Saghir's life, while admitting that he was compromised.[32] There is little doubt that there were foreign spies in Ankara;[33] but in the case of the British government, their reports did not bring enlightenment to policy-makers.

Pending a formal agreement, some of the Turkish detainees in Malta were released. Others escaped. One of the first to reach Ankara was Ziya (Gökalp), the chief ideologist of Turkish nationalism. He was followed by Mustafa Kemal's close collaborator Ali Fethi (Okyar).[34] Mustafa Kemal needed help to control the assembly. On 10 May he held a meeting with his supporters and decided to set up his own political party: he called it the Group for the Defence of National Rights, the name under which he had failed to rally nationalist deputies in the last Ottoman parliament. This meant turning the Anatolia and Rumelia Society for the Defence of National Rights from a national into a party organization, which was free to exclude assembly members of whom it disapproved.[35] Mustafa Kemal became the chairman of the new party.

As head both of the legislature and the executive, Mustafa Kemal could now rely on a parliamentary majority which took decisions in private and could then push them through the assembly. The members excluded from his party now came together under the name of the Second Group, which became the opposition party. The leaders of the opposition represented constituencies in the east of the country: in Erzurum, the Society for the Defence of National Rights added to its title the words 'and for the Protection of the Sacred Heritage' (*Muhafaza-yı Mukaddesat*).[36] The heritage was the sultanate, the caliphate and Islamic law (*şeriat*). The first two were not mentioned in the Law of Fundamental Organization – the constitution passed by the assembly – but the implementation of the *şeriat* was specified as the first duty of the assembly. Nevertheless, conservative nationalists had no difficulty in recognizing the modernist ideas of Mustafa Kemal and his friends and the authoritarian intentions behind their professions of populism.

Mustafa Kemal was less disturbed by the official opposition than by the lack of cohesion of his own party. In May, the prime minister Fevzi Paşa had to resign when the assembly expressed doubts about the wisdom of passing an unbalanced budget. He was re-elected at the head of a new government, in which Fethi (Okyar) became interior minister. Bekir Sami was replaced as foreign minister by one of Mustafa Kemal's loyal supporters, Yusuf Kemal (Tengirşenk), who had signed the Moscow agreement with the Bolsheviks. Mustafa Kemal now had a stronger political team.

The victory at İnönü had been greeted with joy by the Turkish population of Istanbul. Even the sultan had prayers read for the soldiers killed in the fighting and sent a donation to the Red Crescent for the relief of victims.[37] The heir apparent, Abdülmecit, who took special care to express nationalist sentiments, went a step further and despatched his son Ömer Faruk to join the nationalists in Anatolia. The prince arrived by sea in İnebolu, where, like any other traveller, he was made to wait until instructions were received from Ankara. On 27 April he was handed a polite telegram from Mustafa Kemal. It was, he said, in the national interest that he should return to Istanbul; the time had not yet come when the country could make use of the services of all the members of the 'exalted' dynasty.[38] Mustafa Kemal was proceeding step by step, but the direction of his moves was becoming clear.

Mustafa Kemal showed his preoccupations at a speech he made at the opening of a teachers' convention in Ankara on 16 July. The new generation had to be endowed with a strong feeling of order and discipline, he declared. The culture which should be taught should be free of old superstitions and of 'foreign ideas, of all influences, whether from the east or the west, which are alien to our innate character'.[39] Again it was a first step. The move from the east (both Islamic and Bolshevik) had begun, the move to the west would follow.

The pause on the western front was brief. Greece made a supreme effort to win the war: more recruits were called up and the strength of the army in Anatolia was brought up to 200,000 men.[40] On 12 June, King Constantine arrived in İzmir to decide with General Papoulas the plan for a major offensive. It was launched on 10 July. As the Turks had also brought in reinforcements, the two opposing armies were once again roughly equal in numbers. Some 126,000 Greek troops took part in the attack on Turkish lines which were defended by 122,000 men. But again, the Greeks were better armed. They had 410 field guns against the Turks' 160, some 4,000 machine-guns against the Turks' 700, and 20 aircraft against the Turks' four.[41]

The main Greek thrust was directed from the south against Kütahya in the central sector. Its object was to cut the railway line between Afyonkarahisar and Kütahya, and then move north to surround the Turkish headquarters in Eskişehir. The Turkish commander, İsmet Paşa, who had kept the bulk of his forces in the northern sector round İnönü, was caught off-balance. Coordination between the four groups into which his forces had been divided was weak, and the despatch of reinforcements from the two wings was too slow and disorganized to help the crucial central sector. An investigation carried out later by the assembly revealed that of eighteen Turkish divisions, all but five took little part in the fighting, and spent their time on pointless marches.[42] Two of the Turkish commanders – 'Bear-keeper' Arif and 'Mad' Halit – were brave, impetuous, but headstrong, and looked askance at İsmet's orders. The Greeks broke through to Kütahya, which fell on 17 July. They then swung north-east towards Eskişehir.

On the day Kütahya fell, İsmet received a brief telegram from Mustafa Kemal. It read: 'If it's no trouble, I propose to set out immediately to discuss the situation with you.' At five in the morning on the following day İsmet met Mustafa Kemal at Eskişehir station and drove him to his headquarters, to the south of the town. According to an officer present at the meeting, Mustafa Kemal asked İsmet, 'Haven't we lost the battle *déjà*?' (slipping in his favourite French word). 'That's what it looks like,' replied İsmet. 'Then,' said Mustafa Kemal, 'our job is to save the army and prepare a new position. We must withdraw step by step behind the Sakarya river. Let's write the order immediately.'[43] İsmet's account is different. According to him, the meeting took place after his troops had evacuated Eskişehir on 19 July. He proposed, he says, a counter-attack against the Greeks in Eskişehir. If it failed, he would withdraw his troops east of the Sakarya river. Mustafa Kemal agreed and returned to Ankara.[44]

A major Turkish counter-attack was in fact launched on 21 July. It was beaten back and Turkish forces were further weakened. In the evening, front commanders were told by Mustafa Kemal that if counter-attacks made no progress, the entire army should withdraw. But he still hoped that an enemy column further south could be stopped.[45] This sector of the front, south of the curve of the Sakarya river, was defended by cavalry units, under the command of Colonel Fahrettin (Altay). Originally placed in the northern sector, covering Eskişehir against a Greek advance from Bursa, they had been rushed to the open steppe south-east of Eskişehir, country ideally suited to rapid cavalry movement. The trouble was that in July the land was parched, and it was difficult to provision men and horses. Fahrettin's cavalry succeeded in covering the retreat of the Turkish left flank,[46] which abandoned Afyonkarahisar to the Greeks once again on 23 July.[47] The bulk of Turkish troops in the northern sector also escaped encirclement; but the retreat was disorderly. Stores were abandoned in Eskişehir, the railway line stretching east from Eskişehir to the Sakarya was left undamaged, and thousands of men deserted, joining the crowds of civilian refugees fleeing from the Greek advance.[48] In the aftermath of the Greek victory at Kütahya and Eskişehir, the number of Turkish deserters was estimated at 31,000. Soon it was to reach 48,000.[49] The army of the Grand National Assembly emerged from the battle with the loss of some 40,000 men.[50]

Whether or not Mustafa Kemal was as trenchantly decisive when he learnt of the defeat of his forces at Kütahya and Eskişehir as he and his admirers were later to claim, there is no doubt that he approved a rapid withdrawal. His experience had taught him that the army was more important than territory. But it was not easy to explain this in Ankara, which had suddenly become an endangered front town. The assembly was in uproar, the civilian population in panic. On 24 July, the prime minister Fevzi (Çakmak) told the assembly that it had been decided to evacuate Ankara within a week and to move the government to Kayseri. The army, he said, had withdrawn to new positions after suffering heavy losses. If necessary, it would withdraw further to fight on until victory was won. The speech was met with demands that commanders responsible for the defeat should be punished: 'I am the only commander responsible,' Fevzi replied. The assembly then decided to send some of its members to investigate the position at the front. In any case, Ankara was to be defended; while offices and documents would be sent to Kayseri, the assembly would remain in session in Ankara.[51]

Military escorts were provided for the evacuation of the families of ministers and of prominent deputies.[52] The wife of one commander – Colonel (later General) İzzettin (Çalışlar), Mustafa Kemal's chief of staff in the Great War – rushed to Mustafa Kemal's house. She had, she said, two children and needed money for the flight from Ankara.

Mustafa Kemal gave her 50 lira, which was all the money he had on him.[53] At the same time, military members of the assembly obtained permission to serve at the front.[54] The front commander, İsmet, had let it be known that he could give battle west of Ankara if he were provided with 15,000 fresh troops. Deputies rushed to recruitment offices and levies soon began arriving in Ankara. They were then sent by train to Polatlı, the station nearest the Sakarya river.[55] Mustafa Kemal himself paid a brief visit to Polatlı on 26 July.[56] A crucial decision awaited him on his return.

Many members of the assembly had long argued that instead of devoting himself to politics, Mustafa Kemal should take over direct command of the army. A proposal to name Mustafa Kemal commander-in-chief came up for discussion at a closed meeting on 4 August. It could be seen as a revolutionary move, for under the Ottoman constitution, the title of commander-in-chief was vested in the sultan. But Mustafa Kemal saw a threat as well as an opportunity. He was to argue in 1927 that his opponents in the assembly hoped to discard him if he failed in the field. Mustafa Kemal rose to the challenge. He tabled his own proposal, accepting the post of commander-in-chief for a period of three months, on condition that he should be endowed with the full authority of the assembly. This was too much for many members who feared that they would be pushed aside. After lengthy discussions, a compromise was reached on 5 August. Mustafa Kemal would exercise the authority of the assembly in military matters;[57] his appointment as commander-in-chief would be valid for three months, but the assembly could revoke it earlier.[58]

As soon as the law was passed, Mustafa Kemal proposed that the prime minister, Fevzi (Çakmak), should become substantive chief of the general staff and Refet (Bele) minister of war. The assembly agreed, while rejecting Mustafa Kemal's nominee for the interior ministry which was also given to Refet, but on a temporary basis.[59] Mustafa Kemal was to say later that Refet wanted to become chief of the general staff. This Mustafa Kemal refused, telling Refet that he had not proved his capacity for the job.[60] The truth of the matter is that Refet and İsmet could not work successfully together at the front. Under the new arrangement, İsmet reported to Fevzi, while Refet was in charge of supplying the army at the front. It was a difficult job. Not only was equipment scarce but, as it came from various sources, it was difficult to match the ammunition to the weapons. Fortunately for the Turks, a shipment of Russian arms and ammunition had just arrived by sea in Zonguldak. It was rushed to the front in oxcarts, many of them driven by peasant women, whose story now forms part of the epic of

the Turkish War of Independence. Refet was a good organizer and the
subsequent success of Turkish arms owed much to his hard work as war
minister.[61]

As soon as he was appointed commander-in-chief, Mustafa Kemal
issued a proclamation to the nation. The enemy, he declared, would be
'throttled in the inner sanctuary (*harim-i ismet*) of the fatherland'.[62] He
followed it up with ten orders requisitioning supplies from the civil
population: every household was to provide one set of underclothes
and boots for the army; 40 per cent of all stocks of cloth, leather, flour,
soap and candles were to be delivered immediately; all owners of transport were to move army supplies over 100 kilometres a month free of
charge; all weapons had to be surrendered to the army; one fifth of all
horses, carts and carriages had to be given to the military.[63] The impoverished population of a country which had been at war for close on ten
years, and which had lost its most fertile regions, was being asked to
yield up its last supplies.

On 12 August, Mustafa Kemal travelled with Fevzi to İsmet's headquarters at Polatlı. But as he was inspecting the troops, he fell off his
horse and cracked a rib. He returned to Ankara for treatment, and it was
not until 17 August that he finally assumed his command.[64] Three days
earlier, the Greek army had left its positions at Eskişehir and began to
march towards Ankara. The decision to seek out and destroy the
Turkish army was taken at a Greek council of war at Kütahya on 28
July.[65] The Greeks' aims were confused and envisaged the possibility of
having to return to Eskişehir, in which case they would destroy the
railway line running east from that town, and then sit tight hoping that
possession of a large tract of Anatolia would put them in a strong position to force the Turks to agree to the cession of the İzmir area and of
Thrace. It was a forlorn hope. In any case, the Greek plan did not take
account of the devastating effect on their prestige and morale of the
failure of the enterprise to which they committed the bulk of their
troops.

Papoulas tried to repeat the enveloping manoeuvre which had
worked well the previous month in Kütahya. While one army corps
moved east along the railway line to Ankara, two corps marched further
south across the central Anatolian steppe to engage the Turkish left
flank. The Turks had dug in on the edges of the Haymana plateau – a
rolling plain south-east of Ankara, at an altitude of some 3,000 feet. The
plateau is dominated by a number of hills: chief among them Mount
Mangal (Mangal Dağı, literally Mount Brazier) overlooking the Ilıca

valley in the south, and Mount Çal (Çal Dağı, meaning 'bare, stony mountain') in the centre, west of the small town of Haymana. The Turkish positions followed the Sakarya river from north to south until its confluence with a tributary, the Ilıcaözü, where they swung east along the Ilıca valley. They thus formed a right angle. Papoulas planned to break through the base of the angle by crossing the shallow Ilıca stream and then thrust north-east to Haymana and Ankara. This would cut off Turkish troops on the east bank of the Sakarya.

Mustafa Kemal established his headquarters at Alagöz, a village overlooking the plateau from the north, and situated roughly half-way between Ankara and Polatlı. Fevzi amd İsmet had their staffs in near-by houses. They both visited front-line units, checking the execution of orders and trying to raise morale, while Mustafa Kemal was immobilized by his injury and stayed at Alagöz, exercising overall control. He had allowed Halide Edip to enrol as a corporal and join him at his headquarters. Her eye-witness account, written years later in exile after her quarrel with Mustafa Kemal, describes the meticulous attention to detail of the commander-in-chief, his changing moods, his strength of purpose, but also what she saw as his moments of despair.[66] Mustafa Kemal entered the fray with considerable forebodings. In view of the sentiment of the assembly, so he cabled to Karabekir in Erzurum, he had no choice but to give battle west of Ankara; however, he added, 'our position is unfavourable'.[67] As an Istanbul lady, Halide Edip could not fail to be struck by the primitive conditions of life at head-quarters. İsmet, a seasoned provincial soldier, had a different view. 'Alagöz,' he wrote, 'was a pretty village ... The western front head-quarters was large enough for us and our staff officers ... Mustafa Kemal slept even less than usual, dropping off just before dawn ... The pain of his broken rib robbed him of such little rest as he had time for.'[68] Mustafa Kemal's undisciplined companion, 'Bear-keeper' Arif, was at his side.

The Greeks had a slight numerical superiority, as they moved some 100,000 men into battle against 90,000 Turkish troops.[69] But their fire-power was much greater. On the other hand, the Turks had a three-to-one advantage in cavalry, which they used to harass the Greek right flank. The Greeks scored an important success on the first day of the battle on 23 August. Climbing up from the Ilıca valley they captured Mount Mangal against weak Turkish opposition. Mustafa Kemal was furious: he threatened to court-martial the commanders of the Turkish 5th division which failed to defend the peak and ordered the unit to retrieve its honour by holding fast to its new positions.[70] The Greeks continued to make progress, capturing several hills as they swung north towards Mount Çal. On 26 August, İsmet proposed a retreat to a new line. Fevzi decided to hold on round Mount Çal, and brought in reinforcements from the northern flank. In the evening the Greek commander-in-chief Papoulas and Prince Andrew, King Constantine's younger brother, who commanded his 2nd army corps, had a narrow escape when the Turkish cavalry, commanded by Colonel Fahrettin, stumbled on their headquarters at Uzunbeyli village, lying in the steppe to the south of the Ilıca valley. Unaware of the prize awaiting them, Fahrettin called off the attack in response to a call by İsmet to help his troops further north.

The situation there was serious, and Mustafa Kemal ordered work to begin on preparing a new line of defence on the outskirts of Ankara. But while he was determined to save his army if the front were broken, he demanded that every inch of territory should be defended. On 27 August he explained his principle of defence in depth, in an order which proclaimed that what was to be defended was not a line, but the country as a whole. Every unit was to stand its ground, even if neighbouring units were forced to fall back.[71] Nevertheless, he was to report later to the assembly that the initial Greek advance had worked in his favour, as his front line was now shorter and more easily defensible – instead of fighting on two sides of a right angle, Turkish troops now held the hypotenuse.[72] In Ankara, anxious deputies were given two daily briefings by Mustafa Kemal's comrade, Hüsrev (Gerede), who kept insisting that there was no need to worry as long as Mount Çal remained in Turkish hands.[73] After several days of fierce fighting, the Greeks captured Mount Çal on 2 September. But they had reached the limits of their endurance: they had suffered heavy losses; they were often hungry, as their supplies were interrupted by Fahrettin's cavalry; nor were they used to fighting in the summer heat of the Anatolian plateau. But the Turks were not to know this immediately.

According to Halide Edip, the news of the loss of Mount Çal pushed Mustafa Kemal into a state of depressive indecision.[74] Karabekir, writing also after his break with Mustafa Kemal, claims that Fevzi told him that Kemal ordered a general withdrawal, but that Fevzi delayed carrying out the order.[75] According to another version, Fevzi said simply, 'We may be drenched, but then the enemy is not basking in the sun',[76] and argued that there should be no withdrawal. In his victory speech to the assembly on 19 September, Mustafa Kemal claimed that the loss of Mount Çal left him unconcerned. 'For an army that keeps its head, a single position is of no importance,' he said. 'A soldier can fight anywhere – on top of a hill, below a hill, down in a valley. Accordingly, our army was not worried by the loss of Mount Çal. It established itself along a stronger line, five hundred metres, a thousand metres to the east.[77] But the loss of the mountain had certainly worried the assembly: when Hüsrev (Gerede) announced it, he was manhandled by the deputies, and decided to put an end to his briefings.[78]

İsmet believed he knew why the tide turned. He had observed Papoulas closely ever since the first battle of İnönü. His adversary was a good field commander, but he lacked perseverance. Aiming at quick results, he became nervous when he failed to achieve them, and his anxiety affected his judgement. Fearing disaster, he withdrew his troops prematurely. 'Papoulas,' İsmet wrote in his memoirs, 'avoided disaster. But he never won a battle.'[79] On the banks of the Sakarya, as at İnönü, Greeks and Turks contemplated withdrawal at the same time. On both occasions, the Greeks were the first to lose their nerve. But then the Turks were at home, and the Greeks in hostile territory, where they felt menaced at every turn.

Two days after capturing Mount Çal, Papoulas advised the Greek government that it was pointless to go on.[80] As the Greeks began to withdraw, the Turks counter-attacked, winning back Mount Çal on 8 September. But they too were exhausted; the order to pursue the enemy was not given until 13 September. By then there were no Greeks left east of the Sakarya river. Lacking motor transport, the Turks could only harry the retreating enemy with their cavalry. On 14 September they raided the Greek headquarters at Sivrihisar and got away with Papoulas's five war medals: it was small consolation for the fact that the bulk of the Greek army got back to its starting positions at Eskişehir in the north-west and Afyonkarahisar in the centre.

The battle of Sakarya had lasted for twenty-one days. It was fought along a front of sixty miles, to a depth of twelve miles. But by Great War standards casualties were low: the Turks lost 3,700 dead and 18,000 wounded; the Greeks 4,000 and 19,000 respectively. While the figure for Turkish prisoners and missing was under a thousand, the retreating Greeks left nearly 15,000 men behind. For the Turks, the most serious loss was of young officers, many of them newly trained. The Turkish army had just over 5,000 officers in all; nearly 300 of them were killed and over a thousand wounded in the battle of Sakarya.[81] It was, Mustafa Kemal told the assembly, 'an officers' battle'.[82]

But men were also needed. On 13 September, the day on which he announced that the battle had been won, Mustafa Kemal ordered a general mobilization;[83] it was a final repudiation of the 1918 surrender terms, and it had fearsome associations in the popular mind. For the peasants, 'mobilization' (*seferberlik*) was synonymous with the Great

War, in which millions of their brothers had perished. Only after the battle of Sakarya did Mustafa Kemal feel strong enough to face down residual domestic opposition to a renewal of the war. He sugared the bitter pill by declaring that mobilization was needed in order to eliminate from the soil of Anatolia the last remaining soldiers of 'the defeated enemy'. In fact, the enemy had only been checked. Nevertheless, Papoulas's march on Ankara was the last offensive operation undertaken by the Greeks in Anatolia.

Mustafa Kemal returned to Ankara on 18 September, having spent a month at the front. The following day he made his victory speech in the assembly. His optimistic and selective account of military operations ended with an eloquent plea to the Allies. The Turks wanted peace, he said. But like any other civilized nation, they insisted on their freedom and independence. Their true purpose had been concealed from the civilized world. If the Allies accepted Turkey's independent existence, there would no longer be any cause for conflict with them, as there was no longer any cause for conflict between Turkey and Russia.[84] This claim to a common civilization was at the heart of Mustafa Kemal's thinking. It rebutted Western prejudice which took him for a champion of a hostile Asian, Islamic world or for an ally of a destructive Bolshevik onslaught on civilized values. True, anti-Western feeling was strong in the assembly, both among conservative and radical members. But Mustafa Kemal's message, which presaged the domestic reforms he was to impose, was not explicit enough to outrage them.

As soon as the speech was over, two identical bills were put forward – the first by sixty-five deputies, the second by Fevzi and Ismet. They proposed that Mustafa Kemal should be promoted Marshal (*Müşir*) and awarded the title of *Gazi* (which combined conveniently the meanings of 'hero' and of 'warrior for Islam'). This was in keeping with Ottoman practice; several generals who had distinguished themselves in the Russian wars had been given the title of *Gazi*, while army commanders usually held the rank of Marshal. But this traditional recognition raised Mustafa Kemal well above the mass of his followers: he now signed himself 'President of the Turkish Grand National Assembly, Commander-in-Chief, Gazi Mustafa Kemal Paşa'. In popular parlance he became simply 'Gazi Paşa'. In the bill drawn up by the sixty-five deputies he was described as 'saviour of the country and author of the latest victory'. Mustafa Kemal could not have put it better himself.

The presentation of two identical bills could be seen as a competition in flattery. But Fevzi and İsmet had a message to convey. It was that they were and would remain loyal to Mustafa Kemal and that they would not dispute his claims to pre-eminence. Success at the battle of Sakarya confirmed the emergence of a new triumvirate – of one leader and two chief lieutenants – which was to bring a new order out of the chaos of the Turkish national rising. The assembly passed the bill without a debate.[85]

A Turkish national state would probably have emerged even if the Greeks had broken through to Ankara. But Mustafa Kemal might not have been its leader. During the battle of Sakarya he received unsolicited tactical advice from Karabekir in Erzurum.[86] Had he lost the battle, leadership might have passed to Karabekir, 'the Conqueror of the East'. There was another danger. Enver had left Berlin and was making his way to Batum in the hope of crossing into Turkey, where he was bound to challenge Mustafa Kemal's leadership of the nationalist movement. On 24 May, Fevzi had asked Karabekir to arrest Enver or any of his emissaries, should they turn up in eastern Turkey.[87] Enver's uncle, Halil (Kut), who had arrived in Trabzon, was deported. This prompted an angry letter from Enver; writing to Mustafa Kemal from Moscow on 16 July, Enver threatened to disregard any ban on his presence and turn up in Turkey, the moment he came to the conclusion that his absence endangered Turkey and the Muslim world.[88]

Enver arrived in Batum in August and made contact with sympathizers in Trabzon. He held a convention of the ambitiously named People's Soviets Party, which consisted of himself, his uncle Halil and a handful of CUP militants, and which communicated its decisions to Ankara on 9 September under the seal of the old CUP. But by then the Sakarya battle had been won, and Enver's demand that he and his comrades should be allowed into Turkey fell on deaf ears. Prompted by Ankara, Karabekir appointed a cavalry colonel, Sami Sabit (Karaman), as acting governor in Trabzon with strict instructions to repress CUP activity.[89] Deprived of a role in Turkey, Enver travelled to Baku and then on to central Asia, where, instead of heading a movement against the British in India, he joined the Muslim bands (called Basmachi) who opposed the Bolsheviks. He was killed in present-day Tajikistan in a clash with the Red Army on 4 August 1922.[90] He was the last of the CUP triumvirs to die: Talât had been killed in Berlin in March 1921 and Cemal in Tiflis in July 1922, both victims of Armenians intent on avenging the massacres visited on their people under CUP rule in 1915.

The disappearance of the old, defeated leaders made it easier for Mustafa Kemal to unite the forces of Turkish nationalism. On 29 December 1921, he wrote to Ali Fuat in Moscow: 'I cannot call on the nation to gather under the banner of the CUP.'[91] To show that his movement transcended the old political divisions, Mustafa Kemal had taken care to include in his government opponents of the CUP, like Rıza Nur and Ahmet Ferit (Tek), alongside the more numerous former Unionists. Now, his unifying role could no longer be questioned. The battle of Sakarya saved Turkey from further Greek encroachment and Mustafa Kemal from the ghosts of a tragic past.

16

Victory in War

I N THE SPRING of 1921, Mustafa Kemal moved out of the stationmaster's house in Ankara. He had earlier arranged for a more comfortable residence to be built for him not far from the farm school at Keçiören, but a better choice came up. There were pleasant summer houses on the hill of Çankaya, lying in the opposite direction, south-east of the town. The houses had been built among orchards and afforded a good view of the countryside. The air was clean, and the hill position secure. Security was important as bandits were still roaming round the nationalist capital.[1] According to one report, Mustafa Kemal's friend, the journalist Ruşen Eşref (Ünaydın), took Fikriye to the largest house near the top of the hill. She liked it, and Mustafa Kemal approved the choice.[2]

The house was built of stone, with a garden on two terraces and a fountain.[3] It belonged originally to an Armenian, and was then acquired by the local Turkish family of Bulgurzade. The nationalist *müftü* of Ankara, Rıfat Börekçi, organized a collection to purchase the house, which was then donated to Mustafa Kemal. He, in turn, transferred the title-deeds to the Turkish army, and, as a result, his residence became known as the Army Mansion (*Ordu Köşkü*).[4] Mustafa Kemal's mementoes – pictures of his mother, photographs showing him in action in Cyrenaica – were displayed on the walls. Photographs of three – and only three – of his supporters, İsmet, Fevzi and Kâzım (Özalp), were later added, and gifts arrived from well-wishers at home and abroad. The style of decoration was Victorian oriental, with arabesque ceilings and decorative braziers for heating, but also a billiard-table and an upright piano.[5] Quarters were found near by for Mustafa Kemal's bodyguard of Laz irregulars – a company of foot soldiers and a company of cavalry.

Mustafa Kemal's closest friends and collaborators moved into houses lower down the hill. They included childhood friends from Salonica, like his ADC Salih (Bozok) and Lieutenant-Colonel Fuat (Bulca); senior commanders, political supporters (such as interior minister Fethi (Okyar), economy minister Celal (Bayar), the journalist Ruşen Eşref and others. (İsmet was at the front and did not move into his house in Çankaya – the Pink Mansion – until 1925.) Most of the prominent nationalists in Çankaya had their wives with them. The men drank in the evenings as they discussed current developments; the wives kept house. It was a middle-class settlement, with servants and batmen, but no luxuries. Mustafa Kemal had a small generator for his residence. The others made do with paraffin or carbide lamps.[6] Although communications were difficult, family members of Çankaya residents travelled to Istanbul and received visitors from the sultan's capital. It was not an atmosphere conducive to debauch – the charge usually made by Mustafa Kemal's enemies. Nor was Çankaya an 'eyrie', as the nationalist poet Faruk Nafiz (Çamlıbel) described it. But it was removed from the hurly-burly of old Ankara. It was the gathering of an élite which was shaping a new Turkey: there was constant politicking, but no disloyalty to Mustafa Kemal. 'Gazi Paşa' was the approachable, friendly, but unquestioned leader of the Çankaya set.

The town of Ankara was also filling up with officials, officers and nationalist sympathizers. Houses, however inconvenient, were hard to find, and rents were high. For people used to Istanbul cooking, food was bad. The English journalist Ward Price, who visited Ankara in 1923, found that 'mutton was the invariable dish, and had the unmistakable flavour of goat. For three weeks ... I lived almost entirely on eggs and yoghurt, the highest point of my egg-consumption reaching the figure of a dozen a day.'[7] Ward Price was preceded to Ankara by two European women, the French journalist Berthe Georges-Gaulis, who first visited Ankara in 1920 (and who was thanked by the assembly for her reporting the following year),[8] and the English traveller Grace Ellison. They were both impressed by Mustafa Kemal and by the idealistic fervour of his supporters. Foreign visitors spoke of Mustafa Kemal's piercing blue eyes; domestic detractors pointed out that he was cross-eyed.

The battle of Sakarya was a turning point in the fortunes of Mustafa Kemal and of the Turkish nationalists he led. They had stopped the Greeks and proved that only they could deliver peace to Turkey. The Bolsheviks had been the first to help Turkish nationalists openly – the Italians had done so discreetly. Now they were the first to settle outstanding issues. On 13 October, representatives of the Soviet Socialist

Republics of Armenia, Azerbaijan and Georgia, as well as of Soviet Russia, were received by Karabekir in Kars and signed with him an agreement confirming the frontier fixed the previous March by the Russian-Turkish treaty.[9]

Franklin-Bouillon had arrived in Ankara even earlier – on 20 September, in the company of two French officers. But bargaining was tougher and negotiations longer. An agreement was finally signed on 20 October.[10] It was officially called an 'accord' to distinguish it from a peace treaty, and thus preserve the fiction that France was keeping faith with Britain by not signing a separate peace. But it was a peace treaty in all but name, providing for the end of hostilities and an exchange of prisoners, and fixing the frontier between Turkey and French-mandated Syria. There were no direct economic concessions, but France obtained promises that its schools and companies in Turkey would not be harassed and that its investments and advisers would be welcomed. The agreement had a difficult passage in the assembly, some of whose members did not want to cede the district of İskenderun to French rule, even under special status guaranteeing the rights of its Turkish inhabitants. Mustafa Kemal was content to let a minority of members vote against the agreement:[11] it was a useful marker for the future.

The majority was convinced by the government argument that, apart from the immediate return of Cilicia to Turkish rule, the agreement had important military advantages: Franklin-Bouillon had promised that the French army would sell at give-away prices such equipment as it did not need, and Turkish forces tied down in the south would now be able to take this equipment with them to the Greek front.[12] The Armenians who had returned to Cilicia with French troops, left with them once again, in spite of assurances that they would be well treated. On 21 December 1921 Turkish troops entered Adana; on 25 December 1921 Gaziantep was Turkish once again. On 5 January 1922, a 105-metre long Turkish flag was unfurled from the minaret of the largest mosque in Adana to mark the arrival of the Turkish commander.[13] Except for the district of İskenderun, Mustafa Kemal had regained the territory he held in the south at the end of the Great War.

The signing of the French agreement worried the Bolsheviks, who sent to Ankara the Red Army commander Mikhail Frunze, theoretically as ambassador of Soviet Ukraine.[14] He was treated to some choice specimens of Mustafa Kemal's oratory: the day would come, he was told, when oppression would end and there would be neither oppressors nor oppressed.[15] After Frunze's departure, Soviet Russia appointed S.I. Aralov as its ambassador in Ankara. He arrived on 30 January 1922, and pressed his views assiduously on the Kemalist leadership.[16] Mustafa

Kemal responded by asking that Soviet aid should be speeded up.[17] Aralov's unsmiling face became even more depressed when the wooden house in which he had established his embassy was destroyed in a fire, which cost the life of his pet bear.[18] In his memoirs, he was to accuse Rauf (Orbay) of complicity in the disaster, while also quoting the view of his embassy secretary that the French representative in Ankara, Colonel Mougin, was behind the arson.[19] Fires were frequent in Turkey, and there is no evidence to justify the Bolsheviks' suspicions.

In Moscow, the Turkish ambassador Ali Fuat (Cebesoy) had more solid grounds for complaint. On 21 April 1921, agents of the Cheka political police broke into the flat of his military attaché, led away his assistant and confiscated his documents. Unable to obtain satisfaction, Ali Fuat returned to Ankara on 2 June. The matter was settled by a compromise: the Soviet government expressed its regrets, while the Turkish government promised to find out whether any of its officials had committed any offence in Moscow.[20] Mustafa Kemal did not want a break with the Bolsheviks, but he had no illusions about them: a year later he was to say that Communism was nonsense.[21] Even as they helped the Kemalists, the Bolsheviks were unable to obstruct Turkey's ties with the West, but they were given repeated assurances that this would not be at their expense. Mustafa Kemal wanted friendly relations with Soviet Russia. However, he would never allow Russian interference in his country's affairs.

The British government did not find it easy to understand and then come to terms with Mustafa Kemal's ideal of national independence. Lloyd George, who tended to run his own foreign policy over the head of his Foreign Secretary, Lord Curzon,[22] was determined not to follow the French example, which Sir Horace Rumbold, the British High Commissioner in Istanbul, described as dishonourable.[23] Nevertheless, Rumbold assured Hamit Bey, Mustafa Kemal's representative in Istanbul, that the British government was now ready to release all remaining Turkish detainees in Malta in exchange for all British detainees in Anatolia. On 23 October, Hamit Bey announced the agreement of the Ankara government.[24] On 2 November, the most famous of the Turkish prisoners, Rauf (Orbay), landed in İnebolu, together with the Unionist politician Kara Vasıf (founder of the *Karakol* secret society), General Yakup Şevki (Sübaşı) and others.[25] Colonel Rawlinson, the most important British captive, boarded a British warship, travelling the other way. A prominent Turkish general, Ali İhsan (Sabis), also released from Malta, had arrived earlier at Kuşadası, south of the Greek zone of occupation on the Aegean coast:[26] the small town was then still under the control of Italians, who facilitated the movement of Turkish nationalists.[27] Mustafa Kemal, who was the only nationalist of note in Ankara when the last Ottoman parliament met, was now surrounded by prominent and ambitious personalities. He had more help, but also many more arguments.

In the West perceptions were changing not only of the physical strength of the Kemalist movement, but also of the rights and wrongs of the conflict in Anatolia. As they retreated after the two battles of İnönü and then from the banks of the Sakarya, Greek troops burned down towns and villages, driving out and sometimes killing their inhabitants. In their zone of occupation round İzmir they sought security from Turkish irregulars by deporting Muslims sympathetic to them. But it was near Istanbul that the sufferings of Turkish civilians caught the eye of Western observers. To reinforce their thrust into the interior, the Greeks evacuated İzmit and its hinterland. Before they left, they made a point of ransacking or destroying Turkish property. Bands of Greek irregulars (known as *Mavri Mira*, 'Black Fate') murdered Turkish villagers, as they fought with Turkish irregulars. When Greek troops were transferred to the south shore of the gulf of İzmit, the area between Yalova and Gemlik suffered the same treatment.

An Inter-Allied Commission of Enquiry reported: 'There is a systematic plan of destruction of Turkish villages and extinction of the Moslem population.'[28] In Britain, the facts were brought to public notice by Arnold Toynbee, whose reports for the liberal, and therefore traditionally Philhellene, *Manchester Guardian* cost him his chair of Medieval and Modern Greek at King's College, London, endowed by Greek shipowners. Writing from Istanbul in May 1921, Toynbee observed that in the Yalova area 'the malignity and inhumanity of the Greek military authorities are undisguised'. In *The Western Question in Greece and Turkey*, the book he published the following year, Toynbee came to the conclusion that Greece had proved 'as incapable as Turkey (or for that matter any Western country) of governing well a mixed population containing an alien majority and a minority of her own nationality'.[29]

Things were no better in the area controlled by Turkish nationalists. Some 380,000 Greeks lived along the Black Sea coast and its hinterland just before the Great War.[30] Their number was swollen by Greeks fleeing from the Bolshevik revolution. In December 1920,[31] the position of the Black Sea (Pontic) Greeks took a turn for the worse when 'Bearded' Nurettin Paşa was appointed commander of a new central army of some 10,000 men[32] and given the task of pacifying northern Anatolia, where Greek and Turkish irregulars were at each other's throats, and east-central Anatolia, where Kurds and assorted brigands were attacking weak detachments of Turkish troops. Nurettin was a forceful, ambitious, xenophobic and cruel soldier, who had fought the British in Mesopotamia in the Great War and was governor of İzmir after the armistice, before being removed at Allied insistence. He joined the nationalists in Anatolia in June 1920, but sulked after turning down the first command offered to him.[33] Soon after his appointment to the central army, Nurettin turned his attention to the college set up by American missionaries for Greek and Armenian students at Merzifon, inland from Samsun. A Turkish teacher had been killed in the college, which was suspected of being a centre of Christian subversion. No arms were found when the college was searched, but the American missionaries were expelled, and some local Christians put on trial for treason.[34]

Nurettin's first military operation as commander of the central army was directed against the Kurdish Koçgiri tribe which had risen in March 1921 in the area between Erzincan and Sivas on the edges of the Dersim mountains. The rebels sent a telegram to the assembly in Ankara demanding that their land should become an autonomous province under a Kurdish governor.[35] Mustafa Kemal took great care to enlist the support of Kurdish chieftains, and saw to it that some of them became deputies in the assembly. This policy isolated chieftains who hankered after autonomy and sought Allied support. The fact that the Koçgiri tribe was Shiite (Alevi) also helped stop the spread of the rebellion among the majority of Sunni Kurds. When the Koçgiri disobeyed a government order to lay down their arms, Nurettin led against them a force of some 3,000 cavalrymen and irregulars, including Lame Osman's Laz cut-throats. The rebels were crushed by 24 April.[36] The severity of the repression led to angry debates in the assembly. One member said that atrocities committed against the people of Dersim would have been unacceptable even for 'African barbarians'.[37] The assembly decided to send a commission of enquiry and to put Nurettin on trial. Nurettin was relieved of his command in November 1921, but Mustafa Kemal prevented a trial by persuading the assembly that further enquiries were needed.[38] By that time, the resistance of the Pontic Greeks had been broken.

On 9 June 1921, a Greek warship bombed İnebolu, which served as the harbour of the nationalists in Ankara. Nurettin advised the general staff in Ankara that, in view of the danger of a Greek landing in Samsun, all male Greeks aged between 15 and 50 years should be deported to the interior. Mustafa Kemal and his government in Ankara agreed on 16 June.[39] According to the official report on the activities of the central army, nearly 25,000 persons were deported.[40] The deaths and miseries caused by the deportation were compounded by the arrival of an Independence Tribunal in Samsun. Between August and December 1921, the tribunal passed 485 death sentences: this represented nearly half of all the death sentences pronounced by these tribunals during the entire War of Independence.[41] It seems that many of those sentenced in Samsun were leaders or assumed leaders of Greek and Armenian irregulars;[42] many more perished at the hands of Lame Osman's band. On 7 June 1922, a Greek warship bombed Samsun.[43] This served only to worsen the lot of the remaining local Greeks. Greeks in areas of western and southern Anatolia under Turkish nationalist control were also deported by order of the Ankara government.[44]

Mustafa Kemal did his best to counter Western indignation at the treatment of Pontic Greeks. An occasion was provided by the visit to Turkey of the French novelist Claude Farrère, who, like his better-known contemporary, Pierre Loti, had been captivated by the oriental exoticism of Muslim Istanbul, and had lent his support to the Turkish cause. Mustafa Kemal arranged to meet Farrère in İzmit, where he greeted him on 18 June as 'the distinguished son of a noble nation which has wrought revolutions and shed its blood to acquaint the whole world with the ideals of freedom and independence'.[45] Mustafa Kemal genuinely admired French revolutionary ideals, just as he respected British power. He found it easy, therefore, to appeal to the former: the fault for the sufferings of both Greek and Turkish civilians lay with those who had used the Greek army to extinguish Turkish freedom and independence. Some Western politicians refused to acknowledge the civilized capacity of the Turks, but 'the noble French nation' had understood and shown the way to others. The message was clear: Turkey, under Mustafa Kemal's leadership, sought the friendship of the civilized world. At a reception held by Colonel Mougin in Ankara on Bastille Day, 14 July 1922, Mustafa Kemal compared his war with the Greeks with the French resistance to foreign invasion after the revolution.[46]

The trip to İzmit served also a family purpose. Mustafa Kemal had brought Fikriye with him and had arranged for his mother Zübeyde and his sister Makbule to meet them in İzmit. Both women considered Fikriye to be an unsuitable bride, but while Zübeyde was content to put up with her, Makbule did not hide her feelings. After a quarrel with Fikriye, Makbule returned to Istanbul, while Zübeyde went on to Ankara and became the respected matron of Mustafa Kemal's household in Çankaya.[47] There was also a child in the house: an orphan schoolboy called Abdürrahim, whom Mustafa Kemal had adopted and entrusted to Zübeyde's care probably during the Great War.[48] Zübeyde took part in the social life of Çankaya, in accordance with the conventions of middle-class Turkish society: she was an honoured guest at the party celebrating the circumcision of Cemil, the son of Mustafa Kemal's ADC Salih (Bozok), and presented the boy with a gift of an expensive Longines watch.[49]

By the middle of 1922, the risings were over and the authority of the Grand National Assembly extended over most of the territory of Turkey, east of the area under Greek and Allied occupation. But the demography of the land had changed. It was well on the way to becoming a homogeneously Muslim country. The Armenians were largely gone and the Greeks on their way out. Muslim solidarity survived Kurdish and Circassian risings. An attempt by the Greeks to enlist the Circassians against the Turks failed. A Circassian congress, held in Greek-occupied İzmir, made little impression. It proclaimed that the Circassians were Aryans and, as such, members of the white race which had created modern civilization. They were grateful, the congress claimed, for the protection extended to them by the Greek occupation authorities in Anatolia.[50] After the war, the Ankara government expelled seventeen Circassians who had taken part in the congress, as well as Ethem and eight of his followers.[51] It was a tiny number compared with the mass of the Circassians who sided with the Turkish nationalists, and provided many of their officers.

The mood of gratitude which pervaded the assembly after the battle of Sakarya did not last long. True, Mustafa Kemal's appointment as commander-in-chief was extended by three months without too much difficulty on 31 October.[52] But soon afterwards, opposition members in the assembly tried to limit their president's power by defining the rights and duties of ministers. Mustafa Kemal defeated the attempt on 1 December. In a speech that lasted three hours,[53] he argued that the power of the assembly was absolute and that a system based on the separation of powers would diminish it.[54] He carried the day, although his opponents were well aware that the absolute power of the assembly translated itself into the absolute power of its president, Mustafa Kemal. To criticism that there were no precedents for the system of direct government by the assembly, Mustafa Kemal responded with the words: 'We are proud not to be like anyone else. We are like ourselves (*Biz bize benzeriz*).'[55] The speech was also notable for Mustafa Kemal's repudiation of both Pan-Islamism and Pan-Turkism, the idea that all Muslim or all Turkic peoples should come together in one state. All of

Turkey's enemies would join forces to stop such an attempt, he said, which Turkey neither needed nor was strong enough to carry through. 'We must know our limitations,' Mustafa Kemal declared, 'and expend our lives only in the cause of our independence.'[56] This was to be the basis of his foreign policy and that of his successors.

In March, after the powers of the commander-in-chief had once again been extended by three months, Karabekir tried another approach to rein in Mustafa Kemal. Would it not be a good idea, he argued, to set up a senate, albeit under another name? No, it would not, Mustafa Kemal replied. A senate would limit the powers of the assembly. If the object was to improve legislation, then the best way was to make sure that better qualified people were elected as deputies.[57] It would not be long before Mustafa Kemal would decide himself who was best qualified to stand for election to parliament.

Matters came to a head in May 1922, when the assembly again tried to limit Mustafa Kemal's powers as commander-in-chief. The usual critics, headed by the Erzurum lawyer Hüseyin Avni (Ulaş), were now joined by the veteran conspirator Kara Vasıf, newly released from detention in Malta. Mustafa Kemal says that he was ill at the time and that it was his absence from the debate which turned the scales against him. Two days later, on 6 May, he delivered an uncompromising speech in the assembly. The army facing the enemy could not be left leaderless, he declared. 'This is why I did not, I do not and I will not give up the post of commander-in-chief.' The assembly took the hint, and agreed by 177 votes to 11, with 15 abstentions, to extend Mustafa Kemal's full powers by another three months.[58]

Rauf (Orbay), who had been elected minister of public works on his return from exile, says in his memoirs that he did his best to smooth out disagreements between Mustafa Kemal, on the one hand, and Karabekir and critics in the assembly, on the other.[59] In July 1922, the assembly tried once again to clip Mustafa Kemal's wings. This time it deprived the government of the right to nominate candidates for election to ministerial office. Fevzi Paşa thereupon resigned as prime minister, in order to allow the election of a cabinet under the new rules. Rauf was the most popular candidate for the succession. Though a member of Mustafa Kemal's party, he was prepared to listen to critics. However, he had reservations. According to his memoirs, he told Mustafa Kemal: 'If I accept the job, you will still interfere. I don't want to fall out with you, as I believe that you are the right man to save the nation at the head of the army.' Mustafa Kemal promised not to interfere, and on 12 July 1922 Rauf was endorsed as prime minister by 197 votes out of 204.[60] Fevzi remained chief of staff with a seat in the cabinet, while the war

ministry went to Mustafa Kemal's friend from Macedonia, and unquestioning supporter, Kâzım (Özalp).

Rauf succeeded in controlling the opposition. When the powers of
the commander-in-chief had to be extended again on 20 July, the assembly did not set any time limit. Mustafa Kemal declared that, in any case,
he needed the powers only until victory was won; thereafter he would
be happy to revert to the position he had before taking up 'the sacred
cause', for 'Is there a happiness greater than that of returning to the
bosom of the nation as a free man?'[61] No one had any doubt, of course,
that Mustafa Kemal would always be his own master; the question
rather was who was to be the people's master. On 1 March 1922,
opening the third annual session of the assembly, Mustafa Kemal had
declared: 'It is the peasant, the true producer, who is also the true owner
and master of Turkey.'[62] This admirable sentiment was to be repeated
many times during the years of Mustafa Kemal's absolute rule.

It was not enough to control the assembly. Military commanders,
many of whom were, in any case, members of the assembly, were as
argumentative as the politicians. In the years of Ottoman decline, Paşas
often became autonomous warlords. Mustafa Kemal himself did as he
pleased, at least whenever he could, in the Great War. Controlling commanders in the new army of the Grand National Assembly was even
harder than in the old Ottoman army. Seniority in rank did not always
correspond with seniority in the resistance. Most commanders accepted
the authority of Fevzi, who, although a latecomer to the resistance, had
both seniority and a distinguished war record. But İsmet, another latecomer, had been appointed commander of the western front over the
heads of more senior officers. He had fallen out with Refet, then with
Mustafa Kemal's boon companion, 'bear-keeper' Arif, who was relieved
of his command of the 3rd corps in June 1922.[63]

A more serious conflict developed when the forces on the western
front were reorganized in two armies. The 1st Army held the line from
Afyonkarahisar to the south; the 2nd north of Afyon. Ali İhsan (Sabis)
was appointed commander of the 1st Army soon after his return from
Malta. Army pay was often in arrears: when Ali İhsan distributed as pay
money he had received for supplies, the 2nd Army complained of being
unfairly treated. Ali İhsan criticized orders from front headquarters,
took his own counsel in conducting small-scale operations and tried to
rally political support against his superiors. İsmet's objections to Ali
İhsan's unorthodox practices were upheld by Mustafa Kemal and Fevzi,
and Ali İhsan was dismissed and sent to Konya to await court martial.[64]

Command of the 1st Army was then offered to Ali Fuat, who had
become leader of Mustafa Kemal's parliamentary group after his return

from Moscow. Ali Fuat refused. So did Refet (Bele), who was approached next.[65] As neither man wanted to serve under İsmet, the command of the 1st Army went to 'Bearded' Nurettin, the hammer of the Anatolian Greeks and Kurds. İsmet clashed also with Kemalettin Sami, one of the heroes of the battle of Sakarya, when the latter refused to accept an officer appointed to his 4th corps. Kemalettin Sami resigned, but was reinstated. The 2nd Army was given to Yakup Şevki (Sübaşı), another returnee from Malta, who argued ceaselessly against the subordinate role assigned to him in the plans which were being drawn up for the final offensive.[66]

The date of the offensive was the most contentious point at issue between Mustafa Kemal and the assembly. Critics complained that the army was ready, but that it was kept waiting as Mustafa Kemal devoted more time to politics than to the war. No, Mustafa Kemal declared when his mandate was renewed in May, the army was not yet ready.[67] In March he had visited İsmet's new headquarters in Akşehir on the railway line between Konya and Afyon.[68] Accompanied by the Russian ambassador Aralov and the ambassador of the Azerbaijan Soviet Republic, İbrahim Abilov, he was present at the manoeuvres of Fahrettin (Altay)'s cavalry corps. Its strength had been brought up to 10,000 men and it was preparing for the last battle to be fought by a large cavalry formation in modern war.[69]

Mustafa Kemal was prudent in diplomacy as in military strategy. To equip the Turkish army, he secured the help of the Bolsheviks and the collusion of the French and the Italians. In addition to the equipment left by the French in Cilicia and by the Italians in Antalya, war material was purchased from French and Italian private firms. Weapons were also smuggled from stores in Istanbul, as French and Italian sentries looked the other way.[70] But there was still the danger that Britain would enter the fray on the side of the Greeks or agree with France and Italy at the expense of the Turks. Nimble footwork was needed to keep Britain on the sidelines.

On 4 February 1922, Mustafa Kemal's foreign minister Yusuf Kemal (Tengirşenk) asked the assembly's permission to travel to Europe to defend Turkey's national cause. Permission was granted, and Yusuf Kemal proceeded to İzmit, from where he went to Istanbul by special train shadowed by a French torpedo-boat.[71] In Istanbul, he called on the Allied High Commissioners. The British High Commissioner, Sir Horace Rumbold, was impressed by Yusuf Kemal's determination not to be deflected from the goal of a unified and independent Turkey. A few days later, Rumbold learnt that the French High Commissioner, General Pellé, had apparently told Yusuf Kemal that 'France would be the advocate of Turkey against Great Britain who is supporting Greece.'[72]

But Yusuf Kemal did more than exploit distrust among the High Commissioners. He called on the grand vizier Tevfik Paşa and his foreign minister Ahmet İzzet Paşa. Then on 20 February he was received by Sultan Vahdettin. He assured the sovereign of the loyalty of the Ankara government and repeated Mustafa Kemal's request that the sultan should recognize it. Vahdettin shut his eyes and said nothing;[73] he thus threw away the last chance of retrieving his position. There was outrage in the assembly when it heard of the interview. Mustafa Kemal admitted that Yusuf Kemal had been entrusted with a special mission in Istanbul: he was told that he could see the sultan if the latter promised to be bound by the decisions of the assembly. But, Mustafa Kemal claimed, his minister had been misled: he was informed that the sultan wanted to see him and was then put in the position of a petitioner.[74] It was not a convincing argument. Mustafa Kemal would not have authorized the mission if he did not believe that the sultan's support was still worth having.

Yusuf Kemal and the sultan's foreign minister Ahmet İzzet then went to Paris by different routes for a meeting of the French, British and Italian foreign ministers. On the eve of the conference, the position of the British Foreign Secretary, Lord Curzon, was weakened by the publication of a despatch from Lord Reading, the Viceroy of India, calling for the withdrawal of the Greeks from İzmir and the restoration of Istanbul and of eastern Thrace to Turkey.[75] This reinforced the argument put by Yusuf Kemal to Curzon on 18 March, that the evacuation of Anatolia by the Greeks was the precondition of any settlement.[76] On 22 March, the Allied foreign ministers proposed an armistice between Greece and Turkey.[77] The Greeks accepted, subject to minor reservations.[78]

Mustafa Kemal was away inspecting the western front when the Allied proposal reached Ankara via Istanbul. He met his ministers at Sivrihisar, west of Ankara, on 24 March and agreed the terms of a reply: the proposal was accepted in principle, but the Greeks had to start their withdrawal the moment the armistice came into force. However, any discussion of Ankara's response was pre-empted by the publication on 26 March of the Allied recommendations for a peace settlement. These provided that Edirne and a slice of eastern Thrace should go to Greece, while İzmir should revert to Turkey, that any changes in foreign privileges should be subject to negotiation, and that the maximum strength of the Turkish army, which the treaty of Sèvres had fixed at 50,000 men, should be raised to 85,000. It was the crowning absurdity, since the army of the Grand National Assembly was about to number 200,000 men. However, Mustafa Kemal did not break off exchanges with the Allies. Pending agreement on an armistice, he proposed a meeting in İzmit. This led to a pointless discussion on the merits of other venues. Would Beykoz, a suburb of Allied-held Istanbul, be better, or perhaps Venice?[79]

Mustafa Kemal was right to drag out the negotiations. While his army was being built up, the morale of the Greeks was collapsing. Papoulas resigned on 25 May and was replaced as commander-in-chief by General George Hatzianestis, who was widely thought to be of unsound mind. Hatzianestis toured the front, and concluded that a Turkish offensive could be repulsed without difficulty. Fortified by this illusion, he allowed the transfer from Anatolia to Thrace of three regiments and two battalions for a last desperate move by the Athens government.[80] Thus reinforced, the Greek army in Thrace was ordered to march on Istanbul. The Greek foreign minister, George Baltazzis, informed Allied representatives in Athens that only the Greek occupation of the Ottoman capital could now bring about the conclusion of peace.

This was too much even for the British government, which warned Greece on 29 July that any violation of the neutral zone of Istanbul and the straits would be resisted by Allied forces.[81] British and French troops were sent to man the Çatalca lines, guarding Istanbul, under the command of the French General Charpy. A powerful British fleet put out to sea to intercept any Greek warships. The Ottoman government offered 20,000 troops to help defend the capital. They were not needed. The Greeks pulled back their troops, and were rewarded by a friendly, but dangerously misleading statement by Lloyd George. Speaking in the House of Commons on 4 August, he declared: 'we are not allowing the Greeks to wage the war with their full strength. We cannot allow that sort of thing to go on indefinitely, in the hope that the Kemalists entertain, that they will at last exhaust this little country . . .'[82]

This threat that Britain might take concrete action to succour the Greeks destroyed any Turkish hope that the Allies would force a Greek withdrawal from Anatolia. In July, just as the Greeks and the Allies were squaring up for a confrontation outside Istanbul, Mustafa Kemal had despatched his friend, the interior minister Fethi (Okyar), to Paris and London. In Paris, where he was received by the French prime minister Raymond Poincaré, Fethi declared: 'We are capable of winning a military victory, but we are trying to avoid bloodshed.'[83] But in London, neither Curzon nor his deputy A.J. Balfour would see him. According to Mustafa Kemal, Fethi reported to Ankara: 'Our national aims can be

realized only by military means. The matter needs no further elaboration or interpretation.'[84] Fethi was to claim later that the purpose of his
trip was to gain time and make sure that Britain took no concrete steps
to interfere with the coming Turkish offensive. However, as late as 19
August, the Turkish nationalist representative in Paris asked Fethi to be
ready to go to Venice for discussions with the Allies on the conclusion
of an armistice.[85] It appears, therefore, that the decision that diplomacy
had to wait on the Turkish offensive was not prompted either by Fethi
or by Turkish nationalist representatives in Paris and Rome: these were
reporting on likely Allied reactions, while negotiating in good faith. It
was Mustafa Kemal who drew from their reports the conclusion that
the time to strike had come.

Plans for an offensive had been under discussion since the previous
autumn. They were repeatedly revised, as İsmet asked for more time to
strengthen the western front. During his trip to İzmit in June, Mustafa
Kemal discussed the military situation with İsmet, Fevzi and the war
minister Kâzım (Özalp). Then, on 23 July, he travelled to the western
front headquarters in Akşehir. The following day he went to Konya for
a meeting with the British General Townshend, who had set up the
armistice negotiations in October 1918 and who continued to work for
peaceful relations with Turkey; the meeting provided convenient cover
for Mustafa Kemal's inspection of the front. Mustafa Kemal then went
back to Akşehir: Turkish senior commanders had gathered there on 28
July under the pretext of watching a football match between two teams
of officers. Work on the final plans for an offensive took several days.
On 4 August Mustafa Kemal returned to Ankara. He was as prudent as
he was determined, and wanted to cover himself at home and abroad.
The government chaired by Rauf (Orbay) minuted a decision that it
associated itself with the commander-in-chief's plans for an offensive,
bearing in mind all its possible consequences. On 6 August İsmet issued
secret orders to army and corps commanders to prepare for the
attack.[86]

The Turkish and Greek armies in Anatolia were of roughly equal
strength. The Greeks had 225,000 men, the Turks 208,000. But the
Greeks were better equipped, with more machine-guns and field guns,
and infinitely better motor transport.[87] The Turks had two advantages:
they had more heavy guns than the Greeks and a much stronger cavalry.
The Greeks were holding a front 400 miles long, enveloping the whole
of north-western Anatolia from Gemlik on the sea of Marmara to
fortified positions east of Eskişehir, Kütahya and Afyonkarahisar,

where the Greek line turned south-west to follow the Menderes (Meander) valley to the Aegean sea. The Greek army was organized in three corps – the 3rd in the north, the 2nd in the centre and the 1st in the south – under the overall command of General Hatzianestis who had his headquarters on board a ship anchored in İzmir harbour. The plan worked out in İsmet's western front headquarters provided for a concentrated thrust from the south against the Greek forces holding the Afyon salient; the objective was to cut off the bulk of Greek forces in and around Afyon. The sector chosen for the attack ran through difficult mountainous terrain. Here the Turks held the highest peak, Kocatepe (literally Big Hill), which rises to nearly 6,000 feet. Facing it, the Greeks held fortified positions on a series of lower, but steep and well-fortified peaks, rising to a height of some 5,000 feet. The attackers had to come down into narrow valleys and then storm up the Greek positions. Before they could do so, the Greek lines had to be softened with artillery fire. It was a daring plan aiming at what should have been the strongest section of the Greek front.

Conscious of the difficulties of resupply, the Turkish high command relied on delivering a single knock-out blow. The main instrument was to be the 1st Army under Nurettin Paşa, reinforced by units transferred from Yakup Şevki Paşa's 2nd Army further north. It took three weeks to move these troops and to bring up Fahrettin Paşa's 5th cavalry corps from the south-east. Yakup Şevki complained that his sector was left exposed to a Greek push in the direction of Ankara, but his objections were overruled. The Turkish army could not sustain an offensive along the entire front and had to achieve preponderance in one sector.[88]

Mustafa Kemal left Ankara by car in the night of 17/18 August, arriving in the western front headquarters at Akşehir on 20 August. Great care was taken to preserve secrecy. An announcement was put out that a tea party would be held in the commander-in-chief's residence at Çankaya on 21 August; the post office in Konya was subjected to strict censorship; all army movements were executed at night, and a decision was taken to underplay any successes in military communiqués. On 25 August when Mustafa Kemal joined the 1st Army battle headquarters, all communications between Anatolia and the outside world were cut. At dawn the following day, Mustafa Kemal, İsmet, Fevzi and Nurettin gathered on the peak of Kocatepe which dominated the sector chosen for the breakthrough. The attack started with an artillery barrage, concentrated in the southern Afyon sector, but extended also to the front held further north by the depleted 2nd Army, which had been ordered to join in the attack in order to pin down superior enemy forces facing it.

The strength and accuracy of the Turkish fire delighted Mustafa Kemal. After a time, Greek guns stopped responding, because, as it transpired later, their observation posts had been knocked out.[89] But when the Turkish infantry advanced, the Greeks entrenched on the peaks facing Kocatepe put up strong resistance. Some hilltop positions changed hands several times. By the evening, the Turks had made significant gains, but there was no breakthrough. However, the offensive spirit of the Turks was obvious. When the 57th division failed to capture its target (the peak of Çiğiltepe), Mustafa Kemal demanded an explanation from its commanding officer, Colonel Reşat, a comrade from the Great War. Reşat promised to capture the hill in half an hour. The second time Mustafa Kemal called the divisional headquarters, he was read Reşat's suicide note: 'I have decided to end my life because I have not kept my word.' Reporting the incident to the assembly, Mustafa Kemal declared: 'It is not because I approve Reşat's action that I am telling you this. Such behaviour is not acceptable. But I wanted to illustrate the spirit in which our officers and our commanders discharged their duty.'[90]

The situation changed dramatically on the second day of battle, 27 August. The 4th corps of the 1st Army, commanded by Colonel Kemalettin Sami, of Sakarya fame, broke through the Greek lines, and captured the 5,000-feet high peak of Erkmentepe. At the same time, Fahrettin's cavalry found a way through the mountains and appeared in the rear of the Greeks. Having lost the mountainous bastion which covered his right flank, the commander of the Greek 1st corps, General Trikoupis, beat a hasty retreat from Afyon in the plain below, leaving behind the bulk of his stores. Two divisions under General Frangou retreated west so rapidly that they lost touch with the 1st corps. Further north, the Greek 2nd corps, under General Dighenis, was slow to come to the aid of Trikoupis. Communications between Greek units broke down. From İzmir, Hatzianestis issued irrelevant commands to launch a counter-offensive, at a time when only an orderly retreat could have saved the Greek army. The Turkish breakthrough in the mountains south-west of Afyon on 27 August knocked out the Greek army in Anatolia at one blow. Although it was not clear at the time, all the Turks had to do now was to mop up the retreating Greeks.

On 28 August, Mustafa Kemal moved his headquarters to the municipal offices of the newly liberated town of Afyonkarahisar. There he received reports that the bulk of the Greek 1st and 2nd corps was milling round Dumlupınar, some thirty miles to the west. The small town of Dumlupınar, round which the Greeks had built up a fortified position, lies in an upland valley hemmed in by mountains – Murat Dağı in the north and Ahır Dağı in the south. The valley affords a passage for the single-track railway from Afyon to İzmir, which the Greeks wanted to use for their withdrawal. A small Turkish detachment which had attempted to cut it had been beaten back, but stronger Turkish forces – the 1st Army from the west and south and units of the 2nd Army from the north – were closing in, while Fahrettin's cavalry was active in the Greeks' rear to the west. The Turks had thus the opportunity to close the ring round the Greeks. But a Greek division which had not had time to come to the aid of Trikoupis, and the whole 3rd corps further north, were still intact, and if the Turks committed the bulk of their forces at Dumlupınar, their right flank could be dangerously exposed. A more cautious course would have been to swing north and deal with the Greeks there, while allowing the Greek 1st and 2nd corps to retreat in some order to İzmir.

Mustafa Kemal discussed the options with Fevzi, İsmet and Nurettin. İsmet says in his memoirs that it was he who proposed that the encirclement of the Greeks at Dumlupınar should go ahead, while weaker Turkish forces harried the Greeks in the northern sector.[91] However that may be, it was Mustafa Kemal who decided in the evening of 28 August to go for the kill at Dumlupınar.[92] He sent Fevzi to the north, to command the right arm of the pincer movement, while he took personal command of the forces massed in the south and west, leaving İsmet behind at Afyon. It took a day for Turkish troops to complete the encirclement. On 30 August, Mustafa Kemal moved his headquarters to a low hill, since named Zafertepe (Victory Hill), rising just above the railway line, a little to the east of Dumlupınar, to direct the final assault on the encircled Greeks. Subjected to heavy artillery fire and then to bayonet charges by Turkish infantry, the Greek troops disintegrated. As the group commanded by General Frangou abandoned the Dumlupınar fortified position, Generals Trikoupis and Dighenis, commanders of the Greek 1st and 2nd corps, tried to save their remaining troops by leading them north-west across the northern slopes of Murat Dağı. The battle on 30 August destroyed the Greek 1st and 2nd corps as effective fighting forces. Troops which had evaded death or capture round Dumlupınar had only one thought in mind – to escape from Anatolia as quickly as possible.

In the north, the Greek 3rd corps, which had stood by while its neighbours were being mauled, prepared to beat a hasty retreat to the shores of the sea of Marmara. On 31 August, Mustafa Kemal, Fevzi and İsmet met in the yard of a village house near Dumlupınar. Leaning against an oxcart, they discussed what they should do next. İsmet urged that both the 1st and 2nd Armies should pursue the retreating Greeks to İzmir, and prevent them from establishing a new line of defence, which they could then try to hold with reinforcements from Thrace. İsmet wanted to avoid at all costs having to fight another battle. 'We have no arms factories to rely on. I cannot prepare for another battle,' he recalled saying.[93] Fevzi wanted to detach the 2nd Army to clear the north, while ordering the 1st Army alone to advance to İzmir. Mustafa Kemal decided in favour of İsmet. On 1 September he issued an army order, announcing for the first time that victory had been won. The order ended with the words: 'Armies! The Mediterranean is your immediate objective. Forward!'[94] The Mediterranean was 250 miles away from Dumlupınar.

On 2/3 September, the two Greek corps commanders, Generals Trikoupis and Dighenis, surrendered when they found that they had walked into a trap as they came down from the slopes of Mount Murat to the Banaz plain below. Their surrender was accepted by a Turkish captain. In all, nearly 500 Greek officers and 5,000 men were taken captive; hundreds of machine-guns and 12 field guns passed into Turkish hands.[95] This did not represent a large proportion of the total Greek deployment in Turkey, but the morale of the Greek army was broken. It had been kept too long on a front deep in hostile territory; its discipline had been sapped by the feud between Venizelists and royalists; it had been asked to shed its blood to hold a territory that the Allies had already in principle assigned back to Turkey. It is not surprising that the mass of Greek soldiers refused this pointless task. Just as Mustafa Kemal's lightning military victory had been the fruit of more than two years of prudent political activity, so the Greek defeat in Anatolia was the result of political miscalculation based on little more than wishful thinking.

The captives were brought to the Turkish front headquarters which had now moved to Uşak. İsmet recalls:

> They [the Greek generals] were exhausted. Their lips were swollen. I offered them tea, but they were not able to drink it. We treated them well, like comrades. We told them that they had fought well, but that luck was against them ... When we finished chatting, I put on my belt and sword, and said that I would present them officially to the commander-in-chief ... Atatürk treated them magnanimously, and tried to console them. They were very touched.[96]

Mustafa Kemal offered coffee and cigarettes to the captive generals and asked whether there was anything he could do for them. Trikoupis requested only that his family should be informed of his fate.[97] Mustafa Kemal, to whom all manner of vices had been imputed, relished this opportunity to demonstrate that he was a civilized officer and gentleman. Trikoupis learnt in captivity that he had been appointed commander of the entire front. It was a joke in bad taste.

On the same day, İsmet issued an order naming the Dumlupınar battle 'The Battle of the Commander-in-Chief'.[98] The inspiration may have come from *Kaiserschlacht*, the name given by the German high command to their final – and unsuccessful – push on the Western Front in the Great War. The purpose was to nip in the bud any attempt by individual commanders to claim the main credit for the victory. All the commanders had been honoured, both İsmet and his 1st Army commander Nurettin being promoted from Brigadier to Major-General. But Nurettin refused to add a star to his uniform, saying that he had been badly treated by Mustafa Kemal. Nor did he want the 2nd Army to accompany his 1st Army on the march to İzmir, even though the 2nd Army commander, Yakup Şevki, had been transferred to take charge of the pursuit of the Greeks retreating in the north to the sea of Marmara. Mustafa Kemal had indeed imposed his authority on Nurettin and even issued orders directly to his troops, finding that Nurettin's ambition exceeded the bounds of prudence.[99] Mustafa Kemal did not spend long at the head of the army, but when he did so he would allow no doubt that he was in charge.

As early as February, the British representative in İzmir, Sir Harry Lamb, had warned: 'The Greeks have realized that they have got to go, but they are decided to leave a desert behind them, no matter whose interests may suffer thereby. Everything which they have time and means to move will be carried off to Greece; the Turks will be plundered and burnt out of house and home ...'[100] The Turkish victory had been so rapid – it took no more than six days – that the Greeks were unable to evacuate their stores, let alone cart off any plunder. But the rest of Sir Harry Lamb's prophecy came true. In Afyonkarahisar, the Turks were able to put out the fires started by the retreating Greeks.[101] But hundreds of villages and a whole string of market towns – from Uşak to İzmir – were burned down. In Alaşehir (ancient Philadelphia) 4,300 out of 4,500 houses were destroyed with the loss of 3,000 lives. In Manisa (ancient Magnesia) only 1,400 out of 14,000 houses remained standing. In the north, the neighbourhood round the railway station at Eskişehir was destroyed.[102]

As Turkish troops, spearheaded by cavalry, rushed headlong towards İzmir, Mustafa Kemal had to make sure that he retained control of the military as well as of the political situation. Even with the help of İsmet and Fevzi, it was not easy to rein in the boundless ambition of Nurettin, who was in direct command of the 1st Army. Pockets of resistance by the retreating Greeks and the local Greek population were quickly mopped up. However, the bulk of the Greek forces succeeded in reaching the coast. On 5 September a Greek division arrived by sea in İzmir to help hold the city: but the troops mutinied. The following day, the Greek high command decided that Nif (the ancient Nymphaion, now Kemalpaşa), lying in a gap in the last barrier of mountains east of İzmir, should be abandoned, and that retreating troops should be directed to the Urla peninsula, south-west of İzmir, for embarkation to Greece.

Surprised by the speed and extent of the Turkish victory, the Allies renewed their plea for an armistice. From Ankara, Rauf (Orbay) passed on the request to Mustafa Kemal at his travelling headquarters. On 5 September, Mustafa Kemal replied that since the Greek army in Anatolia had suffered a total defeat, there was no longer any need to negotiate an armistice there. Negotiations should, therefore, be confined to the return to Turkish rule of Thrace up to the 1914 Ottoman boundaries. Mustafa Kemal asked that this area should come under the military and civil authority of the Ankara government within fifteen days of the conclusion of the armistice, and that Greece should free all Turkish prisoners and guarantee to pay compensation for the damage it had inflicted in the previous two and a half years. The Turkish offer to negotiate these conditions would remain valid until 10 September.

Responding to a direct approach by Allied consuls in İzmir, Mustafa Kemal offered to meet them in Nif on 9 September.[103] Mustafa Kemal made the rendezvous, but the consuls were not there. Turkish troops had reached İzmir the previous night and on 9 September they occupied the city. Mustafa Kemal, who had his first sight of the promised shore that day, made his entry into the city on 10 September. The last Greek troops in western Anatolia left the Urla peninsula on 16 September.[104]

Three days later the Greeks completed their evacuation of northwestern Anatolia. Bursa, the first capital of the Ottoman Turks, had reverted intact to Turkish rule a day later than İzmir, on 9/10 September. Anticipating the event, the Grand National Assembly had voted on 6 September to remove from its tribune the black drape which had been placed as a sign of mourning at the capture of the city by the Greeks two years earlier.[105]

The Turkish War of Independence was won. Mustafa Kemal's strategy of stopping and then destroying the Greek army in the 'inner sanctuary' of Anatolia had paid off. By delaying the final blow and avoiding foolhardy operations he had reduced military casualties to a minimum.

In three years of warfare, the Turkish army lost just over 13,000 officers and men killed and 35,000 wounded.[106] In the final offensive, the Turks lost 13,000 men killed, wounded and missing. Greek losses amounted to nearly 70,000, including 35,000 prisoners. The Greeks left behind half their guns and most of their stores.[107] The biggest loss was suffered by the civilian population of Anatolia.

Until the re-entry of Turkish troops into İzmir it was Muslim civilians who had suffered most at the hands of the Greeks. Now it was the turn of the Christians. Greek authorities had left İzmir on 7 September. On 9 September when Turkish cavalry rode along the waterfront, one shot was fired wounding a Turkish soldier; there was also some firing in the prosperous European suburbs of İzmir. Otherwise the city was quiet. But although the Turkish military authorities had put up warnings against looting, the Armenian quarter came under attack almost immediately. Hatred between Turks and Armenians was intense. The Armenians were Turkish-speaking; they were natives of Anatolia. But within a generation they had turned their backs on their Muslim neighbours and made common cause with the Muslims' foreign enemies. It was like a murderous family quarrel. Much poorer than their Christian neighbours even before the Great War, the Turks were now largely destitute. Muslim irregulars, many of them outlaws of long standing, poured into the city, joining Turkish soldiers whose sole worldly possessions were their tattered uniforms. Local Muslims, living in poor neighbourhoods round the citadel of Kadifekale, were eager to make use of the opportunity to better their lot.

Only a determined, impartial commander could have prevented large-scale disorder. But Nurettin, who became military commandant of İzmir, was determined only on revenge. Soon after entering the governor's residence, he summoned the Greek archbishop Chrysostom, with whom he had a personal score to settle, for it was the archbishop who had procured Nurettin's dismissal from İzmir in 1919. Having accused the archbishop of treason, Nurettin pushed him out of the residence and invited the assembled crowd of Muslims to deal with him. He was lynched before the eyes of a French patrol.[108] It was an invitation to mob rule. Attacks, mainly on the Armenians, intensified. On 13 September, a fire broke out in the Armenian quarter and quickly spread to other Christian neighbourhoods by the waterfront. Soon they were almost entirely destroyed. The Turkish quarter up the hill, and the small Jewish quarter, were spared in the fire which consumed three-quarters of the city.

Tens of thousands of Christians fled to the waterfront. A large fleet of Allied warships and transports had assembled in the harbour to

evacuate the citizens of Allied states which had theoretically been
neutral in the Greek-Turkish war. Many had already left by the time the
fire broke out. Allied and Turkish patrols tried at first to prevent
Christians who were Ottoman citizens from boarding the ships, but
the suffering of the refugees was such that Allied officers started accepting everyone they could accommodate. In all some 213,000 men,
women and children – the majority of the population of the city – were
evacuated.[109]

Ethnic conflict had raged almost without interruption since 1912.
Having won their War of Independence and thus prevented the loss of
their land to their neighbours, most Muslims in Turkey wanted to see
the last of the Christian minorities. Two months after the fire of İzmir,
Mustafa Kemal criticized Nurettin for trying to attribute to himself
alone 'the patriotic effort of all members of the army to expel non-
Muslims from western Anatolia'. But, clearly, care was needed.
Nurettin's 'readiness to exile and destroy the Greeks and Armenians
in Anatolia', Mustafa Kemal went on to say, was 'nothing more than
demagogy, which should be avoided for fear of damaging the national
interest'.[110]

Mustafa Kemal did not mention the great fire of İzmir in the long
report which he presented to the assembly in Ankara on 4 November
1922, although he did refer to the fire started by the Greeks in
Afyonkarahisar.[111] Nor did he speak of the İzmir fire in his six-day
speech in 1927. Some things are better left unsaid. İsmet is a little more
forthcoming. He speaks in his memoirs both of the fires started by the
Greeks and of the great conflagration in İzmir. 'The cause of these
fires,' he says, 'should be sought in the great events of history.
Subordinates say that they carried out orders; senior figures that there
was a breakdown in discipline. In those days when joy struggled with
pity in our feelings, I remember Atatürk, seated under a lean-to in
Alaşehir or Salihli [on the way to İzmir] saying that one day we might
find ourselves making an alliance with the Greeks.'[112] But, when he contemplated the conflagration in İzmir, Mustafa Kemal could only say,
'Let it burn, let it crash down.'[113] It was not an order; it was the acceptance of the consummation of ethnic conflict.

Falih Rıfkı (Atay), the Turkish nationalist journalist who had come
from Istanbul to İzmir to interview Mustafa Kemal, noted in his diary
that looters had helped the fire to spread. He went on:

Why were we burning down İzmir? Were we afraid that if waterfront mansions, hotels and restaurants stayed in place, we would never be free of the
minorities? When the Armenians were deported in the First World War, this

same fear made us burn down all the neighbourhoods fit to live in, in Anatolian towns. This did not derive from a simple urge to destroy. A feeling of inferiority had a part in it. It was as if anywhere that resembled Europe was destined to remain Christian and foreign and to be denied to us … I believe that but for Nurettin Paşa, known as a thorough fanatic and a rabble-rousing demagogue, this tragedy would not have run its course.[114]

The eastern part of Turkey had been devastated in the Great War. Now western Anatolia, by far the richest and most developed area, lay in ruins, its population uprooted. The Muslims who had fled from the Greeks were returning; the Greeks and Armenians, on whose skills the Ottoman economy was largely dependent, were lucky to escape. Such was the result of the policy advocated by Lloyd George to improve security in an area which had been, by and large, at peace under Ottoman administration when the armistice was concluded in October 1918. True, the tensions engendered by that war had made it difficult, if not impossible, for Christians and Muslims to go on living together in a multi-ethnic society. But the disengagement of the ethnic communities could have been more gradual and infinitely less bloody if a Greek army of occupation had not been allowed in. Andrew Ryan, the dragoman of the British High Commission, justified British policy in retrospect by arguing that it had sought to protect the Christian communities.[115] It ended by destroying them. But to Mustafa Kemal the devastation of Anatolia offered the opportunity to realize his ambitions for his country and himself. Turkey had to be rebuilt. He was determined to be its architect.

17

Winning Without Fighting

———————◆———————

'NOW, GENTLEMEN, WE can move on to the diplomatic stage,'
Mustafa Kemal said in his six-day speech after describing the victorious march of his armies to İzmir.[1] As soon as he entered İzmir, he
set his sights on the next objective – the withdrawal of foreign armies
from Istanbul and eastern Thrace. Istanbul was still under Allied –
British, French and Italian – occupation, while Greek troops in eastern
Thrace had been joined by the forces withdrawn from the Asian shores
of the sea of Marmara. Allied, including Greek, warships barred passage
across the straits.

In theory, the Allies were still bound by their offer of March 1922,
which provided that Greece should keep part of eastern Thrace, including Edirne, the second Ottoman capital.[2] However, Mustafa Kemal
knew that France and Italy were ready to hand back to Turkey all the
territory in Europe which the Ottomans held at the end of the Great
War, in the hope that, at the peace conference, other – mainly economic
– matters would be settled to their satisfaction. Freedom of navigation
through the straits was not a major problem, since the Turkish National
Pact, in all its recensions, had allowed for it. The problem was Lloyd
George, who still fancied that he could secure some gains for his Greek
protégés and treat Turkey as a state defeated in the World War.

British troops and warships were now the only obstacle to the realization of the original aims of the National Pact. Mustafa Kemal was
determined to remove this obstacle by any means short of war. To do so
he had to make use of dissension among the Allies, while appealing to
realists and well-wishers in Britain over the heads of the British government, which, unlike the French and Italian governments, refused to deal

directly with him. It took Mustafa Kemal exactly one month to reach his objective – a month in which his cool pressure tactics made nonsense of the excited responses of Lloyd George and his ministers.

On 10 September, the day he entered İzmir, Mustafa Kemal informed his prime minister Rauf (Orbay) in Ankara that the British consul in İzmir, Sir Harry Lamb, and the admiral commanding British warships in the harbour, Sir Osmond Brock, had told the Turkish 1st Army commander, Nurettin Paşa, that the state of war between Britain and the Ottoman state had ended with the 1918 armistice and that Britain was not at war with the government of the Turkish Grand National Assembly.[3] According to Mustafa Kemal, Nurettin Paşa replied that diplomatic relations needed to be established, but that this depended on the two governments – in London and Ankara – going through the proper formalities.[4] However, the British government did not take the hint.

Mustafa Kemal spent his first night in İzmir at Karşıyaka, across the bay from the centre of the city. According to a story which has become part of the Atatürk legend, a Greek flag had been laid down in front of the entrance to the house, but Mustafa Kemal refused to step on it.[5] In any case, the stench from the bay – into which corpses and dead horses had been thrown – was such that Mustafa Kemal and his party had to leave Karşıyaka the following day and move to a doctor's house on the quayside in the city centre.[6] The journalist Falih Rıfkı (Atay) reports that on arrival, Mustafa Kemal turned up at Kramer's, the smartest hotel on the quayside. At first he was not recognized and was told that no table was available. However, the hotel staff were quickly informed of the identity of their distinguished visitor. As he ordered *rakı*, Mustafa Kemal asked, 'Did King Constantine ever come here to drink a glass of *rakı*?' It had never happened, he was assured. 'In that case,' said Mustafa Kemal, 'why did he bother to take İzmir?'[7] The stories may be apocryphal, but they are true to character: Atatürk liked to be seen as generous in victory; he enjoyed jokes and did not hide his fondness for *rakı*.

On 12 September, Mustafa Kemal gave an interview in his headquarters to the *Daily Mail* correspondent Ward Price. 'He talked for half an hour in fluent French, quietly, but with emphasis. One gold medal on his khaki tunic was the only decoration he wore,' Ward Price remembered.[8] Mustafa Kemal restated his aims, explaining that Turkey claimed neither Syria nor Mesopotamia, and would not fortify the straits. He said that he would prefer to obtain possession of Istanbul by negotiation, but added that he could not wait indefinitely. It was an important interview, and, having carried it, the *Daily Mail* came out strongly against any British attempt to oppose the Turks by force.

Later that day, Mustafa Kemal met the British consul Sir Harry
Lamb. The latter had been instructed to have no official dealings with
him,[9] but as the consul called on the civil governor, Abdülhalik (Renda),
to discuss the safety of British subjects, Mustafa Kemal joined them.[10]
Angered by Lamb's demand for assurances, Mustafa Kemal questioned
his right to negotiate pending the conclusion of peace;[11] Turkey and
Britain were still at war, so Mustafa Kemal said. As the evacuation of
British subjects was speeded up, Admiral Brock sent an emissary to
Mustafa Kemal to ask whether Nurettin Paşa's earlier statement about
the desirability of diplomatic relations still stood. Yes it did, Mustafa
Kemal replied, his words had been misunderstood. Lamb returned to
Istanbul, when the evacuation not only of British subjects but of all
Christians who could save themselves from İzmir was completed. The
question of recognition was still unresolved. Turkish troops gradually
moved north from İzmir towards Çanakkale on the Asian shore of the
Dardanelles, and from İzmit towards İstanbul. Their approach to the
neutral zone, established on both sides of the straits, caused acute
apprehension in London.

Mustafa Kemal stayed on in İzmir savouring the fruits of his military
victory. When the great fire which swept the city on 13 September
threatened his house, he moved to a mansion in the seaside suburb of
Göztepe, on the south side of the bay. The mansion belonged to a rich
and well-connected Turkish merchant, Muammer Uşakîzade (later
Uşaklıgil), whose cousin, the writer Halit Ziya, had served as chief of
chancery to Sultan Mehmet V before the Great War. When the Greeks
occupied İzmir, Muammer prudently removed himself and his family to
France, and waited for the dust to settle. But his 24-year-old eldest
daughter Lâtife decided to interrupt her law studies in France and
returned to İzmir after the Turkish victory at Sakarya. In the family
mansion she was chaperoned by her grandmother.

Lâtife was an ambitious young woman, who had received a good
education. Along with a pretty face and attractive brown hair, she had a
small and rather dumpy body, and a strong will. When Mustafa Kemal
decided to move from the house assigned to him in Karşıyaka, he
checked over other possible residences, including the Uşakîzade
mansion, where he was received by Lâtife. He was impressed by her
easy and direct manners and her European accomplishments. But he
did not immediately take up her insistent invitation to stay in her
house.[12] When he finally moved there, Lâtife so dazzled him with her
organizing ability that he referred to her jokingly as 'the lady commander of the headquarters'.[13] Having set her sights on Mustafa Kemal,
Lâtife did her best to demonstrate the accomplishment most sought

after in Turkish women – the ability to serve a husband. But there is another feminine accomplishment sought by the prospective bride-groom's family and friends – the ability to manage a husband, and keep control over his varying moods. In Turkish as in other traditional cultures, skill in man-management is the essence of feminine wisdom. Mustafa Kemal's entourage considered long and hard whether Lâtife had this essential quality.

The fire had cast a shadow over Turkish joy at the recapture of İzmir. As İsmet recalled in his memoirs, a mood of sadness set in, summed up in the words, 'We have taken İzmir, but what's the use? The city and half of Anatolia have been reduced to ruins.' Mustafa Kemal would have none of this. The cause had triumphed, and repairing the damage was no problem. His optimism was infectious.[14] When the commander of the French squadron in İzmir, Admiral Dumesnil, who did not share the British admiral's reservations, called on him, Mustafa Kemal described the great fire as 'a disagreeable incident'. The Frenchman thought this an understatement, but agreed realistically that 'it was only an episode'.[15]

While Mustafa Kemal relaxed in İzmir, London panicked. At a Cabinet meeting on 15 September, Lloyd George declared that Britain must not 'run away from Mustafa Kemal'.[16] He was supported by the Colonial Secretary, Winston Churchill, who asked that reinforcements should be despatched immediately to the Allied garrison in the neutral zone, which numbered only 7,600 men. British warships and troops were rushed to the straits, and Allied governments were pressed to help. Only New Zealand sent a favourable reply.

France swung into action to avert the danger of renewed war with Turkey. On 18 September, the French High Commissioner, General Pellé, left Istanbul for İzmir without informing his British colleague Sir Horace Rumbold.[17] Pellé urged Mustafa Kemal to stop the movement of Turkish troops towards the neutral zone of the straits. Mustafa Kemal refused, saying that his government had never recognized the existence of the neutral zone,[18] nor could he hold back his victorious armies. Unless an armistice was signed, they would march rapidly on Istanbul. But when Pellé had left, Mustafa Kemal turned to the Turkish journalist Falih Rıfkı (Atay) and said with a smile, 'Our victorious armies ... I don't even know where they are. Who knows how long it would take us to reassemble them.' And he confided that he would not risk the life of a single Turkish gendarme by moving to Thrace before the conclusion of an armistice.[19] On 22 September, Mustafa Kemal cabled to Karabekir in his eastern headquarters: 'Although we are very strong, we are pursuing a very calculating and moderate policy ... We are trying to isolate the British. Our troops are concentrating in the direction of Istanbul and Çanakkale, but we prefer a political solution, and are managing the situation accordingly.'[20]

On 21 September, Mustafa Kemal received in İzmir his prime minister Rauf (Orbay) and General Ali Fuat (Cebesoy), now leader of the parliamentary group of his party. He had decided how to deal with the Allies, and he had to make sure that the assembly in Ankara would not obstruct him. But the first purpose of the invitation was to celebrate the victory. Falih Rıfkı describes a party to which he was invited at the Uşakîzade mansion. Mustafa Kemal appeared in a white belted Russian shirt, sang songs of his native Rumelia, and joined in folk dancing. 'His movements were masculine and dignified. He avoided unnecessary gestures. His manner was not *alla franca* (European-like), but Western, not *alla turca* (Turkish-like), but genuinely Turkish.' What impressed Falih Rıfkı most was Mustafa Kemal's table-talk. He spoke fluently, eloquently, with the wide command of language of an Ottoman gentleman. Conversation turned on the relative merits of love and pity, a subject suggested by the devastation of the city. 'The discussion brought home to me for the first time,' Falih Rıfkı remembered, 'that this determined warrior and calculating politician was also a very human man of the world.'[21]

In the meantime, the British government was fast losing support at home and abroad. On 18 September, the *Daily Mail* came out with the headline 'Stop This New War', reflecting the popular mood. Three days later, the small French and Italian detachments sent to join the British in Çanakkale in a show of Allied unity were withdrawn to Istanbul. Curzon rushed off to Paris, where he had an undignified row with Poincaré, which left him in tears. Count Sforza, now the Italian ambassador in Paris, helped smooth bruised feelings, and on 23 September the Allies agreed on the text of a joint note which they despatched to Ankara. It declared that they 'viewed with favour' Turkey's desire to recover Thrace as far as the Meriç (Maritza) river, including Edirne, but that the area had to remain neutral for the time being. Similarly, the Turks could have Istanbul, but only after peace was signed.[22]

Mustafa Kemal took his time in replying. He had extracted a half-promise; he had to exert pressure to turn it into a firm commitment. On 19 September, Turkish troops had been ordered to resume their advance.[23] On 23 September, the day when the Allies despatched their note, Turkish cavalry entered the neutral zone near Çanakkale. They were reinforced and pressed forward, pushing the British behind the barbed-wire perimeter of Çanakkale.[24] Neither side opened fire, but the risk of an armed clash was ever present. Turkish pressure was directed solely against the British: there was no movement towards Istanbul, where the weak Allied garrison included French and Italian, as well as British troops.

The French now made another effort to keep the peace. On 28 September, Franklin-Bouillon, self-proclaimed friend of Mustafa Kemal, arrived in İzmir bearing the Allied note, which he proceeded to interpret. The Allies, he said, would make sure that the Greeks evacuated eastern Thrace, including Edirne, and would man a buffer zone between Greeks and Turks. Turkish civil authorities, backed up by gendarmes, would take over.[25] Mustafa Kemal was thus promised what he had striven for, before the beginning of negotiations. He promptly seized the opportunity. He had sent two telegrams to Harington: on 26 September, he assured him that while Turkish troops had every right to pursue the defeated Greeks, he was doing his best to avoid incidents with the British;[26] two days later, he welcomed Harington's assurance that the Greek fleet had been ordered to leave Istanbul, and offered to pull back his troops if British troops were withdrawn from the Asian shore of the Dardanelles.[27] Finally, on 1 October he informed Poincaré that Turkish troops had been ordered to stop their advance, and proposed that armistice negotiations on the basis of the assurances given by Franklin-Bouillon should begin on 3 October in Mudanya, the port of Bursa on the sea of Marmara. The Ankara government would be represented by İsmet, the commander of the western front.[28] However, Mustafa Kemal did not offer to withdraw his troops from the neutral zone; they were still needed to exert pressure until a satisfactory settlement had been achieved. Having made his decision, Mustafa Kemal left İzmir, arriving in Ankara on 2 October. He was met as a conquering hero.

Back in İzmir, Lâtife was desolate at losing sight of her hero. 'In spite of my begging requests, His Excellency the Paşa did not wish to take me with him and employ me even in the humblest capacity in Ankara,' she wrote to Mustafa Kemal's ADC, Salih (Bozok), adding hopefully, 'But one evening, he looked at me with his piercing eyes, deep as the sea, and said: "Don't go anywhere. Wait for me. This is an order." '[29] It was a forward move, registering Lâtife's credentials as an obedient bride.

On 29 September, unaware of the content of Mustafa Kemal's discussions with Franklin-Bouillon, the British government ordered General Harington to present an ultimatum to the Turks demanding an immediate withdrawal from the neutral zone, failing which British troops would open fire. To Lloyd George's fury and Poincaré's relief,

Harington did not deliver the ultimatum. It was a wise decision. On 1
October he was informed that Mustafa Kemal had agreed to armistice
negotiations in Mudanya. The British Cabinet, which had been in
almost continuous session for three days, put off war plans and began
drafting instructions for the negotiations.[30]

The conference began, as planned, on 3 October in the house belonging to a Russian merchant in Mudanya.[31] Three Allied generals,
Harington for Britain, Charpy for France and Mombelli for Italy,
arrived in their warships, and were met by a Turkish guard of honour.
They were willy-nilly the guests of the Ankara government. The Greek
representative, General Mazarakis, joined them later. The Turkish chief
of the general staff, Fevzi Paşa, and the ever-helpful Franklin-Bouillon
stood by in the neighbouring city of Bursa, in case of need. The Turkish
team in Mudanya was led by İsmet, whose toughness and meticulous
attention to detail became immediately apparent to the Allied negoti-
ators. İsmet was hard of hearing, particularly when it suited him; neither
threats nor sweet words impressed him. He was also extremely prudent
and referred all contentious points to Mustafa Kemal.

The Turks had good reason to be careful. In Greece, the defeated
army had staged a revolt. King Constantine was forced to leave on 30
September, and a military triumvirate took over.[32] Its leading spirit,
Colonel Plastiras, declared his determination to fight for eastern
Thrace. Venizelos reappeared on the scene and tried to enlist Lloyd
George's help. Disenchantment with Greece was now strongly felt in
London, but Lloyd George still clung to the shreds of his bankrupt
Philhellene policy.[33]

The negotiations at Mudanya were long and hard. The Turks wanted
firm dates for the Greek withdrawal and equally firm arrangements for
the establishment in Thrace of the authority of the Ankara government.
They demanded that eastern Thrace, including Karaağaç, a suburb of
Edirne on the west bank of the Meriç river, should be handed over to
them immediately; the British wanted a secure transition. There were
frequent adjournments and interruptions. On 6 October, Mustafa
Kemal instructed İsmet to tell Harington, 'preferably in the presence of
the French and Italian generals', that Turkish troops would march on
Istanbul immediately if the return of eastern Thrace to the Ankara
government was not accepted; Harington should make sure that his
troops did not provoke any incident.[34] Instead, the British general made
ready for his troops in Çanakkale to open fire on the Turks.

But the handover of eastern Thrace to the Ankara government was accepted, and on 10 October Mustafa Kemal authorized İsmet to sign the armistice terms.[35] The following day, the text was signed by all parties except the Greeks, and the armistice came into force on 15 October when the Greek government notified its agreement. Having achieved his aim, Mustafa Kemal immediately extended an olive branch to the British. 'I have the honour to inform you of the great pleasure which I feel at the mutual understanding achieved at the Mudanya conference between Your Excellency and the Turkish delegate, General İsmet,' he cabled to Harington on 11 October, adding: 'On behalf of all humanity, I desire and hope that the efforts expended in the cause of peace will be crowned with success.'[36]

The armistice agreement provided that the withdrawal of Greek troops from eastern Thrace would start immediately and would be completed within fifteen days. Allied troops would take over from the Greeks and would then hand over the territory to the Ankara government within thirty days. Up to 8,000 Turkish gendarmes would be allowed in to keep order. The Allies would man a buffer zone on the western (Greek) bank of the Meriç, including the disputed suburb of Karaağaç. Turkish troops would withdraw to a distance of 15 kilometres from the Dardanelles and 40 kilometres from the Bosphorus. And, of course, all hostilities between Greece and Turkey would cease.[37]

The Turkish high command immediately detached a force of 6,000 infantry and 1,000 cavalry from the western front and redesignated them as gendarmes.[38] On 19 October, General Refet (Bele), who was given command of these troops, arrived in Istanbul as the special representative of the Ankara government. The Muslim population of the Ottoman capital welcomed him enthusiastically. The following day the first detachment of Turkish troops disembarked, as a military band played the march 'Mustafa Kemal Paşa is our commander' (*Mustafa Kemal Paşa Serdarımız*).[39]

The handover of eastern Thrace proceeded smoothly and was completed by 26 November.[40] The territory was spared material devastation, but lost much of its population, for by a quirk of history, while there were many more Turks than Greeks in western Thrace, Greeks were numerous in eastern Thrace. They all left, with such possessions and animals as they could take with them, in a mass migration, made even sadder by the early onset of winter. It took a long time to repeople the land with Turkish migrants from Greece and Bulgaria. Vineyards tended by the Greeks were replaced by plantations of tobacco and then of sunflower. The frontier city of Edirne, with its dazzling array of Ottoman monuments, lost its importance as the commercial centre of the whole of Thrace, and its population dropped from 83,000 at the outbreak of the Balkan war to 35,000 in 1927.[41] In Turkey-in-Europe, as in Turkey-in-Asia, the land and the people were changing, and the first phase of the change brought security in return for poverty.

The international scene had also changed. On 19 October, the day when Refet arrived in Istanbul, British Conservatives met at the Carlton Club in London and decided to withdraw from Lloyd George's wartime coalition. The following day Lloyd George resigned, never to return to office again. His fall cannot be attributed solely to his disastrous Near Eastern policy. But his defeat in the duel of wills he had fought with Mustafa Kemal was the last straw which brought down the coalition government. The Conservative leader, Bonar Law, who had declared during the Çanakkale crisis that the British could not 'alone act as the policemen of the world',[42] assumed office on 24 October. Lord Curzon remained Foreign Secretary, having finally taken a stand against Lloyd George. Winston Churchill, who had changed his policy disastrously at the last moment and advocated an armed response to the Turks at Çanakkale, was defeated in the general elections on 15 November. His experience – from the Gallipoli campaign in 1915 to the Çanakkale crisis in 1922 – taught him to appreciate the importance of the Turks and of their leader Mustafa Kemal. But his unsuccessful efforts to persuade Turkey to enter the Second World War on the Allied side suggests that he never understood that the experience of the same years had taught Kemalist Turkey the skill to work out its own national interest.

A more profound change took place in Italy, where Benito Mussolini became prime minister on 31 October, after the melodramatic march on Rome of his Black Shirts. Count Sforza, the friend of Turkish nationalists, refused to serve under him.

On 27 October the Allies invited Turkey to a peace conference in Lausanne, in the agreeable surroundings of neutral Switzerland. The invitation was addressed both to the Ankara government and to the sultan's phantom government in Istanbul. Mustafa Kemal was not surprised. On 17 October the grand vizier Tevfik Paşa had asked him to send a representative to Istanbul to concert the action of the two governments. The following day he received a curt reply from Mustafa Kemal: the Turkish Grand National Assembly was the only legitimate authority in Turkey; any other bodies would do well to refrain from causing confusion in the country's policy.[43] However, it was not enough to push aside elderly meddlers from Istanbul with ideas well above their station: Mustafa Kemal needed a skilled and loyal representative in Lausanne. His choice fell inevitably on İsmet who had proved himself in the field and in the conference room in Mudanya, and whose loyalty he could trust.

It was a controversial choice. Kâzım Karabekir, who had negotiated the Gümrü treaty with the Bolsheviks, wanted the job for himself.[44] Moreover, since other countries would be represented by their foreign ministers, the foreign minister of the Ankara government, Yusuf Kemal (Tengirşenk), seemed the proper person to lead the Turkish delegation. Mustafa Kemal found an easy solution. On 24 October he sent a telegram to Yusuf Kemal saying that he understood his 'insistent wish to resign', and asking him to recommend İsmet as his successor.[45] Yusuf Kemal did as he was told, and the assembly duly elected İsmet, first, foreign minister, and then leader of the Turkish delegation.[46] One of his two assistants was the health minister, Dr Rıza Nur, an anti-Unionist politician who was to end his chequered career as an opponent of Mustafa Kemal. The delegation's advisers included the former Ottoman finance minister and prominent Unionist politician, Cavit, and the Chief Rabbi Nahum.

Theoretically, the delegation was to work to the instructions of the prime minister Rauf (Orbay), who was to interpret the wishes of the assembly. But Mustafa Kemal knew that he could rely on İsmet to carry out his wishes and his policy. The territorial aims of the National Pact had been, by and large, achieved at Mudanya. The Lausanne conference was to complete the process by securing international recognition of a fully independent Turkish state. While İsmet struggled with the details, Mustafa Kemal turned his attention to domestic politics once again. He had completed the military task and delegated the diplomatic work to İsmet. He could now concentrate on the job of fashioning a new Turkey.

PART IV

Republic and Reforms

18

The End of the Monarchy

———————◆———————

ON 4 OCTOBER 1922, two days after his return to Ankara from İzmir,[1]
Mustafa Kemal gave his report to the assembly on the victory won
over the Greeks and the decision to hold armistice talks in Mudanya.
He singled out for praise only three of his commanders – his loyal supporters Fevzi, İsmet and the defence minister Kâzım (Özalp).[2] As commander-in-chief, he had, it is true, promoted all the commanders who
had taken part in the final campaign. But this left out two of his original
companions in Anatolia, Ali Fuat (Cebesoy) and Refet (Bele), who had
refused to serve under İsmet. They made common cause with the other
two prime movers of Turkish national resistance – the prime minister
Rauf (Orbay)[3] and the eastern front commander, Kâzım Karabekir. The
latter had flooded Mustafa Kemal with unwanted advice during the
course of the war, and had now arrived in Ankara to congratulate his
commander-in-chief.[4] All four felt that they had the right to a share in the
government of the country. Rauf claims that when Mustafa Kemal left for
the front in August 1922, he told him, 'I leave the country in your care.'[5]

Although personal relations were becoming strained, Mustafa Kemal
still needed the support of his original companions against the parliamentary opposition. On 4 September, as soon as news was received that
successful generals had been promoted on the battlefield, the leader of
the opposition Second Group, Erzurum deputy Hüseyin Avni (Ulaş),
complained that the authority of the assembly had been usurped. Rauf
had to deploy all his political skills to persuade the assembly to approve
the promotions.[6] Rauf was loyal, but he resented İsmet's growing
influence. Mustafa Kemal needed to prevent an alliance between his original companions and the Second Group, made up of provincial notables,

some of whom had supported Enver's attempts to take over the Turkish resistance movement.[7] When his powers as commander-in-chief were extended on the eve of the final offensive, he had promised to return to 'the bosom of the nation', once victory was won. In his mind, this meant assuming the country's political leadership when the military task was over. His companions wanted collective leadership; the Second Group upheld direct government by the assembly, the principle which Mustafa Kemal had proclaimed for tactical reasons in 1920, but which now stood in the way of his designs.

The struggle for power was bound up with the choice of policies to tackle the immense task of reconstruction. Large tracts of the country lay in ruins; its social fabric had been torn apart by the expulsion and flight of Christians and the civil war among the Muslims; the survivors were tired after a decade of war. Although Mustafa Kemal had been circumspect in his speeches during the course of the War of Independence, rival politicians sensed that he stood for a forced march to modernity, a march that he alone would lead. Not surprisingly, their mood was summed up in the words, 'We have got rid of the Greeks. Now let's get rid of Mustafa Kemal.'[8] Mustafa Kemal responded by creating his own political base of unquestioning supporters, inspired, where possible, by the same ideals, but in any case bound by personal loyalty. Favours would thin out the ranks of his critics. It was a slow process. In the meantime, the susceptibilities of his original companions had to be managed. But he also went outside the circle of civilian and military politicians, and appealed directly to 'the people', or rather to the still small, but rising, caste of Turks educated in Western ways. They were to be his new army.

As soon as the Mudanya armistice had been signed, Mustafa Kemal left Ankara for Bursa, where İsmet and Fevzi were waiting. Karabekir and Refet travelled with him; so did Fikriye, who had been diagnosed as suffering from tuberculosis.[9] Mustafa Kemal was thinking seriously of marrying Lâtife. He had asked her to join him in Bursa, and then countermanded his instructions.[10] In accordance with custom, he had discussed his intentions with his mother Zübeyde, who was by that time a very sick woman. Doctors had suggested that Zübeyde would profit from a change to the milder climate of İzmir. There she would have an opportunity of forming her own opinion about Lâtife's suitability as a daughter-in-law. Zübeyde was despatched to İzmir in the company of Mustafa Kemal's ADC, Salih (Bozok), and was taken to a clinic in the suburb of Karşıyaka. Lâtife was in constant attendance. As for Fikriye, Mustafa Kemal sent her on from Bursa for treatment in Munich. She had become an encumbrance.

Mustafa Kemal says that it was in Bursa that he decided to give Refet the job of representing the Ankara government in Istanbul and leading Turkish forces in Thrace.[11] According to Ali Fuat, Mustafa Kemal and Rauf had agreed jointly on the choice of Refet, as a person known and popular throughout the country and, particularly, in Istanbul, and had obtained the assembly's approval for the appointment.[12] In any case, it was in Bursa that Mustafa Kemal asked an unsuspecting İsmet to lead the Turkish delegation to the peace conference.[13] 'The problem of Istanbul', in other words the liquidation of the Ottoman government, had to be solved immediately to give Ankara a free hand in Lausanne. After discussing it with Mustafa Kemal, Refet moved quickly and with a sure hand.

Welcomed on arrival by the sultan's ADC, Refet asked him to convey 'the pious feelings he entertained for the exalted office of the caliph'.[14] There was no mention of the sultanate. Clearly, the decision to abolish the monarchy, but retain the caliphate, had already been taken, even before the matter had been brought to the assembly.[15] Similarly, in reply to the greetings of the grand vizier Tevfik Paşa and the Ottoman interior minister, Refet declared that he did not recognize their titles, but thanked them for their kind words.[16] Refet's behaviour displeased some members of the assembly in Ankara, who questioned his right to speak on their behalf.[17] On 29 October, Refet had a four-hour audience with Sultan Vahdettin. He asked that the sovereign should dismiss the phantom government in the capital and recognize the Ankara government. He also explained that feeling in Ankara favoured the abolition of the monarchy, and the retention of the separate office of the caliph. The sultan played for time and refused to dismiss his ministers.[18] On the same day, the grand vizier Tevfik Paşa appealed directly to the assembly to send a delegate to Istanbul or receive his representative to discuss a joint response to the Allied invitation to the peace conference.[19]

The matter came up before the assembly on 30 October in the presence of Mustafa Kemal, who had returned from Bursa the previous day. Dr Rıza Nur, who had been chosen as İsmet's assistant in the Turkish peace delegation, tabled a motion declaring that the Grand National Assembly, founded as a people's government, was sole heir to the Ottoman empire within Turkey's frontiers, that the institution of the monarchy had therefore lapsed, but that the institution of the caliphate was legitimate and would be freed from foreign domination.[20] However, not enough votes were cast for the motion, and the debate was resumed on 1 November.

Mustafa Kemal intervened with a long account of the history of Islam. He pointed out that there had been impotent Arab caliphs under

the rule of Selçuk (Seljuk) Turks in Baghdad from the eleventh century
to the Mongol invasion two hundred years later, and then under the
Mamluks in Egypt until the Ottoman conquest in the sixteenth century.
The functions of caliph, as successor to the Prophet, and of the temporal ruler, or sultan, could therefore be separated. Now temporal rule
in Turkey had passed to the assembly, which had the power to designate
– and protect – a caliph.

> On the one hand, the people of Turkey will become daily stronger as a
> modern and civilized state, and realize increasingly their humanity and iden-
> tity, without being exposed to the danger of individual treachery, and, on the
> other, the institution of the caliphate will be exalted as the central link of the
> spirit, the conscience and the faith of the Islamic world ...[21]

A committee of the assembly was then asked to draft the necessary
resolution.

Mustafa Kemal said in 1927 that he cut the debate short, telling the
committee:

> Sovereignty and kingship are never decided by academic debate. They are
> seized by force. The Ottoman dynasty appropriated by force the government
> of the Turks, and reigned over them for six centuries. Now the Turkish nation
> has effectively gained possession of its sovereignty ... This is an accomplished
> fact ... If those assembled here ... see the matter in its natural light, we shall
> all agree. Otherwise, facts will still prevail, but some heads may roll.

Thereupon, Mustafa Kemal went on, a cleric who spoke for the committee said: 'Sorry, we had approached the matter from a different angle.
Now you have put us right.' That settled the matter, Mustafa Kemal
claimed in 1927.[22]

However, the official collection of his speeches makes no mention of
a threatening intervention in the discussions of the joint committee.
The record shows only that in the early hours of 2 November 1922, the
assembly passed a resolution (dated 1 November) declaring that the
sultan's government had ended on 16 March 1920, when Istanbul was
occupied by the Allies, that the government of the Grand National
Assembly was the only legitimate authority in the country, that the caliphate was vested in the Ottoman dynasty, but that the assembly had the
right to choose the caliph. The text which was adopted was based
largely on the proposal put forward two days earlier by Dr Rıza Nur.
There was only one vote against the resolution: it was cast by Ziya
Hurşit, a deputy from Trabzon, who was emerging as Mustafa Kemal's
most obstinate opponent in the assembly.[23]

There was no mention of Vahdettin in the decision abolishing the monarchy and creating a separate caliphate. He stayed on in Yıldız palace, abandoned by all but his family and a handful of staff and servants. On 4 November, Tevfik Paşa arrived at the palace to announce the resignation of his government. The following day, Refet closed down all the Ottoman ministries and announced that Istanbul would henceforth be administered as a province of the Ankara government.[24] A few days later he moved to the grand vizier's office in the Sublime Porte.[25] Opponents of the nationalists in Istanbul were seized by panic. On 4 November,[26] the day Tevfik Paşa resigned, Ali Kemal, who had been interior minister in one of Damat Ferit's governments and had criticized the Anatolian resistance in his newspaper *Peyam-ı Sabah* (Morning Message), was kidnapped by nationalist agents outside the Cercle d'Orient club in the European quarter of Istanbul. He was bundled into a boat and taken to İzmit, where Nurettin had transferred his headquarters as commander of the 1st Army. Nurettin dealt with Ali Kemal as he had treated the Greek archbishop Chrysostom in İzmir: he pushed him into the arms of a hostile crowd, which finished him off with sticks, stones and knives.[27]

As news of Ali Kemal's lynching became known, the British High Commission was flooded with requests for asylum. On 5 November, the High Commissioner had his final audience with the sultan, who voiced fears for his personal safety.[28] On 10 November, Vahdettin appeared for the last time at the *selâmlık* ceremony, when the sultan presents himself to his people for Friday prayers. In some mosques in the capital, prayers were still offered for Sultan Mehmet VI (Vahdettin). In others, the congregation was asked to pray for an unnamed caliph.[29] On 16 November, Vahdettin, signing himself as 'Caliph of the Mussulmans', asked General Harington to transfer him as soon as possible from Istanbul, where he considered his life to be in danger. At dawn on 17 November, the sultan, his young son Ertuğrul, and a handful of courtiers and servants,[30] were smuggled from the palace in two British army ambulances and taken aboard HMS *Malaya*. After stopping briefly in Malta, Vahdettin spent some time in Mecca, as the guest of Husayn, the Hashemite king of Hejaz. He finally settled in San Remo, where he was joined by his three wives and his sister, and where he died on 15 May 1926. Refet was to say later that he had thanked Harington for relieving him of the burden of the sultan's presence.[31]

As soon as the news of Vahdettin's flight reached Ankara, the government obtained a canonical decision (*fetva*) from the minister of canon law (Mehmet Vehbi) declaring that the post of caliph had become vacant and that a successor had to be appointed. The assembly confirmed the decision unanimously and elected Vahdettin's cousin

Abdülmecit to be the new caliph.[32] Abdülmecit, who had been heir
apparent before the sultanate had been abolished, had been prudently
sympathetic to the nationalist cause during the War of Independence.
An accomplished painter in the French classical manner, he set his heart
on a fancy-dress caliphate, which, he hoped, would not annoy Ankara.
Would it be all right, he asked Mustafa Kemal through Refet, if he
appeared at the *selâmlık* ceremony dressed in robes and a turban, as
worn by Mehmet II, the conqueror of Istanbul?[33] No it would not, he
was told: he should wear a frock coat, and on no account a military
uniform.[34]

Refet, whose brother was a palace ADC, proved a respectful control-
ler of the new caliph. He presented him with a horse named 'Konya',
after the town which Refet had secured for the nationalist cause in
1919.[35] Refet's attentions to the caliph cost him his job. On 16
December, he was replaced as nationalist envoy in Istanbul by Dr
Adnan (Adıvar), the husband of Halide Edip and a vice-president
(deputy speaker) of the assembly.[36] Refet remained commander of
Turkish troops in Thrace, but he lost any possibility of establishing an
alternative centre of power in Istanbul. However, political opponents of
Mustafa Kemal persisted in attempts to pit the caliph against him. In
Ankara, the new printing press set up by a member of the Second
Group, Ali Şükrü, to publish the opposition newspaper *Tan* (The
Dawn), produced a pamphlet arguing that the caliph should become the
head of the Turkish state, the post held by Mustafa Kemal as president
of the Grand National Assembly.[37]

The peace conference opened in Lausanne on 21 November. Curzon,
who retained his job as Foreign Secretary after the Conservative victory
in the general elections five days earlier, took the chair at the first
plenary session. Mussolini and Poincaré made brief appearances; then
the bargaining began. Earlier agreements with France and the Soviet
republics had defined most of Turkey's frontiers. In Europe, the
Mudanya armistice agreement had implicitly recognized the Meriç river
as Turkey's frontier with Greece. There remained Turkey's claim to the
province of Mosul, which the British had occupied in the days following the 1918 armistice. The British proposed – or rather, threatened –
from the start that if there were no agreement on Mosul, the matter
should go to the newly founded League of Nations, of which Turkey
was not yet a member.

İsmet fought tenaciously for Mosul: the province was known to
contain rich oil deposits, and, perhaps more importantly, if its predom-

inantly Kurdish population were severed from the more numerous Kurds in eastern Turkey, separatists among the latter would find support across the border. Neither Mustafa Kemal nor any other leading Turkish nationalist denied at the time that there were Kurds in Turkey. But they argued that Turks and Kurds were indissolubly linked by a common history and interests, and should be considered an indivisible national entity. To detach Mosul from Turkey would bring division. As İsmet was to say to the British ambassador in Ankara in 1925: 'So long as any large number of Kurds are included in Iraq the Turkish government would have perpetual trouble in their eastern provinces and trouble would arise automatically, however loyally the British authorities might act as neighbours.'[38] This was Mustafa Kemal's opinion from the start. But he was a realist. Speaking to journalists in İzmit in January 1923, he put the question, 'Is it reasonable to continue the war for Mosul?' Turkish troops could capture the town, but one had to think of the danger in the west, where Greek troops were massing. 'It is impossible,' he concluded, 'to regain Mosul by war.' But he hastened to add that this was his personal view.[39]

Mustafa Kemal was prepared in the last resort to sacrifice Mosul. He disagreed also with those who wanted to gain possession of western Thrace by insisting on a referendum among its predominantly Muslim population. The area, he argued, was militarily indefensible. It was better that Greeks and Bulgarians should fight over it, and that all Turks in Macedonia and western Thrace should be repatriated to reinforce the depleted population of Turkey. 'We should give up all thought of mounting expeditions in Europe to return there,' he declared.[40] Eastern Thrace and, with it, the European portion of Istanbul could be defended only by diplomatic and not by military means. This is why negotiations on the straits were nearing agreement.[41] But on one point Mustafa Kemal was adamant: the capitulations had to go, and with them all unequal concessions to foreigners and minorities, all interference in Turkey's internal affairs. Turkey's total independence was not negotiable.

Disagreements on economic matters and the limitations the Allies wished to impose on Turkey's internal jurisdiction led to an adjournment of the negotiations in Lausanne on 4 February 1923. The French, whose economic interests in Turkey were more extensive than those of the other Allies, wanted to improve on the terms of the draft treaty presented by Curzon. İsmet rejected it. Sir Horace Rumbold, who assisted Curzon, was furious. 'I have never run up against such a lot of pig-headed, stupid and irritating people,' he wrote to Nevile Henderson, his deputy in Istanbul.[42] It did not occur to Rumbold that İsmet was a much better judge of Turkey's national interest than he was. Two years earlier Rumbold had raged in similar terms against the Turks' refusal to ratify the treaty of Sèvres: 'I have never dealt with people who have so little political sagacity as the Turks ... I told them they ought to show good will in the matter of ratification, and thereby acquire merit in the eyes of the Allies ... But they could not or would not see this.'[43] But the crux of the matter was not the comic inappropriateness of Rumbold's advice to the Turks. It was, as he observed on another occasion, that 'the Kemalist Turk ... thinks that he can run his country himself without any foreign intervention.'[44] The Allies could not believe that Orientals were capable of providing civilized government. Mustafa Kemal was determined to prove them wrong.

It was no easy task. Muslim Turks lacked the most basic technical skills. Famous as cavalrymen, they had to rely on Armenian farriers to shoe their horses. The official collection of Mustafa Kemal's speeches records only one address to a popular audience during the entire course of the War of Independence: it was given at the diploma ceremony of the newly established school of military farriers in Konya.[45] Speaking four months before the final offensive, Mustafa Kemal told the story of a sultan who was hard put to find a single tradesman in the army which he led to Belgrade. Yet when one was found, the sultan was sad: even one tradesman, he feared, could dilute the martial spirit of his soldiers. It was this attitude, said Mustafa Kemal, that made the nation dependent on outsiders for everything 'from needles to thread, from nails to pegs'. 'The simplest trade is the most honourable,' Mustafa Kemal told his simple audience. 'Shoemakers, tailors, carpenters, tanners, blacksmiths, farriers – these are trades most worthy of respect in our social and military life.' They were all trades reserved by tradition for non-Muslims.

Victory allowed Mustafa Kemal to spell out his objectives more clearly. The first public meeting he addressed was in Bursa, after the signature of the armistice at Mudanya. His audience, which had gathered at the Orient cinema, was made up of teachers, many of whom had come from Istanbul, leading parties of schoolchildren to congratulate the commander-in-chief. It was a gathering of people educated in Western knowledge, with whom Mustafa Kemal shared a common language. He spoke frankly of the 'general ignorance' which had to be remedied. Ignorance was the disease which had brought the nation to the brink of disaster. The country could not live in isolation, it had to become a progressive member of the civilized world. This was only possible through the acquisition of scientific knowledge. 'We will acquire knowledge and science wherever they are to be found and we will stuff them into the head of every individual in the country. No limits, no conditions can be attached to knowledge and science.' The speech contained a warning of the cultural revolution to come. 'If social life is permeated with irrational, useless and harmful doctrines and traditions, it becomes paralysed,' Mustafa Kemal declared.[46]

The abolition of the sultanate on 1 November, Vahdettin's flight on 17 November and the election on the following day of Abdülmecit as a caliph subservient to the assembly had opened the way to radical change. But first Mustafa Kemal had to organize his supporters and intimidate opponents in the assembly. On 26 November, the radical nationalist journalist Yunus Nadi, himself a member of the assembly, published in his newspaper *Yenigün* a warning that there was no room for 'rotten and harmful thinking' even within the assembly, adding for good measure that many heads had to roll before the French Revolution triumphed. *Hakimiyet-i Milliye* (National Sovereignty), the organ of the Group for the Defence of National Rights in Anatolia and Rumelia, published a telegram from the provinces calling on Mustafa Kemal to kick out the assembly, which had come together in an emergency.[47] On 2 December Mustafa Kemal himself threatened his opponents in the assembly with the power of the people.

His attack was occasioned by a proposal to amend the electoral law. Under the terms of the amendment, candidates for election had to be born within the current borders of Turkey and be resident in a specific constituency. 'Turkish or Kurdish' refugees could stand for election only after five years' residence in a constituency. In an angry speech, Mustafa Kemal claimed that the amendment was specifically directed against his person. He was born in a city lost to Turkey through no fault of his. Instead of residing quietly in a Turkish constituency, he had fought in the Gallipoli peninsula to save Istanbul, then in eastern Turkey to win back Bitlis and Muş, then again in the south to form an army out of the troops fleeing from Syria. He went on:

> I think that my subsequent endeavours are known to you all ... and that they have won me the love and sympathy of my nation . . . I had expected foreign enemies to attempt to isolate me, but I could never imagine that members of the assembly ... would act in the same way ... Who has given these gentlemen the right to strip me of my civic rights? ... I demand an answer from you and from these gentlemen's constituents.[48]

Hüseyin Avni (Ulaş), the leading member of the Second Group, pleaded in vain that the amendment was meant to exclude Arabs or Albanians, and not Gazi Paşa, whose home was 'in everyone's heart'. The offending article was removed during the committee stage.[49]

On 6 December, Mustafa Kemal made his own intentions clear. In an interview carried by *Hakimiyet-i Milliye* and *Yenigün*, he declared that 'in order to justify the sympathy and trust extended to me by people of all classes, even to the furthest corners of the world of Islam, I intend to form a People's Party ... after the establishment of peace, in order to devote my life to the good of my country as a humble individual.'[50] The opposition was not silenced, but it knew that the 'humble individual' could rely on the army of which he was commander-in-chief. Another of Mustafa Kemal's publicists, Yakup Kadri (Karaosmanoğlu), was to write later: 'Had it not been for his influence in the army, Mustafa Kemal would not have been able to get his way in the assembly, or even live in Ankara. The vigilant guard which surrounded him, as if he were in constant danger, was proof of this.'[51] True, some of Mustafa Kemal's political opponents still held effective commands: Refet (Bele) in Thrace, Nurettin in İzmit, on the eastern outskirts of Istanbul, and Kâzım Karabekir in the east. But Mustafa Kemal controlled the high command through the chief of the general staff, Fevzi (Çakmak), and he could rely on the loyalty of the non-political young generals who had won their spurs in the War of Independence.

Mustafa Kemal lost no time in taking his message to a wider audience. On 14 January 1923, he left Ankara for a tour of western Anatolia. On the same day, his mother died in İzmir; he received the news from his ADC Salih (Bozok) the following day, at his first stop in Eskişehir. Flouting convention, Mustafa Kemal decided to go on with his tour. A brief telegram instructing Salih to make appropriate arrangements for the funeral ended with the words, 'May God grant the nation a long life.'[52] He had been a dutiful son, but his mission came first. His speech in Eskişehir contained a detailed survey of the local and national scene. Once again he repudiated Pan-Islamism and Pan-Turanianism: independence within the new national boundaries was the proper aim of Turkish foreign policy.[53] Turning to domestic politics, he mentioned the possibility that the assembly might fall out of step with its constituents and harm the nation. 'Legal measures' were needed to prevent this. But the usual remedy was to hold fresh elections.[54]

From Eskişehir, Mustafa Kemal went on to İzmit. The leading journalists of Istanbul had gone there, accompanied by Adnan (Adıvar), the new nationalist representative in the capital, and his wife Halide Edip. Mustafa Kemal gave them a frank and extensive briefing. If the assembly did not proceed to new elections 'the nation would take its own decision'.[55] 'The law of the revolution is above all existing laws. As long as they do not kill us ... our revolutionary renewal will not pause.'[56] Speaking to like-minded modernists, Mustafa Kemal did not hide his anticlericalism. 'I do not like the *hocas* (clerics),' he said and proceeded to tell the story of a visit to a *medrese* (religious school) in Konya, which he had made during the War of Independence in the company of envoys from Soviet Russia and Azerbaijan. The local *müftü* embarrassed them all by complaining loudly that religious students were being conscripted. 'I told him in a loud voice,' Mustafa Kemal went on, 'that he had gathered deserters in his school.' He was then thanked for his frankness by local people who declared that they had now realized that the *hocas* were a worthless lot.[57] True, the nation was attached to Islam, and there was no question of rejecting religion as the Communists had done: the government was materialist, not irreligious. In any case, no one was obliged to think like the government. Nor was there any need to fear the award of the caliphate to the Ottoman dynasty. The nation had defeated the armies of the caliph (Vahdettin). 'Why should we fear the paralysed remains [of the dynasty]? We shall send them all where they need to be sent.'[58]

From İzmit, Mustafa Kemal went to Bursa to deliver a fighting speech at a public meeting, held once again at the Orient cinema. Turkey, he said, would put up statues to its heroes. The Islamic ban on human representation was no longer relevant; it had been directed against the worship of idols: the assumption that educated people were capable of worshipping pieces of stone today was an insult to Islam. 'A nation which does not make pictures, a nation which does not make statues, a nation which does not practise science, such a nation, one must admit, has no place on the highroad of civilization. But our nation with its true qualities deserves to become and will become civilized and progressive.' However, one must not forget that every effort at renewal met with opposition. One must therefore expect reactionary movements in Turkey. Mustafa Kemal went on:

> Bloody revolutions are solid; bloodless ones are not permanent. But we have shed sufficient blood to come to this revolution. It has been shed not only on battlefields, but within the country ... There have been many risings, all of which have been suppressed. Let us hope that there will be no more bloodshed. The first duty of our educated people is to enlighten and guide the opponents of our happy revolution.[59]

Mustafa Kemal was determined to carry out a cultural revolution, by persuasion if possible, by force when necessary.

The tour went on through the devastated regions of western Anatolia. A visit to his mother's grave at the İzmir suburb of Karşıyaka gave Mustafa Kemal the opportunity to attack the despotism of the sultans. In a dramatic soliloquy, he described Zübeyde as the victim of the sultans: first of Abdülhamit's rule, which had imprisoned and exiled her son, then of Vahdettin's government which harassed her while her son led the struggle in Anatolia. She had been blinded by tears. 'When recently, I finally saved her from Istanbul, she was dead in body and lived on only in spirit.' But the sacrifice has had its reward: national sovereignty had been established for ever. Mustafa Kemal concluded with a rhetorical flourish: 'I swear in front of my mother's grave and in the presence of God, that I shall not hesitate to join her if this be necessary for the defence of the sovereignty which the nation has won at the cost of so much blood. I deem it a debt of conscience and honour to give my life for the sake of national sovereignty.'[60]

Two days later, Mustafa Kemal married Lâtife. As soon as he had arrived at Karşıyaka, he told his ADC Salih (Bozok): 'I have taken the decision to marry Lâtife. If her father is in town' – he had not yet met Muammer Uşakizade/Uşaklıgil – 'inform him of my decision and add that he is not to tell anyone.'[61] Muammer, who should have been asked for his daughter's hand, was overjoyed at Lâtife's success. The wedding was disguised as a tea party at Muammer's house (known as the White Mansion). The brief ceremony was performed by the *müftü* of İzmir.

At a Muslim wedding, the bridegroom stays silent, while a relative or friend offers on his behalf to take the bride at a given price, part of which is paid as an immediate settlement (*mihr-i muaccel*) and part held in reserve as indemnity in case of divorce (*mihr-i müeccel*). The consent of the absent bride is similarly expressed by a representative. Mustafa Kemal had arranged that the chief of the general staff, Fevzi Paşa, should speak for him, and that İsmet's chief of staff Asım (Gündüz), a newly promoted brigadier, should represent Lâtife. He offered the symbolic sum of ten silver *dirhems* (an ancient Muslim coin) as the bride price and an unspecified agreed sum as a divorce indemnity. 'You've got the girl on the cheap,' joked Fevzi. If Asım (Gündüz) is to be believed, Mustafa Kemal said that he looked forward to the day when the old forms would be discarded and marriage would be performed 'in a modern manner' by the civil authority, represented at his wedding by the governor of İzmir, Abdülhalik (Renda).

Mustafa Kemal had already broken with tradition: Lâtife was present at the ceremony, and, although she wore a headscarf, her face was not veiled.[62] Kâzım Karabekir, Mustafa Kemal's critical supporter, was a guest at the wedding. Mustafa Kemal was willing to give Karabekir every honour, but no power, and had chosen him as the chairman of an economic congress, which was about to open in İzmir to map out the country's reconstruction. Like the other authors of the Turkish resistance movement, Karabekir was prepared to perform the tasks which Mustafa Kemal gave him so long as he retained the hope that he would also be given a part in shaping policy. But the hope was fast fading.

There was no honeymoon. Mustafa Kemal had no time to lose if he was to turn military prestige into personal political power. After their first meeting, Mustafa Kemal had described Lâtife as his female ADC, and even addressed her playfully as Lâtif, the masculine form of her name.[63] This fitted in perfectly with Mustafa Kemal's conception of a wife: a wife was there to help him, to share, applaud and encourage his vision, not to make demands on him. Lâtife was too young and headstrong to play the role for long; but she tried, and at first Marshal and Mrs Mustafa Kemal were the picture of a modern husband-and-wife team. As in the wedding ceremony, the break with Muslim religious tradition was gradual: Lâtife covered her head in public with a headscarf or the *çarşaf* (the Turkish chador). She appeared at her husband's side, but kept her mouth shut, as her husband hit the campaign trail.

On 30 January, the day after his wedding, Mustafa Kemal received the editors of local newspapers.[64] On 2 February, he spoke for six hours at a public meeting in İzmir.[65] The Lausanne conference was deadlocked. Mustafa Kemal put the blame in the first place on the French and the Italians, who had put forward economic demands incompatible with Turkey's full independence.[66] He restated the Turkish claim to Mosul, while stressing his country's desire for peace.[67] Anti-Western feeling was prevalent in the country, and dominant in the assembly. It had been expressed by the poet Mehmet Âkif in the lines: 'The West's cruel brow, I have not forgiven you. / I'm your enemy, down to the last man.' Mustafa Kemal quoted the verse, but substituted 'I'm a Turk and a Muslim' for 'I'm your enemy' and added: 'Down to the last man, we will root out cruelty from our enemies' heart and we shall then say that our heart too no longer harbours feelings of revenge.'[68] But his thoughts were already centred on the new Turkey which would emerge after the conclusion of peace.

The Turkish nation, he explained, was the main component of the Turkish state, but there were other components, people who had linked their endeavours and their destinies with those of the Turks. They did not have to share the Turks' Muslim religion. The Jews would continue to find security in Turkey. Members of other communities, who would stay on after an exchange of population, would also benefit from the accepted rules of humanity.[69] The principle of solidarity would apply also to the People's Party. There were few rich people in Turkey; the vast majority were peasants; there were probably no more than 20,000 industrial workers. The People's Party would encompass all classes. It would be a school for the political education of the people. But there was one class, on which the nation and the state had to rely in order to be able to work in safety. 'That class is the army.'[70]

The principles of the Kemalist state were emerging. But Mustafa Kemal still hoped to include Islam in his design. True, traditional religious schools, known as *medreses*, were not needed. Mustafa Kemal once again referred to his visit to a *medrese* during the War of Independence. He found the local *müftü* teaching Arabic, but neither he nor his students had a useful knowledge of the language. 'I do not know Arabic,' Mustafa Kemal said, 'but as I had served in Arab lands, I knew more of the language than the *müftü* ... Let us send people to Syria or Arabia to learn Arabic, but let us not waste time in all our *medreses*, where people who neither know nor can teach are uselessly occupied.'[71] If religious text-books were written in Turkish there would be no need to learn Arabic. In fact, to do research on religion one needed to know French, English and German. 'We should realize that these [foreigners] have studied our religion better than we have.' Everybody has a religion, even the person who denies having one. 'But this general rule is true of all religions.'[72] As for Islam, it is the most natural and reasonable of all religions and it enjoins on everyone the pursuit of knowledge:[73] religious education should become part of a general curriculum, which would be followed by men and women together.[74] This was in fact the practice in many European states which had an established religion. But the French revolutionary ideal was closer to Mustafa Kemal's heart.

Still, when he pursued his tour of Anatolia by going to Balıkesir on 7 February, he took the unusual step of preaching a sermon in the main mosque. He started with the pious invocation, 'God is one, and great is his glory!' He then developed the argument of Islamic modernists. Islam was the perfect religion, because it was in conformity with reason and truth. Mosques were not only for worship, but should also serve as a venue for the discussion of secular affairs. Sermons should therefore be in Turkish and should reflect the requirements of the day. Mustafa Kemal went on to commend the project of forming the People's Party. Some of his friends had advised him not to form a political party; it would have been in his personal interest to retire and rest after completing his duty to the nation: but to do this, he would have to be confident that the results he had achieved were safe. That, however, was not yet the case.[75]

Kâzım Karabekir, who was present in the mosque, was to claim later that Mustafa Kemal's sermon was inspired by his ambition to become caliph and sultan. According to Karabekir, it was only when this hope was disappointed that Mustafa Kemal turned against religion.[76] The accusation is inconsistent with the evidence: Mustafa Kemal had spoken against the monarchical principle the moment military victory was won.[77] He had also made no effort to prevent the election of Abdülmecit to the shadowy office of spiritual caliph. Moreover, his attempts to enlist religious feeling in the Turkish national cause continued for some time after the military victory. At the very least, he wanted to persuade his people that modern civilization and Islam were compatible. Then he lost interest in the argument, not because he had been denied the caliphate, but because he decided that Islamic feeling hindered the realization of his project.

From Balıkesir, Mustafa Kemal returned to İzmir to open the country's first economic congress on 17 February 1923. The idea had been suggested by Mahmut Esat (Bozkurt), the minister responsible for the economy, who explained to the assembly that such congresses had helped other countries develop their economies, and cited the specific example of Hungary after the constitutional settlement of 1867. The minister denied that the congress had been summoned in a spirit of hostility towards foreign capital; the government was ready to give it all the facilities it enjoyed in civilized countries, but no more, as Turkey was not 'a country of slaves'.[78] The subject of foreign privileges was acutely topical, as it was largely responsible for the breakdown of the Lausanne conference on 4 February. Mustafa Kemal turned to it when he addressed the thousand delegates who had assembled in İzmir.

They were divided into four sections: farmers, workers, manufacturers, and merchants. Room was scarce in the devastated city, and the Jewish community, whose district had survived the fire, helped by lodging some of the delegates in its orphanage. 'I shall not describe the state the country is in. You know it,' Mustafa Kemal told the delegates. His message was that knowledge of the backwardness of the country should be a spur to united action by all classes of people, whose interests coincided. The capitulations would go. They had been the result of the negligence of sultans who pursued, first, imperial ambitions and then a life of ease and luxury at the expense of the Turkish people. Though offering a materialist explanation of history – the rise and decline of the Ottoman state had both been due to economic factors – Mustafa Kemal clothed his materialism in bright oratory. Ringing phrases followed one another: 'Those who conquer by the sword are destined to be defeated by those who conquer by the plough'; 'The economy is everything: it is the totality of what we need to live, to be happy.'[79]

It was a star performance in a year of incessant speech-making. During the War of Independence, Mustafa Kemal's oratory was confined to the cramped quarters of the Grand National Assembly. Now, as he sought supreme political power, it rang throughout the country. His ideas had a long pedigree in the history of Ottoman reform. Many of them had been expressed by his rivals, but none could match his charisma or the eloquence of his vision. The İzmir economic congress may have been suggested by others. But it remains linked with Atatürk's name.

A few hours after opening the congress, Mustafa Kemal left İzmir to meet İsmet who had returned from Lausanne to seek fresh instructions on how to make peace with the Allies. Karabekir saw the congress through to the final proclamation of the Economic Pact, designed as a counterpart to the National Pact, the original charter of the Turkish resistance.[80] Unlike Mustafa Kemal's opening speech, this document has left no mark on Turkey's consciousness.

19

Peace and the Republic

———◆———

ACCOMPANIED BY HIS young bride, Mustafa Kemal travelled from İzmir to Ankara by train, stopping on 18 February 1923 in Eskişehir, where he met İsmet who was on his way back from Lausanne after the suspension of the peace conference. The chief of the general staff, Fevzi, was present at the meeting.[1] A renewal of hostilities was still possible. In any case, Mustafa Kemal needed the army's support. İsmet wished the couple happiness in their married life, and then turned to the political business in hand. The *Daily Mail* correspondent Ward Price, who travelled with İsmet on his way back from Lausanne, noted that 'The Ghazi ... was dressed in a tweed suit, breeches and cycling stockings, which contrasted oddly with patent-leather shoes', while Lâtife was wearing riding breeches, with high boots and spurs, and had a bright silk handkerchief over her hair. According to Ward Price, 'Turkish onlookers were startled by this costume, which no other woman in Turkey would have dared to adopt.' The costume served to keep the wearers warm in a train with broken windows, no heating and no electric light.[2]

The journey from Eskişehir to Ankara was spent in a discussion of the tactics to be followed in the peace negotiations. The party's arrival in Ankara brought little joy to Lâtife. The simple villa in Çankaya, with three modest reception rooms on the ground floor, and a bedroom, a living room and a tiny rest room upstairs,[3] was much smaller than her father's waterside mansion in İzmir. The staff were untrained in domestic duties. Lâtife found the food awful and asked her father to send a cook from İzmir. Much worse, Mustafa Kemal had little time for his young wife. The very first night, he asked Lâtife to take her dinner alone upstairs, as he wanted to spend his evening with his male friends; their convivial discussion of politics went on until half-past three in the morning, when Mustafa Kemal finally turned up in the bedroom, with a song on his lips.[4] In the days that followed, Lâtife was introduced to the wives of Mustafa Kemal's companions, who put up with their lot with better grace than she did, and she found some solace in making domestic improvements. These included the acquisition of furniture in the French style and the introduction of a yellow colour scheme in the bedroom.

Mustafa Kemal had more pressing concerns. Domestic politics revolved round the conduct of peace negotiations. The prime minister Rauf (Orbay) wanted İsmet to work to his instructions, and resented the fact that his foreign minister had concerted tactics with the commander-in-chief and president of the assembly before reporting to the cabinet.[5] Nevertheless, a joint response to the Allies was agreed in cabinet, and Rauf loyally commended it to the assembly after it had heard İsmet's report on 21 February.[6] Mustafa Kemal had imposed his thinking on the government. In exchange for the best possible terms for Turkey's independence, the Mosul problem could be left over for bilateral negotiations with Britain. Arbitration by the League of Nations would follow if there were no agreement. Mustafa Kemal tried to persuade the assembly that this did not mean giving up Mosul, but rather waiting for a time when Turkey might be stronger. Rauf added the argument that by tabling compromise proposals, Turkey would demonstrate its desire for peace, and influence world public opinion in its favour.[7] But the assembly was not easily persuaded.

Mustafa Kemal's diplomatic tactic was as ever to split the Allied ranks. A compromise on Mosul would satisfy Britain. It would then be easier to resist the economic demands of the French and the Italians. Turkey had earlier insisted that the Soviets should be included in negotiations on the straits. The Allies had therefore to take into account the possibility that if they pressed Turkey too hard, it might make common cause with the Soviets and deny states which did not have a coastline on the Black Sea full freedom of navigation through the straits. Mustafa Kemal sought to balance Russia against the Allies, Britain against France, even Bulgaria against Greece. It was a delicate diplomatic game, well beyond the comprehension of critics in the assembly. These took their stand on the National Pact. Did not the Pact include Mosul in Turkey? Did it not demand a plebiscite in western Thrace? Well then, the assembly which had accepted the Pact should itself authorize any departure from it. Deputies went further, and mentioned claims to Greek islands in the Aegean, to Cyprus, to compensation from Britain for failing to deliver warships to the Ottoman state on the eve of the Great War.[8]

Opposition to Mustafa Kemal's leadership was wrapped in nationalist rhetoric. Rather than attack Mustafa Kemal directly, opposition politicians targeted İsmet, as leader of the Turkish delegation at Lausanne, and accused him of exceeding his powers. Tension boiled over in the secret session of the assembly on 6 March. Mustafa Kemal defended İsmet and accused the fiery opposition spokesman Ali Şükrü of harming the national interest. Ali Şükrü's protests were backed by another Black Sea politician, Ziya Hurşit. As Mustafa Kemal left the podium, deputies pressed round him, their hands gripping the guns in their pockets. Angry contestants faced each other in the small, crowded, low-ceilinged meeting hall. Fisticuffs, even a shooting match, threatened between Mustafa Kemal's supporters and the opposition Second Group. The situation was saved by Ali Fuat who was chairing the session. Unable to make himself heard, he threw his handbell between the opposing ranks and suspended the session. When it was resumed, government supporters tabled a resolution authorizing the cabinet to instruct the Turkish delegation to pursue negotiations in Lausanne. It was accepted by 170 votes to 20, with many members of the opposition abstaining in protest.[9]

Mustafa Kemal had won the day thanks to the help of his prime minister Rauf (Orbay) and the deputy chairman of the assembly, Ali Fuat (Cebesoy). He knew that peace with the Allies could not be achieved without concessions, which would probably include the loss of Mosul. The assembly was likely to play politics by obstructing agreement; it was therefore essential to hold new elections and produce a more compliant membership. Until this was achieved, Rauf, Ali Fuat and Refet had to be kept sweet.

A few days after the vote of the assembly, Turkish counter-proposals for the peace settlement – a detailed document of about one hundred pages – were handed to the Allied representatives in Istanbul.[10] The British High Commissioner, Sir Horace Rumbold, who had returned to Istanbul from Lausanne, was impressed by the speed and the 'businesslike form' of Turkish diplomacy.[11] To soften the French, who were defending the economic concessions granted to them by Ottoman governments, the Ankara government launched a propaganda campaign accusing French troops of atrocities against the Muslim population of İskenderun and Antakya, the district ceded to French-mandated Syria by the Ankara accord of 1921.[12]

A united Allied response was agreed in London on 21 March, and on 31 March the Ankara government was invited to send its delegates back to Lausanne for a resumption of the conference. As Anglo-French unity was restored, the Ankara government tried to set the United States against the European Allies. On 9 April, the assembly, prompted by the government, granted a wide-ranging concession to a group of American businessmen, headed by Commander Arthur Chester. The Chester concession was, in Curzon's words, a 'megalomaniac' scheme, involving a monopoly of railway construction over a wide area, with the right to exploit adjacent mineral resources, construct ports, make use of forests and agricultural land and import huge amounts of farm machinery.[13] It was an attempt to enlist American support for the Turkish claim to Mosul, whose oil was the only natural resource that could have covered the vast investment envisaged.

The attempt failed, as the United States was not yet ready to involve itself in Near Eastern territorial disputes. Nevertheless, the concession worried both the French and the British, whose interests it infringed. After these tactical preliminaries, the Lausanne conference reopened on 23 April. Curzon did not attend, and Rumbold took the chair in his absence. He hoped for a quick settlement, but he had reckoned without İsmet and the latter's difficulties in obtaining the agreement of his government to such concessions as he could not avoid. Bargaining over the final terms was to extend over three months.

As soon as he had imposed his will on the assembly, Mustafa Kemal set off on a second provincial tour in the company of Lâtife. This time he went to Adana and other towns which had been occupied by the French in the southern part of the country. He spoke at meetings of young educated people, who were his chosen constituency, of their teachers, but also of farmers and tradesmen. He made long impassioned speeches full of confidence in the ability of his people to acquire the knowledge necessary for progress. But he was also realistic. The nation had fallen behind, while its enemies had progressed in all branches of learning. 'Let us realize the state we are in,' he urged his audience. 'Let us learn what needs to be learnt. Religion and God demand it.' There was no real need to seek the advice of religious scholars. Everyone could apply a general criterion: whatever was in conformity with reason and the public interest was also in conformity with Islam.[14] Islam and the national interest coincided.

Islam was the religion of army chaplains, and Mustafa Kemal still found it politic to appeal to it. But at the same time, he warned that the evils which had sapped the nation's strength had all been wrought in the name of religion. While recommending a rational form of Islam,

Mustafa Kemal was beginning to sketch out his own version of history. The parts round Adana, he said, were originally Turkish and Turanian, before the arrival of the Persians, of Alexander's Greeks and of subsequent invaders. Later they reverted to their original Turkish owners: Armenians and others had no rights to these lands.[15]

On his way back, Mustafa Kemal stopped in Konya where he addressed the nurses working for the Red Crescent. Konya was, and still is, a conservative town, and Mustafa Kemal chose his words carefully. He was proud to note that Turkish women did not lag behind their menfolk, even in unfavourable conditions. In conditions of equality they might even outpace the men. But women's most important duty was to be good mothers and to shoulder the difficult task of training their children in accordance with modern needs. To do this they had to be better educated than the men. Although clothes were of secondary importance, he advised a middle way between exaggerated Islamic dress and the fashions of Europe, which some Turkish women in Istanbul were wrong to imitate. Islamic dress should not prevent women from playing a full part in social, economic and academic pursuits. They should dress in a reasonable way in accordance both with the rules of religion and with national customs.[16]

In Kütahya, his last stop before Ankara, Mustafa Kemal reverted to his favourite theme when he addressed a gathering of women and men teachers. An army's worth resided in its officers, he said. Teachers were the officers of the army of education. He had full confidence in their ability to dispel the cloud of general ignorance which had settled on the people.[17] It was a call to a crusade, whose impact is still felt in Turkey today. But in Ankara the politicians had other worries.

On 26 March, two days after Mustafa Kemal's return to Ankara, his critic Ali Şükrü made his last appearance in the assembly. He then disappeared. On 29 March, Ali Şükrü's colleague in the Second Group, Hüseyin Avni, brought the matter to the attention of the assembly, and attacked the government for its failure to find the missing deputy. He was backed by another opponent of Mustafa Kemal, Ziya Hurşit. Accusing the authorities of complicity, he cited the earlier murder of the boatmen's leader Yahya in front of the army barracks in Trabzon.[18] The nationalist press in Istanbul, with Hüseyin Cahit (Yalçın) in the lead, demanded firm action. Mustafa Kemal provided it.

The search ordered by the government discovered the body of Ali Şükrü in a shallow grave not far from Mustafa Kemal's villa on Çankaya hill. It had been suspected from the start that the deputy had been kidnapped by Lame Osman's Laz irregulars, who served as Mustafa Kemal's personal bodyguard. Lame Osman had an agent in the assembly by the name of Mustafa Kaptan. Detained and questioned by the police, Mustafa admitted that Ali Şükrü had accepted an invitation to visit Lame Osman and that he had escorted the deputy to Osman's house in the old city of Ankara. No sooner had Ali Şükrü sat down than men sprang from behind and strangled him. His body was then smuggled out and buried near Osman's country house, known as Papaz Bağı (The Priest's Vineyard), on the slopes of Çankaya hill. Searchers were led to the grave by a swarm of flies circling round newly dug ground. As soon as Osman heard of his agent's arrest he barricaded himself in the Priest's Vineyard.

When he learned the news on 31 March, Mustafa Kemal ordered Major İsmail Hakkı (Tekçe), the regular officer commanding the battalion guarding the assembly, to serve an arrest warrant on Lame Osman.[19] Then, taking Lâtife with him, Mustafa Kemal slipped out of the villa in Çankaya and moved to his old quarters in the stationmaster's house. As İsmail Hakkı's troops began to surround the Priest's Vineyard, Osman's men opened fire, killing one soldier. But the Lazes proved no match for regular soldiers, who overran the Priest's Vineyard, killing a number of their opponents and wounding Osman mortally. The surviving Lazes were taken to Mustafa Kemal for questioning.[20]

Dealing with Lame Osman was a minor matter. As far as Mustafa Kemal was concerned, the assembly, which was in uproar at the murder of one of its members, presented the major problem. As soon as he had arrived in the stationmaster's house, Mustafa Kemal held a cabinet meeting at which it was agreed that fresh elections should be held. He then persuaded his supporters, who controlled the majority in the house, to vote for dissolution. The proposal was immediately taken to the assembly and approved *nem. con.* Congratulating the members on the decision, Mustafa Kemal declared that the Turkish state had neither a crowned head nor a dictator.[21] This was true so far as it went, but any hopes the opposition Second Group may have had of surviving the elections were dashed when the assembly voted the text of the new electoral law, which had finally emerged from committee stage.

The provisions which would have prevented Mustafa Kemal from standing in the elections had, of course, been removed. But the opposition protested strongly and unsuccessfully at two other clauses. The first allowed serving corps commanders to become deputies, while retaining their commands: it was Mustafa Kemal's gift to his supporters and also his potential rivals in the armed forces, whose good will he still needed. More seriously, the law authorized the government to conduct the elections and rule on any allegations of impropriety. This was passed against the united opposition of the Second Group.[22] The way to electoral manipulation was now wide open.

On 2 April, the day after it had decided on new elections, the assembly finally heard prime minister Rauf (Orbay)'s report on the murder of Ali Şükrü by Lame Osman's men. After an angry debate, the deputies voted that Osman's body should be exhumed and exhibited on a gallows outside the assembly building. Government supporters did not oppose the decision. But Mustafa Kemal prevented an attempt by the Second Group to send the body of the murdered deputy Ali Şükrü via Istanbul for burial in his native city of Trabzon. Fearing opposition demonstrations, the government arranged for the cortège to go by road to the small port of İnebolu and then by sea to Trabzon. Ali Şükrü's burial in Trabzon was attended by a large crowd of mourners. The authorities then did their best to draw a veil over his murder: Mustafa Kemal did not mention it in his six-day speech; he also avoided describing Lame Osman as the murderer.[23]

One explanation offered for the murder was that Lame Osman was infuriated by Ali Şükrü's harassment of his patron, Mustafa Kemal, and acted on his own initiative. But many found this difficult to believe. Karabekir was to say later that when he heard the news of the murder he could not help remembering Mustafa Kemal's earlier angry denunciation of Ali Şükrü and the opposition press which he had established in Ankara. This does not prove that he was privy to the murder, particularly as, according to Karabekir, Mustafa Kemal was initially worried that regular troops might refuse to fight Lame Osman's men.[24] Clearly, his main concern at the time was that the murder might be exploited by the opposition. But even if Mustafa Kemal was taken by surprise, his supporters in the assembly showed their feelings by preventing the award of a pension to Ali Şükrü's family.[25]

There were in the ranks of government supporters hard men who had joined Mustafa Kemal as junior officers and who were ready to advance his cause and their own interests by eliminating those who stood in their way. The killing both of Ali Şükrü and of Lame Osman suited them: the opposition was deprived of an effective orator and given a warning that it was dangerous to stand in the way of Mustafa Kemal's party. At the same time, the last detachment of irregulars was eliminated. Lame Osman, a sadistic ethnic cleanser of Armenians and Greeks, and the hammer of Mustafa Kemal's Muslim opponents, had served his purpose: there was no room for him in the new order. There was also no need to inform Mustafa Kemal of any plot to use and then do away with Lame Osman. Mustafa Kemal would understand, and his hands would remain clean. İsmet, who had initiated the process of the absorption of nationalist guerrillas in the regular army, refers to the incident as an explosion of the hatreds which had accumulated over the years in domestic politics, and adds: 'Atatürk emerged successfully from all these controversies ... His political ability was actually greater than his military ability.'[26] In recent years, a modest memorial was put up over Ali Şükrü's grave; Lame Osman has long had an impressive monument over his grave in his native port town of Giresun.[27]

Mustafa Kemal demonstrated his political ability in the run-up to the elections of the second assembly. On 8 April he announced that the Society for the Defence of National Rights in Anatolia and Rumelia would be transformed into a People's Party, which would seek a majority in the new assembly. A party programme would be prepared in due course, but in the meantime Mustafa Kemal announced nine guiding principles. They proclaimed that the abolition of the sultanate was irreversible, that the caliphate was supported by the assembly as a supreme body for all Muslims, that law and order would be ensured, and that the country's full independence was a precondition of the peace settlement. There was no mention of the National Pact. Other principles set out economic measures in line with the recommendations of the İzmir congress.[28]

One of the principles was immediately put into effect. On 15 April, the government forced through the assembly a change in the law on high treason. As voted in 1920, it was directed against any action seeking to impugn the legitimacy of the assembly, which had come together to 'save from foreign forces the august institution of the caliphate and sultanate and the Ottoman realm'. Now any activity by word or deed directed against the abolition of the sultanate and the supremacy of the assembly was to be punished as high treason.[29] Mustafa Kemal had forecast the change in his speech to the assembly on 1 March, when he declared that there was unlimited freedom in the country, except for the enemies of national sovereignty.[30] The opposition argued in vain that the law limited freedom of thought, and drew parallels with the fascist regime which had been installed in Italy. The newspaper *Yenigün*, published by Mustafa Kemal's supporter Yunus Nadi, retorted that there was nothing to fear in fascism, which, on the contrary, contained principles applicable to Turkey.[31] Mustafa Kemal never went that far, preferring to get his way in the name of national sovereignty.

The First Assembly held its last meeting on 16 April 1923. Mustafa Kemal then proceeded to pick his candidates for the elections. There was little external opposition, as the Second Group decided against presenting its own list of candidates, on the grounds that it was part and parcel of the original undivided Society for the Defence of National Rights. Mustafa Kemal's main problem was with unruly Unionists within the Society, some of whom wanted to revive the old CUP, and all of whom wanted an effective role in government. They were particularly strong in Trabzon, where a local paper warned 'those who had recourse to the dirty hands of Lame Osman' that the nation would defend its freedoms, just as it had defended its independence.[32] Taking this as an attack on his person, Mustafa Kemal sent emissaries to Trabzon who dissolved the local branch of the Society and found acceptable substitutes. In Istanbul, which was still under Allied occupation and where Unionists could make their voices heard in the opposition press, a government spokesman announced that no one need trouble to come forward as a candidate, as a list would be drawn up in Ankara without reference to the local branch of the Society.[33]

Mustafa Kemal tried to associate his original comrades with the selection of candidates in what, everybody saw, would be an uncontested election. Kâzım Karabekir claims in his memoirs that he refused at first, after Mustafa Kemal had told him, 'I do not want an opposition', but that he finally gave way to entreaties and agreed with a heavy heart.[34] Rauf refused after arguing unsuccessfully that Mustafa Kemal should stand above the parties.[35] It was a demand that Mustafa Kemal had faced from the moment he had set foot in Anatolia, and which was to be repeated in subsequent years. But he had no intention of being a figurehead or even an arbiter of a political process which was bound to reflect the chaotic state of the country. He wanted to lead it and establish a new order, and for this he needed a pool of loyal supporters among whom he could pick his executives for years to come. He took immense trouble over the choice of candidates, weighing up their record, their ability and above all their loyalty. Of the 202 members of the government majority, only 114 satisfied these criteria. They were, of course, all elected, and more than half of them continued to serve as deputies in the assembly until the end of Atatürk's life.[36]

The election itself, which took place in two stages, first of local electoral colleges and then of deputies, was a formality. An exception showed the rule. In the constituency of Gümüşhane, inland from the Black Sea, the gendarmerie commander, who was also the acting district governor, had this to say to the electoral college: 'We shall be present at the election, and every member of the college will show us the slip on which he will have written the names of the candidates of his choice. You may vote only for those the government wants to be chosen.'

When the local notables refused, insisting on one Zeki, a local favourite son, Mustafa Kemal called the mayor and promised that a job would be found for Zeki, if the government's candidates were all chosen. But for once the offer was refused. Mustafa Kemal then called the gendarmerie commander and ordered him to leave the electors alone, saying, 'One cannot put more pressure on people who are so determined.' However, local people compromised by electing the government's candidates for the other seats in the province.[37]

Mustafa Kemal could afford to be magnanimous in one isolated case, as his candidates were endorsed everywhere else without trouble. However, they did include a small number of rivals and critics, whom he could not yet eliminate or whom he still hoped to win over. Rauf (Orbay), Kâzım Karabekir, Ali Fuat (Cebesoy), and other prominent leaders of the national resistance, were included in the government's list and elected. Later, bearded Nurettin Paşa, the notorious user of lynch mobs, succeeded in winning a by-election against Mustafa Kemal's wishes. But of the sixty-three members of the Second Group, not one was elected.[38] Now only independent-minded supporters stood between Mustafa Kemal and absolute power. They were few in number, but prominent in public esteem as leaders of the national resistance.

Rauf (Orbay) was the first to fall by the wayside. From Lausanne, İsmet sent him daily reports on the progress of the conference, asking the government's authorization for agreement on specific points.[39] This was not easily given. Having agreed to set Mosul aside, Rauf took a stand on the Turkish demand for compensation from Greece for the destruction wrought in western Anatolia. İsmet was prepared to waive compensation in exchange for Karaağaç, a suburb of Edirne, west of the Meriç river, which he had conceded to Greece during the first stage of the conference. He pointed out that Greece was bankrupt and that the Allies would not stump up the money on behalf of the Greeks. When Rauf rejected the argument, İsmet appealed to Mustafa Kemal and threatened to resign if his disagreement with the government were not resolved. The telegram was sent through Rauf, as İsmet had no means of communicating directly with the president of the assembly.[40]

Mustafa Kemal sided with İsmet, while trying to manage Rauf's susceptibilities. But another disagreement cropped up, this time on the repayment of the Ottoman Public Debt. İsmet complained that by depriving the delegation of any freedom of initiative, the government was behaving like Sultan Abdülhamit who tried to direct from the palace the disastrous war with the Russians in 1878. Mustafa Kemal, who now involved himself directly in the exchanges, reproved İsmet for his outburst, but encouraged him to bring the negotiations to a successful conclusion. One by one the remaining problems were resolved, and at 1.30 a.m. on 17 July final agreement was reached on the text of the treaty.[41] On 15 July, anticipating agreement, İsmet asked the government in Ankara for authority to sign. Three days later there was still no reply. Again, İsmet appealed to Mustafa Kemal, cabling:

> If the government is determined to reject what we have accepted, then do not ask us to do it. After long thought the only way I can suggest is that the Allied High Commissioners in Istanbul should be informed that we [the Turkish delegation] have been stripped of the authority to sign. True, this would cause an unprecedented scandal. But since the supreme interests of the country are above personal considerations, the national government can act according to its conviction. We expect no thanks from the government. The nation and history will be our judge.

However, Mustafa Kemal decided to be the judge himself. On 19 July he cabled to İsmet: 'Please advise that [the treaty] has been signed in due form to enable us to present to you our warmest congratulations on your success.' İsmet abandoned his usual formal language to express his joy. 'Whenever I am in a corner, you come to my aid,' he cabled to Mustafa Kemal. 'You can imagine what I've been through in the last four to five days. You have done and made others do great deeds. I am more than ever attached to you, my beloved brother and leader.'[42]

The treaty of Lausanne was signed on 24 July. İsmet, who was invited to sign first, used the pen which Mustafa Kemal had given him specially for the purpose.[43] There were a great many documents to sign: the lengthy peace treaty itself, which contained 141 articles; conventions on the Turkish straits, on trade, on the exchange of populations between Greece and Turkey, agreements, binding letters. The United States and Soviet Russia, though not directly involved in the negotiations since they were not at war with Turkey, signed the final act, accepting the peace treaty and sixteen agreements appended to it.[44] It was a signal success for Turkish diplomacy, as the Soviets looked askance at any agreement between Turkey and the West. The Lausanne treaty made peace between Turkey and the major Allies – Britain, France and Italy, and between Turkey and Greece; it recognized Turkey as an independent state, fixed its frontiers, and applied to it principles and standards current in 'the civilized world', as Mustafa Kemal had always insisted. The limitations on Turkish sovereignty were few: the demilitarization of the straits, which in the event lasted for thirteen years; the temporary presence of a handful of legal and health advisers; a temporary ban on increasing customs duties. Turkey promised a political amnesty, which would exclude only 150 people who were to be exiled by the Ankara government. But these concessions were insignificant when compared with the final abolition of the capitulations. Lausanne ended the unequal treatment of Turkey.

Outside Turkey, the treaty was seen for what it was – a victory for the Turks, reversing the roles of vanquished and victor, whereby a people defeated in the Great War obtained satisfaction of its basic demands. 'None of us can pretend that the Treaty is a glorious instrument,' the British signatory Rumbold wrote to Nevile Henderson, his deputy in Istanbul. 'Even if the Peace of Lausanne is not perfect peace ... the great relief that peace affords is quite likely to give the mentality of the Turks a new turn,' Henderson responded.[45] In fact, the treaty of Lausanne has outlasted all the other international arrangements made after the First World War. Its annexes are detailed to the point of absurdity, promising, for example, that Turkish snails would benefit from most-favoured-nation treatment when exported to France.[46] But the agreements have stood the test of time, because they were freely negotiated, even by Greece, whose chief delegate, the former prime minister Venizelos, accepted them as a renunciation of his irredentist past and the foundation on which a new relationship could be built between his country and Turkey.

From today's perspective it seems strange that Rumbold's reservations should have been mirrored in Turkey. Three years after the signature of the treaty, Mustafa Kemal deemed it necessary to include in his six-day speech a lengthy comparison between its provisions and those of the treaty of Sèvres and of the various proposals made by the Allies in the course of the Turkish War of Independence, before concluding that Lausanne spelled the defeat of an attempt pursued over several centuries to destroy the Turkish nation. 'It was,' he said, 'a political victory unequalled in the history of the Ottoman era.'[47] To mark it, he instituted commemorative ceremonies on the anniversary of the signature. But while the treaty of Lausanne is the outcome of Mustafa Kemal's leadership of the forces of Turkish nationalism, it is İsmet who is remembered in Turkey to this day as 'the hero of Lausanne' rather than as the commander of the western front in the War of Independence. İsmet stayed on in Lausanne until 6 August when he signed a separate agreement with the United States, whose open-door policy was a useful counterweight to the Allies' demands for preferential treatment. But the US Senate refused to ratify the agreement, and in December 1923 Turkey annulled the Chester concession.[48]

The prospect of İsmet's triumphal homecoming was too much for

Rauf, who was not allowed to forget that he had been the chief signatory of the armistice of Mudros, the act of capitulation of the Ottoman
empire. On 25 July he went to Çankaya in the company of Ali Fuat to
confirm to Mustafa Kemal that the peace treaty had been signed. The
preliminaries over, Rauf announced that he had decided to resign as
prime minister, and that he would go to his old constituency in Sivas,
leaving the chief of the general staff Fevzi as his deputy.[49] It was an
unwise first move in the struggle for leadership. In his six-day speech,
Mustafa Kemal said that Rauf had asked him during the meeting to
strengthen the position of the head of state, and that he had agreed to
do so. According to Mustafa Kemal's interpretation, Rauf meant that
the office of the caliph should be strengthened, whereas, in agreeing,
Mustafa Kemal had in mind the proclamation of the republic (with a
strong president).[50]

In fact, Rauf had repeated diplomatically his old demand that, as
head of state, Mustafa Kemal should stand above the parties, which
meant above the personalities struggling for power. This is confirmed
by Ali Fuat's question, 'Can we be told who are your *apôtres* [apostles]
today?', to which Mustafa Kemal said he replied, 'I have no *apôtres*.
Whoever serves the country, and is capable of doing so, is the *apôtre*.'[51]
What Rauf and Ali Fuat wanted to know was whether Mustafa Kemal
would give his backing to İsmet in the struggle for the job of chief executive. By resigning, Rauf showed that he intended to oppose İsmet's
elevation, and that he counted on Ali Fuat to help him. The struggle for
power between the leading personalities of the national resistance came
into the open when Rauf absented himself from the welcoming ceremony arranged for İsmet in Ankara. In his memoirs, İsmet claims that
he was surprised by the dispute.[52] If he was, his naivety was uncharacteristic.

Rauf's resignation took effect on 4 August; he was succeeded by
Fethi (Okyar). On 13 August, the day of İsmet's return to Ankara, the
second Grand National Assembly elected Mustafa Kemal as its president. He was unopposed. In an eloquent opening speech, he commended the Lausanne treaty. Negotiations had inevitably been difficult,
he said, because they had to settle the accounts not of the four years of
the War of Independence, but of four centuries with their legacy of evil.
The success which had been achieved had opened the road to progress
and civilization, but these ideals had not yet been reached. The country
had been reduced to bare earth lacking any sign of a prosperous life. But
there were treasures beneath and a noble and heroic people above
ground. The new Turkish state was a people's state, animated by the
same wind of freedom which had brought low the Austrian, German,

Russian and even the Chinese empires. But it was also the fruit of the development of Turkey's own history.[53] It was one of Mustafa Kemal's greatest speeches, presenting with all the resources of Ottoman oratory the vision of a Turkey at peace, respecting those who respected it, and drawing on its own inner strength as it took part in the universal march of progress.

The vision was noble, but the circumstances were bleak. A Turkish woman socialist, Sabiha (Sertel), who went to Ankara in August 1923, after graduating from the New York School of Social Work, was shocked when her neighbours begged her not for clothes or shoes, but for bits of rag to patch up their own poor clothes. Sabiha had brought a pram for her two small daughters. Seeing it, the women of Ankara decided that she must have come from the sultan's palace. 'Only princesses can have such a carriage,' they declared.[54]

On 14 August, the assembly chose Mustafa Kemal's liberal supporter Fethi (Okyar) as prime minister, while the hard-liner İsmet remained foreign minister. Nine days later, the assembly ratified the Lausanne treaty, after a spirited debate. The cession of İskenderun and Antakya to French-mandated Syria was once again criticized, and fourteen deputies, most of them from constituencies in the south of the country, voted against the treaty:[55] it was a reminder of unfinished business. But ratification was not in doubt. An overwhelming majority of 213 deputies came out in favour of the treaty.

Ratification set in train the compulsory exchange of populations between Turkey and Greece. The agreement signed on 30 January 1923[56] used religion as a definition of ethnicity. As a result, some 1,100,000 former Ottoman citizens professing the Greek Orthodox faith moved to Greece, while 380,000 Muslims, mainly from Macedonia and Crete, were transferred to Turkey.[57] Many of the Greeks had fled before the signature of the treaty, but the Turkish-speaking Greek Orthodox community in central Anatolia (known as *Karamanlı* in Turkish and *Karamanlidhes* in Greek), as well as Greeks cut off along the Black Sea coast and elsewhere, had to seek a new homeland. Muslims in western Thrace and Greeks resident within the municipal boundaries of Istanbul before the end of the Great War were exempted. But some 150,000 Greeks chose or were forced to leave the old Ottoman capital and its environs,[58] changing its character irrevocably. The departure of the Greeks compounded the shortage of skills, which had arisen when the Armenians were expelled.

While the compulsory exchange affected many more Greeks than Turks, the total number of immigrants which Turkey received was swollen by refugees from other Balkan countries – Bulgaria, Yugoslavia and Romania.[59] The vast majority of these immigrants were peasants. The exchange of population and the settlement of property claims took four years to complete. Immigrants into Turkey were supposed to receive abandoned property to the value of the assets they left behind; but much of the property formerly belonging to Greeks and Armenians passed into the hands of friends of the government in Ankara, becoming in some cases the foundation of business fortunes.[60] Mustafa Kemal himself paid the treasury 36,000 lira for a 3,000-acre estate originally belonging to a Greek called Bodosakis, near Silifke on the south coast.[61] Elsewhere, he did not have to dip into his own pocket: in Trabzon and Bursa, the town councils generously presented him with houses left behind by rich Greek owners.

Thanks to İsmet's insistence, it had been agreed in Lausanne that Allied forces would be withdrawn from Istanbul and the straits within six weeks of the ratification of the treaty by the assembly in Ankara, without waiting for its ratification by all the other signatories.[62] The British commander, General Harington, was aware of the exposed position of the 22,000 troops under his command,[63] and had no wish to procrastinate. Mountains of stores were sold to the Turkish Red Crescent at knock-down prices. For £32,000, the British Army sold equipment worth some £600,000. One British artillery unit had to spend its last nights in Anatolia sleeping in the open air, because its tents had been sold to the Turks, while the Coldstream Guards fitted out with boots a whole Turkish regiment for the handover ceremony. The ceremony took place on 2 October, orchestrated by Harington. Contingents of British Guards regiments paraded down to the harbour; Harington saluted the Turkish flag, and the Coldstream band played the Turkish march 'Long live Mustafa Kemal Paşa',[64] which had been composed during the Great War under the title 'Long live Enver Paşa'. On 6 October, the Turkish army marched into the city, which had been decorated with Turkish flags and garlands. Prohibition was still in force in Turkey, and Istanbul went officially dry.

Mustafa Kemal did not travel to the old capital when it reverted to Turkish rule. As Sabiha (Sertel) noted, opposition to the Ankara government was widespread in Istanbul, where some Turkish journalists were stirring up feeling against Mustafa Kemal.[65] The wave of elation which swept over the Turkish inhabitants of Istanbul when Turkish troops arrived from Anatolia to replace the Allied army of occupation did not erase the certain knowledge that the privileges enjoyed by their city, which had long absorbed a large part of the country's wealth, were coming to an end. As early as 27 September, Mustafa Kemal had told the correspondent of the liberal Viennese newspaper

Neue Freie Presse that Turkey would become a republic and Ankara would be its capital.[66] The palace and central government had been major employers of Muslims in Istanbul. Now senior civil servants were faced with the prospect of exchanging the comfort of their metropolis for the austerity of a bleak Anatolian market town.

The departure of thousands of Europeans and local Christians and the loss of the bulk of Russian transit trade, as a result of the Bolshevik revolution, had already disrupted the city's economy. The transfer of central government would compound the loss. A great metropolis was becoming a backwater, whose inhabitants had to live by their wits, trying to guess the decisions of the country's new rulers in Ankara. The demand for democracy came naturally to the lips of people who had lost their privileged access to power: it was answered with angry denunciations of the Byzantine intrigues and the effete cosmopolitanism of the old Ottoman capital, which were contrasted with the youthful, self-reliant and straightforward spirit of Anatolia, embodied by Mustafa Kemal and his band of reformers in Ankara. The contrast was largely a myth, as many of the reformers slipped to Istanbul as often as they could. But the fact remained that the old capital was a hotbed of opposition and of snide disparagement. The Gazi (derided *sotto voce* by his Istanbul opponents as *Gazöz Paşa*, or Pop Paşa, from the French *limonade gazeuse*) punished it with his absence.

On 9 October, İsmet tabled a resolution proposing that Ankara should become Turkey's capital. Among its fifteen signatories was one deputy for İstanbul as well as Refet, who had been elected deputy for Konya. The resolution declared that İstanbul would remain for all time the seat of the caliphate, but that the country's administrative capital was best situated in the centre of Anatolia, not least for reasons of security. Only one deputy, Zeki, elected against the government's wishes, spoke against the resolution, which was approved overwhelmingly on 13 October, as part of an as yet unfinished new constitution.[67] The People's Party had been registered a month previously, on 9 September 1923, and two days later it had elected Mustafa Kemal to be its leader.[68] The leader now had a political instrument to control the assembly and, through it, the country.

Mustafa Kemal was not content to wait on the slow deliberations of the constitutional commission of the assembly. He had already made it clear that he wanted the country to become a republic, and as the leader of the national movement he had no credible rivals for the presidency. What concerned him were the powers of the president and his ability to rule the country. During the War of Independence, he had been able to impose his will on the assembly as commander-in-chief; but it had not been easy. Now, direct rule by the assembly stood in the way of his designs for himself and his country. It was difficult to introduce fundamental changes or even provide effective government so long as ministers were elected separately and could dissociate themselves from cabinet decisions. Even the decision to make Ankara the capital had been secured on a private motion, as İsmet knew that the agreement of the cabinet could not be easily obtained: the prime minister, Fethi (Okyar), had not been consulted beforehand.[69] Lack of consultation was particularly resented by Mustafa Kemal's original companions in Anatolia. When İsmet returned from Lausanne he had been asked by the chief of the general staff Fevzi (Çakmak) to support a joint plea to Mustafa Kemal to discuss major decisions beforehand with the authors of the national movement. İsmet refused. He believed that the attempt to circumscribe the authority of the head of state violated the rules of orderly administration. Mustafa Kemal thought it a plot against his person;[70] he foiled the attempt by striking first.

Ali Fuat and Rauf unwittingly provided the opportunity. When peace was signed at Lausanne, the army command was reorganized. The headquarters of the military fronts were dissolved and the system of three army inspectorates, devised after the World War, was reintroduced. One result was to leave 'Bearded' Nurettin Paşa without a command. Welcome as this was to Mustafa Kemal, the appointment of Kâzım Karabekir as 1st Army inspector in Istanbul and of Ali Fuat as 2nd Army inspector in Konya carried some risk for him, a risk which he contained by keeping the chief of staff, Fevzi, on his side. Both Ali Fuat and Karabekir were deputies in the assembly; in addition, Ali Fuat was deputy speaker. Mustafa Kemal asked him to retain this post, but Ali Fuat indicated his displeasure at the rise in power of Mustafa Kemal's personal entourage by resigning to take up his army post. Before going to Konya he stopped in Istanbul where he met Rauf, Refet and Adnan (Adıvar), the last representative of the Ankara government in the old capital. On 25 October, the assembly elected Rauf to replace Ali Fuat as deputy speaker, as well as a new interior minister. Mustafa Kemal was not pleased and decided to impose his authority on the assembly. He responded by convening a cabinet meeting in Çankaya and persuading Fethi and all his ministers to resign and to refuse re-election to a new administration: unlike Rauf, Fethi could not stand up to Mustafa Kemal. In any case, he agreed that as long as ministers were elected individually by the assembly, orderly government was impossible. The People's Party, left to its own devices, was unable to agree on a new cabinet.

On 28 October, Mustafa Kemal was to relate later in his six-day speech, he 'came across' two generals, Kemalettin Sami, the hero of the battles of Sakarya and Afyon, and ('Mad') Halit, who had fallen out with Karabekir during his service on the eastern front. He invited them to dinner at Çankaya together with the minister of defence, Kâzım (Özalp), a friend from Macedonia. They were joined by two deputies, another Macedonian friend and distant relative Lieutenant-Colonel Fuat (Bulca), commandant of Ankara, and Mustafa Kemal's first publicist, Ruşen Eşref. Fethi was there too, as was İsmet, who was a house guest at Çankaya. During dinner, Mustafa Kemal later related, he told his guests, 'Tomorrow we shall proclaim a republic.' He then outlined his tactics and apportioned roles among his friends.

After they had all left, Mustafa Kemal and İsmet drafted a short amendment to the 1921 constitution. Its provisions were simple: the Turkish state was a republic; its president was to be elected by the assembly from among its members; his term of office would coincide with that of the assembly and he could be re-elected; the president would appoint the prime minister and the latter would choose ministers from among the members of the assembly, which would then be called upon by the president to approve the cabinet; and, as head of state, the president would be entitled to chair the assembly and the cabinet whenever he wished.[71] This last provision made the president the head of both the legislature and the executive. Two further articles were to be added to the constitution, specifying Islam as the official religion and Turkish as the official language. Mustafa Kemal was later to describe the reference to official religion as 'superfluous',[72] explaining that its introduction had been tactically necessary at the time.

The following day, the executive of the People's Party met to discuss the formation of the new government. Fethi was in the chair, while Mustafa Kemal waited in Çankaya. After an inconclusive debate, General Kemalettin Sami proposed that as party leader, Mustafa Kemal should be asked to resolve the crisis. When the proposal was accepted, Mustafa Kemal arrived from Çankaya and read the constitutional amendment which he had drafted with İsmet. There were some faint objections that the constitution required further thought. But when İsmet insisted that delay would weaken the state, the executive approved the amendment, which was then immediately passed on to the full assembly. It was adopted, almost without a debate, among cries of 'Long live the Republic'. A cleric who represented the conservative city of Urfa volunteered the explanation that the republic was fully in conformity with Islam. 'We are returning to the days of the first caliphs,' he added hopefully.[73]

The rest of the plan was carried out without a hitch. Having changed the constitution, the assembly unanimously elected Mustafa Kemal president of the republic. He accepted graciously and nominated İsmet as prime minister. The latter had already prepared the list of his cabinet, in which he retained the ministry of foreign affairs. Fevzi remained chief of general staff with a seat in the cabinet, and Kâzım (Özalp) kept the defence ministry. They were the pillars of the regime. Fethi was con-soled with the chairmanship of the assembly. On 19 November, Mustafa Kemal appointed İsmet acting leader of the People's Party.[74]

The shape of Turkey's government was thus settled for a generation. Supreme power rested with the president of the republic. The prime minister was his chief executive. Legislation was discussed by the People's Party behind closed doors, and then formally approved by the assembly. The attempt to pen in Mustafa Kemal had failed, and he had now obtained the administrative instruments he needed to reshape the country. On 4 October, before the proclamation of the republic, a small humorous magazine, *Kahkaha* (Laughter), which appeared in Trabzon, published a cartoon, showing three faces representing the nation, the assembly and the government. All three bore the identical features of the Gazi, Mustafa Kemal Paşa.[75] But his critics and rivals were still at large, and it would take another four years to silence them.

20

The End of the Caliphate

———————◆———————

MUSTAFA KEMAL WAS 42 years old when he achieved his ambition and became the first president of the Turkish republic. But the challenge to his power had not been removed. Mustafa Kemal strove for personal power, but power was not an end in itself. It was a means to refashion the country, to make it civilized in the way that France and the other major Western states were civilized. He was convinced that he alone was capable of doing this: what was good for him was good for his country. Mustafa Kemal was an accomplished tactician who knew how to wait for the propitious moment. Once the moment had arrived, he did not delay. He was a practical man of action, a realist with a vision. He believed his people had the potential to create and sustain a civilized state: though many were still burdened with ignorance, they could be educated, and he would be their teacher.

On 29 October 1923, a few hours before the republic was proclaimed, Mustafa Kemal explained his ideas to a sympathetic French writer, Maurice Pernot.[1] France, he said, had inspired the struggle for freedom throughout the world; he himself had briefly attended a French school. Turkish nationalists were not xenophobic: they were the friends of all civilized nations, while remaining jealous of their independence. Throughout history, the Turks had moved from east to west; a modern government meant a Western government. 'Can one name a single nation that has not turned to the West in its quest for civilization?' he asked. The Islam he professed contained nothing contrary to reason and progress. But 'this Asian nation which has won Turkey's freedom' had a second religion – a mass of irrational superstitions. The 'ignoramuses, the wretches', professing this second religion, would become enlightened in due time. If they failed to see the light, they would destroy themselves. 'But we will save them.' Mustafa Kemal chose his words carefully when he spoke of the caliph. He could see no historical or pragmatic justification for the office, so much so that if he had been appointed caliph, he would have resigned immediately. The caliphate had been preserved out of respect for an old tradition. But, as a result, the Turks were the only Muslim nation to bear the costs of the office or be subject to its influence. This was indefensible.

The caliph, Abdülmecit, found himself on the front line immediately the republic was proclaimed. He rushed off a telegram of congratulations to Mustafa Kemal. On three previous occasions – when the caliph had sent him his condolences on the death of his mother, and then when he congratulated him on his marriage and followed it up with a gift – Mustafa Kemal had sent flowery, respectful replies wishing the caliph a long and healthy life. This time, he responded with a single dry sentence thanking the caliph for his good wishes.[2]

The proclamation of the republic had taken Mustafa Kemal's rivals by surprise. When the 101-gun salute announced the birth of the new regime on the night of 29/30 October, Rauf (who was in effect without a job) and Refet were in Istanbul, Kâzım Karabekir in Trabzon on his way to take up his new appointment as 1st Army inspector in Istanbul. Although all three were members of the assembly, they were not informed when the order to fire the salute was sent to garrison commanders.[3] In Istanbul, the commander was Şükrü Naili Paşa, a native of Salonica and an old friend of Mustafa Kemal. He was handed the official telegram from Ankara during a reception by the municipal authorities in the old city. He read the proclamation to the guests, who responded with loud applause. In his 1927 speech, Mustafa Kemal described this as an expression of the true feelings of the people of Istanbul, and contrasted it with the grudging reaction of Rauf.[4]

The latter was visited on 30 October by two prominent editors, Ahmet Emin (Yalman) and Velit Ebüzziya. In the interview which was published the following day, Rauf argued that the change of name to republic would make a difference only if the new regime respected the wishes of the people.[5] On 10 November, when Kâzım Karabekir arrived in Istanbul, he was greeted by Rauf, Refet and a group of journalists, who told him that news from Ankara showed that Mustafa Kemal had acquired a new entourage and was moving to a full-blown dictatorship. According to his memoirs, Karabekir explained to the journalists that it was Mustafa Kemal's companions who had stopped him becoming sultan and caliph, and for this reason he had jumped the gun and become president. Now Mustafa Kemal would describe his old comrades as enemies of the republic and partisans of the sultan, thus ensuring he remained president for life.[6] Karabekir's memory may have been coloured by subsequent events, and he probably spoke more cautiously than he recorded. However, it was clear that Mustafa Kemal's original comrades had joined forces to thwart him and that they had the support of the most influential newspapers in Istanbul. Mustafa Kemal's supporters in the assembly responded on 8 November by electing from among their members an Independence Tribunal and despatching it to Istanbul to root out subversion, particularly in the press.[7]

On 12 November, Karabekir was received by the caliph Abdülmecit. It was a sad occasion. 'All I have here is my painting equipment and two bundles of personal effects,' said the caliph, his eyes fixed firmly on the ground. 'If they don't want me, I'll pick up my things and go.'[8] As rumours spread of Abdülmecit's willingness to resign, the head of the Istanbul bar association, Lütfü Fikri (Düşünsel), published on 15 November an open letter in *Tanin* in which he appealed to the caliph to remain at his post even at the cost of personal peril.[9] On the same day, the caliph received Rauf and Adnan (Adıvar), reinforcing the impression that he was siding with Mustafa Kemal's critics.

At this critical moment, as tension between Ankara and Istanbul was building up, Mustafa Kemal was struck down by illness. On 11 November, after lunch at Çankaya with his undemanding companions, Salih (Bozok), Recep Zühtü and Kılıç Ali, he felt suddenly ill. His personal doctor Refik (Saydam) was summoned, and diagnosed a cardiac spasm; the diagnosis was confirmed by a senior military doctor, Neşet Ömer (İrdelp) Paşa, who was rushed from Istanbul. But official silence was maintained for six days. Then Neşet Ömer gave a reassuring statement to journalists, saying that Mustafa Kemal's illness was nothing more than exhaustion, and not angina, and that after six days' rest the president had made a full recovery. The doctors prescribed rest and 'a light diet', which meant that, at the very least, Mustafa Kemal was to moderate his drinking. Lâtife tried to enforce the regime, and banned visitors. Mustafa Kemal was furious. He was already irritated by his wife's attempts to regulate his domestic life and institute an official protocol at Çankaya. He now overruled her arrangements and made sure that such visitors as he wished to see were admitted. However, he agreed to travel with his wife for a rest in her family mansion in İzmir, when his health and urgent business allowed it.[10] Just when Mustafa Kemal became partially incapacitated, Istanbul newspapers added to the uncertainty by giving currency to rumours that Enver was still alive in central Asia.[11]

The day-to-day management of the political crisis fell to the lot of

İsmet, as prime minister and deputy leader of the People's Party, and of the chief of the general staff, Fevzi. The army's role was, as ever, crucial. Karabekir claims in his memoirs that Ankara had begun to fear that he would assemble an army in Istanbul and march on the new capital. He adds that, as a precaution, Fevzi ordered back to the east a division previously under Karabekir's command which had been transferred to Istanbul, and that General Kemalettin Sami received secret orders to lead his army corps from Eskişehir to Istanbul at the first sign of trouble.[12] But Mustafa Kemal's original companions recoiled before a frontal challenge to the country's leader. They laboured under the illusion that it was İsmet who had sown division in the happy band of prominent nationalists and who was promoting the president's new entourage. Mustafa Kemal, they thought, could still be persuaded to take them into his confidence.

Rauf attempted a reconciliation. A motion had been tabled in the People's Party parliamentary group demanding a debate on his statements to the Istanbul press.[13] The debate was fixed for 22 November, and Rauf went to Ankara to defend himself. He first called on Mustafa Kemal, but, finding him ill in bed, refrained from talking politics.[14] When the deputies met to debate the motion, İsmet announced that as a party to the argument he would not take the chair. Atatürk's publicist and admirer, Falih Rıfkı (Atay), was to note later in his memoirs that both Rauf and İsmet spoke effectively and displayed self-control. Rauf declared that he supported the republic, but not one that trampled the people's will, as was the case in some Latin American countries.[15]

İsmet dwelt on Rauf's visit to the caliph, and warned that any attempt by the latter to play a part in Turkish politics would be deemed high treason; but caliphs who kept within the limits of their position in Turkey would always enjoy respect.[16] This last sentence was omitted by Mustafa Kemal when he quoted İsmet in his six-day speech in 1927. İsmet then put a question to Rauf: would he work with the party or against it? The decision, he said, was his. But neither the party nor Rauf was as yet ready for the break, and the debate ended inconclusively on a motion that misunderstandings had been cleared and that the fact would be announced in the press. However, a second motion allowed the party leadership to omit from the press release any statements which were politically sensitive;[17] Rauf's reference to banana republics was not publicized. In his 1927 speech Mustafa Kemal complained that the result of the debate was to give Rauf and his friends more time to continue subverting the party from within.[18]

In Istanbul, Karabekir met the new speaker of the assembly, Fethi (Okyar), and asked him to help repair relations between Mustafa Kemal and his original companions. He also proposed formally on 7 December that commanders be asked to choose between their military career and politics, and that officers on active service should no longer be allowed to serve as deputies in the assembly. Fethi replied that Karabekir's proposal could not be processed as the matter was already under discussion in committee. On 19 December 1923 the assembly did in fact vote a law to end military involvement in politics.[19] But it allowed commanders who had been elected to the assembly to serve out their term. However, they could not take part in parliamentary debates so long as they held effective commands.[20] This provision applied to Karabekir and Ali Fuat, but not to Refet (Bele), whose appointment as commander in Thrace was terminated in October 1923.[21] Nor did it apply to Mustafa Kemal, who ceased being commander-in-chief when the republic was proclaimed.[22] The prime minister, İsmet, the defence minister, Kâzım (Özalp), and some other members of Mustafa Kemal's team were similarly placed: they were still members of the armed forces, but they could be active in parliament, as they did not hold military commands. Mustafa Kemal thus retained his rank of Marshal as he laid the foundations of the republic. His retirement from the army was postponed until the 1927 elections, by which time commanders sympathetic to the opposition had been purged.

After a trip with Fethi to Edirne in Thrace, Karabekir travelled to Ankara, where he dined with Rauf on 17 December. They discussed the common front which they saw being formed against them by Mustafa Kemal, İsmet and Fevzi. The following day Karabekir was invited to lunch at Çankaya, where he appealed to Mustafa Kemal to trust him with a clear statement of his intentions. He also repeated his argument that commanders should relinquish their seats in the assembly and that the Independence Tribunal should be recalled from Istanbul, where there were no plots to uncover.[23]

The plea fell on deaf ears. The government had found a new stick with which to beat the opposition. Two prominent Indian Muslims, the Agha Khan, leader of the main subdivision of the Ismaili sect, and Ameer Ali, had addressed a plea to İsmet asking that the caliphate should be safeguarded and arguing that this would redound to Turkey's honour. The letter was published in three Istanbul newspapers on 5 and 6 December, before it had reached İsmet. The government in Ankara seized on this as an act of interference in Turkey's internal affairs to which the Istanbul press had lent itself. On 9 December the Independence Tribunal ordered the arrest of the bar association president Lütfü Fikri and of the editors of the three newspapers, and charged them with high treason.[24]

The trial turned into farce, as the tribunal chairman, Major İhsan (Eryavuz), tried and failed to impress a sophisticated audience. At the end of one session, one of the accused, Hüseyin Cahit (Yalçın), editor of *Tanin*, remarked loudly: 'Curtains for tonight's performance.' On 27 December, Lütfü Fikri was sentenced to five years' imprisonment; but the tribunal chairman dissented and said that he would try to secure a pardon, which was duly voted by the assembly on 11 February 1924. The journalists were acquitted on 2 January 1924 on the grounds of absence of malicious intent. Falih Rıfkı (Atay), who was present at the proceedings, was to comment later: 'It would have been better if the Independence Tribunal had never been sent [to Istanbul]. The weakness of İhsan and his comrades had made a bad impression, and led to the tragedy of the deadly İzmir Independence Tribunal [in 1926] with its gallows.'[25]

On 1 January 1924, as the problem of the caliphate and of its supporters rumbled on, Mustafa Kemal left for İzmir for a rest in the Uşakizade (Uşaklıgil) mansion.[26] Three weeks later, on 22 January, he received a telegram from his prime minister. İsmet reported that the caliph was disturbed by press attacks on his person and by the fact that official visitors from Ankara were boycotting him. He had considered sending a member of his court to Ankara or asking for an emissary from Ankara to discuss the situation, but decided not to do so for fear that his initiative might be misunderstood. However, the caliph asked the government to send him the funds it had promised on 15 April to cover expenses which he could not meet from his treasury. İsmet added that the request would be discussed in cabinet.

Mustafa Kemal decided that the time to strike had come. But, as usual, he kept his own counsel and prepared the ground carefully. First, he sent an immediate reply to İsmet's implicit request for instructions. He declared that the caliph had only himself to blame for the criticism to which he was subjected. Abdülmecit appeared to be following in the steps of the sultans in domestic and foreign affairs: he was in touch with foreign representatives and lent an ear to complaints of reserve officers; he surrounded himself with pomp and ceremony in his palaces. He should realize that his function had no religious or political justification. The suggestion that officials of the republic should contact him was a challenge to the republican government. His budget should be lower than that of the president; he had no right to a personal treasury; his staff should be reduced, and his assets registered to prevent unauthorized sale. The telegram ended with a reminder that a century after the revolution, France refused to admit exiled members of the royal family, and that the Turkish republic should not be sacrificed to meaningless civility in its relations with a dynasty which still hoped for the return of the sultanate. The government should act accordingly and keep him informed.[27] Cast as a Bourbon pretender, Caliph Abdülmecit had in fact more in common with King Lear in his plight.

Mustafa Kemal then turned his attention to the opposition press in Istanbul. The president of the Independence Tribunal, İhsan (Eryavuz), had arranged for the editors of Istanbul newspapers to visit Mustafa Kemal in İzmir. The visit, which Mustafa Kemal did not mention in his 1927 speech, was to lead to a press truce. The editors were graciously received by Mustafa Kemal, who conferred with them for two days. At the final reception on 5 February Mustafa Kemal declared that the press should form a fortress of steel round the republic. The republic had a right to demand this from journalists. The struggle was not over; the press had a duty to convey this truth to the nation and safeguard its unity.[28]

Replying on behalf of his colleagues, Hüseyin Cahit declared diplomatically: 'Freedom is won by violence, but needs mutual tolerance to survive. I am happy to see this spirit in the Gazi.'[29] Hüseyin Cahit was to say in his memoirs that he had parted from the Gazi as a happy and convinced supporter, but that Mustafa Kemal still believed that he would stab him in the back.[30] Hüseyin Cahit owed his fame and fortune to the acerbity of his journalism: he could be tempted with favours or, alternatively, cowed temporarily, but he was not to be controlled. He was a modernist, and even proposed that Turkey should switch from the Arabic to the Latin script.[31] But Mustafa Kemal had his own order of priorities.

First he had to make sure of the support of the army. On 9 February 1924, Kâzım Karabekir was surprised to learn that İsmet and the defence minister Kâzım (Özalp) had gone to İzmir to supervise army manoeuvres. The chief of the general staff, Fevzi (Çakmak), was also going, and Karabekir decided to join him.[32] Mustafa Kemal addressed the commanders twice: on 15 February, at the start of the manoeuvres, and on 22 February, when they ended. He explained his military principles: the need to determine clear objectives, to conserve forces and to concentrate them for a decisive strike. He added significantly that the republic relied on two forces: the determination of the nation and the courage of the army. His only reference to politics was a cryptic sentence: 'we have taken up positions,' he said, to remove obstacles which lay in the way of the nation's safety and happiness.[33] As Mustafa Kemal was to reveal in his six-day speech, it was during these manoeuvres that he decided with İsmet, Fevzi and the defence minister, Kâzım (Özalp), to go ahead with the abolition of the caliphate. Two other measures would be taken at the same time: a unified education system would be set up and the ministry which dealt with the application of Muslim canon law and the administration of pious foundations would be abolished.[34]

The decisions amounted to a cultural revolution, for which Mustafa Kemal had canvassed the army's support. A unified education system implied the closure of *medreses* – the religious schools which trained the *ulema* in Arabic, the scriptures and traditions, and canon law. To replace them with secular, Turkish-language schools would put an end to the transmission of the Islamic religious and cultural heritage. There were to be other consequences. Non-Turkish Muslims never had secular schools providing education in their own languages, but in the *medreses* local teachers could provide explanations in their own vernacular, such as Kurdish. Now they would be educated exclusively in Turkish. The ministry which supervised the application of canon law and the administration of pious foundations was the successor of the office of the Şeyhülislâm, the head of the official clerical hierarchy; this office issued canon law decisions (*fetva*) on matters of current concern. Now the secular government would rule on faith and morals and employ the clergy. The Islamic establishment had always been subject to the sultans, but enjoyed a certain autonomy and applied its own rules. Now religion, religious endowments and education were all to be national-ized and subjected to secular criteria. The change was bound to shock. İsmet was to say in his memoirs:

> We encountered the greatest resistance when we abolished the caliphate. Abolishing the sultanate had been easier, as the survival of the caliphate had satisfied the partisans of the sultanate. But the two-headed system could not go on for ever. It nourished the expectation that the sovereign would return under the guise of caliph ... and gave hope to the [Ottoman dynasty]. This is why the abolition of the caliphate ... had deeper effects and was to become the main source of conflict.[35]

The decision was taken, but it was not announced immediately. Mustafa Kemal returned to Ankara on 23 February.[36] On 1 March he opened the new session of the assembly with a speech which outlined the government's activities. The resettlement of immigrants from Greece was proceeding; military service had been reduced to eighteen months; work was about to start on the extension of the railway from Ankara to Sivas in the east. Looking ahead, Mustafa Kemal asked that a uniform system of education should be created without delay. The deputies had been prepared for this, and Mustafa Kemal's words were greeted with applause. He spoke of the press, and asked that it should always have the national interest in mind. But, he added to prolonged cheers, 'We believe that the remedy to any harm resulting from press freedom lies in press freedom itself.' The ideal was stated: its implementation was another matter. The principle of keeping the army out of politics, Mustafa Kemal went on to say, would be respected. So, too, would the religion of Islam be elevated by ceasing to be a political instrument, as had been the case in the past. But there was not a word about the caliphate.[37] Mustafa Kemal who had argued in the assembly in favour of the institution of the caliphate, divorced from the sultanate, now left it to the assembly to put an end to its existence. Forms were preserved: he was the president, but parliament was supreme.

Parliament took the hint. On 2 March, the parliamentary group of the People's Party met to approve formally three bills. The first abolished the ministry of canon law and pious foundations and the ministry of the general staff, removing from the cabinet the chief of the general staff. The second instituted a single system of public education. The third deposed the caliph, abolished the institution of the caliphate, and exiled from Turkey all members of the Ottoman dynasty. The following day, the three bills were presented to parliament. The proposal to abolish the two ministries and subordinate the clergy to a department of religious affairs, responsible to the prime minister, was made in the name of a cleric, Halil Hulki, deputy for the conservative town of Siirt in eastern Anatolia. The bill was approved after a brief discussion of the title of the new department.[38] Islam remained the official religion of the republic, but it was placed under direct government control. The foundations of secularism were thus laid with hardly a murmur of dissent in a compliant parliament.

The law setting up a single system of public education, and thus putting an end to religious schools, was then passed on the nod. Another cleric, Şeyh Safvet, deputy for Urfa, also a conservative eastern town, known to Muslims as the city of Abraham, was chosen to present the bill putting an end to the caliphate and exiling the Ottoman dynasty. One deputy who was not a member of the People's Party, Zeki from Gümüşhane, spoke against it. He reminded the assembly that on 1 November 1922, when it had put an end to the sultanate, it had declared that the Ottoman dynasty would for ever fill the post of caliph. He argued that a referendum, or at least new elections, were needed before this decision could be reversed. Zeki's arguments made no impression. Nor did a milder protest from one other deputy, Halit, who argued that the office of the caliphate should be preserved even if its present holder were deposed.

The government's case was put by the justice minister, Seyit, who had received a clerical education. He argued that the caliphate was synonymous with temporal power, and that there were no religious grounds for its survival once it was divorced from power. Then the prime minister, İsmet, assured the assembly that Turkey would suffer no harm abroad if it put an end to the caliphate. One deputy proposed that women members of the dynasty should be allowed to stay, as they would be exposed to moral danger if sent abroad with no means of subsistence; his plea was brushed aside. A prominent member of the People's Party, Major İhsan (Eryavuz), the chairman of the Independence Tribunal sent to Istanbul, proclaimed his hatred of the Ottoman dynasty by telling the assembly: 'Even the bones of their dead should be dug up and scattered.'[39] The outcome was never in doubt, as the People's Party had already decided to vote in favour of the law.[40]

Mustafa Kemal kept quiet as the assembly did his will, and as clerics competed with each other in revolutionary fervour. According to the journalist Falih Rıfkı, one *hoca* rushed into Mustafa Kemal's office in the assembly, crying, 'Paşa, if it is your intention to do away with the Holy Book, say so, and we'll find a way to do it. But don't make the deputies talk the way they do.'[41] Sunni Islam enjoins obedience to the ruler: before 1923, the ruler was the sultan; for a few months it was the caliph and the president. Now it was the president alone. Not only did the clerical establishment fail to fight the institution of a secular state; its members competed in currying favour by facilitating the process. Only a few simple provincial *hocas* rebelled. After listening to the speech of Seyit, the cleric who, as minister of justice, advocated the abolition of the caliphate, Mustafa Kemal remarked, 'He has performed his last duty.'[42] Seyit was dropped from the cabinet in a reshuffle three days later.[43] The episode illustrates the contempt in which the clerics were held by the reformers led by Mustafa Kemal. But at this crucial moment, when the framework within which Turks lived their lives was being changed, Mustafa Kemal made only one brief public statement. Speaking to the editors of Istanbul newspapers, assembled at the railway station in Ankara, he said: 'The decisions taken by the assembly these last few days were what the nation had wanted, naturally and genuinely. There is no need to look at them as something extraordinary.'[44] It was a strange way to describe what was happening in Istanbul and elsewhere.

The law had given Ottoman princes ten days to pack up and go. But there was to be no delay for the caliph himself. As soon as the law was passed, the governor and the police chief of Istanbul went to Dolmabahçe palace and told Abdülmecit to prepare to leave immediately. Outraged, the caliph ordered the governor out. The police chief thereupon announced that he had orders to remove the caliph, by force if necessary. As the palace was surrounded and telephones were cut off, Abdülmecit had no option but to comply. He was told that he would be taken to Sirkeci station, the terminus of the Orient express in the old city, and put on the train to Europe. In fact, different arrangements had already been made. Worried by popular feeling in the metropolis, the authorities decided on a less conspicuous exit. They made arrangements to take the caliph and his immediate family and staff by car to the station of Çatalca, outside Istanbul.

At 5 a.m. on 4 March 1924, Caliph Abdülmecit left Dolmabahçe palace, accompanied by two of his four wives, by his son and daughter, and by his chief chamberlain, private physician and secretary. The small party was kept waiting at Çatalca station until midnight, when the Orient express finally drew up. A special coach had been attached to it: the governor of Istanbul had travelled in it to meet the exiles. He handed them an envelope containing £2,000 in British banknotes, and the temporary entry visas which had been granted by the Swiss consulate. Abdülmecit responded by issuing a press statement saying that he would obey the nation's verdict and that he intended to devote himself to fine arts. But the caliph's resignation did not last long. As soon as the train had crossed the Bulgarian border, he issued a second statement declaring that he considered the decision to depose him to be null and void. Sadly, he was to discover that few people cared. He was held up at the Swiss frontier, as the authorities arranged to exempt him from a law which barred polygamous immigrants. He soon found Switzerland too expensive, and moved to Nice. He died in Paris in August 1944, and was buried in Medina. Requests by Abdülmecit's descendants to have his remains transferred to Turkey were turned down repeatedly.

A few days after Abdülmecit's expulsion, another 116 members of the dynasty followed him into exile.[45] Most of them never saw Istanbul again. The ban on re-entering Turkey was lifted for female descendants of the Ottoman dynasty in 1952 and for male descendants only in 1974 – fifty years after the expulsion.[46]

The subjection of the Islamic establishment to the secular state was and remains controversial in Turkey. But there has never been any movement to restore the monarchy. Mustafa Kemal's policy of denouncing the dynasty as, at best, irrelevant and, at worst, treacherous, has left a lasting impact. The sultans and princes were not missed, except by their servants who were left destitute. Most of the palaces stood empty, and deteriorated over the years. The imperial monograms – the bird-shaped *tuğra* – faded or were removed from the fronts of buildings. Only in recent years has there been a serious effort to restore the artistic and architectural heritage of the Ottoman dynasty. In 1924, Turkey had other worries.

Mustafa Kemal remarked in his 1927 speech that when the assembly abolished the caliphate, the leader of a Turkish delegation which had gone to India to thank Indian Muslims for their support of Turkish nationalists informed him that Muslims abroad wanted him to become caliph. Mustafa Kemal said that he rejected the proposal as ridiculous. A caliph was a head of state, and foreign Muslims had their own governments and were in no position to implement the orders of a caliph residing outside their borders.[47] This was as true in March 1924 as it had been in November 1922, when Mustafa Kemal had decided for tactical reasons to put up with a caliph for a little longer.

The abolition of the caliphate signalled Mustafa Kemal's determination to exclude Islam from the public domain. Barely a month later, on 8 April 1924, religious courts, which applied Muslim canon law in matters of personal status – marriage, divorce, inheritance – were closed down.[48] The following day, the ban on alcohol, to which Mustafa Kemal and his companions had paid scant attention, was lifted.[49] True, the first full republican constitution, which was adopted on 20 April, still described Islam as the official religion and retained the formula, used in the 1921 law of fundamental organization, enjoining on the assembly the duty to give effect to the provisions of the *şeriat*.[50] But, as Mustafa Kemal was to say in 1926, these were 'superfluous formulations, incompatible with the modern character of the new Turkish state and of the republican regime, even though the revolution and the republic saw no harm in allowing them as a concession at the time'.[51]

The assembly dutifully endorsed the changes demanded by Mustafa Kemal, but made a careful attempt to guard its own rights. The constitutional commission had proposed that the president be allowed to dissolve parliament and order early elections. This conjured up unpleasant memories: Abdülhamit II had suspended parliament indefinitely, while retaining the constitution, at least in theory; Vahdettin had dissolved parliament twice to please himself and the Allies. In a show of independence, the Grand National Assembly of the republic refused to grant the president the power of dissolution. But, after a debate, it allowed him to send back laws (but not the budget law) for reconsideration.[52] These provisions had little practical significance at the time, as Mustafa Kemal controlled the assembly through his nominees. But they laid the ground rules for parliamentary government.

There was a lively debate on 16 April, when the assembly met to draw up the list of opponents of Turkish nationalist resistance who were to be exiled and lose their Turkish citizenship. The treaty of Lausanne had limited their number to 150 and provided for an amnesty for all others who had fallen foul of the nationalist regime. The assembly implemented this provision by passing two amnesty laws, but then found it difficult to decide who were the worst offenders deserving exile. When the list was finally drawn up, the Istanbul press published documents proving that the interior minister Ahmet Ferit (Tek), who had first selected the candidates for exile, had himself opposed Mustafa Kemal at the beginning of his campaign in Anatolia. The accusation was endorsed by Refet, one of Mustafa Kemal's original companions, who, for all his protestations to the contrary, was happy to find new grounds to embarrass the regime in Ankara.[53] Ferit was forced to resign. But it was a pyrrhic victory for the opposition, as the new minister, Recep (Peker), was one of Mustafa Kemal's most authoritarian supporters.

Mustafa Kemal kept a low profile in the weeks which followed the abolition of the caliphate. The destruction of the old order had shocked the country, but incidents of open rebellion were few. There was a riot in the small Mediterranean coastal town of Silifke, and minor disturbances in Bursa; a provincial *hoca* was sentenced to death for inciting the people against the godless government.[54] But popular reaction was ineffective without educated leadership, and, as Ali Fuat was to note in his memoirs, the small educated class was divided.[55]

Opposition papers, published in Istanbul, spoke of rampant corruption in the ranks of government supporters and attributed it to autocratic rule by the People's Party. Allegations of corruption involved the disposal of property left by departing Christians and attempts by rich Greek and Armenian fugitives to regain control of their assets with the help of persons close to the government. Ruined by wars, Turkey was not producing new wealth. It was the division of spoils – of the old wealth which had been accumulated by the minorities and foreigners – which led to quarrels among the Turkish élite. The Istanbul newspapers had small circulations, which seldom exceeded 15,000 copies. But the semi-official government mouthpiece, *Hakimiyet-i Milliye*, published in Ankara, had a print run of only 6,000.[56] In May 1924, the government acquired a mouthpiece in Istanbul, when Mustafa Kemal's faithful supporter, Yunus Nadi (Abalıoğlu), himself a radical deputy of the People's Party, founded the newspaper *Cumhuriyet* (The Republic). It became the voice of authoritarian, and sometimes xenophobic, Turkish nationalism, as it defended Mustafa Kemal's reforms, whose inspiration was, in fact, more humane.

Political troubles were compounded by a personal drama in Mustafa Kemal's private life. Fikriye, whom Mustafa Kemal had sent for treatment to a tuberculosis clinic in Europe, had returned to Istanbul as soon as she had heard of his marriage to Lâtife. On 6 March 1923, Adnan (Adıvar), the representative of the Ankara government in Istanbul, which was then still under Allied occupation, asked the Gazi whether she should be allowed to travel on to Ankara. Mustafa Kemal replied the same day with an angry telegram. Fikriye had returned without his permission; he had given her enough money for her needs; she should stay in Istanbul and explain her conduct. To make the matter doubly sure, the governor of İzmit was instructed to stop Fikriye, if she attempted to travel by train to Ankara.[57]

Fikriye spent the next fourteen months in Istanbul and Gallipoli. She sent letter after letter to Mustafa Kemal and, it seems, even to İsmet, begging to be allowed access to Çankaya. Then, at the end of May 1924, she left Istanbul undetected and travelled to Ankara. According to the officially sanctioned story published on 1 June 1924, Fikriye declared on arrival at Ankara station the previous day that she had come to visit Lieutenant-Colonel Fuat (Bulca), Mustafa Kemal's friend and distant relative (and therefore her own even more distant relation) from Salonica. But instead of going to Fuat's house, she took the carriage to Çankaya and asked to see the president and his wife. Told that this was impossible, she returned to the carriage. On her way back, she took out a handgun from her bag and shot herself. Informed, Mustafa Kemal ordered his personal doctor Refik (Saydam) to do his best to save the young woman. The surgeon of the Ankara hospital was told that Fikriye should not be allowed any visitors, and that if the treatment was successful, arrangements would be made for her recovery, in Switzerland if necessary. But the treatment was not successful. Within a week of admission, Fikriye developed pneumonia. Two days later she was dead.[58]

The tragedy of discarded wives (and concubines) was a staple of Turkish life and literature. But this did not make things easier for the Gazi. Fikriye herself was overlooked, as Mustafa Kemal's opponents attributed her tragic death to his loose morals. His staff did their best to stop the scandal spreading. In Istanbul, plainclothes police searched Fikriye's lodgings and removed all her personal effects.[59] In the absence of any revelations or compromising material, the incident was gradually forgotten. Atatürk's adopted daughter, Sabiha Gökçen, was to say later that Atatürk had felt great affection for Fikriye, who would have made a better wife for him than Lâtife.[60] In fact, neither woman realized that while Mustafa Kemal did not wish to give pain to his female companions, he would not allow anyone to stand in his way. As Falih Rıfkı (Atay) noted, Atatürk went against his natural inclinations when he championed women's emancipation – 'his tendency was towards the harem'.[61] Years later, he is reported to have said to a foreign lady, who tried to lead him on the dance floor, 'Madam, when a man and a woman are together, it is best to give the lead to the man.'[62]

Fikriye, a desperately unhappy, sick woman, paid with her life for her inability to understand Mustafa Kemal's character. Lâtife was about to make the same mistake, but at a lesser cost. Mustafa Kemal had wanted to leave her in İzmir, when he returned to Ankara at the end of February. She would have none of it, and instead summoned her father, Muammer, and her mother to hold her hand in Çankaya. Muammer tried to make use of the opportunity to establish a business partnership with Mustafa Kemal, who had control of the money collected by Indian Muslims for Turkey's needs. But wiser counsels prevailed, and Mustafa Kemal used 250,000 lira of the money to put up the initial paid-up capital of the Turkish Business Bank (*Türkiye İş Bankası*), which was to introduce Turkish entrepreneurs to the foreign-dominated field of banking. Celal (Bayar), the bank clerk who had become CUP organizer in İzmir and then a leader of the national resistance in the area, became the first director of the Business Bank when it was founded on 26 August 1924.[63]

Mustafa Kemal's six months' silence ended in late August. On the 25th he addressed a meeting of the Turkish union of teachers in Ankara and restated his principles: education should produce free-thinking people, capable of playing a successful part in economic life. National morals should be founded on the principles of civilization.[64] He then set off on an extensive provincial tour in the company of Lâtife. On 30 August he laid the foundation of a monument on the battlefield of Dumlupınar, where the Greek army had been destroyed two years earlier. In a long speech, he described how he had won the victory: he praised the services of Fevzi and İsmet; he mentioned by name General Kemalettin Sami whose troops had broken through the Greek positions, but not the latter's superior officer, 'Bearded' Nurettin, the commander of the 1st Army. Nurettin had been banished to the outer darkness, a fate he richly deserved.

Mustafa Kemal then turned to the future. The existence of all nations depended on their ability to produce the works of civilization. Success in the field of civilization demanded renewal. Centuries-old ways of thinking and reverence for the past should be abandoned. Mustafa

Kemal's recent private problems appear to have been reflected in the next step in his argument. Family life, he said, was the foundation of civilization. Men and women should possess their natural rights and be capable of carrying out their family duties. He then returned to the theme that the battle for economic progress was even more important than the military victory which they were commemorating. The peroration ended with an appeal to the young, which prefigured the coda of his 1927 six-day speech. 'Members of the rising new generation! The future is yours. The republic has been founded by us. It is up to you to guard and exalt it.'[65]

The monument, whose foundations were laid, was made by a local artist, who sculpted an arm holding a Turkish flag. It gave rise to the story that the design had been chosen by Mustafa Kemal, who had seen a Turkish standard-bearer buried in a shell hole, but still clutching the flag in his arm which protruded from the earth. A more likely explanation is that the Dumlupınar monument was a first step towards the representation of human form in sculpture. Earlier monuments, which respected the Islamic ban on human representation, were usually in the shape of a column, tapering at the top. The arm of the unknown soldier, showing above ground, was the harbinger of full-length statues of Mustafa Kemal which were soon to dot the country. In recent years a more grandiose monument was erected on the hill from which Mustafa Kemal had conducted the battle, and the 'monument to the unknown standard-bearer' was moved outside Dumlupınar village, now dominated by a large standard-issue neo-Ottoman mosque.

From Dumlupınar, Mustafa Kemal went to Bursa. He chose this conservative city of mosques, built by the early sultans, for an attack on the Ottoman dynasty, declaring on slender historical evidence that the city had been repeatedly ruined and plundered in dynastic quarrels between Ottoman princes, whose last descendants had let in the Greek occupiers by stirring up rebellion behind the nationalist lines. Now the town lacked any signs of prosperity, but it had the resources to become a centre of civilization in the new republic.[66] Bursa had in fact been lucky, as fleeing Greek troops did not have the time to damage it; but, like other Anatolian towns, its commerce had been disrupted by the departure of local Greeks and Armenians.

From Bursa, Mustafa Kemal went to the port of Mudanya to board the cruiser *Hamidiye* (named after the Sultan Abdülhamit II) which was to take him on a tour of the Black Sea coast. The ship sailed through the Bosphorus, but Mustafa Kemal did not set foot in the old capital. On 16 September he arrived in Trabzon. The opposition had in the meantime begun to organize. His old comrade Ali Fuat, who had attended the commemoration ceremonies at Dumlupınar, had gone on to İzmir, where he met Karabekir and Rauf.[67] The three then met again in Istanbul. They were joined by two prominent Unionists, Rahmi, who had been governor of İzmir in the Great War, and İsmail Canbulat: Mustafa Kemal had distanced himself from both men, who thus found themselves on the margins of political life. All agreed that they were being followed and that their correspondence was opened. Karabekir and Ali Fuat decided that they could no longer perform their duties as army inspectors in these conditions, and that the only course open to them was to take their opposition to autocratic government to the floor of the assembly. They argued that the president should behave as an impartial arbiter in the political struggle between them and the People's Party.[68]

It was precisely this suggestion that Mustafa Kemal rejected when he spoke at the People's Party club in Trabzon on 16 September, saying:

> I take pride in the position of chairman of the People's Party, which is led day-to-day by our prime minister, İsmet Paşa ... Those who discuss constantly the relationship between the presidency of the republic and the leadership of the party ... should know that I am partisan – partisan for the republic, for reform in thinking and society. I do not wish to believe that there is anyone in the new Turkey who does not share these principles of the People's Party.[69]

Mustafa Kemal's original companions were thus given notice that if they opposed the majority in the People's Party, of which they were still members, they would have to fight the president, who had hand-picked and who controlled that majority.

From Trabzon, Mustafa Kemal went to Samsun, the town where he had started his Anatolian campaign. At a reception in the town hall, the mayor proudly produced the armchair on which Mustafa Kemal had sat in May 1919[70] – the collection of relics had begun. Speaking next at a meeting of teachers, Mustafa Kemal made his celebrated statement: 'For everything in the world – for civilization, for life, for success – the truest guide is knowledge and science. To seek a guide other than knowledge and science is [a mark of] heedlessness, ignorance and aberration.'[71] The traditional terms used softened the message: the word for knowledge, *ilim*, like *scientia* in medieval Europe, started its career as theological knowledge; the word for guide, *mürşit*, connoted the leader of a Muslim brotherhood. But by the time the words were engraved on the front of the main building of Ankara University, the uncompromising positivist message was clear: science is the best guide in life.

The speech threw light also on Mustafa Kemal's opinion of foreign Muslims. There were, he said, more than 300 million Muslims in the world, and these millions were all subject to the will and the contempt of others. Why? Because the education they had received had not given them the human qualities needed to break their chains; their education was not national. This showed how necessary it was to refrain from stuffing young minds with 'rusty, numbing, fanciful superfluities'. To make his point plain, Mustafa Kemal then referred to a previous speaker, a *hoca* who had expounded a passage in the Muslim scriptures comparing the olive, which had one stone, with the fig, with its multitude of pips. The olive, said the *hoca*, symbolized unity, the fig plurality. But another *hoca*, whom Mustafa Kemal had questioned on the meaning of the verse, said that he needed half an hour to explain it. What was the point of tiring young minds with such conundrums? Tell them the plain truth.[72] The implication was clear: the old, religious knowledge was useless in the new age. As for Muslim subjects of foreign powers, they had only themselves to blame for their subjection.

From Samsun, Mustafa Kemal retraced his 1919 itinerary. He went to Havza, Amasya and, finally, to Erzurum. Erzurum had not figured in his travel plans, but the town had been badly shaken by an earthquake, and Mustafa Kemal went to give assurances of government aid. But, as elsewhere, he took the opportunity to defend the latest changes: the removal of 'persons and institutions which had damaged the nation's true sovereignty, freedom and independence' – in other words, of the caliphate and the Ottoman dynasty.[73] During the War of Independence, Erzurum had been the home of a 'society for the defence of the sacred heritage', and its chief deputy Hüseyin Avni was a leading member of the opposition Second Group in the assembly. Now, Mustafa Kemal declared that he was happy to see that his actions had reflected the true feelings of the people of Erzurum, as of other parts of the country. There was no one to contest the claim.

Everywhere, Mustafa Kemal spoke of the need to build railways and roads to knit the country together. Nowhere did he speak of his companions in 1919. Karabekir's victory over the Armenians went unmentioned in his speech in Erzurum, in contrast with the regular commemoration of İsmet's victory at İnönü.[74]

Lâtife was at Mustafa Kemal's side as he toured the devastated eastern provinces. She had insisted on accompanying him, when the wives of other officials returned by ship from Samsun. It was an unfortunate decision. Lâtife was jealous of Mustafa Kemal's companions. Husband and wife quarrelled publicly in Tokat, on the way to Erzurum, when Lâtife tried to break up a convivial gathering and drag Mustafa Kemal away to bed. There was another row at a dinner in Erzurum, where Lâtife accused Mustafa Kemal of paying too much attention to the pretty wife of the local commander. The following day Mustafa Kemal despatched his wife back to Ankara by car, in the company of his ADC, Salih (Bozok). Salih was given a sealed letter to İsmet. It read:

Mme Lâtife is preceding me to Ankara. I decided that it would be wrong for us to continue the trip together, as the experience of the last two years has convinced me that we cannot live together. I have informed her of my decision. She is desperately sad and may ask you or Fevzi Paşa to bring us together again, but my decision is final. However, I do not wish to harm the honour and standing of herself and her family, for whom I retain my respect and my feelings of true friendship. The manner of separation will be decided in Ankara. She must be made to agree to return quietly to İzmir.[75]

Before leaving, Salih had asked Mustafa Kemal's companion, Kılıç Ali, to let him know by code if the president changed his mind. If he did, Kılıç Ali would cable, 'He is in good health'; otherwise, the message would be, 'His sickness continues.' Lâtife wrote an imploring letter to Mustafa Kemal from her first stop at Erzincan. When the car reached Kayseri, Salih was handed an order from Mustafa Kemal to interrupt the journey and await his arrival. He checked with Kılıç Ali and was assured that the patient had recovered. Overjoyed, Lâtife turned back to meet Mustafa Kemal fifty miles east of Kayseri. When Mustafa Kemal arrived, he ordered Salih to tear up the letter to İsmet. Then, changing his mind, he told him to keep the pieces. Lâtife had been granted a reprieve, not a full pardon. Mustafa Kemal had decided on a truce with Lâtife, just as his battle with the opposition, led by his original companions, was about to erupt.

21

Imposing Law and Order

M USTAFA KEMAL WAS back in Ankara on 17 October 1924. The assembly had been summoned to meet the following day to discuss a crisis in relations with Britain over the Mosul dispute. In 1922, a Turkish officer had been sent to stir up the Kurds against the British in the Süleymaniye (Sulaimaniyya) area, in what is now Iraqi Kurdistan. He was unsuccessful. Then, local Nestorian Christians, known anachronistically as Assyrians, who had made common cause with the Allies in the Great War, tried to return to their mountain villages in the province of Hakkâri, where the authority of the Turkish government was tenuous. After they had briefly detained the Turkish governor, they were thrown back by a Turkish punitive column, which, the British claimed, crossed the ceasefire line. On 9 October, the British government delivered an ultimatum to Turkey threatening hostilities unless Turkish troops withdrew within forty-eight hours. Turkey appealed to the League of Nations, of which it was still not a member, and the British ultimatum was suspended. A meeting of the League on 27 October 1924 defined the line, which became known as the Brussels line, between areas of British and Turkish occupation, pending a full enquiry into the Mosul dispute.[1]

Both sides pretended to be ready to go to war, which neither in fact wanted. The decision to summon a special session of the assembly, a fortnight before its annual session was due to begin, was meant to publicize Turkey's determination to defend its claim to Mosul. But Mosul was not Mustafa Kemal's main concern as he contemplated the scene from his house in Ankara. During his absence it had changed aspect from a square Anatolian summer house to a turreted suburban

European villa. Near the railway station in Ankara a new parliament building had been erected in time for the new session. It was in the oriental colonial style, which has become known in Turkey as 'first-phase national style', adopted for the first republican public buildings in Ankara. Next door, the old parliament building, which had started its career as a CUP club, was taken over by Mustafa Kemal's People's Party for its headquarters. Another decade was to pass before Austrian and German architects were to bring modern brutalism and dot Ankara with unadorned rectangular buildings; in the first years of the republic, the Orient had not yet been cast aside, and the first generation of Turkish shopkeepers taking over from Greeks and Armenians still chose names such as 'The East' for their grocery stores.

Throughout the summer the opposition press had subjected the government to a sustained campaign of criticism. There was indeed much to criticize. Refugees streaming in from the Balkans complained both of administrative inefficiency and of corruption as they were being resettled. Demobilized officers and war invalids pressed their claims for jobs and pensions. The closure of religious schools had left gaps in education. Many of Mustafa Kemal's original companions seized on these complaints as they fought for a role in decision-making. Though still members of the People's Party, they formed within it an opposition faction, which was numerically weak, but strong in its record of service and in intellectual weight.

Two leading members of the opposition faction, Rauf (Orbay), formerly speaker of the assembly and prime minister, and Dr Adnan (Adıvar), formerly assistant speaker and government representative in Istanbul, hurried to Ankara for the special session. Mustafa Kemal was to say in 1927 that he was surprised that neither had joined the welcoming party which met him when he returned from his tour of the eastern provinces; he had concluded there and then that he was faced with a plot.[2] What faced him in fact was a determined last stand by some of Turkey's leading nationalists asserting their right to have a say in the country's transformation.

On 26 October, Kâzım Karabekir resigned as inspector of the 1st Army, saying that since his reports on the reorganization of the army had been disregarded, he had decided to devote his time to his duties as member of the assembly. Four days later, Ali Fuat (Cebesoy) followed suit, resigning as inspector of the 2nd Army, and giving no reasons. Mustafa Kemal complained in 1927 that he had invited Ali Fuat to dinner as soon as the latter had arrived from 2nd Army headquarters in Konya on 30 October, but that Ali Fuat was met by Rauf (Orbay) and did not turn up at Çankaya. The resignations were clearly prompted by the ban, introduced the previous December, on participation in assembly debates by holders of army commands.

Mustafa Kemal responded on the same day, 30 October 1924, by sending a telegram to six senior army commanders who held seats in the assembly. It was couched in personal terms. 'Relying on the confidence and affection which you feel towards my person, I have deemed it essential that you should immediately inform the presidency of the assembly by telegram that you are resigning as deputies,' Mustafa Kemal wrote, adding that the chief of the general staff, Marshal Fevzi (Çakmak), had already done so at his request.[3] Four corps commanders complied immediately, while two generals asked for time to consider their position. Of the two, the 3rd Army inspector in Diyarbakır, Cevat (Çobanlı), who had been senior to Mustafa Kemal until the latter was promoted Marshal, gave way and resigned from the assembly after going to Ankara. But his subordinate, the 7th corps commander, Cafer Tayyar (Eğilmez), the nationalist commander captured by the Greeks in Thrace in 1920, decided to throw in his lot with Karabekir and Ali Fuat as a deputy in the assembly and resigned his command.[4]

The three generals who had resigned their commands, but who still remained on the army's payroll, were in a hurry to take part in assembly debates; the government, however, insisted that they wait until they had handed over their duties to their successors. By the time they arrived in Ankara, elections had taken place to parliamentary committees and they had lost the chance of a place on them. They complained they had been tricked, while Mustafa Kemal waxed indignant that they had been intent on leaving their commands at a moment's notice at a time when hostilities threatened with Britain.[5] The arguments were less important than the fact that Mustafa Kemal had asserted his control over the armed forces: officers could henceforth look forward to secure careers before and after retirement, provided they were loyal to the president. The armed forces had not been removed from the political arena; they had been subsumed as a corporate element in the Kemalist regime. Mustafa Kemal continued, of course, to take an interest in the army and made a point of attending manoeuvres, but he did not interfere in the day-to-day running of the large military establishment, which he left in the care of Marshal Fevzi (Çakmak), his loyal chief of staff. Relations between civil and military authorities were cooperative, but formal. To this day all over Turkey senior local commanders pay their respects to the civil authority on Republic Day, 29 October, and local governors return the compliment to garrison commanders on Victory Day, 30 August. It is an orderly arrangement.

The next battle was for control over the People's Party. The loyalty of many of its members was suspect. According to the Kemalist writer, Yakup Kadri Karaosmanoğlu, at one private meeting of the party so many members were denounced as opposition sympathizers that Mustafa Kemal expressed the fear that he might find himself in a minority.[6] Although he wanted to shape the party into an effective instrument for his policies, he decided against a purge; it was better to let outright opponents leave of their own free will, and win over the rest.[7] A censure motion provided the opportunity to sort out the party. Criticism had originally been directed at the minister responsible for the resettlement of refugees; the minister was removed, and his department given to the interior minister, Mustafa Kemal's tough lieutenant Recep (Peker). As more and more departments were criticized, the prime minister, İsmet, proposed that the motion to set up a parliamentary enquiry should be debated as a general vote of censure.[8]

The debate started on 5 November 1924. Recep and other radical supporters of Mustafa Kemal mounted personal attacks on Rauf and Refet, accusing them of failing to support the republic and of hankering to reinstate the sultan and caliph. They responded by saying that they were opposed to all forms of authoritarian government. Mustafa Kemal's personal rule was the real, but unspoken, subject of the debate. On 8 November the censure motion was rejected by 148 votes to 18. Forty-one deputies did not vote.[9] Whatever the arguments, the majority of the People's Party, which held all but one seat in the assembly, chose Mustafa Kemal against his critics.

The minority, having come out into the open, decided to leave the party. The following day, 9 November, Rauf, Refet, Dr Adnan and others resigned, and on 17 November they formed the Progressive Republican Party – the name of the party being chosen to rebut the accusation that its leaders were reactionary enemies of the republic. This first official opposition party in the parliament of the republic eventually acquired twenty-nine supporters in the assembly, all but one former members of the People's Party.[10] In his speech opening the regular assembly session on 1 November 1924, Mustafa Kemal had declared that the Turkish nation was 'firmly determined to advance fearlessly on the path of the republic, civilization and progress'.[11] Karabekir, Ali Fuat, Refet, Adnan and other leaders of the opposition wanted to make it clear at the outset that they shared that determination. The party programme[12] pledged support for a liberal, democratic republic, and argued the advantages of decentralization, free enterprise and low tariffs. Mustafa Kemal was to accuse the Progressive Republican Party of encouraging religious reactionaries by declaring in its programme that it respected 'religious thought and beliefs' (article

6).[13] But the programme stated uncompromisingly that laws should meet the needs of the age, as well as the requirements, interests and wishes of the people (article 3) and that there should be a uniform system of education (article 49). Both propositions were anathema to conservative Muslims.

However, principles could not prevent malcontents of all kinds from seeking a home in a legal opposition party. The core of the Progressive Republican Party was formed by Mustafa Kemal's original companions in the War of Independence: Karabekir, who became party leader, Ali Fuat, who became secretary-general, Rauf, Refet, Adnan, Mustafa Kemal's estranged ADC Colonel Arif ('the Bear-keeper') and his first foreign minister Bekir Sami (Kunduh). They were joined by CUP militants, such as Kara Vasıf and İsmail Canbulat, and by Hüseyin Avni and other members of the Second Group, who had been eliminated from the assembly.[14] They were all Turkish nationalists, and most of them modernizers. Their liberal credentials were doubtful; the common link was opposition to the monopoly of power exercised by Mustafa Kemal through his chief executive İsmet.

A by-election held in Bursa in December, to fill the vacancy caused by the departure from parliament of the local military commander in accordance with Mustafa Kemal's wishes, showed that there was discontent in the country. The candidate put up by the People's Party was defeated by 'Bearded' Nurettin Paşa, who stood as an independent. Although the first result was invalidated on a technicality, when the election was held again in March 1925 Nurettin increased his vote.[15]

The reaction of the People's Party was at first uncertain. On 10 November, it tried to steal a march on the new party by adding the word Republican to its name;[16] it also tightened discipline by deciding that members would need the party's permission to table motions critical of ministers, and that they were not to make statements against party policy.[17] On 21 November, at a secret meeting of the party leadership, İsmet asked that the country should be placed under martial law. Mustafa Kemal spoke in support, saying, 'I can smell powder and blood. I hope I am wrong.' But the majority of the members present were not yet ready for a policy of repression. İsmet thereupon resigned.[18] He notes in his memoirs that he was exhausted by his work, particularly as he was suffering at the time from amoebic dysentery.[19]

As İsmet left Ankara to recuperate and bide his time in Heybeliada, an agreeable summer resort in the Princes Islands near İstanbul, Mustafa Kemal asked Fethi (Okyar), the speaker of the assembly, to form the new government. Fethi, a loyal friend of Mustafa Kemal, was himself a liberal reformer, but his cabinet included hard-liners, such as

Recep (Peker) and İhsan (Eryavuz), the unfortunate president of the Istanbul Independence Tribunal.[20] Even so, Fethi attempted a more moderate approach. But when he suggested that the mayor of Istanbul should be elected,[21] in line with the programme of the opposition, this was too much for Recep who resigned from the interior ministry to become secretary-general of the People's Party.[22]

Mustafa Kemal took care not to show his worries. On 11 December, his mouthpiece, the Ankara newspaper *Hakimiyet-i Milliye*, published his replies to questions sent in writing by the correspondent of the London *Times*. Political parties, the Gazi declared, were a natural feature of republican regimes; he would remain at the head of the Republican People's Party (RPP), but would delegate the leadership to a deputy as long as he was president. The programme of the Progressive Republican Party offered nothing new; religious feeling had always been respected. There were no grounds for believing the contrary.[23]

On 1 January 1925, as domestic political tensions mounted, Mustafa Kemal left Ankara for another provincial tour, taking Lâtife with him. This time, he made only one notable speech – in Konya on the anniversary of İsmet's victory at İnönü. He praised the army and described his guiding principle in these words: 'Victory is won by the man who says "Victory is mine", success belongs to him who starts by saying "I will be successful" and can then say "I have succeeded".'[24] He was clearly in a determined mood.

Mustafa Kemal had been presented with a house in Konya, as in several other towns. It was the scene of a lunch party, where, unusually, women mingled with men, discarding their veils. But, as Fahrettin (Altay), the newly appointed 2nd Army inspector, noted: 'Embarrassment and timidity were not yet banished.' After lunch, Mustafa Kemal took his friends for a walk as far as a local hotel. No sooner had they settled down to coffee than Lâtife arrived unannounced. 'Kemal,' she said, 'I have come to take you home for tea.' Mustafa Kemal, who hated being called 'Kemal', got up furious. Lâtife had clearly decided to prevent a drinking session. 'I was surprised,' General Fahrettin wrote in his memoirs, 'that this cultured and sensitive lady did not realize that her behaviour would upset a man like Atatürk.'[25] Discord within the president's family appeared to echo political discord in the country.

From Konya, Mustafa Kemal went to the Mediterranean coast to inspect an estate formerly owned by a Greek at Taşucu, near Silifke. Today this is an area of prime tourist development, attracting thousands of visitors. But in 1925 access was difficult. From the port of Mersin, where Mustafa Kemal stayed in a mansion formerly belonging to a rich Greek merchant, the road to Silifke had to be rebuilt before the party could proceed by car. Local people had good reason to be pleased with this result of the president's visit: for many years, until the modern coastal highway was built, the Gazi's road was to serve their needs. When the party finally reached the farm, they found it in a sad state of repair. Mustafa Kemal decided to buy it and convert it into one of the model 'Gazi's farms', which he was setting up in the country.[26] Leaving the warm coast of the Mediterranean, the Gazi returned to the rigours of the Ankara winter on 2 February 1925. He found the assembly in a state of nervous excitement.

One deputy wanted to know why Hungarian students on an exchange visit to Istanbul had been allowed to dance in a Turkish girls' school. There was no law against dancing, replied the education minister (and future prime minister) Şükrü (Saracoğlu), but school regulations had been broken. Turks, he added, had a strong moral sense, but some educators were wrong-headed.[27] Other deputies asked for an end to university autonomy, a suggestion which the Kemalist regime was later happy to take up. Soon arguments became more ominous. As critics raised their voices, some members of the Republican People's Party threatened physical violence. Many deputies carried handguns, although this was forbidden by house rules. On 9 February there was a quarrel between 'Mad' Halit Paşa, a hero of the War of Independence, and a deputy who had offended him by asking to read his proposal to extend aid to war invalids before signing it. A group of RPP deputies, known for their violent disposition, joined the fray, ostensibly to break it up. Shots were fired, and Halit Paşa was mortally wounded. An enquiry found that the RPP deputy, 'Bald' Ali (Çetinkaya), who was soon to become the hanging judge of the regime, had fired in self-defence. The finding was disputed by critics who alleged that the RPP had reverted to CUP methods to silence its opponents.[28] Mustafa Kemal's premonition of 'powder and blood' was coming true. As in the recent past, freedom had brought out the guns.

Guns were particularly plentiful in the Kurdish areas in the south-east of the country. The Mosul dispute had an unsettling effect on the Kurdish tribes living on either side of the Brussels line. The treaty of Lausanne had made no mention of the Kurds, and had thus closed the prospect of eventual independence which the treaty of Sèvres had held out for them. But a small group of Kurdish nationalists – army officers and some tribal and religious leaders, with whom they had a family relationship – continued to agitate for a separate Kurdistan.

In September 1924, a number of Kurdish officers and men deserted from Turkish units engaged against the Nestorian Assyrians and fled to the area under British occupation in northern Iraq. The deserters had links with the Kurdish secret nationalist society, *Azadî* (Freedom), whose existence was known to the Turkish authorities.[29] A founder member of the organization, Colonel Halit Cibran, was arrested and sent to face a court martial in the Kurdish town of Bitlis.[30] The enquiry implicated Cibran's relative by marriage, Şeyh Sait, a leader of the strictly orthodox Nakşibendi (Naqshibandiyya) Muslim fraternity, and at the same time an active member of *Azadî*. The Nakşibendis had numerous followers throughout the Kurdish areas, and their sheikhs wielded great influence, particularly after the dispossession of Kurdish feudal lords by the reforming sultans. Şeyh Sait was influential among Sunni Kurds; by contrast, Alevi (Shiite) Kurds, who had suffered under Sunni domination and favoured Mustafa Kemal's increasingly secular republic, would have nothing to do with him. But although Kurdish society was deeply divided, all sections had grounds for disaffection.

The establishment of the republic was bringing tighter controls. The authorities had begun to act in earnest to collect taxes and enforce conscription after the interregnum which had followed the collapse of Ottoman rule. There were few, if any, countervailing material benefits: the republic was poor, the officials sent to the Kurdish east were sometimes venal and oppressive. Official subsidies dried up, since the republic had no need of tribal regiments. The closure of the *medrese* religious colleges had deprived religious leaders of status and revenue. As the Mosul conflict dragged on, Kurdish nationalists followed the old tribal tradition by trying to enlist British help against the Turkish government:[31] but London had decided as early as December 1921 against instigating a Kurdish rebellion outside the area of the British mandate in Iraq. However, the British were 'to keep in with Kurdish revolutionaries as a necessary precaution'[32] against Turkish encroachment into the disputed province of Mosul. Although this policy was ultimately to contribute to a settlement of the Mosul dispute, it could easily be misunderstood both by the Turkish government and by disaffected Kurds.

Fearing that the net was closing in on him after the arrest of Colonel Halit Cibran, Şeyh Sait called a gathering of tribal and religious leaders, at which the decision was taken to raise the standard of rebellion in April 1925. But trouble broke out earlier, on 11 February, when local people overcame a detachment of gendarmes sent to arrest deserters in the village of Piran (north of Diyarbakır), where Şeyh Sait was visiting his brother.[33] The mountainous area, separating the valleys of the Tigris and of the upper Euphrates (known here as Murat water), was almost devoid of government troops. Weak military detachments sent in to the trouble spot were unable to break through the mountains. As the rebellion spread, Şeyh Sait declared himself Commander of Warriors for the Faith (*Emirülmücahidin*) and made it known that his aim was to restore the holy law of Islam, violated by a godless government. It was a call Turkey's nationalist leaders had heard when troops had mutinied against the Young Turks in 1909 and when risings were instigated against the nationalists during the War of Independence. None of them had any doubts that 'religious reaction' had raised its head once again, and had to be crushed.

As the Kurdish rebels had cut telegraph lines, it was not until 16 February that news of the rebellion was published in the Turkish press.[34] A week later, prime minister Fethi (Okyar) signed an order proclaiming martial law throughout the Kurdish area south of Erzurum.[35] On 25 February the proclamation was endorsed by the assembly, which passed unanimously a law declaring that whoever exploited religion for political purposes was guilty of high treason.[36] Prime Minister Fethi acknowledged that in this case the political purpose was Kurdish separatism (*Kürtçülük*)[37] – a fact which later official pronouncements passed over in silence. Promising the opposition's full support, Karabekir said that the whole country would unite against the internal and external danger.[38] Fethi was ready to tackle the Kurdish rebels, but the president denied him the chance.

Mustafa Kemal's immediate response to the rebellion was to summon İsmet to Çankaya; he arrived on 21 February.[39] News from the Kurdish area grew more ominous. After taking a number of provincial centres, Şeyh Sait set up his headquarters north of Diyarbakır on 28 February, and began preparations to attack this chief city of Turkey's Kurdish area. The attack began on 2 March. A few days later, some rebels managed to enter Diyarbakır; but they were beaten back, and Şeyh Sait retreated, although the city remained under siege until 27 March. By then İsmet was back in the saddle in Ankara.

On 2 March, five days after the assembly had endorsed Fethi's policy, İsmet called a meeting of the parliamentary group of the RPP, of which he was still deputy leader. Accused of lack of firmness in the emergency, Fethi replied, 'I will not dip my hands in blood by choosing unnecessary violence.'[40] According to Halide Edip, writing as a critic of Mustafa Kemal, the Gazi made it clear that his was a policy of firmness, saying, 'The nation has to be led by the hand. The man who has begun the revolution[41] will also complete it.'[42] A vote was then taken: 60 deputies voted in support of Fethi, 94 against him. Disowned by his party, Fethi announced his resignation in the assembly. The following day, 3 March, Mustafa Kemal appointed İsmet to replace him. His government,

which included Recep (Peker) as defence minister, was endorsed by 154
votes to 23. Speaking for the opposition, Ali Fuat (Cebesoy) asked that
the natural rights and freedoms of the nation should not be restricted
as the 'reactionary movement' was being suppressed.[43] But this was
precisely the course of action for which Mustafa Kemal had selected
İsmet.

On 4 March the assembly was asked to approve a draconian law
giving the government the right, subject only to the president's
approval, to close down any organization or publication which it
deemed subversive. Known as the 'Maintenance of Order Law' (*Takrir-
i Sükûn Kanunu*), this notorious measure was approved by 122 votes to
22. Karabekir, Rauf and other opposition speakers protested in vain:
the Gazi's mind was made up. On the same day, the assembly set up two
Independence Tribunals, one in Diyarbakır, the other in Ankara, and
selected their members from among deputies known for their devotion
to Mustafa Kemal. 'Bald' Ali (Çetinkaya) was chosen to head the Ankara
tribunal, while Mazhar Müfit (Kansu) became president of the tribunal
in Diyarbakır. Death sentences handed down by these political courts
were not subject to appeal. On 6 March, the government used its new
powers to close down publications which had dared to criticize the
regime. *Vatan*, the newspaper edited by the liberal Ahmet Emin
(Yalman), was spared until 11 August, when it too was closed down, the
government having realized that it was attracting the readers of banned
publications.

Mustafa Kemal made no public statement on the rebellion until 7
March when he issued a proclamation attributing it to criminals who
tried to hide their intentions under the mask of religion, and who had
relied on activities all over the country aimed at weakening the authority of the state.[44] What these activities were, and what intentions the
rebels pursued the Gazi did not specify. But it could easily be inferred
that he blamed the opposition for creating conditions which Kurdish
separatists sought to exploit. The burden of the proclamation was that
law and order would be re-established with a firm hand, and that no
criticism of security forces would be countenanced. 'The precondition
of all happiness ... and particularly of economic and commercial development is tranquillity, security and order beyond the reach of any violation,' declared the Gazi. İsmet had advocated the imposition of martial
law even before Şeyh Sait's rebellion. The Gazi now made it clear that
events had proved him right.

Evidently worried by the military threat posed by the rebels, the
government ordered a partial mobilization. Kemalettin Sami, one of the
most successful generals of the War of Independence, arrived from

Berlin, where he had been appointed ambassador, to organize the shipment of German guns.[45] But even before newly mobilized troops
reached the south-east of the country, Şeyh Sait's tribal forces had run
out of steam. On 24 March, 300 rebels entered the provincial centre of
Elâzığ (then Mamuretülaziz, or Elâziz in brief) and proceeded to sack
the town. They were driven out by local people two days later.[46] By the
end of March, the rebels were in retreat everywhere. On 15 April, Şeyh
Sait was captured by a battalion of Turkish soldiers, assisted by Kurdish
tribesmen, as he was trying to escape to Iran. By 10 May all the leaders
of the rebellion had been caught and were sent for trial to the
Independence Tribunal in Diyarbakır.[47] Şeyh Sait had raised no more
than 15,000 Kurdish fighters; 25,000 Turkish soldiers, assisted by
Kurds who sided with the Turkish state, routed them in a couple of
months.[48]

Nevertheless, the prospect of general disaffection among the Kurds
shook Turkish nationalists. On 8 March, a military communiqué attributed to Şeyh Sait's supporters the intention of establishing a Kurdish
government in Diyarbakır and of asking for foreign recognition and
aid.[49] On 7 April, Prime Minister İsmet assured the assembly that the
government would take measures to prevent the repetition of political
subversion under the guise of religious reaction in an area that laid itself
open to it.[50] In the course of his trial in Diyarbakır, Şeyh Sait insisted
that his sole aim was to establish an Islamic order based on the *şeriat*.
But one of his former supporters, Major Kasım Cibran, who defected
to the authorities and may have assisted in Şeyh Sait's capture,[51] said in
evidence that the real aim of the rebellion was to create an independent
Kurdistan; he also tried to implicate the opposition Progressive
Republican Party by claiming that the rebels believed that if it came to
power it would grant autonomy to the Kurds.[52]

This was precisely what the government wanted to hear. The prosecution sought to prove that by distinguishing between Kurds and
Turks, the accused had tried 'to make trouble between brothers who
belonged to the same nation'. Anticipating the government's intentions,
the prosecution also pointed out that the Muslim brotherhoods had
served as centres of secret political plotting.[53] In its verdict, the
Diyarbakır Independence Tribunal declared that Şeyh Sait had intended
all along to establish an independent Kurdistan and split the Turkish
fatherland.[54] The tribunal was determined to punish the attempt:
according to official Turkish records, it handed out fifty-seven death
sentences. The veteran Kurdish leader Seyit Abdülkadir was sentenced
to death on 27 May; Şeyh Sait and forty-six others on 29 June. All were
hanged in Diyarbakır.[55] Earlier, Colonel Halit Cibran had been hanged

in Bitlis.[56] The Independence Tribunal ordered the closure of all dervish lodges (*tekke* and *zaviye*) throughout the eastern provinces.[57]

Mustafa Kemal's toleration of a legal opposition ended as soon as news of the Kurdish revolt reached Ankara. On 25 February, Fethi, who was still prime minister, visited Kâzım Karabekir, the leader of the Progressive Republican Party, and said to him: 'I have been instructed to ask you to dissolve your party. If you don't, I fear for the future: blood will be shed.' Karabekir replied that if the government wished to close down the party, it should do so itself.[58] In his 1927 speech, Mustafa Kemal confirmed that the warning had come from him, and was motivated by the opposition party's 'harmful stand which encouraged rebellion'.[59]

On 25 April, the Ankara Independence Tribunal ordered that the Istanbul offices of the Progressive Republican Party should be searched.[60] When the newspaper *Tanin* described the search as 'a raid', it was closed down and its editor, Hüseyin Cahit (Yalçın), was arrested and sent to Ankara to be tried by the Independence Tribunal. Hüseyin Cahit had already angered the authorities by announcing, as soon as the Maintenance of Order Law was published, that he would no longer write leading articles, but would publish his memoirs instead.[61] In Ankara prison he joined Zekeriya (Sertel), the well-known left-wing journalist who had been briefly press director of the regime. Hüseyin Cahit was sentenced to exile in the provincial town of Çorum.[62] Hearing the decision, he said: 'I would rather be judged by this court, than be a judge in it.' Zekeriya was exiled to Sinop;[63] other Marxist writers received prison sentences – among them the poet Nazım Hikmet (Ran), who went into hiding, then fled to Bolshevik Russia. According to Ali Fuat (Cebesoy), closures had reduced the number of daily newspapers in Istanbul from fourteen to six, and total sales to only 49,000 copies. It was, he says, an unprecedented fall: 'As the press was deprived of the right to criticize and control the government, people stopped buying newspapers or treating them seriously. It was a kind of protest.'[64]

On 3 June 1925, the government closed down the Progressive Republican Party; the decree cited the opinion of the Independence Tribunals in both Ankara and Istanbul that the reference to 'respect for religious beliefs' in the party's programme had been used to encourage religious reaction.[65] Left-wing workers' organizations in Istanbul were also suppressed. No one could accuse them of sympathy for either religious or Kurdish tribal 'reactionaries',[66] but they were, at least potentially, a threat to the regime. Nine leading journalists, including Ahmet

Emin (Yalman) and Velit Ebüzziya, were arrested and sent for trial to
Diyarbakır, where the Independence Tribunal accused them of attacking the government 'unfairly and unnecessarily' and thus creating
conditions propitious for Şeyh Sait's rebellion. The journalists were
encouraged to express regret for their actions and to plead for the
president's intercession. They did as they were told. Mustafa Kemal
responded by saying that he was not disposed to make any personal
accusations, even if there were legal grounds for them, and asking that
the tribunal should exercise 'tolerance'.[67] The journalists were freed and
returned to Istanbul chastened. Press criticism of the government
stopped. On the anniversary of the republic the following year, an
amnesty allowed Hüseyin Cahit (Yalçın) and Zekeriya (Sertel) to return
from exile. Seeking to benefit from the amnesty, the romantic
Communist poet Nazım Hikmet came back from Russia in 1928, but
his troubles were not over. He was briefly imprisoned, set free and then
exposed to the regime's prolonged cat-and-mouse tactics.[68]

Mustafa Kemal had been stung to the quick by opposition journalists, and two years later he devoted a lengthy portion of his six-day
speech to answering their criticisms, which he quoted at length. But his
government found it comparatively easy to frighten the press into
silence or compliance; it was more difficult to dispose of the threat of
Kurdish separatism. Mustafa Kemal had fought the Russians in 1916 in
the area where Şeyh Sait started his rebellion. He had put his knowledge
of Kurdish tribal leaders to good use in the War of Independence, when
he tried, and often succeeded, in enlisting their help in the Turkish
national resistance. He had promised them rights and privileges within
a system of local self-government.[69] The second assembly, elected, or
rather selected, in 1923 – like the first, which had come together in 1920
– counted Kurdish notables among its members; there were many
ethnic Kurds among the thirty-seven representatives of eastern and
south-eastern provinces who voted in favour of the Maintenance of
Order Law.[70] But the rebellion led the government to conclude that it
was not enough to rely on the traditional policy of co-opting cooperative Kurdish notables.

Reports were commissioned from Fethi's finance minister (and
future assembly speaker) Abdülhalik (Renda), and the interior minister
Cemil (Uybadın). Abdülhalik was a native of Yanya (Yanina, now in
Greece), and probably of Albanian origin; Cemil came from Süleymaniye.[71] But they both came out in favour of a policy of assimilation,
which was to be promoted by suppressing the Kurdish language, settling Turks among Kurds, and moving some Kurds to the west. Interior
minister Cemil proposed in his report that 'colonial administration

should be introduced in the east under a governor-general'.[72] It was not a shocking idea at a time when the British were using aircraft to bomb the Kurds into submission in northern Iraq and the French and Spanish were suppressing Abdelkrim's Moroccan tribesmen in the Rif. The difference was that Britain and France had the money to bring material improvements to tribal areas in their colonies; Turkey did not. But this did not affect the presumption that civilized government had a duty to control unruly tribesmen whether it was on the north-west frontier of India or the south-east frontier of Turkey.

The conclusions of the enquiry reports were embodied in the Reform Plan for the East (*Şark Islahat Plânı*), submitted to the government in September 1925. It provided for special administrative arrangements for the Kurdish areas under an Inspector-General, the settlement of 50,000 Turks in properties earlier belonging to Armenians, the exile of 'dangerous' Kurdish families, and the exclusion of ethnic Kurds from government service in their home areas.[73] İsmet, whose family came from the east Anatolian town of Malatya – a fact which led to speculation that he was himself, at least partly, of Kurdish origin – implemented the Eastern Reform Plan. But the ethnic character of the Kurdish areas, where, according to Abdülhalik (Renda), there were almost a million Kurds, against 250,000 Turks and 117,000 Arabic-speakers,[74] did not change appreciably. With time, railways and the improvement in government services knit the country closer together, but most Kurds retained a sense of separateness, and their home areas continued to be poor and backward – a place of exile for unwilling civil servants.

Mustafa Kemal, a westerner in origin and orientation, backed what Kurdish nationalists called later 'the policy of denial' (of the existence of a separate Kurdish people). There was, in any case, no argument about it among modernizing Turkish nationalists, whether they supported or opposed Mustafa Kemal. Their ideal was the creation of a single nation, united by the Turkish language and Turkish culture, in the same way that the French language and French culture had moulded the French nation. In December 1926, the ministry of education decreed that ethnic names such as Kurd, Laz or Circassian should not be used, as they harmed Turkish unity.[75]

Mustafa Kemal never mentioned the Kurds by name in his public speeches after the proclamation of the republic. Opening the new session of the assembly in November 1925, he described the rebellion in the east as the result of 'reactionary tendencies and preparations'.[76] In the closing passage of his six-day speech he spoke of the rebellion as 'an uprising of ignorance, fanaticism and general hostility towards the republican administration and the modern movement' and accused the opposition Progressive Republican Party of becoming a source of hope for reactionaries.[77] It is true that Şeyh Sait had made use of religious discourse to mobilize the Kurds. But he and many other Kurdish leaders had sought a separate dispensation for their people, and had tried to enlist foreign help in this project, long before the abolition of the caliphate.

The Kurdish problem preceded Mustafa Kemal's access to power and he brought no insights to its solution. He left its management to İsmet, along with other administrative problems. Mustafa Kemal's interest lay elsewhere, in the cultural revolution which was to lead his country into the mainstream of human civilization. In 1927, he defended the Maintenance of Order Law as a necessity at a time of revolutionary change.[78]

Şeyh Sait's rebellion hastened both the imposition of single-party rule and the pace of cultural change. But even outside periods of profound cultural change, democracy and good government are difficult to combine in Turkey, as the history of the years following the Second World War has shown. In 1925 it was much more difficult: the population was largely illiterate and disparate, reconstruction had barely started, poverty turned easily to violence. Mustafa Kemal was a conservative revolutionary. He believed that civilization and law and order were inseparable.[79] He opted for both.

22

Reforms and Repression

T HE KURDISH REBELLION and the political struggle with the opposition did not stop the work of building a new Turkish state. Mustafa
Kemal was fascinated by the commercial and military potential of aviation. 'The future is in the sky,' he was to say later. On 16 February 1925,
the Turkish Aviation Society was set up to train pilots and produce
simple small aircraft.[1] Mustafa Kemal appointed his childhood friend
Fuat (Bulca) to head the new society. All the hides of sheep sacrificed
by pious Muslims had to be donated to it; all petitions to the authorities,
handbills and posters had to carry its revenue stamps; and it was given
the right to operate the national lottery.[2] The Aviation Society became
ubiquitous in Atatürk's republic as a symbol of self-help and modernity.

On 17 February, in the midst of Şeyh Sait's rebellion, the assembly
voted to abolish tithes;[3] they had been a heavy burden on the peasantry
which accounted for most of the country's population. This relief
measure was taken at a time when, in the Soviet Union, the Bolsheviks
were starving the peasants for the sake of rapid industrialization. In
contrast, in Turkey the economic development of the young republic
had to rely on reduced tax revenue. Mustafa Kemal saw himself as a
pioneer of agricultural improvement, and on 5 May 1925 work began on
the Gazi's Forest Farm (*Gazi Orman Çiftliği*), four miles south-west of
Ankara.[4] Marshes were drained, trees planted, a smart farmhouse and
sheds for livestock were built. Over the years other features were added:
two large ponds, one in the shape of the sea of Marmara, the other of
the Black Sea; a restaurant, a brewery. The Gazi was frequently seen on
his farm – driving a tractor or entertaining guests. He had been brought
up in the well-watered Macedonian countryside; now he sought to

create green vistas in the dry steppe which surrounded his new capital. He was furious when an oleaster – a thorny tree of the Anatolian plateau – was cut down in his absence. On another occasion, he insisted that some willows which stood in the way of a projected cottage should be moved rather than cut down, and oversaw the job himself.[5]

Lack of resources did not stop the drive to nationalize the economy. A 'national economy' – the transfer of enterprises from foreigners and non-Muslims to Muslims and the Turkish state – had been a prime object of the CUP; like all nationalist Turks, Mustafa Kemal remained wedded to this policy in his pursuit of economic independence. On 26 February 1925, the *Régie*, the French-run tobacco monopoly, which had been part of the administration of the Ottoman Public Debt, was taken over by the Turkish state. On 5 April a law was passed authorizing the state to set up sugar mills. On 17 April, the first section of the railway which was to link Ankara with Sivas and then Erzurum in the east was opened.[6] For Atatürk, as for his supporters, railways and modernization were synonymous.

Mustafa Kemal found relief from frantic public activity in the company of his friends. Work on the model farm helped him reduce his drinking, but kept him away from his wife more than ever. Lâtife grew increasingly frustrated. Two years earlier, an Istanbul newspaper suggested that she should be elected deputy; Mustafa Kemal ruled it out, even for the future when women would be given political rights.[7] Lâtife was not content to be a ceremonial wife in public and a companion of last resort at home. While entertaining guests one evening, she complained that she had not been able to complete her university education. 'Madam,' Mustafa Kemal interjected, 'you are free to do so any moment you choose.' He himself was capable of spending the whole night reading, if a book interested him. Stories began to circulate that Lâtife spied outside the closed doors of Mustafa Kemal's study, that in her jealousy and frustration she tried to keep out his friends and quarrelled with their wives. One night, Mustafa Kemal returned late to the villa and chatted with the sentries before turning in. Their conversation was cut short when Lâtife appeared on the balcony and shouted: 'Kemal, come in at once. Aren't you satisfied with your chums in the neighbourhood? Do you have to make friends of your sentries too?'[8] The story may be apocryphal, but all accounts agree that mutual irritation had become the strongest feeling in the presidential household. Mustafa Kemal was fond of children and was to say later that he would have liked to have children of his own. But the marriage was barren.

One evening in August, possibly after the balcony scene, Mustafa Kemal stumped out of his villa in Çankaya and was driven to his old office in the railway station. There he wrote a letter to Lâtife saying that it would be better if they lived apart for a time, and suggesting that she should take a rest in her family mansion in İzmir. An ADC delivered the letter the following day, with instructions to escort Lâtife to İzmir. Meanwhile, Mustafa Kemal and four companions took the train along the uncompleted line east of Ankara. He waited until he heard that his instructions had been carried out and the coast was clear; he then returned to the capital. On 11 August, Mustafa Kemal informed the government that, six days earlier, he had divorced his wife according to Muslim canon law. The divorce documents (*talakname*) had been served on Lâtife in İzmir and, on the day of the announcement, husband and wife had formally agreed to end their marriage.[9]

Lâtife, who had no choice in the matter, spent the rest of her life regretting what she called her 'childishness'.[10] First, she asked Mustafa Kemal for an appointment as a teacher or a secretary in a Turkish embassy.[11] When neither was forthcoming, she travelled to Europe, and spent some time in a sanatorium in the Tatra mountains (in Czechoslovakia) and then in the south of France. Returning to Turkey, she appealed to Mustafa Kemal's friend Salih (Bozok) to repair the breach with her husband, which she blamed on another companion, Kılıç Ali.[12] It was no use. Lâtife settled finally in Istanbul, in a flat belonging to her family, which continued to enjoy the Gazi's favour.[13] She never remarried, and died in July 1975, a little old lady, known for her masterful disposition, and praised for the total discretion she maintained even after Atatürk's death in 1938. There were rumours that she had left an account of her thousand days with the founder of the Turkish republic, but no such document has turned up.

It was said that Mustafa Kemal was shaken by the divorce and was heard crying in his room as he played the record of the song 'I have become a distraught nightingale'.[14] If so, he shook off the mood quickly. Şeyh Sait's rebellion had given a new sense of urgency to Mustafa Kemal's cultural revolution. The changes which he had in mind in order to modernize the country had been discussed by Ottoman and Turkish reformers for decades. As the victorious commander of armies which had saved the country from partition, he had acquired the power and prestige to turn talk into action. But the critical attitude of the Istanbul press and the rise of the opposition, culminating in open rebellion, had shown that the capital of victory was quickly exhausted. Speaking of change, Mustafa Kemal said to İsmet, 'If it can be done at all, it must be done now.'[15] Now, with the Maintenance of Order Law in force, and Independence Tribunals meting out summary justice, Mustafa Kemal set out to introduce the most visible, personal and controversial of his measures. On 23 August 1925,[16] little more than a fortnight after seeing off Lâtife, Mustafa Kemal left Ankara to tell his people that they were to wear European-style hats.

Headgear had been a distinguishing mark of rank, profession and religion throughout the history of Turkey, as of other countries. The turbans, fezes, bonnets and head-dresses surmounting Ottoman funerary steles show the sex, rank and profession – civil or military – of the deceased. They allow us also to date the grave, for headgear changed both by edict and by the evolution of fashion. In the first half of the nineteenth century, the reforming Sultan Mahmut II restricted the turban to religious dignitaries, and introduced the fez for civil and military officials. The fez had evolved out of the red, soft felt cap of Mediterranean sailors and derived its name from Fez or Fès, one of the four capitals of Morocco. The fact that it did not have a rim or peak made it particularly suitable for Muslims, whose foreheads have to touch the ground as they prostrate themselves in canonical prayer. Imposed by edict, the fez had been taken to heart by the Ottoman Muslim middle class, although it was sometimes worn also by Ottoman Christians. However, as the latter fell under the spell of Europe, many of them adopted the rimmed European hat, known in Turkey by the Russian word *şapka* (*shapka*), derived from the French *chapeau*. For the majority of Ottoman Turks, *şapka* was the distinguishing mark of the infidel.

But the fez had a disadvantage, particularly for soldiers in hot countries. Lacking a rim or a peak, it did not shade the eyes from the sun. In the Great War, Enver Paşa addressed the problem by introducing a sloping, rimless topee, which became known as the *enveriye*. Modernizers, who wanted to go a step further, advocated cautiously the European cap under the euphemism 'headgear with sun-shield'. Mustafa Kemal rejected the euphemism and called a hat a hat. He wanted it as part of 'civilized dress', the common dress of civilized people, banishing distinctions of culture. He was convinced that all civilized people should have the same way of life, that culture and civilization were synonymous. So too were 'orientalism' (*şarklılık*) and backwardness, which exoticism only served to mask. Where Marxists combated distinctions of class, Mustafa Kemal, the most consistent and radical of Turkish modernizers, set out to destroy distinctions of way of life, and therefore of dress. Only then would it become clear that a Turk was a man for a' that.

Mustafa Kemal decided to take this message first to a provincial backwater – the wooded, mountainous area, north of Ankara, known in classical times as Paphlagonia, where the traditions of Muslim brotherhoods were still strong. His first stop was in Kastamonu, 160 miles north of the capital. The town had been festooned with decorations for the visit. When Mustafa Kemal got out of his car, he was bareheaded and held a panama hat in his hand. The crowd responded by removing fezes and turbans. The following day, 24 August, Mustafa Kemal donned his marshal's uniform for a visit to the barracks.[17] Then, outside the town hall, he turned his attention to a delegation of farmers. 'I too am a farmer,' he declared. 'Farming requires machinery ... Come together and buy machines!' Tradesmen were next in line. 'What is cheaper,' Mustafa Kemal asked a tailor, 'local dress with baggy trousers or international clothes?' 'International clothes,' replied the tailor, who was clearly no fool. 'Quite so,' said Mustafa Kemal, 'and you'll have enough cloth for two suits.' 'Take off your fez,' he told another tradesman. Seeing the skullcap underneath, Mustafa Kemal commented, 'Skullcaps, fezes, turbans – it all costs money which goes to foreigners.' He ended with a peroration: 'We will become civilized ... We will march forward ... Civilization is a fearful fire which consumes those who ignore it.'[18]

From Kastamonu, Mustafa Kemal went on to İnebolu, the small port on the Black Sea which had served as a supply base for Turkish nationalists in the War of Independence. Addressing a meeting at the local Turkish Hearth, the nationalist society, he told his audience that there was no need to revive ancient Turkish forms of dress. 'Internationally accepted civilized dress suits us too,' he declared. He went on to describe it: 'Shoes or boots on your feet, trousers on your legs, then shirt, collar and tie, waistcoat, jacket and, to complete it all, headgear with a sun-shield, which I want to call by its proper name: it's called a hat.' He then introduced a second, more delicate subject. Not only in villages, but also in towns, he had seen women cover their faces and their eyes as his party passed by. This habit, which caused particular discomfort in the heat of the summer, was, at least to some extent, the result of male selfishness, of scruples for purity. 'But, friends, our women have minds too.' So teach them morals and then stop being selfish. 'Let them show their faces to the world, and see it with their eyes ... Don't be afraid. Change is essential, so much so that, if need be, we are prepared to sacrifice lives for its sake.'[19]

Lives were indeed about to be sacrificed for the sake of the hat. As for the veiling of women, it was officially discouraged, but not banned. In any case, veiling had been largely a middle-class custom, and the middle classes discarded it. The generality of women wore long headscarves, which they drew across their faces in the presence of male strangers. The government of the republic banned headscarves in official premises, including schools, under civil service regulations. Elsewhere they were tolerated and they have remained a feature of the Turkish scene to this day, while the ban on women's headscarves in official premises is challenged every time that official pressure is relaxed.

Mustafa Kemal stopped once more in Kastamonu on his way back to Ankara. His thoughts again turned to dress reform.[20] Pointing to a man in the crowd, he said: 'He has a fez on his head, and a green turban wound round the fez, a traditional waistcoat [*mintan*] on his back, and on top of it a jacket like mine. I can't see what's below. Now I ask you, would a civilized man wear such peculiar clothes and invite people's laughter?' 'Of course, they'd laugh at him,' responded the crowd, entering into the spirit of unkind fun.

Muslim brotherhoods were another target. In the same speech, he went on:

In the face of knowledge, science, and of the whole extent of radiant civilization, I cannot accept the presence in Turkey's civilized community of people primitive enough to seek material and spiritual benefits in the guidance of sheikhs. The Turkish republic cannot be a country of sheikhs, dervishes and disciples. The best, the truest order is the order of civilization. To be a man it is enough to carry out the requirements of civilization. The leaders of dervish orders will understand the truth of my words, and will themselves close down their lodges [*tekke*] and admit that their disciples have grown up.

He referred to the shrines of Muslim saints, saying, 'It is a disgrace for a civilized society to appeal for help to the dead.' It was an uncompromising positivist message, which struck at the roots of popular religion. Mustafa Kemal had ended his first great speech to the Erzurum congress, at the start of the War of Independence in 1919, with an eloquent prayer to the Prophet Muhammad. He was as dead as the most obscure Anatolian dervish saint, whose shrine was about to be closed.

On 2 September, the day after Mustafa Kemal returned to Ankara, the government issued a decree closing down all dervish lodges, restricting the wearing of turbans and robes to Islamic officials, and regulating the dress of civil servants for whom hats became compulsory. A month later, another decree stipulated that tails and top hats should be worn on ceremonial occasions. Opening the new session of parliament on 1 November, Mustafa Kemal declared that 'the nation had taken the final decision to adopt in essence and in form the life and the resources which contemporary civilization grants to all nations.' He warned the press that its abuses would be punished by the 'educative and firm hand of the assembly', adding that the republic would itself create a press inspired by its ideals.[21] A few months later, his general factotum, Mahmut (Soydan), was given the money to publish the newspaper *Milliyet* (Nationality): the regime thus acquired a second mouthpiece in Istanbul, in addition to Yunus Nadi's *Cumhuriyet*. However, the venture was not a success, and the newspaper changed owners, reappearing as *Tan*,[22] which moved gradually to a discreet liberal, and then left-wing posture. As ever, sales depended on criticism.

Mustafa Kemal did not mention hats specifically in his opening speech in the assembly. But when the government's decree was converted into law on 25 November, its terms were widened. 'The hat is the common headgear of the Turkish people,' the law declared, 'and the government forbids habits to the contrary.'[23] When 'Bearded' Nurettin argued that the law violated the constitution, deputies competed in denouncing him as an enemy of the popular will. 'Freedom is not a toy in the hands of reactionaries,' declared the justice minister, Mahmut Esat (Bozkurt), while the representative of the deeply conservative province of Muş, in the Kurdish area, warned, 'The revolution is a torrent which sweeps aside those who resist it.'[24] It was the last significant debate in the assembly, whose function was henceforth restricted to rubber-stamping decisions reached by the Republican People's Party at the government's behest.

As usual, while senior clerics kept a prudent silence, some provincial *hocas* came out in open protest, and the Ankara Independence Tribunal was sent out to deal with them. There was a riot in Erzurum, where the government declared martial law. Another trouble spot was Rize near the Soviet border, where the people saw themselves as the frontiersmen of Islam. Courts charged prisoners with rebellion rather than with violation of the new hat law, and the tribunal took care to implicate the dissolved Progressive Republican Party, whenever possible. The Ankara Independence Tribunal pronounced 138 death sentences, between March 1925 and March 1926. Of that total, twenty or so can be attributed directly to the hat riots. Their suppression served also to eliminate opposition to the regime among provincial notables. The worst case of judicial terror concerned one Atıf Hoca, who was hanged for publishing a tract long before the hat law was passed, denouncing 'imitation of the Franks'.[25]

Mustafa Kemal had argued that fezes and turbans had put money in foreigners' pockets. But, as Turkey had no factories to produce European hats, foreign – mainly Italian – manufacturers made a killing. Foreign observers had a field day giggling as they noticed some Turks wearing hats back to front, or, on occasion, men donning ladies' hats as they hastened to obey the new law. Many men found an acceptable way out, choosing to wear berets, which did not interfere with their prostrations, instead of rimmed hats. Many more bought peaked cloth caps, which could be turned back to front – like modern 'IQ-shrinker' baseball caps – during prayers. The prevalence of cloth caps gave Istanbul a proletarian appearance. Red fezes had been a symbol of the gorgeous East; the new look struck European observers as universally grey. A law requiring that public employees should wear suits of locally made cloth, which was also to be used for all uniforms,[26] depressed the standards of dress, as the Turkish textile industry was not yet capable of producing quality materials. Schoolboys wore peaked caps, as in Germany, with ribbons in school colours. Black pinafores became compulsory for primary schoolchildren, boys and girls. The republic reinforced habits of discipline in Turkish society.

The avalanche of secularizing laws went on. On 30 November, all dervish lodges, shrines and mausolea, including the tombs of sultans, were closed and their staff dismissed.[27] On 26 December 1925, the assembly adopted the international Christian era, and the twenty-four hour clock. This replaced the Muslim solar calendar, which had been used for administrative purposes, and the system of numbering hours from sunset, which regulated the times of the five canonical daily prayers. Thus, 1 January 1342 (Muslim solar Gregorian, corresponding to 19 December 1341, Muslim solar Julian, or 16 Jumada II, 1344, in the religious Muslim lunar calendar) became 1 January 1926. But as birth certificates were not changed, one can still come across elderly Turks who say 'I was born in 1340'. The Young Turks had changed the administrative calendar from Julian to Gregorian, but they did not dare date the year from Christ's birth, instead of the date of Muhammad's flight from Mecca to Medina. Mustafa Kemal had no such scruples.

On 17 February 1926, the assembly adopted a new civil code of personal status. It was based on Swiss law, and gave women new rights. It ended divorce at the husband's discretion – the Muslim rule from which Mustafa Kemal had benefited six months previously. Women acquired equal inheritance rights, where, under Muslim law, a woman's share was half that of a man. But, as in many European countries at the time, men retained a privileged position as heads of household: women could not take outside work or travel abroad without the permission of the *chef de famille*. Nevertheless, the adoption of the civil code was the most important step in the emancipation of Turkish women. In towns, practice followed the law. There were already women teachers, but only in girls' schools, and during the Great War women had been employed in hospitals and, more than ever, in workshops. As a result of Atatürk's reforms, women teachers became ubiquitous in mixed primary and 'middle' schools (for 12- to 15-year-olds), and began to make careers in law, medicine and public services.

Atatürk, who encouraged the process from the start, deserves his fame as the hero of women's emancipation in Turkey, even though social change was, inevitably, gradual and limited. In the countryside life went on much as before. The law did not recognize religious or polygamous marriages, but rural society did. There were also disadvantages. Muslim canon law stipulated the sum of money settled on a woman on marriage (the bride-price), and the sum which had to be paid to a divorced woman – safeguards absent from European law. Traditionalists denounced change as an invitation to immorality. In fact, emancipated Turkish women moved in a strait-laced society; there were no flappers in interbellic republican Turkey. For Atatürk, religion was a matter of personal choice, but, as he was to say later, 'morals are sacred.'[28]

On 1 March 1926 a new penal code was introduced. It was adapted from Italian law, and its provision banning Marxist activity was attributed by critics to Mussolini's practice. But it retained the death penalty, which Italy had discarded. Judges had to be trained to apply the new laws. Although Istanbul University had a law faculty, Mustafa Kemal decided it was insufficient and founded a law school in the capital. Inaugurated by the president on 5 November 1925, it became the nucleus of Ankara University.

Mustafa Kemal had by then returned from another provincial tour. Everywhere he carried the same message. As he told an audience in Akhisar in western Anatolia on 10 October: 'The civilized world is far ahead of us. We have no choice but to catch up. It is time to stop nonsense, such as "should we or should we not wear hats?" We shall adopt hats along with all other works of Western civilization. Uncivilized people are doomed to be trodden under the feet of civilized people.'[29] Mustafa Kemal was not romantic about modern civilization: he saw it as the prerequisite of his country's survival.

It was to be Mustafa Kemal's last major speaking tour. It also gave him an opportunity to rearrange his domestic life. In Bursa, where he arrived on 22 September,[30] he was approached by a young girl, called Sabiha, who asked for help in her schooling.[31] Sabiha was an orphan, and Mustafa Kemal decided to adopt her. At roughly the same time, he adopted two slightly older girls, Zehra and Rukiye. There was soon to be a significant addition to their number. In İzmir, which he visited in October 1925, he was impressed by the looks and polite manners of a young fair-haired woman teacher. Her name was Afet, and she was 18 years old.[32] Mustafa Kemal introduced her to his friend, the 2nd Army inspector Fahrettin (Altay), saying:

> Her family was so close to ours in Salonica, they were almost like relatives. I was happy to meet her here. Her mother is dead and her father has married a young bride. She became a teacher to make a living. She is very keen on education, but lacks the means to pursue her studies. So she has accepted to become my daughter. She will come to Ankara where she will continue to teach, and, at the same time, I shall make it possible for her to continue her education.

General Fahrettin noted in his memoirs, 'We were all pleased that Atatürk had found a friend to dispel his sadness, as we were afraid that his nerves would give way. This lady rendered a great service to the country by preventing a nervous crisis.'[33] Afet, who was later given by Atatürk the surname İnan (meaning 'Believe!'),[34] became Mustafa Kemal's lifelong favourite woman companion. She was content to serve as his amanuensis, working to his dictation, amplifying his theories, and falling in with all his views. Everyone agreed that she knew how to manage Mustafa Kemal: she was there when he needed her, but left him free to pursue his irregular life. It was not until 1937 that Afet went to Europe to study for a doctorate in Geneva.[35] After Atatürk's death she was appointed professor of the history of civilization at Ankara University. Her published reminiscences reflect the picture which Atatürk wanted to present of himself. She married, had two children, and died in the 1980s.

It was deemed meritorious in Turkish society for rich people to adopt and bring up poor children, especially, although not necessarily, orphans. Mustafa Kemal had earlier adopted a boy, whose presence in the household was hardly noticed. But the adoption of young girls by a divorced man was bound to cause gossip. To train his new charges in European manners, Mustafa Kemal employed a Swiss woman, Madame Bauer, who joined the staff in Çankaya.[36] General Fahrettin, who was a house guest in Çankaya at the end of October 1926, described an evening spent in the presidential palace: 'The drawing room was crowded. Atatürk's daughters, in silk dresses of various colours, surrounded him like a circle of flowers. Madame Bauer was very smart, made up and wearing a black décolleté dress. Afet's black silk evening dress, embroidered in silver-gilt, suited her well.'

After dinner Madame Bauer danced with Mustafa Kemal, confiding to Fahrettin that her purpose was to stop him drinking. There were waltzes, and then Atatürk performed solo the Turkish *zeybek* male dance. Afet stayed on, looking tired, after the young girls had been sent to bed. 'She is a good girl,' Mustafa Kemal said in French, 'and she will be better still. I'll give her an excellent upbringing. She's finding this behaviour of mine hard to take, but she'll get used to it. I want my friends to see me as I really am.' Then, changing to Turkish, he went on, 'Madame [Bauer] complains I've drunk too much. But all I've had is a couple of *rakıs* and a glass or two of champagne.' The party was then entertained by a handsome young waiter dancing in drag. Mustafa Kemal joined Afet on a settee, saying to all and sundry, 'My daughter Afet loves me very much, but she also wants to study. Sometimes my behaviour makes her sad. She's right. I love her too. I shall give her the best education and make her learn languages. She'll become the great lady of the future. The little ones are my pearls. I want my guests to have a good time, rather than myself.' Afet replied tactfully, 'Paşa, don't be upset, next to my deep respect and love for you, my greatest pleasure is reading. You're giving me this opportunity and I'm very grateful to you.' The party broke up at three in the morning.

Another evening, the presidential dinner party was entertained by a plump woman in her thirties, performing Indian dances, 'almost naked', as General Fahrettin noted, adding, 'Purple marks on her thighs suggested that she was a morphine addict.' Mustafa Kemal danced with Afet, 'very smart in a pink silk décolleté gown'. He then suggested that his prime minister İsmet should dance with the artiste. İsmet declined politely. One guest proposed that the artiste should strip off her scanty clothes. 'No,' said Mustafa Kemal, 'there are limits.' Conversation suddenly turned to education, as Mustafa Kemal told İsmet, 'You must improve education, starting right at the beginning.' İsmet asked leave to go, as he had a busy day before him. It was two in the morning.[37]

The following day was 29 October, the third anniversary of the proclamation of the republic, and a ball was organized in Fresco's restaurant. Madame Bauer was there escorting Mustafa Kemal's adopted daughters. So was the Indian dancer, whose performance, General Fahrettin noted, 'was a novelty for Ankara'. Mustafa Kemal opened the ball, dancing with the pretty daughter of the French ambassador Albert Sarraut. After drinking champagne with a group of young Turkish officers, he returned to the ambassador's daughter and dragged her off to dance again, kissing her as he did so.[38] As soon as his back was turned, the French ambassador escaped with his daughter, without taking his leave. At four in the morning, Mustafa Kemal passed out in his car, which took him and General Fahrettin back to Çankaya. 'It was the first time,' noted the general, 'that I had seen him a little the worse for drink. It was the officers' fault.'[39]

The French ambassador was not amused but, as İsmet reported two days later, he accepted the explanation that the president's behaviour towards his daughter was not ill-intentioned, but was inspired by his appreciation of her beauty.[40] Naturally, rumours began to spread that no woman was safe from the president's attentions, and that place-seekers offered their wives to him. But Mustafa Kemal's fun with the ladies appears to have been confined to parties from which he returned the worse for wear. As for his adopted daughters, Mustafa Kemal had a black eunuch to serve them.[41] Old habits died hard.

23

Measured Terror

MUSTAFA KEMAL STAYED in Ankara between November 1925 and May 1926. It was a busy time. Society was being refashioned by a stream of legislation emerging from a compliant parliament. At the same time the new Turkish republic was regularizing its relations with neighbouring states. The commission which the League of Nations set up to look into the Mosul dispute recommended that the province should go to Iraq, provided that it remained under British mandate for twenty-five years and that the wishes of local Kurds were respected. In September 1925 Britain accepted these conditions.[1] In December the Council of the League decided that the award was binding.[2]

Turkey tried to resist it nevertheless, and negotiated treaties with its other neighbours in the hope of isolating Britain. On 17 December there was a new treaty of friendship and neutrality with the Soviet Union; on 22 April 1926 a treaty with Iran; on 30 May a convention with France, regulating relations with Syria and Lebanon, which were under French mandate.[3] But these did not affect the essentials of the Mosul dispute: British troops remained in occupation, and Mustafa Kemal was unwilling to risk war to dislodge them. Negotiations resumed in Ankara between İsmet's foreign minister Tevfik Rüştü (Aras), an old associate of Mustafa Kemal, and the British ambassador Sir Ronald Lindsay. Finally, on 5 June 1926, the dispute was settled by a tripartite treaty. The new kingdom of Iraq was the third party, and by ceding Mosul to it rather than to Britain, nationalist Turkey could be said to have saved face.

The official frontier between Turkey and Iraq was based on the Brussels line, which had separated areas under British and Turkish

control. Turkey, starved as it was of resources to cover current expend-
iture, converted its 10 per cent share in the oilfields into a lump sum of
£500,000. But to save face once again, the payment was mentioned only
in the protocol annexed to the treaty.[4] The British government later
wriggled out of the conditions in the League's award: the mandate over
Iraq was terminated in 1932, and the wish of the Kurds to escape Arab
rule was disregarded. However, the treaties with the Soviet Union,
Britain, France and Iran gave Turkey secure frontiers during the forma-
tive years of the republic, and denied Turkish Kurds the prospect of
foreign intervention.

The concessions which Mustafa Kemal had accepted as the cost of
good relations with Britain could have been exploited by the domestic
political opposition, but organized opposition had been suppressed the
previous year. Individual opposition politicians were, however, still at
large. But their options were stark: participation in the Kemalist regime,
withdrawal from politics or conspiracy. On 22 October 1925, Mustafa
Kemal agreed to receive Kâzım Karabekir and Ali Fuat, the leaders of
the dissolved Progressive Republican Party.[5] The meeting was fruitless.
The two generals had accepted Mustafa Kemal's cultural revolution, but
they continued to plead for a democratic government. They could not
shake Mustafa Kemal's determination to be his country's unquestioned
ruler. İsmet shared his leader's conviction. Government, he believed,
was like command in war: objections could be heard only before a plan
of operations was decided. Thereafter, decisions should be obeyed. A
political struggle could be allowed only if the country were sufficiently
civilized and politicians mature.[6] This was not yet the case.

In August 1925, Rauf, one of Mustafa Kemal's four original companions, asked the assembly's permission to go abroad for medical treatment;[7] unfortunately, he did not leave at once. At the end of the year,
Ziya Hurşit, the impassioned orator of the Second Group, arrived in
Ankara.[8] He had been a consistent opponent of Mustafa Kemal's rise to
absolute power. In 1921, when members of the assembly had rushed
out of the parliament building to welcome Mustafa Kemal after the
battle of Sakarya, he stayed behind and scrawled on the blackboard the
sentence, 'A nation creates its own idol and then worships it.'[9] He had
been a friend of the opposition MP, Ali Şükrü, murdered by Mustafa
Kemal's Laz bodyguards, and after demanding justice in the assembly,
had taken the body for burial in Trabzon.[10] He had been furious at
being excluded from the assembly in the 1923 elections in favour of his
brother Faik (Günday).[11]

Ziya Hurşit arrived in Ankara, accompanied by a professional criminal, İsmail, known as 'the Laz'. He met an opposition politician, Ahmet

Şükrü, once a prominent member of the CUP, and then a member of the Progressive Republicans in parliament; he appears also to have visited Mustafa Kemal's estranged friend, Arif the 'Bear-keeper', again a member of the dissolved party, who, like other members, retained his seat in parliament as an independent.[12] One morning, yet another opposition MP, Sabit, went to see Rauf and reported that the previous night Ahmet Şükrü had confided in his cups that he had discussed with Ziya Hurşit a plot to assassinate Mustafa Kemal. Hurşit's brother, Faik, was also an opposition MP, and Rauf appealed to him to stop the plotting. Approached by his brother, Hurşit denied all knowledge of the plot and returned to Istanbul. The leadership of the dissolved Progressive Party was disturbed, fearing that they would all be compromised, but did not report the rumours to the authorities. However, it seems that Sabit did so.[13] Soon afterwards, Rauf went abroad. Another opposition MP, Adnan (Adıvar), and his wife, the writer Halide Edip, had already left the country. Yet another MP and former minister, Rıza Nur, who had assisted İsmet at Lausanne, went abroad a little later, fearing for his life.[14] At the beginning of 1926, General Fahrettin (Altay) received instructions that military training exercises were being suspended; he deduced that there was political trouble afoot. However, a little later the order was rescinded.[15]

In May, Mustafa Kemal set out on another provincial tour. First he went south to Mersin, where the sultan's yacht *Ertuğrul*, now available for his use, had been sent to await him and take him to İzmir. But he changed his plans, and went by train to Konya and then on to Bursa, where he arrived on 31 May. In the meantime, Ziya Hurşit had returned to Istanbul, where he conferred with Ahmet Şükrü and the key figure in the plot, Abdülkadir, a CUP militant who had been governor of Ankara during the War of Independence. When they heard that Mustafa Kemal had arrived in Bursa, they sent İsmail the Laz to see whether the assassination could be staged there. A few days later, İsmail reported that, in the absence of a local contact, an attack on the president would be suicidal. The three conspirators – Ziya Hurşit, Abdülkadir and Şükrü – then decided to kill Mustafa Kemal at his next destination, İzmir, where Şükrü had a contact, Edip, known as *Sarı Efe* (the Yellow Brave). Şükrü had worked with him in covert CUP operations in Serez (Serres), in eastern Macedonia, before the Great War; so too had the assembly speaker, General Kâzım (Özalp), who says in his memoirs that he was considering helping the Yellow Brave as a reward for his services to the nationalist cause during the War of Independence, and that he had discussed the matter with Mustafa Kemal.[16] This suggests that Edip, like other irregular fighters, had found it difficult to make a successful

transition to peacetime farming and that he had applied to the government for help. It was slow in coming, and he expressed his anger by
joining the conspiracy.

Ziya Hurşit travelled by boat to İzmir, accompanied by İsmail and
another hitman, Yusuf the Georgian. He had brought with him four
handguns. The Yellow Brave agreed to cooperate and recruited a third
desperado, Pock-marked Hilmi, and a boatman, Şevki, a refugee from
Crete, who was to take the conspirators to the Greek island of Chios
after the deed was done. They first planned to make the attempt along
the road from İzmir to Çeşme, the small town opposite Chios, where a
mansion was being prepared for Mustafa Kemal. But when they heard
that 500 gendarmes had been sent to Çeşme, they decided to kill the
president in the centre of İzmir, near the hotel where Ziya Hurşit had
put up. The main road was narrow at that point and the president's car
would have to slow down. Hilmi was to open fire with a handgun, while
the others would follow suit with guns and grenades which the Yellow
Brave had obtained. Having helped the conspirators, Edip, the Yellow
Brave, left İzmir by boat for Istanbul on 15 June in the company of
another opposition MP, Abidin. Ziya Hurşit was to state later that he
had met Abidin in İzmir, but that he did not know whether the latter
was privy to the conspiracy.

On 14 June, Mustafa Kemal arrived by train in Balıkesir on his way
from Bursa to İzmir. He decided to break his journey there, although he
was expected in İzmir the following day. Towards eleven o'clock at
night on 15 June, the Cretan boatman Şevki informed the police that he
knew of a conspiracy to murder the president.[17] It seems he had decided
to denounce it when he learned that Edip, the Yellow Brave, who had
recruited him, had left for Istanbul. This may have led him to believe
that the plot was about to be uncovered. The governor of İzmir,
General Kâzım (Dirik), a member of the staff which Mustafa Kemal
had taken with him to Anatolia in May 1919, swung into action. Ziya
Hurşit, and the three hitmen – İsmail the Laz, Yusuf the Georgian, and
Pock-marked Hilmi – were arrested in the middle of the night.
Handguns and grenades were found in Ziya Hurşit's hotel room.

Mustafa Kemal arrived in İzmir the following day, 16 June. Ziya
Hurşit, who had already been questioned by a prosecutor, was taken to
the president. He admitted the conspiracy and described how his
brother Faik had earlier stopped him making an attempt on Mustafa
Kemal's life in Ankara. Earlier in the day, Mustafa Kemal had sent a tele-
gram to İsmet asking him to despatch the Ankara Independence
Tribunal to İzmir, but to stay in Ankara himself.[18] As the governor of
İzmir informed İsmet on the same day, only four people had been

arrested – Ziya Hurşit and the three hitmen. But before leaving Ankara by special train on 17 June, and therefore before hearing any of the evidence,[19] the Independence Tribunal ordered that all the members of parliament of the dissolved Progressive Republican Party should be arrested and their houses searched.[20] This suggests that the decision had been taken by Mustafa Kemal as soon as he had heard of the plot, if not earlier.

The loose cannons of the CUP had worried Mustafa Kemal ever since the beginning of the War of Independence. Most had cooperated with him against the foreign enemy. Some, like Bald Ali and Kılıç Ali, had transferred their allegiance from Enver to Mustafa Kemal. They indulged their propensity to violence as they carried out his commands or interpreted his will. Mustafa Kemal enjoyed their rough companionship and was open to their influence. But some CUP desperadoes and veterans of ethnic cleansing would not be tamed; they remained loyal to the surviving old leaders of the CUP. Others wanted more riches, influence or, simply, adventure than the Kemalist regime was prepared to allow them. Mustafa Kemal suspected them of conspiring with his political opponents, even respectable ones. The desperadoes who had joined him could be relied upon to fan these suspicions. Mustafa Kemal allowed them to dominate the Independence Tribunal. The tribunal was chaired by Bald Ali (Çetinkaya). He was seconded by Kılıç Ali, another veteran of irregular warfare. A third Ali, Necip Ali (Küçüka), had some legal training and was chosen as prosecutor. The fourth member was an ambitious nationalist doctor, Reşit Galip, who had impressed Mustafa Kemal by his flowery flattery[21] and was made a member of the assembly in 1923.[22]

İsmet did his best to narrow the target of Mustafa Kemal's suspicions, which the three Alis had widened beyond the bounds of reason or prudence. He was shocked to hear that the Progressives' leader, Kâzım Karabekir, had been arrested and, having discussed the matter in cabinet, ordered his release.[23] The arrest of the opposition MPs had, in any case, violated the constitution, as parliament had not lifted their immunity. The speaker of parliament, Mustafa Kemal's friend General Kâzım (Özalp), later argued that immunity could not be claimed when MPs were caught red-handed engaged in crime. The argument was absurd since the MPs were nowhere near the scene of the crime.

The Independence Tribunal arrived in İzmir on 18 June. The first official announcement of the failed plot appeared the same day.[24] The following day the press published a statement in which Mustafa Kemal expressed his gratitude for the messages of support which, he said, had reached him from all classes of the population. He went on, 'My humble body will surely turn to dust one day, but the Turkish republic will live on for ever.'[25] The rhetoric concealed Mustafa Kemal's concern; as İsmet was to say in his memoirs, the safety of his republic and of his person preoccupied Mustafa Kemal constantly.[26] Mustafa Kemal summoned İsmet to İzmir as soon as he heard that he had ordered Karabekir's release. In his memoirs İsmet denies the story that the Independence Tribunal had ordered his arrest for countermanding its orders,[27] but there is no doubt that Mustafa Kemal made him apologize to the tribunal. Karabekir was re-arrested and brought to İzmir together with twenty-six other members of the Progressive Party, five of them generals on the army's payroll. When some of the arrested MPs, including Mustafa Kemal's former companion Ali Fuat (Cebesoy), arrived by boat in İzmir, they were kept aboard until nightfall.[28] The authorities clearly feared that they might be met with demonstrations of sympathy.

The Independence Tribunal targeted two overlapping groups: the parliamentary members of the dissolved Progressive Republican Party and those members of the CUP who had not sided with Mustafa Kemal or had broken with him after the War of Independence. Among the latter there were formidable professional plotters, none more so than Kara Kemal (Black Kemal), the organizer of Muslim tradesmen in Istanbul. Early in 1923, in the interval between the first and second phases of the Lausanne conference, Mustafa Kemal had met Kara Kemal in İzmit; he had decided to hold elections and wanted to know the intentions of surviving CUP members in Istanbul, which was then still under Allied occupation. Kara Kemal promised to canvass the views of his friends.

On 8 April 1923, Mustafa Kemal published his party's nine principles as an election manifesto. This seems to have concentrated the minds of CUP leaders in Istanbul, who held a meeting in the flat of Cavit, minister of finance in CUP governments before, and then at the end of, the Great War. The meeting produced its own nine principles, one of which was that Istanbul should remain the capital of Turkey. However, the document was never published, as participants in the meeting decided to offer their support to Mustafa Kemal, generally, and otherwise act individually. On 14 April 1923, Mustafa Kemal put out a statement in response to reports that the CUP had offered its cooperation; the CUP, he declared, of which 'most of us' had been founders and members, no longer existed, and its entire membership as well as that of its successor (the short-lived Renewal Party) had joined his Society for the Defence of National Rights in Anatolia and Rumelia and accepted its programme.[29] It was an exaggeration, although many former CUP members did stand as candidates of the new People's Party in the 1923 elections.

The Independence Tribunal claimed that the meeting in Cavit's house was the starting point of the plot which, three years later, culminated in the attempt on the president's life. Cavit, it argued, was at the head of a secret committee which sought first to penetrate the People's Party, then, when this failed, set up the Progressive Republican Party, and finally organized the assassination attempt in İzmir. This could have been said of Ahmet Şükrü, but the allegation was manifestly false with regard to most participants in the meeting in Cavit's house. Some of them, including Cavit, had quit politics; most of them confined their political activity to ineffectual criticism and indiscreet denunciations of the regime in private gatherings. But the Independence Tribunal did not require hard proof; its 'considered opinion' was sufficient, and its opinion rested on guilt by association: Ziya Hurşit had stayed in the Progressives' club in Ankara; the Progressive leaders had heard of the plot or a plot; they had links with discontented former members of the CUP; they were all critics of the regime and, sometimes explicitly, of Mustafa Kemal. So they were all guilty.

The trial opened in İzmir on 26 June 1926 in the Alhambra cinema (which later became a branch of the National Library). The prisoners were accused of conspiracy to overthrow the government, a charge which carried the death penalty. Ziya Hurşit was questioned first. He repeated his confession, and did not implicate any politicians other than Ahmet Şükrü and Abdülkadir. The latter and Kara Kemal were not in the dock: they had gone into hiding as soon as the arrests were ordered. The prosecutor tried to implicate the arrested generals, reminding Ziya Hurşit that his trip to Ankara to organize the assassination coincided with the publication of rumours during the hat riots in Rize that both Mustafa Kemal and İsmet had been shot and that 'pious generals had taken over power'.[30]

Edip, the Yellow Brave, gave more satisfaction to the tribunal. Asked where Ahmet Şükrü had found the money for the plot, he replied, 'I believe he was in touch with Kara Kemal, who was, in turn, in touch with the Second Group and the Progressives. Cavit helped with money.'[31] However, he did not produce any evidence for his belief. It later transpired that Cavit's wealth consisted of a life insurance policy for £1,000.[32] Both Karabekir and Ali Fuat were to say that Edip had been used by the government as an *agent provocateur*.[33] 'My services have not been taken into account,' Edip shouted when he was sentenced to death.[34] The words, however, probably referred to his willingness to implicate opposition politicians, rather than to the organization of the plot itself. Mustafa Kemal's shock at its discovery seems genuine.

Mustafa Kemal did not attend the trial. Making an effort to appear unconcerned he went to a tennis match, then a football game in İzmir.[35] On 29 June, the chief of the general staff, General Fevzi (Çakmak), arrived in İzmir.[36] The attitude of the army to the trial of some of its most famous commanders was crucial. Their interrogation began on 3 July. Karabekir took up the challenge. 'When we all joined forces in sad circumstances at the end of the Great War and brought the Gazi to the leadership,' he declared, 'mine was the only force on which he could rely. But, as in all revolutions, those who begin by working together see their unity destroyed by parasites who come up once the original aim is reached.'[37] Furious that Karabekir had been allowed to speak out, Mustafa Kemal summoned the tribunal to Çeşme. For the sake of appearances, the summons was presented as an invitation to a ball. But the judges did not stay to dance: after hearing Mustafa Kemal's comments, they slipped out through a French window and returned to İzmir.[38] Mustafa Kemal had decided that in the circumstances he had to spare the accused generals, but he wanted it to be known that it was his intervention that had saved them from the judges' severity.

After despatching the judges, he called in İsmet and General Fahrettin (Altay) and said: 'Ali (Çetinkaya) will hang our generals along with the others.' Fahrettin replied tactfully: 'You think and act better than any of us. You must have already reached a merciful decision.' 'Fine,' said Mustafa Kemal, 'but can we be confident of the consequences?' It was İsmet's turn to work on Mustafa Kemal. 'Pasha,' he said, 'you can be sure that as long as you are alive, your government will always be strong. The whole nation worships you. Ingratitude is confined only to a few deviants. If punishment is limited to them, your justice will increase the nation's loyalty to you.' 'All right, let us speak to Ali again,' Mustafa Kemal concluded. On 9 July, Mustafa Kemal left İzmir by train for Ankara. On the way he read a romantic novel entitled *The Chatelaine of Mount Lebanon*.[39]

Two days later the prosecutor Necip Ali asked for thirteen death sentences and eight sentences of imprisonment, for the retrial of some former CUP politicians in Ankara, and for the acquittal of the rest, including Mustafa Kemal's military companions in the War of Independence – Generals Karabekir, Ali Fuat, Refet and Cafer Tayyar. The defendants then made their last statements. Ziya Hurşit argued that since he had made arrangements to escape to Greece, he could not be convicted of trying to overthrow the government, but only of attempted assassination, which was punishable by imprisonment: it made no difference. On 12 July, the tribunal announced its final verdict. It had increased the number of death sentences to fifteen, adding to the list two opposition deputies (Halis Turgut and İsmail Canbulat), who had objected to the prosecution's demand that they should be sentenced to prison. At dawn on 13 July, thirteen of the condemned men were hanged at prominent points in İzmir. They included Mustafa Kemal's former friend, 'Bear-keeper' Arif; his letter to Mustafa Kemal, pleading for mercy, was not delivered until after the execution.[40] Ziya Hurşit went bravely to his death. Most of the others protested their innocence to the last. A price was put on the head of the two fugitives. Kara Kemal committed suicide when he was found hiding in a chicken coop. Abdülkadir was caught as he tried to escape to Bulgaria and was hanged in Ankara.

When the acquitted commanders made their way on foot from the improvised courthouse, they were surrounded by a crowd shouting, 'Praise be to Allah who has spared our Pashas.' Turning to Karabekir, Ali Fuat said: 'Now we have been acquitted properly.'[41] Eight months later, Ali Fuat returned to the Gazi's favour. He was invited, incongruously together with the president of the Independence Tribunal, to the president's table. 'It was for your sake that I secured a pardon for all the Pashas,' Mustafa Pasha declared in the hearing of the whole party.[42] Mustafa Kemal was fond of Ali Fuat; what is more he did not fear him. Lapsing into French, he is said to have described him as *'simple soldat'*. This did not prevent his election as a deputy in 1933 and a subsequent appointment as minister of public works. Refet's rehabilitation took longer, but he too became a member of the assembly in 1935. Rauf and Karabekir never made their peace with Mustafa Kemal.

With the exception of Ziya Hurşit, his henchmen, and two politicians – Ahmet Şükrü and Abdülkadir – the judges had failed to prove that the men they sent to the gallows bore any responsibility for the attempted assassination in İzmir. But most of the accused stood to profit by Mustafa Kemal's death, and many wished it. This was enough. It was a political, but not a show trial, as the accused were allowed to defend themselves. Mustafa Kemal had decided to impose a measured dose of terror: of the twenty-seven accused members of parliament of the dissolved Progressive Republican Party, six were hanged, the others went free.

Bad as the İzmir trial was, its sequel in Ankara was worse. It opened on 2 August and became known as the trial of the Unionists. The government press preferred to call them 'the Black Band' (*Kara Çete*), a word play on the surnames Kara Kemal (Black Kemal) – the Unionist who had committed suicide after the İzmir verdict; Kara Vasıf (Black

Vasıf), the CUP militant who collaborated with Mustafa Kemal in the War of Independence, and Karabekir (Black Bekir), the acquitted general. The title of the secret nationalist organization *Karakol* (The Sentry, literally the Black Arm),[43] set up by the CUP in Istanbul at the end of the Great War, had also been a pun on these names.[44] There were forty-six defendants, three of them absent in Europe – Rauf, Adnan and Rahmi, the wartime governor of İzmir. The prosecutor, Necip Ali, produced no evidence linking them to the assassination attempt in İzmir; instead, he dwelt on the irresponsible behaviour of the Unionists in entering the Great War, and the corruption of the rulers and the sufferings of the population during its course.

Cavit was the key figure in the indictment, since he was described as the head of the secret committee responsible for the assassination attempt. He had no difficulty in rebutting charges of war guilt, as he had resigned in protest at the unorthodox way in which Enver had dragged the Ottoman empire into the war. He had no private fortune and was known as an honest man. The meeting of Unionists in his flat in 1923 was concerned with the elections held that year. Thereafter, he had devoted himself to his family and his work as representative of Ottoman bondholders in the Public Debt Administration. But since he had continued to meet Mustafa Kemal's opponents, including Kara Kemal and Ahmet Şükrü, the regime had decided he was dangerous: his eloquent defence was disregarded.

On 26 August the tribunal announced its verdicts. Four leading Unionists, Cavit, Dr Nazım, Hilmi (an opposition MP) and Nail, were sentenced to death. Five defendants, including two refugees in Europe – Rauf and Rahmi – were condemned to ten years in prison for incitement to murder. Rauf responded with a long angry letter to the assembly speaker, Kâzım (Özalp), describing the tribunal as a nest of bandits, and challenging parliament to do its duty and safeguard the nation's liberties.[45] He stayed abroad until 1935, returning finally after an amnesty had been proclaimed. Thirty-seven defendants were acquitted, among them Adnan (Adıvar), who preferred to stay abroad, and the journalist, Hüseyin Cahit, who had been brought from exile in Çorum to face new charges. Journalists were frequently threatened under Mustafa Kemal's rule; but, though often silenced, they survived. The intellectual's pen conferred a modicum of immunity.

The four condemned men were not in court when the sentences were read, learning their fate only when they were taken from their cells in the middle of the night. After they were hanged, the bodies were buried in unmarked graves in the prison yard. It was judicial murder. Three of the four – Dr Nazım, Hilmi and Nail – had been revolutionaries who had, in their time, sanctioned the use of violence. Rıza Nur remarked acidly: 'Most of the hanged men had earlier been guilty of massacres and other crimes. But they were hanged for a crime they did not commit.'[46] Cavit was in a different category. He was a rational middle-class politician who had set his face against violence; he had been taken from his wife, whose first husband was an imperial prince, and from his baby son, dragged to prison from his summer house in the Princes Islands, and executed after a travesty of a trial. In his memoirs, İsmet gave a characteristically pragmatic explanation: 'When one becomes a leader of a political organization, one assumes an unlimited responsibility. Cavit's fate represents the worst possibility implicit in the nature of politics.'[47] But Cavit was a leader only in the sense that he had hosted a legal political gathering, three years before his execution. The Kemalist writer, Falih Rıfkı, is more candid in his account:

> Cavit was not a revolutionary terrorist, he was a civilized man. Starting with the Lausanne conference [where he had been adviser to the Turkish delegation], he moved to the opposition because he believed that without the help of the European great powers and without corresponding concessions to them, we were incapable all by ourselves of establishing a viable state in the middle of Anatolia. Mustafa Kemal and İsmet were, after all, soldiers, just like Enver. The government in Ankara was bound to become an arbitrary military dictatorship, for which the republic would serve as a mask. Cavit was an Ottoman who could not tear himself away from the world of business and finance, who considered nationalism as an all-round narrowing down of life, and who was temperamentally unsuited to revolution. He was patriotic and honest. His only defect was arrogance.[48]

Cavit was killed because he was capable of appealing for foreign support for an alternative, gradualist strategy of development. Like most other nationalists, Mustafa Kemal was afraid of foreign interference. Cavit was a freemason – a member of a secret society with strong foreign links. He had connections with French financial circles, and both the French government and the house of Rothschild appealed to Ankara on his behalf.[49] The fact that he came from a Salonica *dönme* family, and was called 'Jew Cavit' by his enemies, did not endear him to backwoodsmen among Mustafa Kemal's supporters. But Mustafa Kemal was free of anti-Semitic prejudice. 'Some people imply I am a Jew, because I was born in Salonica,' he said one day to his childhood friend Nuri (Conker). 'But one must not forget that Napoleon was an Italian from Corsica. Yet he died a Frenchman and has passed into history as a Frenchman. People must serve the society in which they find themselves.'[50]

Mustafa Kemal is said to have been saddened by Cavit's fate,[51] although he could have averted it, as he had prevented a similar fate being visited on the four generals who had worked with him in the War of Independence. After the verdict, Mustafa Kemal told his secretary Hasan Rıza (Soyak) that he had intended to intervene on behalf of the defendants, but gave up the idea when Rauf, Ahmet Şükrü and others claimed that the assassination attempt had been staged by the regime in order to liquidate the opposition – an accusation which was taken up abroad. 'In the circumstances,' Mustafa Kemal went on, 'my intervention would have been construed as a confirmation of these claims. So I had no choice but to change my mind and let things take their natural course. But I did not hand over the commanders.'[52]

The authorities had probably expected a plot by the Unionists, whose renewed activity had been noticed by both foreign and domestic observers,[53] but their failure to stop Ziya Hurşit in his tracks appears to have stemmed from inefficiency rather than complicity. However, there is no doubt that the assassination attempt was used as a pretext to liquidate the opposition. Regretting that the authority of the new regime came to be based on the gallows erected in İzmir and Ankara, Falih Rıfkı justified it, on the grounds that 'this thorough purge took the wind out of the sails of all opponents and reactionaries and made it possible for Mustafa Kemal to complete the revolution he had started.'[54] The claim that the hangings were the price Turkey had to pay for its rapid modernization has been repeated by many Turkish writers, some of whom note that, in comparison with the French, let alone the Bolshevik, revolution, Atatürk's cultural revolution cost few lives.

However, the victims of the 1926 purges were themselves modernists. Describing Bald Ali's rudeness to Cavit in court, Falih Rıfkı calls it an explosion of hatred by an old, backward Unionist against an old, progressive Unionist, 'a friend of civilization, just like us'.[55] In his unpublished memoirs, Cavit admits that he had no religious beliefs: he was a liberal agnostic, Mustafa Kemal an authoritarian one. He had doubts about his people's capacity for rapid unaided progress, Mustafa Kemal had none. The struggle between the two was about methods rather than aims. But essentially, the purge was a manifestation of the struggle for power which was bound to accompany the birth of a new state. The Turkish people were used to authority; Mustafa Kemal provided it. If he was saddened by the verdict, he did not show it. He spent the evening following the executions in his usual manner, drinking with his friends.[56] The anodyne effects of alcohol did not come amiss that night.

PART V

Unrivalled Ruler

24

The Leader is Always Right

THE ASSASSINATION PLOT strengthened Mustafa Kemal's determination to stamp his personality on the new Turkish state. As early as 1925, the Austrian sculptor Heinrich Krippel was commissioned to work on a victory monument[1] for what was then the central square of Ankara (now Ulus square), at the foot of the citadel hill. It consisted of an equestrian statue of the Gazi in uniform, standing on a six-metre high pedestal, surrounded by smaller statues of two soldiers, a peasant woman, and a relief showing the Gazi instructing İsmet and Fevzi to pursue the enemy.[2] Having prepared his plans, Krippel went to Istanbul to work on another statue. It went up on Seraglio Point (Sarayburnu) in Istanbul on 3 October 1926. Mustafa Kemal was not present at the unveiling, but he sent a telegram to the mayor thanking the citizens for expressing their appreciation by putting up his first statue.[3] Krippel went on to make further statues for Konya and then Samsun. The Ankara victory monument was unveiled in 1927.

In the meantime, another fashionable European sculptor, the Italian Pietro Canonica, who had specialized in busts of European royalty and nobility, arrived in Ankara. Mustafa Kemal posed for him in his villa in Çankaya, which Canonica described in a report to Mussolini as 'a middle-class home [*una casa borghese*], in the best sense of the term'. Mustafa Kemal, Canonica added, was a simple man, but distinguished, 'like our Lombard and Piedmontese soldiers of old'. He had a great heart; he had clearly suffered much; he had been disappointed in love and friendships. Canonica was struck by a portrait on the wall which reminded him of his poor *mamma*. Mustafa Kemal told him it was his mother. 'She was my best friend,' he said. 'Losing her, I lost everything.'

'You know,' he went on, 'I was married, but, it seems, marriage was not made for me. In any case, it is difficult to find a lady capable of grasping the delicacy of her position when her husband has a mission in politics. My wife did not understand this. So we had to part.' 'I have the impression,' concluded Canonica, 'that rumours about his moral conduct are greatly exaggerated.'[4]

Canonica worked hard. He produced an equestrian statue, which stands outside the Ethnographic Museum in Ankara; one of Atatürk, erect in his military uniform, for the main boulevard in the capital; another equestrian statue for İzmir, and, his best-known work, the monument to the republic in Taksim square in Istanbul. On one side, Mustafa Kemal is in civilian clothes, flanked by İsmet and Fevzi, the only companions whose aid he acknowledged; on another, he is in uniform at the head of his soldiers. The Taksim monument was unveiled in 1928. It is now overlooked by a large international hotel, while in 1997 the city's Islamic mayor threatened to build an equally large mosque to hem it in further.

Planned before the purges, these statues became a monument to the new order. They shocked pious Muslims and they confirmed the impression that Mustafa Kemal had become a dictator. For who else would put up statues to himself? They were financed by public subscription, spurred on by a mixture of gratitude, admiration, place-seeking and sycophancy. Sycophancy had a free rein in the assembly. When Mustafa Kemal spoke of the assassination attempt in his speech opening the new session on 1 November 1926, Refik (Koraltan), who, some thirty years later, became one of the founders of the liberal Democrat Party, interjected, 'Oh great genius! These wretches do not belong to the Turkish nation.' 'Even hell will not accept them,' chipped in another member.[5] In the circumstances, Mustafa Kemal was lucky to have at his side İsmet, whom Canonica described to Mussolini as 'a man of singular and elastic intelligence, of exceptional cunning, a profound observer, full of brio, of a happy disposition, animated by the highest ideals, most cultivated, who makes up for the Gazi's shortcomings'.[6]

It was İsmet who, by dint of tactful insistence, persuaded Mustafa Kemal to dissolve the Independence Tribunals. The president announced his decision to Bald Ali, suddenly during a ball held at the Ankara Palace, the new hotel built across the road from the parliament building. The following day, 7 March 1927,[7] the tribunals ceased to exist. The MPs, who had served on them as judges, were rewarded with Benz motor cars.[8] Bald Ali continued to frequent the president's table and served several terms as minister. He held his seat in parliament until his death in 1949, although he was said to have lost his reason, tormented by guilt for having sent Cavit to the gallows.[9] Kılıç Ali too remained a member of the president's set, which official circulars described as 'the usual gentlemen' (*mutat zevat*). The third judge, Reşit Galip, was left without a job for three years. 'I was half-starved,' he noted in his diary.[10] It was an exaggeration, as he continued to receive an MP's salary until his death in 1934. But it shows that in a poor country, such as Turkey was then, politics was a means to a livelihood. Falih Rıfkı (Atay), the chief publicist of the regime, was to complain that membership of the assembly had become a modest salaried position. İsmet had his work cut out keeping at arm's length shady businessmen (known as *affairistes*) and their political contacts in Ankara.[11]

On 2 March 1927, a few days before the Independence Tribunals were abolished, the assembly extended the Maintenance of Order Law.[12] The prime minister, İsmet, explained that the main danger had not been the Şeyh Sait rebellion; it was disorder, which had become rooted in the country. The law would make it possible to carry out with the least pain reforms which had been discussed for centuries.[13] But order also made for a dull assembly. Many members refrained from voting; those who did – usually less than half – backed unanimously, and usually without discussion, the bills presented by the government. On 26 June, the assembly met for the last time before the elections. 'The honour of the session's achievements,' the speaker, General Kâzım (Özalp), declared in his closing speech, 'belongs to our honourable president, the Gazi Mustafa Kemal Paşa, our true guide, who after delivering the country from danger, opened the nation's path to prosperity and happiness.'[14]

On 30 June Mustafa Kemal retired from the armed forces at his own request. So did İsmet and Kâzım (Özalp). The law passed in 1923 had allowed them to remain on the army's payroll until the following elections: the time for these had come. Mustafa Kemal was now entitled to an army pension of 40 lira a month (worth 20 dollars at the time). It was later raised to 150 lira. He did not touch his pension and saved it as an insurance for the future. His salary and allowances as president amounted at the time to some 13,000 lira a month (6,500 dollars), and had to pay for the food, and other expenses, of his staff. Presidential accounts were kept separate from the state budget.[15] Mustafa Kemal lived comfortably; he liked good clothes and he was a generous host. But both he and İsmet took care to abide by the rules of financial accountability. Mustafa Kemal was a careful middle-class ruler, not an irresponsible oriental potentate.

*

The purges restored order, as İsmet had predicted. Mustafa Kemal grew more relaxed. In the interval between the İzmir and the Ankara trials he had already told his secretary Hasan Rıza (Soyak): 'We must not become agitated or suspicious ... we must master our nerves. Otherwise we are done for.'[16] Firmness elicited popular admiration, and Mustafa Kemal was mobbed whenever he showed himself in public. The time had come for him to visit Istanbul, until recently the stronghold of his opponents. However, relaxation for Mustafa Kemal was synonymous with drinking, smoking and tossing back innumerable cups of Turkish coffee. On 22/23 May 1927 he had a second attack of angina. Doctors advised him to cut down on drink and tobacco. He agreed 'with an ironic look on his face'.[17] He kept to the regime for a month, but reverted to his old habits in the excitement of the visit to Istanbul.

On 1 July 1927 he arrived in the old capital aboard the imperial yacht *Ertuğrul*. The city was festooned with bunting, and a large crowd had gathered on the quays. Mustafa Kemal received civic representatives in the ceremonial hall of Dolmabahçe palace. He spoke of his happiness at seeing the city after an absence of eight years, but did not explain why he had not come earlier. His audience understood that controversy, in which many of them had taken part, had to be stilled before the president could stage his triumphal return. 'This palace,' Mustafa Kemal declared, 'belongs no longer to the Shadows of Allah on Earth, but to the nation, which is a fact and not a shadow, and I am happy to be here as an individual member of the nation, as a guest.'[18] He was to be a regular guest.

Mustafa Kemal's first visit as president to Istanbul was marked by a violent incident. The police discovered that a group of Armenians had entered the country and stockpiled arms in a house near the Tokatlian hotel in Beyoğlu (Pera), which the president liked to visit. The house was raided and three members of the group were killed. The authorities announced that the Armenians were preparing to rob the casino which had opened in Abdülhamit's Yıldız palace. Inevitably, there were rumours that Mustafa Kemal and not the casino was the target of the Armenians, who were alleged to be Communists probably financed by Russian Bolsheviks. The fact that Armenian avengers had killed prominent CUP leaders in exile and that Mustafa Kemal had himself been the object of an assassination attempt the previous year lent credibility to the rumours, even though Russian involvement was hard to explain. The interior ministry congratulated the police on 19 September for foiling a raid on the casino.[19]

His apprehensions overcome, Mustafa Kemal returned to Istanbul every summer to escape from the heat of his new capital. In later years, he built for himself a villa, projecting into the sea of Marmara, at the sandy beach of Florya. Sea-bathing was a modern fashion, brought to Istanbul by White Russian refugees after the revolution. Mustafa Kemal, who had earlier swum off Çeşme, near İzmir, became a regular swimmer at Florya. He loved the sea: he rowed, and took trips to the Bosphorus and the sea of Marmara. He had a hotel built at the thermal springs of Yalova, at the mouth of the gulf of İzmit – a distance of two hours by boat from Istanbul – and acquired two farm estates near by. He was addicted to modern pleasures – swimming, dancing, visits to hotels, restaurants and night-clubs, but also the traditional Ottoman custom of sundowners – in his case, convivial gatherings which could last from sunset to sunrise.

The summer of 1927 marked the beginning of these pleasures. But there was still unfinished business, and the modern message was well to the fore. In his address in Dolmabahçe palace, he warned that true contentment would come only when thought and emotion were moulded by knowledge and science. Receiving a delegation of teachers, six days later, he told them that they should master their charges through (modern) knowledge, as their predecessors, the *hocas*, had done through religion.[20]

The first unfinished business was to provide his own version of his achievements. He had started this in 1918 in the interview he gave to the journalist Ruşen Eşref (Ünaydın), in which he portrayed himself as the saviour of Istanbul in the Gallipoli campaign. In 1922 he described the budding of his genius in childhood and youth in a conversation with the liberal editor, Ahmet Emin (Yalman).[21] In 1924, there were more reminiscences in an interview with his publicist Yunus Nadi (Abalıoğlu).[22] Finally, in March 1926, in a long interview with two other favourite editors, Falih Rıfkı (Atay) and Mahmut (Soydan), he spoke of his early disagreements with the leaders of the CUP.[23] Now he decided to give a full account of his leadership of the national resistance in the War of Independence, the proclamation of the republic, the reforms and their sequel. The occasion was the convention of the Republican People's Party, which was due to open in Ankara on 15 October to draw up the party statutes.[24]

Mustafa Kemal returned to Ankara on 10 October after a break of three months in Istanbul, and set to work immediately, dictating his text to a relay of secretaries. The long and detailed account was not complete on 15 October, when he read the first section. The opening sentence set the tone: 'On the nineteenth day of May of the year 1919, I landed in Samsun.' It was to be a history of the birth of modern Turkey as a personal story, as the achievement of one man who discovered and embodied the will of the nation. The speech occupied six consecutive sessions of the convention. At the end of each session, the Gazi went back to his desk to work through his archive and prepare the text for the following day. Finally, on 20 October, he came to the coda – the address to the youth of Turkey, demanding that future generations should defend the republic and its independence even if they found themselves in conditions as difficult as those which he had overcome at the end of the Great War. 'The strength you need,' the Gazi concluded, 'exists in the noble blood in your veins.' Noble blood was often on the lips of contemporary politicians all over the world.

The address to the country's youth is learnt, usually by heart, by everyone who has been through a Turkish school – but not in the original version. Mustafa Kemal wrote his speech in the eloquent, flowery Ottoman language, of which he was a master, but which, after the language reforms which he instituted, has become incomprehensible to his fellow-countrymen. The speech has been published in successive versions, each one simplifying the vocabulary used in the preceding one. Revision has not been easy. The original text, published in Latin characters, runs to 600 pages[25] and is accompanied by a volume of 300 documents. Immensely detailed at first, it glides over the closing events: the Şeyh Sait rebellion and the assassination attempt in İzmir. The address to the youth of Turkey is preceded by a justification of the Maintenance of Order Law and the Independence Tribunals as a necessity for the forward march of the reforms.

The Speech (*Nutuk*), as it is invariably referred to in Turkey, is an apologia and a polemic. Mustafa Kemal argues that from the beginning he had sought to establish the sovereignty of the nation, which implied the proclamation of the republic, but that he had to conceal his project until the nation was ready, and implement it stage by stage. He goes on: 'In the development of national life to the present-day republic and its laws, some of the travellers who had set out together on the path of the national struggle came up against the limits of their emotional and intellectual understanding and began to resist and oppose.'[26] These words, and the account of specific events which follows, are ungenerous to those who had become Mustafa Kemal's opponents. After his death they published their own stories, usually professing great respect for the Gazi, while rebutting some of his claims. Kâzım Karabekir, the only nationalist commander who could have disputed Mustafa Kemal's claim to the leadership, tried to publish a first short version of his memoirs during the Gazi's lifetime, but the publisher was raided and his stock of copies burnt. However, a copy was saved for submission to Mustafa Kemal, who annotated it in the margin, sometimes with angry remarks, such as 'infantile!' or 'blackmail!', at other times writing coolly 'must find out'.[27] Karabekir republished his short book in 1951, and followed it up with a hugely detailed account in 1960. The publisher was sued and it was not until his acquittal in 1969 that Karabekir's full story became generally available. Refet (Bele) was blunt and brief. Invited, years later, to the Gazi's table, he interrupted the Gazi's reminiscences with the admonition, 'Don't fib, Kemal!' (*Atma, Kemal, atma!*). A member of the Çankaya secretariat, who reports the incident, comments that the Gazi was unruffled by the interruption.[28]

Mustafa Kemal later supplemented the Speech and the interviews which preceded it by relating further reminiscences to his adopted daughter, Afet, and to the friends who gathered round his table. He thus shaped his own legend, just as he established his own cult by encouraging the erection of his statues. Nevertheless, the Speech remains an important source for the history of the foundation of the modern Turkish state, a monument to its founder, and the eloquent expression of his determination to propel his country into the modern world.

The programme which Mustafa Kemal had set out to implement was not yet complete when he stepped down from the rostrum. On 29 August 1927 he had presented his party's candidates in the elections. He said that he had chosen them himself with great care to discharge the trust which the nation had shown him.[29] The candidates were unopposed, and on 1 November the new assembly, finally purged of Mustafa Kemal's opponents, re-elected him to the presidency by a unanimous vote. The ritual was to be repeated on a further two occasions, in 1931 and 1935. On 9/10 April 1928 the assembly removed from the constitution all references to Islam, as he had forecast in his speech. Islam ceased to be the official religion; parliament no longer had to give effect to Muslim canon law, and oaths of office were secularized.[30] The process of secularization, which had taken a big step forward with the abolition of the caliphate, was now complete.

The new secular republic reflected Mustafa Kemal's personal philosophy. In a book published in 1928, Grace Ellison quotes him as saying to her, presumably in 1926–7:

I have no religion, and at times I wish all religions at the bottom of the sea. He is a weak ruler who needs religion to uphold his government; it is as if he would catch his people in a trap. My people are going to learn the principles of democracy, the dictates of truth and the teachings of science. Superstition must go. Let them worship as they will; every man can follow his own conscience, provided it does not interfere with sane reason or bid him act against the liberty of his fellow-men.[31]

Yet, like many rationalists, Mustafa Kemal was himself superstitious and sought omens in dreams.[32] When he inspected the front in March 1922, during the War of Independence, he had portions of the Koran recited during evening gatherings with commanders.[33] But now he was out of the wood.

Sane reason marched on. On 24 May 1928, international numerals replaced Arabic numerals, from which they had originally evolved.[34] The next step was to break the link between Turkish and Arabic and Persian, the languages of Islamic culture. Their role in Ottoman Turkish was, if anything, more important than that of Latin and Greek in English. It was promoted by the use of the Arabic script, which preserved the original spelling and made clear the derivation of Arabic words. Script and religion went together: Turkish-speaking Greeks wrote Turkish in Greek characters, Armenians and Jews in their own alphabets. Adopting the Latin script, as some Turkish reformers had advocated even before the Great War, would put Turks in the same camp as Western Christians. What made it easier was that Western Christians were becoming progressively secularized.

The Arabic script had disadvantages: letters could have four shapes (initial, medial, final or free-standing) and short vowels were omitted. The Arabic script reflected the phonetic structure of classical Arabic; it did not suit Turkish, which has fewer consonants and more vowels than Arabic. At the beginning of the Great War, Enver had introduced a modified Arabic script, employing only free-standing forms of letters. Mustafa Kemal, like most other educated Turks, thought it was worse than useless.[35] It destroyed the main advantage of joined-up Arabic writing – the shape of the written word which could be read at a glance, while preserving letters not needed to render the sounds of Turkish. Above all, like unreformed Arabic script, it hampered intercourse between Turkey and the advanced nations which used the Latin script.

In June 1928, Mustafa Kemal set up a committee in Ankara to recommend the best way of adapting the Latin alphabet to Turkish phonetics.[36] The journalist Falih Rıfkı presented the commission's conclusions to the Gazi in Istanbul, who simplified them further. One recommendation was that the letter 'q' should be used to render the sound of the soft (palatalized) 'k': since Mustafa Kemal preferred to spell his name with a 'K', the proposal was dropped.[37] It was decided to adopt a purely phonetic spelling, based on Istanbul educated speech, which was close to Mustafa Kemal's native Balkan Turkish dialect. Most letters would have the values they had in French or German, and there would be a separate single letter for all the main sounds of spoken Turkish. This required the use of marks (cedilla, circumflex, breve) to modify the standard Latin alphabet. Foreign words, including borrowings from Arabic, would be written as pronounced in Turkish.[38]

The new spelling took time to settle down: the older generation was often influenced by Arabic spelling; others spelled words differently, because they pronounced them differently. In the seventy years which have passed since the adoption of the Latin alphabet, total consistency has not been achieved in written Turkish. It may come in our time with computer spell-checks. This has not detracted from the value of Atatürk's reform: Turkish is infinitely easier to read and write now than it had been when the Arabic script was used, and the millions of Turks who learn European languages do not have to start by learning a new alphabet. But, by the same token, it has become much harder for Turks to master the languages of Islam. New terms were no longer derived from Arabic roots; loan words of Arabic and Persian origin became ossified; the Latin script, which does not differentiate between long and short vowels, affected their pronunciation and usage. But what purists still deplore as linguistic solecism has become part of standard Turkish.

The commission thought that the change to the Latin alphabet would take between five and fifteen years. 'It will be done in three months or not at all,' Mustafa Kemal retorted, adding that if both scripts were used in parallel, people would stick to the script which they knew best. He chose a popular gathering in Istanbul on 9 August 1928 to announce the adoption of the Latin alphabet. He decided to present it as a change from Arabic to 'Turkish letters': the script of the infidel Franks thus became the alphabet of patriotic, nationalist Turks.

Mustafa Kemal had been invited to an open-air night entertainment centred round a restaurant in the gardens of Seraglio Point, where his statue had earlier been put up. Music was provided by a Western dance band, and an oriental ensemble with an Egyptian singer, Munira al-Mahdiyya, as vocalist. A large crowd had gathered to see the Gazi and listen to the music. Mustafa Kemal was in a happy mood. He started by asking a young man to read some notes which had been written in the Latin alphabet. The young man failed to make sense of them. 'He can do it,' Mustafa Kemal said encouragingly. 'I want you all to learn it in five or ten days.' By way of demonstration, he showed the text to Falih Rıfkı, who, of course, read it with great aplomb.

Mustafa Kemal then took his cue from the music. 'Madame Munira al-Mahdiyya, who came out first to adorn the stage with her presence,' he said gallantly, 'has successfully demonstrated her artistry.' But, he went on,

> this music, this simple music, can no longer satisfy the highly developed soul and feelings of the Turk, of a Turk like myself. And now we hear coming to us the sounds of the music of the civilized world, and people who looked life-less as they listened to oriental melodies have gone into action: they have started to behave naturally, to dance and enjoy themselves ... The nation has shed its blood to correct its errors: it is now at peace and can give vent to its natural joy.

Mustafa Kemal was speaking of himself: he enjoyed dancing and he liked oriental Turkish music. But he believed that the young should be taught only Western music, 'the music of civilization'. It was Western music he had in mind when he said, 'There can be no revolution without music.'[39] Mustafa Kemal explained his ideas to the German pianist Wilhelm Kempff, when the latter gave a recital in Ankara in 1927. Classical music, he said, was an integral part of the Western culture which was the source of his reform movement. Without reforms in music, Mustafa Kemal thought that his reforms in other areas would remain incomplete. The conversation led eventually to the choice of the composer Paul Hindemith to help set up the state conser-vatoire in Ankara and organize musical education in Turkey.[40]

Mustafa Kemal had long been accused of being a debauched drinker. Now he turned the tables on his accusers. Before leaving the gathering at Seraglio Point, he raised his glass to the crowd, saying, 'Hypocrites and frauds of old used to drink a thousand times more, secretly in hovels as they indulged in all sorts of nastiness. I am not a fraud. I drink in my nation's honour.'[41] Then, having tossed back a glass of *rakı*, he made his way through the crowd to board the boat which was to take him to a formal dinner at the Büyükada club in the Princes Islands. As he was met by guests in evening dress, he turned to Falih Rıfkı and said, 'Listen, boy, we couldn't have done here what we did at the other place.'[42] Resistance to the Latin alphabet was naturally strongest in the educated élite. But the population, which the first census held in 1927 put at 13,650,000, was largely illiterate. Most Turks thus first learnt to read in the new Latin alphabet.

On 11 August 1928 Mustafa Kemal gave the first class in the new letters in Dolmabahçe palace.[43] He enjoyed the role of teacher and on 23 August he set out on a tour to extend the lesson to provincials. All MPs were asked to follow suit. The law making the use of the Latin alphabet compulsory from 1 January 1929, was passed as soon as the assembly met for the new session on 1 November. All over Turkey 'national schools' were opened to teach reading and writing in the new alphabet. By 1936, when their functions were transferred to the new People's Houses, they had issued 2,500,000 diplomas of literacy.[44] The literacy rate doubled from 10 to 20 per cent in a population which had by that time increased to over 16 million.

But although progress was steady, Mustafa Kemal ruled until the end of his days a country which was predominantly illiterate, and where the ruling class was small. The reforms which came in a rush between 1923 and 1929 had a gradual effect and hardly touched the villages until after the Second World War. What Mustafa Kemal did was to create the framework within which his country developed. Like all revolutions, his was seen at first as a total transformation. But its initial effect was limited to the lives of the ruling class, whose composition was largely unchanged, as the republic inherited Ottoman officialdom almost *in toto*. The biggest break in Turkish social history came not with Atatürk's reforms, but earlier with the departure of the Christians, on whose skills the country had long depended. Atatürk's republic was indeed a new Turkey, but the essence of its newness was that for the first time in its history it was a homogeneously Muslim country.

25

The Depression

———————◆———————

THE YEAR 1929 started well for Mustafa Kemal. Opposition to his rule had been broken, and the regime felt confident enough to repeal the Maintenance of Order Law on 4 March. Banditry, which used to be endemic in Anatolia, had been suppressed.[1] Although Kurdish nationalists continued to stir up trouble among tribes living astride the border with Iran, a rectification of that border was about to isolate the insurgents, while the extension of the railway network made it easier to bring order to the whole country.[2] An obedient assembly continued to pass laws imported from Europe: court procedure was reformed; the German commercial code and the Swiss law on bankruptcy were adopted; agricultural credit cooperatives were established.[3] A docile press proclaimed the successes of the regime; members of the assembly assured it that their constituents were happy; the welcome given to government leaders touring the country gave the same impression.[4]

Mustafa Kemal could devote time to his cultural interests. He wanted to see the country's political and economic independence buttressed by the creation of a truly national language and history. A committee was set up to establish new terms for technical concepts: the Ottomans had coined them from Arabic roots; now they were to be derived from Turkish or imported from Europe. On 17 February, İsmet made an effort to confine himself to words of Turkish origin when he addressed the committee.[5] Mustafa Kemal had long been disturbed by the European stereotype of the Turk, as a member of a conquering, barbarous tribe, spreading destruction wherever he went. In 1928, this concern was brought to the fore, when he was told by his adopted daughter, Afet, who had begun her training as a scholar by going to the smart French convent school, Notre Dame de Sion, in Istanbul, that the history textbook she had been given classified Turks among the yellow races.[6] To rebut this slur, Turkish scholars were invited to the Gazi's table at the seaside resort of Yalova, where he spent the summer. Work began on producing a version of world history centred on the Turks.

The Gazi set out the terms of reference in a manual of civics which he dictated to Afet. 'There is no nation in the world greater, older or more honourable than the Turkish nation, nor has one been seen in the history of humanity,' the manual declared on its first page. 'The Turkish language,' the manual went on, 'is the most beautiful and the richest in the world; it could also be the easiest.' Islam was put firmly in its place: 'the Turks were a great nation even before they adopted the Muslim religion ... The religion founded by Muhammad was based on a policy of setting Arab nationalism above all other nationalisms.' Islam had been replaced by Turkish nationalism: the Turk no longer thought of heaven but of the sacred heritage of his ancestors and the defence of the last remaining Turkish lands. Every adult was free to choose his own religion, but fanaticism had to be fought lest freedom perish.[7] Mustafa Kemal's manifesto was both nationalist and liberal. Practice fell short of it, but he felt it was important to set an ideal. The cultural revolution took a step forward on 2 September 1929 when the first contest was held in Istanbul to choose a Turkish beauty queen.[8]

The happy interlude ended in the autumn when the Wall Street crash ushered in the great depression. The Turkish economy, based largely on agriculture, was hit hard by the fall in commodity prices. Turkish agriculture had made a good recovery after the War of Independence. In the eight years to the end of 1930, the value of farm production increased by over 11 per cent a year.[9] But the country was still desperately poor. Cash crops, mainly tobacco and dried fruit, made up the bulk of exports. Even before prices fell, they could not cover the cost of essential imports – cloth and sugar, cement and paper, iron and steel. By the end of 1929, the trade deficit approached 50 million dollars, or roughly a quarter of total foreign trade.[10] The resources of the state were strained by the nationalization of foreign-owned utilities and the railway-building programme. Mustafa Kemal and İsmet were at one in promoting these projects: they had seen military operations hampered by bad communications; they wanted to knit the country together; and they feared foreign control of the economy. But there was a price to pay for economic nationalism.

The British consul-general in Istanbul, Sir Alexander Telford Waugh, wrote on his return to London in 1930:

Turkey's priceless possession of the great trading port of Constantinople has been deliberately sacrificed, partly to jealousy of foreign enterprise there and partly to resentment at the city's failure to identify itself with the national struggle. The coal-bunkering trade has been driven to the Piraeus, and foreign shipping has been so harassed by police regulations that shipmasters avoid stopping at Constantinople when passing through the Straits.[11]

Waugh believed that Turkey's nationalist leaders had failed to realize that 'generations of tradition and hard work are required to form a nation of traders'.[12] But Mustafa Kemal was determined that his people should start learning on the job right away.

The beginnings were inevitably ragged. Take-over by the state meant mismanagement by People's Party stalwarts, veterans of ethnic conflict who had friends in the government, but knew nothing of management or business. Employees, workers, consumers – all suffered. As the government believed in balanced budgets, prices had to reflect the costs of unskilled operations. It was sometimes cheaper to move goods by caravan than by newly built railways.[13] Taxes had to be raised. The tithes were gone, but there was a land tax, which was difficult to estimate equitably in the absence of registers, a tax on cattle, and a tax to finance the building of roads and bridges. The peasantry found it hard enough to pay these taxes in good years: the depression made things worse. The price of cereals dropped by more than two-thirds between 1929 and 1933. Turkish exports, which had peaked at 105 million dollars in 1925, dropped to less than 50 million in 1932.[14] As the depression spread to Turkey in 1930, Mustafa Kemal realized that his young republic was in crisis: the country could not finance essential imports; its currency was shunned; zealous revenue officials seized the meagre possessions of peasants who could not pay their taxes. Popular misery and resentment could no longer be ignored, although sycophancy still obscured their extent.

In March 1930 Mustafa Kemal travelled south – to İzmir and then to Antalya on the Mediterranean coast.[15] He was depressed by what he saw. He told his secretary Hasan Rıza (Soyak):

There are complaints wherever we go. Poverty, and material and moral misery, are everywhere. There is little to cheer us. Unfortunately, this is the true state of the country. It's not our fault: unthinking rulers, ignorant of the way of the world, have run this country for years, not to say centuries, and reduced a paradise to this sorry state. Most of our officials are inexperienced and at a loss. Our poor people have ability, but they have fallen under the influence of superstitions which have been presented as sacred dogma.

Worst of all, the people expected him to put everything right. 'But,' Mustafa Kemal went on, 'I have no talisman.'[16]

The depression had brought political upheaval in most countries. It undermined democratic institutions, particularly where they were weak. It confirmed or brought to power dictatorships from the Baltic to the Mediterranean, confining European democracy to the northern and western fringes of the continent. In Turkey, where the opposition had earlier been liquidated, it started by having the opposite effect.

Mustafa Kemal decided that political discontent should be provided with a legal but controlled outlet. But there was a difficulty. He was convinced that opposition to his rule came from religious reaction, which was manipulated by dishonest politicians. Now he wanted to allow criticism, but make sure that religious reaction did not benefit from it. However, the mass of Turks had always expressed their discontents in religious terms. In their eyes, misery was the fruit of impiety, prosperity the reward of obedience to the law of Islam. The spectacle of People's Party officials scrambling for public favours reinforced this view. Even a secular opposition party was bound to attract conservative Muslims whose religious feelings the Kemalist regime had offended.

As in 1924, Mustafa Kemal turned to Fethi (Okyar) to help the regime out of trouble. Fethi, the Gazi decided, was an ideal person to lead a loyal opposition. He was a personal friend from Macedonia, an honest modernizer, untainted by scandal, and a nationalist. He was known and liked as a politician more liberal than İsmet. After losing power to İsmet in 1925, as a result of the Şeyh Sait rebellion, Fethi had been appointed ambassador in Paris. He arrived in Istanbul on leave on 22 July 1930 and was told by Mustafa Kemal's Salonica friend, Fuat (Bulca), that the 'usual gentlemen' of the Gazi's company, such as Kılıç Ali and Recep Zühtü, were grumbling against İsmet's government. 'They'll ask you to form an opposition party,' Fuat warned Fethi. 'Don't accept on any account or you will be doing yourself a disservice.'[17]

The offer did indeed come a few days later, when Fethi paid his respects to the Gazi in Yalova. Mustafa Kemal argued in favour of greater parliamentary control of the government. An opposition party would provide it by stimulating free debate in the assembly. If Fethi were to lead it, he could speak freely and help correct errors in policy implementation. 'Don't pit me against İsmet,' Fethi pleaded. But Mustafa Kemal would not be put off. He had been upset when the popular German historian, Emil Ludwig, whom he had received the previous December, had described him as a dictator. 'I do not want to be recorded in history as a man who bequeathed a tyranny,' he said.[18] Mustafa Kemal had even chosen the name of the new opposition party – the Free Republican Party. He promised that although he would remain titular leader of the ruling Republican People's Party, he would be impartial in his dealings with government and opposition.[19]

Fethi accepted the offer, and drew up the new party's programme, which the Gazi vetted. The Gazi also chose his close friend Nuri (Conker) as the general secretary of the party, enrolled in it his sister Makbule (who was more interested in gambling than in politics), and discussed the names of the members of the assembly who would be transferred from the ruling party to the opposition. When the Free Republican Party was officially set up on 12 August, it seemed that every precaution had been taken to produce a tame liberal opposition. 'Are you not pleased with what you have achieved?' Mustafa Kemal asked Fethi.[20] In fact both were pleased with their work in the relaxed atmosphere of the spa in Yalova. But the pleasure was short-lived.

On 4 September, Fethi arrived in İzmir to set up the Free Republicans' provincial organization. A large crowd had come together to welcome him. The governor, Mustafa Kemal's friend General Kâzım (Dirik), tried to stop an opposition meeting, but was instructed to let it go ahead. Sensing official indecision, the crowd took the bit between its teeth. The offices of the People's Party and of its newspaper were stoned, and İsmet's photographs were torn up. Security forces guarding the building opened fire, and killed a 14-year-old schoolboy. The father laid the bleeding body at Fethi's feet, with the words: 'Here is a sacrifice for you. We are ready to give others. Only save us.' On 7 September, an opposition meeting drew a crowd of more than a hundred thousand.[21]

Two days later, the ruling party's Istanbul mouthpiece, *Cumhuriyet*, published an open letter to the Gazi, complaining that new parties were trying to appropriate his name and asking that he should make his position clear. The following day, Mustafa Kemal replied that he intended to remain leader of the Republican People's Party, but that this would not affect his impartiality as president.[22] But when the Free Republicans went ahead to contest local government elections, they came up against official obstruction and fraud. 'Who's winning?' Mustafa Kemal asked his secretary Hasan Rıza. 'Our party, of course, Pasha,' the secretary replied. The Gazi laughed. 'Not so,' he said, 'I'll give you the name of the winning party: it's the party of the administration, boy. In other words, the gendarmes, the police, the district officers and the governors. Do get it right!'[23]

Nevertheless, the opposition was allowed to win in a few places. One was Samsun, where the governor, General Kâzım (İnanç), who had been present at Mustafa Kemal's Yalova meeting with Fethi, had followed his leader's example and enrolled his daughter in the opposition party. Fethi claims in his memoirs that when he returned to Istanbul and saw the Gazi, his complaints were met with the words, 'I'll show a little partiality from now on. Otherwise, the People's Party will be wiped out and once again we'll be left with a single party. This will not do.'[24]

Nevertheless, the 1930 local elections did mark a step forward in the development of democratic institutions. Votes were cast directly for candidates and not for members of electoral colleges. (Direct parliamentary elections did not take place until 1946,[25] when the authorities manipulated the outcome, as they had done in 1930. Progress came in two stages: first rights with fraud, then rights without fraud.) More significantly, women were given the right to vote and to be elected in the 1930 local elections. Afet was the first woman to enrol as a member of the People's Party.[26] Women's suffrage was extended to village councils on 26 October 1933[27] – a truly radical measure to which conservative rural society submitted in form but not in spirit. Finally, on 5 December 1934, women won the vote in parliamentary elections.[28] All these changes were imposed from above; all had no immediate political significance, since the People's Party chose whom it willed to serve on elected bodies. But the official recognition of women's political rights had a psychological effect, and reinforced the gradual improvement in the social position of Turkish women.

Having seen the sorry performance of his party in the local elections, Mustafa Kemal toyed with the idea of forming a national bloc, within which parties would be allocated parliamentary seats in proportion to their vote in the forthcoming general elections. The idea did not make sense, since uncontested elections would not test the parties' support; but Fethi accepted it with alacrity. However, the People's Party executive refused outright.[29] This meant that Fethi would have to fight the elections against Mustafa Kemal, as leader of the People's Party. On 15 November, Fethi brought his accusations of impropriety in the local elections to the floor of the assembly. But only ten members of his party voted for his motion criticizing the interior minister, Şükrü Kaya.

Fethi had had enough. Two days later he wrote to the Gazi saying that he was dissolving the Free Republican Party. He had founded it with 'the encouragement and approval of our Great Gazi', and he would not lead it against him.[30] The experiment in liberal democracy had lasted barely three months. The Free Republican members of the assembly returned to the ranks of the People's Party, except for a handful who had taken their opposition role too seriously. Fethi went abroad again, this time as ambassador to London. He felt that Mustafa

Kemal had let him down, and that İsmet had outsmarted him, but he kept his thoughts to himself.

İsmet had kept his head down in the weeks which followed the establishment of the Free Republican Party. Turkish politicians, well used to the ways of absolute rulers, had seen the limited experiment in democracy simply as a contest between İsmet and Fethi for the Gazi's favour, and waited for the outcome before declaring themselves. İsmet was convinced that the experiment would fail and that the Gazi would call on him to pick up the pieces, as he had done in 1925. He was proved right. Even before the Republicans dissolved their party, İsmet was back at the Gazi's dinner-table discussing how government could be improved in the absence of an opposition, which, although loyal at the outset, had created a threat to law and order. Before making up his mind, Mustafa Kemal set out on a tour of the provinces to find out why his party had failed to live up to his expectations.

First he travelled east by presidential train. He was accompanied by the toughest advocates of law and order in the cabinet, by senior civil servants and specially selected advisers. The Gazi liked to question his subordinates. Some questions were rhetorical. 'Were we right to do away with the Free Republican Party?' he would ask, expecting a reasoned justification. He also liked to test the wits of his companions. Unfortunate officials stumbled when ordered to define such terms as 'the economy', 'liberalism' or even 'poetry'. But a clever reply could earn favours. 'Define zero,' the Gazi asked Hasan-Âli (Yücel), an education inspector attached to his suite. 'Your humble servant in your presence,' replied Hasan-Âli.[31] It was the first step to his appointment as minister of education, a job in which he did more than most to realize Atatürk's ideal of bringing world culture to Turkey.

General Kâzım (İnanç), the governor of Samsun, had less wit. Having allowed an opposition candidate to be elected mayor, he filled the town with troops to avoid hostile demonstrations when the Gazi arrived, and failed to invite the mayor to the banquet of welcome. Mustafa Kemal demanded that the mayor should be summoned. He came, but refused the proffered glass of *rakı*. 'Is it a sin in your eyes?' asked the Gazi. 'No,' said the mayor, 'but I've already had dinner.' Mustafa Kemal then suggested that the mayor should resign, since his party had been dissolved. The mayor refused, saying that he had a duty to serve his electors; however, if the government did not want him, it could get the election annulled by an administrative court. He then took his leave. Mustafa Kemal vented his anger on the governor, saying,

'Have you seen the behaviour of the man you have elected mayor? He has no manners. We come as guests to his city and he has dinner before joining us at table. We offer him a drink, and he refuses. Finally, he leaves the president's table before we get up.' But when a member of the president's suite joked, 'The mayor is going to cost the governor his job. That's not bad going,' Mustafa Kemal backed General Kâzım, saying, 'He has acted on our orders.'[32] The mayor's election was annulled in due course.[33]

The results of the fact-finding tour were discussed at a meeting in Dolmabahçe palace. Then Mustafa Kemal went on to tour Thrace, while leading members of his People's Party visited the rest of the country. Mustafa Kemal was in Edirne, on the border with Greece and Bulgaria, when he learnt that religious fanatics had started a bloody riot in the market town of Menemen near İzmir.

It was a small-scale incident. A dervish, Mehmet, a refugee from Crete, and five companions, entered Menemen on 23 December. They had with them a dog they called Kıtmir, the name of the magical dog which had guarded 'the men of the cave' in the Koranic version of the Christian legend of the Seven Sleepers of Ephesus. The strangers seized the green religious flag of Islam, which was kept in the local mosque, and planted it in the main square. There the dervish Mehmet proclaimed himself *mehdi* (the messiah), sent to overthrow godless rulers. A crowd of some hundred locals gathered in support, while the majority of the townspeople gaped undecided. Mehmet brandished a gun, announcing that the town was surrounded by the magical number of seventy thousand supporters.[34] Two officers pleaded unsuccessfully with the rioters to disperse, and then sent a platoon under the command of a young second lieutenant, who bore the pure Turkic (or rather Mongol) name of Kubilay. Kubilay drew his gun and fired on dervish Mehmet, using a blank cartridge with which he had been issued for manoeuvres. Unharmed, the dervish declared that he was impervious to bullets, and drawing his gun in turn, wounded Kubilay mortally. The lieutenant's body was then carried to the mosque courtyard, where the dervish cut off his head and stuck it on a pole to the applause of his supporters. Two watchmen who fired on the crowd were killed. A little later, a near-by regiment arrived on the scene, and dispersed the rioters, killing the dervish Mehmet and five of his supporters.[35]

Although the riot had been quickly suppressed, Mustafa Kemal was outraged. He was particularly shocked by reports that the people of Menemen had applauded the murderers of the young second lieutenant.[36] The government declared martial law over a wide area of western Anatolia and sent a court martial under a tough general, Mustafa

Muğlalı. Returning from Edirne, Mustafa Kemal held a meeting in Dolmabahçe palace in Istanbul, and then went on to Ankara where he chaired a cabinet meeting. He was in a furious mood, having convinced himself that the riot was part of a wider conspiracy, possibly linked with the dissolved Free Republican Party, incited by newspapers which had recently been allowed to voice criticism, and proving once again that any loosening of the reins would be exploited by religious fanatics, whom politicians could not be relied upon to disown.

Borrowing his terminology from French, he demanded that Menemen should be declared a *ville maudite* (accursed town) and razed to the ground and its inhabitants transported,[37] that no mercy should be shown to religious fanatics, even women, that executions should not be delayed, and that opposition journalists should, at least, be frightened by being made to appear before the court martial. The government had heard that the dervish Mehmet belonged to the banned Nakşibendi order: the order, Mustafa Kemal declared, should be *écrasé* (crushed). True, not all Nakşibendis were 'awful', but those of them who were *convaincus* (convinced supporters) were dangerous and should be eliminated. To make matters worse, French newspapers had suggested that the incident had been staged by him and İsmet to discredit the Free Republicans.

İsmet agreed tactfully that the *convaincus* should be shown up as traitors and their links with the Free Republicans should be investigated.[38] This narrowed the target and saved Menemen at the expense of the Nakşibendis. Mustafa Kemal made no further references to accursed towns, and soon set out on another provincial tour, while the court martial hunted down suspects. No evidence could be found to incriminate either the Free Republicans or the press. But the Nakşibendis were found guilty by association: the dervish Mehmet had, it seems, first made his messianic claims at one of their meetings. Their provincial leader knew the son of the head of the order, 'the Supreme Pole of Attraction' (*kutbülaktap*), the elderly Şeyh Esat, a native of Erbil (Irbil) in Iraqi Kurdistan, who lived in a mansion in Istanbul. The fact that the strictly orthodox Nakşibendis were unlikely to approve the messianic claims of a dervish, who, according to witnesses, was addicted to drugs, did not impress General Muğlalı's court martial. The elderly sheikh died in detention, while his son was hanged along with twenty-seven others on 4 February 1931. Most of them were poor refugees from the Balkans, newly settled in the area[39] – one a Jewish shopkeeper who had sold a piece of rope to the rioters. A measured dose of terror was thus imposed once again, this time to discourage any further challenge by religious enthusiasts.

The newspaper *Cumhuriyet* opened a campaign to finance a monument to Kubilay. It was unveiled in Menemen in 1934 to commemorate an exemplary hero of the revolution: a young teacher, married to a young teacher, who was doing his national service as a second lieutenant. The name of Kubilay became instantly popular with Turkish parents. Mustafa Kemal, speaking in Konya in February 1931, linked teachers and officers in a common encomium. There were few countries, he declared, where the nation and the army were as closely identified as they were in Turkey. The people's progress had always been led by the army.[40] These words of the founder of the republic are to this day displayed proudly in officers' messes. General Muğlalı's career ended sadly: when the People's Party lost power in 1950, he was court-martialled for having ordered the shooting of thirty-three Kurdish tribesmen accused of smuggling cattle to Iran. He died in detention before the end of the trial.[41]

The impact of the depression and the brief contest between two political parties stirred up an ideological debate in the country's small ruling caste. The Free Republicans had come out with a liberal programme and proposed that state monopolies should be ended, that foreign capital should be attracted, and that state investment should be curtailed. On 30 August 1930, İsmet gave his reply when he opened the extension of the railway to Sivas. He argued that it had proved impossible to attract foreign capital for essential development, and described the government's policy as 'moderate state intervention' (for which the Turkish term was *devletçilik*, translated into French as *étatisme* or 'statism').[42] İsmet won the debate, because he had won the political battle, as the ideals of a free market and free politics went down together.

The next step was to work out a philosophy and define the limits of state intervention. In 1932 İsmet went to Russia, where he was impressed by Bolshevik industrialization. He secured the services of a Soviet planner, Professor Orlov, who helped draw up a five-year economic development programme. A Soviet loan of 8 million dollars in gold was negotiated to finance the building of textile mills by Soviet engineers.[43] To raise more funds, the government invited citizens to subscribe to a development loan. The experiment succeeded.[44] Statism did not replace capitalism: it proved to be a form of state capitalism, which often worked together with private enterprise, though limiting its scope.

Mustafa Kemal always had radical left-wing supporters, most of whom gradually lost their radicalism. After the depression, a group which included the writer Yakup Kadri (Karaosmanoğlu), one of Mustafa Kemal's chief publicists, and a number of former Marxists started a magazine called *Kadro* (The Cadre), promoting the view that Kemalism was a third way between capitalism and socialism, particularly suited to developing countries where power had to be exercised by the enlightened élite – the cadre of the revolution. Its ideas were influential, but before long it was disowned by the authorities. Mustafa Kemal was a pragmatist, and anyone whom he labelled as an impractical visionary (*hayalperest*) was cast out.[45] In any case, ideology mattered less than official appointments, favours and opportunities for enrichment. As politicians fought for them, they changed their views.

In the event, Turkey followed the world trend in the era of the New Deal. State intervention increased in the economy. So did protectionism in trade, much of which was conducted under clearing arrangements, which meant that Turkish products were bartered against foreign manufactures at artificial prices. The chief foreign beneficiary was not Bolshevik Russia, but Germany, which became Turkey's main trading partner. Taxes were increased and salaries cut. Patriotic campaigns were launched to urge the public to save and to buy locally produced goods. Unions and strikes were not allowed. In a largely rural country the problem was not unemployment but warding off starvation and ensuring the flow of essential supplies. İsmet's government did this. The depression was contained. The state and a few state-aided private individuals built the first factories which not only produced simple necessities like cloth, sugar, cement and, at the end of the decade, paper and steel, but trained the first generation of Turkish engineers and managers. Private suppliers and sub-contractors, working for the state, became the first Turkish entrepreneurs and started business dynasties which later came to dominate the Turkish economy.

Mustafa Kemal had always stressed the importance of economic development, but had no fixed views about the means to achieve it. His interest lay in the acquisition and dissemination of knowledge, which, he knew, would have to come from abroad. İsmet would run the government and Fevzi the army; Mustafa Kemal would do the thinking and, of course, keep an eye on his subordinates.

The dissolution of the Free Republican Party inaugurated unopposed single-party rule by Mustafa Kemal's Republican People's Party. He spelled out the new order in a speech in İzmir on 27 January 1931. 'Our party,' he declared, 'is not like any party in any other country ... It is an institution which seeks to benefit all classes equally, without harming any of them ... Its programme is wholly democratic and populist, but at the same time statist in economic management.' In his speech in Konya, a few days later, he said that he wanted all young people above the age of 18 to become active members of the party, and younger people to be deemed candidates for membership.[46]

Independent societies were dissolved. Freemasons declared that they no longer needed a separate organization, since they shared the aims of the People's Party. The nationalist Turkish Hearths joined the People's Party and were transformed into People's Houses, whose number was eventually raised to nearly five hundred.[47] Many became active social clubs, with drama and music groups and sports facilities. Their mission was to bring Western civilization to the people, but they were also a source of salaries and perks for bureaucratic party officials. The task of propagating Western values and manners was shared by girls' institutes, the first of which was opened in Ankara in 1930 and named after İsmet Paşa. Here modern Turkish young women were taught not only child care, dress-making and household management, but also how to make paper flowers. Mustafa Kemal's ideal of national development was all-encompassing. In a speech in Bursa in 1925, he had declared that one of the country's main needs was to train waiters to provide table service in a manner suited to civilized people. Too many dishes should not be served: it was bad for the economy and bad for health.[48] The Gazi was not greedy for food.

On 4 May 1931, Mustafa Kemal was re-elected president for a third term by the new single-party assembly. On 10 May, he opened the convention of his Republican People's Party, asking delegates to be frank, but friendly towards each other.[49] The convention confirmed what Mustafa Kemal had already decided. It defined the party's six principles as republicanism, nationalism, populism, statism (state intervention in the economy), secularism and attachment to the process of revolution (or reform). To symbolize them, a party flag was devised showing six arrows against a red background. The six arrows thus joined other symbols fashionable at the time: the hammer and sickle, the fasces, the swastika.

But Mustafa Kemal drew a line between single-party rule, which he had come to see as inevitable, and a full-blown totalitarian dictatorship. He had refused Fethi (Okyar)'s proposal that he should relinquish the leadership of the Republican People's Party and become president for life. Now he opposed attempts to put the party above the state. As he told his secretary Hasan Rıza (Soyak) he did not want to repeat the mistakes of the CUP which had allowed irresponsible politicians to interfere in the work of responsible officials.[50] As he saw it, the task of the People's Party was to inculcate the ideas and habits of universal civilization, and not to run the state.

The party had a flag, but no uniforms or shock troops. Totalitarian ideas seeped in, but Mustafa Kemal did not allow them to dominate the country. Turkey in the 1930s, in the last phase of his rule, was a disciplined country under an unopposed pragmatic government which respected the forms of constitutional democracy.

26

Table Talk

BANISHED FROM THE assembly and the press, the political game continued to be played round Mustafa Kemal's drink-loaded dinner-
table. True, it was not the centre of government, as Turkey was ruled by
İsmet and his ministers in Ankara. But the Gazi was the fount of new
ideas and the arbiter of disputes: careers were made and unmade round
his table. In one of the many stories about his parties, he asks one of his
guests, 'Tell me what goes best with *rakı*?' 'Roasted chick-peas (*leblebi*),'
the guest replies, knowing the host's frugal tastes. 'Wrong,' says Mustafa
Kemal, 'the best accompaniment to *rakı* is good conversation.'

At a party in Dolmabahçe palace in 1932, Dr Reşit Galip, the excit-
able former member of the Independence Tribunal, criticized the education minister Esat Mehmet who had stopped women teachers from
appearing on the stage of the Ankara People's House. Mustafa Kemal
asked Reşit Galip to show more respect for a minister who had been his
teacher. Emboldened by *rakı*, Reşit Galip refused, and Mustafa Kemal
asked him to leave the table. 'No,' said Reşit Galip, 'this is not your table,
it belongs to the nation.' 'In that case,' replied Mustafa Kemal, 'I shall
go myself.' And he left, followed by the other guests.[1] Nevertheless, he
was so impressed by Reşit Galip's boldness and his support for the
reforms that, shortly afterwards, he imposed him on İsmet as minister
of education.

It was during Reşit Galip's tenure of the ministry that Istanbul
University was reorganized, and shed its faculty of theology, as well as a
large part of its old staff. The gaps were filled by German Jewish academics displaced by the Nazis' anti-Semitic laws. Their contribution to
the development of higher education in Turkey, and of the country in

general, has been immense. Istanbul University which under its Ottoman name of *Darülfünun* (House of Sciences) had sunk into provincial mediocrity, became a genuine centre of learning. Other German refugee professors went to Ankara to help set up a new university in the capital, or to advise the government on taxation and other matters. They trained a generation of Turkish scholars and specialists who applied Western thought and practice to the solution of the country's problems.[2] The Ottomans had long employed foreign advisers, and Mustafa Kemal continued the practice with a greater sense of urgency. But it was Reşit Galip who seized the opportunity to enlist outstanding foreign talent, at a time when the country's poverty, not to mention its grinding bureaucracy, might have deterred a more cautious administrator. Like Mustafa Kemal, he was a Turkish nationalist who realized that the windows to the outside world should be flung open if the country was to progress.

Inevitably, Reşit Galip made enemies and he was dismissed after eleven months in office. As he sulked in retirement, Mustafa Kemal invited him to his table at Çankaya. After a few drinks, Mustafa Kemal winked at two soldiers who proceeded to lift Reşit Galip in his chair and, after taking him to Mustafa Kemal, set him back in his place. 'Doctor,' said the Gazi, 'that is how we raise people up and then put them down.'[3]

Mustafa Kemal had adopted a mongrel to which he gave the English name of Fox. Contrary to Muslim custom, Fox slept in Mustafa Kemal's bedroom, and lay under the president's dinner-table. One day the dog chewed Reşit Galip's trouser leg; Mustafa Kemal made amends by ordering a new suit for his guest. But Fox came to a sad end. It bit its master's hand, and Atatürk agreed to have it put down. The director of the forest farm in Ankara thought he would endear himself to the president by having the carcass stuffed and exhibited in a glass case. Mustafa Kemal was outraged and ordered its immediate removal.[4] He loved animals. Told at dinner one day that a foal had been born in his stable, he ordered that the mare and foal should be brought into the reception hall of Çankaya palace, where the horses slid on the parquet floor.[5] On another occasion, Mustafa Kemal's rough companion Salih Bozok took it into his head to amuse the company by releasing a live quail while roast quail were being served for dinner. When the bird landed in the president's lap, he vowed never to eat quail again.[6]

There were also long-running feuds fought round the Gazi. The most notable was between 'the Business Bank (*İş Bankası*) set' and İsmet. Mustafa Kemal held shares in the bank, and some of 'the usual gentlemen' – Salih (Bozok), Kılıç Ali, Mahmut (Soydan) – had secured appointments on its board. İsmet blocked suggestions that the Business Bank should take over the issue of currency from the foreign-owned Ottoman Bank. Instead, the Turkish Central Bank was founded on 11 June 1930[7] to implement İsmet's strict anti-inflationary monetary policy. The Business Bank was open to partisan abuse: it financed publishers who were in with the regime,[8] and favoured friends of the government. Nevertheless, the letter of banking rules was respected.

Some time before Reşit Galip's outburst at Dolmabahçe palace, Mustafa Kemal took his friends to *Rose Noire*, a night-club in Beyoğlu, the European district of Istanbul, owned by a White Russian refugee, known as Madame Vera. Night-clubs, Madame Vera told her distinguished customer, were providing a useful service keeping up the spirit of the public. But she had been denied a bank loan to refurbish her establishment. Mustafa Kemal wrote there and then a letter to the Business Bank asking it to lend the lady 15,000 lira. The following morning, the Istanbul branch manager asked Mustafa Kemal's secretary for confirmation, and was told to follow normal procedure. Madame Vera was unable to provide collateral or name a guarantor, and credit was refused.[9] But the story that Mustafa Kemal was showering money on bar ladies was spread, allegedly, by the president's chief secretary, Tevfik (Bıyıklıoğlu). Conveniently, proof was found that Tevfik had asked the Egyptian prince Abbas Hilmi for a bribe to advance the latter's application for a concession to prospect for oil. Tevfik was despatched as ambassador to Afghanistan, to the satisfaction of his enemies in the president's court.[10]

The director of the Business Bank, Celal (Bayar), was open to proposals by businessmen who came to him with projects, sometimes backed by foreign firms. All projects had to be approved by the government, and applications were turned down if İsmet thought that the entrepreneurs intended to get rich at the expense of the state, distorting the five-year plan in the process. Disappointed applicants would then put their case to the Gazi through 'the usual gentlemen', arguing that the government's fanatical adherence to 'statism' was holding back the country's development. One such incident caused the first public quarrel between Mustafa Kemal and İsmet.

In August 1932, Mustafa Kemal forced the resignation of the minister of national economy, Mustafa Şeref, whose mistake was to have defended an official who had turned down a business application. İsmet was incensed. Later that month, Mustafa Kemal and İsmet argued about the wording of a denial of a newspaper story, according to which King George V had offered the Turkish president the Order of the Garter. When Mustafa Kemal insisted that the denial should state that he would not accept the honour, were it offered, İsmet objected that such a denial was unnecessary since no offer had been made. Mustafa Kemal said that İsmet was being obstreperous because of his treatment of the minister of national economy a few days earlier. Guests at the Gazi's table at Yalova noticed that president and prime minister parted without shaking hands.[11]

However, the breach was quickly repaired. İsmet Paşa sent Mustafa Kemal a handwritten note expressing his undying devotion. Mustafa Kemal replied:

> İsmet you are a great man; you feel and inspire emotion. It seems you cry when you read my words. Would you believe it if I said that I sob when I read yours? I am expressing these feelings in writing, not in company at the dinner-table, but after retiring to my bedroom with my intimate companion (*mahremim*). I am certain that you love me very much. I love you too.[12]

The intimate companion was probably Afet. Mustafa Kemal's handwriting, no less than the emotional tone of the letter, betrays the effects of the evening's entertainment. But a hand-written directive which Mustafa Kemal issued at roughly the same time put across the same message soberly: 'To resolve your difficulties you should always apply to the prime minister İsmet Paşa, and no one else.'[13]

On 9 September 1932, Celal (Bayar) was appointed minister of national economy. He sent Mustafa Kemal a sycophantic telegram: 'I will work as your idealistic labourer on the radiant road opened by your great genius, which comprehends better than anyone the needs of the people and the country.' Mustafa Kemal replied with an unusually long telegram saying that the economic burden falling on the state would be lightened if everybody could be drawn into the task of development: it was a criticism of extreme 'statism', with which İsmet was associated in the public mind. İsmet was disturbed, even though Mustafa Kemal made a point of thanking him formally for appointing the new minister.[14] But he was too canny to resist, and worked with Celal in the cabinet.

Present-day Kemalists like to compare the Gazi's evening gatherings with Plato's symposium. To do them justice, there were frequent discussions of general ideas – largely on language and history, but also politics and economics. The Gazi's four favourite writers – Ruşen Eşref (Ünaydın), Falih Rıfkı (Atay), Yunus Nadi (Abalıoğlu) and Yakup Kadri (Karaosmanoğlu) – were frequent guests. But so too were 'the usual gentlemen', who formed an unofficial bodyguard. One evening at the Park Hotel in Istanbul the electric lights went out; when they were switched on again Kılıç Ali and one other companion were seen covering the president with their bodies, guns in hand.[15] All but one of the band were kept at the Gazi's side until he (or they) died. The exception was Recep Zühtü, who was banished from the Gazi's table in 1935 when he shot his mistress, wounding her mortally. He was acquitted on the grounds that his mental balance was disturbed, and was allowed to keep his seat in parliament.[16] Mad or bad, Recep Zühtü needed his salary as an MP.

Some guests were invited for observation. 'See that man over there,' Mustafa Kemal said one evening to Afet. 'He is real filth – the kind of filth that sticks to the bottom of a dustbin when you tip it out.' 'Why then did you invite him?' asked Afet. 'You wouldn't understand that, my girl,' Mustafa Kemal replied cynically.[17] He was skilled at puncturing pretensions. One evening as he was discussing with İsmet a report from the Turkish ambassador in London, a guest chipped in: 'The English are notorious for thinking specially, even exclusively, of their own interests in their dealings with other countries.' 'Is that all you have to say?' asked Mustafa Kemal. 'Yes, sir,' replied the guest. 'In that case,' Mustafa Kemal concluded, 'I thank you for your distinguished advice, in my name and that of the republic.' 'Don't mention it,' said the guest, failing to see the joke.[18]

Mustafa Kemal's symposia were platonic in the sense that few of the guests had the capacity to turn general principles into effective action. As Falih Rıfkı (Atay) was to write in his memoirs, 'When Mustafa Kemal founded the new state, he had the smallest and least qualified staff seen in the country's modern history. The brainy set did not turn up in Ankara. Many were opposed to the new regime.' The revolution was born in chaos, another Kemalist writer, Yakup Kadri Karaosmanoğlu noted.[19] Sensing this, Mustafa Kemal respected foreign experts and defended their work. But, at the same time, he reacted furiously to any suggestion that Turks were incapable of learning, and always encouraged newly trained local professionals, praising them beyond their merits.[20]

One frequent guest at the Gazi's table was Tevfik Rüştü (Aras), who held the foreign ministry for thirteen years from 1925 to the end of Atatürk's life. Foreign policy can be the undoing of absolute rulers, tempted to foreign adventure in order to compensate for failure at home or spurred on by domestic adulation. Mustafa Kemal did not fall into the trap. He had witnessed the failure of Enver's adventures, which had hastened the destruction of the Ottoman empire, and he was determined not to jeopardize the fruits of his victory in the Turkish War of Independence. Satisfied as he was with the gains achieved in Lausanne, his main concern was to safeguard the post-war settlement. In his 1931 election manifesto he said that his aim was 'Peace at home and peace in the world'[21] – a formula which was repeated many times. As Bolshevik Russia was still building up its strength, the main danger to the settlement came at first from Mussolini's ambitions and the grievances of two small countries – Hungary and Bulgaria – which had lost territory in the Great War.

The position of Greece was at first uncertain. It had gained territory, but had been disappointed in its wilder ambitions at the expense of Turkey. The understanding which İsmet had achieved with Venizelos in Lausanne helped prevent any Greek moves against Turkey, and with his return to power in Athens in 1928, there followed the rapid settlement of property claims and disputes about the exact terms of the exchange of population agreed at Lausanne. Agreement was hastened by the Turkish decision to modernize the battleship *Yavuz*. Unwilling to engage in an arms race in the Aegean, Venizelos visited Ankara in October 1930, where a comprehensive settlement[22] was signed amid organized demonstrations of friendship. Mustafa Kemal had no time for historic enmities or atrocity-mongering. When a painting showing a Turkish soldier plunging his bayonet into the body of his fallen Greek enemy was put up in his house in Çankaya, he is said to have exclaimed, 'What a revolting scene!', and ordered its immediate removal.[23]

Venizelos's visit was returned the following year by İsmet, who was surprised by the warmth of his welcome in Athens,[24] although he took care to point out that friendship did not mean that Greek refugees would be able to return to Turkey.[25] Venizelos's fall from power did not halt the improvement in relations. His successor, Panayotis Tsaldaris, went to Ankara in September 1933, where a more comprehensive *Entente Cordiale* was signed.[26] It was a stepping stone to a wider Balkan Pact. But first, İsmet had to reassure Stalin.

Under a protocol signed in Ankara in December 1929, Turkey and the Soviet Union undertook not to conclude treaties with any of their neighbours without obtaining each other's agreement. A secret protocol named Greece, Bulgaria, the British empire and France among Turkey's neighbours.[27] When İsmet visited Moscow in 1932, he informed Stalin that he meant to work for an inclusive Balkan Pact, which would not be directed against the Soviets, and also to join the League of Nations, without waiting for a similar move by the Soviet Union. Stalin expressed misgivings, but did not object.[28] Having discharged its obligation, Turkey accepted in July 1932 the invitation of the League of Nations to become a member. Membership of the International Court of Justice at The Hague followed three years later.[29]

Negotiations with the Balkan states were pushed forward, and led to the signature of the Balkan Pact on 9 February 1934.[30] However, Bulgaria refused to join. The pact was hedged in by reservations: Turkey promised that it would never be directed against the Soviets; Greece made it clear that action would be taken only against a Balkan country which attacked another Balkan country, and never against a great power; a secret protocol spelled out that the pact guaranteed only the frontiers between Balkan states.[31] Bulgaria was the only country which the pact could conceivably restrain, and in July 1938 it signed an agreement with the pact as a whole, renouncing the use of force.[32] It was to prove an empty promise in the Second World War, when Bulgarians were allowed by Nazi Germany to occupy Greek, Yugoslav and Romanian territory. The Balkan Pact was a false dawn, but it shone brightly for a time. There were Balkan sports, games and folklore festivals, visits and banquets. The treatment of Turks in Greek western Thrace and of Greeks in Istanbul improved for a few years. Venizelos put up Atatürk for the Nobel peace prize,[33] but with no success. The pink house in Salonica where Atatürk is supposed to have been born was donated to the Turkish state, and a plaque outside described Atatürk as the 'architect of the Balkan Pact'.

Mustafa Kemal certainly took it all seriously. There were even rumours that he was thinking of a Balkan confederation of which he would become president, leaving a trusted lieutenant to be president of Turkey.[34] If he did think of it at all, it was a daydream, like the passing fancy attributed to him by his secretary Hasan Rıza (Soyak) to leave the presidency to Nuri (Conker) and lead the Republican People's Party against the Free Republicans in 1930. If his party were then defeated he would have been happy, Hasan Rıza claims, to go on a world tour and pursue his study of Turkish language and history in the company of foreign scholars.[35] But there was always unfinished business at home, and the consolation of the nightly gathering of admiring followers, obedient ministers and eager petitioners. Rather than go abroad himself, foreigners could come to him.

In September 1932, the US army chief of staff, General Douglas MacArthur, visited Istanbul. Mustafa Kemal received him in Dolmabahçe palace.[36] In August 1951, at the height of the Cold War, an American magazine, *The Caucasus*, published an unsigned article purporting to quote verbatim some remarks which Mustafa Kemal had addressed to the general. According to this account, Mustafa Kemal told MacArthur that Germany had the means to create an army capable of occupying the whole of Europe, that England could no longer rely on France, which had lost its martial spirit, and that 'civilization, and even the whole of mankind', was threatened by the new and terrible power of Bolshevik Russia, which would emerge as the victor in a new European war. The report is suspect, for it was in 1932 that İsmet negotiated the Russian loan; and the following year, when Mustafa Kemal opened the new session of parliament, he stressed the deep sincerity of Turkey's friendship with the Soviet Union – a friendship which he described as a valuable contribution to international peace.[37] İsmet admits in his memoirs that he held at the time the mistaken belief that Bolshevik Russia would not be a threat to Turkey for another twenty-five years – a prediction which was falsified as a result of Hitler's aggression.[38] This implies that he, and probably Mustafa Kemal as well, entertained the possibility that Russia might one day be a threat; but in the meantime they took every care not to antagonize Stalin.

There are other stories attributing prophetic powers to Mustafa Kemal. He is said to have objected to the construction of a Turkish embassy in Warsaw on the grounds that the future of Poland was uncertain.[39] As for his documented predictions, his record was mixed. He told Turkish journalists in 1923 that the next war would be fought between France and Russia and that England would seek to profit by it.[40] He was luckier in 1935 when he told the American journalist Gladys Baker that the United States could not stand aside if war broke out. The Americans would be like occupants of the most luxurious apartment in a block of flats set on fire by some of its other tenants.[41]

There were other foreign visitors. In 1929, King Amanullah of Afghanistan became the first foreign head of state to make a state visit to the Turkish republic.[42] He was to return twice after losing his throne – in 1933, when Mustafa Kemal received him in the Dolmabahçe palace,[43] and in 1938 to attend Atatürk's funeral. In January 1931 Prince Takamutsu came to promote Japanese industrial exports. Later that year, King Faysal of Iraq spent a few days in Ankara under the watchful eye of the British ambassador. In October 1933, King Alexander of Yugoslavia arrived by warship in Istanbul and was received by the president. These were not world figures of the first rank, but Mustafa Kemal made the most of each visit to display the achievements of his republic.

The tenth anniversary of the proclamation of the republic on 29 October 1933 was the occasion of proud celebrations. There was a big military parade in Ankara. Most countries were represented by their ambassadors, but Stalin sent his commissar for defence, Kliment Voroshilov, and the inspector of the Red Cavalry, Marshal Budenny, to publicize Soviet-Turkish friendship, newly reinvigorated with Russian gold. A French-trained young Turkish musician, Cemal Reşit (Rey), composed a catchy tune for the Tenth Anniversary March. The opening line of the lyrics – 'We have come out of ten years of struggle, heads held high' – reflected the confidence of those lucky members of the rising generation, educated in new Western knowledge, who were preparing to take charge of the country. Their last survivors remember the tenth anniversary as a dawn of hope and promise; in their eyes, Mustafa Kemal had made a reality of the positivist motto 'order and progress'.

The Gazi marked the anniversary with his last memorable speech. It was brief, putting in a few words his belief that Turkey would not only join the ranks of the most prosperous and civilized nations of the world, but would surpass them thanks to its unity of purpose and its choice of 'positive science' as a guiding light. The speech ended with the words, 'Happy is he (or she) who calls himself (or herself) a Turk.'[44] It is today the most familiar of all Turkish quotations. It has been incised in huge letters on the Kyrenia range in Cyprus for the eyes of Greek Cypriots, and it taunts Kurdish nationalists in Diyarbakır, the chief city of Turkey's Kurdish-speaking area. But if Mustafa Kemal's favourite journalist Falih Rıfkı (Atay) is to be believed, the author of the quotation was himself unmoved. As guests at his dinner-table gave vent to the emotion which the anniversary stirred in their breasts, Mustafa Kemal said: 'As for me, I feel nothing.' Falih Rıfkı was to say that this was the first sign of Mustafa Kemal's exhaustion.[45]

Mustafa Kemal abided by the rules he had made. 'In our country,' he complained to his secretary Hasan Rıza (Soyak), 'the president's only function is to sign documents.' He went on:

I'm bored to tears. I am usually alone during the day. Everybody is at work, but my work hardly occupies an hour. Then I have the choice of sleeping, if I can, reading or writing something or other. If I want to take the air for a break, I must go by car. And then, it's back to prison, where I play billiards by myself as I wait for dinner. Dinner doesn't bring variety. No matter where it is, it's roughly the same people, the same faces, the same talk. I've had enough, boy.[46]

Atatürk was often described as a dictator – a description he hated above all others.[47] It was, in fact, inappropriate, for he behaved not like a modern dictator, but like a latter-day king, who had delegated government to his chief minister, and then sought to amuse himself as best he could. The logbook, kept by the presidential guard, reveals a clear pattern: the gathering round the dinner-table was usually the high point, and night was turned into day. The Gazi was in Ankara in December 1931. The logbook notes:

8 December. His Excellency the Gazi got up at 15.25 hours; at 17.00, he went to Marmara [the house on his Ankara Forest Farm], returning at 19.15. He retired at 3.30 a.m. He received [the interior and foreign ministers] ...

9 December. H.E. the President got up at 13.15 hours; at 16.15 he went for a drive in town, returning to Çankaya at 18.00 hours and retiring at 4.30 a.m. He received [a list of eleven names follows, including two ministers and 'the usual gentlemen'] ...

10 December. H.E. the President got up at 17.30 hours. He did not go out and received guests in the evening, retiring at 5 a.m. ...

11 December. H.E. the President got up at 15.30. He went to the Bulgarian operetta at 21.15, returning at 00.30 and retiring at 3 a.m. ...[48]

Mustafa Kemal began his day, or afternoon, by sitting cross-legged on a sofa. Dressed in a linen nightshirt, he sipped Turkish coffee and smoked cigarettes as he glanced at the day's papers. According to his secretary, he consumed up to fifteen cups of coffee and almost three packets of cigarettes a day. Unlike most Turks of his generation, he bathed daily.[49] He was particular about his clothes. In Istanbul he employed a Greek tailor and shoemaker. The underclothes exhibited in the house he occupied in Istanbul in 1919 were made in France of crêpe de Chine. He had a Jewish dentist, Sami Ginsberg, who had earlier looked after the teeth of members of the Ottoman dynasty. As a member of the Çankaya secretariat noted in his memoirs, skilled jobs were in the hands of non-Muslims when the Gazi took over from the Ottomans in Istanbul.[50]

Mustafa Kemal was only 50 years old in 1931, the year to which the logbook entries refer. Two years later, his chief secretary Hikmet (Bayur), who was writing down the text of the tenth anniversary speech with its promise of new and greater achievements, burst out: 'If you worked the way you did during the National Struggle you would certainly get there quickly, but if you go from dinner-table to bed and from bed to dinner-table, the way you do now, the job will be long and hard.' Mustafa Kemal's response was to whisper to his private secretary Hasan Rıza (Soyak): 'We would be offended if we did not know him for an honest man.'[51] To vary his life, Mustafa Kemal spent some evenings out at the Ankara Palace hotel and, when he was in Istanbul, in the Pera Palace, the new Park Hotel, and the *Rose Noire* and *Garden Bar* night-clubs.[52] There he would mingle with other customers and invite some of them to his table. But 'the usual gentlemen' went with him too.

The Ankara Palace was the venue for official balls and receptions. At the Republic Day Ball on 29 October 1932, Mustafa Kemal was offended by the sight of the fez worn by the Egyptian ambassador. According to the official Turkish explanation furnished later, he suggested politely that the ambassador would feel more comfortable without his fez, when the official part of the reception was over. But press reports claimed that the ambassador had been ordered to remove his fez and place it on a silver tray held by a waiter, and that he did so to avoid an incident. Egypt protested; Turkey insisted that no insult had been meant, and the matter was closed. On subsequent official occasions, the ambassador wore his red fez with impunity.[53]

It was also in October 1932 that Mustafa Kemal acquired a proper presidential palace in Ankara. Built next to the old villa in Çankaya by the Austrian architect Clemens Holzmeister, the palace was a plain two-floor pink building in the modern style, with strong horizontal lines and large windows looking on to the growing new city below. The population of Ankara had risen to 150,000, and a German specialist Hermann Jansen was commissioned that year to prepare a city plan to accommodate 300,000 people within fifty years. In fact, fifty years later the population of the capital exceeded two million, and Jansen's neat model of a modern city of tree-lined residential streets was buried in concrete.[54]

Mustafa Kemal's routine was interrupted by state occasions, visits by foreign dignitaries, conferences, provincial tours and military manoeuvres. His behaviour could be eccentric. The composer Paul Hindemith, who was invited to Turkey in 1935 to advise on musical education, was woken up at 3 a.m. one night and taken by car to Çankaya palace to play for the president.[55]

Outwardly, Mustafa Kemal led a pleasant and relaxed life. He told the American journalist Gladys Baker in 1935: 'I am happy, because I have been successful.'[56] But Yakup Kadri (Karaosmanoğlu), a frequent guest at the Gazi's table, believed that his host was not a happy man, because reality never measured up to his ideals.[57] Kâzım Karabekir, the disgraced rival seething in retirement, claimed that, although he was followed by plainclothes police for fifteen years, he led a happier life than Mustafa Kemal, who was surrounded by 'unquestioned pomp'.[58] It was sour grapes. Mustafa Kemal had fun the moment the cloud of alcoholic depression lifted, and his enthusiasm, diverted from boring office work, found new fields of endeavour.

27

Last Battles

THE YEAR IN which Turkey celebrated the tenth anniversary of the republic, 1933, was also the year in which Hitler came to power. As Nazi Germany took the lead in efforts to destroy the Versailles settlement, its defenders looked for partners in collective security. Turkey was already active in what was known as the 'anti-revisionist' camp in the Balkans. Now it moved to a wider stage. The League of Nations had been set up to safeguard the post-war settlement, and the Turkish government took an active part in its, ultimately fruitless, deliberations. But Turkey had to tread warily. The main concern of both Mustafa Kemal and İsmet was to safeguard their country's independence and territorial integrity, and to find resources to develop its economy and strengthen its new institutions. Beyond that, Mustafa Kemal was more conscious of opportunities, İsmet of dangers in the new unstable situation. İsmet sought to avoid commitments which might antagonize one or other of the great powers.[1] He was a man of extreme prudence, and he was worried that 'the usual gentlemen' and other habitués of the president's court might tempt Mustafa Kemal into an unwise move.

Fortunately for İsmet, Mustafa Kemal's interest in language and history had become a passion, which consumed much of his time and energy. He discussed foreign and domestic policies with İsmet and his foreign minister, Tevfik Rüştü (Aras); he lent an ear to complaints against the government conveyed to him by the 'usual gentlemen', but he respected İsmet's judgement and stood by him. İsmet for his part was a convinced believer in the Gazi's blueprint for a modern Turkey.

Mustafa Kemal's interest in history had practical aims. Racist theories were rife in his lifetime, and President Wilson's advocacy of national self-determination had not displaced the belief that ownership of territory had to be justified in terms of 'historic rights'. The territory of Turkey was littered with monuments left by Hittites, Phrygians, Lydians, Greeks, Romans, Byzantines, Armenians. Did this mean that the Turks, who were latecomers to the land, had no 'historic right' to it? The main Turkish monuments were either mosques or fortifications. Did that mean that the Turks' contribution to civilization was restricted to a Muslim culture, frozen in its medieval mould, and to the art of war, and that they were incapable of anything else? For all their currency in contemporary Western discourse, these were silly questions. Inevitably, they produced a silly answer.

This posited that all the peoples who had lived in and around Turkey were of Turkish origin – Elamites and Sumerians, Akkadians and Scythians, Achaeans and other early Greek tribes, not to mention Hittites, Phrygians, Lydians, Carians, the people of Urartu and anyone else who left a civilized memorial behind. *Ergo*, the Turks had a historic right to their land, had created great civilizations, and were capable of contributing to the one, universal, modern civilization. It would have been simpler to say that the Turks had a right to the land because they lived in it and formed the overwhelming majority of its population, and that they were as capable of acquiring and contributing to the sum of human knowledge as any other community which is given the chance.[2] Mustafa Kemal did his best to give his people that chance, but he could not step outside a debate whose terms had been dictated by the masters of the contemporary universe. In any case, he was an avid reader of history and believed in its value. Unfortunately, this led him to promote the production of fantastic tales.

The task of writing a history centred on the Turks was entrusted in 1930 to a committee of the nationalist Turkish Hearths. It was then taken over by the Turkish Historical Society, set up in 1931. Turkey had a number of competent Ottoman historians, but knowledge of world history came to it from foreign works. Scholarly specialist studies or popular books, like Mustafa Kemal's favourite *Outline of History* by H.G. Wells (which he read in French translation), were combed for anything that could be construed as a favourable reference to the Turks. Starting in 1930, Turkish historians worked with Mustafa Kemal in Ankara, Yalova and the Dolmabahçe palace, where they had their own office. A first *Outline of Turkish History* (*Türk Tarihinin Ana Hatları*) was produced quickly in 1930. Mustafa Kemal dictated some passages and corrected others. The following year the *Outline* formed the basis of textbooks for 15- to 18-year old pupils. They were given maps showing how the Turks had moved out in prehistoric times from their original homeland in central Asia to people and civilize the world; they had to memorize unpronounceable names of Hittite kings; they learnt that Islam was an incident in Turkish history and the multinational nature of the Ottoman empire an aberration. The proposition that the Turks were second to none led to the claim that they were better than anyone else.

Unscientific history, made up to serve political purposes, was the exotic fruit of a rationalism which rejected all religious and other metaphysical doctrines. 'One must accept,' the *Outline of Turkish History* declared, 'that life is the natural and necessary outcome of chemical and physical processes, unaffected by any external intervention from outside nature.'[3] Nevertheless, religion is an important social and psychological phenomenon, subject to evolution. But now that man has discovered his strength, society has become the source of contentment and security, and the basis for humanity's further progress in maturity.[4] Mustafa Kemal's historiography was the product of his clash with domestic Islam and foreign detractors. He hoped that apart from giving his people confidence in their abilities, it would make them better and more knowledgeable guardians of the artistic monuments that form the pre-Islamic heritage of their country. To some extent this has happened.

His interest in language was also initially functional. The movement to simplify Ottoman Turkish and to narrow the gap between the official and the spoken language had started before the Great War. This movement gained strength from the adoption of the Latin script in 1928/9. The next step was to imitate French and other European languages in vocabulary and word-formation. But, just as the Latin alphabet was called officially the Turkish alphabet, so borrowings and imitations were given a Turkish dressing. Linguistic engineering reflected cultural engineering. The new names picked for educational establishments – *okul* (school: an amalgam of the French *école* and the Turkish *oku*, meaning 'read'), *lise* (*lycée*), *üniversite* – proclaimed the fact that they taught Western knowledge. The international trade fair, first held in İzmir in 1936, was called *İzmir Enternasyonal Fuarı*, making it international in name as well as in intended scope. Linguistic nationalism was a European invention, practised widely by Germans, Hungarians, Russians, Finns and others, and not unknown in France and even England. Mustafa Kemal pushed it to extreme lengths. In 1930 he set out his aim: 'The Turkish nation, which has proved its ability to defend its country and its full independence, should also free its language from the yoke of foreign languages.'[5]

Two years later, a Turkish Language Society[6] was founded as a sister organization of the Turkish Historical Society. Mustafa Kemal gave it the task of simplifying and purifying the language by bringing written Turkish closer to the spoken tongue and by trawling dictionaries of various Turkic languages (composed mainly by foreigners) for 'pure' Turkish words which had fallen into disuse. In addition, researchers were asked to travel the length and breadth of the country to record Turkish words which had survived only in provincial usage. In fact the laudable aim of simplification was compromised by the ideal of purification. An adequate 'pure' Turkish vocabulary could not be formed by reviving old-fashioned and provincial words and quarrying central Asian Turkic languages (and sometimes importing from them words of Mongol or Indo-European Sogdian origin under the misapprehension that they were 'pure' Turkish). There were 92,000 words in the French *Larousse Universel*, Mustafa Kemal was informed, while the most complete Turkish dictionary contained only 40,000 words.[7] To make up the shortfall, words were coined in Mustafa Kemal's dining-room, where a blackboard stood ready for the purpose. Guests came up with ideas for new Turkish words, which the Gazi then discussed, adopted or adapted. The outcome was a private language, at least as remote from everyday usage as high Ottoman Turkish. The high point of the process was a short, totally incomprehensible speech with which Mustafa Kemal greeted the Swedish Crown Prince Gustav Adolf in Ankara in October 1934.[8]

A complementary approach was found fortuitously the following year. Mustafa Kemal was shown a paper sent in by a Dr Hermann Kvergić of Vienna who argued that all languages derived from exclamations made by primitive man as he contemplated nature, and that the original sounds so uttered were embedded in Turkish. With Mustafa Kemal's enthusiastic support, this unprovable hypothesis was developed into the Sun-Language Theory (*Güneş Dil Teorisi*), named thus because 'it is among us Turks that, in the journey of history, the inspiration of the Sun has left its most abundant marks. The Turkish race found its culture in a place where the Sun was most beneficent. When the Turks were forced to move out of their first homeland, the Sun served as their guide along their paths of migration.'[9]

The Sun-Language Theory, like the Turkish history thesis, was a wayward product of rationalism: of nineteenth-century theories about 'the great migration of peoples', applied first to the Indo-Europeans and now transposed to the Turks; of animism as the origin of religion ('The Turk worships only nature,' Mustafa Kemal told a German journalist in 1929[10]); of the Marxist theory (developed by Nikolay Marr, who visited Turkey) that language was part of the 'superstructure' determined by the economic 'infrastructure' of society. Mustafa Kemal's wishful thinking shaped the conclusion that the Turks, as Sun-worshippers *par excellence*, were also the originators of language. It was a convenient conclusion. If all languages derived from Turkish, the Turks were only getting their own back when they borrowed words from other languages, and, particularly, from the languages of civilized Western peoples. Sycophants fell over each other in their enthusiasm for the Sun-Language Theory. Mustafa Kemal was convinced, and ordered that the theory should be taught at the new university in Ankara. He told a young French financial expert, Hervé Alphand, that his name was Turkish as it comprised the words *alp* (champion) and *han* (or khan, a ruler). In confirmation, Mustafa Kemal felt Alphand's skull: it was, he decided, brachycephalic, the characteristic skull-shape of the Turkish race.[11]

At the third congress of the Turkish Language Society, in 1936, foreign linguists damned the Sun-Language Theory with their silence. But Mustafa Kemal was not deflected, and he pursued to the end of his life the campaign to derive from Turkish roots foreign words which had entered the language. The Sun-Language Theory is remembered today by an absurd example: the derivation of the name of the river Amazon from the Turkish words *ama* ('but' – the word is in fact of Arabic origin) and *uzun* ('long'), on the grounds that the first migrants to South America, who were, of course, Turkish-speaking, exclaimed on seeing the river, 'But (isn't it) long!'[12] A library attendant, whose job it was to dust the shelves, was allowed to publish his contribution to Turkish etymology. One of Atatürk's linguistic advisers was to say in his memoirs that this was a joke.[13] In fact the whole of the Sun-Language Theory became a joke, and it was laid to rest quietly when Atatürk died.

The 'purification' of Turkish survived the demise of the Sun-Language Theory. Begun by edict, it was taken up by the young generation, educated in Western knowledge and seeking to express in Turkish the ideas it was taught. 'Pure' Turkish became a badge of progressive attitudes, and it spread with them. Like the languages of other developing societies, which import knowledge, Turkish has become largely a translated language. The names of new imported objects and concepts enter the language either in their original form or in literal Turkish translation. It would have been pointless to go on translating them into Arabic, as the Ottomans had done.[14] 'Pure' Turkish has not displaced all words of Arabic and Persian origin. Many remain in current use, sometimes as synonyms of 'pure' Turkish words, sometimes expressing a different shade of meaning.

Atatürk's linguistic policy made high Ottoman, the language which he himself used until the 1930s, largely unintelligible. But his linguistic revolution was followed by the evolution of a language, rich in borrowings from all sources and in neologisms, largely adequate to serve the needs of a modern society, and refined by imaginative writers. What was linguistically extreme in his day is now commonplace. True, many of his coinages did not survive, but his policy of using Turkish roots to form new words did, and it made the language more accessible. The introduction of the Latin script and of 'pure' Turkish cut off the people from a literary past – a past that was largely medieval and oriental in spirit. After the change of script, 'a cultured Turk' predicted to Telford Waugh that it 'would destroy the Turkish language in ten years'.[15] It did not. Instead it gave birth to a new form of Turkish, which has not yet totally shed its artificial origins. The same is true of Atatürk's other reforms.

The Gazi's policy of encouraging the use of Turkish in Muslim worship caused controversy which has lasted to this day. Arabic is the liturgical language of Islam. The Koran may be translated as an aid to understanding, but the Arabic original alone must be used in worship, and all canonical prayers must also be said in Arabic. Mustafa Kemal desisted from a frontal attack on this deeply held doctrine. Instead, he decided that Turkish should be used on the edges of the liturgy – in the call to prayer (*ezan*), the opening prayer (*kamet*) and the formal homily (*hutbe*).

A homily was delivered in Turkish for the first time on 3 February 1928. Then, on 22 January 1932, a portion of the Koran was recited in Turkish in an Istanbul mosque, again for the first time. It was meant for the edification of the faithful. On 18 July of the same year, religious authorities in Istanbul announced that the call to prayer (both *ezan* and *kamet*) would have to be recited in Turkish within a few months.[16] Implementation was patchy, and, as usual, uncertainty led to trouble. On 1 February 1933 a small group of faithful protested against the introduction of the call to prayer in Turkish in the great mosque (*Ulu Cami*) in Bursa, and pointed out that Arabic was still permitted elsewhere. The police stopped a march to the governor's office and arrested the leaders of what was immediately described as a 'hateful reactionary incident'. The press reported that the government had received hundreds of telegrams denouncing the reactionaries.

Mustafa Kemal, who had insisted that an example should be made of the religious fanatics in Menemen a year earlier, was more relaxed this time. Arriving in Bursa on 6 February, he declared that the incident was not particularly important. Language, and not religion, was the crux of the matter. Everybody should realize, Mustafa Kemal went on, that the Turkish national language and identity would infuse the whole of life. Meanwhile, no tolerance would be extended to anyone who used religion for political purposes, and 'ignorant reactionaries' would be punished. A few local officials were dismissed, and the ringleaders of the protest were imprisoned. There are no reports of any executions. On 6 March 1933, the department of religious affairs ordered that the call to prayer should be recited in Turkish everywhere 'in accordance with the national purpose of our exalted government'.[17] However, this was an administrative ordinance and not a law. The faithful continued to use Arabic in canonically prescribed prayers (*namaz*). The Bursa incident showed that it was not safe to go further in Turkishing Muslim worship.

In June 1934, in the midst of strenuous efforts to create a new history and a new language, Mustafa Kemal made surnames compulsory for all Turkish citizens. The usefulness of the measure was hard to dispute. A few families had acquired surnames; some individuals had nicknames. But the majority of Muslim Turks were known only by their forenames. To help identify them, documents specified their parents' names. In military schools cadets were known by their forenames and places of birth. This traditional system could not serve the needs of a modern society, and the obligation to adopt surnames was readily accepted. Inevitably, the change caused some confusion.

Mustafa Kemal thought long and hard about the surname he should adopt. Finally, in November he chose for himself the name Atatürk, literally Father Turk – that is, father of the Turks. It shed light on his state of mind: the innovator was now 53 years old and felt paternally middle-aged. With no children of his own, he could be father to all Turks. The description of the ruler as father of his people was commonplace: Abdülhamit II, reviled by Western liberals as the Red (bloody) Sultan, was known to Muslim Turks as *Baba Hamit*, Daddy Hamit. *Ata* was grander, signifying not only a father, but the progenitor of a line. The assembly passed a law restricting the surname Atatürk to the person of the Gazi Mustafa Kemal Paşa, who thereafter signed himself simply as 'K. Atatürk'. His relatives had to have different surnames: his sister Makbule was called Atadan (literally 'from [the family of] the father'), and his adopted daughters each had a different surname.

Atatürk then amused himself by devising surnames for his friends and associates. İsmet was named after İnönü, the battlefield where on two occasions he had checked the Greek advance. But as the surname started with him, his mother and brothers had to choose a different name (Temelli). Like İsmet, many generals chose to be called by the places where they had won their battle honours, and all the peaks round Afyon, the scene of the final Turkish victory in the War of

Independence, were appropriated by commanders who had taken part in the battle. As amongst other peoples, presumed places of origin or trade names were adopted by many families. But most had recourse to the list of approved pure Turkish names, which was helpfully circulated. It stressed masculine qualities: Hard (*Sert*), Tough (*Çetin*), Uncowed (*Yılmaz*), Iron (*Demir*), Steel (*Çelik*), Rock (*Kaya*). These were so popular that they were chosen both as surnames and as forenames for newborn boys. They could be combined as in Çetinkaya (Tough Rock) or Demirel (Iron Hand). They were supplemented by 'pure' Turkish coinages of which Atatürk was a prolific producer, as witness the scraps of paper, preserved by proud Turkish families, on which the founder of the republic wrote the name he had chosen for them and its alleged significance. Even so, there were not enough descriptions of masculine qualities, other virtues, or claims to patriotic origin or devotion to go round. As a result, a common claim to the name Öztürk (Pure Turk) is no more a proof of a family relationship than is the common possession of the surname Smith among English-speaking people. But in Turkey, surnames, being of more recent origin, shed greater light on the claims of close ancestors and the spirit of their age.

The egalitarian impact of the general adoption of surnames was reinforced by two further measures. In November 1934, a law was passed abolishing all traditional titles and distinctions – including Pasha, Bey, Efendi, Hanım (for ladies) and Hoca (for clerics and teachers). All citizens were to be known thenceforth as Mr (*Bay*, a central Asian Turkic word for a rich man) and Mrs/Miss (*Bayan*, a neologism, the second syllable -*an* echoing that of Madame). Adopted immediately for official purposes, these two simple titles, which precede the name as in the West, unlike their predecessors which followed it, are to this day rarely used in everyday life. Generals are still informally called Pasha, while in polite conversation Bey and Hanım continue to follow the forenames of men and women respectively, and academics address each other as 'My hoca' (*hocam*) as readily as Catholic priests call each other 'Father'. But civility is one thing, and the theoretical equality of all citizens, decreed by Atatürk, another.

The second measure, introduced in December 1934,[18] banned clerical dress outside places of worship and religious ceremonies. It had already been restricted to officially recognized clerics. Now it vanished from public view. On 2 February 1935, the great basilica of St Sophia, a mosque since the conquest of Istanbul by the Turks in 1453, was opened to the public as a secular museum.[19] Finally, in May 1935, a new law on official holidays made Sunday a day of rest instead of Friday, the Muslim day of congregational prayer.[20]

Atatürk's reforms were complete: not only was the state secular; it looked it. Similarly, not only was it national, but it looked it, as notices in foreign languages were banned; and it sounded it, as citizens were urged to speak only Turkish, particularly in public.

A resettlement law passed in 1934[21] classified the territory of the republic under three headings: areas where the number of people of Turkish culture should be increased; areas where people who were to be assimilated to Turkish culture were to be transferred; and areas to be evacuated. Immigrants who were not of 'Turkish race' were to be settled at the discretion of the government. People who were not 'attached to Turkish culture', anarchists, spies and nomadic gypsies, were not allowed into the country. The following year, permanent military government was established in the Dersim mountains (renamed the province of Tunceli, literally 'Bronze-land' on the assumption that it had been inhabited by Turks since the Bronze Age). The military governor was authorized to relocate the population and ratify death sentences.[22] The local tribes – Alevi (Shiite) Kurds, speaking the Zaza (Dımılî) language – rose in revolt. It was suppressed ruthlessly, and the area was pacified. For the next fifty years, the Kurds of Dersim gave little trouble to the government in Ankara.

Atatürk had little time for administrative detail and it cannot be assumed that he thought out these and similar measures, to which he gave his formal assent. Faced since its foundation with the Bolshevik and the Italian fascist models, the Turkish republic was now exposed to the influence of German Nazis. The economic crisis had, in any case, increased anti-foreign prejudice everywhere, along with protectionism, and Turkey was not alone in restricting jobs to its nationals.

The nationalization of foreign-owned railways, harbours and utilities was completed. There was a pervasive fear of spies, and social contacts with foreigners were discouraged. The chief of the general staff, Marshal Fevzi Çakmak, was a keen proponent of military security areas from which foreigners were excluded: foreign sailors could be arrested if they strayed near Atatürk's summer house at Yalova, near the İzmit naval base. The Marshal objected to the use of radio aerials in Istanbul, in case they were used for spy transmissions.[23] Potential domestic opponents were kept under close surveillance. There was a crack-down on Marxists in 1932, and the poet Nazım Hikmet (Ran) was arrested and kept in prison until 1934. Two persons were closely involved in these repressive policies: Recep Peker, secretary-general of the Republican People's Party, and Şükrü Kaya, interior minister from 1931 to the end of Atatürk's life.

Elections to the assembly were held in February 1935. There was a single list of candidates, but the People's Party allowed sixteen independents to be returned unopposed. The most notable was Atatürk's estranged companion General Refet Bele. Women took part for the first time, and eighteen were elected, or rather appointed, in a parliament of nearly 400 members. The number of women MPs decreased subsequently, particularly when elections became genuinely free. Another innovation was the appointment of four non-Muslim deputies – two Greeks, one Armenian and one Jew (one of Atatürk's private doctors).[24] They knew they were in parliament for presentational purposes. On 1 March 1935, Atatürk was re-elected president of the republic for the fourth and last time.

His next move was to make his Republican People's Party totally subservient to the state. The party's powerful secretary-general Recep Peker had been to Nazi Germany, and on the eve of the party convention in May 1935 he drew up a proposal to put the single party in charge of the administration. According to Atatürk's secretary, Hasan Rıza Soyak, İsmet İnönü countersigned the proposal. Atatürk was horrified. 'Who is to elect these bullies?' he asked his secretary.[25] Peker had already angered Atatürk by trying to undermine the position of the latter's friend, General Kâzım Dirik, governor of İzmir at the time of the attempt on Atatürk's life and now Inspector-General for Thrace. Dirik had imposed levies on the peasants to finance local improvements; the local party official had opposed the measure. Atatürk sided with General Dirik, and the official was transferred.[26]

This was not enough for Atatürk. At the evening gathering in Çankaya which coincided with the party convention on 15 May, he told Peker that he should be more careful in his choice of party officials: the man transferred from Thrace should not be let loose in any part of the country. Peker was infuriated by the public rebuke and took the unprecedented step of stalking out of the gathering. Atatürk sacked him there and then.[27] The following day, İnönü, as deputy leader of the party (Atatürk was the nominal leader), announced a new dispensation: the interior minister, Şükrü Kaya, would become secretary-general of the party, which would henceforth be run by a triumvirate consisting of the president of the republic, the prime minister and the interior minister; regional inspectors-general and provincial governors would be in charge both of the administration and of party organization in their respective areas.[28]

Atatürk prevented the spread to Turkey of totalitarian party rule which held sway in the Soviet Union, Germany and Italy. In Turkey, it was the state and not the party which was the master. But, at the same time, Atatürk's administration was totally shielded from criticism – first the opposition was silenced, and then the official single party itself. The fusion of state and party was enshrined in the constitution the following year. Two amendments were voted on 5 February 1937: under the first, the six principles ('arrows') of the Republican People's Party were given constitutional force; the second provided that political counsellors, selected from the membership of the assembly, should be attached to ministers.[29] But soon afterwards, Atatürk decided that political counsellors were interfering busybodies. In November 1937, their posts were abolished; the assembly was informed that this had been done at its own request.[30] Members of the assembly did not have to believe this: what they saw was that all along the line the state had triumphed over the party to which they belonged.

Peker was not alone in pushing his luck too far. Atatürk's obedient companion, General Kâzım Özalp, who had been speaker of the assembly since 1924, was unwise enough to allow triumphal arches to be erected for himself when he visited Antalya in February 1935, and to stay in the mansion usually reserved for the president. His enjoyment of the facilities was cut short when Atatürk turned up unexpectedly in the town.[31] But Özalp was luckier than Peker, who, after being dismissed, had to go and teach the history of Atatürk's reforms. Deprived of the speakership of the assembly, Özalp was given the ministry of defence, a job of genuine importance at a time of frantic rearmament in Europe.[32] However, as the constitution provided that the speaker of the assembly stood in for the president of the republic, Özalp's transfer was a demotion, which distanced him from the line of succession.

One intrigue which shook the country concerned the deputy for Urfa, Ali Saip Ursavaş, a former gendarmerie captain of Kurdish origin who had commanded guerrilla bands against the French during the War of Independence. After the war, Ursavaş acquired a large estate near the porous Syrian frontier, and became, by all accounts, a local tyrant. In the autumn of 1935 Ursavaş was accused of plotting with the disgraced guerrilla leader, the Circassian Ethem, by then a refugee in Jordan, to assassinate Atatürk. The accusation was based on the alleged confessions of a Circassian, said to have contacted Ethem before returning to Turkey. Ursavaş was put on trial together with seven others, who, like many local people, made their living by smuggling. This activity had brought them into contact with Ursavaş. After a long trial, all were acquitted in February 1936, on the grounds that the confessions were inconsistent, lacked corroboration and seemed to have been extracted under pressure. Atatürk accepted the verdict. An intrigue against – rather than by – a local bully did not threaten him, as the opposition had done ten years previously at the time of the İzmir assassination attempt.

His only reaction was to stop receiving Ursavaş, who, however, kept his seat in parliament.[33]

Through all these distractions, Atatürk kept an eye on foreign policy, which was conducted by Tevfik Rüştü Aras. The president appeared on the international stage only to receive foreign visitors and ambassadors. Reza Shah Pahlavi of Iran came for a long visit in the summer of 1934 and was duly impressed by Atatürk's achievements. A new opera, extolling the friendship of Turanians and Iranians – the progenitors of Turks and Persians -was staged in his honour in the Ankara People's House. Named *Özsoy* (The Pure Breed), the opera was composed in record time by Ahmet Adnan (Saygun), a member of the group of young, Western-trained composers encouraged by Atatürk to orchestrate Anatolian folk melodies in a Western manner.[34] At a time when the Bolsheviks sought to create a culture 'socialist in content and national in form', Atatürk's aim was that Turkish culture should become national in content, but Western in form, for only thus could it enter the field of universal culture. He wanted Turks to shine in music, painting, sculpture, the theatre. But Atatürk's encouragement had its price: the arts had to serve the cause of progress. Plays which did not damn 'reaction', or which were deemed insulting to Turkey's neighbours and new friends, were banned.[35] Atatürk himself corrected the text of an epic work, *Bayönder* ('The Leader'), written to glorify him. The author, he decided, was not sufficiently discriminating in his choice of 'pure' Turkish words. In another play, he objected to the description of women as 'an adornment' and of love as 'amusement'. 'This is not how we look at women: they are the foundation of the nation,' Atatürk wrote in the margin, and again, 'To think of love as amusement is to devalue it.'[36]

Reza Shah was taken by train to İzmir and then to Istanbul. When the train stopped at Uşak, Atatürk was infuriated by the sight of the local *müftü*, wearing a turban. According to one account, he pushed the turban off the cleric's head, but, discovering later that the *müftü* was a man of enlightened views, sent him a present as a peace offering.[37] The ban on clerical dress was decreed five months after the Uşak incident.

After a banquet held in the Shah's honour at the Ankara Palace on 17 June, the new British ambassador, Sir Percy Loraine, was invited to stay on for a game of poker which went on until the following morning. Atatürk 'played the game with utmost zest and thoroughly enjoyed himself. He played skilfully and was a big winner, but when he terminated the game, he insisted on mixing up all the chips so that there should be no winners and no losers.'[38] The president had behaved in the same way when he had invited the US ambassador Joseph Grew to a game of poker on 20 February 1928.[39] Loraine admired Atatürk, but it would be an exaggeration to say that he had developed a special relationship with the president. After the game, Atatürk spoke to Loraine of his desire for friendly relations with Britain, and was reassured when Loraine said that these need not conflict with Turkey's friendship with Russia. Mussolini helped matters along by threatening simultaneously Britain's interests and Turkey's security in the Mediterranean.

After the Italian invasion of Ethiopia in October 1935, Turkey joined in League of Nations sanctions,[40] all the more readily for the fact that Italy had fortified the Dodecanese islands off the Turkish coast. Mussolini's speeches expounding Italian ambitions in Asia and Africa brought to mind the Italian occupation of Antalya after the Great War. In February 1935 Atatürk had toured the western and southern shores of Anatolia on board a destroyer,[41] beating the bounds of his country in the Mediterranean. Stories about Atatürk's rebuffs to the Italian ambassador – how he put on his marshal's uniform when the ambassador mentioned his country's claim to Antalya, how he challenged the ambassador 'to go and get Antalya', how he predicted that Mussolini would be hanged by his own people[42] – are almost certainly apocryphal. But there is no doubt that he despised Mussolini, as a man who strutted around in a commander's uniform, although, unlike Atatürk, he had never commanded a victorious army.[43] Nevertheless, rather than challenge Mussolini directly, Turkey attempted to draw him into an agreement with the Balkan Pact.[44] The attempt, which failed, illustrates the tactful prudence of Turkish foreign policy.

While Mussolini's threats presented the more immediate danger, it was Hitler's reoccupation of the Rhineland in March 1936 that gave Turkey the opportunity to resume full military control over the straits. 'The situation in Europe,' Atatürk declared, 'is highly appropriate for such a move. We shall certainly achieve it.'[45] In April, the Turkish government sent a memorandum to all the signatories of the Lausanne treaty (plus the Soviet Union and Yugoslavia) suggesting that a conference should revise the provisions governing the Turkish straits. The conference met on 22 June in Montreux, not far from Lausanne on the shores of the lake of Geneva. The Soviet Union was this time a full participant, while Italy, which was the object of sanctions, stayed away. A new convention on the straits was signed on 20 July. Turkey was allowed to fortify the straits area and introduce troops into it, and was given the job of applying the terms of the convention, which provided for unlimited freedom of passage for commercial shipping while regulating the movement of warships, to the advantage of Black Sea states.[46]

The Turkish government had achieved all its aims by legal means, without harming its relations with Britain, France, and its Balkan neighbours. The Soviet Union was not fully satisfied and saw in the convention a sign of Turkey's closer alignment with Britain and France;[47] the Soviet delegate signed it nevertheless. It was a notable diplomatic victory. There were celebrations as Turkish troops took possession of fortifications in the straits. The following year (in August 1937), Atatürk was present at military manoeuvres held in Thrace, outside Istanbul. In 1923 he had expressed the opinion that the area was militarily indefensible. Now fortifications, named the Çakmak line (after the chief of the general staff, Marshal Fevzi Çakmak), began to be built to protect Istanbul and the straits from the west.[48]

The improvement of relations with Britain was symbolized by the private visit of King Edward VIII. He was on a cruise in the Mediterranean with Mrs Wallis Simpson on board the yacht *Nahlin*, and it was arranged that he should stop in Istanbul. The king arrived on 4 September 1936, and Atatürk met him on the quay of Dolmabahçe palace. The following day he accompanied the king in an open car to the British consulate-general, before taking him on the ageing yacht *Ertuğrul* to the new presidential summer house in Florya. In the evening, Atatürk and his guests watched a regatta off Moda, the suburb on the Asian shore favoured by English merchants. The visit produced a crop of apocryphal stories meant to illustrate Atatürk's dignified patriotism. We are told that when a Turkish waiter dropped a plate, Atatürk apologized, saying, 'We can train our people for any job, except that of a lackey',[49] and that when the king steadied himself by placing his hand on the quayside as he landed, Atatürk said, 'Don't worry, the soil of our country is clean.'

The visit of King Edward VIII became an important ingredient of the Atatürk legend: the British monarch had come in person to bury the hatchet, disown the legacy of Gladstone and Lloyd George, and pay homage to the new Turkey. Atatürk had a high opinion of British power and skills. He believed that in world wars, 'Britain had always won and would always do so.' It 'was not merely a power, but a world power; it was ubiquitous; its interests lay everywhere.'[50] The fact that he had worsted the British, militarily in Gallipoli and diplomatically in the War of Independence, made it easier to love the old enemy. The British government was not slow to cultivate the image of chivalrous enemies renewing the bond of friendship. A specially bound copy of General Aspinall-Oglander's official history of the Gallipoli campaign, with its retrospective tribute to Mustafa Kemal, had been presented in Çankaya in 1932. However, the effect was somewhat spoiled later that year by the publication of *Grey Wolf*, H.C. Armstrong's biography of Mustafa Kemal.

Grey Wolf was a sensational mixture of gossip and men's club racism.[51] According to yet another apocryphal story, Atatürk had the book translated for his own eyes, and, after listening to the translation, concluded: 'The government has made a mistake in banning the book. That fellow has made too little of our pleasures. Let me complete the account, and then the book can be allowed and everyone will be able to read it.'[52] The fact is that *Grey Wolf* remained banned in Turkey, and that a first translation appeared only in the 1990s. A rebuttal of the many mistakes in the book was serialized in the newspaper *Akşam* (The Evening), starting from 7 December 1932. It was written by the paper's owner, Necmettin Sadık (Sadak), an MP of the ruling party. However, in his eagerness to flatter Mustafa Kemal, Necmettin Sadık himself strayed into fantasy. The president's father, he claimed, had been a senior officer; he owned six houses in Salonica, as well as forests and timber shops; the president's mother had come from a rich and famous old family.[53] Had Mustafa Kemal been stung by the imputation of modest origins? Or was it his official advocate who believed that a poor background was a disgrace?

Atatürk's appreciation of Britain's cunning use of power did not detract from his admiration of French culture, which had moulded his intellectual development. During the War of Independence, he had detached France from Britain. Now British friendship was useful in wringing an important concession from France. At the end of the Great War, Turkey had ceded the district of İskenderun (Alexandretta) and Antakya (Antioch) to French-mandated Syria. It was done with a heavy heart. Mustafa Kemal had himself kept the Allies out of İskenderun until after the armistice was signed. This meant that the district was part of the territory claimed by Turkish nationalists in their National Pact. Under the 1921 accord, the French had promised to make special arrangements for the protection of Turkish culture in the district of Alexandretta. They respected the promise, and governed the area under a special statute which recognized Turkish as an official language.

The special district (*sancak*, in French spelling *sandjak*) of Alexandretta led a peaceful and prosperous existence under French rule, particularly before the onset of the world depression. According to French statistics, out of a total population of 220,000 in the mid-1930s there were 85,000 Turkish-speaking Sunni Muslims living in the *sancak*; they were the single largest community, numbering many landowners, whose estates were worked by Arabic-speaking heterodox Muslims (properly called Nusayris, but known to the French as Alaouites and to the Turks as Alevis). These formed the second largest community. Armenians, Kurds and others made up the rest of the population. Although feelings of Turkish and Arab nationalism spread gradually, there was little trouble in the *sancak* so long as French rule looked permanent. That prospect disappeared in 1936 when the French Popular Front government signed an agreement with Syrian representatives as a first step towards relinquishing the mandate.

On 26 September 1936, the Turkish foreign minister Tevfik Rüştü Aras told the League of Nations that while his country backed the independence of Syria, the people of the *sancak* should continue to govern themselves. The French declared that they were ready to discuss the necessary arrangements, provided the unity of Syria was safeguarded.[54] Turkey was willing to negotiate, but its aim was different. It saw itself and not Arab Syria as the residuary legatee of the French in the *sancak*. Atatürk decided to make the claim his own. It was to be the last great cause in his life, and it occupied him constantly until his death.

Atatürk staked out his claim when he opened the new session of the assembly on 1 November 1936. The Turks, he said, were the true owners of İskenderun, Antakya and their environs. Their resolve should be appreciated, and this last problem between Turkey and France solved accordingly.[55] Uncertainty about the future disturbed the peace in the disputed territory. Bloody riots erupted as Turkish nationalists clashed with local people – Arabs and Armenians – who wanted their territory to remain part of Syria. At Atatürk's instigation, his secretary and attorney, Hasan Rıza Soyak, was appointed representative of the Turkish community in the *sancak*, and a local Turk, Tayfur Sökmen, was made deputy in the assembly in Ankara. Soyak joined the Turkish delegation which conducted negotiations with France at the League of Nations in Geneva. Before he left, Atatürk told him: 'An independent Turkish state should be formed there [in the *sancak*] under our guarantee.'[56] It was the first step to the annexation of the territory – which Atatürk decided to call Hatay, after Khitai, the name of a medieval grouping of Turkic (or perhaps Mongol) tribes on the northern confines of China. Hatay also brought to mind the Hittites, the Turks' ancestors in Anatolia according to Atatürk's version of history.

In the middle of November 1936, Atatürk fell ill. Pulmonary congestion was diagnosed and he was advised to take a rest and give up drink.[57] At the same time, he developed a rash, a symptom of cirrhosis of the liver, which his doctors had failed to diagnose, and which Atatürk attributed to the presence of ants or perhaps other insects in his

Çankaya mansion. He decided to go to Istanbul and take the waters in Yalova, while Çankaya was disinfected. Illness served only to make him more determined to wrest the *sancak* from Syria. Before leaving Ankara, he invited the French ambassador and military attaché to his table in the night-club of the Ankara Palace. After describing at length his friendly feelings for France, he explained that he had promised his nation that he would win Hatay, and win it he would. To underline his point, he asked two young Turkish officers (who, the French military attaché was convinced, had been kept waiting for the purpose) to join them: they too loved France and would hate to fight it.[58]

Some Turkish troops had already been sent to the border. Now Atatürk decided to give currency to reports that he was about to lead them into the disputed territory. On 6 January 1937, the Turkish press announced that the president had left Istanbul by train to go 'for the present' only as far as Konya, and that the prime minister, other ministers and the chief of the general staff had set out to meet him on his way in Eskişehir.[59] The official announcement appeared under the headline: 'We are not incapable of defending our rights. If the need to defend our honour leads us into a state of war, the responsibility will fall on France.'[60]

İnönü was alarmed. France was facing troubles at home and abroad; French forces in and around Alexandretta were weak. But hostilities with France would do Turkey no good. After a stormy meeting, Atatürk promised that he would neither undertake nor allow military action.[61] He went on to Konya, spent only twenty minutes there, and returned to Istanbul on 9 January.[62] Having discarded the military option, he launched a psychological offensive against France. He inspired a series of virulently anti-French articles in a party newspaper in Istanbul.[63] A smart café in Istanbul changed its name from Pâtisserie Parisienne (*Parizyen* in new Turkish spelling) to Hatay. The rest and abstention from alcohol, which doctors had prescribed for Atatürk, went by the board. The guardroom logbook records visits to the Garden Bar and the Pera Palace, as well as more salubrious trips to Yalova, Florya, the Princes Islands and the Bosphorus.[64]

The process of prising the *sancak* from French-mandated Syria was proving slow. Atatürk returned to Ankara on 10 March 1937, determined to speed it up. His methods were at times theatrical. One evening he asked his adopted daughter Sabiha Gökçen to put on her uniform – she had trained as a military pilot – and express her patriotic feelings of exasperation in the face of French delays by firing in the air when the French ambassador was eating his dinner in Karpich's restaurant. Sabiha did as she was told, and was hustled out by the police, summoned by Atatürk himself. She was charged with causing a breach of the peace and this gave her another opportunity to give vent to her patriotic fervour. Sentenced to one night in prison, she was joined by Atatürk's plump, middle-aged sister Makbule who had similarly declared herself ready to fight for the liberation of Hatay. Such, at least, is the story told by Sabiha Gökçen in her old age.[65]

According to another story, Atatürk tried further to impress the French ambassador by saying that he was ready to resign the presidency and fight as a volunteer in Hatay.[66] While the threat was hardly credible, serious calculations of the national interest, not to mention British efforts at mediation, induced France to give way. On 29 May 1937, the League of Nations resolved that the *sancak* should become a 'separate entity'. On the same day, France and Turkey agreed to guarantee its integrity jointly.[67] But Turkey wanted to make sure that its writ would run in the new 'separate entity'. Elections, held under the supervision of an international commission, threatened to produce a non-Turkish majority. Ankara decided to boycott them as unfair. In November 1937, Atatürk, ravaged as he was by illness, travelled to Adana and Mersin, north of the Syrian frontier.[68] The visit underlined his decision to win the *sancak*. The French made another concession, and agreed that the disputed territory should be policed jointly by French and Turkish troops. A Turkish contingent entered the *sancak* on 5 July 1938. Its arrival was followed by fresh elections, after the international commission had been dismissed.

The elections produced a suitable result: Turks secured 22 out of 40 seats in the parliament of the new state. Tayfur Sökmen, a member of the assembly in Ankara, became president of Hatay. The local assembly severed one by one the links with Syria which had been stipulated in the agreement setting up the 'separate entity'. Atatürk did not live to see the final act: the agreement under which France ceded the 'separate entity' to Turkey on 23 June 1939.[69] But the entry of Turkish troops into what was about to become the Turkish province of Hatay had settled the matter in his lifetime. İnönü was happy too: war had been avoided and Turkey had got its way without breaking the letter of international law. As far as today's Turks are concerned, Hatay, whose population has increased fivefold to over one million, is Atatürk's last gift to his country.

At the time, much attention was also given to a toothless agreement, known as the Saadabad Pact, which Turkey signed with Iran, Iraq and Afghanistan on 8 July 1937.[70] It was meant to deter Mussolini from adventures in the Middle East, and is remembered today only by diplomatic historians. A month earlier, Atatürk received in Ankara

Abdullah, the amir of Transjordan (later the king of Jordan). It was a sign of Turkey's importance in the region.

Ill as he was, Atatürk remained the arbiter of his country's policies. İnönü notes in his memoirs that at the birth of the republic, Atatürk's original companions feared his unpredictability and sought constantly to put the brakes on him.[71] As the danger of a new war in Europe grew imminent, İnönü himself began to harbour the same fear. He had tried to curb Atatürk's impetuous pursuit of the claim to the *sancak* of Alexandretta. As the claim was pushed to a successful conclusion, a minor disagreement on another foreign policy issue prepared the ground for the final rift between a temperamentally decisive head of state and his temperamentally prudent chief minister.

Britain and France had summoned a conference in Nyon in Switzerland to determine measures against pirate submarines which had attacked ships bringing supplies to the Republicans in the Spanish civil war. A ship loaded with Soviet arms was torpedoed outside the entrance to the Turkish straits, and there were reports that unidentified submarines had been sighted in the sea of Marmara. Soviet Russia accused Italy of engaging in piracy. The accusation was well-founded, although the diplomats of most other countries were too careful to say so. Russia was Turkey's friend, at least in theory; Italy a potential enemy, in view of Mussolini's declared ambitions. But neither Atatürk nor İnönü wished to be drawn into a European war.

The foreign minister Tevfik Rüştü Aras was sent to Nyon with instructions to support collective security, while avoiding dangerous commitments. A satisfactory agreement was reached: Mediterranean countries would guard their own territorial waters, while British and French fleets would patrol the open seas. But İnönü was alarmed by the stipulation that parties to the agreement would assist British and French naval units wherever possible. Could that mean that they might have to join in action on the high seas? Tevfik Rüştü Aras explained that assistance meant shore supplies. Atatürk, who was at the time at his beach house in Florya, was satisfied and authorized Aras to sign the agreement. But from Ankara, İnönü demanded that he should do so only if he received a written assurance that Turkey was not committed to military action outside its coastal waters.

İnönü brought the disagreement to the cabinet on 13 September 1937, complaining that Atatürk's entourage had prevented direct contact between them. According to the president's chief secretary, Hasan Rıza Soyak, who was the intermediary involved, Atatürk was worried that Aras would be put in an impossible position in Nyon if he followed İnönü's instructions. It was a replay of the difficulties İnönü himself had experienced in Lausanne in 1923 at the hands of the prime minister, Rauf Orbay. In any case, Atatürk was not averse to the idea of sending a Turkish naval vessel to join the British fleet, if this were requested. 'It's no small thing,' he said, 'to show that we are in a position to cooperate with the great powers.'[72]

In the event, Aras signed the agreement on 14 September, and then obtained the written guarantee on which İnönü had insisted. The matter was resolved, but only at the cost of increased mutual irritation between Atatürk and İnönü. 'Is it possible to rule a state with a mentality that goes well beyond the needs of prudence?' Atatürk exclaimed when he saw İnönü's final instructions to Aras.[73] The days of İnönü's premiership were numbered.

28

Apotheosis

T HE SUMMER OF 1937 was the second and last holiday Atatürk was to spend in his new beach house at Florya. He looks fit in photographs showing him swimming off the uncompleted pier in 1935. By the following summer he had put on weight. In 1937, his face is drawn, his body unhealthy. In spite of many years of hard drinking and irregular hours, the strength of his constitution had tided him over two episodes of heart trouble, malaria, and other diseases. In the mid-1930s, as Falih Rıfkı Atay noted, Atatürk was still able to stay up all night and inspect army manoeuvres the following morning. He could race up the steep slope of Dikmen hill in Ankara like a young man, when games were played after a picnic.[1] He was fond of outdoor life, and spent much time on his model farms. After he had given up riding, his main exercise was playing billiards before dinner, and swimming in the summer.

His daily drives, frequent boat trips in the Bosphorus and the sea of Marmara, and provincial tours were in marked contrast with the sedentary, secluded life of the last sultans. These showed themselves to the people briefly once a week when they drove the short distance to the nearest mosque for Friday prayers. Atatürk was frequently surrounded by crowds at railway stations, in hotels and restaurants, at exhibitions and meetings, on the beach. But as the French military attaché, Colonel Courson de la Villeneuve, noted already in 1934: 'The Gazi is 53 years old, an age at which health gives way suddenly if one makes excessive demands on life.' Courson had been observing Atatürk at the Park Hotel in Istanbul in the early hours of the morning. The president was in his shirtsleeves, pressed close to a young Hungarian woman, who was staying at the hotel while her husband was away.[2] His hand was ruffling her platinum-blonde hair, while his arm was clasping her waist. When he got up to dance 'he looked haggard'.[3]

A few days earlier,[4] as the president was dancing in the hotel, the band stopped playing when the *müezzin* of a small neighbouring mosque recited the call to prayer. Soon afterwards, the mosque was closed and the minaret pulled down. The hotel had been built on land belonging to the last Ottoman grand vizier, Tevfik Paşa. His grandson says tactfully in his memoirs that the order to close the mosque was given by an over-zealous official who misinterpreted Atatürk's remark that there should be a decent distance between places of worship and places of entertainment.[5] The French military attaché attributed the decision to demolish the minaret to Atatürk himself.[6] In any case, in a choice between a little undistinguished mosque and a large modern hotel, the president's preference was clear.

Atatürk made no attempt to conceal his way of life. According to one story, when he was in İzmir in 1930, the governor ordered that blinds should be drawn closed when the president and his friends settled down to their evening's drinking in the ground-floor restaurant of the local hotel.[7] Mustafa Kemal objected, saying, 'Let the people see how we eat and drink.' According to another version, he added that secrecy would only stimulate stories of debauchery. Later, when he was drinking aboard a yacht off Moda point in Istanbul,[8] he raised his glass to people crowding round in rowing boats, and shouted, 'Fellow-countrymen, this drink is called *rakı*. You must know that I have long been in the habit of drinking it. Now, I raise my glass and drink in your honour.'[9]

Particularly in his later years, Atatürk made no distinction between work and pleasure. Decisions were made round the dinner-table; state documents were brought to him during picnics or as he was driving round.[10] He signed the law ratifying the Montreux convention while he was drinking in the beer garden of the Ankara model farm; he then invited a young girl student to his table and asked her to prove that her (Arabic) name, Melâhat, was derived from a Turkish root. When the girl excused herself saying that she had not been taught the Sun-Language Theory, Atatürk ordered that there should be lectures on it in all departments of the Ankara faculty of language and history. Then, tiring of the subject, he demanded that the band should play a waltz. The musicians' efforts disappointed him, but he finally took to the floor when they struck up a Hungarian csardas.[11] Atatürk's behaviour could be odd, but, as long as his health held up, his company was fun.

As he grew weaker, he drew closer to his sister Makbule, who had a house in the grounds of Çankaya palace, and who began to accompany him on his trips. The guardroom logbook refers to her as 'the Great

Lady' (*Büyük Bayan*). Of the five girls whom he had adopted in the late 1920s, two – his trainee scholar Afet İnan and Sabiha Gökçen – stayed close to him. One of the girls, Zehra, fell to her death from a train in France in 1936. A French police enquiry concluded that it was suicide.[12] Sabiha had a disappointing school career, interrupted by illness, but then found her calling as a pilot. She was sent to Russia for training, and was later allowed exceptionally to enrol as a military pilot. Sabiha says in her memoirs that Atatürk tested her by asking her to press a gun against her head and pull the trigger. She did not flinch, and was allowed to take part in a bombing mission against Kurdish rebels in the Tunceli (Dersim) mountains in 1937. She was given a gun – which was loaded this time – to defend herself if her plane crashed and she fell into rebel hands. At the end of the operation, Atatürk and Makbule met her at the Ankara military airfield.[13] The following June, Sabiha was sent on a demonstration flight to the Balkan countries. The high point of the tour was the flight to Salonica, where Sabiha was shown the house where Atatürk was reputedly born. She flew on to Yugoslavia and Romania, where her aircraft developed a fault, and she returned to Turkey by train. By that time Afet had finally been allowed to go abroad, first to Paris and then to study for a doctorate in Geneva.

Atatürk's paternal interest in little girls found a new focus in his youngest adopted daughter, Ülkü. Born in Ankara in 1932, she was the child of a retainer of Atatürk's mother and of the stationmaster of the Ankara model farm.[14] In 1935, Atatürk held her by the hand as he got off the train at Haydarpaşa station in Istanbul, at the start of his usual summer visit. She stayed at his side, as his inseparable pet, until a few weeks before his death three years later.

As Atatürk's health worsened, İnönü became worried by a change in his leader's mood. Earlier, hasty decisions taken at night under the influence of drink were reversed the following morning. Now, Atatürk would continue to insist on such decisions even after sobering up. İnönü resented also the president's habit of criticizing his ministers individually.[15] The disagreements about the handling of the Hatay claim and the Nyon negotiations were compounded by friction over the disposal of Atatürk's model farms. These had cost the treasury a great deal of money.[16] Though in his six-day speech in 1927, the Gazi had indicated that he would turn over his farms to the People's Party, he was unable to bring himself to do so: every plant had become dear to him. In any case, he did not like giving things away.[17]

The farms grew into a large enterprise, with their own workshops, a small brewery in Ankara and a number of farm shops to market produce. Inevitably, their staff and patrons in Çankaya had a vested interest in keeping the farms as Atatürk's private property. Early in 1937, they decided to enlarge operations by extending the existing brewery, and building others. Money was obtained from the state Agricultural Bank by mortgaging the farms.[18] However, before the new breweries could be built, courts had to hear an appeal from a private brewery in Istanbul against the ending of its concession. İnönü insisted that the result of the case should not be anticipated.[19] Some of Atatürk's close companions countered this by spreading rumours that İnönü's relatives and associates had an interest in the private brewery in Istanbul.

In May 1937, Atatürk finally decided that the farms should be handed over to the state, but against payment, the proceeds going to the People's Party.[20] But İnönü rejected the idea that the state should pay for property which it had helped finance, and Atatürk gave way.[21] İnönü was warned that he had hurt his chief's feelings. It made no difference. On 11 June, Atatürk, who was on a visit to the Black Sea port of Trabzon, sent a telegram to İnönü declaring that he was presenting the farms to the state as an unconditional gift.[22] İnönü informed the assembly, which passed a vote of thanks.[23] However, the brewery was not included in the gift. It could make a profit only if it sold its production to the state monopoly; but since Atatürk was still the legal owner, the contract would have to be between the president and the state. Once again İnönü refused to countenance it.[24]

Atatürk was loath to break with İnönü. In a second telegram from Trabzon on 11 June, he spoke of his certainty that İnönü would share his delight at the warmth of his reception and would wish to tell the whole country about it.[25] However, after his return to Istanbul, the disagreement over the Nyon negotiations gave supporters of the Ankara brewery scheme a chance to press their case. On 17 September, Atatürk travelled back to Ankara, going on arrival to the model farm in the company of 'the usual gentlemen'. He decided that it had been neglected since its transfer to the state three months earlier, and summoned the cabinet to meet him round the dinner-table in Çankaya the same evening. Informed that the brewery would come up for discussion, İnönü is said to have bucked himself up by having a couple of whiskies on the way to the palace. Atatürk chose to drink tea.

When İnönü and the ministers arrived, Atatürk accused the agriculture minister of not looking after the farm properly. İnönü lost his temper. The president, he declared, should address his complaints to the farm managers he had appointed, and who had kept their jobs. In a clear reference to gossip that his family had an interest in the private brewery in Istanbul, he accused the president of lending an ear to rumours circulated by his enemies. 'You issue orders from your dinner-table and make trouble for us,' İnönü complained. He had good reason for this uncharacteristic outburst. He had been the object of incessant intrigue; his brother had died recently; his gall bladder was giving him trouble. But he had gone too far. Atatürk got up and put an end to the meeting.[26] The row had taken place in public, and the president decided that he could no longer keep his chief minister without losing face. It was a hard decision to take. He had often told his friends, 'It is thanks to İsmet that I am free from care in Çankaya.'[27] He decided that the break should come gently and hoped his friendship with İnönü would survive.

On 19 September Atatürk and İnönü both travelled by train to Istanbul to attend the second conference of the Historical Society at Dolmabahçe palace. On the way, Atatürk summoned İnönü to his compartment, and told him that it would be better if they stopped working together for a time. As parliament was in recess, he would be given leave of absence for reasons of health; in the meantime, Celal Bayar, the minister of national economy, would become deputy prime minister. İnönü raised no objections. When the party arrived at Dolmabahçe, İnönü slipped away to his family summer house in the Princes Islands. Returning to the palace for the conference, he passed to Atatürk a piece of paper with the words: 'So, you're not too angry with me?' 'No, I've forgotten it all,' Atatürk scribbled in reply. 'As you know, you're my friend and my brother.' 'May I keep this paper?' İnönü asked. 'As you wish,' Atatürk wrote back.[28] The following month, Atatürk invited İnönü to accompany him to army manoeuvres near İzmir. Later that year, Atatürk is reported to have said to the wife of his journalist friend Falih Rıfkı, 'Keep it a secret, but I've made trouble for myself by opening up the question of who is to be prime minister.'[29] Nevertheless, he stuck to his choice of Bayar, who became prime minister on 25 October.

At the opening of the new session on 1 November, the assembly was informed that İnönü had resigned, and that Bayar had been appointed to succeed him at the head of an almost identical cabinet.[30] Atatürk made no reference to the change of government in his opening speech. It ended on a note of secularist pragmatism. 'We do not consider our principles,' he said, 'as dogmas contained in books said to come from heaven. We derive our inspiration, not from heaven or the unseen world, but directly from life.'[31] Bayar, on the other hand, made it clear in his first speech as prime minister that the source of his inspiration was none other than Atatürk. The speech was notable for its use of the word Leader (the French word *chef*, spelled in Turkish *şef*, was adopted, as

Turkish was still mercifully free of its own term for the concept in its modern meaning of dictator): it occurred nineteen times in his text.[32]

Bayar and his allies among 'the usual gentlemen' did their best to block İnönü's return to favour. A few days after the change of government had been announced, İnönü was loudly cheered when he went as a private citizen to watch a match between the football teams of Ankara and Budapest (the Hungarians won). Atatürk is said to have been disturbed. Was İnönü trying to whip up popular support? On 6 November, as the People's Party parliamentary group met to discuss the new government's programme, Atatürk's boon companion Salih Bozok challenged İnönü to explain his disagreements with the president. İnönü apologized for his outburst at Atatürk's table, and explained that he had been tired and had asked for leave to take a rest. He was in no way responsible for the demonstration in his favour at the Ankara stadium, which, he said, had taken him by surprise; he continued to consider Atatürk his benefactor, and instanced the president's habit of passing on to him part of his own allowance. Bozok declared himself satisfied. A couple of days later, Falih Rıfkı Atay reported to İnönü that Atatürk had described the demonstration at the stadium as a proper expression of the nation's gratitude for services rendered, and had said that İnönü should always be treated with respect.[33] İnönü was invited to dinner at Çankaya on several subsequent occasions.

In November 1937, Atatürk travelled on the newly built railway line to the Kurdish areas in the south-east of the country, which he had last seen when he was an Ottoman general fighting the Russians in 1917. Easier access had allowed the government to strengthen its grip on the Kurds. Atatürk's stay was brief, but it left a mark. He decreed that Diyarbekir, the chief city of the area, where he had his headquarters in 1917, should be renamed Diyarbakır, in accordance with the Sun-Theory, which declared that every name had a Turkish origin (*bakır* is Turkish for copper).[34] Speaking after a concert in the local People's House, he declared: 'In this most modern and most beautiful building I have listened to fine, modern music in the presence of a civilized portion of humanity.'[35] Civilization had not been brought without a struggle. North-west of Diyarbakır, the Turkish army had only just defeated the rebellion of the Kurds in the Dersim mountains.

It had started when the local tribal and religious leader, Seyit Rıza, destroyed a bridge leading to his inaccessible territory and wiped out the Turkish detachment guarding it. He was captured with his companions and put on trial, just as Atatürk had set out for the area. Fearing that Kurds would demonstrate in hope of a pardon for their leaders, the authorities arranged for Seyit Rıza and six of his companions to be hanged summarily, just before Atatürk's arrival. The president came by train to the chief city of the province, changed its name from Elâziz to the allegedly Turkish Elâzığ, walked through a crowd of thoroughly cowed Kurds, drove on to inaugurate the rebuilt bridge, and then continued his journey back to Ankara.[36] On his way, he stopped briefly in Adana to admire the statue put up to him in the town gardens. He also found time to explain that the near-by town of Tarsus derived its name from an ancient Turkish people called Terkeş.[37] Describing his impressions of the trip on his return to Ankara, Atatürk said that he was happy to witness the willingness with which local people handed over to the treasury whatever was surplus to their requirements in order to strengthen the republic.[38] This claim was as unreal as Atatürk's etymology of local place names.

Although his health was deteriorating rapidly, Atatürk stuck to his habits. On 25 November 1937, he sat up until dawn, drinking with friends at the Ankara Palace hotel. In December, there were two all-night sessions at Karpich's restaurant. On 9 December, he received a representative of the Hitler Youth.[39] But the rash induced by cirrhosis made him increasingly uncomfortable. In January 1938, the death of his childhood friend and regular companion Nuri Conker sapped his morale. But he clung to life, and at the end of the month decided to undergo a course of treatment at the Yalova spa.

The establishment was headed by Nihat Reşat Belger, a distinguished doctor who had worked for many years in Paris, where he had served as Turkish nationalist representative during the War of Independence. Dr Belger examined Atatürk and concluded that the rash was a symptom of cirrhosis of the liver. He put the diagnosis as tactfully as he could. 'The itch,' he said, 'is the result of your eating, and particularly your drinking.' Atatürk took the hint and spent a quiet week in Yalova, where the new prime minister Celal Bayar joined him for dinner every night. But rumours of the president's illness could not be stopped. On 24 January, the newspaper *Cumhuriyet*, the party's mouthpiece in Istanbul, carried a strange story. Purporting to quote a non-existent radio station in Yalova, it declared that Atatürk's advice was a cure for all ills, his measures an effective medicine. It was therefore incumbent on the nation to pray for his health.[40] It was a first, oblique reference to the president's mortal illness.

On 1 February Atatürk decided to go to Bursa to open a new

merino-wool mill. There was a ball at which Atatürk joined in the energetic *zeybek* folk dance, and sat up drinking until 4 a.m. The following
day he donated to the Bursa town council his shares in the modern spa
hotel (which he had named *Çelik Palas*, or Steel Palace on the assumption that the hot spring, which fed the spa pool, contained iron), and the
adjoining house given to him in 1923.[41]

Back in Istanbul, Atatürk slipped off to the Park Hotel for another
night-long session. The following day he developed a fever. Pneumonia
was diagnosed.[42] But a fortnight later, he was well enough to receive both
Celal Bayar and İnönü. On 24 February Atatürk decided to go to Ankara
for a Balkan Pact council meeting. İnönü travelled with him by train.

The Balkan Pact, like the European Union today, was notable for the
number of meetings it spawned. On 27 February 1938 Atatürk welcomed the Greek dictator, General Ioannis Metaxas, and the Yugoslav
prime minister, Milan Stojadinović. Both were moving to a policy of
propitiating Nazi Germany. As on previous occasions, views were
exchanged, but to little purpose. Nevertheless, Atatürk told visiting
journalists: 'History has witnessed unions between various peoples,
who have lived together for centuries. But the *union* [Atatürk used the
French word] we are planning, will be something greater.'[43] In fact, the
Balkan Entente melted away at the outbreak of the Second World War
eighteen months later.

Atatürk was late for the meeting, delayed by a nosebleed which
proved hard to stop. It was another symptom of advancing cirrhosis.
Celal Bayar asked the president's permission to call in a specialist from
abroad. Atatürk, he believed, was more likely to listen to a distinguished
foreigner than to his local medical friends. The president agreed after
some argument, and a French specialist, Professor Fissenger,[44] arrived
in Ankara and confirmed the belated diagnosis of cirrhosis. On 30
March, the official Turkish news agency published a statement declaring
that the president had been ill with influenza, and that he had been
examined by Professor Fissenger who had found no cause for alarm.
Fissenger, the statement went on, had left the country after advising the
president to rest for a month and a half.[45]

It was the first official news of the president's illness, although
rumours of it had come from French sources the previous December.
Questioned about them, the Turkish foreign minister, Dr Tevfik Rüştü
Aras, succeeded in misleading the British ambassador, Sir Percy
Loraine, who sent the Foreign Office optimistic reports about Atatürk's
health prospects.[46] Aras had good reason to spread hope: he had fallen
out with İnönü and dreaded the possibility that the ex-prime minister
might succeed to the presidency. Besides, he believed, like Atatürk, that

news of the illness might weaken Turkey's hand in the Hatay problem.
As for Loraine, he seems to have shared the tendency of British diplomats to disbelieve anything the French say. Atatürk followed Fissenger's
advice and spent a couple of months quietly at Çankaya, keeping regular
hours. On 13 April, he received İnönü for the last time, in the company
of Celal Bayar.[47]

Atatürk made one last attempt to play a public role. He watched a
parade in the capital on 19 May, the anniversary of his arrival at Samsun
at the start of the War of Independence. He then took the train south.
Turkey had massed 30,000 troops on the border with Syria to put pressure on France, as elections were being organized in the *sancak* of
Alexandretta.[48] Atatürk gave added publicity to the campaign by
inspecting troops in Mersin and Adana, not far from the border.[49] He
made no speeches, but his presence helped persuade France to allow
Turkish troops into the disputed district. The trip exhausted him, but
he did not give up: he even found time to visit an archaeological site
near Mersin. As he returned to Ankara, a minister in the party which
welcomed him at the station turned to Falih Rıfkı Atay and said: 'Look
at his skin – it is the skin of a dead man.'[50]

A day later, on 26 May 1938, Atatürk left Ankara for Istanbul for the
last time. From Dolmabahçe palace, on the shores of the Bosphorus, he
drove to his house on Florya beach. He was taken ill and had to be
rushed back to the palace. Liver failure had produced an oedema in his
abdomen, which was causing him acute discomfort. Bayar had in the
meantime found another means to endear himself to Atatürk. The
Sultan's old yacht *Ertuğrul* was too old to sail outside the sheltered
waters of the sea of Marmara, and the president had to use ordinary
passenger steamers for his trips to the Black Sea and the Mediterranean.
He would be happy to have something grander. The new prime minister was informed that a luxury yacht, the *Savarona*, was lying idle in its
German shipyard. It had been built in 1931 at the order of an American
millionaire, who, however, refused to take delivery of it when the US
government decided to levy import duty on the vessel. The Turkish
government bought the *Savarona* in March 1938 for one and a quarter
million dollars,[51] and presented it to Atatürk as a gift from the nation. It
was an implicit reproach to İnönü, who had preached austerity during
his long tenure of office. The *Savarona* arrived in Istanbul on 1 June
1938. The bizarre suggestion that it should be renamed *Sun-Language*
was fortunately abandoned.[52]

Atatürk moved from the palace to his new yacht. He agreed to follow
medical advice and take a complete rest. On 8 June, Professor Fissenger
was summoned again. To avoid alarm, Atatürk was told that the French

professor had come to treat İnönü, who was at the time seriously ill with gall-bladder inflammation, and would use the opportunity to examine the president again.[53] After the examination, Fissenger warned the interior minister Şükrü Kaya that the president had at most two years to live, but could die at any moment.

On 14 June Atatürk sent a letter from the *Savarona* to Afet in Geneva. It was the doctors' fault, he complained, that his illness had not been cured. He had been allowed to get up and walk about too early. Nevertheless, his general state of health was good and he had high hopes of a complete recovery; Afet had no cause for worry.[54] Five days later, King Carol of Romania who had arrived in Istanbul on his yacht was allowed to visit Atatürk on board the *Savarona*. As they discussed the Sudeten crisis, the Romanian king said that President Beneš of Czechoslovakia was not proving sufficiently accommodating. 'How can one expect a head of state,' Atatürk riposted, 'to oblige by abandoning territory entrusted to his safe keeping?'[55] Illness had not affected Atatürk's judgement or sense of duty.

Another visitor was Fethi Okyar, who had come from London, where he had been appointed ambassador after the closure of the Free Republican Party. He noted that Atatürk's body was clearly affected by illness, but that his mind was as clear as ever, and was even livelier as he had stopped drinking. Atatürk said he felt tired and thought that it would do him good to breathe some country air on the Asian shore of the Bosphorus.[56] He was thinking of the sultans' hunting lodge at Alemdağ, which he had visited as a young cadet with Ali Fuat Cebesoy. The lodge was inspected and was found to be in a ruined state; repairs would take time.[57]

Atatürk continued to conduct business with his new prime minister. In view of the approaching fifteenth anniversary of the republic, he agreed to amnesty the 150 opponents of the Turkish nationalist movement who had been exiled at the end of the War of Independence. Rauf Orbay, one of Atatürk's critics, had already returned, under the terms of the tenth anniversary amnesty. Ali Fuat Cebesoy had become a frequent visitor during Atatürk's illness. Refet Bele was a deputy. Now the slate was to be wiped clean. Only members of the Ottoman dynasty were kept out. The law amnestying the 150 was passed by the assembly on 29 June.[58] No one voted against it, but some of the leading figures of the nationalist movement, including İnönü and 'the usual gentlemen', stayed away.[59] Unfortunately, repression found other victims. On 29 August, the Communist poet Nazım Hikmet was sentenced to twenty-eight years in prison on a trumped up charge of inciting a mutiny in the navy. He appealed to Atatürk.[60] The president was by then in the last stages of his illness; in any case, military courts were the province of the chief of the general staff, Marshal Fevzi Çakmak, a strict disciplinarian who had no time for Communists. Nazım Hikmet remained in prison until after the end of the Second World War.

Atatürk was kept informed of new government initiatives. The economy had gradually revived after the crisis of 1929–30, and Bayar hoped that private merchants would work hand in hand with state banks in the framework of a second five-year plan. 'The Business Bank set' was briefly in the ascendant. More importantly, Turkey began to be courted as a new European war drew near. Britain gave Turkey a loan of £16 million to establish its first steel mill and to buy arms; immediately afterwards, a Nazi German minister arrived in Ankara with the offer of a credit of 150 million marks.[61] Bolshevik Russia was no longer the only source of foreign aid.

To distract the patient, the *Savarona* made short trips to the Bosphorus and the sea of Marmara. But as his illness progressed, she remained anchored off Dolmabahçe palace. Her generators were noisy, and energy was supplied from a submarine berthed alongside. 'I had waited for this yacht like a child waiting for a toy,' Atatürk is reported to have said. 'Will it now become my grave?'[62] The answer was 'no'. On 24 July, the president's doctors decided that he should be transferred to the shore. To avoid publicity, the move was made after dark, and lights were switched off when Atatürk was carried in an armchair from the yacht to a palace bedroom facing the Bosphorus. Opposite his bed there was a painting sent by the Turkish ambassador in Moscow: it showed spring in the mountains, probably the Caucasus.[63] Pictures of trees amid green mountain scenery are to this day popular with Turks who long for a change from the dry Anatolian plateau.

The extended family gathered round. Afet had returned from Geneva. Makbule and Sabiha were in constant attendance. So too were 'the usual gentlemen', Kılıç Ali and Salih Bozok. Only little Ülkü was sent back to Ankara.

A committee of six Turkish doctors was formed to treat the president, and medical bulletins began to be issued. These spoke optimistically of the president's rest and convalescence. Ahmet Emin Yalman, the liberal editor of the newspaper *Tan* (The Dawn), was the first to challenge official optimism on 7 August. But his polite request for genuine information was met by the decision to close down his paper for three months.[64] Far from the public eye, Fissenger was called again, this time together with a German and an Austrian professor. They decided that liquid should be drawn off from the patient's abdomen.

Atatürk agreed. But realizing it was a risky operation, he decided that the time had come to write his will. The document drawn up on 5 September was brief. It bequeathed all his property to the People's Party. The revenue would cover modest monthly payments to his sister and his surviving five adopted daughters. Makbule was to keep her house in Çankaya for life, and money would be provided to acquire a house for Sabiha Gökçen, the adopted daughter who had become a pilot. The balance would go to the Historical and Language Societies, except for the sum needed to help İnönü's children to complete their education.[65] Atatürk knew that İnönü was not rich, and he may have exaggerated the gravity of his former prime minister's illness; but the provision looks also like a peace offering, and confirms the impression that Atatürk felt guilty at dismissing a man whose discipline he resented, but whose services he appreciated.

İnönü stayed on in Ankara. In a note he penned three months after Atatürk's death, he claimed that Atatürk no longer wanted to keep in touch with him, fearing that any contact might weaken his authority and that of the new government. According to İnönü, Atatürk said repeatedly that he wanted his former prime minister to regain his health in the capital.[66] İnönü's argument, that he stayed away from Istanbul because the president did not want him by his sickbed, makes sense. The presence of the aide he dismissed might well have disturbed Atatürk. But it was also rumoured that İnönü decided to keep away because Recep Zühtü, who had been expelled from the ranks of 'the usual gentlemen' when he shot his mistress, threatened to kill him if he turned up to see Atatürk in Istanbul.[67] From Ankara, İnönü sent his best wishes to Atatürk by letter;[68] he corresponded with the president's close friend Salih Bozok; he was visited regularly by Sabiha Gökçen, who kept him informed of the president's illness. The foreign minister, Tevfik Rüştü Aras, offered to send İnönü as ambassador to Washington. İnönü refused.[69] The struggle for succession had begun, and İnönü played a shrewd waiting game in Ankara, where the assembly was about to meet.

On 13 October Atatürk's abdomen was again drained.[70] Three days later he fell into a coma. His secretary, Hasan Rıza Soyak, his friends Kılıç Ali and Salih Bozok, the commander of the presidential guard and an ADC, took turns to keep watch round his bed. The speaker of the assembly, Abdülhalik Renda, who had the duty of deputizing for the president, and the cabinet rushed from Ankara. The interior minister Şükrü Kaya tried to persuade İnönü to come too. He refused again.[71]

On 17 October, Şükrü Kaya briefed the editors of Istanbul newspapers. When Atatürk died, he warned, no meetings or religious services in mosques would be allowed, as these could easily get out of hand. The regime would carry on according to the constitution, and the assembly would choose the new president. Şükrü Kaya did not expect more than a couple of candidates, and he added significantly, 'Let us see whether the candidate acceptable to the assembly can be persuaded to stand.'[72] As no one had any doubt of İnönü's desire to succeed, this was a reference to the efforts of Şükrü Kaya, Tevfik Rüştü Aras and some of 'the usual gentlemen' to push forward Marshal Fevzi Çakmak as an alternative candidate.

Atatürk's secretary Hasan Rıza Soyak, who was opposed to İnönü, claims in his memoirs that, after signing his will, Atatürk told him that Çakmak would be a good choice, as İnönü, for all his virtues, was not liked in the country.[73] İnönü's memoirs throw light on the incident. He says that after his opponents had failed to get Atatürk to name a successor, Soyak tried to make up an 'oral testament', but that Celal Bayar would have none of it.[74] The fact remains that even after signing his will – which his entourage took as an acceptance of impending death – Atatürk would not name a successor. Was it because he genuinely believed that the assembly should have a free hand? Did he still hope to survive? Or did he feel that İnönü would be chosen in any case, and that to endorse him would be tantamount to an admission that he had been wrong to dismiss him as prime minister a year earlier? All three thoughts would have been in character.

On 22 October, Atatürk came to, and appeared to have recovered. Following an announcement that no further medical bulletins would be issued, the ministers returned to Ankara. Professor Fissenger is said to have advised that the president would be able to go to the capital for the celebration of Republic Day on 29 October, and a lift was ordered to take him up to the saluting stand.[75] However, Atatürk's health took a turn for the worse, and he agreed that Bayar should deputize for him at the opening of the new session of the assembly on 1 November.

Istanbul celebrated Republic Day as Atatürk lay on his deathbed. Military cadets sailed past Dolmabahçe palace, a military band playing on their beflagged boat. It is often said that Atatürk was lifted from his bed and taken in an armchair to the window from which he waved his hand at the cheering cadets. But the president's secretary, Hasan Rıza Soyak, reports in his memoirs that it was Kılıç Ali who appeared at the window and that he signalled to the boat to move on quickly. Similarly, instructions from the palace put an end to a fireworks display which disturbed the president's rest.[76]

On 8 November Atatürk fell into a final coma. According to Hasan Rıza Soyak, he addressed his last words to his doctor Neşet Ömer

İrdelp. They were, '*Aleyküsselâm*' (Peace to you) – the Muslim reply to a greeting.[77] Medical bulletins were issued again, and this time they did not conceal the gravity of the president's illness. At five past nine on the morning of 10 November 1938, Atatürk died in his bedroom in Dolmabahçe palace. Three Turkish doctors, the commander of the presidential guard and the secretary Hasan Rıza Soyak were at his bedside. At midday, the news was announced in an official communiqué. Order would be safeguarded, the government promised, and the republic would live on. The assembly was to meet immediately to elect a new president.[78]

Moments after Atatürk's death, his friend Salih Bozok burst into the president's bedroom. After seeing the body of his patron, he stepped outside and shot himself in the chest. The bullet missed the heart, and Bozok survived until 1941.[79] Haldun Derin, who worked in the presidential secretariat, was to write acidly: 'None of the other usual gentlemen was disposed to commit hara-kiri.'[80] Afet and Sabiha were immediately packed off to Ankara.[81] Arrangements were made for Atatürk to lie in state in the throne room of Dolmabahçe palace. This went against Muslim custom which enjoins burial within twenty-four hours of death.

On 11 November, the assembly met in Ankara to elect a new president. Marshal Çakmak had decided not to stand, and İnönü was the only candidate. He was elected unanimously.[82] İnönü asked Bayar to stay on as prime minister. All the ministers retained their posts, except for the foreign minister, Tevfik Rüştü Aras, and the interior minister, Şükrü Kaya, who had done their best to stand in İnönü's way. In his acceptance speech, İnönü praised his predecessor's 'extraordinary services' to the country. It was a measured and brief encomium.[83] The assembly then voted the money needed to cover the expense of Atatürk's state funeral. The debate gave members an opportunity to compete in the eloquence of their tributes to the founder of the republic.[84]

After Atatürk's body had been embalmed, the doors of Dolmabahçe palace were thrown open to the waiting crowd on 12 November. For seven days, mourners filed past the catafalque guarded by officers with drawn swords. Official organizations, associations, schools took their turn. In the evening of 17 November, police failed to control a huge crowd of mourners and eleven people were trampled to death.[85] Telegrams of condolence poured into the presidential secretariat. There was one even from the Circassian Ethem, who decided not to return to Turkey when the 150 exiles were pardoned. But the most piquant came from General Ali İhsan Sabis, who had been dismissed from his command during the War of Independence. It was addressed to İnönü, and read, 'Now that the obstacle has been removed, we can work together.'[86] The offer was not taken up.[87]

Atatürk's friend General Fahrettin Altay, who was at the time commander of the 1st Army in Istanbul, was put in charge of the military ceremonial. He says in his memoirs that he insisted that Muslim funeral prayers should be said: this was agreed after some hesitation. The secular government was worried that prayers might lead to religious demonstrations; it was therefore decided that the religious ceremony should be held not in a mosque, but privately in the palace, after the general had reminded the government that a Muslim may worship anywhere.[88] When the brief religious ceremony was completed, the coffin was taken in procession to the battleship *Yavuz*, for the short trip to İzmit on the Asian shore of the sea of Marmara. It was then placed on a special train, which slowed down at stations on the way to Ankara, to allow local people to pay their respects. Recep Zühtü, the gun-toting former companion of Atatürk, who had apparently threatened to kill İnönü, had boarded the train in Istanbul. The government in Ankara ordered that he should be asked to leave.[89]

The train arrived in Ankara on 20 November, and İnönü was invited to pay his respects in the railway carriage before the coffin was removed. The official funeral took place the following day. The procession started from the courtyard of the Grand National Assembly and covered the short route to the Ethnographic Museum, which was chosen as a temporary resting place until a proper mausoleum was built. Atatürk, his companions reported, wanted to be buried in the grounds of his mansion at Çankaya. But, as one of İnönü's friends is alleged to have said, 'Çankaya cannot become a shrine, with the president of the republic as its keeper.'[90]

Atatürk's state funeral was an event such as the country had never seen. It called forth both sorrow and pride. Seventeen countries had sent special representatives, nine contributed armed detachments to the cortège. Britain was represented by Field-Marshal Lord Birdwood of Gallipoli fame, France by its interior minister, Albert Sarraut (whose daughter had been the object of Atatürk's attentions), Nazi Germany by Baron von Neurath. British marines had come on board HMS *Malaya*, on which the last sultan had made his getaway in 1922. İnönü had represented Turkey at the funeral of King George V in 1936. Now, Britain along with the rest of the world was paying tribute to Turkey's first president. Atatürk's aim of making Turkey a fully independent, respected member of the community of civilized nations had been achieved.

What of the Turkish people themselves? Crowds, first at Dolmabahçe palace and then along the route of the cortège, were large. Many wept. İnönü caught the public mood with his proclamation to the nation on the day of the funeral. It ended with the words: 'Peerless hero Atatürk! The fatherland is grateful to you.'[91] Atatürk's status as a Turkish national hero was not in doubt. Even those who disliked his regime acknowledged him as *Halâskâr Gazi*, the Saviour Gazi, who had expelled the foreign invader from the national territory. The question was how many shared his vision and supported his reforms. The British ambassador, Sir Percy Loraine, reported: 'The mourning for him is very real. During the funeral ceremonies it was pathetically evident among the common people and patently genuine.'[92] But outpourings of national grief are ephemeral. The test came quickly.

One of İnönü's first acts as president was to conciliate two of Atatürk's original supporters, who had become consistent political opponents – Rauf Orbay and Kâzım Karabekir. Early in 1939, the Istanbul newspaper *Tan* announced that it would serialize Karabekir's memoirs, which had been confiscated in Atatürk's lifetime. When they heard the news, Istanbul university students stoned the newspaper's offices and demanded that the serialization should be stopped. The newspaper complied. A pattern was thus set for the future. Atatürk had won over the segment of society to which he had appealed throughout his life. The young, who were educated in the new Western knowledge, remained loyal to him and his twin ideals of full independence and participation in the one universal civilization. Irrespective of divisions among the republic's rulers and the discontents of the ruled, they would not allow any criticism of the Great Reformer (or Revolutionary – *İnkılâpçı*, later *Devrimci*).

As in France, the model Atatürk knew best, the revolution had found a solid constituency. But in Turkey the revolution had one author in whose person it was embodied. Loyalty to the ideals of the revolution thus became synonymous with loyalty to an idealized memory of Atatürk. Inevitably, the struggle between the defenders and the critics of Atatürk's cultural revolution became centred on his person. The defenders saw it as a struggle between light and darkness. So had Atatürk himself. In May 1918, as the Ottoman empire was fighting its last battles, he gave his photograph to the journalist Ruşen Eşref (Ünaydın) with this inscription:

In spite of everything, I am certain we are moving towards the light. The strength which animates my faith derives not only from my infinite love for my dear country and people, but from the young people I see, who are moved purely by love of country and of truth in their efforts to find and to spread light amid today's darkness, immorality and fraud.[93]

Atatürk was a competent commander, a shrewd politician, a statesman of supreme realism. But above all he was a man of the Enlightenment. And the Enlightenment was not made by saints.

29

Aftermath

O N 26 DECEMBER 1938, the Republican People's Party, meeting in a special convention, bestowed on Atatürk the title of Eternal Leader (*Ebedî Şef*). İnönü was named the party's leader for life, and accorded the title of National Leader (*Millî Şef*).[1] Atatürk, who had no doubts that he was Turkey's leader, had seen no need to proclaim it formally.[2] On 25 January 1939, the prime minister Celal Bayar resigned at İnönü's request, and was succeeded by Refik Saydam, the army doctor who had accompanied Mustafa Kemal on his fateful journey to Samsun in May 1919.[3] Atatürk's picture was replaced by İnönü's on the walls of government offices, on stamps, coins and banknotes. Reparations were made to Atatürk's first companions in the War of Independence: Ali Fuat Cebesoy and Kâzım Karabekir were given in turn the honorific post of speaker of the assembly; Rauf Orbay became Turkish ambassador in London. But none of the three wielded power. İnönü shared Atatürk's misgivings about their ambitions and their political abilities.[4]

In his private life, İnönü was a conventional Muslim, who carried a miniature Koran in his pocket.[5] He saw to it that his children received private religious lessons from an official of the department of religious affairs.[6] But he was scrupulously loyal to Atatürk's principle of a secular republic, in which religion was banned from politics. He even made the law stricter in 1941 when it became a criminal offence to recite the call to prayer in Arabic.[7] Atatürk's policy of reducing the use of Arabic and Persian loanwords was pushed forward, and in 1945 the constitution was rewritten in pure Turkish, and Turkish names were invented for four calendar months (October to January), which had previously borne Arabic names.[8] Efforts begun in Atatürk's lifetime to extend basic secular education to the countryside and give it a practical slant led in 1940 to the creation of a network of Village Institutes, where young peasants were trained as schoolteachers. An energetic education minister, Hasan-Âli Yücel, was encouraged by İnönü to commission translations of world classics. Atatürk's ideal of bringing 'modern' (that is, Western) culture to Turkey was served by the opening of a Turkish state conservatoire, which held its first lectures in 1936, and the establishment in 1940 of permanent opera and ballet companies.[9] Atatürk's cultural revolution thus marched on in the years following his death.

İnönü was as determined as had been his mentor and predecessor that Turkey should become a modern country. But in Nazi Germany, Bolshevik Russia and militarist Japan, modernity had assumed a threatening shape. As the modern world began to tear itself apart, İnönü's main preoccupation was to safeguard the achievements of the Turkish republic. He sought to serve this aim, first by signing an alliance with France and Britain, then, after the fall of France, by concluding a non-aggression treaty with Germany, and finally by stalling in the face of Winston Churchill's efforts to bring Turkey into the war on the Allied side. It was a skilful and sustained balancing act which required domestic discipline. This was ensured by the monopoly of power exercised by the Republican People's Party. The single-party regime helped İnönü maintain armed neutrality until it was safe to come down on the side of the victorious Allies, shortly before the war ended.[10] İnönü's success in keeping his country out of the war, yet steering it into the safe haven of the Western alliance at the war's end, was the product of the prudence and astuteness which he had developed as Atatürk's prime minister. But if Turkey's neutrality was respected it was also because Atatürk had demonstrated between 1918 and 1923 that the country was capable of defending itself. Memories of the victory won in the Turkish War of Independence helped deter aggression.

The war froze Turkish politics. But in 1945, the Allied victory brought internal and external pressure to relax the single-party regime. The United States and Britain, whose help Turkey needed to resist Stalin's expansionist designs, preferred democratic allies. Their advocacy of democracy was echoed inside Turkey. Cultural conservatives and supporters of political and economic freedom joined forces, as they had been on the point of doing in Fethi Okyar's short-lived Free Republican Party in 1930. İnönü made concessions to both sets of opponents. Village Institutes, criticized by conservatives as nests of Communist subversion, began losing their distinctive status in 1947.

Two years later, religious education was introduced on a voluntary basis in primary schools and a faculty of theology was opened in Ankara.[11] These 'concessions to religious reaction', as many Kemalists see them to this day, did not decrease the pressure from İnönü's political opponents. They came in the main from within the People's Party.

On 7 June 1945, Celal Bayar and three other party members – Adnan Menderes, who was until then relatively unknown,[12] the nationalist historian Fuat Köprülü, and Refik Koraltan, whose sycophancy of Atatürk had been a byword in the assembly – signed a motion asking for free party politics. Expelled from the People's Party, they formed the opposition Democrat Party in January 1946. They were joined briefly by Marshal Fevzi Çakmak, the strict disciplinarian who had retired from the post of chief of the general staff in 1944, and who together with Atatürk's former foreign minister, Tevfik Rüştü Aras, became incongruously a founder of a Human Rights Association.[13] In 1946, the ruling People's Party allowed the Democrat Party to win sixty-six seats in elections of doubtful fairness. İnönü then tried to contain the agitation by appointing Recep Peker, one of Atatürk's toughest lieutenants, as prime minister. But measured repression was no longer effective, and İnönü opted for democracy. Peker resigned in 1947. The first genuinely free elections in the history of the republic were held on 14 May 1950. The Democrat Party won 408 out of 487 seats in the assembly, but only on 53 per cent of the total poll.[14] The Republican People's Party never won an absolute majority in the assembly again.

İnönü resigned with good grace. Bayar became president, Menderes prime minister. The change was hailed as a triumph of smooth democratic transition and the consummation of Atatürk's ideal of national sovereignty. In 1937, Bayar had sought to outdo İnönü in his adulation of Atatürk. Now the Democrat Party government outdid him in signs of respect for Atatürk's memory. Atatürk's picture returned to coins, banknotes and postage stamps. His body was transferred to a grandiose mausoleum in 1953. A law was passed in 1951 making it a criminal offence to insult Atatürk's memory.[15] It had been prompted by incidents in which members of a banned dervish brotherhood had mutilated busts of Atatürk. The attacks were an extreme sign of the reappearance of Islam as a social and political force. The Democrat Party took it into account: one of its first acts in government was to allow the call to prayer to be recited in Arabic once again.[16] Thousands of mosques were built all over the country, mainly by voluntary subscription. Although, in formal terms, the government's departures from the Kemalist canon were few, Islamic feeling was expressed more freely and loudly.

The Democrat Party stayed in power for ten years which changed the face of Turkey. Atatürk's statement that the peasant was the country's master had remained a dead letter. Now the voter, or rather the political party which drew his support, became the real master. But in seeking to satisfy its supporters' demand for immediate material improvements, the Menderes government upset the balance which İnönü had maintained in the economy. At the same time, as it responded to demands that it should respect its supporters' culture, the government antagonized those whose culture had changed before, and particularly after, Atatürk's reforms.

The fall from power of the Democrat Party was not caused by 'concessions to religious reaction'. It lost support because it debauched the economy. And it was overthrown by the military on 27 May 1960, because it tried to cling to power by repressing the legal opposition. But the defence of Kemalism served as a banner for the Democrats' opponents, and the preamble of the 1961 constitution, enacted after the coup, proclaimed its loyalty to '[Atatürk's] principle of "Peace at home and peace in the world", the spirit of the National Struggle and Atatürk's reforms'.[17]

The armed forces now saw themselves as guardians of Kemalism, which, they believed, was endangered by vote-seeking and self-seeking politicians. The military changed the civilian government in March 1971; they took power themselves in September 1980; they helped change another civilian government in June 1998. But as they now accepted the principle of rule by a freely elected parliament, they kept on returning to their barracks after each incursion into politics. Each time they devised new rules for the political game, but the rules failed to deliver Kemalist stability. So, was the model flawed or are today's discomforts the growing pains of a body restored to health by Atatürk three-quarters of a century ago?

Atatürk earned his place in history by directing the successful resistance of the Muslim inhabitants of Anatolia against the occupation and attempted partition of their country. Many others took part in the preparation, planning and execution of the struggle. But from the moment he was chosen chairman of the Erzurum congress in 1919 to the time when the victory of the Turkish resistance received international recognition at Lausanne in 1923, he was in charge of the forces of Turkish nationalism.

His second fundamental achievement was to have given his country peace and a degree of internal order it had not known before. What others would have done in his place we do not know. But it is a matter of record that he insisted on setting clear aims and limits for the nationalist movement and that, having achieved the full independence of his country and won most of the territory claimed at the outset of the struggle, he resisted the pressure of some of his companions to go further. It was by means of negotiations that he achieved full control over the straits and won the territory he named Hatay. He set his face against irredentism whether of a pan-Islamic or pan-Turkist nature. He worked consistently for peaceful relations with all his country's neighbours and took part in international efforts to preserve peace.

The Muslim population of Anatolia had been depleted by war. It was ravaged by disease. It lacked basic skills. Communications were primitive. The absence of war and the presence of an administration which made a genuine effort to fight malaria and other endemic diseases allowed the population to climb from 13.6 million in 1927, when the first census was held in the republic, to 17.8 million in 1940 (the first census after Atatürk's death).[18] Literacy doubled from one tenth to more than one fifth of the population.[19] An adequate railway network was constructed (while roads were neglected). The state built factories to produce basic manufactures such as cloth and sugar. In spite of the increase in population, the national income per person doubled between 1923 and 1938.[20] The economic policies pursued during Atatürk's lifetime were conservative: budgets were balanced; so was foreign trade after the 1930 crisis. Progress was the fruit of domestic effort: Turkey received almost no foreign aid during Atatürk's lifetime. There was only one loan (from Soviet Russia) until a few months before his death. The control exercised by the state over the economy dampened private initiative, but it saved the nationalist regime from sinking in corruption.

It is true that when Atatürk died, Turkey was still a poor and backward country. It was largely rural. Some four-fifths of the population lived in villages, many in primitive houses built of mud brick. To the peasants, the state provided order and little else. But law and order – the end of banditry, the presence of a stable administration – were the prerequisite of progress. The world outside the village was slowly changing, and foundations were being laid for the rapid rise in material standards in the countryside as well as in towns in the years which followed the Second World War.

Atatürk did not work a social revolution. Under his authoritarian rule, landowners and notables continued to dominate provincial society. In towns, officials formed the backbone of a small middle class. Muslims were gradually learning trades, but the small remaining Christian and

Jewish communities were still prominent in skilled occupations. The republic Atatürk founded was run by officers and officials who had served under the sultans, as he had himself.

The change of political principles had a limited impact on practice. Theoretically, sovereignty had passed from the sultan to the nation, represented by the Grand National Assembly, but it was exercised by Atatürk as president. The prime minister was his chief vizier in all but name. Governors were masters of provinces, inspectors ruled over regions. Discipline was, if anything, tighter than it had been under the last sultans. True, the president, his ministers and his officials were not above the law, but then neither had been the sultan and his ministers. Nevertheless, Atatürk's republican principles mattered, just as the Declaration of the Rights of Man mattered, however much it may have been violated in the turmoil of the French revolution which gave birth to it. During the War of Independence parliamentary government had some substance. Later, the substance drained away, but the form survived. The first republican constitution of 1924 enshrined the principles and set up the structures which allowed genuine parliamentary government to emerge from free elections in 1950. Atatürk left behind him the structure of a democracy, not of a dictatorship.

Atatürk was not a social revolutionary – and certainly not a socialist. His political revolution was formal. But the cultural revolution he wrought was genuine and wide-ranging. Secularism was central to it. True, the secularization of the Turkish ruling class and of the state which it ran had started in the nineteenth century. It was pushed forward vigorously by the CUP after 1908. But it was Atatürk who decided that religion should have no say at all in government. None of his predecessors in power had dared go that far; most of his companions would have preferred to fudge the issue. Atatürk's secularism, like that of his Turkish predecessors who had toyed with the theory, was inspired by the French principle and practice of *laïcisme*, the separation of church from state in post-revolutionary France. But the Turkish practice was different. The republic declared its independence from Islam, while continuing to control it, as the sultans had done before it.

French *laïcisme* could not be applied logically to a Muslim society. The principle that religion is a private matter is inconsistent with historical Islam. The Koran is not only a compendium of moral principles; it is also the constitution of the state created by Muhammad – its civil and criminal law. The practice of the Prophet, his *sunna*, which together with the Koran forms the basis of Muslim religious law, prescribes details of social and individual behaviour. Ingenious religious scholars can, of course, interpret, even explain away, the holy law. But to deny its validity is a revolutionary act for a Muslim. This is what Atatürk did after abolishing the caliphate in 1924.

His publicist Falih Rıfkı Atay has described Kemalism as the reform of Islam, a reform which abrogated all the rules of the religion except those which relate to worship.[21] This is indeed what happened in practice. Turkish Muslims continued to worship – and Mustafa Kemal did not interfere with the private religious practices of his closest companions, let alone of the people at large. It is true that as metropolitan society took its cue from the leader, the practice of Islam became for a while unfashionable and mosques emptied. It was a passing phenomenon. But it was also the harbinger of slow organic secularization. The idea that religion was a matter of private choice gained ground, aided by the state which applied secular law to regulate social behaviour. As a result, a new form of Islam, illogical in theory but viable in practice – Islam-within-secularism – gradually developed in Turkey. However, Atatürk did not see himself as a religious reformer. He was a rationalist, and at least after 1924, the books he sponsored promoted a materialist and determinist ideology. An attempt to reform Islam was quickly abandoned in 1928. The view prevailing in Atatürk's circle was that a reform of Islam would be as useless as a graft on dead wood.[22]

It was because Atatürk broke the tie with religious law that he was able to decree the equality of the sexes. Turkish women had achieved a considerable degree of freedom in sophisticated Ottoman society in the capital. Female emancipation progressed during the Great War, when the government of the Young Turks had no choice but to enlist women's labour. But as long as Islam affected civil law, full equality was impossible, and any advance in their freedom could be challenged and ultimately reversed. Turkish women owe their rights to Atatürk.

The adoption, without any reservations, of Western laws, of the Latin alphabet, of the well-nigh universal Christian calendar and weekend, facilitated intercourse with advanced societies. Atatürk believed that his people had been denied knowledge – positive, secular knowledge. He sought to dispel ignorance – which was palpable in Muslim society – by promoting the inflow of knowledge from those countries where its frontier was being pushed forward. The basic difference between him and most of his domestic opponents was that he was not afraid of the outside world, while they were. His nationalism looked outwards; theirs was inward-looking. Unlike them, he was able to combine a realistic recognition of his countrymen's backwardness with total faith in their ability to overcome it.

It is true that he often failed to practise what he preached. In his private life, he could not accept women as equals. He did not travel abroad, probably because he would have felt uncomfortable in a world to which he was leading his fellow-countrymen. His rationalism and attachment to 'positive science' did not stop him inventing fantastic historical and linguistic theories. A democrat in theory, he created his own cult and was convinced that he was always right. He worshipped reason, while persisting in unreasonable personal habits. No matter, his vision was humanist and universalist. His cult of youth – a widespread contemporary phenomenon – served to combat ignorance and not presumed national, racial or class enemies as in Italy, Germany and Soviet Russia. His advice 'Be proud, confident and hard-working' brought the philosophy of Samuel Smiles to Turkey. When restraints on private initiative were relaxed after the Second World War, the spirit of self-reliance, which Atatürk had fostered, helped transform a backward country into the world's seventeenth largest economy.[23]

Today, Atatürk is criticized on three main grounds – that he did not establish democratic government, that his policy of secularism divided Turkish society and severed the link between the rulers and the ruled, and that he suppressed ethnic diversity and, in particular, denied the rights of the large indigenous Kurdish population.

The first criticism is easiest to answer. Parliamentary democracy requires agreement on essentials – on the nature of the state and of society, whose rulers are to be chosen by free ballot. In the absence of such agreement, party politics become a battleground for conflicting ethnic, religious and local groups, clans and tribes. There was no agreement on essentials in Atatürk's day. What is more, between the two wars, democracy could not be sustained in many richer and better educated societies. Atatürk's enlightened authoritarianism left a reasonable space for free private lives. More could not be expected in his lifetime.

Critics of Atatürk's secularism argue that he should have allowed room for Islam in the governance of the republic. However, recent experience suggests that political Islam is exclusive in its claims. Egypt has not prevented fundamentalist terrorism by recognizing Islam as the official religion. It can, of course, be argued that Atatürk could have treated organized Islam with more respect, while denying its secular claims. There is no doubt that he was fiercely anticlerical: he despised the *hocas* and could not stand their company. But without passion there could have been no cultural revolution. One's assessment of Atatürk depends ultimately on one's view of the worth of the modern civilization which was shaped largely by anticlericals in the European Enlightenment. Atatürk felt like them.

On the Kurds and other ethnic groups in Turkey, Atatürk shared the views of reforming Turkish nationalists. Namık Kemal, the 'poet of liberty' who had inspired Mustafa Kemal in his youth, had written as early as 1878: 'We must try to annihilate all languages in our country except Turkish ... Language ... may be the firmest barrier – perhaps firmer than religion – against national unity.'[24] During the War of Independence, Mustafa Kemal made separate mention of the Kurds, but always as 'brothers' whose fate was indissolubly linked with that of the Turks;[25] he said that he envisaged autonomy for the Kurds within a general system of local self-government.[26] But in 1924, after the war had been won, the new republican constitution set up a centralized state, and pressure was brought to bear on all citizens to speak Turkish.[27]

The policy of considering all citizens of the republic as Turks succeeded in relegating ethnic background to the private sphere, except for the vestigial Christian minorities and the Kurds, millions of whom clung to their ethnic identity. The persistence of the Kurdish problem is thus a failure of the Turkish nationalist approach, which Atatürk shared, but did not initiate. Later, however, his theories of history provided a spurious justification for a policy of assimilation. He could, of course, have tried to implement his original promise of local autonomy; but as the Kurds were (and remain) divided, and fought each other with as much gusto as they resisted attempts at control from outside, it is doubtful that autonomy would have been compatible with law and order. It would certainly have made it more difficult to carry out modernizing reforms throughout the country. Like the French revolutionaries before him, Atatürk opted for modernity and law and order, imposed from the centre. But whatever the cause, he bequeathed the Kurdish problem to his successors.

Atatürk inspired nationalists among colonial peoples, particularly in French North Africa and British India. But he was an anti-imperialist only with regard to his own country, which he deemed worthy of independence and capable of achieving civilized status through its own efforts. He admired the civilization of European imperial powers. As for their colonial subjects, he believed that they could become independent nations only through their own exertions.[28] During the War of Independence, Mustafa Kemal kept in touch with Muslim nationalists grouped round the Hashemites in Syria and the Khilafat movement in British India. He gave refuge to the Senusi leader, who had fled from the Italians in Cyrenaica. But after Lausanne, the European powers were given no grounds to fear that the Turkish republic might encourage subversion within their empires or spheres of influence. Foreign revolutionaries were not welcome in Atatürk's Turkey. Anti-imperialism

was not for export. Atatürk believed that self-improvement applied
as much to communities as to individuals, and that its aim should be
participation in the one, universal modern civilization.

Memorials to Atatürk continue to multiply in Turkey. But it is the
Republic of Turkey, which he founded and shaped, which is his main
monument. Today it is a regional power, often, and unjustly, a source of
fear for immediate neighbours and of hope, tinged with apprehension,
for more distant countries. The creation of the 'separate' entity of Hatay
in Atatürk's last days, and at his instance, has been mirrored by the proclamation of the Turkish Republic of Northern Cyprus. Both are post-
imperial adjustments in territories of Turkish presence: the first a
response to the French withdrawal from Syria, the second to the British
withdrawal from Cyprus. Neither is a sign of Turkish expansionism.
Atatürk's policy of looking to Turkey's development and the defence of
its independence and integrity, while avoiding foreign adventure, has
prevailed. Nor is Turkey's current interest in the newly emancipated
Turkic republics of the former Soviet Union a reversal of Atatürk's
renunciation of Pan-Turkism. He had sponsored the Saadabad Pact
with neighbouring Arabs, Persians and Afghans. Close relations with
Turkic kinsmen in today's changed circumstances would have met with
his entire approval.

The outside world took a long time to understand Atatürk's policy. It
is still finding it hard to place the country he has shaped. He is said to
have steered Turkey towards Europe and the West. This is true to the
extent that the civilization to which he aspired had, and still has, its
centre in the West. But his allegiance was to an ideal, not a geographical
area. The ideal of catching up with modern civilization wherever it may
be found, and of contributing to its further development, continues to
inspire most Turks. Atatürk showed first that Turks could hold their
own as soldiers. Now thousands of them are doing so too in the international environment of culture and business. This suggests that
Atatürk's ideal was not an idle dream.

Turkish society today can give an impression of disorder and division. Atatürk admired order; he was obsessively neat and tidy; he longed
for a well-ordered, green environment. The urban mess in which most
of his compatriots live today seems to belie his aspirations. Falih Rıfkı
Atay noted thirty years ago that Atatürk created a government strong
enough to make people wear hats and use the Latin alphabet, yet incapable of implementing a town plan.[29] But this means only that social
development has its own pace.

Atatürk's belief that there was only one culture in the world, just as there was only one civilization, may be true of high culture – of literature and the arts. But this is manifestly not the case when culture is understood in the anthropological sense as the way of life of a people. The social class to which Atatürk belonged found it easy to adopt European ways. But he underestimated the difficulty of leading the mass of his countrymen in the same direction.

However, the fact that it is taking Turkey a long time to settle down after Atatürk's cultural revolution does not invalidate it. It is only within living memory that French Catholics and secularists took to celebrating Bastille Day together as the anniversary of a common achievement. All the while, the French Revolution is reassessed by each passing generation. So too in Turkey, an impassioned debate has begun round the person of Atatürk and the subject of his revolution. It will go on for a long time.

In the meantime, the Bolshevik revolution has been reversed. The secularization of society begun by Atatürk's contemporary, Reza Shah of Iran, has been undone. At the very least, Atatürk's reforms have withstood hostile pressures better than many contemporary attempts at radical change. The West which Mustafa Kemal sought to emulate has changed. Kemalism can change with it, shedding its authoritarian past, while preserving its openness to new knowledge.

Atatürk's message is that East and West can meet on the ground of universal secular values and mutual respect, that nationalism is compatible with peace, that human reason is the only true guide in life. It is an optimistic message and its validity will always be in doubt. But it is an ideal that commands respect.

Biographical Notes

The following list of principal Turkish personalities mentioned in the text is arranged in the order of the Muslim forenames by which they were known; additional Muslim forenames and surnames are given in brackets.

(Abdülhak) Adnan (Adıvar) (1882–1955)
Trained as a doctor. Fled to Europe to oppose Abdülhamit II. After the Young Turk revolution in 1908, he organized the Red Crescent Society, and served in Libya during the war with Italy in 1911; was in charge of a hospital during the Great War. Married the writer Halide Edip (*q.v.*) in 1917. After the armistice, became active in the nationalist cause and fled to Ankara in 1920. Was a member of the assembly, health minister, deputy speaker and representative of the Ankara government in Istanbul after the nationalist victory. Joined the opposition Progressive Republican Party and moved to Europe in 1926 after the party's dissolution. Although acquitted of involvement in plot to assassinate Mustafa Kemal, he stayed abroad until 1939. He spent his last years as an academic writer.

Ahmet Emin (Yalman) (1888–1972)
Prominent liberal journalist and editor. Born in Salonica, he started work as a journalist in Istanbul before going to study in New York. On his return, he co-founded the newspaper *Vakit* (Time) in 1917. His defence of Turkish national interests led to his exile in Malta by British occupation authorities after the armistice. In 1923 he founded the newspaper *Vatan* (The Fatherland), which was closed down when all opposition activity was repressed in 1925. With a group of friends he then bought the newspaper *Tan* (The Dawn), which he left to relaunch *Vatan* in 1940. He escaped an attempt on his life in 1952, and was imprisoned in 1959 by the Democrat Party government he had helped bring to power a decade earlier. Freed after the 1960 coup, he lost control of *Vatan*, and had to content himself with freelance work. He remained throughout a consistent defender of Western democracy and the free market.

Ahmet İzzet Paşa (Furgaç) (1864–1937)
Ottoman soldier and statesman of Albanian origin. After working with von der Goltz Paşa and training in Germany, he served in the Greek war of 1897, and was then posted to Syria and Yemen, where he found himself at the outbreak of the Balkan war.

Returning to the capital he became in turn chief of the general staff, deputy commander-in-chief and war minister, ceding this last job to Enver in 1914. He opposed the Ottoman entry into the war and did not accept a field command until 1916 when he was given the 2nd Army on the eastern front. After the armistice, he served as grand vizier for twenty-five days. Appointed interior minister in Tevfik Paşa's cabinet, he was sent to negotiate with Mustafa Kemal, who removed him forcibly to Ankara. He resigned to obtain his release, but agreed to serve as Tevfik Paşa's foreign minister a little later. He retired from public life at the end of the War of Independence.

Ahmet Rıza (1859–1930)

Ideologist of the positivist, centralist and nationalist tendency of the Young Turks. Developed his ideas in Paris where he first went to study farming and where he became chairman of the CUP local branch and published its organ *Meşveret* (Consultation), whose French edition attracted Western notice. Rejected an appeal for intervention by the great powers adopted at the congress of the Young Turks in Paris in 1902, and made common cause with Turkish nationalist revolutionaries inside the Ottoman state. Returning after the Young Turk coup of 1908, he was acclaimed as 'the father of freedom' and elected speaker of the chamber of deputies. Shortly afterwards he quarrelled with the CUP and was ejected from its central committee. After the Great War he was briefly speaker of the senate. In touch with Mustafa Kemal and other Turkish nationalists, he was sent to publicize their cause in Europe. His ideas were influential in shaping the Turkish republic, but he was ineffective as a politician.

Ali (Çetinkaya) (1878–1949)

Known as Bald Ali (*Kel Ali*). Studied in the War College; joined the CUP in 1907; served as a *fedaî* (volunteer on dangerous missions) in the war with Italy and then in the Great War, as member of Enver's Special Organization (*Teşkilât-ı Mahsusa*). On 29 May 1919, he ordered his regiment to resist Greek troops in Ayvalık on the Aegean coast. Joining Mustafa Kemal in Ankara, he became deputy leader of the parliamentary group of the Society for the Defence of National Rights. President of the Independence Tribunal which sentenced to death alleged plotters against Mustafa Kemal in 1926. Minister of public works and then of communications from 1934 to 1940.

Ali (Kılıç) (1888–1971)

Born Emrullahzade Asaf, he served as an adjutant of both Enver Paşa and of the latter's half-brother Nuri Paşa. He acquired the *nom de guerre* Kılıç Ali (Ali the Sword) in 1919, when he was sent by Mustafa Kemal to command irregulars against the French in southeastern Anatolia. One of 'the usual gentlemen' – the set of Mustafa Kemal's close friends; member of the Independence Tribunal in 1926; MP for Gaziantep from 1920 until Mustafa Kemal's death in 1938.

Ali Fuat (Cebesoy) (1882–1968)

Born in Istanbul, son of Ottoman general İsmail Fazıl Paşa. Classmate of Mustafa Kemal in the War College; served with him in Syria and Macedonia. Military attaché in Rome, 1908–10. Served on Palestine front in Great War; promoted Brigadier in 1917. After the armistice he was appointed commander of 20th corps in Ankara and became one of Mustafa Kemal's chief companions in the Turkish resistance. Commander of national forces (militia) in western Anatolia, then commander of western front between June and November 1920, when he was appointed ambassador in Moscow. On his return he became head of the parliamentary group of the Society for the Defence of National Rights. Deputy speaker of the assembly between December 1922 and October 1923, when he was appointed inspector of 2nd Army in Konya. Resigning his command in November 1924, he became one of the founders of the Progressive Republican Party. Tried for complicity in attempt on Mustafa Kemal's life in 1926, he was acquitted;

returned to the assembly as independent MP in 1933 and served as minister. Speaker of the assembly in 1948. Elected independent MP on Democrat Party list in 1950, he retired from politics when that party was ousted by the military in 1960.

Ali Fuat (Türkgeldi) (1867–1935)
Born into family of Ottoman senior officials, he served as chief secretary of the household (*mabeyn*) of Sultan Mehmet V and of his successor Mehmet VI (Vahdettin) from 1912 to 1920, and was then under-secretary (*müsteşar*) of the last grand vizier, Tevfik Paşa.

Ali İhsan (Sabis) Paşa (1882–1957)
Turkish general. Graduated top of his class from the Staff College; trained in Germany. Distinguished himself in Mesopotamia in the Great War, and was commander of the 6th Army with headquarters in Mosul when the armistice was signed. Removed at British insistence, he was exiled to Malta. Joined the nationalists in Anatolia in September 1921 and was appointed commander of the 1st Army. Dismissed for disregarding orders, he was forced to retire in 1923. During the Second World War he was editor of the Nazi German newspaper *Türkische Post*. An opponent of İnönü, he was elected to the assembly in 1950.

Ali Rıza Paşa (1860–1932)
Ottoman soldier and statesman. Unsuccessful commander of Western Army in Balkan war. Having been briefly war minister in 1908, after the Great War (in which he took no part) he served in three short-lived governments, before becoming grand vizier in October 1919. Unable to satisfy either the Allies or Mustafa Kemal, he resigned five months later. A member of the last Ottoman cabinet of Tevfik Paşa, he retired from public life when the Istanbul government was dissolved in 1922.

Ali Rıza Paşa (1854–1921)
Known as *Topçu* (the Gunner). Trained in Germany. In charge of Bosphorus forts in 1905. Navy minister after 1908 revolution. Led Ottoman observers to Picardy manoeuvres in 1910. Commander of the straits in war with Italy and of Çatalca lines in Balkan war. Abstained when crown council recommended the signature of the treaty of Sèvres in 1920.

(Mehmet) Arif (1883–1926)
Known as 'the Bear-keeper'. Born in Adana into a leading family of the Karakeçili tribe, he graduated from Staff College, where he became Mustafa Kemal's close friend. Travelled with him to Samsun in May 1919, and took part in suppression of Circassian rebellions. Attached to Mustafa Kemal's suite on the eve of the battle of Sakarya, but fell out with İsmet (İnönü) and was subjected to disciplinary proceedings in June 1922. As a member of the assembly, he joined the opposition in 1924, and was hanged for alleged involvement in the plot to assassinate Mustafa Kemal in İzmir in 1926.

Bekir Sami (Günsav) (1879–1934)
Regular officer. As deputy commander of 17th corps, he organized nationalist forces in and around Bursa; served briefly as a nationalist commander before being sent on a mission to the Bolsheviks; retired soon afterwards.

Bekir Sami (Kunduh) (1867–1933)
Born in the Caucasus and educated in Istanbul, he served as provincial governor before the end of the Great War. He joined Mustafa Kemal in Anatolia in 1919, became a member of the executive of the Society for the Defence of National Rights, and was the first foreign minister of the Ankara government. Resigned in May 1921 when the assembly rejected agreements he had signed in London; joined the Progressive

Republican Party in 1924; was tried and acquitted on charges of involvement in the plot to assassinate Mustafa Kemal in 1926. Retired from politics the following year.

(Mehmet) Cavit (1875–1926)
Born in Salonica into a *dönme* family, he became a teacher of economics. A freemason, he joined the CUP in his native city and in 1909 served his first term as economy minister. Resigned from the Sait Halim government in November 1914 in protest at the country's entry into the Great War. Became economy minister once again in February 1917, keeping the job briefly after the armistice. Sentenced for war guilt, he fled to Europe, and advised the Ankara government at the London conference in 1921 and at Lausanne in 1922–3. Then retired from active politics, but was known as a critic of Mustafa Kemal. Tried on the trumped up charge of organizing the attempt on Mustafa Kemal's life, he was hanged in Ankara in August 1926.

(Mahmut) Celal (Bayar) (1883–1986)
Started career as bank clerk in Bursa. Joined CUP in 1907 and was put in charge of its branches, first in his native city, then in İzmir, where he promoted Muslim commercial activity at the expense of Christians. After the armistice, he moved into the interior under an assumed name and organized resistance to the Allies. Elected to the assembly, he served as economy minister and then as adviser of the Turkish delegation at Lausanne. Founded the Turkish Business Bank in 1924 and managed it until 1932, when he was again appointed economy minister. Took over from İnönü as prime minister in October 1937. Resigned in 1939, became leader of the Democrat Party in 1946, and president of the republic when the party won the 1950 elections. Removed from office in the 1960 military coup, sentenced to death and amnestied in 1964. Spent last years of his life as a respected elder statesman.

(Ahmet) Cemal Paşa (1872–1922)
(Djemal, Jemal or Jamal in Western sources) Known as 'the Great Cemal Paşa'. One of the CUP triumvirs in the Great War. Joined CUP while serving as chief of staff of 3rd reserve division in Salonica. Worked with Fethi (Okyar) (*q.v.*) and Mustafa Kemal on the staff of 3rd Army. As a member of the CUP central committee, he was sent to restore order in Adana after a pogrom of the Armenians. Military governor (*muhafız*) of Istanbul after the CUP 'raid on the Sublime Porte' in 1913. Appointed navy minister in March 1914, he doubled as commander of the 4th Army and governor-general of Syria when the Ottoman state entered the Great War. Made two unsuccessful attempts to cross the Suez Canal; repressed Arab nationalist plotters in Syria, which he left after the formation of the Lightning Group of Armies in 1917. On 1/2 November 1918, he fled to Germany with Enver and Talât (*q.v.*). Plotted against the British in central Asia, and was assassinated by an Armenian in Tiflis (Tbilisi), Georgia, in July 1922.

Cemal Paşa (Mersinli) (b. 1873)
Known as 'the Lesser Cemal Paşa'. Ottoman general. Served alongside Mustafa Kemal in Syria in 1918; though senior in rank (he was a Major-General), he was passed over when Brigadier Mustafa Kemal succeeded Liman von Sanders at the head of the Lightning Group. After the armistice, appointed 2nd Army inspector in Konya. Unlike Mustafa Kemal, he returned to Istanbul when his nationalist stance led to a British demand for his recall. Became war minister in Ali Rıza Paşa's pro-nationalist government in October 1919. Theoretically the representative in the capital of the Society for the Defence of National Rights, he angered Mustafa Kemal by resigning in January 1920 in response to Allied pressure. Exiled to Malta after the Allied occupation of Istanbul in March 1920. Unlike most other exiles, he did not join Mustafa Kemal on his return to Turkey. In 1926, he was arrested for alleged involvement in the plot to kill Mustafa Kemal, but was acquitted by the İzmir Independence Tribunal.

Cevat Paşa (Çobanlı) (1871–1938)
Born into a military family, he graduated top of class from the Staff College in 1894. Won fame as commander of the Gallipoli Straits Fortified Area in 1915, when he was responsible for the defence of the southern (Cape Helles) sector. After the armistice, he served twice as chief of the general staff and once as war minister. Exiled to Malta in March 1920, he became on his return commander of the Mesopotamian (Elcezire) front and then 3rd Army inspector. He was tried and acquitted by the İzmir Independence Tribunal in 1926, and ended his military career in 1935 when he retired from the Army Council.

Enver Paşa (1881–1922)
Leading triumvir of the CUP, who took the Ottoman state into the Great War. Entered military preparatory school in Manastır, graduated from Staff College in 1902 and was posted to 3rd Army in Salonica, where he won fame fighting Balkan guerrillas, and joined the CUP. Emerged in 1908 as 'champion of freedom' after proclaiming the constitution in Macedonia. Appointed military attaché in Berlin; returned and commanded leading detachment of Operational Army which suppressed the Istanbul mutiny in 1909. Volunteer and commander in Cyrenaica against the Italians in 1911. Fought in the Balkan war and became known as 'second conqueror' of Edirne in 1913, having seized power as the leading personality in CUP. Married sultan's niece. Became war minister and chief of general staff in January 1914; concluded secret treaty with Germany and led the state into the Great War, when he assumed the title of acting commander-in-chief. Launched disastrous attack on the Russians in Sarıkamış in December 1914. Fled to Germany in November 1918, tried to cooperate with Bolsheviks in raising Muslims worldwide against the British. Refused entry into Anatolia by Mustafa Kemal, went to Tajikistan to lead Muslim irregulars against the Bolsheviks and was killed in a clash with the Red Army.

Çerkes (Circassian) Ethem (1886–1948)
With his two brothers, Reşit and Tevfik, a leader of Circassian irregulars in northwestern Anatolia. Fought as a non-commissioned officer and cavalry commander in the Balkan war, and served in Enver's Special Organization in the Great War. After the armistice he resisted the Greek advance in Anatolia and commanded the cavalry Mobile Forces based on Kütahya. He suppressed anti-nationalist risings, took part in the establishment of the Green Army, sponsored pro-Bolshevik activity in his area, and refused to integrate his forces in the regular army built up by the Ankara government. Having failed to conciliate him, Mustafa Kemal authorized İsmet (İnönü) to move against Ethem, who thereupon crossed over to the Greeks with some of his followers. He settled in Jordan after the War of Independence and died there, having refused the offer of an amnesty in 1938.

Fahrettin (Altay) (1880–1974)
Commander of Turkish cavalry in the War of Independence. Born in Albania and a graduate of the Staff College in Istanbul, he took part in operations against Kurdish tribesmen and reorganized their levies after 1908. After leading a Kurdish tribal cavalry brigade against the Bulgarians in 1913, he served in the Great War as divisional and then corps commander. After the armistice, he commanded the 12th corps in Konya and organized resistance against advancing Greeks. He hesitated before breaking with the sultan's government, but having decided to back Mustafa Kemal, contributed to the Turkish victory at the head of his 5th cavalry group and was the first Turkish commander to re-enter İzmir in 1922. Under the republic he was close to Mustafa Kemal as inspector of the 2nd Army and then commander of the 1st Army.

Falih Rıfkı (Atay) (1894–1971)
Began journalistic career in CUP newspaper *Tanin* (The Echo) in 1913. Served in the office of 'Great' Cemal Paşa in Syria during the Great War. Founded the nationalist

newspaper *Akşam* in 1918. A member of the Ankara assembly from 1922, he became one of Mustafa Kemal's closest companions and favourite writers. His reminiscences are a major source of information on Atatürk's life. He continued to defend Kemalist reforms in the newspaper *Dünya* which he founded in 1952.

(Mehmet) Ferit Paşa (1853–1923)

Known as *Damat* (son-in-law [of Sultan Abdülmecit]). Born into a family of officials, of Albanian origin, he held junior positions in Ottoman embassies in Europe, married the daughter of Sultan Abdülmecit (and sister of the last sultan Vahdettin), and was a founder of the Freedom and Concord Party formed against the CUP in 1911. Little noticed before the Great War, he formed five governments after the armistice when Istanbul was under Allied occupation. Placing his trust in the British, he opposed all attempts at Turkish national resistance against the Allies, and tried to suppress the nationalist movement in Anatolia. Resigning in 1920, when the Allies realized that nationalist assent was needed for a peace settlement with Turkey, he died in exile in France on the eve of the proclamation of the Turkish republic.

(Mehmet) Ferit Paşa (1851–1914)

Known as *Avlonyalı* (after the town in Albania where his family originated). Abdülhamit's grand vizier at the time of the 1908 CUP coup, he resigned on its eve, unable, and perhaps unwilling, to control his Albanian kinsmen who were inveigled into the constitutional movement. He held minor offices until 1913 when the CUP achieved a monopoly of power, and then spent the last year of his life in Egypt.

(Ali) Fethi (Okyar) (1880–1943)

Turkish soldier and statesman, close companion of Mustafa Kemal, whom he first met at the Manastır military high school. Member of the CUP, he took part in the Italian and Balkan wars. In 1913 he fell out with the leadership of the CUP and was appointed ambassador in Sofia where he stayed until 1917. After the armistice he served briefly as interior minister; published with Mustafa Kemal the newspaper *Minber*; and was exiled to Malta. Returning to Ankara he served as interior minister in 1921–2. The following year he was prime minister for two months on the eve of the proclamation of the republic, when he was made speaker of the assembly. Again prime minister between November 1924 and March 1925. Resigning in the wake of the Şeyh Sait rebellion, he was appointed ambassador in Paris. In August 1930 he was encouraged by Mustafa Kemal to become leader of the Free Republican Party, which he dissolved three months later, refusing to face Mustafa Kemal in a political contest. Appointed ambassador in London in 1934. His last political appointment was as justice minister between 1939 and 1941.

(Mustafa) Fevzi (Çakmak) (1876–1950)

Known as Kavaklı, after his place of birth; the only officer, with the exception of Atatürk, to hold the rank of Marshal in the Turkish republic. Born into a military family, after Staff College he served in the Balkans where he took part in the suppression of Albanian rebellions. Succeeded Mustafa Kemal as commander of the Anafartalar Group in Gallipoli in 1915, and of the 7th Army in Syria in 1917. After the armistice he was appointed chief of the general staff, then 1st Army inspector. Sent on special mission to secure the loyalty of nationalist commanders in Anatolia in November 1919, he was appointed Ottoman war minister the following February. In Ankara by April 1920, he was made a member of the assembly, and appointed defence minister and deputy prime minister, as well as deputy chief of the general staff. In January 1921 he became prime minister (until July 1922), and in August substantive chief of the general staff, keeping the latter job until his retirement in 1944. Promoted Marshal in September 1922, after the defeat of the Greek army at Dumlupınar, he was in charge of the armed forces of the republic until his retirement. In 1946 he joined the opposition to President İnönü, but died before he could make a mark in politics.

(Ahmet) Fuat (Bulca) (1881–1962)
Member of Mustafa Kemal's family and political circle. Born in Salonica. Joined Mustafa Kemal in Cyrenaica. Commanded a company guarding the deposed sultan Abdülhamit in Istanbul. Served with Mustafa Kemal on the eastern front and then in Syria in 1918 when he was captured by the British. Freed, he joined the nationalist forces in Anatolia in December 1920, and became in 1921 military commandant of Ankara. Under the republic he was president of the Turkish Aviation Society, as well as member of the assembly.

Halide Edip (Adıvar) (1882–1964)
(Edib in English publications) Politically active writer. Educated in the American College. Her first articles appeared in the CUP newspaper *Tanin*. Established a society to promote women's participation in social life. After the armistice, she was a founder of the Wilson Society (advocating national self-determination) and became famous for her speeches protesting against the country's partition. She fled to Ankara with her husband Adnan (*q.v.*), and was given the rank of Sergeant to enable her to witness fighting at the front in Mustafa Kemal's company. After the nationalist victory, she became critical of Mustafa Kemal and went abroad, returning in 1939 to take up the chair of English at Istanbul University.

Halil (Menteşe) (1874–1948)
Joined the faction of Young Turks under Ahmet Rıza (*q.v.*), while a student in Paris. In 1898 he returned to the family estate south of İzmir and was active in plots to reintroduce constitutional government. When this was achieved in 1908 he was elected to parliament and became leader of the CUP parliamentary group. During the Great War, he served first as foreign and then as justice minister, in the latter capacity restricting the power of Islamic courts and introducing a new family law. After the armistice he was tried for war crimes and exiled to Malta. Returning to his family estate, he took part in the establishment of the opposition Progressive Republican Party, but failed to be elected to the assembly. When the attempt on Atatürk's life was exposed in 1926, he was interrogated, but not charged. Making peace with the regime, he entered the assembly in 1931 and remained a member until 1946.

Halit Paşa (1883–1925)
Known as 'Mad Halit', he fought as a volunteer in Tripolitania in 1912, and commanded a detachment of Special Organization troops on the Caucasian front. He served uneasily under Kâzım Karabekir at the outset of the War of Independence and attributed to himself the glory of the capture of Kars from the Armenians. He was then transferred to the western front where his wilful behaviour is said to have contributed to the loss of Eskişehir in 1921. Made a member of the assembly for Kars, he was shot dead by another former member of the Special Organization, Ali (Çetinkaya), during an altercation in February 1925.

Hüseyin Hilmi Paşa (1855–1922)
Civil inspector-general of Macedonia between 1902 and 1908, when he won the trust of the CUP to whose clandestine activity he had closed his eyes. When the constitution was reinstated, he became, first, interior minister and then grand vizier in February 1909. Ousted in the mutiny of 13 April, he was reappointed when the Operational Army entered Istanbul. Fell out with the CUP and resigned; held office briefly in the 1912 anti-CUP government, and was appointed the same year ambassador in Vienna, where he remained until his death.

İbrahim Hakkı Paşa (1863–1918)
Ottoman statesman. After a career in central government, he achieved ministerial office under the CUP. Appointed ambassador in Rome, he was recalled and made grand vizier in 1910 on the eve of the war with Italy. Pessimistic about its outcome he resigned when the CUP decided to launch a guerrilla war against the Italians. Died in Berlin, where he had been appointed ambassador in 1916.

(Mustafa) İsmet (İnönü) (1884–1973)
Trained as an artilleryman; graduated top of class from Staff College in 1906. Posted to 2nd Army in Edirne, where he joined the CUP. Served as chief of staff in Yemen in 1912, then in Balkan war, after which he was a member of commission of enquiry into responsibility for Ottoman defeats. Head of department in general staff at outbreak of the Great War, he later saw service on eastern and Syrian fronts, largely as subordinate of Mustafa Kemal. War office under-secretary after the armistice. Visited Mustafa Kemal in Ankara, then joined him permanently after Allied occupation of Istanbul in March 1920. Nationalist chief of general staff with seat in the cabinet, deputy war minister, and western front commander in War of Independence, when he won two battles at İnönü and planned final offensive in August 1922. In October the same year he was named foreign minister and led the Turkish delegation in Lausanne, signing the peace treaty in July 1923. Prime minister when the republic was proclaimed, he resigned the following year, but was reappointed after the Şeyh Sait rebellion in March 1925, and kept the post as Mustafa Kemal's chief executive until a rift developed between them in 1937. Elected second president of the republic on 11 November 1938, he kept Turkey out of the Second World War, and presided over introduction of free parliamentary rule after it. Leader of opposition after 1950. Prime minister once again between November 1961 and March 1965, when he led the country back to democracy after the 1960 military coup. He retired from politics when his Republican People's Party rejected his political programme in May 1972.

İzzettin (Çalışlar) (1882–1951)
Turkish general, born in Yanya (Yanina in Greece). Trained as a gunner, he became Mustafa Kemal's chief of staff in Gallipoli and then on the eastern front. He joined the nationalists in Anatolia in July 1920, served with distinction in the War of Independence, and rose in the military hierarchy, becoming inspector of the 3rd and then of the 2nd Army.

(Mehmet) Kâmil Paşa (1832–1913)
Ottoman statesman. Born in Cyprus, he served first in provincial government, and then as minister in Istanbul, becoming grand vizier for the first time in 1885. After a second term in 1895 he fell out of favour with Abdülhamit. Returning to power in 1909, after the constitution had been reinstated, he soon fell out with the CUP, and achieved office for the fourth and last time when the CUP lost control in 1912. He was removed from office in the 'raid on the Sublime Porte' the following year, and retired to Cyprus. Known as a liberal and an Anglophile, Kâmil Paşa was a prudent statesman who did his best to safeguard the territory of the Ottoman state.

(Mehmet) Kâzım (Dirik) (1881–1941)
Turkish general. Held the rank of Colonel when he became chief of staff of Mustafa Kemal's mission in Anatolia in May 1919. Took part in War of Independence as corps commander and director of transport. Governor of İzmir in 1926 when the attempt on Mustafa Kemal's life was uncovered, he continued in the post until 1935, when he was appointed Inspector-General of Thrace.

Kâzım (İnanç) (1880–1938)
Turkish general. Chief of staff of Lightning Group in Great War. Joined Mustafa Kemal in Ankara and served in War of Independence. Appointed governor of Samsun in 1926.

(Musa) Kâzım Karabekir (1882–1948)
Born into a military family; top graduate of Staff College in 1905. Joined Enver in founding CUP cell in Manastır. A prominent officer with political ambitions, he fought in Gallipoli, Mesopotamia and on the eastern front. After the Bolshevik revolution, he commanded Turkish troops which recaptured Erzurum and went on to occupy Iranian Azerbaijan. Appointed commander of 15th corps in Erzurum in 1919, he sponsored the congress of the Eastern Anatolia Society for the Defence of National Rights, helping Mustafa Kemal to assume the leadership of the nationalist resistance. Appointed commander of the eastern front, he defeated the Armenians and imposed on them the agreement assigning the region of Kars to Turkey. After the War of Independence he became inspector of 1st Army. Disagreements with Mustafa Kemal led him to help found the opposition Progressive Republican Party, which was dissolved in 1925. The following year he was tried and acquitted of involvement in the plot to assassinate Mustafa Kemal. He withdrew from politics until 1939 when he re-entered the assembly as an MP, becoming speaker in 1946.

(Mehmet) Kâzım (Orbay) (1887–1964)
Turkish general. Enver's chief adjutant in the Great War. He joined the resistance in Anatolia in May 1920, served in the War of Independence and rose in the military hierarchy, becoming chief of the general staff in 1944.

Kâzım (Fikri) (Özalp) (1882–1968)
Soldier and statesman. Born in Macedonia, he graduated from Staff College, and served in the Balkan and Great Wars. A member of the CUP, he set about organizing resistance to the Allies when he found himself commander of a division in north-western Anatolia in 1919. Elected to the assembly, he was put in charge of the İzmit front, facing Istanbul, and then distinguished himself in the Sakarya battle. Promoted Brigadier, he was chosen as defence minister in 1922, a post he kept until 1924 when he was elected assembly speaker. Again defence minister 1935–9; in 1943 he became deputy leader of the Republican People's Party. Retired from politics in 1954.

Kemalettin Sami (1884–1934)
The most dashing Turkish general in the War of Independence. Wounded in the defence of Yanya in 1912 and in Gallipoli, he ended the Great War as chief of staff of the Ottoman Northern Caucasus Army. After the armistice he commanded the 10th Caucasian division quartered in Istanbul. His headquarters were overrun when the British occupied the city in March 1920, but he managed to escape and joined the nationalist army in Anatolia. He distinguished himself at the head of the 4th group (later corps) in the battles of Sakarya and Afyonkarahisar. He spent the last ten years of his life as ambassador in Berlin.

Lütfü Fikri (Düşünsel) (1872–1934)
Lawyer and politician who fought to uphold the rule of law. Born into a prominent family of Ottoman officials, he studied law in Paris, opposed Abdülhamit's regime, the CUP, and finally Mustafa Kemal's Republican People's Party. Twice tried by Independence Tribunals and briefly imprisoned, he withdrew from politics.

Mahmut Şevket Paşa (1856–1913)
Born in Baghdad of Chechen ancestry. After Staff College, posted as an aide to Goltz Paşa and then sent for training in Germany. Appointed governor of Kosova in 1905

where he won the trust of the CUP. Became commander of 3rd Army in Salonica in 1908 and commanded the Operational Army which re-established CUP rule in Istanbul the following year, when he became war minister. Resigned, but was brought back by the CUP as grand vizier when it seized power in the middle of the Balkan war in January 1913. Assassinated in June the same year.

Mehmet V (Mehmet Reşat) (1844–1918)
Sultan between April 1909 and July 1918. Son of Sultan Abdülmecit, he led a secluded life as heir apparent to Abdülhamit II, developing an attachment to the Mevlevi (Whirling Dervish) brotherhood. Brought to the throne by the Young Turks in 1909, he was a weak constitutional monarch, frightened by the CUP into doing its bidding.

Mithat Şükrü (Bleda) (1874–1956)
Joined CUP in Paris after science studies in Switzerland. Returned to his native Salonica under an amnesty in 1897 and founded with Talât (*q.v.*) the Ottoman Freedom Society which later merged with the CUP. Became its secretary-general in 1916, was exiled to Malta and later refused to work with Mustafa Kemal. Was tried and acquitted of involvement in the plot to kill Mustafa Kemal in 1926. Made his peace with the regime and entered the assembly, keeping his seat until 1950.

Mustafa Suphi (1883–1921)
Born into a family of senior officials, he studied in Paris, opposed the CUP and fled to Russia in 1914. Drew close to Bolsheviks in internment camp and set about converting Turkish POWs and Turkic Muslims. Joined Third International and founded Turkish Communist Party in Baku in September 1920. Entered Turkey in December and was murdered together with his companions in a boat off Trabzon.

(Abdüllâtif) Naci (Eldeniz) (1875–1948)
Regular officer. Trained in Germany; assistant academic director at War College when Mustafa Kemal was a cadet. Travelled with Mustafa Kemal to Germany in Prince Vahdettin's suite in December 1917. Joined nationalists in Ankara in 1922 in his old capacity of inspector of military academies. Served two terms as member of the assembly.

Dr Nazım (1870–1926)
Leading Young Turk revolutionary and co-founder with Ahmet Rıza (*q.v.*) of the CUP in Paris in 1895. Returned secretly to Salonica and helped fuse the local revolutionary society with the CUP; served on its executive until the party's dissolution. Fled to Germany and travelled to Russia after the armistice, returning to Turkey after the War of Independence. His attempts to revive the CUP led to his hanging at the orders of the Ankara Independence Tribunal in 1926.

Nazım Hikmet (Ran) (1902–63)
Turkey's best-known modern poet. Born in Salonica into a family of senior officials, he studied in the naval academy in Istanbul. His first poems, of nationalist inspiration, appeared under Allied occupation in Istanbul. Travelling to Ankara in 1921 in the company of young Turkish Communists, he disturbed nationalist authorities with his radical views, and was sent to the provinces as a teacher. Soon afterwards he made his way to Moscow where he studied in a Communist college and came under the influence of Mayakovsky and other iconoclastic modernists. Returning secretly in 1924, he was sentenced to prison the following year, but escaped back to Russia. Home again in 1928, he was briefly imprisoned before benefiting from an amnesty. He won fame – and many enemies – as a controversial modernist in Istanbul; was imprisoned again in 1934, released after eighteen months, rearrested in 1938, and sentenced to 28 years in prison on

a trumped up charge of inciting a mutiny in the navy. Released in 1950 with the help of an international campaign of solidarity, he fled to eastern Europe the following year, was an active member of the Soviet-sponsored peace movement, and died in Moscow. A romantic figure, blue-eyed, tall with flowing fair hair, attracting a host of adoring women, he left behind a large body of inspired poetry, modern in style, direct in diction and distinguished by pervasive sympathy for the oppressed, as well as not a few propaganda poems.

Nihat Reşat (Belger) (1882–1961)

Distinguished Turkish doctor, active in the nationalist cause. Trained in Paris, where he had fled after being denounced to Abdülhamit. Returning to Turkey in 1908, he fell out with the CUP, and made his way again to Paris in 1913. Devoted himself to medical research until 1919 when he published the review *Écho de l'Orient* to defend Turkish national rights. Served as representative of the Ankara government in Paris and then in London, and advised the nationalist delegations at the London and Lausanne conferences; later divided his time between Paris and Turkey, where Atatürk put him in charge of the Yalova spa, near Istanbul. He was the first to diagnose Atatürk's fatal cirrhosis of the liver.

Nurettin Paşa (1873–1932)

The son of Marshal İbrahim Paşa, he served in his father's headquarters in Salonica at the time of the 1908 CUP coup. In the Great War, he commanded Ottoman troops in Mesopotamia and acted as governor of Basra and Baghdad in 1915–16. After the armistice, he was appointed governor of İzmir. Removed at Allied insistence, he joined the nationalists in Anatolia, becoming commander of the Central Army (fighting insurgents in the interior), and then of the 1st Army in the final offensive against the Greeks. Responsible for the persecution of Greeks and Kurds in northern and central Anatolia, for the lynching of the Greek archbishop in İzmir and the journalist Ali Kemal in İzmit, and for failing to prevent the great fire of İzmir in September 1922. Elected to the assembly against Mustafa Kemal's wishes in 1925, he was denounced in the latter's six-day speech in 1927.

(Mehmet) Nuri (Conker) (1882–1937)

A member of Mustafa Kemal's family circle. Graduated from Staff College in 1905; joined Mustafa Kemal in Cyrenaica in 1911, in Thrace in 1913 and on the eastern front in 1916. Went to Ankara in June 1920; was briefly city commandant, then governor of Adana. Member of the assembly under the republic and close companion of the president.

Osman Ağa (1883–1923)

Known as 'the Lame' (*Topal*). Notorious leader of irregulars. Served CUP in the Balkans (where he was lamed) and in his native Black Sea area, and then Mustafa Kemal for whom his band provided a bodyguard. Persecuted Armenians, Greeks and Muslim opponents of the nationalists. Shot by regular troops after he had abducted and murdered an opposition member of the assembly.

Ömer Naci (1878–1916)

The 'orator of the CUP'. A revolutionary from his early youth, he first met Mustafa Kemal in the military high school at Manastır. Played a part in the formation of CUP, was a member of its central committee and entered its Special Organization. Fought against the Italians in Cyrenaica. Died of typhus contracted in Iran where he was sent to stir up trouble against the Allies.

(Hüseyin) Rauf (Orbay) (1881–1964)
One of the leaders of Turkish national resistance. Of Caucasian origin, he trained as a naval officer and won fame as the commander of the battleship *Hamidiye*, which harried enemy shipping during the Balkan war. In the Great War, he was assigned to covert operations in Afghanistan and western Iran, but was soon afterwards appointed naval chief of staff. A member of the Ottoman delegation at Brest Litovsk in 1918, he was appointed navy minister later that year, and led the Ottoman delegation which signed the armistice at Mudros. Retiring from the navy, he moved to Anatolia where he joined Mustafa Kemal in issuing nationalist proclamations at Amasya, Erzurum and Sivas. A member of the executive of the Society for the Defence of National Rights, he organized its supporters in the last Ottoman parliament, and was arrested and deported to Malta by the British in March 1920. On release, he joined the Ankara government, becoming prime minister in July 1922. Resigned a year later after disagreements with his foreign minister İsmet (İnönü), and became one of the founders of the Progressive Republican Party in November 1924. When the party was closed down, he moved to Europe. Sentenced *in absentia* to prison for alleged involvement in the plot to assassinate Mustafa Kemal. Returned to Turkey in 1935, but did not make peace with Mustafa Kemal. Under İnönü, became a member of the assembly in 1939 and ambassador in London in 1942. He retired two years later.

Recep (Peker) (1889–1950)
Fought in Yemen, Libya and the Balkan war. Graduated from Staff College during the armistice and joined Mustafa Kemal in Ankara in February 1920, becoming chief secretary of the assembly. Chosen secretary-general of Mustafa Kemal's Republican People's Party in 1923, and served as minister of the interior, defence and public works. One of the toughest members of the Kemalist regime, he lost Atatürk's trust in 1936, but returned to favour under İnönü, serving as interior minister during the Second World War, and as prime minister from August 1946 to September 1947, when his resignation signalled the genuine liberalization of the regime.

(İbrahim) Refet (Bele) (1881–1963)
One of Mustafa Kemal's original companions in the War of Independence. Graduated top of class from Staff College in 1912; served mainly on Syrian front in Great War. Appointed 3rd corps commander after the armistice; accompanied Mustafa Kemal to Samsun in May 1919. Signed nationalist proclamation in Amasya; became member of executive of Society for the Defence of National Rights; suppressed rising in Konya. Interior minister, briefly commander of southern sector of western front, then defence minister to January 1922. Appointed Istanbul representative of Ankara government in October that year, also commander in Thrace until October 1923. One of the founders of the opposition Progressive Republican Party in November 1924. Tried and acquitted by İzmir Independence Tribunal in 1926. Retired from politics until 1935 when he was re-elected to the assembly. His last job was as a member of the Palestine Refugee Commission in Beirut after the Second World War.

(İbrahim) Refik (Saydam) (1881–1942)
Military doctor, trained in Germany. He joined Mustafa Kemal on his journey to Samsun in 1919 and took part in the congresses at Erzurum and Sivas. Elected to the assembly and made health minister in 1921, he kept the job until 1937, becoming the author of the republic's advances in public health. He founded the institute and school of hygiene in Ankara, named after him. He was often at Atatürk's side as his medical adviser. İnönü made him prime minister in January 1939.

Reşit Galip (1893–1934)
Notable reforming education minister under the republic. Studied medicine, worked in villages, joined nationalist movement and was elected to the assembly in 1923. Member

of the Independence Tribunal after the Şeyh Sait rebellion in 1925, and of Republican People's Party executive. Established modern university in Istanbul and recruited German refugee academics during his brief tenure of the education ministry in 1932–3.

Rıza Nur (1878–1942)
Born in Sinop, he trained as an army doctor. Joining the CUP, he was elected deputy in 1908, but soon moved to the opposition. Arrested after the mutiny of 13 April 1909, he became a founder of the Freedom and Concord Party in 1911. Fled abroad in 1913, returning to Istanbul when the CUP lost power in 1918. Joined the nationalists in Ankara, serving as minister of health and of education, but fell out with Mustafa Kemal and moved to Paris, where he wrote his memoirs (published after his death); he returned to Turkey in 1939. A man of violent passions, and a racist nationalist, he is remembered as one of Atatürk's main detractors.

(Hasan) Rıza Paşa (d. 1912)
Trained in Germany and worked on the staff of von der Goltz Paşa. Commandant of Staff College when Mustafa Kemal was a student. Killed defending İşkodra (Shkodër, northern Albania) against the Montenegrins in the Balkan war.

Ruşen Eşref (Ünaydın) (1892–1959)
Turkish journalist who published in 1918 Mustafa Kemal's account of his achievements in Gallipoli. He joined the nationalists in Ankara, was press adviser of the Turkish delegation at Lausanne, served as member of the assembly, chief secretary of the president, and ambassador. A staunch defender of Kemalism.

Sabiha (Sertel) (1895–1968)
Turkish left-wing woman journalist. Born into a *dönme* Salonica family and married to another journalist, Zekeriya (*q.v.*), she studied social work in New York. A leading figure in Istanbul intellectual society between the wars, she moved to eastern Europe after the Second World War, joined the Turkish Communist Party and died in the Soviet Union.

(Mehmet) Sait Paşa (1838–1914)
Known as 'the Lesser'. Ottoman statesman who served Abdülhamit as grand vizier for eight terms, yet presided over the special meeting of parliament in 1909 at which his sovereign was deposed, before himself becoming grand vizier for the ninth and last time in 1911–12. He is remembered for his pragmatism, and for pushing through Abdülhamit's large-scale school-building programme.

(Mehmet) Sait Halim Paşa (1863–1921)
A member of the Egyptian royal family, he joined the CUP in 1906 and was made senator in Istanbul after the 1908 coup. He became speaker of the senate in 1912, nominal chairman of the CUP in 1912, foreign minister and then grand vizier in 1913. Kept in ignorance when Enver propelled the Ottoman state into the Great War, he soldiered on as a figurehead grand vizier until 1917. After the armistice he was exiled to Malta. Freed, he settled in Italy where he was assassinated by an Armenian.

Salih (Bozok) (1881–1941)
Born in Salonica. A contemporary, distant relative and close companion of Mustafa Kemal. A trusted member of CUP, he served (with Nuri Conker) in the guard posted at Beylerbeyi palace in Istanbul, where the deposed sultan Abdülhamit was transferred from Salonica during the Balkan war. Joined Mustafa Kemal as an adjutant in Syria in 1917, returning with him to Istanbul a few months later. Rejoined Mustafa Kemal in Ankara in 1920; his inseparable companion, he was rewarded by membership of the assembly. Shot himself on the day Atatürk died, but survived in retirement until 1941.

Şükrü (Kaya) (1883–1959)
Minister of the interior between 1927 and 1938 and a pillar of the Kemalist regime. Trained as a lawyer in France, he joined the nationalists after the armistice, was exiled to Malta, escaped to Ankara in 1921 and was an adviser of the Turkish delegation in Lausanne. His ministerial career began in 1924. Becoming interior minister in 1927, after the liquidation of the opposition, he was a stern enforcer of the new order, and an uncompromising secularist. When he lost office after Atatürk's death, İnönü, whose succession he had tried to thwart, noted that the country had drawn a sigh of relief.

(Mehmet) Talât Paşa (1874–1921)
Coming from a humble background in Thrace, he started life as a postal clerk and soon joined the CUP cell in Edirne. Transferring to Salonica, he prepared the ground for the CUP coup in 1908. Elected MP for Edirne, he became deputy speaker of the Ottoman parliament. He dominated the CUP central committee, and held several ministerial posts, including that of interior minister at the time of the Armenian deportations in 1915. Becoming grand vizier in 1917, he resigned when the Ottoman state was defeated the following year, and fled to Germany where he was assassinated by an Armenian in 1921.

(Ahmet) Tevfik Paşa (Okday) (1845–1936)
Last Ottoman grand vizier. Received a military education before entering the civil service. Served as ambassador in Athens and Berlin before becoming foreign minister in 1895. Briefly grand vizier after the mutiny of 13 April 1909, then ambassador in London. Grand vizier during the armistice, in 1918–19 and 1920–2 until the dissolution of the Ottoman state. A conciliator, he did his best to bring together the governments in Istanbul and Ankara.

Tevfik Rüştü (Aras) (1883–1972)
Studied medicine in Beirut; joined CUP. First met Mustafa Kemal in 1907–8, and became a lifelong follower. One of the founders of the 'official' Turkish Communist Party set up by Mustafa Kemal. Elected to the assembly in 1923, he became foreign minister in 1925 and kept the post until Atatürk's death. İnönü, whose succession he tried to prevent, made him ambassador in London where he served from 1939 to 1942. Supported the Democrat Party against İnönü after the Second World War, when he became an advocate of rapprochement with the Soviets.

Vahdettin (Sultan Mehmet VI) (1861–1926)
(Vahideddin in Western literature) Last Ottoman sultan (July 1918–November 1922). A son of Sultan Abdülmecit, he succeeded on the death of his brother Mehmet V, and tried to reassert the monarch's power which had passed to the CUP. Fearful for his throne, he put his trust in British protection at the end of the Great War, bringing to power his brother-in-law Damat Ferit Paşa (*q.v.*) believing that the Ottoman state could be saved only if it cooperated with the Allies. Outwitted by Mustafa Kemal, on whose loyalty he thought he could rely, he found himself isolated in the palace when the nationalist cause triumphed. Fled on board a British warship in November 1922 after the assembly had voted to abolish the sultanate, and ended his days in the south of France.

Yakup Kadri (Karaosmanoğlu) (1889–1974)
Prolific Kemalist writer. Born into a feudal family, he spent the last years of the Great War in Switzerland. On his return, he defended the nationalist cause and was summoned to Ankara to publicize Greek atrocities. Under the republic, he served in the assembly and as an ambassador. Founded the review *Kadro*, which gave its name to a movement advocating planned development. His novels and reminiscences glorify the War of Independence and Atatürk's reforms.

Zekeriya (Sertel) (1890–1980)
Leading Turkish publisher and left-wing journalist. Born in Salonica, his first writings appeared in the CUP organ in that city. Studied in Paris and New York, where he travelled with his wife Sabiha (*q.v.*). On his return he served as press director of the Ankara government, then moved to Istanbul, where he published the influential magazine *Resimli Ay* (Monthly Illustrated) and then the newspapers *Son Posta* (Latest Mail) and *Tan*. When *Tan*, which advocated cooperation with the Soviet Union, was wrecked in a demonstration condoned by the authorities, he moved with his wife to eastern Europe. After her death, he settled in Paris, returning finally to Turkey in 1977 where he took up journalism once again.

Chronology

1876	*1 September.* Accession of Abülhamit II
	23 December. Promulgation of Ottoman constitution
1877	*19 March.* Opening of first Ottoman parliament
	24 April. Russian troops enter Ottoman territory
1878	*14 February.* Ottoman parliament dissolved
	3 March. Russian victory confirmed by treaty of San Stefano (Ayastefanos)
	13 July. Treaty of Berlin replaces treaty of San Stefano
1880/1	*Winter.* Mustafa (Kemal Atatürk) born in Salonica
1881	*24 May.* Thessaly ceded to Greece and new frontier established
c. 1888	Death of Ali Rıza, Mustafa's father
1893	Mustafa enters military preparatory school in Salonica; acquires second name of Kemal
1895	Mustafa Kemal enters military high school at Manastır
1897	Brief war with Greece ends with Ottoman victory
1899	*13 March.* Mustafa Kemal enters infantry class of War College in Istanbul
1902	*10 February.* Commissioned Second Lieutenant, and enters Staff College
1903	Promoted First Lieutenant
1905	*11 January.* Passes out as Staff Captain and is posted for training to 30th cavalry regiment, 5th Army in Syria; revives secret opposition group in Damascus
1906	Makes clandestine trip to Salonica
1907	*20 June.* Promoted Adjutant-Major
	13 October. Posted to 3rd Army headquarters in Salonica
1908	*22 June.* Appointed to inspectorate of eastern railways in Rumelia
	24 July. CUP forces Abdülhamit II to reintroduce constitutional rule
	September. Mustafa Kemal travels to Tripoli and Benghazi to re-establish CUP authority
1909	*13 January.* Appointed chief of staff of 17th reserve division in Salonica
	13 April. Mutiny in Istanbul; CUP organizes Operational Army to regain power; Mustafa Kemal travels with his division to the outskirts of Istanbul
	27 April. Abdülhamit II deposed and succeeded by Mehmet V, following occupation of Istanbul by Operational Army
1910	*September.* Visits French army manoeuvres in Picardy; takes part in suppression of Albanian revolt

1911	*15 January.* Appointed to 5th army corps headquarters, then commander 38th infantry regiment
	13 September. Posted to general staff in Istanbul; volunteers for service against the Italians in Cyrenaica
	27 November. Promoted Major
1912	*11 March.* Appointed commander of Derne sector in Cyrenaica
	8 October. Beginning of first Balkan war; Salonica falls to the Greeks
	24 October. Mustafa Kemal leaves Cyrenaica and returns to Istanbul
	21 November. Appointed director of operations of Straits Composite Force
1913	*23 January.* CUP seizes power in 'raid on the Sublime Porte'
	24 March. Edirne falls to the Bulgarians
	29 June. Beginning of second Balkan war
	21 July. Ottomans reoccupy Edirne
	29 September. Treaty of Istanbul fixes Turkish-Bulgarian frontier
	27 October. Mustafa Kemal appointed military attaché in Sofia
1914	*1 March.* Mustafa Kemal promoted Lieutenant-Colonel
	28 July. Austria declares war on Serbia; beginning of First World War
	2 August. Ottoman empire signs secret alliance with Germany
	29 October. Ottoman navy under German command shells Russian targets
	2 November. Russia declares war on Ottoman empire (Britain and France follow suit on 5 November)
1915	*20 January.* Mustafa Kemal leaves Sofia to take up appointment as commander of 19th division for service in Gallipoli
	18 March. Allied navy fails to force the straits
	25 April. Allied troops land at Arıburnu (Anzac); Mustafa Kemal plays major role in stopping their advance
	1 June. Mustafa Kemal promoted Colonel
	6 August. Allies land at Suvla bay (Anafartalar)
	8 August. Mustafa Kemal appointed commander Anafartalar Group; checks Allied advance
	10 December. Mustafa Kemal leaves Gallipoli for Istanbul
	20 December. Allies evacuate Suvla/Anzac beachhead
1916	*9 January.* Allies complete evacuation of Gallipoli
	27 January. Mustafa Kemal appointed commander of 16th corps, which is transferred to eastern (Caucasian) front
	1 April. Mustafa Kemal promoted Brigadier
	5–6 August. Mustafa Kemal recaptures Bitlis and Muş from the Russians (but is forced to evacuate Muş at the end of September)
1917	*7 March.* Appointed commander of 2nd Army
	5 July. Appointed commander of 7th Army in Syria
	4 October. Resigns his command and returns to Istanbul
	20 December. Accompanies heir apparent Vahdettin on visit to Germany
1918	*25 May.* Leaves Istanbul for medical treatment in Vienna and Karlsbad
	3 July. Sultan Mehmet V dies and is succeeded by Vahdettin (Mehmet VI)
	7 August. Mustafa Kemal is reappointed commander of 7th Army in Syria/Palestine
	16 September. British begin offensive and drive out Ottoman troops from Syria and Palestine
	26 October. Mustafa Kemal checks British advance at Katma, north of Aleppo
	30 October. Ottoman state signs armistice with Allies at Mudros
	31 October. Mustafa Kemal appointed commander Lightning Group with headquarters in Adana
	7 November. Lightning Group dissolved
	13 November. Mustafa Kemal returns to Istanbul

1919   *30 April.* Mustafa Kemal appointed inspector of 9th (later 3rd) Army in Anatolia
15 May. Greeks occupy İzmir
19 May. Mustafa Kemal lands in Samsun
22 June. Meets nationalist commanders in Amasya and issues first resistance proclamation
8 July. Mustafa Kemal leaves the Ottoman army
23 July–7 August. Nationalist congress in Erzurum; Mustafa Kemal elected chairman
4–11 September. Nationalist congress in Sivas; Mustafa Kemal becomes leader of permanent executive of countrywide resistance organization
27 December. Mustafa Kemal arrives in Ankara, which becomes his headquarters

1920   *12 January.* Last Ottoman parliament opens in Istanbul; proclaims the National Pact on 17 February
16 March. British troops complete occupation of Istanbul
18 March. Ottoman parliament adjourns
23 April. Grand National Assembly opens in Ankara; Mustafa Kemal elected assembly president
22 June. Greek troops cross Milne line round İzmir and proceed to occupy western Anatolia and eastern Thrace
10 August. Treaty of Sèvres signed
27/28 September. Turkish troops launch offensive against Armenians in the east
30 October. Kars captured from Armenians
14 November. Venizelos defeated in Greek elections, King Constantine returns; General Papoulas assumes command of Greek forces in Anatolia
2 December. Turkish victory over Armenians confirmed by treaty of Gümrü

1921   *5 January.* Circassian Ethem crosses over to the Greeks; end of nationalist militias
9–11 January. Turks win first battle of İnönü
20 January. Assembly votes first (provisional) constitution
21 February–2 March. London conference (on revision of treaty of Sèvres)
16 March. Treaty of friendship with Russia signed in Moscow
1 April. Turks win second battle of İnönü
10 July. Greeks launch offensive and capture Eskişehir and Kütahya
5 August. Assembly appoints Mustafa Kemal commander-in-chief; his military career resumes officially
23 August–13 September. Greeks thrown back at battle of Sakarya
19 September. Assembly awards Mustafa Kemal rank of Marshal and names him *Gazi*
13 October. Treaty of Kars fixes Turkey's eastern frontier
20 October. French-Turkish Accord signed in Ankara; French withdraw from southern Turkey

1922   *12 July.* Rauf (Orbay) becomes prime minister of government of Grand National Assembly
26 August. Turks launch final offensive against Greek forces in Anatolia; break through the following day; win decisive victory on 30 August
9 September. Turkish troops occupy İzmir; Mustafa Kemal arrives in the city the following day
23 September. Turkish troops enter straits neutral zone
3–11 October. Mudanya conference; armistice signed
31 October. Handover of eastern Thrace to Turkey begins
1 November. Assembly abolishes the sultanate, keeps the caliphate
17 November. Last sultan, Vahdettin, flees from Istanbul on board a British warship

18 *November.* Assembly elects Abdülmecit caliph

21 *November.* Turkish peace conference opens in Lausanne

1923   14 *January.* Mustafa Kemal's mother, Zübeyde, dies in İzmir

29 *January.* Mustafa Kemal marries Lâtife in İzmir

4 *February.* Lausanne conference suspended

17 *February–4 March.* Economic congress in İzmir

1 *April.* Assembly votes to hold elections

23 *April.* Lausanne conference resumes

24 *July.* Turkish peace treaty signed in Lausanne

4 *August.* Rauf (Orbay) resigns as prime minister

11 *August.* Second assembly convenes; Fethi (Okyar) becomes prime minister

23 *August.* Newly elected assembly ratifies Lausanne treaty

9–11 *September.* People's Party (later Republican People's Party/RPP) founded with Mustafa Kemal as overall leader

2 *October.* Allies evacuate Istanbul

13 *October.* Ankara becomes capital of Turkey

29 *October.* Republic proclaimed; Mustafa Kemal elected president; the following day İsmet (İnönü) becomes prime minister

1924   3 *March.* Caliphate abolished, Ottoman dynasty exiled, religious schools closed, organized Islam comes under state control

8 *April.* Religious courts closed

20 *April.* Assembly votes first republican constitution

30 *October.* Mustafa Kemal forces commanders to choose between the army and opposition politics

17 *November.* Progressive Republican Party formed as the republic's first opposition party

21 *November.* Fethi (Okyar) replaces İsmet (İnönü) as prime minister

1925   11 *February.* Beginning of Şeyh Sait's Kurdish rebellion in the east

3 *March.* İsmet (İnönü) returns as prime minister: Maintenance of Order Law voted the following day

15 *April.* Şeyh Sait captured; tried and executed in Diyarbakır on 29 June

3 *June.* Progressive Republican Party dissolved

5 *August.* Mustafa Kemal's marriage to Lâtife dissolved

23 *August–1 September.* Mustafa Kemal travels to northern Anatolia and announces his decision to ban the fez and close down dervish orders

25 *November.* Hat Law passed

30 *November.* Muslim brotherhoods dissolved, their lodges and shrines closed

1926   17 *February.* New civil code enacted: women gain equal civil rights

1 *March.* New criminal code

5 *June.* Treaty with Britain and Iraq resolves Mosul dispute and fixes Turkey's south-eastern frontier

15 *June.* Attempt to assassinate Mustafa Kemal uncovered in İzmir

13 *July.* Independence Tribunal in İzmir sentences fifteen alleged plotters to death

26 *August.* Four former CUP politicians hanged in Ankara for alleged involvement in İzmir assassination plot

3 *October.* First statue of Mustafa Kemal unveiled in Istanbul

1927   7 *March.* Independence Tribunals abolished

30 *June.* Mustafa Kemal retires from the army

1 *July.* Mustafa Kemal visits Istanbul for the first time since the start of the War of Independence

15–20 *October.* Mustafa Kemal gives an account of his leadership in six-day speech at a convention of the RPP

28 *October.* First census held: population 13.6 million

1 November. Mustafa Kemal re-elected president

1928   *3 February.* Formal homily recited in Turkish for the first time in Istanbul

9 April. Reference to Islam as official religion removed from the constitution

24 May. International numerals adopted

9 August. Mustafa Kemal announces in Istanbul that the Latin alphabet is to be adopted (and teaches it for the first time in Dolmabahçe palace on 11 August)

1 November. Assembly passes law adopting Latin alphabet

1929   *1 January.* 'National schools' opened to teach new alphabet

4 March. Maintenance of Order Law repealed

13 May. New commercial code adopted

2 September. Beauty queen chosen in Turkey for the first time

1930   *3 April.* Turkish women given the vote in local elections

29 April. First women judges appointed

11 June. Turkish Central Bank established

12 August. Free Republican Party founded by Fethi (Okyar) as second opposition party in republic's history

27 October. Mustafa Kemal receives Greek leader Venizelos in Ankara (friendship treaty signed on 30 October)

17 November. Free Republican Party dissolves itself after clashes in İzmir and allegations of fraud in local elections

23 December. Riot in Menemen: court martial orders the hanging of twenty-eight persons allegedly involved in the murder of Lieutenant Kubilay by Islamic fanatics

1931   *26 March.* International weights and measures adopted

15 April. Turkish Historical Society founded to produce a nationalist version of history

4 May. Mustafa Kemal re-elected president for third time

10–18 May. State intervention in the economy (*étatisme*) adopted at RPP convention

1932   *19 February.* People's Houses founded

12 July. Turkish Language Society established to promote 'pure' Turkish

18 July. Turkey admitted to League of Nations. Official announcement in Istanbul that the call to prayer would be recited in Turkish

1933   *1 February.* Disturbances in Bursa over decision to recite the call to prayer in Turkish

31 May. New Istanbul University established (with the help of refugee German professors)

29 October. Celebration of tenth anniversary of the republic

1934   *9 February.* Balkan *Entente* (Pact) signed in Athens

16 June. State visit by Reza Shah of Iran

21 June. Surnames made compulsory

24 November. Mustafa Kemal adopts the surname Atatürk

3 December. Clerical dress banned outside places of worship

5 December. Women given the vote in parliamentary elections

1935   *2 February.* St Sophia, the Byzantine basilica in Istanbul converted into a mosque in 1453, is opened as a museum

1 March. Atatürk voted president for the fourth time by newly elected assembly which includes eighteen women MPs

27 May. International weekend adopted

1936   *6 May.* State conservatoire opened in Ankara

20 July. Signature of Montreux convention allows Turkey to re-militarize the straits

4–6 September. King Edward VIII is received by Atatürk in Istanbul during an unofficial visit

9 October. Turkey raises with France the status of *sancak* of Alexandretta (later, province of Hatay)

14 December. League of Nations begins discussions on Alexandretta

1937 *5 February.* RPP principles (The Six Arrows), including secularism, are made part of the constitution

March–April. Kurdish rising in Dersim (Tunceli): rebel leader surrendered on 12 September, hanged on 15 November (a second outbreak was suppressed in September 1938)

29 May. Agreement that Alexandretta should become a 'separate entity'

11 June. Atatürk donates his farms to the state

25 October. Celal Bayar replaces İsmet İnönü as prime minister

1938 *30 March.* First official bulletin on Atatürk's state of health

26 May. Atatürk leaves Ankara for the last time

1 June. Atatürk boards the yacht *Savarona*, newly bought for him

5 July. Turkish troops enter the *sancak* of Alexandretta, which becomes the independent state of Hatay

2 September. Hatay parliament opens

5 September. Atatürk draws up his will in Dolmabahçe palace, where he is transferred from the *Savarona*

17 October. Official medical bulletins issued as Atatürk sinks into coma; bulletins cease when his condition improves

8 November. Atatürk sinks into coma for a second time

10 November. Atatürk dies at 9.05 hours in Dolmabahçe palace

11 November. İsmet İnönü elected president

21 November. Atatürk buried in the Ethnographic Museum in Ankara

26 December. RPP meets in extraordinary convention and proclaims Atatürk 'Eternal Leader' (and İnönü 'National Leader')

1939 *29 June.* Hatay becomes part of Turkey (following Franco-Turkish agreement of 23 June)

1953 *10 November.* Atatürk's remains transferred to new mausoleum

Notes

References to works cited in full in the Bibliography (p. 623ff.) are given here in short-ened form under the author's surname.

INTRODUCTION

1. *Histoire de l'Empire Ottoman*, Hachette, Paris 1881, 637.
2. Claude Cahen, *Pre-Ottoman Turkey*, Sidgwick & Jackson, London 1968, 145.
3. Kemal Karpat, 'Ottoman Population Records and the Census of 1881/2–1893' in *International Journal of Middle Eastern Studies (IJMES)*, May 1978, Vol. 9, No. 2.
4. Aydemir, *Suyu Arayan Adam*, 9, 19–22.
5. Ibid., 47.
6. Ibid., 17.
7. Gürün, 167–8.
8. McCarthy, 117.
9. Aron Rodrigue, *French Jews, Turkish Jews*, Indiana University Press 1990, 169–70.
10. McCarthy, 140, n. 4.
11. Ibid., 118.
12. *Rıza Nur Kendini Anlatıyor* (Rıza Nur Tells His Own Story), ed. Abdurrahman Dilipak, İşaret, Istanbul 1992, I, 217.
13. Yavuz Özgüldür, 'Yüzbaşı Helmut von Moltke'den Müşir Liman von Sanders'e Osmanlı Ordusunda Alman Askeri Heyetleri' (German Military Missions in the Ottoman Army from Captain Helmut von Moltke to Marshal Liman von Sanders), in *OTAM*, Ankara University 1993, No. 4, 301–3.
14. The Greek nationalist historian, K. Paparrigopoulos, ascribes the war to 'the encouragement given to the sultan by German organizers in the Turkish general staff' (VII, 78).
15. In 1913, the Ottoman empire imported 16 kg of flour, 5 kg of rice, 8 kg of sugar and 2.6 kg of cotton goods per head of population. Consumption of these goods was, of course, much higher in towns than in the countryside. Vedat Eldem, 'Cihan Harbinin ve İstiklâl Savaşının Ekonomik Sorunları' (Economic Problems in the World War and the War of Independence), in Osman Okyar (ed.), *Türkiye İktisat*

Tarihi Semineri: Metinler, Tartışmalar (Turkish Economic History Seminar: Papers and Debates), Hacettepe University, Ankara 1975, 374.

16. Karpat, *IJMES*, Vol. 9, No. 2, 258–74. The figures for the provinces refer to the population of the central districts (*merkez kaza*), which covered the urban area and adjoining suburbs and villages.

17. Zeynep Çelik, *The Remaking of Istanbul*, University of Washington Press 1986, 38.

18. Ziya Paşa writing in the émigré weekly *Hürriyet* (Freedom), published in London, No. 21, November 1868, quoted by İhsan Sungu, 'Tanzimat ve Yeni Osmanlılar' (The Tanzimat [Reforms] and the Young Ottomans) in *Tanzimat*, T.C. Maarif Vekâleti (Turkish Ministry of Education), Istanbul 1940, I, 836–7.

CHAPTER I   A HOME IN EUROPE

1. Aydemir, *Tek Adam*, I, 22.
2. Soyak, I, 5.
3. Cebesoy, *Sınıf Arkadaşım Atatürk*, 3.
4. Aydemir, *Tek Adam*, 24; Kılıç Ali, *Atatürk'ün Hususiyetleri*, 7. On the other hand, Atatürk's ADC, Salih Bozok, notes that they were both descended from the same maternal and paternal grandfathers, whom he names as Hacı İslâm Ağa and Hacı Salih Ağa (*Hep Atatürk'ün Yanında*, 9). However, since Bozok says that the relationship was 'in the third generation', he is probably referring to great-grandfathers. According to Atatürk's surviving relatives, his paternal grandparents were Ahmet and Ayşe. In addition to Ali Rıza, they had two other children Mehmet Emin and Nimeti (the latter, a boy's name, could be a mistake for Nimet, a girl's name). Mehmet Emin's grandchildren were frequent visitors to Dolmabahçe palace when Atatürk was president (*Milliyet*, 28 February 1995, 5; genealogical tree in Göksel, 19).
5. *AnaBritannica*, IX, 213.
6. *Milliyet*, 28 February 1995, 5.
7. Şapolyo, 20.
8. Aydemir, *Tek Adam*, I, 25–7. Aydemir says these battalions were also called *asakir-i mülkiye* (civil [servants'] troops). This suggests that civil servants either volunteered or were drafted to serve in these reserve units. According to Şapolyo (19), the Salonica volunteer battalion visited Istanbul. Its presence worried Sultan Abdülhamit II who put an end to the use of civil servants as military volunteers.
9. According to Aydemir, Ali Rıza died at the age of 47. He quotes Zübeyde as saying that she was then 27 years old (*Tek Adam*, I, 35).
10. Some biographers have substituted the Turkish ending *-oğlu* or *-oğulları* for the Persian *-zade*, meaning 'son/s of'; *-zade* was the more common form in Ottoman times.
11. Bozok, 7–8.
12. Şapolyo, 15.
13. Tevetoğlu, 163. Abdülhamit II believed that the Karakeçili were related to the Ottoman dynasty (*AnaBritannica*, XII, 585). A part of the tribe settled in south-eastern Anatolia, where it was assimilated by the Kurds (Bayrak, 70, quoting the memoirs of the Ottoman grand vizier Sait Paşa). Arif, who was born in Adana (ATASE [Turkish General Staff Military History Department], *Türk İstiklâl Harb'ine Katılan ... Komutanların Biyografileri*, 163) may have come from this Kurdish-speaking part of the tribe.
14. Bozok, 7.
15. Ibid., 160.
16. Aydemir, *Tek Adam*, I, 29; Volkan and Itzkowitz, 21.
17. Aydemir, *Tek Adam*, I, 27–31.

18. Ibid., 25–7; Volkan and Itzkowitz, 21–2.
19. Şapolyo (17) says that Papaz Köprüsü was in the district of Katarin (Katerini), on the frontier between Greek Thessaly and Ottoman Macedonia.
20. Anderson, 222.
21. A Turkish researcher, İhsan Sungu, quoted by Atatürk's biographer Şapolyo (19), is clearly aware of the difficulty of reconciling dates when he says that he was unable to determine whether Ali Rıza had become a timber merchant before or after his appointment as a customs officer. The difficulty is resolved if we assume that Ali Rıza was engaged in the timber trade while he worked in the customs service.
22. Aydemir, *Tek Adam*, I, 32.
23. Ibid., 34.
24. The house was in Islahhane (Reformatory) street, a name which was sometimes applied to the neighbourhood (Özel, 16).
25. Aydemir, *Tek Adam*, I, 35. This would fix the date of Ali Rıza's death at 1887/8. Hikmet Bayur gives it as '1888 or a little later' (8). Given that Zübeyde was 27 years old when her husband died, she would have been born *c.* 1861, and would have married at the age of 16 or 17. A caption in the memoirs of Afetinan, Atatürk's adopted daughter, giving the date of Ali Rıza's death as 1893 cannot be right, since according to Afetinan herself (10), Atatürk was at that time at the military preparatory school (*rüştiye*), which by all accounts he entered after his father's death.
26. The first link in Salonica's rail connection with Europe was established as early as 1871 (Yitzchak Kerem, 'The Effects of Physical Disasters on the Jewish Community of Salonika in the Nineteenth Century' in *Scripta Hierosolymitana*, Vol. 35, 60, Hebrew University, Jerusalem 1994.)
27. A French company began building a modern port in 1889 (ibid., 60).
28. Sources vary widely in their estimates of the population of Salonica and its communal composition. According to the Ottoman census of 1893 the central administrative district of Salonica, which included near-by villages, had a population of 103,000, of whom 37,000 were Greeks, 35,000 Jews and 29,000 Muslims. Since all Eastern Orthodox who gave their allegiance to the Greek patriarch in Istanbul, rather than to the Bulgarian exarch, were classified as Greeks, the latter must have included Slav-speaking Macedonians in and around Salonica. Chambers Encyclopaedia of 1904 estimates the population of Salonica in 1900 at 100,000, including 50,000 Jews, 35,000 Turks and 15,000 Greeks. Lucy Garnett who lived in the city in the late 1880s puts the number of Salonica Jews at 60–80,000 (II, 3). The Paris-based Alliance Israélite Universelle (AIU) listed the Jewish population as 75,000 in 1905 and 90,000 three years later (Yitzchak Kerem, 58). There is no doubt that the Jewish community grew quickly in numbers and prosperity during the stable years of Sultan Abdülhamit's reign.
29. Yitzchak Kerem, 52.
30. Garnett, II, 19–20.
31. Ibid., II, 102.
32. According to Şapolyo (16), the term *Molla* was applied among Salonica Muslims to those (few) women who could read and write. Their reading was, of course, of a pious nature.
33. This well-known passage occurs at the beginning of a long interview granted in January 1922 to Ahmet Emin Yalman, editor of the Istanbul daily *Vakit* (*ASD*, III, 39).
34. Garnett, II, 104.
35. The chronology of Atatürk's childhood is uncertain. We know that he was born in 1880/1 and that he entered the military high school in Manastır in 1895/6. His adopted daughter Afet (who later called herself Afetinan, joining her given name and her new surname, İnan, in order to keep her place in bibliographies) writes that he was enrolled in the military preparatory school in 1891 at the age of 10 (*Atatürk*

Hakkında Hâtıralar ve Belgeler, 10). Before that, he is unlikely to have started his education at Şemsi Efendi's before the age of 6 or, more likely, 7, i.e. in 1887/8. Hikmet Bayur writes that Ali Rıza died 'in 1888 or a little later' (8), i.e. when Atatürk was 7 or 8 years old. His stay on Hüseyin Ağa's farm is said to have lasted for only a few months (five or six months, according to Falih Rıfkı Atay, *Çankaya*, 18). His unhappy period in the state civil preparatory school in Salonica probably accounted for the school year 1889/90.

36. According to the 1893 census, there were 30,000 Muslims as compared with 20,000 Greeks in the district of Langaza (Karpat, 266).
37. *ASD*, III, 40.
38. *Ağabeyim Mustafa Kemal*, 24.
39. Aydemir names him as Kâmil Efendi (*Tek Adam*, I, 45). On the other hand, Cebesoy gives his name as Karabet Efendi (*Sınıf Arkadaşım Atatürk*, 5), which would make him an Armenian.
40. Atatürk uses the word *teyze* (maternal aunt) (*ASD*, III, 40). His companion Kılıç Ali gives her name as Fatma (*Atatürk'ün Hususiyetleri*, 10). But another friend, Ali Fuat Cebesoy, says that young Mustafa returned to Salonica at the invitation of his paternal aunt (*hala*), Emine (*Sınıf Arkadaşım Atatürk*, 5). In any case, Mustafa's effective guardian in Salonica at that time seems to have been Zübeyde's mother, Ayşe (Kılıç Ali mentions her, but does not specify the degree of parentage).
41. *ASD*, III, 40.
42. Kılıç Ali, *Atatürk'ün Hususiyetleri*, 18–19.
43. Soyak, I, 19.
44. He graduated from the War College (*Harbiye*) in 1903, a year after Atatürk, but did not go on to the Staff College.
45. Kılıç Ali, 10.

CHAPTER 2   THE MAKING OF AN OTTOMAN OFFICER

1. From the interview given to Falih Rıfkı (Atay) and Mahmut (Soydan), published in the newspaper *Milliyet* on 13 March 1926 (*ASD*, III, 16).
2. According to Atatürk's adopted daughter Afet, who gives these dates, he was 10 years old when he entered the school, and 14 when he moved on to the military high school at Manastır.
3. From the interview with Ahmet Emin (Yalman), published in the newspaper *Vakit* on 10 January 1922 (*ASD*, III, 40–1).
4. Quoted by Volkan and Itzkowitz, 36–7.
5. Kılıç Ali, *Atatürk'ün Hususiyetleri*, 14.
6. Aydemir says that her name was Rukiye and that she was the wife of a customs official, called Hacı Hasan Efendi, who would have been in that case a colleague of Atatürk's father Ali Rıza (*Tek Adam*, I, 58). Falih Rıfkı Atay, who was Atatürk's main publicist, says, on the other hand, that when Zübeyde remarried, Atatürk moved to the house of his paternal aunt Emine, in a different neighbourhood (*Çankaya*, 20).
7. Ibid., 20.
8. Belli, *Fikriye*, 66–7.
9. Ibid., 20–9.
10. Kılıç Ali, *Atatürk'ün Hususiyetleri*, 19–20.
11. Ibid., 19.
12. Belli, *Fikriye*, 26.
13. Şapolyo, 31.
14. Atay, *Çankaya*, 19.
15. According to Ali Fuat (Cebesoy), who became his friend in the War College in

Istanbul, Atatürk wanted to study at the prestigious military high school at Kuleli on the Asian shore of the Bosphorus (*Sınıf Arkadaşım Atatürk*, 8).

16. Ibid.
17. *Encyclopaedia of Islam*, 2nd edn (*EI²*), VI, 372a.
18. *AnaBritannica*, IV, 286a.
19. Cebesoy, *Sınıf Arkadaşım Atatürk*, 9.
20. *ASD*, III, 41.
21. *Atatürk'ten Anılar*, 1.
22. Aydemir, *Makedonya'dan Ortaasya'ya Enver Paşa*, I, 177–95.
23. Atay, *Çankaya*, 21.
24. *Sınıf Arkadaşım Atatürk*, 11.
25. Ibid., 12.
26. Ibid., 9.
27. Ibid., 13.
28. *Çankaya*, 31. Falih Rıfkı Atay, who relates the story on the authority of Hakkı Kılıçoğlu, whose family were close to Atatürk's mother Zübeyde, believes that these ceremonies inspired in Atatürk a liking for classical Turkish music rather than religious feelings. Mustafa Kemal's attendance at a dervish ceremony would not have shocked his friends: the Mevlevi order of dervishes was 'very popular in westernized, cosmopolitan circles', and had been praised in *Gonca-i Edeb* (The Bloom of Letters), a magazine published by members of the *dönme* community (İlber Ortaylı, 'Ottoman Modernization and Sabetaism' in Tord Olsson *et al.* (eds.), *Alevi Identity*, Swedish Research Institute in Istanbul, Istanbul 1998, 101).
29. Cebesoy, *Sınıf Arkadaşım Atatürk*, 14.
30. *ASD*, III, 41.
31. *Atatürk'ten Hatıralar*, I, 19.
32. Cebesoy, *Sınıf Arkadaşım Atatürk*, 14.
33. Ibid., 32; *Çankaya*, 31.
34. Kılıç Ali, *Atatürk'ün Hususiyetleri*, 20–1.
35. *ASD*, III, 42.
36. Cebesoy, *Sınıf Arkadaşım Atatürk*, 32–3.
37. *Kemal Atatürk: Les chemins de l'Occident*, 324.
38. Erikan, 72 and Ali Fuat Cebesoy, *Sınıf Arkadaşım Atatürk*, 27, 38. Ali Fuat gives Mustafa Kemal's ranking at the end of the first and second years as 7th and 6th.
39. Cebesoy, *Sınıf Arkadaşım Atatürk*, 41.
40. Ibid., 44–5.
41. Anderson, 271–2.
42. *ASD*, III, 42.
43. Cebesoy, *Sınıf Arkadaşım Atatürk*, 46.
44. Özalp, 2.
45. Emre, 337.
46. *Sınıf Arkadaşım Atatürk*, 52–7.
47. The suspicion arose following Enver's meeting with Abdülmecit's Austrian teacher of German and a correspondent of the Viennese newspaper *Neue Freie Presse* (Aydemir, *Makedonya'dan Ortaasya'ya Enver Paşa*, I, 191–5).
48. *ASD*, III, 42–3.
49. Şapolyo, 34.

CHAPTER 3   PRELUDE TO A MILITARY COUP

1. Kemal Salibi, *The Modern History of Lebanon*, Weidenfeld & Nicolson, London 1965, 116, quoting Philip Hitti.
2. Ibid., 115.

3. Cebesoy, *Sınıf Arkadaşım Atatürk*, 86–100.
4. Afetinan, *Atatürk Hakkında Hâtıralar ve Belgeler*, 4th imp., 41–51.
5. Cebesoy, *Sınıf Arkadaşım Atatürk*, 88.
6. Afetinan, *Atatürk Hakkında Hâtıralar ve Belgeler*, 49.
7. *EI*², II, 637.
8. Ibid., III, 364.
9. Atay, *Çankaya*, 41–2.
10. Philip S. Khoury, *Urban Notables and Arab Nationalism: The Politics of Damascus 1860–1920*, CUP 1983, 53.
11. Zürcher, 33.
12. Ibid.
13. *ASD*, III, 43.
14. Cebesoy, *Sınıf Arkadaşım Atatürk*, 92. Atatürk himself said: 'We laid our hands on a leave permit doubtless issued by mistake. We can call it a mistake, but it occurred through the efforts of Committee members working in various places' (*ASD*, III, 43–4).
15. Afetinan, *Atatürk Hakkında Hâtıralar ve Belgeler*, 53.
16. Ibid., 54.
17. Quoted by Bayur, 19; *Atatürk'ün Bütün Eserleri*, 32.
18. Anderson, 272.
19. *Atatürk Hakkında Hâtıralar ve Belgeler*, 57.
20. Kâzım Nami (Duru), who passed out of the War College in 1897, joined the Şkodra branch soon after his first posting in Tiran (Tiranë, the capital of Albania), see Aydemir, *Makedonya'dan Ortaasya'ya Enver Paşa*, I, 271–3.
21. Quoted by Bayur, 22.
22. Zürcher, 34, n. 69.
23. Şapolyo, 65.
24. *ASD*, III, 44.
25. Gövsa, 162a.
26. *Sınıf Arkadaşım Atatürk*, 108.
27. Writing in Sofia in 1914, Mustafa Kemal referred to a journey he made by boat from İzmir to Crete and then on to Catania in Sicily. In Crete the boat picked up a foreign lieutenant serving with the international force on the island. Chatting over a drink in Catania, the lieutenant told Mustafa Kemal that he was lucky to have picked up the latest military manuals, as his superiors had reproved him for not keeping up with developments in military science. Mustafa Kemal cited the story as an example to be followed (*Atatürk'ün Bütün Eserleri*, I, 166). He describes the incident as an 'old memory'. Mustafa Kemal made four journeys by boat before the outbreak of the war with Italy in 1911: when he was first posted to Syria in the company of Ali Fuat (Cebesoy), who does not mention any detour to Crete and Catania; then from Alexandria to Salonica via Piraeus for his unauthorized visit to his home town; thirdly, the return to Jaffa; and, finally, the journey to Salonica when he was officially posted there in 1907. The meeting in Catania is most likely to have taken place during this fourth voyage. The choice of an itinerary from Beirut to İzmir and then on to Crete, Catania and, finally, Salonica suggests that Mustafa Kemal was in no hurry to take up his post.
28. Bayur, 23; Gövsa, 43.
29. According to the Grand Lodge of the State of New York, quoted in the *New York Times*, 29 March 1998, 5.
30. Atatürk's waiter Cemal Granda says in his reminiscences that at a party in İzmir Atatürk described how he had been taken by a friend to a masonic lodge in Beyoğlu (Pera) in Istanbul. He was initiated as a member, but he claimed never to have visited the lodge again or encountered any of the men he had met there (Granda, 294). According to the account, he walked under crossed swords during the initi-

ation. This suggests that he was enrolled as a military member. In the words attributed to him, Atatürk played down the incident, which, he said, he had found boring.
31. Tunaya, 113; Zürcher, 38. Halil Menteşe, a prominent member of the CUP, who was to become speaker of the Ottoman parliament, says that the Ottoman Freedom Society was founded 'in the summer months of 1906' (*Halil Menteşe'nin Anıları*, 9).
32. İnal, 1933–4.
33. Bleda, 14ff.
34. Gövsa, 238.
35. Bleda, 21–2.
36. Şapolyo, 5.
37. Menteşe, 121–2.
38. Bleda, 22–3.
39. İnal, 1934.
40. Şapolyo, 64.
41. Zürcher, 17.
42. Lewis, 199.
43. Bleda, 26–7.
44. Menteşe, 9. At first the order of the words in the title was reversed as 'Progress and Union' (*Terakki ve İttihat*).
45. Menteşe, 118–20.
46. Yalçın, 5–6.
47. Aydemir, *Makedonya'dan Ortaasya'ya Enver Paşa*, I, 196.
48. Ibid., 489.
49. Ibid., 484.
50. See Enver's official record of service given at the end of Vol. III of *Makedonya'dan Ortaasya'ya Enver Paşa*. Earlier (I, 474), Aydemir gives the date of assignment erroneously as October 1907.
51. Ibid., 483.
52. Zürcher, 42.
53. Cebesoy, *Sınıf Arkadaşım Atatürk*, 110ff.
54. Şapolyo, 66.
55. *Nutuk*, 487.
56. Cebesoy gives the date of the incident as 29 May 1908 (*Sınıf Arkadaşım Atatürk*, 126).
57. Bleda, 33–9.
58. *Nutuk*, 487–8.
59. He won fame in the Turkish War of Independence as 'Bearded' Nurettin Paşa.
60. *Nutuk*, 489; Cebesoy, *Sınıf Arkadaşım Atatürk*, 128–9.
61. Bayur, 23.
62. Cebesoy, *Sınıf Arkadaşım Atatürk*, 119.
63. Letter dated 27 April 1960, quoted in *Tek Adam*, I, 109.
64. *ASD*, III, 114.
65. Ibid., 115.
66. *Sınıf Arkadaşım Atatürk*, 107.
67. Ibid., 115–17.
68. *Hep Atatürk'ün Yanında*, 145.
69. Atay, *Çankaya*, 50.
70. İnal, 1623, 1637.
71. Anderson, 272–3.
72. Ahmad, 2.
73. Ibid., 11.
74. See photocopy of the proclamation signed by Enver, under that title, in Aydemir, *Makedonya'dan Ortaasya'ya Enver Paşa*, I, 527–8.

75. Aydemir, *Makedonya'dan Ortaasya'ya Enver Paşa*, I, 547.
76. İnal, 1617–18.
77. Ibid., 1071.
78. Aydemir, *Makedonya'dan Ortaasya'ya Enver Paşa*, I, 530.
79. *Nutuk*, 490.

CHAPTER 4   AN IMPATIENT YOUNG TURK

1. Aydemir, *Makedonya'dan Ortaasya'ya Enver Paşa*, I, 561–2.
2. Bleda, 53.
3. Ibid., 50. Şapolyo (64) says that two 'palace agents', Captain İbrahim of the military police and cavalry Lieutenant Ali, were killed at the time of the 1908 revolution.
4. Bleda, 50–2.
5. Ibid., 53.
6. *Nutuk*, 490–1. Marshal İbrahim Paşa was then appointed commander of the 4th Army in Erzurum, where his authority was once again challenged by the CUP (Ertürk, 72–3). He was sent as governor to Tripolitania, only to be removed in 1911 in a vain move to placate the Italians (İnal, 1777).
7. Ibid., 1887.
8. Bleda, 54–5.
9. Cebesoy, *Sınıf Arkadaşım Atatürk*, 140.
10. Afetinan, *Atatürk Hakkında Hâtıralar ve Belgeler*, 57–72.
11. *ASD*, III, 45.
12. Aydemir, *Makedonya'dan Ortaasya'ya Enver Paşa*, II, 126.
13. Ibid., 34. Major Niyazi's resignation appears to have taken effect after he had led a group of volunteers from his home town in the suppression of the mutiny in Istanbul in April 1909.
14. İğdemir, 13–15.
15. Quoted by Rachel Simon, 'Prelude to Reforms: Mustafa Kemal in Libya', in Landau (ed.), 22–3.
16. ATASE, *Türk İstiklâl Harbi'ne Katılan ... Komutanların Biyografileri*, 2.
17. Afetinan, *Atatürk Hakkında Hâtıralar ve Belgeler*, 77.
18. Ibid., 72–4.
19. Menteşe, 12; Aydemir, *Makedonya'dan Ortaasya'ya Enver Paşa*, II, 93. Stanford J. and Ezel Kural Shaw give slightly different figures (II, 278).
20. Aydemir, *Makedonya'dan Ortaasya'ya Enver Paşa*, II, 127–9.
21. Ahmad, 40.
22. Menteşe, 15–17; Ahmad, 39. The assassin is believed to have been Abdülkadir, a military member of the CUP, who had shot the *müftü* of Manastır in Salonica before the revolution (Bleda, 39). Abdülkadir was later assumed to have been the murderer of another liberal journalist, Ahmet Samim, killed in June 1910 (Ahmad, 82). During the War of Independence, Abdülkadir served for a time as governor of Ankara. In 1926 he was found guilty of involvement in the plot to assassinate Atatürk, and was executed. Atatürk is said to have remarked at the time: 'If Abdülkadir had made the attempt all by himself, he would have been successful' (Aydemir, *Makedonya'dan Ortaasya'ya Enver Paşa*, II, 130, n. 1).
23. 31 March 1325 in the *Rumi* calendar, hence the name 'Incident of 31 March', by which the revolt is known in Turkish.
24. Menteşe, 17, and Sina Akşin, *31 Mart Olayı*, Sinan, Istanbul 1972, 125ff. Akşin, whose monograph provides the best account of the revolt, argues that it was partly the result of a plan by Prince Sabahattin to get rid of Sultan Abdülhamit, but that nascent Albanian nationalism was also a factor (given that the troops in whose midst the mutiny started were largely of Albanian origin).

25. *ASD*, III, 45.
26. Aydemir, *Makedonya'dan Ortaasya'ya Enver Paşa*, II, 164–5.
27. Erikan, 92.
28. Aydemir, *Makedonya'dan Ortaasya'ya Enver Paşa*, II, 167.
29. Ibid., II, 168.
30. ATASE, *Türk İstiklâl Harbi'ne Katılan … Komutanların Biyografileri*, 178; Karabekir (ed. Bozdağ), *Paşaların Kavgası*, 31.
31. Menteşe, 17.
32. The disagreement arose when the CUP opposed the award to the British Lynch company of navigation rights on the Euphrates, in present-day Iraq (Menteşe, 21).
33. Aydemir, *Makedonya'dan Ortaasya'ya Enver Paşa*, II, 173–4.
34. Bayur, *Atatürk Hayatı ve Eseri*, 38–9. Texts and notes on sources in *Atatürk'ün Bütün Eserleri*, I, 47–50.
35. Cebesoy, *Sınıf Arkadaşım Atatürk*, 142.
36. Gürün, *The Armenian File*, 166–70; Walker, 182–8; Arıkoğlu, 45–59.
37. *Takımın Muharebe Talimi* (Combat Training for Squads). The introduction, which is dated Salonica, 10 February 1324 (23 February 1909), presents the brochure as an adapted summary of a work by 'General Litzman, former director of the military academy of Berlin' (*Atatürk'ün Bütün Eserleri*, I, 34–6; Afetinan, *Atatürk Hakkında Hâtıralar ve Belgeler*, 82–6).
38. In a letter which he sent to his friend Salih (Bozok) on 8/9 May 1912 from his headquarters in Ayn-ı Mansur (Ayn Mansur) in Cyrenaica, Mustafa Kemal wrote: 'You know that what I love above all in military life is its artistry (*sanatkârlık*). If we had the time and the means to apply this art properly here, a military scene would emerge which would satisfy the wishes of the nation and dazzle the eyes of the whole world' (Bozok, 165).
39. Op. and loc. cit.
40. Cebesoy, *Sınıf Arkadaşım Atatürk*, 153.
41. *Nutuk*, 298; Cebesoy, *Sınıf Arkadaşım Atatürk*, 154.
42. *Cumalı Ordugâhı, Süvari Bölük, Alay, Liva, Talim ve Manevraları* (The Camp at Cumalı: Training and Manoeuvres of Cavalry Companies, Regiments and Brigades), 41 pp., Salonica, 30 August 1325 (12 September 1909) (text in *Atatürk'ün Bütün Eserleri*, I, 52, 83; İğdemir, 17).
43. *Atatürk Hakkında Hâtıralar ve Belgeler*, 75.
44. Bayur, 42.
45. Ibid., 43–6.
46. Bayar, *Atatürk'ten Hatıralar*, 15.
47. Ibid., 14–20.
48. Kâzım Karabekir later claimed that it was he who had proposed to the congress that the army should not be involved in politics (Karabekir (ed. Bozdağ), *Paşaların Kavgası*, 214).
49. *Atatürk'ün Bütün Eserleri*, I, 142–3; Bayur, 46.
50. *Çankaya*, 57–8. Halil (Kut), who was to become Ottoman commander in Mesopotamia in the First World War, was only three years older than Enver. See also Bayur, 45, n. 42.
51. *ASD*, III, 45.
52. İğdemir, 21–2.
53. Aydemir, *Makedonya'dan Ortaasya'ya Enver Paşa*, III, 195, where the year is given erroneously as 1909.
54. II, 286.
55. *ASD*, III, 46.
56. *Atatürk'ten Anılar*, 4–5.
57. ATASE, *Türk İstiklâl Harbi'ne Katılan … Komutanların Biyografileri*, 2; Bayur, 47.

58. *Osmanlı Sarayının Son Günleri*, 134–7.
59. Bayur (30–1) gives November 1908 as the date of the clandestine trip to Bosnia, and implies that Mustafa Kemal met Fevzi at some unspecified later date, after the settlement of the problem caused by the Austrian annexation of Bosnia-Herzegovina. It is more likely that the meeting and the clandestine trip (if it took place at all) occurred during Mahmut Şevket's punitive expedition against the Albanians.
60. Özalp, 4–5.
61. Bıyıklıoğlu, 93, n. 36.
62. Uriel Heyd, *Foundations of Turkish Nationalism*, Luzac, London 1950, 32ff.
63. Gövsa, 152.
64. Şapolyo, 68–9.
65. This was founded in Manastır as *Hüsn-ü-Şiir* (Beauty and Poetry). It moved to Salonica in 1910 and was published until the end of Ottoman rule in October 1912 (*AnaBritannica*, IX, 368).
66. Lewis, 345.
67. *ASD*, III, 45–6.
68. *Sınıf Arkadaşım Atatürk*, 155.
69. Text in *Atatürk'ün Bütün Eserleri*, I, 105–24.
70. ATASE, *Türk İstiklâl Harbi'ne Katılan … Komutanların Biyografileri*, 2.
71. *Atatürk'ün Bütün Eserleri*, I, 125; Bozok, 153.
72. *Atatürk'ün Bütün Eserleri*, I, 127–8.
73. Ibid., 126–7; Bozok, 154–5.
74. *Atatürk'ün Bütün Eserleri*, I, 142–3; Bayur, 49.
75. In a telegram to the mayor of Salonica on 12 February 1937, Atatürk declared himself profoundly touched by this 'generous gesture' (*ATTB*, 659).

CHAPTER 5   ADVENTURE IN THE DESERT

1. ATASE, *1911–1912 Osmanlı-İtalyan Harbi ve Kolağası Mustafa Kemal*, 33.
2. İnal, 1774.
3. Ibid., 1976–7.
4. C.D. Haley, 'The Desperate Ottoman: Enver Paşa and the German Empire', in *Middle Eastern Studies*, XXX, No. 1, 2ff.
5. Aydemir, *Makedonya'dan Ortaasya'ya Enver Paşa*, II, 226, says that Naciye Sultan was born in 1899.
6. Ibid., 227. Enver arrived on 15 October, but was detained on board for four days, as the ship was kept in quarantine following an outbreak of cholera in Istanbul.
7. Stoddard, 70.
8. Memorandum to the war ministry, dated 3 August 1919, quoted in Karabekir, *İstiklâl Harbinin Esasları*, 110.
9. İnal, 1089.
10. A convenient summary of the events in 1911–12 is given in the introduction to the memoirs of Halil Menteşe (24–37).
11. When Mustafa Kemal wrote from Derne to his friend Salih (Bozok) in Salonica and asked what was happening at home, the latter sent him a despairing account of the plight of Unionist officers and of the army in general. Salih argued that the army was being destroyed under the pretext of eradicating politics from it (Bozok, 167–9).
12. The date is given in a letter sent by Mustafa Kemal to Salih (Bozok) on 17 October 1911 from the quarantine station at Urla, near İzmir (Bozok, 155), and repeated in another letter dated 22 May 1912 to (Abdül) Kerim from Ayn Mansur in Cyrenaica (ATASE, *1911–1912 Osmanlı-İtalyan Harbi*, 134).

13. Bayur, 51.
14. Mustafa Kemal's letter of 9/22 May 1912 to (Abdül) Kerim (later Paşa), in ATASE, *1911–1912 Osmanlı-İtalyan Harbi*, 134–6; *Atatürk'ün Bütün Eserleri*, I, 139–40.
15. Bayur, 50. Thirteen days should be added to the dates in the Julian calendar supplied to Bayur by the Turkish department of military history. Some dates are suspect. Thus Bayur says that Mustafa Kemal left Istanbul on 21 October, while we know that the true date is 15 October. Even allowing for delays in quarantine both in Urla and Alexandria the journey to Alexandria is unlikely to have taken a fortnight. On the other hand, arrival in Alexandria late in October fits in with the dates of Mustafa Kemal's subsequent movements: an abortive trip to the frontier, followed by return to Alexandria, a fortnight in hospital, and finally departure once again for Cyrenaica at the beginning of December 1911.
16. An Egyptian officer, Salih Harb (later Paşa, and in Egyptian usage Salih Basha Harb), claims that as commander of a border patrol provided by the Egyptian camel corps, he was instrumental in smuggling Ottoman officers across the frontier with Libya against the instructions of British authorities. Salih Harb had been trained both in Egypt and in the Istanbul War College, where he graduated in 1907. Later he fought in the ranks of Turkish nationalist troops in Anatolia before resuming his military career in Egypt (Stoddard, 70 and n. 178).
17. In writing to his friend (Abdül) Kerim on 22 May 1912 (*1911–1912 Osmanlı-İtalyan Harbi*, 134–5) Mustafa Kemal says that he had fallen ill after first leaving Alexandria. But in a letter which he had sent from Alexandria on 15 November 1911 to Salih (Bozok), Mustafa Kemal, still signing himself Şerif, says cryptically, 'At one point on the journey I was shot at by a mounted man (*hayvandan vurularak*, lit. 'hit from an animal'), and I have come for treatment in Alexandria' (Bozok, 160). In his next letter to Salih on 28 November 1911, he says, 'I have got rid of the wound (*mecruhiyet*), which I suffered in the first phase of the journey. We are now embarking on a second journey' (ibid.). Given that Salih was a close friend and that the two letters were written almost immediately after the event, it is likely that the 'illness' which Mustafa Kemal mentioned to Kerim, was indeed the result of an attack by an unknown assailant in the desert.
18. ATASE, *1911–1912 Osmanlı-İtalyan Harbi*, 134–5.
19. Bozok, 161–2.
20. Ibid., 162–3.
21. Şıvgın, 83. According to Atatürk's service record, the promotion was promulgated on 27 November 1911 (ATASE, *Türk İstiklâl Harbi'ne Katılan … Komutanların Biyografileri*, 1)
22. Telegram from Ethem Paşa to the general staff in Istanbul, dated 16 December 1911 (Şıvgın, 151).
23. Haley, 11.
24. İğdemir, 33.
25. Bayur, 51.
26. Ibid., 50.
27. *Atatürk'ün Bütün Eserleri*, I, 137.
28. Letter to Mithat (Denli), in ibid., I, 146.
29. Stoddard, 75.
30. *Atatürk'ün Bütün Eserleri*, I, 140.
31. John Wright, *Libya*, Ernest Benn, London 1969, 109–17.
32. Enver's telegram to the war ministry, quoted by Şıvgın, 151.
33. ATASE, *1911–1912 Osmanlı-İtalyan Harbi*, 115–17, 140–2.
34. Stoddard, 75.
35. *Atatürk'ün Bütün Eserleri*, I, 134.
36. ATASE, *1911–1912 Osmanlı-İtalyan Harbi*, 101–7, 137–9.
37. Bozok, 165.

38. ATASE, *1911–1912 Osmanlı-İtalyan Harbi,* 47.
39. Bozok, 166–7.
40. Şıvgın, 153–4.
41. Ibid., 149.
42. Ibid., 154.
43. Bayur, 52.
44. Şıvgın, 85.
45. *ASD*, III, 81.

CHAPTER 6   FIGHTING DISASTER

1. For text, see Paparrigopoulos, VII, 137.
2. Türkgeldi, 57ff.; Paparrigopoulos, VII, 137–8.
3. Türkgeldi, 64.
4. Ibid., 60.
5. Quoted by Erikan, 106.
6. Aydemir, *Makedonya'dan Ortaasya'ya Enver Paşa,* 304.
7. Ibid., 336–41.
8. Anderson, 298.
9. *EI²*, VIII, 340a.
10. For a Turkish account of Bulgarian atrocities, see İlker Alp, *Belge ve Fotoğraflarla Bulgar Mezalimi (1878–1989)* (Bulgarian Atrocities in Documents and Photographs (1878–1989)), Trakya Üniversitesi Yayınları, Ankara 1990.
11. Aydemir, *Makedonya'dan Ortaasya'ya Enver Paşa,* II, 341.
12. İnal, 1823.
13. Türkgeldi, 66.
14. Text in Aydemir, *Makedonya'dan Ortaasya'ya Enver Paşa,* II, 269–74.
15. İnal, 1977.
16. Anderson, 293.
17. Bozok, 170.
18. Paparrigopoulos, VII, 139.
19. Okyar (ed. Kutay), *Üç Devirde Bir Adam,* 161ff.
20. Bozok, 21–4.
21. Bayur, 53.
22. Aydemir, *Makedonya'dan Ortaasya'ya Enver Paşa,* II, 373.
23. Ahmad, 117.
24. Bayur, 53.
25. Türkgeldi, 76.
26. Text in ibid., 97–8.
27. Aydemir, *Makedonya'dan Ortaasya'ya Enver Paşa,* II, 381. Aydemir says that even if these were not the exact words used, they sum up the tenor of Enver's intervention.
28. Ahmad, 117.
29. Bayar, *Ben de Yazdım,* 1091–2.
30. Türkgeldi, 77.
31. Ibid., 80.
32. Ibid., 78–9.
33. Bayur, 54.
34. Anderson, 296.
35. Altay, 62–3.
36. Bayur, 55.
37. This account is based on the sometimes mutually contradictory details given in Aydemir, *Makedonya'dan Ortaasya'ya Enver Paşa,* II, 388–91; Bayur, 54–5; Erikan, 107–8; Zürcher, 57–9.

38. Text in *Atatürk'ün Bütün Eserleri*, I, 147–9. The memorandum is addressed to the war minister. Mahmut Şevket Paşa combined at the time the job of grand vizier with that of deputy war minister (*Halil Menteşe'nin Anıları*, 36).
39. İğdemir, 27–32.
40. Altay, 63.
41. Erikan, 108.
42. Bayar, 1205.
43. Anderson, 296.
44. İsmet İnönü, *Hatıralar*, I, 80.
45. İlker Alp, 134.
46. Orbay (ed. Kutay), *Yüzyılımızda Bir İnsanımız*, II, 295.
47. Bayar, 1211; Anderson, 297.
48. İğdemir, 32–3.
49. Ahmad, 129.
50. Ibid., 129.
51. Türkgeldi, 106.
52. İğdemir, 34.
53. Atay, *Çankaya*, 76.
54. *Halil Menteşe'nin Anıları*, 166.
55. Belli, *Fikriye*, 67.
56. Özverim, 23.
57. Belli, *Fikriye*, 56–62, 115–19.
58. Atay, *Çankaya*, 70.
59. Ibid.
60. Okyar (ed. Kutay), *Üç Devirde Bir Adam*, 193.
61. Bayur, 56.
62. İğdemir, 34; Bayur, 61; Atay, *Çankaya*, 70–1.
63. *Hatıralar*, I, 83.
64. The willingness of the Ottoman high command to submit to German direction is spelled out in the commentary by the Ottoman military history commission on the memoirs of Liman von Sanders (*Türkiye'de Beş Sene*, 309–10).
65. Bayur, 59–61.
66. Liman von Sanders, 4.
67. Ibid., 8; Menteşe, 40–1.
68. Aydemir, *Makedonya'dan Ortaasya'ya Enver Paşa*, II, 427.
69. Menteşe, 41.
70. Türkgeldi, 111.
71. Bayur, 61–2.
72. Menteşe (177–9) dismisses accusations that İsmail Hakkı abused his post for personal profit, and says that he died a poor man.
73. İsmet İnönü, *Hatıralar*, I, 87.
74. Liman von Sanders, 10–12.
75. İsmet İnönü, I, 87.
76. Bayur, 60.

CHAPTER 7   A DIPLOMATIC INTERLUDE

1. Bayur, 61. The following day, 21 November, he wrote his first letter in French to Corinne Lütfü (photocopy in Özverim, 103–6.)
2. Atay, *Çankaya*, 79.
3. Bozok, 154.
4. Letter to Corinne Lütfü, dated 3 December 1913, in Özverim, 37–8.
5. Belli, *Fikriye*, 39–40.

6. Letter of 3 December 1913 (Özverim, 37–8).
7. Belli, *Fikriye*, 37–55.
8. Özalp, 8–9.
9. Aydemir, *Tek Adam*, I, 188.
10. Bozok, 171–3.
11. Okyar (ed. Kutay), *Üç Devirde Bir Adam*, 214–15.
12. Derin, 81.
13. *Among the Turks*, Robert Carter, New York 1878, 261.
14. İsmet İnönü, I, 91–4.
15. ATASE, *Türk İstiklâl Harbi'ne Katılan ... Komutanların Biyografileri*, 2.
16. *Atatürk'ün Bütün Eserleri*, I, 183.
17. Ibid., 151, which gives the date of the report incorrectly as 5 November 1913, before Mustafa Kemal's arrival in Sofia. Since the report is given the number 3, 5 December is a more likely date.
18. ATASE, *Türk İstiklâl Harbi'ne Katılan ... Komutanların Biyografileri*, 178.
19. Letter from Mustafa Kemal to Kâzım Karabekir, sent from Sofia in January 1914, in *Atatürk'ün Bütün Eserleri*, I, 179.
20. Ibid., 168. The commentary was published in Istanbul in 1918 by the newspaper *Minber*, with which Mustafa Kemal was associated, under the title 'A Chat with an Officer and Commander' (*Zabit ve Kumandan ile Hasbihal*). It draws on Mustafa Kemal's experience during badly conducted Ottoman manoeuvres in 1911, in Cyrenaica in 1912 and, finally, in the Balkan war. Mustafa Kemal blames his superiors in Macedonia for the defeat of the Ottoman armies in the Balkan war. 'I heard one day,' he writes, 'that my home town of Salonica, and my mother, sister, and all my relatives and those who were close to me were given as a gift to the enemy by people who had chased me out of my home town because I had shown them up for what they were. I heard one day that bells had been installed in the minaret of the Hortacı Süleyman mosque, and that the bones of my father laid to rest there had been trodden under the feet of Greek bully boys' (ibid., 165).
21. Özalp, 9.
22. Gürün, *The Armenian File*, 179–85.
23. Cemal Paşa claims in his memoirs (115) that neither Enver nor Talât had approved of his trip to Paris.
24. İsmet İnönü, I, 313–17.
25. Türkgeldi, 114.
26. Quoted by Aydemir in *Makedonya'dan Ortaasya'ya Enver Paşa*, II, 525.
27. *Hatıralar*, 132.
28. Menteşe, 197.
29. İsmet İnönü, I, 332.
30. Ibid., 325.
31. Menteşe, 49 (introduction by İsmail Arar).
32. Ibid., 53.
33. Stoddard, 24–30.
34. Hikmet Bayur, who summarizes the letter in *Atatürk Hayatı ve Eseri*, 66–7, says that the original has been lost. This raises some doubt about its authenticity. On the other hand, the detail which he gives (e.g. that the letter was written on seventeen small pages) sounds convincing. See also *Atatürk'ün Bütün Eserleri*, I, 200–1.
35. Bozok, 174–5.
36. The letter was published for the first time in the Istanbul daily *Hürriyet* on 10 November 1995.
37. *ASD*, III, 31, 32.
38. Mustafa Kemal, *Eskişehir–İzmit Konuşmaları (1923)*, 86.
39. İsmet İnönü, I, 141.

40. *Atatürk'ten Hatıralar*, I, 75.
41. İğdemir, 34–5; Bayur, 68.
42. Mustafa Kemal had reservations about attempts to stir up Muslims in Macedonia. In a letter he sent from Sofia on 6 November 1914 to İsmail Hakkı, who was deputizing for Enver, he wrote: 'As a result of the operations of our bands in Serbian and Greek-occupied Macedonia, the local Muslim population is facing misery and destruction' (*Atatürk'ün Bütün Eserleri*, I, 205).
43. Bayur, 68.
44. Barker, 76.
45. Stoddard, 101–9.
46. İğdemir, 34, 35.

CHAPTER 8   A MOVE TO THE FRONT

1. İsmet İnönü, I, 333, 335–6.
2. Orbay (ed. Kutay), *Yüzyılımızda Bir İnsanımız*, III, 23–8.
3. Liman von Sanders, 42–3; on Hüseyin Rauf's mission, see Orbay (ed. Kutay), *Yüzyılımızda Bir İnsanımız*, III, 23–7, and *Cehennem Değirmeni*, I, 19–22; on the German agents, see Hopkirk, 63.
4. Liman von Sanders, 46. The Sarıkamış disaster is described in Aydemir, *Makedonya'dan Ortaasya'ya Enver Paşa*, III, 99–157.
5. Ibid., 169–80.
6. Cemal Paşa, 186–7.
7. *Atatürk Hayatı ve Eseri*, 55–6, n. 61.
8. Quoted by İğdemir, 35–6.
9. *Atatürk'ün Bütün Eserleri*, I, 281. On p. 279, the date of the report is given as '12.11.1332 (25 January 1917)'.
10. Liddle, 33–4.
11. Mustafa Kemal's report of 7 March 1915 to the command of the Straits Fortified Area (*Atatürk'ün Bütün Eserleri*, I, 210). In the account dated 25 December 1916, which he sent to the military history department of the Ottoman general staff, Mustafa Kemal said that he had immediately requested that Sergeant Mehmet should be decorated as an example to others (*Atatürk'ün Bütün Eserleri*, I, 282).
12. Altay, 82–3.
13. İğdemir, 37.
14. Ibid., 38.
15. Liman von Sanders, 54.
16. İğdemir, 37.
17. Çalışlar, 34.
18. Quoted by Erikan, 117, from extracts of Mustafa Kemal's reminiscences published in the Ankara daily *Hakimiyet-i Milliye* on 10 April 1926.
19. Mustafa Kemal reports this portion of the words he addressed to the troops in the report which he submitted to the military history section of the general staff in January 1917 (*Atatürk'ün Bütün Eserleri*, I, 292). The additions occur in the interview he gave to Ruşen Eşref (Ünaydın) in March 1918 (Şapolyo, 106, 108).
20. The fullest Turkish account of the fighting, based on Mustafa Kemal's subsequent reports, is in Erikan, 128 *et seq.*
21. İğdemir, 39.
22. Aspinall-Oglander, I, 296, n. 4.
23. Mustafa Kemal's report of 26 April 1915 to 3rd corps headquarters (*Atatürk'ün Bütün Eserleri*, I, 214); Çalışlar, 34, n. 23.
24. Çalışlar, 35, says that 'the German Colonel Kanengiesser came with the 5th divi-

sion' on 30 April 1915. But on 7 August he describes Kanengiesser as commander of the 9th division (50).

25. Altay, 97.
26. Çalışlar, 37.
27. *Atatürk'ün Bütün Eserleri*, I, 218; Aydemir, *Makedonya'dan Ortaasya'ya Enver Paşa*, III, 252–3.
28. Ibid., 244; Çalışlar, 37.
29. *Atatürk'ün Bütün Eserleri*, I, 369–71.
30. Çalışlar, 39.
31. Ibid., 40.
32. Belli, *Fikriye*, 43.
33. Özverim, 52–3.
34. İğdemir, 46–52.
35. Çalışlar, 43.
36. Ibid., 41.
37. Ibid., 44.
38. *Atatürk'ün Bütün Eserleri*, I, 389–96.
39. Erikan, 181, n. 88.
40. Çalışlar, 48.
41. Özverim, 56–7.
42. Liman von Sanders, 77–9.
43. İğdemir, 53–4.
44. Erikan, 152; Altay, 107.
45. İğdemir, 58.
46. Liman von Sanders, 82.
47. Erikan, 156.
48. Çalışlar, 51.
49. Liman von Sanders, 87.
50. Şapolyo, 116.
51. Çalışlar, 50–1.
52. Erikan, 171–2. Mustafa Kemal first told the story of the watch which saved his life in his report to the general staff in January 1917 (*Atatürk'ün Bütün Eserleri*, I, 447).
53. *ATTB*, 10–11.
54. Official record in ATASE, *Türk İstiklâl Harbi'ne Katılan ... Komutanların Biyografileri*, 2. Çalışlar reports the division of the group into two army corps on 24 August 1915 (54). The fact that Mustafa Kemal retained the overall command of the Anafartalar Group is confirmed by his letter to Enver of 4 October 1915, which is signed 'Commander of the Anafartalar Group. Colonel M. Kemal' (*Atatürk'ün Bütün Eserleri*, I, 271).
55. İzzettin Çalışlar noted in his diary that Liman von Sanders was dissatisfied with Selahattin Adil, the commander of the 12th division, and appointed the German Colonel Heuck in his place (56). Another German, Colonel Nicolai, became deputy commander of the 2nd corps in the Anafartalar Group (54).
56. Çalışlar, 57.
57. Ibid., 58.
58. Anderson, 327–9.
59. Text in İğdemir, 75.
60. Text of two telegrams in *Makedonya'dan Ortaasya'ya Enver Paşa*, III, 263; Mustafa Kemal's reply (with the correct date) in *Atatürk'ün Bütün Eserleri*, I, 271.
61. Çalışlar, 59.
62. Bozok, 176; *Atatürk'ün Bütün Eserleri*, I, 272.
63. Liman von Sanders, 90–1.
64. Çalışlar, 65.

65. Ibid., 66.
66. Bozok, 177.
67. Aydemir, *Makedonya'dan Ortaasya'ya Enver Paşa*, III, 264. Total Allied casualties were only slightly lower at 213,980 men (*Encyclopaedia Britannica*, 15th edn, XIX, 951).

CHAPTER 9   FIGHTING ON ALL FRONTS

1. Çalışlar, 71.
2. Ibid., 70.
3. *ASD*, III, 111.
4. Halil became foreign minister on 24 October 1915. Zürcher believes that Ahmet Nesimi (Sayman) was the foreign minister whom Mustafa Kemal met on his return from Gallipoli (*The Unionist Factor*, 61), but Ahmet Nesimi did not become foreign minister until February 1917.
5. Menteşe, 213–22.
6. *ASD*, III, 111–14.
7. Çalışlar, 72.
8. Liman von Sanders, 61.
9. Çalışlar, 78–9.
10. Altay, 116.
11. *Harp Mecmuası*, No. 8, p. 119 (April 1916). It is not clear whether this was a separate ceremony or the one referred to by Fahrettin Altay.
12. *Harp Mecmuası*, No. 2, p. 22.
13. Ibid. The officer in the cover photograph of issue No. 6, showing Ottoman troops planting an Islamic flag on Kanlı Sırt (Bloody Ridge) above Arıburnu, is not Mustafa Kemal. On the other hand, the photograph on p. 84 of the same issue, captioned 'A battery commander at an observation post giving orders by telephone to direct the fire at retreating enemy troops', could conceivably be Mustafa Kemal.
14. Erikan, 183, quotes the story that Enver Paşa prevented the magazine *Harp Mecmuası* from carrying Mustafa Kemal's picture on its cover.
15. Ruşen Eşref first met Mustafa Kemal in 1918 in the house of the latter's doctor, Rasim Ferit (Talay), in the Pangaltı district of Istanbul, near the War College (Ünaydın, 23).
16. Şapolyo, 100. Şapolyo's account confuses the date of the anniversary commemorated (18 March 1915) with the date of publication. However, he says, correctly (100), that the interview appeared in *Yeni Mecmua*, which did not start publication until 1917, and reproduces the text which is dated 28 March 1918 (120). Mustafa Kemal's account is based on the detailed report of his part in the Dardanelles campaign, which he sent to the war history section of the general staff in January 1917 (text in *Atatürk'ün Bütün Eserleri*, 279–462). The report was not published at the time.
17. Liman von Sanders, 96.
18. Ibid., 75.
19. Erikan, 188; Çalışlar, n. 126.
20. ATASE,*Türk İstiklâl Harbi'ne Katılan … Komutanların Biyografileri*, 2. Bayur (96) argues that Enver had delayed the promotion, which was due to Mustafa Kemal when he became Anafartalar Group commander in Gallipoli. But the Group was an *ad hoc* structure. It was not unusual for officers to exercise command authority above their rank: İsmet (İnönü) became acting corps commander on the Caucasus front while he was still a colonel (Erikan, 202), a rank which he kept until the end of the World War. Reacting to Sultan Abdülhamit's practice of creating generals for political reasons, the Ottoman high command was slow to grant substantive promotions during the war.

21. Atay, *Çankaya*, 76.
22. Zürcher, 67.
23. İğdemir, 77.
24. When Halil (Menteşe) returned from Berlin in the summer of 1915, Talât told him that he had decided to settle the Armenian question, rightly or wrongly, before he had returned and had a chance of reporting what the Germans thought about it. Later, when he visited Talât in his house he found the latter extremely upset. 'I have received telegrams about the Armenians from Tahsin [the governor of Erzurum],' he said, 'and they've ruined my nerves. I've been unable to sleep all night. It's more than one can stand, but if I had not done it to them, they would have done it to us. In fact, they had already started. It's a struggle for national survival' (Menteşe, 215–16). Dr Mehmet Reşit, the governor of Diyarbakır, who committed suicide after being charged with war crimes at the end of the war, is reported by another CUP leader, Mithat Şükrü (Bleda), as saying: 'Either the Armenians will clean up the Turks and become masters of this country or the Turks will clean them up.' Asked by Mithat Şükrü whether his behaviour had not troubled his conscience, Dr Reşit replied: 'How could it have failed to? But I didn't do it to satisfy my pride or fill my pockets. I saw that we were on the point of losing our country. So for the sake of my nation, I shut my eyes and went forward without showing restraint' (Bleda, 58–9).
25. Goloğlu, *Trabzon Tarihi*, 259–60.
26. Walker, 405; Erikan, 191, 199.
27. Liman von Sanders, 122–3.
28. Çalışlar, 144.
29. *Çankaya*, 93.
30. Erikan, 201.
31. Çalışlar, 122.
32. Ibid., 124.
33. Ibid., 143–4.
34. Özverim, 65.
35. In a letter which he sent in 1911 to another friend from Salonica, Fuat (Bulca), Mustafa Kemal wrote: 'Tell that precious brother of ours that if I have a true brother whose memory is ever present in my heart and conscience, it is Nuri' (*Atatürk'ün Bütün Eserleri*, I, 127).
36. İğdemir, 80–7.
37. Çalışlar, 130.
38. Ibid., 130–1.
39. Çalışlar, 142. Mustafa Kemal sent his report to the historical section of the Ottoman general staff. It was published by the Turkish Historical Society (TTK) in 1962 and 1968, and then included in *Atatürk'ün Bütün Eserleri*, I (279–462).
40. Çalışlar, 148. The appointment was never gazetted. On 7 March 1917, Mustafa Kemal was made substantive commander of the 2nd Army, while Ahmet İzzet Paşa became overall commander of the Caucasian (eastern) front.
41. Mustafa Kemal's appointment took effect on 7 March 1917 (ATASE, *Türk İstiklâl Harbi'ne Katılan ... Komutanların Biyografileri*, 3).
42. Confirmed by Major İzzettin (Çalışlar, 151), who noted on 12 March that on his return from Damascus, Mustafa Kemal told him that he had achieved a good understanding with Enver and that mutual trust and affection had been established.
43. Erikan, 184.
44. Ibid., 214–15.
45. Bayur, 114.
46. Hopkirk, 129–31.
47. Bayur, 113.
48. Çalışlar, 118.

49. Bozok, 178–9.
50. Liman von Sanders, 199.
51. Çalışlar, 164. The appointment took effect on 5 July 1917 (ATASE, *Türk İstiklâl Harbi'ne Katılan ... Komutanların Biyografileri*, 3).
52. Bozok, 180.
53. Ibid., 181.
54. Liman von Sanders, 112.
55. Bozok, 181–2.
56. *Hatıralar*, 202–4.
57. Bozok, 182–3.
58. Erikan, 217.
59. For the text of this report, its follow-up and subsequent developments, see Bayur, 116–34.
60. İsmet İnönü, I, 113–14.
61. Texts of telegrams exchanged between Mustafa Kemal and Enver in İğdemir, 93–7.
62. Erikan, 223; Liman von Sanders, 199.
63. *Hatıralar*, 207–8.
64. Text of letters in Borak (ed.), *Atatürk'ün Özel Mektupları*, 45–51. Mustafa Kemal submitted his resignation to von Falkenhayn on 4 October. He confirmed it three days later.
65. Interview with Falih Rıfkı (Atay) and Mahmut (Soydan), reprinted in İsmet Bozdağ (ed.), *Atatürk'ün Anıları*, 26–30. This part of the interview is omitted from the text in *ASD*, III, 111–17.
66. See Cemal Paşa's account of Mustafa Kemal's clash with Falkenhayn (*Hatıralar*, 208–10).
67. Bozok says only that he had taken the resignation letter to Falkenhayn and that at the railway station in Aleppo Mustafa Kemal turned his back on Falkenhayn, when the latter tried to shake his hand (184–5).
68. The reappointment to the command of the 2nd Army was made officially on 9 October 1917 (ATASE, *Türk İstiklâl Harbi'ne Katılan ... Komutanların Biyografileri*, 3).
69. Bayur, 134–5.
70. *Hatıralar*, 213–14.
71. İsmet İnönü, I, 123–4.
72. Bayur, 135–6.
73. Salih Bozok claims that Talât was informed by Mustafa Kemal's friend Fethi (Okyar). But the latter did not return from Sofia to Istanbul until 21 December 1917 (Okyar (ed. Kutay), *Üç Devirde Bir Adam*, 229), by which time Mustafa Kemal was already in Germany.
74. Bozok, 185–8.
75. Rıza Nur, III, 23.
76. Orbay, *Cehennem Değirmeni*, I, 30–3.
77. Bayur, 127.
78. Aydemir, *Makedonya'dan Ortaasya'ya Enver Paşa*, III, 372.
79. Orbay (ed. Kutay), *Yüzyılımızda Bir İnsanımız*, IV, 21–2.
80. *ATTB*, 12–13.
81. Önder, 11.
82. Ibid., 12–13.
83. Ibid., 16.
84. Ibid., 56–7.
85. Ibid., 26–7.
86. Ibid., 48.
87. Ibid., 45.
88. Ibid., 55.

89. Borak (ed.), *Atatürk'ün Özel Mektupları*, 60.
90. Önder, 60.
91. Şapolyo, 101.
92. *AnaBritannica*, XXII, 364.
93. Önder, 22.
94. Okyar (ed. Kutay), *Üç Devirde Bir Adam*, 229–35.
95. Gologlu, *Trabzon Tarihi*, 266.
96. The anti-CUP Turkish journalist Ahmet Refik wrote in 1919 that when the Russians captured Erzurum they stopped Armenian troops from entering the city, and that 'after the tyrannical government of the CUP, even the enemy administration of the Russians was a period of prosperity for a population that had not known happiness, security and justice for centuries' (*İki Komite İki Kıtâl*, Kebikeç, Ankara 1994, 50–1).
97. Okyar (ed. Kutay), *Üç Devirde Bir Adam*, 231; Simavi, 390–1.
98. In a letter from Vienna on 5 June 1918, Mustafa Kemal told his Turkish doctor Rasim Ferit (Talay) that his diagnosis had been confirmed and that 'nothing was found other than *bacillus coli*' (Özverim, 68). This throws doubt on the statement by Dr Rıza Nur that when he examined Mustafa Kemal in Ankara in 1920/1, he found 'abundant gonococci' from an old episode of gonorrhoea (*Hayat ve Hatıratım*, III, 56). By the time he wrote his memoirs Rıza Nur had developed a pathological hatred of Atatürk.
99. Önder, 65.
100. Yalçın, 225.
101. See photocopy of a page in Önder, 75.
102. İğdemir, 124, says that these words were addressed to a Turkish lady, whom Mustafa Kemal met in Karlsbad.
103. Önder, 68.
104. Bayur, 151, n. 90.
105. Önder, 78.
106. Simavi, 379–80.
107. Bayur, 151.
108. Ibid., 153.
109. Ibid., 150–5.
110. ATASE, *Türk İstiklâl Harbi'ne Katılan ... Komutanların Biyografileri*, 3.
111. Liman von Sanders, 243.
112. Text of telegram announcing the capture of Baku in Aydemir, *Makedonya'dan Ortaasya'ya Enver Paşa*, III, 448.
113. Liman von Sanders, 252.
114. Ibid.
115. Bayur, 156.
116. Erikan, 236.
117. Photocopy of telegram in Aydemir, *Makedonya'dan Ortaasya'ya Enver Paşa*, III, 265.
118. Liman von Sanders, 276.
119. İsmet İnönü, I, 127.
120. Liman von Sanders, 281–2.
121. Ibid., 282.
122. Elie Kedourie, 'The Capture of Damascus, 1 October 1918' in *The Chatham House Version*, Weidenfeld & Nicolson, London 1970, 33–51.
123. Bayur, 157.
124. Liman von Sanders, 290.
125. İsmet İnönü, I, 134.
126. Quoted by Murat Bardakçı, *Şahbaba*, Pan, Istanbul 1998, 91–2.
127. Liman von Sanders, 299.

128. Ibid., 299–300; Şapolyo, 159.
129. In the proclamation which he issued in 1923 from his exile in Arabia, Sultan Vahdettin accused Mustafa Kemal of having made the conclusion of the armistice inevitable by allowing 'the whole of the main force available to the state to be taken prisoner and himself seeking refuge abjectly in the foothills of the Taurus mountains' (İlhami Soysal, *İşbirlikçiler*, 195). But when Mustafa Kemal returned to Istanbul in November 1918, he had been made welcome in the palace. The bitterness of Vahdettin's subsequent accusation reflects the deposed sultan's disappointment: instead of using Mustafa Kemal, he had been used by him.

CHAPTER 10   FIGURES IN A RUINED LANDSCAPE

1. İnal, 1941.
2. Dyer, *MES*, VIII, 2, 150; Menteşe, 65. According to İnal (1941), Talât returned on 28 September.
3. Aydemir, *Makedonya'dan Ortaasya'ya Enver Paşa*, III, 459, 466.
4. Menteşe, 65.
5. İnal, 1941–2.
6. Dyer, *MES*, VIII, 2, 151–2.
7. Bayur, 164–5.
8. Ibid., 165.
9. İnal, 2015.
10. Bayur, 165.
11. Ibid., 166.
12. İnal, 1987.
13. Türkgeldi, 155.
14. Dyer, *MES*, VIII, 2, 169.
15. Ibid., 3, 313 & nn. 2 and 3; Bayur, 311.
16. Dyer, *MES*, VIII, 2, 169.
17. Ibid., 3, 340–1.
18. Turkish translation of Calthorpe's letter in Bayur, 175.
19. Dyer, *MES*, VIII, 3, 337.
20. Tansel, I, 27, n. 99.
21. Aydemir, *Makedonya'dan Ortaasya'ya Enver Paşa*, III, 493ff., where the date of the flight is given incorrectly as 8/9 November; Akşin, I, 64.
22. Akşin, I, 64–7.
23. İnal, 1980.
24. Akşin, I, 78.
25. İnal, 1715.
26. Tansel, I, 32–6, 64–5.
27. Turkish military records show that Mustafa Kemal was placed at the disposal of the war ministry (i.e. removed from his command) and recalled to Istanbul on 7 November 1918, the day on which the Lightning Group of Armies was disbanded (ATASE, *Türk İstiklâl Harbi'ne Katılan … Komutanların Biyografileri*, 3). But as the following day the grand vizier still addressed him as 'Commander of the 7th Army', it seems that the order was not put into effect until a few days later. Atatürk was to say: 'One day I was summoned by Ahmet İzzet Paşa to stand by the telegraph machine. He told me that his cabinet had resigned and that it would be right for me to go to Istanbul. I realized that there was a crisis in Istanbul and left for the capital, as the army group which I had commanded had been disbanded' (İğdemir, 148). This conversation by telegraph could not have taken place later than 10 November, since Atatürk left Adana for Istanbul that night. Ahmet İzzet resigned on 11 November, but he may have informed Mustafa Kemal of his decision the previous

day. The friendly summons to Istanbul looks like a polite formula for notifying Mustafa Kemal of the loss of his command.
28. Texts of telegrams exchanged between Mustafa Kemal and Ahmet İzzet Paşa between 3 and 8 November in İğdemir, 137–48; also Bayur, 180–7.
29. İğdemir, 136.
30. Ibid., 135–6.
31. Arıkoğlu, 72.
32. Ibid., 72–4; Tansel, I, 50.
33. Tansel, I, 49, n. 68.
34. Allen and Muratoff, 478.
35. Ibid., 498.
36. Karabekir, *İstiklâl Harbinin Esasları*, 35.
37. Selek, 87.
38. Aydemir, *Makedonya'dan Ortaasya'ya Enver Paşa*, III, 285–6, 491–2.
39. Erikan, 275–6.
40. Selek, 90.
41. Bayur, 189.
42. Ibid.
43. Aydemir, *Tek Adam*, I, 323; İğdemir, 148.
44. Karabekir, *İstiklâl Harbinin Esasları*, 35, 41.
45. Erikan, 265.
46. Tansel, I, 54, 56, 58.
47. Llewellyn Smith, 68–9.
48. *ASD*, III, 31.
49. Tansel, I, 56–7.
50. Alexandris, 56–7.
51. This was the rough estimate given in March 1923 by the Greek patriarchate, which had claimed in March 1919 that the Greek population of the Ottoman capital amounted to 450,000. Given that 189,000 Greeks from Istanbul and another 61,000 from the suburbs left after the treaty of Lausanne in 1923, while some 120,000 remained (Alexandris, 60, 107, 142, 191), it is likely that the number of Greeks peaked at around 350,000.
52. Akşin, I, 85ff. According to another report, Mustafa Kemal was accompanied by Fethi (Okyar) when he visited Ahmet İzzet (Bayur, 233).
53. Bayur, 196.
54. An article in issue No. 18 of *Minber* declared that Mustafa Kemal had been the sole saviour of Istanbul through his victory at Anafartalar in Gallipoli, but that his modesty forbade him to divulge this fact, allowing others to usurp the honour and glory of all his successes (Borak (ed.), *Atatürk'ün Özel Mektupları*, 42).
55. Akşin, I, 113.
56. Bayur, 236–8.
57. Akşin, I, 125.
58. Türkgeldi, 171.
59. Akşin, I, 128.
60. Career details in ATASE, *Türk İstiklâl Harbi'ne Katılan … Komutanların Biyografileri*, 217.
61. Bayur, 196.
62. Türkgeldi, 170.
63. Text published in *Vakit* on 18 November 1919 (*ASD*, III, 1).
64. Tansel, I, 76.
65. Ward Price, 104–5.
66. Bayur, 259.
67. ATASE, *Türk İstiklâl Harbi'ne Katılan … Komutanların Biyografileri*, 175.
68. Akşin, I, 131–2.

69. *Nutuk*, 201.
70. Atay, *Çankaya*, 159.
71. *Nutuk*, 5.
72. Akşin, I, 140–1.
73. The treatment of ordinary soldiers was particularly bad: of the 2,600 British other ranks captured, only 900 survived (Barker, 286).
74. Akşin, I, 150.
75. Ibid., 145–6.
76. Bayur, 262.
77. Zürcher, 81.
78. Orbay (ed. Kutay), *Yüzyılımızda Bir İnsanımız*, III, 210–11.
79. Akşin, I, 113. The conversation about the army's loyalty may have occurred at this interview, rather than the previous one on 29 November.
80. Akşin, I, 191, n. 111.
81. Ibid., 153.
82. Yalçın, 259.
83. Bayur, 208.
84. *European Dictatorships*, 201; *Makers of Modern Europe*, 357.
85. Ibid.
86. Ibid., 346. Sforza says that Mustafa Kemal was at the time 'chief of the general staff of Mahmud Shevket Pasha', although it was only in 1909 that Mustafa Kemal served briefly on the latter's staff during the suppression of the Istanbul mutiny against the CUP.
87. *Makers of Modern Europe*, 355.
88. *European Dictatorships*, 203.
89. Atay, *Çankaya*, 160.
90. Aydemir, *Tek Adam*, I, 371, based on Rauf Orbay (see *Yüzyılımızda Bir İnsanımız*, III, 208).
91. Atay, *Atatürk'ün Anlattıkları*, 93.
92. *Makers of Modern Europe*, 356.
93. Akşin, I, 158.
94. Sami Paşazade Sezai quoted in Aydemir, *Makedonya'dan Ortaasya'ya Enver Paşa*, III, 516–17.
95. Jevakhoff, 21.
96. Akşin, I, 148.
97. Ibid., I, 152.
98. Bleda, 62.
99. Akşin, I, 172.
100. Ibid., 174–8.
101. Ibid., 195–200.
102. Bayur, 268.
103. Orbay, *Cehennem Değirmeni*, I, 226.
104. Zürcher, 99.
105. ATASE, *Türk İstiklâl Harbi'ne Katılan ... Komutanların Biyografileri*, 114.
106. Erikan, 282.
107. Bayur, 287.
108. Erikan, 285.
109. Karabekir, *İstiklâl Harbinin Esasları*, 40–3.
110. İsmet İnönü, I, 174.
111. Karabekir, *İstiklâl Harbinin Esasları*, 36.
112. İsmet İnönü, I, 175.
113. Llewellyn Smith, 71–5.
114. Alexandris, 56–7.
115. Akşin, I, 260–1.

116. Tansel, I, 142.
117. Gologlu, I, 18.
118. Tansel, I, 143–4.
119. Altay, 186. Details of the commissions' travels in Mevlüt Çelebi, passim.
120. Akşin, I, 255–6.
121. Euxine Pontus, literally the Hospitable Sea, was the apotropaic name given to the Black Sea in antiquity, to conciliate its treacherous waters.
122. Alexandris, 59.
123. Gologlu, I, 24–6; Yüksel, 5.
124. Akşin, I, 243.
125. Bülent Gökay, 'Turkish Settlement and the Caucasus, 1918–1920' in *MES*, XXXII, 2, 58.
126. Akşin, I, 287.
127. Bayar, 2565.
128. The account of Mustafa Kemal's appointment as 9th Army inspector is based on Akşin, I, 277–89; Bayur, 290–306.
129. Tansel, I, 230–1, n. 35.
130. List and biographical details in Tevetoğlu.
131. Akşin, I, 290.
132. Orbay, *Cehennem Değirmeni*, I, 238.
133. Akşin, I, 283.
134. Bayur, 298–300.
135. Okyar (ed. Kutay), *Üç Devirde Bir Adam*, 281–2.
136. Bayur, 302.
137. Akşin, I, 283.
138. Text in İlhami Soysal, *İşbirlikçiler*, 193–9.
139. Mehmet Ali published the disbursement voucher for 'several thousand liras' in *La République Enchaînée*, the opposition paper which he circulated from Paris after his expulsion from Turkey (Rıza Nur, III, 25). Akşin (I, 293) reports that the sum was said to amount to 25,000 liras. Erikan (286) gives it as 1,000 liras.
140. Llewellyn Smith, 78–9.
141. Ibid., 88.
142. Tekeli and İlkin, *Ege'deki Sivil Direnişten*, 73.
143. Celal (Bayar), the local CUP leader, who was by that time already hiding in the hinterland, quotes an eyewitness report that the shot was fired by a nationalist Turkish civilian, Aziz (*Ben de Yazdım*, 1796–7). The honour of firing the first shot has also been attributed to a Turkish journalist, Hasan Tahsin (Tekeli and İlkin, 76), who was in fact a former *Teşkilât-ı Mahsusa* agent working under an assumed name. Hasan Tahsin had taken the lead in calling for resistance on the eve of the occupation (Tekeli and İlkin, 72).
144. Llewellyn Smith, 90.
145. *ASD*, II, 237.
146. Türkgeldi, 207–10.
147. Statement to *Hakimiyet-i Milliye* on 22 April 1921 (*ASD*, III, 34).
148. *ATTB*, 23–4.
149. Akşin, I, 287–8.
150. Bayur, 304.
151. Bennett, 14.
152. Bayur, 304.
153. *Nutuk*, 7.
154. İsmet İnönü, I, 170.
155. Tansel, I, 76.

CHAPTER 11   MEETING THE PEOPLE

1. Şapolyo (209), quoting İsmail Hakkı Dursun, captain of the *Bandırma*.
2. Tansel, I, 236, n. 46.
3. Gökbilgin, 85.
4. Şapolyo, 223.
5. Since 1981 it has been officially called Atatürk Commemoration, Youth and Sports Day (*AnaBritannica*, II, 496).
6. Ryan, 131.
7. Bayur, 305.
8. For instructions to units, see Apak, 30–5.
9. See the telegram sent by Mustafa Kemal from Amasya on 16 June 1919 to Kâzım Karabekir in Erzurum (ATASE, *Atatürk Özel Arşivinden Seçmeler*, IV, 43).
10. Akşin, I, 309–10.
11. Ibid., 306–7, who corrects the date of 6 June, given by Halide Edip for the first Sultan Ahmet meeting (*The Turkish Ordeal*, 30).
12. Cabinet list in Akşin, I, 300, n. 5.
13. Ibid., 323–4.
14. Ibid., 312–13. Fifty-five detainees were taken to Malta and twelve to Mudros.
15. Gökbilgin, 83–4.
16. *ATTB*, 24–5; Sonyel, 18.
17. Ibid., 18.
18. Karabekir, *İstiklâl Harbimiz*, 32–3.
19. *Nutuk*, 12.
20. Erikan, 363; Bozok, 87.
21. Şapolyo, 206; Kinross, 167; Erikan, 363.
22. Gökbilgin, 85.
23. Sonyel, 21.
24. Evans, 21.
25. Sonyel, 19.
26. British official documents quoted in ibid., 18–22.
27. Akşin, I, 344–5.
28. Sonyel, 22.
29. *ATTB*, 26.
30. *Nutuk*, 18.
31. Ibid., 19.
32. Gökay, 'Turkish Settlement and the Caucasus' in *MES*, XXXII, No. 2, April 1996, 59–60.
33. Karabekir, *İstiklâl Harbimiz*, 59–60.
34. Apak, 64–6.
35. Akşin, I, 29.
36. Apak, 73–4.
37. Gologlu, I, 59.
38. Orbay (ed. Kutay), *Yüzyılımızda Bir İnsanımız*, IV, 352.
39. According to Mustafa Kemal, Rauf went to Bandırma and on to the Aegean region to meet Colonel Bekir Sami (Günsav), commander of the 56th division and acting commander of the 17th corps (*Nutuk*, 23). However, Rauf himself does not mention Bekir Sami, although he says that he met the 14th corps commander, Yusuf İzzet Paşa, in Balıkesir (Orbay (ed. Kutay), IV, 359).
40. Ibid., 369.
41. *Nutuk*, 22.
42. Rauf Orbay's letter to Kâzım Karabekir, dated 4 July 1941, in Karabekir, *İstiklâl Harbimiz*, 1100–1.
43. Tansel, II, 8.

44. Erikan, 315.
45. Ibid., 372.
46. Ibid., 374.
47. Akşin, I, 346.
48. *Nutuk: Vesikalar*, 621–2.
49. Erikan, 374.
50. Akşin, I, 347–9.
51. *Nutuk*, 21.
52. Gökbilgin, 17.
53. Tekeli and İlkin, *Ege'deki Sivil Direnişten*, 169ff.
54. Orbay (ed. Kutay), *Yüzyılımızda Bir İnsanımız*, III, 230.
55. *Nutuk*, 22.
56. Karabekir, *İstiklâl Harbimiz*, 1101.
57. Akşin, I, 204, 428.
58. *Nutuk: Vesikalar*, 628.
59. Karabekir, *İstiklâl Harbimiz*, 54–5.
60. Akşin, I, 347, n. 122.
61. *ATTB*, 45–6.
62. *Nutuk*, 24–5.
63. Tansel, II, 20. Ali Fuat had left earlier for his headquarters in Ankara, taking with him the letters addressed to politicians in Istanbul.
64. *Nutuk*, 26–9.
65. McCarthy, *Death and Exile*, 198–9.
66. Akşin, I, 55.
67. Karabekir, *İstiklâl Harbimiz*, 65.
68. Gologlu, I, 3.
69. Karabekir, *İstiklâl Harbimiz*, 65.
70. Sonyel, 24.
71. Ibid., 25.
72. Akşin, I, 58.
73. *İstiklâl Harbimiz*, 69–71.
74. Akşin, I, 356–8.
75. See Rauf's letter to Karabekir of 4 July 1941, cited at note 42 above.
76. Karabekir, *İstiklâl Harbimiz*, 80.
77. *Nutuk*, 30–1.
78. Kansu, I, 34.
79. Karabekir, *İstiklâl Harbimiz*, 1103–4.
80. Ibid., 50.
81. Rawlinson, 180, 181.
82. *Nutuk*, 47.
83. Ibid., 11.
84. Kansu, I, 131.
85. Rawlinson, 251; Sonyel, 29.
86. Rawlinson, 188–9.
87. Gologlu, I, 65, 68.
88. Ibid., 68–9, 81.
89. Ibid., 81. According to one account the majority was 38 out of 56; another account puts it at 48.
90. *ASD*, I, 1–5.
91. Gologlu, I, 83–6.
92. Ibid., 87–8.
93. Ibid., 89.
94. Ibid., 91.
95. Ibid., 103–4.

96. Ibid., 182.
97. Text in ibid., 201–3.
98. Ibid., 187–9.
99. *Nutuk: Vesikalar,* 643.
100. *Nutuk,* 45.
101. Karabekir, *İstiklâl Harbimiz,* 106. In accordance with the rulebook, Karabekir, as a serving officer, could be only an advisory member (Gologlu, I, 105).
102. *Nutuk: Vesikalar,* 646.
103. *Nutuk,* 47–8.
104. Ibid., 49–50; Kansu, I, 139–41.
105. Ali Fuat informed Karabekir on 21 August 1919 that he had decided not to distribute the instructions issued by *Karakol.* Nevertheless, Karabekir notes that 'some useful articles' of the instructions were circulated to army units as an addition to the rulebook, presumably of the Eastern Anatolian Society for the Defence of National Rights (*İstiklâl Harbimiz,* 136–7).
106. Akşin, I, 399–402, 414, 418–21, 436–7; İnal, 1994–5.
107. Akşin, I, 443.
108. Ibid., 463.
109. ATASE, *Türk İstiklâl Harbi'ne Katılan ... Komutanların Biyografileri,* 99.
110. Karabekir, *İstiklâl Harbimiz,* 110–13.
111. Kansu, I, 155–6.
112. Gologlu, II, 20; Kansu, I, 173–6.
113. Text in Bozok, 191–3.
114. Kansu, I, 174.
115. *Nutuk,* 56–7; Kansu, I, 198–203.
116. List in Gologlu, II, 73–4.
117. Tekeli and İlkin, 184ff., 205, 207.
118. Gologlu, II, 61.
119. Ibid., 78.
120. Quoted by Sonyel, 44.
121. Akşin, I, 518.
122. Rıza Nur, III, 27.
123. Shaw and Shaw, III, 331.
124. Akşin, I, 519–20.
125. Ibid., 528.
126. Karabekir, *İstiklâl Harbimiz,* 165–76.
127. *Nutuk,* 60–77.
128. Gologlu, II, 96–7.
129. Akşin, I, 533. The resolution of the Sivas congress inviting a US Senate committee of enquiry is appended as Exhibit 'F' to the report of the Harbord mission (US Congress, *Conditions in the Near East*).
130. *Conditions in the Near East,* 17.
131. Ibid.
132. *Nutuk,* 77.
133. Gologlu, II, 107–11, 220.
134. Text in ibid., 232–4.
135. The province was also sometimes called Harput, the name of its old chief town which Elâziz replaced.
136. Text in *Nutuk,* 85–7.
137. Akşin, I, 535, n. 266.
138. Akşin, I, 549, n. 303; Karabekir, *İstiklâl Harbimiz,* 225.
139. Telegram from Recep Zühtü to 3rd army corps, sent from Malatya on 15 September 1919 (ATASE, *Atatürk Özel Arşivinden Seçmeler,* IV, 96–7); *The Diary of Major Noel,* 24.

140. Goloğlu, II, 80–1.
141. İlhami Soysal, *150'likler*, 60, 150.
142. Telegram sent on 20 September 1919 (ATASE, *Atatürk Özel Arşivinden Seçmeler*, IV, 124).
143. Akşin, I, 555; Goloğlu, II, 97.
144. *Nutuk*, 92.
145. Ibid., 88.
146. Goloğlu, II, 112.
147. Karabekir, *İstiklâl Harbimiz*, 261.
148. Ibid., 227–8, 232.
149. *Nutuk*, 184.
150. Akşin, I, 581.
151. Ibid., 584; *Nutuk*, 114–15 (where Mustafa Kemal blames Refet for demanding the title of 2nd Army inspector, which was not in the gift of the Sivas congress).
152. Akşin, I, 579.
153. Ibid., 585.
154. İnal, 2122.

CHAPTER 12   THE BIRTH OF KEMALISM

1. Alexandris, 65.
2. Ryan, 135.
3. Goloğlu, II, 178.
4. Ibid., I, 159–60.
5. *Nutuk*, 130.
6. Ibid., 145.
7. *Nutuk: Vesikalar*, 776.
8. *Nutuk*, 144.
9. Ibid., 156.
10. Ibid., 163–6. Text of two protocols in *Nutuk: Vesikalar*, 809–10. Summaries in Goloğlu, II, 186–8; Akşin, II, 43–8.
11. *Nutuk*, 167–71.
12. Ibid., 172.
13. Ibid., 173.
14. He replaced his namesake (Ahmet) Fevzi, a general close to the palace, who was appointed commander of Ali Fuat's 20th corps in Ankara, but who was prevented by the nationalists from taking up his post. In view of Çakmak's later career as chief of staff of the armies of the Grand National Assembly and then of the Turkish republic, Atatürk himself preferred to speak of Ahmet Fevzi as leader of the fact-finding commission (Akşin, II, 164). The last-minute change from Ahmet Fevzi to Mustafa Fevzi has led to persistent confusion (Goloğlu, II, 201–2, 255).
15. Karabekir, *İstiklâl Harbimiz*, 372–4.
16. Ibid., 371.
17. *Nutuk*, 183.
18. Zürcher, 136; Kılıç Ali, *Kılıç Ali Hatıralarını Anlatıyor*, 9–10, 26.
19. *Nutuk: Vesikalar*, 119.
20. Akşin, II, 234–8.
21. *ATTB*, 141–2, 143–4.
22. Kansu, II, 449.
23. Ibid., 447.
24. From the reminiscences of Süleyman Fehmi Kalaycıoğlu, director of the Sivas farm school, in Goloğlu, II, 253–5.
25. Kansu, II, 465–6.

26. Ibid., 481–3, 489.
27. Gologlu, III, 5.
28. *ASD*, II, 2–4.
29. Gologlu, III, 6.
30. Kansu, II, 489–91, 496–7.
31. Bozok, 87.
32. Details of Mustafa Kemal's arrival in Ankara in Gologlu, III, 9–11; Kansu, II, 497ff.
33. *ASD*, II, 4–15.
34. Altay, 205.
35. Özerdim, 33.
36. Altay, 214.
37. İsmet İnönü, I, 177.
38. Ibid., 181–2.
39. Gologlu, II, 216.
40. *Nutuk*, 207–20.
41. Kutay (*Yüzyılımızda Bir İnsanımız*, IV, 613) says that Rauf left Ankara on 2 January. On the other hand, Colonel Mahmut, acting on behalf of Mustafa Kemal, sent a telegram to Kâzım Karabekir in Erzurum on 7 January asking him for his views on the decision of the Representative Committee to send Rauf to Istanbul. Karabekir agreed, but advised that Rauf should not seek to become either speaker or deputy speaker of the chamber (*İstiklâl Harbimiz*, 412–13). On 9 January, reports that Rauf was in the capital were published in the press (Akşin, II, 217). This suggests that the telegram to Karabekir was sent after Rauf's departure. Because of lack of coal, the train journey from Ankara to Istanbul used to take at least forty-eight hours (Kansu, II, 534). It is therefore unlikely that Rauf could have left Ankara later than 6 January.
42. Gologlu, II, 47–51.
43. Akşin, II, 270.
44. Ibid., 295.
45. *Nutuk*, 249.
46. *Nutuk: Vesikalar*, documents 226a and 226b.
47. Ibid., documents 228a and 228b.
48. Akşin, II, 302–5.
49. Ibid., 302–9.
50. *Nutuk: Vesikalar*, document 239b.
51. *Nutuk*, 241.
52. Özerdim, 33.
53. *AnaBritannica*, XVII, 491.
54. Bozok, 193.
55. Kansu, II, 534.
56. Akşin, II, 331–3.
57. Text in modern Turkish wording in Gologlu, III, 80–1; original text, omitting however the controversial addition 'and outside [the armistice lines]' in Selek, 276; commentary in Akşin, II, 315–18.
58. Quoted by Llewellyn Smith, 112.
59. Ibid., 111.
60. Ibid., 120.
61. As in all matters pertaining to Armenian massacres, estimates of the number of Armenian victims in Maraş vary widely – from 1,700 to 16,000 (Akşin, II, 345). There had been some 45,000 Armenians in the district of Maraş in 1914 (McCarthy, 79). One does not know how many survived the 1915 deportations and killings, and how many returned in 1919, but the figure of 20,000 returnees, given by Hovannisian (III, 37), seems excessive.
62. Orbay (ed. Kutay), *Yüzyılımızda Bir İnsanımız*, II, 27–8.

63. *Nutuk*, 273.
64. Orbay (ed. Kutay), *Yüzyılımızda Bir İnsanımız*, II, 31.
65. *Nutuk*, 274.
66. Kemalettin Sami was a founder member of the *Karakol* secret society (Tunaya, 520).
67. A full account of the occupation of Istanbul, drawn from all sources, is given in Akşin, II, 404–16.
68. *Nutuk*, 276–80.
69. Ibid., 281; *ASD*, I, 56; *ATTB*, 274–5.
70. Akşin, II, 443.
71. *Nutuk*, 281–2.
72. List in Gologlu, III, 345–51.
73. Kansu, II, 558–66.
74. Türkgeldi, 257.
75. Akşin, II, 481–2.
76. Türkgeldi, 260–1.
77. Akşin, II, 482.

CHAPTER 13   AN EMBATTLED LEADER

1. Yunus Nadi, 247–56.
2. Rıza Nur, III, 57.
3. Yunus Nadi, 257.
4. Özerdim, 26.
5. Text in Yunus Nadi, 329–31.
6. Goloğlu, III, 159.
7. *ASD*, II, 11.
8. Ergil, 190–1.
9. *Nutuk*, 288.
10. Tansel, III, 94. The Prophet's relics – a hair from his beard and his standard – are in fact kept in the Topkapı palace in Istanbul. The provenance of the relics carried in procession in Ankara on 23 April 1920 seems doubtful.
11. Tansel, III, 93.
12. *ASD*, I, 61.
13. *Nutuk*, 293.
14. Halide Edip calls them 'commissaries' in her memoirs (*The Turkish Ordeal*, 170).
15. *Nutuk*, 294. Mustafa Kemal defended his candidature in a closed session of the assembly. But the public were admitted when he was voted president (Türkiye Büyük Millet Meclisi (TBMM), *Gizli Celse Zabıtları*, I, 10).
16. *ASD*, I, 65.
17. Karabekir, *İstiklâl Harbimiz*, 619.
18. Tansel, III, 96.
19. *ATTB*, 318.
20. Tansel, III, 99.
21. *The Turkish Ordeal*, 169.
22. *Millî Mücadele Hâtıraları*, 371. Cebesoy reproduces the text of the telegram of welcome, while saying that a subordinate had informed him of Mustafa Kemal's original order to send Fevzi back to Istanbul.
23. Goloğlu, III, 164–5.
24. Ibid., 176. This was the second law passed by the assembly. Law No. 1 reversed the decision of the Istanbul government to increase the tax paid by sheep farmers.
25. Tansel, III, 106–7. Alfred Rüstem, the former Ottoman ambassador in Washington, and Kara Vasıf, who was at the time a prisoner of the British in Malta,

were also sentenced to death. The sentences were confirmed by the sultan on 24 May 1920, subject to the proviso that the persons named in the sentences would be retried if they were captured.

26. Gologlu, III, 170–1.
27. *Nutuk*, 297–9; Tansel, III, 115–27; Gologlu, III, 182–95.
28. Tansel, III, 125.
29. Llewellyn Smith, 125.
30. Ibid., 121–3.
31. Ibid., 125.
32. Özerdim, 41, 43.
33. *Nutuk*, 309–11, drawing on Mustafa Kemal's speech on 3 July (text in TBMM, *Gizli Celse Zabıtları*, I, 68–74).
34. *ATTB*, 358.
35. Ethem (ed. Kutay), *Çerkez Ethem Dosyası*, 271–6.
36. Halide Edip believed that although Mustafa Kemal was fearless in battle, he lacked the courage to face a mob (*Turkish Ordeal*, 166). Refet claimed later in a private conversation that Mustafa Kemal contemplated fleeing from Ankara at the time of the Yozgat rebellion, but that he (Refet) persuaded him to stay on. (The conversation was reported privately to the author.)
37. Belen, 206–7.
38. İsmet İnönü, I, 207.
39. Ibid.; *Nutuk*, 314–15; Ethem (ed. Kutay), *Çerkez Ethem Dosyası*, 313–16; Çerkes Ethem, *Hatıralar*, 73–8.
40. Tansel; III, 168.
41. Ibid., 140–1.
42. Ibid., 141–4.
43. Gologlu, III, 190.
44. Bozok, 72.
45. Tansel, III, 168–75.
46. Text in ibid., 191, n. 321.
47. Sultan Vahdettin's proclamation from exile in the Hejaz. Text in İlhami Soysal, *İşbirlikçiler*, 196.
48. Dates in Özerdim, 39, 44, 46.

CHAPTER 14   A FIGHTING DIPLOMAT

1. Llewellyn Smith, 68.
2. *ATTB*, 194.
3. Karabekir, *İstiklâl Harbimiz*, 443.
4. Cämil Häsänov (ed.), *Azärbaycan Beynälxalg Münasibätlär Sistemindä*, Dovlät Näşriyyatı, Baku 1993, 360–1.
5. Erikan, 285.
6. In August 1920, British military advisers were drawing up plans for an Armenian army of 40,000 men (Hovannisian, III, 341). In October, the Armenians had more than 10,000 men on the Kars front (ibid., IV, 241). Earlier, the Turks had estimated Armenian strength round Kars and Gümrü (Aleksandropol) at 8,000 men. In addition, there were Armenian troops in the areas of Erivan (Yerevan) and Karabağ (Karabakh) facing the Azeris (Erikan, 571).
7. Allen and Muratoff, 499, n. 1.
8. Dates in Özerdim, 39, 45.
9. Karabekir, *İstiklâl Harbimiz*, 591–6.
10. Cebesoy, *Moskova Hatıraları*, 166–77; Hovannisian, II, 83.
11. Aydemir, *Makedonya'dan Ortaasya'ya Enver Paşa*, III, 549.

12. Ibid., 574; Hovannisian, IV, 166–74. The Ankara government was represented separately by Colonel İbrahim Tali (Öngören).
13. Cebesoy, *Moskova Hatıraları*, 106–7.
14. *ATTB*, 371–3.
15. Karabekir, *İstiklâl Harbimiz*, 833; *Nutuk*, 325.
16. *ATTB*, 368; *Nutuk*, 321.
17. ATASE, *Türk İstiklâl Harbi'ne Katılan ... Komutanların Biyografileri*, 215.
18. Arıkoğlu, 151–2.
19. Çerkes Ethem, *Hatıralar*, 109.
20. The name of Green Army was first adopted by the forces of the Ukrainian anti-Semitic bandit Makhno in the Russian civil war. As green is the colour of Islam, some Turks thought that the Russian Green Army was a force of revolutionary Muslims. The formation of the Green Army in Turkey seems to have followed the brief appearance of Makhno's bands in the northern Caucasus which gave rise to hopes that the Muslims of the former tsarist empire were marching to help the Turks (Belen, 231–2).
21. *AnaBritannica*, XXII, 390.
22. Çerkes Ethem, *Hatıralar*, 103–6.
23. Gologlu, III, 171.
24. The full title of the newspaper was *Seyyare-yi Yeni Dünya* or 'The Planet of the New World'. Since the word *seyyare* (lit. 'moving') designated also Ethem's Mobile Forces, the title reflected the link between the newspaper and Ethem (Belen, 232).
25. Gologlu, III, 272.
26. *ATTB*, 364–7.
27. Karaosmanoğlu, *Vatan Yolunda*, 107.
28. Gologlu, III, 273.
29. Dates in Özerdim, 47.
30. Aydemir, *Tek Adam*, II, 377.
31. Çerkes Ethem, *Hatıralar*, 110.
32. *AnaBritannica*, XVII, 195. The *Yeni Dünya* press was subsequently used to print *Yenigün*, the title which the Turkish nationalist journalist and Mustafa Kemal's publicist, Yunus Nadi (Abalıoğlu), transferred from Istanbul. *Yenigün* was briefly the organ of the official Turkish Communist Party, created by Mustafa Kemal (*AnaBritannica*, I, 7).
33. Hovannisian, IV, 219, 228–9.
34. Belen, 249–51; Erikan, 577–9.
35. Hovannisian, IV, 259.
36. Ibid. Erikan gives Armenian losses in Kars as 1,100 dead and 1,200 prisoners.
37. Ibid., 268–91, 394–8; full text of treaty in İsmail Soysal, 19–23. It is dated 2 December 1920. Hovannisian says that the treaty was signed at 2 a.m. on 3 December.
38. Hovannisian, IV, 40–4.
39. Reminiscences published in *Hakimiyet*, 14 March–12 April 1926, quoted by Erikan, 244.
40. Hovannisian, IV, 235, 387, 398.
41. The eye-witness report cited by Arıkoğlu (118–23) makes no mention of the peasant woman Hatice and the villager Kumcu Veli who, according to legend, were employed by the French as guides and who led them into the ambush (Aybars, 257).
42. Tansel, III, 197, n. 8. Cooperation with the Arabs worried Kâzım Karabekir who believed that it was contrary to the decision taken at the Sivas congress to leave the Arabs severely alone. In reply, Mustafa Kemal explained that his purpose was to make sure that the country's enemies had their hands full, fighting off the demands for independence of nations outside Turkey's frontiers. Turkey would gain polit-

ical advantage not by lying low but, on the contrary, by proclaiming on every occasion that it enjoyed a dominant influence in both Syria and Iraq.

43. *Nutuk,* 304.
44. Aybars, 258–9; date of surrender of Antep in Özerdim, 52. In the 1980s, two other towns which had resisted the French in 1920 were similarly honoured: Maraş became Kahramanmaraş (the Heroic) and Urfa was renamed Şanlıurfa (the Glorious). These belated honours followed the erection in Marseilles of a monument to the victims of the Armenian genocide.
45. Text in Tansel, III, 181, n. 281.
46. Aybars, 247, who also gives the text of the law (245–6).
47. Kılıç Ali, *İstiklâl Mahkemesi Hatıraları,* 8–9.
48. Aybars, 250. Between 1920 and 1922, Independence Tribunals passed 3,881 death sentences. Of these 2,827 were commuted (Aybars, 313).
49. Dates in Özerdim, 47; *Nutuk,* 331–3; Çerkes Ethem, *Hatıralar,* 110–20; Belen, 216–18; Erikan, 557–8.
50. *Nutuk,* 337.
51. Ibid., 341.
52. İnal, 1996.
53. *Nutuk,* 349–50.
54. Ibid., 339.
55. İnal, 1997.
56. *Nutuk,* 350.
57. İnal, 1997.
58. Ibid.
59. *Nutuk,* 404.
60. Ibid., 401–2.
61. İnal, 1999.
62. Çerkes Ethem, *Hatıralar,* 152.
63. Text in Gologlu, IV, 400–2.
64. *ATTB,* 406.
65. *ASD,* I, 127.
66. Gologlu, IV, 53.
67. *ATTB,* 367.
68. Karabekir, *İstiklâl Harbimiz,* 852–3.
69. Cebesoy, *Moskova Hatıraları,* 50–1.
70. Gologlu, IV, 300.
71. Mustafa Kemal, *Eskişehir–İzmit Konuşmaları,* 98.
72. Gologlu, IV, 54–6. Muhittin (Birgen), whose daughter became Nazım Hikmet's first wife, later returned to Turkey, where he promoted farmers' cooperatives, and was appointed member of parliament by the ruling single party.
73. Belli, *Fikriye,* 69ff.

CHAPTER 15   STOPPING THE GREEKS

1. Llewellyn Smith, 166–7.
2. *Nutuk,* 370, quoting the telegram sent to Mustafa Kemal by the grand vizier Tevfik Paşa on 27 January 1921.
3. İsmet's 12,000 troops had 6,000 rifles, 50 machine-guns and 28 field guns. The attacking Greek force numbered 18–20,000 men armed with 12,000 rifles, 140 machine-guns and 72 field guns (Erikan, 608).
4. Ibid., 611–17.
5. Selek, 92.
6. *Nutuk,* 372.

7. Ibid., 373–4.
8. Tansel, IV, 39, n. 35.
9. Quoted by Llewellyn Smith, 196.
10. Rıza Nur says in his scurrilous memoirs: 'Our respected president has this trait: he is very fond of women, but he is never very fond of the same woman. He changes them quickly. One could call him the chief taster' (III, 71).
11. Tansel, IV, 56–60.
12. Ibid., 50–1.
13. Ibid., 55–6.
14. Ibid., 56; Özerdim, 55.
15. *Nutuk*, 391–5.
16. Llewellyn Smith, 215.
17. Allen and Muratoff, 500.
18. Text in İsmail Soysal, 32–8. Before news of the agreement reached Batum, the Turkish forces in the town came under attack from Russian Bolsheviks. Four Turkish officers and twenty-six men were killed in the clash. Turkish troops evacuated the area allocated to Georgia, when the Moscow agreement was confirmed in Ankara on 21 March 1921.
19. Text in Ergil, 420.
20. Ibid., 416–19.
21. Text in İsmail Soysal, 41–7.
22. *Nutuk*, 386; İsmet İnönü, I, 248–51; Belen, 310–16; Erikan, 636–57.
23. *Nutuk*, 387.
24. Erikan, 663; *ATTB*, 398.
25. Erikan, 653, 666.
26. Özerdim, 55; Jevakhoff, 240.
27. Arıkoğlu, 217–19.
28. *Nutuk*, 416.
29. Özerdim, 55.
30. *Nutuk*, 428–9.
31. Ibid., 428–9; Gilbert, 242–3; Kinross, 286–9.
32. The Turkish version of the affair is given by Kılıç Ali in *İstiklâl Mahkemesi Hatıraları* (79–88); British documents have been examined by Sonyel (74).
33. Martin Gilbert (244) says that an officer at Mustafa Kemal's headquarters figured among the informants of Major Cornwall, who was in charge of General Harington's intelligence.
34. Ziya arrived on 13 June, Fethi on 8 August 1921 (Özerdim, 55, 57).
35. Gologlu, IV, 160–2.
36. Articles of association in Karabekir, *İstiklâl Harbimiz*, 917–18.
37. Tansel, IV, 85.
38. *ATTB*, 400; Tansel, IV, 83–4.
39. *ASD*, II, 19.
40. Llewellyn Smith, 222, note.
41. Erikan, 685.
42. Rıza Nur, III, 185–6.
43. Altay, 290.
44. İsmet İnönü, I, 257.
45. Erikan, 696–7.
46. Altay, *İstiklâl Harbimizde Süvari Kolordusu*, 14–19.
47. Özerdim, 56.
48. Erikan, 699–701.
49. Alkan, 37.
50. Arıkoğlu, 235.
51. Ibid., 237.

52. Terzioğlu, 51.
53. Ibid., 48.
54. Goloğlu, IV, 170.
55. Arıkoğlu, 239.
56. Özerdim, 57.
57. Minutes of debates on 4/5 October 1921 in TBMM, *Gizli Celse Zabıtları*, II, 157–85; *Nutuk*, 406–9; Arıkoğlu, 243–5.
58. Text of law in Tansel, IV, 107, n. 46.
59. On 10 October, Fethi Okyar was elected interior minister (Goloğlu, IV, 173). Mustafa Kemal did not insist on his original candidate for the interior ministry, a certain Haydar, deputy for Van, who, as he admitted, had been the subject of (unspecified) gossip (TBMM, *Gizli Celse Zabıtları*, II, 180; Arıkoğlu, 245).
60. *Nutuk*, 391.
61. *ASD*, I, 198; Arıkoğlu, 251.
62. *ATTB*, 413.
63. Ibid., 414–24.
64. Özerdim, 57.
65. Llewellyn Smith, 229.
66. *The Turkish Ordeal*, 284–310.
67. Karabekir, *İstiklâl Harbimiz*, 933.
68. İsmet İnönü, I, 262.
69. Erikan, 713, 733.
70. İsmet İnönü, I, 262.
71. Erikan, 721–3.
72. *ASD*, I, 193.
73. Arıkoğlu, 250, 253–4.
74. *The Turkish Ordeal*, 297.
75. Karabekir, *İstiklâl Harbimiz*, 934, n. 2.
76. Erikan, 725–6.
77. *ASD*, I, 194.
78. Arıkoğlu, 254.
79. İsmet İnönü, I, 252–3.
80. Erikan, 726.
81. Ibid., 733.
82. *ASD*, I, 197.
83. *ATTB*, 429.
84. *ASD*, I, 200.
85. Goloğlu, IV, 180.
86. Karabekir, *İstiklâl Harbimiz*, 933–5.
87. Aydemir, *Makedonya'dan Ortaasya'ya Enver Paşa*, III, 613.
88. Text in Goloğlu, IV, 270–1.
89. Goloğlu, IV, 277.
90. Aydemir, *Makedonya'dan Ortaasya'ya Enver Paşa*, III, 683. Enver's bones were disinterred in 1996 and transferred to the Eternal Liberty monument built in Istanbul to commemorate the soldiers killed while re-establishing CUP rule in 1909.
91. Aydemir, *Makedonya'dan Ortaasya'ya Enver Paşa*, III, 596.

CHAPTER 16   VICTORY IN WAR

1. Families of prominent nationalists evacuated to Kayseri during the battle of Sakarya had to be protected from bandits during their journey (Terzioğlu, 51–4).

2. Belli, *Fikriye*, 76–9. The house was known as the Bulgurzade mansion. It is now preserved as a museum within the grounds of the presidential palace.
3. Bozok, 98.
4. Akgün, 311–14.
5. See Directorate General of Press and Information, *The 'Köşk' Museum in Ankara*, Ankara n.d.
6. Bozok, 99–100.
7. Ward Price, 140–1.
8. Jevakhoff, 192; Özerdim, 59.
9. Text in İsmail Soysal, 40–7.
10. Text in ibid., 50–60.
11. Arıkoğlu, 267.
12. Mules used to move gun carriages were sold for 5 lira apiece. The Turkish 41st division and volunteer detachment were moved from the south to the western front (Arıkoğlu, 263).
13. Tansel, IV, 52–3.
14. Ibid., 53.
15. *ASD*, II, 32.
16. Aralov, 70ff.
17. On 27 March 1922, Mustafa Kemal noted in his diary, 'Nothing has been given to us [by the Soviets] since Frunze's departure' (Ali Mithat İnan (ed.), 131).
18. Bozok, 86.
19. Aralov, 129. Mougin, who was originally attached to the Ottoman general staff in Istanbul, accompanied Franklin-Bouillon to Ankara. His reports were so favourable to Mustafa Kemal that the French High Commissioner in Istanbul, General Pellé, called him 'Mougin pacha' (Jevakhoff, 323).
20. Cebesoy, *Moskova Hatıraları*, 428–54.
21. Mustafa Kemal, *Eskişehir–İzmit Konuşmaları*, 96.
22. Gilmour, 534–7.
23. Gilbert, 245.
24. Text of letter in Tansel, IV, 60.
25. Orbay, *Cehennem Değirmeni*, II, 56–7.
26. Özerdim, 58.
27. Sabis, V, 36–7.
28. Llewellyn Smith, 213.
29. Quoted by Richard Clogg, *Politics and the Academy*, Frank Cass, London 1986, 56, 57.
30. Adding together the corrected figures for the provinces of Trabzon, Canik, Sivas and Kastamonu (McCarthy, 97).
31. Özerdim, 49.
32. Erikan, 784.
33. *Nutuk*, 305–7.
34. Kurt, 36–79.
35. Text in Bulut, 108–9. The Koçgiri tribal leaders asked for the establishment of a 'privileged (*mümtaz*) province', the term applied in Ottoman administration to such autonomous areas as Mount Lebanon, Eastern Rumelia and the island of Samos (known collectively as *eyalât-ı mümtaze*).
36. Bulut, 110.
37. TBMM, *Gizli Celse Zabıtları*, II, 270.
38. Ibid., 248–56, 262–70, 622–4, 627–30; *Nutuk*, 419–20; Bulut, 39–41.
39. Text in Kurt, 407–8.
40. Karabekir, *İstiklâl Harbimiz*, 1002. The report, which covers the period from 1 January 1921 to 6 February 1922, and refers therefore to operations against both Greeks and Kurds, gives the following figures: arrested 2,841; 'exterminated' (*meyten istisal*) 3,262; executed after trial 231; sent to the interior 24,511; Muslim

deserters arrested 6,809; casualties (suffered by the Central Army) 80. It would seem that the death sentences passed by the Independence Tribunal in Samsun are not included in the total.

41. Aybars, I, 313.
42. On 21 October 1921, the Allied High Commissioners in Istanbul protested at the death sentences passed by the Samsun Independence Tribunal against 168 Greeks and 3 Armenians, of whom 17 had managed to escape (Kurt, 418).
43. Özerdim, 61.
44. Kurt, 406.
45. *ASD*, II, 37.
46. Text in Borak (ed.), *Atatürk'ün Resmi Yayınlara Girmemiş...*, 146–50.
47. Belli, *Fikriye*, 82–3.
48. Bozok, 98. Abdürrahim, to whom Atatürk later gave the surname Tunçak, led an uneventful life. He trained as an engineer in Germany and worked for the town council in Ankara until his retirement in 1977. He died in 1998. The newspaper *Sabah* (20 August 1998, 14) quotes him as saying that he never knew his true parents, and that his first memories were of Zübeyde's house in Akaretler. Given that Zübeyde moved to that house in 1913, Abdürrahim could not have been 90 at the time of his death, as the newspaper claims. He may well have been the orphan picked up by Mustafa Kemal in Bitlis in 1916.
49. Ibid., 107.
50. Text in Ergil, 350–6.
51. İlhami Soysal, *150'likler*, 61.
52. *Nutuk*, 434.
53. Orbay, *Cehennem Değirmeni*, II, 69.
54. *ASD*, I, 202–35.
55. Ibid., 212.
56. Ibid., 216.
57. *Nutuk*, 426–7.
58. Ibid., 434–40.
59. Orbay, *Cehennem Değirmeni*, II, 73.
60. Ibid., 76–7.
61. *Nutuk*, 441.
62. Ibid., 240.
63. ATASE, *Türk İstiklâl Harbi'ne Katılan ... Komutanların Biyografileri*, 164.
64. İsmet İnönü, I, 272–5.
65. *Nutuk*, 446.
66. İsmet İnönü, I, 267–78, 283–5.
67. *Nutuk*, 437.
68. Özerdim, 60–1. Mustafa Kemal spent the whole of March inspecting the front. In his diary he noted deficiencies: '*11 March*. The [3rd] division is very good, like all the others, but regimental and battalion commanders lack experience' (Ali Mithat İnan (ed.), 125). Relations with the 1st Army commander, Ali İhsan Paşa, were already difficult: '*20 March*. İhsan Paşa complained. He was in the wrong. I did not mince my words' (ibid., 128). Mustafa Kemal was intermittently ill during his tour of inspection. His kidneys were again giving trouble; he developed a fever and suffered also from a stomach infection (ibid., 126–30).
69. Altay, 316–19.
70. Details in Tansel, IV, 144–51.
71. Gologlu, IV, 227.
72. Gilbert, 249.
73. Gologlu, IV, 228.
74. Ibid., 231; *Nutuk*, 430.
75. Gilmour, 538.

76. Gilbert, 249.
77. *Nutuk*, 431.
78. Llewellyn Smith, 255, note.
79. *Nutuk*, 431–4.
80. Llewellyn Smith, 264, 273–4, 277.
81. Ibid., 278.
82. Ibid., 282–3; Gilbert, 255–6.
83. Tansel, IV, 157.
84. *ASD*, I, 267.
85. Orbay (ed. Kutay), *Üç Devirde Bir Adam*, 308–9.
86. *Nutuk*, 446–7; İsmet İnönü, I, 283–7; Erikan, 769–95; Tansel, IV, 1544–5.
87. Erikan, 785.
88. İsmet İnönü, I, 283–5.
89. Ibid., 287, 293.
90. *ASD*, I, 271.
91. İsmet İnönü, I, 290.
92. Erikan, 808.
93. İsmet İnönü, I, 290–1.
94. *ATTB*, 473–4.
95. Erikan, 827.
96. İsmet İnönü, I, 292. According to Halide Edip, Mustafa Kemal shook hands with the captive Greek generals, while İsmet and Fevzi refused to do so (Tansel, IV, 174–6). But İsmet had already received the captives, and when they were taken to Mustafa Kemal, he and the other Turkish commanders remained in the background.
97. Tansel, IV, 175–6.
98. Ibid., 168, n. 43.
99. İsmet İnönü, I, 296–8.
100. Gilbert, 251.
101. *ASD*, I, 274.
102. Tansel, IV, 173.
103. *Nutuk*, 449–50.
104. Llewellyn Smith, 311.
105. Tansel, IV, 182.
106. Özakman, 464–5, correcting Selek, 92–3.
107. Erikan, 838.
108. Puaux (22) and Llewellyn Smith (309) give the date of the murder of Chrysostom as 9 September, the eve of Mustafa Kemal's arrival in İzmir. This is more likely than Marjorie Housepian's account which seems to place it on Sunday 10 September (*Smyrna 1922*, 133).
109. Walder, 177.
110. Borak (ed.), *Atatürk'ün Resmi Yayınlara Girmemiş …*, 366.
111. *ASD*, I, 274.
112. İsmet İnönü, I, 300.
113. From Lâtife's letter of 26 October 1922 to Salih Bozok (Bozok, 217).
114. Atay, *Çankaya*, 325.
115. Ryan, 228.

CHAPTER 17   WINNING WITHOUT FIGHTING

1. *Nutuk*, 450.
2. Ibid., 499.
3. *ATTB*, 481–2.

4. *ASD*, I, 283.
5. Soyak, I, 136.
6. Bozok, 203.
7. Atay, *Çankaya*, 321–2.
8. Ward Price, 126.
9. Walder, 175.
10. Bozok, 204. According to Ward Price, the meeting took place by chance in the street.
11. *ASD*, I, 283.
12. Bozok, 203. Bozok, who was at Mustafa Kemal's side as his ADC, does not mention the story found in other biographies (e.g. Araz, 32–8) that Lâtife arrived at Mustafa Kemal's headquarters unannounced, insisted on an interview, in which she expressed her infinite admiration and gratitude, and pressed an invitation on him. On the other hand, Halide Edip, who was also in Mustafa Kemal's suite, says that Lâtife first called on Mustafa Kemal on 10 September, the day he arrived in İzmir (*Turkish Ordeal*, 384).
13. Cebesoy, *Siyasî Hâtıralar*, 70.
14. İsmet İnönü, I, 300.
15. Jevakhoff, 278.
16. Walder, 212.
17. Gilbert, 261–2.
18. *ASD*, I, 284.
19. Atay, *Çankaya*, 329.
20. *ATTB*, 484.
21. Atay, *Çankaya*, 327.
22. Walder, 222, 229.
23. Erikan, 844.
24. Walder, 242–3, 259.
25. Sonyel, 176 (sources in n. 35); Tansel, IV, 209.
26. *ATTB*, 487.
27. Ibid., 488–9.
28. Ibid., 489–90. The British government does not seem to have been aware of the full text of this telegram, and was unpleasantly surprised when İsmet rather than Mustafa Kemal welcomed the Allied generals at the head of the Turkish delegation at Mudanya (Walder, 304). Turkish sources (Tansel, IV, 209, and others) give 29 September as the date of Mustafa Kemal's acceptance of armistice negotiations. This is likely, since Mustafa Kemal left İzmir for Ankara on that day. But there is no telegram of that date in the collected edition of Atatürk's instructions. Harington received the news on 1 October (Walder, 298).
29. Bozok, 216.
30. Walder, 298.
31. Cebesoy, *Siyasî Hâtıralar*, 79.
32. Llewellyn Smith, 311–14.
33. Walder, 267–9.
34. *ATTB*, 495.
35. Ibid., 497–8.
36. Ibid., 500.
37. Text in Tansel, IV, 216–18, n. 216.
38. Belen, 526.
39. Aybars, I, 350.
40. Özerdim, 68–9.
41. Behar, *Osmanlı İmparatorluğunun ve Türkiye'nin Nüfusu*, DİE, Ankara 1996, 33.
42. Gilmour, 554.

43. Cebesoy, *Siyasî Hâtıralar*, 111–13.
44. İsmet İnönü, II, 44.
45. *ATTB*, 502.
46. Cebesoy, *Siyasî Hâtıralar*, 168.

CHAPTER 18   THE END OF THE MONARCHY

1. Özerdim, 67.
2. *ASD*, I, 282.
3. Rauf (Orbay) appealed unsuccessfully to Mustafa Kemal to promote Ali Fuat and Refet, when he went to İzmir soon after the entry of Turkish troops into the city (İsmet İnönü, II, 43).
4. Karabekir, *İstiklâl Harbimiz*, 1095.
5. Orbay (ed. Kutay), *Yüzyılımızda Bir İnsanımız*, V, 52.
6. Orbay, *Cehennem Değirmeni*, II, 85–91.
7. Kâzım Karabekir describes the deputies from Trabzon in the Grand National Assembly as old Unionists who had tried to bring Enver back (*İstiklâl Harbimiz*, 1075, n. 1).
8. Aybars, I, 349.
9. Araz, *Mustafa Kemal'le 1000 Gün*, 89.
10. See Lâtife's letter to Salih Bozok (Bozok, 217).
11. *Nutuk*, 453.
12. Cebesoy, *Siyasî Hâtıralar*, I, 102.
13. *Nutuk*, 453; İsmet İnönü, II, 44.
14. Cebesoy, *Siyasî Hâtıralar*, I, 104.
15. Karabekir says that when he travelled with Mustafa Kemal to Bursa on 16 October the latter asked him how Refet should deal with Abdülmecit. Karabekir replied that Refet should greet him as the caliph (*İstiklâl Harbimiz*, 1027, n. 1). If true, this implies that the decision to send Refet as nationalist representative to Istanbul, to depose Vahdettin as sultan and choose Abdülmecit as caliph, was taken even before the meeting with İsmet and Fevzi in Bursa.
16. Cebesoy, *Siyasî Hâtıralar*, I, 106–7.
17. Ibid., 106.
18. Çetiner, 244–5.
19. Text in *Nutuk: Vesikalar*, 928–9.
20. Text in Goloğlu, IV, 347.
21. Text in *ASD*, I, 287–98.
22. *Nutuk*, 459.
23. Goloğlu, IV, 358–9.
24. Cebesoy, *Siyasî Hâtıralar*, I, 136.
25. İnal, 1743.
26. Lady Rumbold, in a letter dated 6 November 1922, referred to the incident as happening 'two days ago' (Gilbert, 279).
27. Ali Kemal's murder was described to Rauf (Orbay) by Necip Ali (Küçüka), who was at the time legal adviser to Nurettin and later became prosecutor of the Ankara Independence Tribunal. Rauf expressed his shock at the 'tragedy' and brought it to the attention of the chief of the general staff, Fevzi, and the defence minister, Kâzım (Orbay (ed. Kutay), *Yüzyılımızda Bir İnsanımız*, V, 299–301).
28. Gilbert, 278–9.
29. İnal, 1743.
30. List in Goloğlu, IV, 361.
31. Çetiner, 268.
32. Goloğlu, IV, 362.

33. *Nutuk: Vesikalar*, 942.
34. Cebesoy, *Siyasî Hâtıralar*, I, 162.
35. *Nutuk*, 468–9.
36. Özerdim, 71. When Adnan (Adıvar) went to Istanbul, Ali Fuat (Cebesoy) became assembly vice-president (*AnaBritannica*, V, 427).
37. Mustafa Kemal, *Eskişehir–İzmit Konuşmaları*, 126.
38. Quoted by Olson, 141.
39. Mustafa Kemal, *Eskişehir–İzmit Konuşmaları*, 96.
40. Ibid., 90, 113–14.
41. Ibid., 92, 94.
42. Gilbert, 283.
43. Ibid., 225.
44. Ibid., 276.
45. *ASD*, II, 34–6.
46. Ibid., 47–8.
47. Demirel, 492–5, 500.
48. *ASD*, I, 298–300.
49. Demirel, 522–5.
50. *ASD*, II, 50–2.
51. *Atatürk*, 50–1.
52. *ATTB*, 508.
53. Mustafa Kemal, *Eskişehir–İzmit Konuşmaları*, 60.
54. Ibid., 66.
55. Ibid., 166.
56. Ibid., 163–4.
57. Ibid., 144.
58. Ibid., 136, 146, 148.
59. *ASD*, II, 69–74.
60. Ibid., 78–80.
61. Bozok, 211.
62. Araz, *Mustafa Kemal'le 1000 Gün*, 125.
63. Ibid., 57.
64. *ASD*, II, 85–7.
65. Text in Borak (ed.), *Atatürk'ün Resmi Yayınlara Girmemiş...*, 155–225.
66. *ASD*, II, 86, 97.
67. Borak (ed.), *Atatürk'ün Resmi Yayınlara Girmemiş...*, 199.
68. Ibid.
69. Ibid., 225.
70. Ibid., 218–20.
71. Ibid., 214–15.
72. Ibid., 216.
73. Ibid., 216, 214.
74. Ibid., 216.
75. *ASD*, II, 98–103.
76. Mumcu (ed.), *Kâzım Karabekir Anlatıyor*, 75; Karabekir, *İstiklâl Harbimiz*, 917, n. 1.
77. In his proclamation to the nation on 13 September 1922, Mustafa Kemal declared: 'If the King of Greece is not among the prisoners, the reason is that it is a principle with monarchs to share only in national celebrations, and when calamity strikes on the battlefields they find it natural to think only of their palaces' (*ATTB*, 483).
78. Gologlu, V, 91–3.
79. Text in *ASD*, II, 103–16.
80. Text in Gologlu, V, 104–5.

CHAPTER 19   PEACE AND THE REPUBLIC

1. *Nutuk*, 479; Gologlu, V, 86.
2. Ward Price, 140.
3. A turreted extension was added in 1924, when the president's residence changed aspect from an Anatolian summer house to a European suburban middle-class home (see Basın-Yayın, *The 'Köşk' Museum at Çankaya*).
4. From Lâtife's undated letter to her mother, paraphrased by Araz, *Mustafa Kemal'le 1000 Gün*, 134.
5. In his 1927 speech, Mustafa Kemal expressed surprise at Rauf's criticism of İsmet's conduct in meeting him before reporting to the government and the assembly (*Nutuk*, 479).
6. Cebesoy, *Siyasî Hâtıralar*, I, 233, 243.
7. Gologlu, V, 113–15.
8. Ibid., 122; Cebesoy, *Siyasî Hâtıralar*, I, 264.
9. Gologlu, V, 129–39.
10. Özerdim (73) says that the Turkish proposals were communicated on 8 March 1923. Martin Gilbert (287) gives the date as 9 March, as do Sonyel (*Turkish Diplomacy*, 213) and Ali İhsan Sabis (III, 362).
11. Gilbert, 288.
12. Sonyel, *Turkish Diplomacy*, 213.
13. Ibid., 214–15.
14. Speech to the tradesmen of Adana on 16 March 1923 (*ASD*, II, 131–2).
15. Ibid., 130.
16. Ibid., 155–7.
17. Ibid., 169.
18. Gologlu, V, 149.
19. İsmet İnönü, II, 103.
20. İsmail Hakkı Tekçe's reminiscences, quoted by Gologlu, V, 165.
21. Gologlu, V, 187.
22. Demirel, 524.
23. Gologlu, V, 166.
24. Mumcu (ed.), *Kâzım Karabekir Anlatıyor*, 79.
25. Gologlu, V, 168.
26. İsmet İnönü, II, 104, 109.
27. Photographs in Yüksel, 165, 173.
28. Demirel, 525–6.
29. Ibid., 161, 529.
30. *ASD*, I, 326–8.
31. Demirel, 529–30.
32. Gologlu, V, 192.
33. Demirel, 573.
34. Mumcu (ed.), *Kâzım Karabekir Anlatıyor*, 81.
35. Demirel, 572.
36. Ibid., 594.
37. Ibid., 575–7.
38. Ibid., 594.
39. İsmet İnönü, II, 115.
40. Ibid.
41. Gilbert, 297.
42. Text of telegrams in İsmet İnönü, II, appendix 3 (311). Mustafa Kemal described his role in the quarrel between İsmet and Rauf in his six-day speech (*Nutuk*, 511–27).
43. İsmet İnönü, II, 309.

44. Text in İsmail Soysal, 213–17.
45. Gilbert, 297.
46. İsmail Soysal, 227.
47. *Nutuk*, 510.
48. *AnaBritannica*, V, 571.
49. Cebesoy, *Siyasî Hâtıralar*, II, 8.
50. *Nutuk*, 527–8.
51. Ibid., 528.
52. İsmet İnönü, II, 152.
53. *ASD*, I, 330–9.
54. Sertel, 70.
55. Goloğlu, V, 247–75.
56. Text in İsmail Soysal, 176–83.
57. Clogg, 121.
58. Alexandris, 104.
59. The 1935 census showed that 960,000 Turks were foreign-born, of whom some 370,000 had come from Greece, 227,000 from Bulgaria, 158,000 from Yugoslavia, 70,000 from the lands which had become the Soviet Union, and 62,000 from Romania (General Directorate of Statistics, *Small Statistical Abstract of Turkey*, Ankara 1948, 87).
60. 'Transfers to Muslim businessmen of industrial property previously belonging to the minorities have played a non-negligible role' in the development of business enterprises in Turkey (Ayşe Buğra, *State and Business in Modern Turkey*, SUNY, 1994, 187). Hacı Ömer Sabancı, the founder of Turkey's largest holding company, was among Muslims who had been lured from Kayseri to Adana 'by the possibility of taking over the real estate as well as the commercial and industrial establishments left idle after the emigration of their Greek or Armenian owners. Such takeovers were encouraged by the government, and those who had connections with government authorities could benefit greatly from these opportunities' (ibid., 82).
61. Aslan, 172, 180.
62. İsmail Soysal, 204.
63. Ward Price, 140.
64. Walder, 349–51.
65. Sertel, 67.
66. *ASD*, III, 87.
67. Goloğlu, V, 295–302.
68. Özerdim, 77.
69. İsmet İnönü, II, 167.
70. Ibid., 171–2.
71. *Nutuk*, 533–4.
72. Ibid., 476–7.
73. Goloğlu, V, 308–15.
74. *ATTB*, 553.
75. Mumcu (ed.), *Kâzım Karabekir Anlatıyor*, 108.

CHAPTER 20   THE END OF THE CALIPHATE

1. Text of interview, as printed later, on 11 February 1924, in Hüseyin Cahit (Yalçın)'s Istanbul newspaper *Tanin*, in *ASD*, III, 89–93.
2. *ATTB*, 509, 511, 512, 552.
3. Mumcu (ed.), *Kâzım Karabekir Anlatıyor*, 108ff.
4. *Nutuk*, 544–5.
5. Ibid., 546.

6. Mumcu (ed.), *Kâzım Karabekir Anlatıyor*, 112–13.
7. Gologlu, VI, 3.
8. Mumcu (ed.), *Kâzım Karabekir Anlatıyor*, 116.
9. Gologlu, VI, 4.
10. Araz, *Mustafa Kemal'le 1000 Gün*, 163–4.
11. Gologlu, VI, 3.
12. Mumcu (ed.), *Kâzım Karabekir Anlatıyor*, 121–2.
13. Orbay (ed. Kutay), *Yüzyılımızda Bir İnsanımız*, V, 254.
14. Orbay, *Cehennem Değirmeni*, II, 138.
15. Ibid., 139.
16. Seçil Akgün, 145.
17. Orbay (ed. Kutay), *Yüzyılımızda Bir İnsanımız*, V, 264.
18. *Nutuk*, 561.
19. Tunçay, 114.
20. Text of law in Tunçay, 113, n. 8.
21. ATASE, *Türk İstiklâl Harbi'ne Katılan ... Komutanların Biyografileri*, 100.
22. Ibid., 3.
23. Mumcu (ed.), *Kâzım Karabekir Anlatıyor*, 121–5.
24. Gologlu, VI, 4–6.
25. Atay, *Çankaya*, 384–5.
26. Özerdim, 80; Araz, *Mustafa Kemal'le 1000 Gün*, 164–5.
27. *Nutuk*, 562–3.
28. *ASD*, II, 170–1.
29. Gologlu, VI, 7.
30. Yalçın, 276.
31. Ibid.
32. Mumcu (ed.), *Kâzım Karabekir Anlatıyor*, 129–31.
33. *ASD*, II, 175–6.
34. *Nutuk*, 563.
35. İsmet İnönü, II, 188.
36. Özerdim, 80.
37. Text in *ASD*, I, 344–50.
38. The title chosen was *Diyanet İşleri Riyaseti* (later, *Başkanlığı*). *Diyanet*, a derivative of *din* (religion), had the connotation of matters pertaining to religion, rather than religion itself. But the text of the law specified that the authority of the Department of Religious Affairs to administer religious life extended to 'all regulations (*ahkâm*) concerning beliefs and worship (*itikadat ve ibadat*) in the ... religion of Islam' (Aybay, 255). The secular Turkish government thus acquired with regard to Islam rights similar to those vested in the House of Commons in relation to the Church of England.
39. Major İhsan later became navy minister, but his political career ended in 1927 when he was sentenced to two years' imprisonment for accepting bribes from a French company which had won the contract to repair the battleship *Yavuz*. His choice of the surname Eryavuz ('Man of *Yavuz*') was clearly meant to proclaim his innocence.
40. Summary of debate in Seçil Akgün, 182–92.
41. Atay, *Çankaya*, 388.
42. Ibid.
43. List of cabinet announced on 6 March 1924 in Gologlu, VI, 23–4.
44. *ASD*, III, 97.
45. Details of Abdülmecit's expulsion and exile in Seçil Akgün, 195–214.
46. Özerdim, 138–9.
47. *Nutuk*, 565.
48. Özerdim, 83.
49. Ibid., 47.

50. In his six-day speech, Mustafa Kemal said that in 1921 he had tried to omit the reference to 'provisions of the *şeriat* (*ahkâm-ı şer'iye*)' on the grounds that the literal meaning of the Arabic word *şer'* was law, and that it was self-evident that the assembly was to give effect to the law (*Nutuk*, 475). However, he added, he had been unable to convince people who gave the term a different meaning. If he had indeed used the argument, it was a sophism, for whatever the original meaning of *şer'* (and its derivatives *şeriat* and *şer'iye*), the current meaning was Muslim canon law. It was used in this sense in the law of 8 April 1924 'on the abolition of *şeriat* courts ...' (*mehakim-i şer'iyenin ilgası* ...) (Özerdim, 83).

51. *Nutuk*, 477.

52. Goloğlu, VI, 45–6.

53. İlhami Soysal, *150'likler*, 57–8. Ali Fuat Cebesoy (*Siyasî Hâtıralar*, II, 89–91, 96) argues that Refet did not wish to be mixed up in the controversy. When he was attacked by the government press, he submitted his resignation as a deputy, but later withdrew it at Rauf (Orbay)'s instance.

54. Seçil Akgün, 224–5.

55. *Siyasî Hâtıralar*, II, 89.

56. Tunçay, 232.

57. Belli, *Fikriye*, 96–7. Photocopies of telegrams exchanged between Adnan and Mustafa Kemal and of instructions sent to İzmit are reproduced in the book.

58. Ibid., 102–3. In his memoirs attacking Atatürk, Rıza Nur retails rumours that Fikriye did not commit suicide, but was shot (III, 281–2). According to Fikriye's nephew, Abbas Hayri Özdinçer, this was also the conviction of his father (Fikriye's elder brother), Ali Enver, who believed that Fikriye did not suffer from tuberculosis, but had been sent to Europe simply to remove her from Atatürk's household (interview in Istanbul magazine *Aktüel*, No. 352, 16–22 April 1998). Such rumours were encouraged by the attempts of the police to hush up the incident and remove all personal papers. But the conspiracy theory makes no sense. No one would have dared shoot Fikriye without Mustafa Kemal's authorization. To have given it would have been not only out of character, but also senseless: Fikriye did not pose a threat to Mustafa Kemal. Similarly, no credence should be attached to stories according to which Fikriye stayed for some time in Atatürk's villa in Çankaya after her return from Europe, until she was forced to leave by Lâtife. The telegrams exchanged between Adnan (Adıvar) and Mustafa Kemal in March 1923 make it clear that Mustafa Kemal had no intention of seeing her again.

59. Ibid., 99.

60. Ibid., 105–8.

61. Atay, *Çankaya*, 410.

62. Belli, *Fikriye*, 109.

63. Araz, *Mustafa Kemal'le 1000 Gün*, 175; *AnaBritannica*, XXI, 324.

64. *ASD*, II, 179.

65. *Ibid.*, 179–88.

66. Ibid., 189–93.

67. Ali Fuat says in his memoirs that he and Rauf went to İzmir to be present at Karabekir's wedding (*Siyasî Hâtıralar*, II, 94–5).

68. Ibid., 94–7. Ali Fuat says that he and his companions had taken note of a passage in the Gazi's speech in Bursa in which he said: 'The reforms we have made are sufficient (*kâfi*) to ensure Turkey's welfare and happiness for centuries to come. Our duty is to realize this and to safeguard them.' This suggested that Mustafa Kemal did not intend to make any more fundamental changes. However, in the official text of the Bursa speech, Mustafa Kemal's words appear as 'our reforms guarantee (*kâfil*) Turkey's happiness for centuries to come ...' (*ASD*, II, 193). There was thus no suggestion that the reform process was complete.

69. *ASD*, II, 195.

70. Ibid., 199–200.
71. Ibid., 202.
72. Ibid., 206–7.
73. Ibid., 211.
74. *ASD*, III, 95 and II, 213. Karabekir complained to İsmet about this (Mumcu (ed.), *Kâzım Karabekir Anlatıyor*, 128).
75. Araz, *Mustafa Kemal'le 1000 Gün*, 177–83; Bozok, 220–3.

CHAPTER 21   IMPOSING LAW AND ORDER

1. Tunçay, 110–13; Evans, 87.
2. *Nutuk*, 567.
3. Ibid., 569.
4. Ibid., 569–71.
5. İsmet İnönü, II, 191–2; *Nutuk*, 572ff.
6. Quoted by Tunçay, 101, n. 82.
7. İsmet İnönü, II, 196–7.
8. Ibid., 195.
9. *Nutuk*, 574–94; Gologlu, VI, 63–79; Tunçay, 100–1; İsmet İnönü, II, 194–6.
10. Tunçay, 103–9.
11. *ASD*, III, 351.
12. Text in Tunçay, 370–81.
13. *Nutuk*, 591–2.
14. Names in Tunçay, 108–9.
15. Ibid., 117–20.
16. In Turkish the party became known as *Cumhuriyet Halk Fırkası* (CHF). Later, when words of Arabic origin were replaced by Turkish or international terms, this was changed to *Cumhuriyet Halk Partisi* (CHP). The party led an uninterrupted existence until 1980, when, like all other political parties, it was closed down by the military government. It has since been revived.
17. Tunçay, 103.
18. Ibid., 105–6.
19. İsmet İnönü, II, 196. Mustafa Kemal said in 1927 that, a day after he had proposed that the debate should be held on a general censure motion, İsmet was too ill to speak in the assembly, where the government's record had to be defended by the defence minister Kâzım (Özalp) (*Nutuk*, 589).
20. List in Gologlu, VI, 81–2.
21. The mayor of Istanbul was termed Trustee for the City (*Şehremini*), originally trustee on behalf of the sovereign, and, as such, was appointed by the government. Other mayors (called *Belediye Reisi*, i.e. President of the Municipality) were elected.
22. Gologlu refers to the assembly's minutes for 5 January 1925 in reporting the resignation (VI, 83). İnönü is therefore wrong to claim in his memoirs that Recep (Peker) resigned because he believed that Fethi's government had not been sufficiently firm in suppressing Şeyh Sait's rebellion, which broke out in the beginning of February (II, 198).
23. *ASD*, III, 109–10.
24. Ibid., II, 214.
25. Altay, 386–9.
26. For a detailed account of the trip to Silifke, see Aslan, 131–73.
27. Gologlu, VI, 89–90.
28. Ibid., 96–9.
29. Olson, 41–3.
30. Ibid., 92.

31. In 1921, the most influential Kurdish nationalist living in Istanbul, Seyyit Abdülkadir, member of the Ottoman senate and briefly president of the Ottoman Council of State, had pleaded in vain with British representatives to support him in a rebellion against the Turks (Olson, 75). Kurdish officers, who asked for British support after deserting from Turkish units in Hakkâri in September 1924, were similarly disappointed (ibid., 45, 76).
32. Ibid., 76.
33. Bayrak, 255.
34. Ibid., 271.
35. Ibid.
36. Özerdim, 89.
37. Bayrak, 275.
38. Gologlu, VI, 106.
39. İsmet İnönü, II, 198.
40. Gologlu, VI, 110.
41. Revolution is the literal meaning of the word *inkılâp* (and of its Turkish equivalent *devrim*), which was used to designate the modernizing measures taken by Atatürk and, before him, by the CUP. But gradually its connotation softened to 'reform', so that today Turks use it when speaking of Atatürk's reforms. There is another Turkish word for revolution – *ihtilâl*. Meaning literally 'disorder', it was used originally for the French and then for the Russian revolutions. In practice, *inkılâp* came to mean a non-violent, and *ihtilâl* a violent revolution. This useful distinction was lost when the Turkish neologism *devrim* replaced both words.
42. Quoted by Tunçay, 139, n. 18.
43. Gologlu, VI, 110–11.
44. *ATTB*, 562–3.
45. Olson, 118.
46. For an eye-witness account of events in Elâzığ by a European resident, see ibid., 184–6.
47. Ibid., 115–16.
48. Ibid., 126.
49. Bayrak, 284.
50. Ibid., 289.
51. Olson, 116.
52. Bayrak, 323–4.
53. Ibid., 365.
54. Ibid., 383–4.
55. Olson, 124–5.
56. Ibid., 114.
57. Text of verdict in Bayrak, 390–3.
58. Cebesoy, *Siyasî Hâtıralar*, II, 143.
59. *Nutuk*, 593–4.
60. Tunçay, 147.
61. Cebesoy, *Siyasî Hâtıralar*, II, 164–5.
62. Yalçın, 278.
63. Sertel, 111, 121.
64. *Siyasî Hâtıralar*, II, 166.
65. Text of decree in Cebesoy, *Siyasî Hâtıralar*, II, 161–2.
66. Sertel, 107.
67. Indictment and verdict in Bayrak, 394–400; Mustafa Kemal's telegram referring only to Lütfü Fikri (Düşünsel), former president of the Istanbul bar, in *ATTB*, 568.
68. *AnaBritannica*, XVI, 430.
69. Mustafa Kemal, *Eskişehir–İzmit Konuşmaları*, 104.

70. List in Göldaş, 474–5, who notes that only seven deputies from the area voted against the law.
71. Cebesoy, *Sınıf Arkadaşım Atatürk*, 92.
72. Bayrak, 471.
73. Text of reports and plan in ibid., 452–89.
74. Ibid., 453.
75. Özerdim, 93.
76. *ASD*, I, 356.
77. *Nutuk*, 594.
78. Ibid., 595.
79. *ASD*, I, 362.

CHAPTER 22   REFORMS AND REPRESSION

1. Özerdim, 88.
2. Gökçen, 71–2.
3. Özerdim, 88.
4. Nejat Akgün, 208–11; Mamboury, 264–5.
5. Soyak, I, 33–5.
6. Dates in Özerdim, 89.
7. Araz, *Mustafa Kemal'le 1000 Gün*, 156.
8. Ibid., 192.
9. Soyak, I, 10–11.
10. Bozok, 220.
11. Altay, 403.
12. Bozok, 219–20.
13. Soon after the divorce, Mustafa Kemal issued instructions that Lâtife's father, Muammer Uşakizade (Uşaklıgil), should be given help to repay his debts in İzmir (Altay, 403).
14. Ibid., 389.
15. İsmet İnönü, II, 204.
16. Özerdim, 87.
17. Gologlu, VI, 138, who gives details of the trip, says that Mustafa Kemal left Ankara on 24 August and visited the barracks and the town hall on the 25th. However, *ASD*, II, 215 gives the date of the speech outside the town hall as 24 August.
18. Ibid., 216.
19. Ibid., 218–22.
20. Text of speech in ibid., 223–7.
21. Text in ibid., I, 355–61.
22. Özerdim, 94. *Milliyet*, currently one of Turkey's most successful newspapers, revived the title when it was founded as a new venture in 1950.
23. Gologlu, VI, 156; Özerdim, 92.
24. Gologlu, VI, 152–6.
25. Details in Alkan, 83.
26. Gologlu, VI, 166.
27. Ibid., 159–62.
28. Afetinan, *Atatürk'ün Yazdığı Yurttaşlık Bilgileri*, 17.
29. *ASD*, II, 234.
30. Özerdim, 88.
31. Gökçen, 23.
32. Volkan and Itzkowitz, 260.
33. Altay, 390.

34. In order to maintain her place in bibliographies, she joined her given name and new surname, and called herself 'A. Afetinan' (Afetinan, *Atatürk Hakkında Hâtıralar ve Belgeler*, 354).

35. Her thesis on the anthropological characteristics of the population of Turkey was published in Geneva in 1939, with a disclaimer stating that her professors did not necessarily agree with her views (Afetinan, *Atatürk Hakkında Hâtıralar ve Belgeler*, 350–1).

36. According to Atatürk's waiter Cemal Granda, a German housekeeper (*hausdame*) employed in the presidential household was dismissed when it was discovered that she was noting down her experiences (*Atatürk'ün Uşağı idim*, introduction by Turhan Gürkan, 3). It may well have been Mme Bauer.

37. Altay, 399–411.

38. Derin, 47.

39. Altay, 413.

40. Ibid., 415.

41. Derin, 38.

CHAPTER 23   MEASURED TERROR

1. Evans, 89.

2. Ibid., 91.

3. Texts in İsmail Soysal, 268–73, 276–8, 285–303.

4. Text in ibid., 309–17.

5. Altay, 392.

6. İsmet İnönü, II, 206–7.

7. Orbay (ed. Kutay), *Yüzyılımızda Bir İnsanımız*, V, 291; Orbay, *Cehennem Değirmeni*, II, 195.

8. Cebesoy, *Siyasî Hâtıralar*, II, 198.

9. Kılıç Ali, *İstiklâl Mahkemesi Hatıraları*, 64.

10. Gologlu, V, 167.

11. Ibid., VI, 192.

12. Faik (Günday)'s reminiscences published in September 1956 in *Dünya* and quoted by Soyak, I, 357.

13. Ibid., II, 365.

14. Rıza Nur, III, 331–40.

15. Altay, 27.

16. Özalp, 41. Karabekir told the İzmir Independence Tribunal that Edip, the Yellow Brave, had received 8–10,000 lira from government secret funds on the grounds that his house had been burned down, presumably during the War of Independence (Mumcu, *Gazi Paşa'ya Suikast*, 50). He had also been given an estate at Değirmendere, south of İzmir (ibid., 112, n. 30). But he was clearly not satisfied.

17. Zürcher, 144.

18. İsmet İnönü, II, 210.

19. Edip, the Yellow Brave, who was to tell the Independence Tribunal that he 'believed' that the conspiracy involved the Progressive Republican Party, was not arrested until 17 June, in the Bristol Hotel in Istanbul (Mumcu, *Gazi Paşa'ya Suikast*, 45). Mustafa Kemal had previously – presumably on 16 June – instructed the Istanbul police chief to follow Edip's movements and establish his contacts before arresting him. It seems certain that Edip's unsupported evidence did not precede the arrests of the Progressive Republicans, but was used later to justify them.

20. Kılıç Ali, *İstiklâl Mahkemesi Hatıraları*, 40.

21. In a speech of welcome which he made when the Gazi visited Mersin in 1923. The

text (in Elman, 231–3) begins with the words, 'Is it necessary to speak of your victories in your presence? They are known to all, from Eskimos in Greenland to negroes listening to the wind for news in Africa's burning deserts', etc.

22. Ibid., 230.
23. İsmet İnönü, II, 212.
24. Cebesoy, *Siyasî Hâtıralar*, II, 201.
25. *ASD*, II, 119.
26. İsmet İnönü, II, 219.
27. Ibid., 212.
28. Cebesoy, *Siyasî Hâtıralar*, II, 205.
29. *ASD*, III, 85–6.
30. Kandemir, I, 37.
31. Mumcu, *Gazi Paşa'ya Suikast*, 50.
32. Ibid., 116, n. 61.
33. Ibid., 50.
34. Ibid., 15.
35. Goloğlu, VI, 202–3.
36. Altay, 420.
37. Kandemir, I, 69.
38. Goloğlu, VI, 204.
39. Altay, 421–2.
40. Soyak, I, 373.
41. Cebesoy, *Siyasî Hâtıralar*, II, 220.
42. Ibid., 224.
43. The literal meaning is etymologically misleading: *karakol* is in fact a Turkicized adaptation of the Mongolian *karaghul* meaning 'patrol'.
44. Zürcher, 81.
45. Orbay, *Cehennem Değirmeni*, II, 223.
46. Rıza Nur, III, 35.
47. İsmet İnönü, II, 216.
48. Atay, *Çankaya*, 381.
49. Jevakhoff, 371.
50. Reported by Atatürk's waiter Cemal Granda (205). The story that Atatürk was born a Jew or, alternatively, that he came from a *dönme* family of converted Jews surfaced most recently when Ezer Weizman, the president of Israel, visited Turkey in January 1994 (*Forward*, New York City, 28 January 1994, 1). All the evidence is against it.
51. Testimony to the author by Altemur Kılıç, son of Kılıç Ali, judge of the Independence Tribunal.
52. Soyak, I, 375.
53. Jevakhoff (370) quotes a French resident's reminiscences that in 1925–6 'the old Unionists manoeuvred in the corridors, while fearing that their wrists would be slapped'. Rıza Nur claims that, just before the attempt, he saw some fifteen opposition politicians, including Ahmet Şükrü, in the Taksim gardens in Istanbul: 'They looked happy. They laughed a lot. There was something special – hope, confidence, contentment – in their behaviour. There was something afoot, which caught my attention' (III, 332).
54. Atay, *Çankaya*, 406.
55. Ibid., 404.
56. Zürcher (156) corrects Armstrong's claim (279) that Mustafa Kemal held a party to celebrate the executions, and says that the party marked the founding of the model farm near Ankara. But the celebration of the first anniversary of the farm's establishment had taken place on 5 May (Nejat Akgün, 210). Mustafa Kemal did not need a special occasion to spend the night drinking with his friends.

CHAPTER 24   THE LEADER IS ALWAYS RIGHT

1. *AnaBritannica*, XIII, 626.
2. Mamboury, 239–40.
3. *ATTB*, 575.
4. Eyice, 31, 43–4.
5. *ASD*, I, 363.
6. Eyice, 43.
7. Özerdim, 97.
8. Atay, *Çankaya*, 406.
9. Ağaoğlu, *Babamın Arkadaşları*, 104.
10. Elman, 375.
11. Atay, *Çankaya*, 454–5.
12. Özerdim, 97.
13. Goloğlu, VI, 220–1.
14. Ibid., VI, 224.
15. Soyak, II, 683, 691. At the time of his death, Atatürk had accumulated nearly 20,000 lira (approx. 15,000 dollars) in his pension account. His personal account closed with a balance of 53,000 lira. There was also a balance of 1,450,000 lira in the account of the model farms which he had by then made over to the state (Soyak, II, 686).
16. Ibid., I, 376.
17. Reported by his doctor Asım İsmail Arar. The report on the full medical examination mentions that 'the Wassermann test was negative' – in other words, Mustafa Kemal did not have syphilis (726–7).
18. *Atatürk'ün Söylev ve Demeçleri*, II, 265.
19. The incident is related in the newspaper *Milliyet* of 10 November 1998. Rumours that it was an attempt to assassinate the president were believed by the US ambassador Joseph Grew, who reported them to Washington (Grew, II, 725).
20. *ASD*, II, 266.
21. Ibid., III, 35–50.
22. Ibid., 97–102.
23. Ibid., 111–17.
24. It was officially described as the second convention, on the grounds that the founding congress of the Society for the Defence of National Rights in Anatolia and Rumelia, held in Sivas in 1919, was the party's first convention. The claim is controversial, as the Progressive Republicans also saw themselves as heirs of the original all-encompassing nationalist organization.
25. In the 1989 edition.
26. *Nutuk*, 11.
27. Mumcu (ed.), *Kâzım Karabekir Anlatıyor*, 179–86.
28. Derin, 45.
29. *ATTB*, 580.
30. Özerdim, 100–1.
31. Ellison, 24.
32. Halide Edib (Edip), 170.
33. Ali Mithat İnan, *Atatürk'ün Not Defterleri*, photocopies of entries in notebooks in appendices 10–12.
34. Özerdim, 101: the law was passed on 24 May 1928 and came into effect four days latter.
35. Ünaydın, 28–31.
36. Atay, *Çankaya*, 430; Emre, 325.
37. Falih Rıfkı says that Mustafa Kemal was not familiar with the shape of capital letters and did not like the look of the lower-case 'q' (*Çankaya*, 441). This is unlikely, given that he had for years read French printed texts.

38. This led to inconsistencies. Thus 'geometry' was spelled *geometri*, 'geology' became *jeoloji*, while 'geography' kept its Arabic form and was spelled *coğrafya* (pronounced 'jorafia').
39. Atay, *Çankaya*, 410.
40. I owe this information to Şefik Yüksel, the husband of the Turkish virtuoso pianist İdil Biret. He first told the story in a programme on Wilhelm Kempff which Bayerische TV broadcast on 21 November 1995.
41. *ASD*, II, 272–4.
42. Atay, *Çankaya*, 442.
43. Özerdim, 103.
44. *AnaBritannica*, XVI, 94.

CHAPTER 25   THE DEPRESSION

1. İsmet İnönü, II, 257.
2. Ibid., 168–9.
3. Özerdim, 105–6.
4. Başar, 21.
5. Özerdim, 105.
6. Perinçek (ed.), *Türk Tarihinin Ana Hatları*, 17.
7. [Afetinan,] *Atatürk'ün Yazdığı Yurttaşlık Bilgileri*, 13, 14, 18–20, 83–5.
8. Özerdim, 106.
9. Hale, 46.
10. Ibid., 48.
11. Waugh, 284.
12. Ibid., 286.
13. Başar, 39.
14. Hale, 48, 73, 62.
15. Özerdim, 107.
16. Soyak, II, 405.
17. Okyar, 10.
18. Ibid., 14.
19. Ibid., 16.
20. Ibid., 70.
21. Gologlu, VI, 285.
22. Okyar, 71–2.
23. Soyak, II, 436.
24. Okyar, 73.
25. Özerdim, 136.
26. Ibid., 107.
27. Ibid., 116.
28. Ibid., 120.
29. Soyak, II, 437.
30. Text in ibid., 442–3.
31. Başar, 31.
32. Ibid., 36.
33. Gologlu, VII, 6.
34. Eye-witness account in Çetinkaya, 23.
35. Details in Gologlu, VI, 301–5.
36. Soyak, II, 454.
37. Özalp, 47.
38. Altay, 434–40.
39. Gologlu, VI, 308.

40. *ASD*, III, 302–3.
41. *AnaBritannica*, XVI, 275.
42. Gologlu, VI, 282–4.
43. Hale, 56.
44. İsmet İnönü, II, 277–8.
45. This happened to Ahmet Hamdi Başar who had accompanied Mustafa Kemal as an economic adviser on his 1930 fact-finding trip (Başar, 147, n. 1).
46. Quoted in Gologlu, VII, 6–7.
47. *AnaBritannica*, X, 312.
48. *ASD*, II, 282.
49. Ibid., 385–7.
50. Soyak, II, 486.

CHAPTER 26   TABLE TALK

1. Bozdağ, *Atatürk'ün Sofrası*, 77–80.
2. Details in Grothusen, 71–81.
3. Elman, 238–41; Bozdağ, *Atatürk'ün Sofrası*, 77–87; Afetinan, 208.
4. Atay, *Çankaya*, 561–2; Granda, 193–7.
5. Ibid., 224–5.
6. Ibid., 199–200.
7. Özerdim, 107.
8. *Tan*, published by Mahmut (Soydan) as a successor to *Milliyet*, was financed by the Business Bank (Sertel, 189), which also held the account of Mustafa Kemal's farms (Soyak, II, 686).
9. This version told by Hasan Rıza Soyak (I, 22–8) was confirmed by Vladimir, the head waiter of the *Rose Noire* (Bozdağ, *Atatürk'ün Sofrası*, 89–93).
10. Soyak, I, 24–8.
11. Bozok, 231.
12. Photograph of letter in album *Mustafa Kemal Atatürk*, ed. Ülger, I, 188. The caption dates the letter 6 August 1933, but the date is clearly written in another hand below the word '*kapadım*' (lit. 'I have closed it') and refers probably to the date on which the letter was locked away.
13. The photograph of the directive in Aydemir, *İkinci Adam*, II, 469, does not include the date. But as it is signed 'Gazi M. Kemal' rather than 'K. Atatürk', it must have been written before 1934. It probably followed the argument in front of guests in Yalova in August 1932.
14. Bozdağ, *Bitmeyen Kavga*, 123–6.
15. Incident related to the author by Kılıç Ali's son Altemur Kılıç, who had heard it from the chief waiter of the hotel.
16. Gologlu, VII, 170–1.
17. Atay, *Çankaya*, 401. Atay does not name Afet and speaks of 'a lady' at Atatürk's side, but the remark was almost certainly addressed to Afet.
18. Ibid., 541–2.
19. Karaosmanoğlu, *Atatürk*, 140, 163.
20. Atay, *Çankaya*, 544.
21. *ATTB*, 608.
22. Text in İsmail Soysal, 393–6.
23. Soyak, I, 29.
24. According to Atatürk's waiter Cemal Granda (132–3), İnönü feared that his life might be in danger in Greece. Before setting out, he asked the president to look after his children should anything happen to him.
25. İsmet İnönü, II, 240.

26. Text in İsmail Soysal, 433–6.
27. Ibid., 271–2.
28. İsmet İnönü, II, 251.
29. İsmail Soysal, 397–403.
30. Özerdim, 117.
31. Texts in İsmail Soysal, 454–8.
32. Text in ibid., 463.
33. Photocopy of letter which Venizelos addressed on 12 January 1934 to the president of the Nobel Peace Committee (appointed by the Norwegian parliament) in newspaper *Milliyet*, 28 October 1998, 1, 18.
34. Soyak's claim, quoted by Derin (98–9), that Atatürk was thinking of Marshal Fevzi Çakmak as his stand-in, should be seen in the light of his efforts to promote Çakmak against İsmet İnönü.
35. Soyak, II, 443, 445.
36. Özerdim, 112.
37. *ASD*, I, 392.
38. İsmet İnönü, II, 252.
39. Egeli, 123.
40. Mustafa Kemal, *Eskişehir–İzmit Konuşmaları*, 96.
41. *ASD*, III, 138.
42. Altay, 426–9.
43. Özerdim, 115.
44. *ASD*, II, 318–19.
45. Atay, *Çankaya*, 483.
46. Soyak, II, 55, 64.
47. Ibid., I, 53.
48. Özel Şahingiray (ed.), *Atatürk'ün Nöbet Defteri*, 14–15.
49. Soyak, I, 11.
50. Derin, 40.
51. Soyak, I, 43.
52. Ibid., 63.
53. Us, 63–7; Kinross, 462, n. 1.
54. Nejat Akgün, 182, 238, 314; *AnaBritannica*, XII, 219.
55. I owe this story to Mr David Lane, formerly of the British Embassy in Ankara, who had heard it from Mme Praetorius, the widow of the conductor of the Presidential Philharmonic Orchestra (appointed at Hindemith's suggestion).
56. *ASD*, III, 140.
57. *Atatürk*, 123.
58. Bozdağ (ed.), *Paşaların Kavgası*, 320.

CHAPTER 27   LAST BATTLES

1. İsmet İnönü, II, 284.
2. As early as 1927, Turkey's best Ottomanist, Professor Fuat Köprülü, had warned that foreign scholars would deride as absurd the claim that all ancient civilizations had been founded by Turks. The Turkish folklore specialist Mehmet Şakir Ülkütaşır says characteristically: 'I found Fuat Köprülü's view more scientific and rational [than those he criticized] ... But I realized that it would be more pleasing to our Great and Beloved Teacher if I remained silent, and this is what I did' (Ülkütaşır, 103).
3. Perinçek (ed.), *Türk Tarihinin Ana Hatları*, 33.
4. Ibid., 55.
5. Özerdim, 108.

6. It was founded in Ankara in July 1932 as the Society for Turkish Language Research (*Türk Dili Tetkik Cemiyeti*), held its first congress in Dolmabahçe palace the following September, and was then renamed the Turkish Language Society (lit. 'Institution', *Türk Dil Kurumu*) (Afetinan, 215–18).

7. Jevakhoff, 422.

8. Text in *ASD*, II, 320–1.

9. Words spoken by Afet at Atatürk's command (Afetinan, 219–20).

10. *ASD*, III, 124.

11. Jevakhoff, 423–4. The *Outline of Turkish History* (47) declared that 'the skull of the Turkish race is, in the majority of cases, brachycephalic'. According to Atatürk's waiter Cemal Granda, Reşit Galip (education minister in 1932–3) made a habit of measuring skulls: those who measured below 80 cm were classed as dolichocephalic, above 80 as brachycephalic. Atatürk measured 81 cm. So did his waiter, whom Atatürk called 'that animal' (Granda, 57). Racists are to this day known as 'skull merchants' (*kafatasçı*) in popular Turkish.

12. Derin, 125.

13. Emre, 345.

14. When peroxide was first imported into the Ottoman empire as a disinfectant, a name for it was coined from Arabic, the unwieldy term *mâ-i müvellidülhumuzaî* (generator-of-acidity water, a translation of the Greek 'oxygen'). Under the republic, this was changed to *oksijene* ('[eau] oxygénée').

15. Waugh, 275.

16. Dates in Özerdim, 111–12.

17. Topçuoğlu (ed.), VI, 107–12; Dâver, 171. In Istanbul, the order to recite the call to prayer in Turkish was issued on 7 February 1933 (Özerdim, 114)

18. Ibid., 120.

19. Ibid., 121.

20. Ibid.

21. Law No. 2510, *Resmî Gazete*, 14 June 1934.

22. Law No. 3195, published on 2 January 1936. Text in Bulut, 307–18.

23. Atay, *Çankaya*, 545–6.

24. Gologlu, VII, 153–7.

25. Soyak, I, 57–60.

26. According to Kılıç Ali (101–4), Atatürk decided to look into the matter personally and went as far as Çorlu in Thrace in the company of Kâzım Dirik. He visited a village built for immigrants from Romania and decided that Dirik gave good value for the taxes he collected from the peasants. The guardroom logbook (502) records this as a one-day trip on 3 June 1936. This brief visit seems to have inspired a long tale, according to which Atatürk left Florya secretly in the company of Nuri Conker, met an aggrieved peasant whose ox had been seized by tax officials, invited the peasant back to Florya, and confronted İnönü with this evidence of his government's oppressive practices. İsmet Bozdağ devotes some thirty pages to this imaginary escapade (*Atatürk'ün Sofrası*, 9–36), placing it in the autumn of 1936. There is no evidence in the logbook to support the story.

27. Özalp, 63–4.

28. Gologlu, VII, 190–1.

29. Ibid., 208–9.

30. Ibid., 278–9.

31. Ibid., 155–6.

32. Özalp, 55–6.

33. Details in Soyak, I, 377–400, who is intent on justifying the proceedings. For a shorter version, see Gologlu, VII, 171–4. The account given to İsmet Bozdağ by Şükrü Kaya, Tevfik Rüştü Aras and Kılıç Ali (*Atatürk'ün Sofrası*, 208), suggests that the intrigue against Ali Saip Ursavaş was pushed forward by Şükrü Kaya, the inter-

ior minister, and taken up by Kılıç Ali, one of 'the usual gentlemen'. In a letter to his elder brother, Reşit, who returned to Turkey after the 1938 amnesty, the Circassian Ethem described the alleged plot of 1935 as a fabrication and said that he was ill in Egypt at the time he was supposed to have despatched assassins from Jordan (Ethem (ed. Kutay), *Çerkez Ethem Dosyası*, 16).

34. And, 24.
35. Ibid., 32–41.
36. Photographs of corrections in ibid., 76–7.
37. Derin, 75. General Hassan Arfa, who accompanied the shah, gives a more dramatic account of the incident (Arfa, 250). But his claim that Atatürk ordered the destruction of Uşak is almost certainly an echo of the earlier true story of Atatürk's outburst against the citizens of Menemen. General Fahrettin Altay, who acted as the shah's Turkish ADC, does not refer in his memoirs to the Uşak incident, while mentioning Atatürk's earlier threat to raze Menemen to the ground.
38. Sonyel, *Atatürk*, 174.
39. Grew, II, 764–5.
40. Text of agreement in İsmail Soysal, 430–8.
41. Özerdim, 120.
42. Kinross, 460; Millman, 486; Volkan and Itzkowitz, 321.
43. Millman quoting Atatürk's remarks to Georges Bonnet, 504–5, n. 21.
44. Aras, 228–9.
45. İsmail Soysal, 493. Aras claims that, as foreign minister, he launched the initiative to revise the straits regime, and that, after soundings abroad, he obtained, first Atatürk's, and then the government's agreement to summon a conference for the purpose (Aras, 230). This is likely. Aras's direct access to the president – he was a frequent guest at Atatürk's dinner table – did not endear him to the prime minister, İsmet İnönü.
46. Text and introduction in İsmail Soysal, 493–518.
47. On 2 July 1936, the official Bolshevik newspaper *Pravda* noted 'with regret' that the Turkish proposals did not give due weight to Soviet interests. On 10 July, Atatürk wrote a reply, which was published under the name of Yunus Nadi, editor of *Cumhuriyet*. Friends should realize, he declared, that the Turkish nation would insist on measures which ensured the country's full security (Derin, 108).
48. Millman, 498. Given that Atatürk must have approved work on the Çakmak line, it is unlikely that he would have criticized the construction of the Maginot line, as is sometimes claimed. Stories to this effect appear to be another instance of the attribution of prophetic powers to Atatürk, with the certainty of hindsight.
49. Kinross, 482.
50. Millman, 490.
51. To give the flavour of the book, it is enough to quote a sentence such as 'Power brought out in him [Mustafa Kemal] the brute and the beast, the throw-back to the coarse, savage Tartar – the wolf-stock of the central steppes of Asia' (254). Elsewhere, Armstrong refers to the secretary-general of the People's Party, Safvet (Arıkan), an army officer born in eastern Anatolia, as 'Zia Sefet … a capable and quick-witted Jew' (284). The popularity of the book suggests that its tone was acceptable to English taste in the 1930s. It seems that some passages were lifted textually from British government despatches. This compounded the fears of British diplomats that *Grey Wolf* might damage Anglo-Turkish relations (Sonyel, *Atatürk*, 165–71). The Turks were more polite about their British interlocutors. It is instructive to compare the kindly references to Sir Horace Rumbold in İsmet İnönü's autobiography (I, 76) with Rumbold's description of the Turkish delegation in Lausanne as 'a lot of pig-headed, stupid and irritating people' (Gilbert, 283). 'The wild men of Angora', as Rumbold called the Turkish delegates (ibid., 288), and their leader, Mustafa Kemal, had good reason to stand on their dignity.

52. Kılıç Ali, *Atatürk'ün Hususiyetleri*, 80–1. A similar story is told by Volkan and Itzkowitz (259), who add that Atatürk entertained the suspicion that Armstrong may have been in touch with Lâtife to learn details of their intimate life together.
53. Borak (ed.), *Atatürk'ün Armstrong'a Cevabı*, 48–9.
54. İsmail Soysal, 532.
55. *ASD*, I, 410.
56. Soyak, II, 558, 562–3.
57. Ibid., 728.
58. Jevakhoff, 444–5, gives 10 December as the date of the meeting. The guardroom logbook (562) records a visit to the Ankara Palace on that date. According to Soyak (II, 608), the meeting with the French ambassador took place at the reception given in the Ankara exhibition centre in honour of the Balkan chiefs of staff.
59. Soyak, II, 602.
60. Topçuoğlu (ed.), X, 5.
61. İsmet İnönü, II, 283–4.
62. Şahingiray (ed.), *Atatürk'ün Nöbet Defteri*, 371.
63. Texts in Ülger (ed.), II, 103–6.
64. Şahingiray (ed.), *Atatürk'ün Nöbet Defteri*, 572–87.
65. Gökçen, 251–64.
66. Ibid., 252.
67. Texts in İsmail Soysal, 544–72.
68. Özerdim, 125.
69. İsmail Soysal, 573–81.
70. Text in ibid., 584–7.
71. İsmet İnönü, I, 184.
72. Soyak, I, 679.
73. Hasan Rıza Soyak gives a detailed account of the Nyon affair in his memoirs (II, 658–82). According to İnönü's brief version (II, 285–6), his government instructed Aras not to take part in any action against the Italians. This simplifies a complex argument. Falih Rıfkı Atay also summarizes the controversy (*Çankaya*, 495).

CHAPTER 28   APOTHEOSIS

1. Atay, *Çankaya*, 484.
2. The lady may well have been Zsa Zsa Gabor, at that time wife of the journalist Burhan Belge, who was employed in the government's press department.
3. Quoted by Jevakhoff, 432–3.
4. The guardroom logbook (300) notes that the president had been at the hotel between 11.30 p.m. and 4.30 a.m. on 21/22 August 1934. He then took a boat trip on the yacht *Ertuğrul*. He retired on board the following morning at 8 a.m., but at 1.30 p.m. he was already at the Language Conference in Dolmabahçe palace. He did not leave until 3 a.m., when he crossed the sea of Marmara to the spa in Yalova, where he went to bed at 5 a.m. His next visit to the hotel was on 3 September, when he stayed until 3 a.m. It was probably on this occasion that Colonel Courson de la Villeneuve saw him.
5. Okday, 102. As foreign musicians, like other professionals, were not allowed to ply their trade permanently in Turkey, Atatürk arranged for members of the Park Hotel band to be given Turkish citizenship (ibid., 101).
6. Jevakhoff, 433.
7. The hotel was called Naim Palas. Mustafa Kemal stayed there between 26 February and 5 March 1930 (Topçuoğlu (ed.), III, 8–20.)
8. Probably during the regatta held on 1 July 1935.
9. Ünaydın, 49; Atay, *Babanız Atatürk*, 119.

10. Soyak, I, 35.
11. Derin, 108–9.
12. Jevakhoff, 442, n. 1.
13. Gökçen, 115–26.
14. Ibid., 68.
15. İnönü's hand-written autobiographical note, dated February 1939, three months after Atatürk's death (İsmet İnönü, II, 321–8).
16. The sculptor Pietro Canonica reported to Mussolini that the Gazi had told him that in the first three years (1925–7) he had spent two million lira on his model farm in Ankara, with meagre results (Eyice, 44).
17. Atay (*Çankaya*, 527–8) says that Atatürk's companions found it hard to make him share with them gifts he received from well-wishers.
18. Soyak, II, 704.
19. İsmet İnönü, II, 288.
20. Soyak, II, 687.
21. İsmet İnönü, II, 287–8.
22. *ATTB*, 668–72.
23. Gologlu, VII, 239–41.
24. İsmet İnönü, II, 289.
25. *ATTB*, 661–8. The date of 1 June on the telegram is a misprint, since Atatürk arrived in Trabzon on 10 June and left the following day. On 1 June, he was still in Ankara (Özerdim, 125).
26. Accounts of the incident in Atay, *Çankaya*, 495–7; Soyak, II, 707–8; İsmet İnönü, II, 289–90.
27. Atay, *Çankaya*, 400.
28. Derin, 117–18; Aydemir, *İkinci Adam*, I, 497–8.
29. Derin, 119. The conversation is said to have taken place in Atay's home. The guardroom logbook (678) records a visit by Atatürk to Atay's house in Ankara on 4 December 1937.
30. Gologlu, VII, 273.
31. *ASD*, I, 433.
32. Derin, 123.
33. Bozok, 244–53; İsmet İnönü, II, 292–4; Aydemir, *İkinci Adam*, I, 502.
34. The town was originally known as Amid. Atatürk was informed that the Yakuts, a Turkic people in Siberia, called copper *amit*. As the Turkish word for copper is *bakır*, Atatürk decided that Diyarbekir, the Turkish spelling of an Arabic name meaning 'country of the Bakr [Arab tribes]', should be changed to Diyarbakır. Unaccountably, the first part of the name, the Arabic *diyar*, was kept.
35. *ASD*, II, 326.
36. İhsan Sabri Çağlayangil, the future Turkish foreign minister, who was at the time a police official, had been sent to make sure that the leaders of the Dersim rebellion were executed before the presidential visit. He describes the episode in his memoirs (46–55).
37. Toros, 67.
38. *ATTB*, 678–9.
39. Şahingiray (ed.), *Atatürk'ün Nöbet Defteri*, 680.
40. Derin, 127–8.
41. *ATTB*, 680.
42. Gologlu, VII, 305.
43. *ASD*, II, 330.
44. Jevakhoff spells his name as Flessinguer. It appears as Fissinger in all other sources.
45. Soyak, II, 739.
46. Sonyel, *Atatürk*, 185.
47. Şahingiray (ed.), *Atatürk'ün Nöbet Defteri*, 716.

48. İsmail Soysal, 538.
49. Toros, 71–3.
50. Atay, *Çankaya*, 489.
51. According to Ülger (ed.), II, 243, the purchase price is given in one source as 1,700,000 dollars and in another as 1,250,000 lira. If the denominations are reversed, the two figures express the same amount at the rate of exchange in force at the time.
52. Derin, 130.
53. İsmet İnönü, II, 323.
54. Borak (ed.), *Atatürk'ün Özel Mektupları*, 78–9.
55. Aras, 71–2.
56. Okyar (ed. Kutay), *Üç Devirde Bir Adam*, 542.
57. Soyak, II, 747–8.
58. Derin, 135.
59. İlhami Soysal, *150'likler*, 145.
60. Derin, 135.
61. Gologlu, VII, 317 quoting the speech Bayar read in Atatürk's name when he opened the assembly session on 1 November 1938.
62. Atay, *Çankaya*, 580.
63. Soyak, II, 747.
64. Derin, 135.
65. Text in Gologlu, VII, 355. Makbule was to receive 1,000 lira a month, Afet 800, Sabiha 600, Ülkü 200 and Rukiye and Nebile 100 each, 'as before'.
66. İsmet İnönü, II, 323.
67. Us, 307.
68. According to Atay, the letters were addressed in humble high Ottoman 'to the exalted presence of the protector of the presidency' (*huzur-u âli-yi riyasetpenahiye*). They were returned to İnönü after Atatürk's death (*Çankaya*, 499).
69. İsmet İnönü, II, 300, 324.
70. Derin, 136.
71. İsmet İnönü, II, 324. Soyak (II, 761) claims that İnönü was about to go to Atatürk's bedside, but was dissuaded by Refik Saydam (who, a few months later, was to succeed Bayar as prime minister).
72. Us, 300.
73. Soyak, II, 758.
74. İsmet İnönü, II, 324.
75. Derin, 136; Soyak, II, 767.
76. Ibid., 769.
77. Ibid., 771. The doctor had asked Atatürk to show his tongue. This may explain the story that his last words were '*Dil mi?*' (What, the tongue?) The Turkish word *dil* means both 'tongue' and 'language', and this version of Atatürk's last words has given rise to the belief that he continued to be preoccupied by his reform of the Turkish language as he lay dying.
78. Soyak, 771–4.
79. Bozok, 266–7.
80. Derin, 140.
81. Gökçen, 308.
82. Gologlu, VI, 321. Earlier, when the People's Party met to determine its candidate for the presidency, one vote was cast for Bayar.
83. Derin, 141.
84. Text of speeches in Gologlu, VII, 322–30.
85. *Cumhuriyet*, 19 November 1938.
86. Derin, 142.
87. Later, Ali İhsan Sabis became the official editor of *Türkische Post*, subsidized by Hitler's consulate in Istanbul.

88. Altay, 562. According to another version, it was Atatürk's sister Makbule who insisted that prayers be said, saying, 'My brother was not an infidel.'
89. Derin, 142.
90. Bozdağ, *Toprakta Bile Bitmeyen Kavga*, 255.
91. Derin, 143.
92. Quoted by Sonyel, *Atatürk*, 199.
93. Ünaydın, frontispiece.

CHAPTER 29   AFTERMATH

1. Derin, 148.
2. Soyak (II, 788–9) sees İnönü's assumption of the title of National Leader as proof that he had adopted the fascist principles embodied in the party programme prepared by Recep Peker for the 1935 convention, but rejected by Atatürk.
3. Biographical details in Tevetoğlu, 203–12.
4. İnönü remarks acidly in his memoirs that Karabekir tried to have his friends selected for membership of the assembly (II, 27), and implies that he resisted his approaches. Similarly, he dismisses the attempts made by Rauf Orbay, when he was ambassador in London during the Second World War, to have a say in the appointment of Turkish ambassadors elsewhere (II, 184–5).
5. Heper, 80, n. 141.
6. Erdal İnönü, I, 260.
7. Dâver, 171. Earlier, a muezzin who used Arabic to call the faithful to prayer would have been guilty of breaking a departmental order – a disciplinary matter and not a criminal offence.
8. Goloğlu, VIII, 283.
9. *AnaBritannica*, VII, 207, 208.
10. Turkey declared war on Germany and Japan on 23 February 1945, just in time to qualify for an invitation to the founding conference of the United Nations in San Francisco (Selim Deringil, *Turkish Foreign Policy During the Second World War*, CUP 1989, 178–9).
11. Dâver, 78, 136–7.
12. Adnan Menderes was a landowner. He first attracted public attention when he spoke against a land reform bill which the assembly began debating on 14 May and passed on 11 June 1945 (*AnaBritannica*, VII, 108).
13. Sertel, 295, 383.
14. DİE (Turkish State Institute of Statistics), *Türkiye İstatistik Yıllığı*, 1995, 208.
15. Law No. 5816 of 25 July 1951.
16. Law No. 5665 of 16 June 1950 (Dâver, 172).
17. Aybay, 1.
18. DİE, *Türkiye İstatistik Yıllığı*, 1995, 57.
19. According to the earliest available statistics, 89.4 per cent of the total population could neither read nor write in 1927. By 1935–6 the literacy rate had almost doubled and stood at 20.4 per cent of the population (Andreas Kazamias, *Education and the Quest for Modernity in Turkey*, Allen & Unwin, London 1966, 174). The official *Small Statistical Abstract of Turkey*, published by the General Directorate of Statistics in 1948, gives a higher figure, 23.3 per cent, for 1935 (80).
20. From TL 50.3 to TL 111.5 (Hale, 46, 76).
21. Atay, *Çankaya*, 303.
22. Başar, 45; Tunçay, 220, n. 19.
23. World Bank report quoted in *Milliyet*, 25 April 1998, 9. The classification is based on purchasing power parities (PPPs).
24. Quoted by Arai, 3.

25. See for example the telegram Mustafa Kemal sent to the Kurdish sheikh Ziyaettin of Garzan on 15 January 1920: 'Thus, provided that the Turks and the Kurds – these two blood brothers sharing the same religion – work hand in hand, determined to defend our sacred unity, our fatherland and our independence will undoubtedly be saved with God's help' (ATASE, *Atatürk Özel Arşivinden Seçmeler*, IV, 195).

26. In instructions to General Nihat (Anılmış), commander of the Mesopotamian (Elcezire) front, sent sometime after 1920 when he was appointed to this command (ATASE, *Türk İstiklâl Harbi'ne Katılan ... Komutanların Biyografileri*, 69), Mustafa Kemal said: 'Our domestic policy provides for the gradual large-scale establishment of local administrations in the whole country, in a way that would affect all layers of the population directly. As for areas inhabited by the Kurds, we deem it necessary for reasons both of domestic and of foreign policy to set up gradually a local administration.' These instructions were read during a secret session of the assembly in Ankara on 22 July 1922 (TBMM, *Gizli Celse Zabıtları*, III, 551).

27. The 1921 Law of Fundamental Organization provided that local councils (or soviets – the term *şura*, which occurs in the text, was used in that sense at the time; the 1876 Ottoman constitution had used the term *meclis-i umumî*, a literal translation of the French *conseil général*) would be responsible for education, health, the economy, farming, public works and social services (article 11). The 1924 constitution stated briefly and vaguely that 'in provincial administration wider powers will be delegated while duties will be distinct' (*tevsi-i mezuniyet ve tefrik-i vezaif esası*, article 91). See Aybay, 199–200.

28. The manual of civics which Atatürk dictated to Afet describes nation formation as an effort to achieve separate existence, in parallel with other nations. Every nation has the right to claim its territory and demand fair treatment. But, he goes on, the Chinese, the Afghans, the Indians, the inhabitants of Tripoli (in Libya), the Tunisians, Moroccans, and Syrians, the Iraqis, Egyptians and Albanians, are communities, but not nations, because they are neither free nor independent ([Afetinan], *Atatürk'ün Yazdığı Yurttaşlık Bilgileri*, 25–6).

29. Atay, *Çankaya*, 428.

Bibliography

PERSONAL WRITINGS AND SPEECHES

Atatürk, *Atatürk'ün Söylev ve Demeçleri* (*ASD*) (Speeches and Statements by Atatürk), original text in Ottoman Turkish, I–III (in one vol.), Atatürk Kültür, Dil ve Tarih Yüksek Kurumu (AKDTYK) [Atatürk Culture, Language and History Higher Institute], Ankara 1989

——*Atatürk'ün Tamim, Telgraf ve Beyannameleri* (*ATTB*) (Circulars, Telegrams and Proclamations by Atatürk), published as IV of above, separate volume, 1991

——*Nutuk* (Speech), original text, AKDTYK, Ankara 1989, *Vesikalar* (Documents), 1991

——*Atatürk'ün Bütün Eserleri* (Collected Works of Atatürk), I (1903–15), Kaynak Yayınları, Istanbul 1998

——*Atatürk'ün Anıları* (Atatürk's Memoirs), published by Falih Rıfkı (Atay) in *Hakimiyet-i Milliye* and Mahmut (Soydan) in *Milliyet*, ed. İsmet Bozdağ, Bilgi, Ankara 1982

——*Atatürk Kendini Anlatıyor* (Atatürk Tells His Own Story), ed. İlhan Akşit, Kastelli, Istanbul 1981

——Mustafa Kemal, *Eskişehir–İzmit Konuşmaları (1923)* (Speeches in Eskişehir and İzmit (1923)), ed. and pref. by Doğu Perinçek, Kaynak, Istanbul 1993

——*Atatürk'ün Resmi Yayınlara Girmemiş Söylev, Demeç, Yazışma ve Söyleşileri* (Atatürk's Speeches, Statements, Correspondence and Interviews Omitted from Official Publications), ed. Sadi Borak, 2nd edn, Kaynak, Istanbul 1997

——*Atatürk'ün Gizli Oturumlarda Konuşmaları* (Atatürk's Speeches in Closed Sessions [of the Assembly]), ed. Sadi Borak, İnkılâp, Istanbul 1981

——*Atatürk'ün Not Defterleri* (Atatürk's Notebooks), ed. Ali Mithat İnan, Gündoğan, Ankara 1996

——*Atatürk'ün Özel Mektupları* (Atatürk's Private Letters), ed. Sadi Borak, Varlık, Istanbul 1961 (references are to this edition; a more recent and fuller edition was published by Kaynak Yayınları, Istanbul 1998)

——*Atatürk'ün Kurtuluş Savaşı Yazışmaları* (Atatürk's Correspondence During the Liberation Struggle), I, ed. Mustafa Onar, Kültür Bakanlığı, Ankara 1995

Atatürk/Afetinan, *Atatürk'ün Yazdığı Yurttaşlık Bilgileri* (Civics Manual Written by Atatürk), Çağdaş Yayınları, Istanbul 1994

BIOGRAPHIES

Armstrong, Harold C., *Grey Wolf*, Barker, London 1932
Aydemir, Şevket Süreyya, *Tek Adam: Mustafa Kemal* (The Only Man: Mustafa Kemal), Vol. I (1891–1919), Remzi, Istanbul 1963; Vol. II (1919–22), 1964; Vol. III (1922–38), 1995
Bayur, Hikmet, *Atatürk Hayatı ve Eseri* (Atatürk's Life and Work), Vol. I (from his birth to his landing in Samsun), AKDTYK, Ankara 1990
Bircan, Osman, *Belge ve Fotoğraflarla Atatürk'ün Hayatı* (The Life of Atatürk in Documents and Photographs), Milli Eğitim Bakanlığı, Ankara 1993
Blanco Villalta, Jorge, *Atatürk*, trans. William Campbell, Türk Tarih Kurumu (TTK) [Turkish Historical Society], Ankara 1982
İğdemir, Uluğ, *Atatürk'ün Yaşamı* (Life of Atatürk) (Vol. I 1881–1918), AKDTYK, Ankara 1988 (1st impression TTK, Ankara 1980)
İslâm Ansiklopedisi, *Atatürk*, fasc. 10, Istanbul 1960 (trans. Andrew Mango, Turkish National Commission for UNESCO, Ankara 1963)
Jevakhoff, Alexandre, *Kemal Atatürk: Les chemins de l'Occident*, Tallandier, Paris 1989
Kinross, Lord, *Atatürk: The Rebirth of a Nation*, Weidenfeld & Nicolson, London 1964 (5th impression 1971)
Macfie, A.L., *Atatürk*, Longman, London 1994
Orga, İrfan and Margarete, *Atatürk*, Michael Joseph, London 1962
Özel, Mehmet, *Atatürk* (photographs and commentary), Kültür Bakanlığı, Ankara 1991
Sonyel, Salâhi, *Atatürk – The Founder of Modern Turkey*, TTK, Ankara 1989 (references to Sonyel are to this work, unless otherwise specified)
Şapolyo, Enver Behnan, *Kemal Atatürk ve Millî Mücadele Tarihi* (Kemal Atatürk and the History of the National Struggle), Berkalp, Ankara 1944
Ülger, S. Eriş (ed.), *Mustafa Kemal Atatürk* (photographs and commentary), I–II, Kültür Bakanlığı [Ministry of Culture], Ankara 1994
Volkan, Vamık D. and Itzkowitz, Norman, *The Immortal Atatürk: A Psychobiography*, University of Chicago, 1984

GENERAL BIBLIOGRAPHY

Afetinan [Afet İnan], *Atatürk Hakkında Hâtıralar ve Belgeler* (Reminiscences and Documents on Atatürk), T. İş Bankası, Ankara 1984
——(see also under Atatürk)
Ağaoğlu, Samet, *Kuvay-ı Milliye Ruhu* (The Spirit of National Forces), 3rd edn, Ağaoğlu, Istanbul 1964
——*Babamın Arkadaşları* (My Father's Friends), 2nd edn, Nebioğlu, Istanbul n.d.
Ahmad, Feroz, *The Young Turks*, Clarendon Press, Oxford 1969
Akarsu, Bedia, *Atatürk Devrimi ve Temelleri* (Atatürk's Reforms and Their Foundations), İnkılâp, Istanbul 1995
Akgün, Nejat, *Burası Ankara* (This is Ankara), Ankara Kulübü, Ankara 1996
Akgün, Seçil, *Halifeliğin Kaldırılması ve Laiklik* (The Abolition of the Caliphate and Secularism), Turhan, Istanbul n.d.
Akşin, Sina, *İstanbul Hükümetleri ve Milli Mücadele* (The Istanbul Governments and the National Struggle), I–II, Cem, Istanbul 1992
Akşit, İlhan (ed.) (see under Atatürk)
Alexandris, Alexis, *The Greek Minority of Istanbul and Greek-Turkish Relations 1918–1974*, Centre for Asia Minor Studies, Athens 1992
Alkan, Turan, *İstiklâl Mahkemeleri* (Independence Tribunals), Ağaç, Istanbul 1993
Allen, W.E.D. and Muratoff, Paul, *Caucasian Battlefields*, CUP 1953

Altay, Fahrettin, *On Yıl Savaş ve Sonrası* (Ten Years of War and After), İnsel, Istanbul 1925 (references are to this work, unless otherwise specified)
——*İstiklâl Harbimizde Süvari Kolordusu* (The Cavalry Corps in Our War of Independence), İnsel, Istanbul 1925
And, Metin, *Atatürk ve Tiyatro* (Atatürk and the Theatre), Devlet Tiyatroları, Ankara 1983
Anderson, M.S., *The Eastern Question*, Macmillan, London 1972
Apak, Rahmi, *İstiklâl Savaşında Garp Cephesi Nasıl Kuruldu* (How the Western Front was Formed in the War of Independence), TTK, Ankara 1990
Arai, Masami, *Turkish Nationalism in the Young Turk Era*, Brill, Leiden 1992
Aralov, S.I., *Bir Soviet Diplomatının Türkiye Anıları* (A Soviet Diplomat's Reminiscences of Turkey), Turkish translation, Birey ve Toplum, Ankara 1985
Aras, Tevfik Rüştü, *Görüşlerim* (My Views), Istanbul 1968
Araz, Nezihe, *Mustafa Kemal'le 1000 Gün* (One Thousand Days with Mustafa Kemal), Apa, Ankara 1993 (references are to this work, unless otherwise specified)
——*Mustafa Kemal'in Ankara'sı* (Mustafa Kemal's Ankara), Apa, Ankara 1994
Arfa, Hassan, *Under Five Shahs*, John Murray, London 1964
Arıburnu, Kemal, *Atatürk'ten Anılar* (Reminiscences of Atatürk), T. İş Bankası, Ankara 1969
Arıkan, Zeki, *Tarihimiz ve Cumhuriyet: Muhittin Birgen (1885–1951)* (Our History and the Republic: Muhittin Birgen (1885–1951)), Tarih Vakfı, Istanbul 1997
Arıkoğlu, Damar, *Hatıralarım* (My Memoirs), Tan, Istanbul 1961
Aslan, İzzet, *Atatürk Silifke'de* (Atatürk in Silifke), Kemal Matbaası, Adana 1981
Aspinall-Oglander, C.F., *Military Operations: Gallipoli*, 2 vols., Heinemann, London 1929–31
Atadan, Makbule, *Ağabeyim Mustafa Kemal* (My Elder Brother Mustafa Kemal), ed. Şemsi Belli, Ayyıldız Matbaası, Ankara 1959
ATASE [Military History Department of Turkish General Staff], *1911–1912 Osmanlı-İtalyan Harbi ve Kolağası Mustafa Kemal* (The 1911–1912 Ottoman-Italian War and Adjutant-Major Mustafa Kemal), Kültür Bakanlığı, Ankara 1985
——*Atatürk Özel Arşivinden Seçmeler* (Selections from Atatürk's Private Archive), IV, Ankara 1996
——*Türk İstiklâl Harbi'ne Katılan Tümen ve Daha Üst Kademelerdeki Komutanların Biyografileri* (Biographies of Divisional and More Senior Commanders in the Turkish War of Independence), Ankara 1989
Atay, Falih Rıfkı, *Çankaya*, 2nd edn, Bateş, Istanbul 1984 (references are to this work, unless otherwise specified)
——*Atatürk'ün Anlattıkları* (Told by Atatürk), Sel, Istanbul 1955
——*Babanız Atatürk* (Your Father Atatürk), Bateş, Istanbul 1990
Ateş, Nevin Yurdsever, *Türkiye Cumhuriyetinin Kuruluşu ve Terakkiperver Cumhuriyet Fırkası* (The Establishment of the Turkish Republic and the Progressive Republican Party), Sarmal, Istanbul 1994
Avcıoğlu, Doğan, *Milli Kurtuluş Tarihi (1838'den 1995'e kadar)* ('The History of National Liberation (from 1838 to 1995)), I–II, Istanbul Matbaası, Istanbul 1974
Aybars, Ergun, *İstiklâl Mahkemeleri* (Independence Tribunals), Bilgi, Istanbul 1975
——*Türkiye Cumhuriyeti Tarihi* (History of the Turkish Republic), I, 3rd edn, Dokuz Eylül Üniversitesi, Ankara 1994 (references are to this work, unless otherwise specified)
Aybay, Rona, *Karşılaştırmalı 1961 Anayasası* (Comparative [Text of] 1961 Constitution), Fakülteler Matbaası, Istanbul 1963
Aydemir, Şevket Süreyya, *İkinci Adam* (The Second Man), I–II, 6/7th edn, Remzi, Istanbul 1992–3
——*Makedonya'dan Ortaasya'ya Enver Paşa* (Enver Paşa – from Macedonia to Central Asia), I–III, Remzi, Istanbul 1971–2
——*Suyu Arayan Adam* (A Man in Search of Water), Remzi, Istanbul 1967
——(see also under Biographies)

Baltacıoğlu, İsmail Hakkı, *Atatürk: Yetişmesi, Kişiliği, Devrimleri* (Atatürk: His Education, Personality and Reforms), Atatürk Üniversitesi, Erzurum 1973

Barker, A.J., *The Neglected War: Mesopotamia 1914–1918*, Faber, London 1967

Basın-Yayın [General Directorate of Press and Information], *The 'Köşk' Museum at Çankaya*, Ankara n.d.

Başar, Ahmet Hamdi, *Atatürk'le Üç Ay* (Three Months with Atatürk), Ankara İktisadi ve Ticari İlimler Akademisi, Ankara 1981

Bayar, Celal, *Ben de Yazdım* (So I Wrote Too), I–VIII, Baha, Istanbul 1968–72 (references are to this work, unless otherwise specified)

——*Atatürk'ten Hatıralar* (Reminiscences of Atatürk), Sel, Istanbul 1955

Bayrak, Mehmet, *Kürtler ve Ulusal-Demokratik Mücadeleleri* (The Kurds and Their National-Democratic Struggles), Öz-Ge, Ankara 1993

Belen, Fahri, *Türk Kurtuluş Savaşı* (The Turkish Liberation Struggle), Başbakanlık, Ankara 1973

Belli, Şemsi, *Fikriye*, Bilgi, Ankara 1995

——(see also under Atadan)

Bennett, John G., *Witness*, Omen, Tucson Arizona 1974

Bıyıklıoğlu, Tevfik, *Atatürk Anadolu'da 1919–1921* (Atatürk in Anatolia 1919–1921), 2nd edn, Kent, Ankara 1981

Bilgehan, Gülsün, *Mevhibe*, Bilgi, Ankara 1994

Bleda, Mithat Şükrü, *İmparatorluğun Çöküşü* (The Collapse of the Empire), Remzi, Istanbul 1979

Borak, Sadi (ed.), *Atatürk'ün Armstrong'a Cevabı* (Atatürk's Reply to Armstrong), Kaynak Yayınları, Istanbul 1997

——(see also under Atatürk)

Bozdağ, İsmet, *Atatürk'ün Sofrası* (Atatürk's Table), Kervan, Istanbul 1975

——*Gazi ve Lâtife* (The Gazi and Lâtife), Emre, Istanbul 1991

——*Toprakta Bile Bitmeyen Kavga: Atatürk–İnönü, İnönü–Bayar* (A Quarrel Which Did Not End Even In the Grave: Atatürk–İnönü, İnönü–Bayar), Emre, Istanbul 1993

——(see also under Atatürk, Cavit and Karabekir)

Bozok, Salih and Cemil, *Hep Atatürk'ün Yanında* (Always at Atatürk's Side), Çağdaş, Istanbul 1985

Bulut, Faik, *Belgelerle Dersim Raporları* (Dersim Reports Documented), Yön, Istanbul 1991

Cavit, *İdama Beş Kala* (Five [Minutes] to Execution), letters ed. İsmet Bozdağ, Emre, Istanbul 1993

Cebesoy, Ali Fuat, *Siyasî Hâtıralar* (Political Memoirs), Vatan, Istanbul, I, 1957; II, 1960

——*Moskova Hâtıraları* (Moscow Memoirs), Kültür Bakanlığı, Ankara 1982

——*Millî Mücadele Hâtıraları* (Memoirs of National Struggle), Vatan, Istanbul 1953

——*Sınıf Arkadaşım Atatürk* (My Classmate Atatürk), İnkılâp, Istanbul 1981

Cemal Paşa, *Hatıralar* (Memoirs), Selek, Istanbul 1959

Cemal, Yüzbaşı, *Yüzbaşı Cemal'in Anıları* (The Memoirs of Captain Cemal), ed. Kudret Emiroğlu, Kebikeç, Ankara 1996

Clogg, Richard, *A Short History of Modern Greece*, CUP 1979

Çağlayangil, İhsan Sabri, *Anılarım* (My Memoirs), 3rd edn, Yılmaz, Istanbul 1990

Çalıka, Ahmet Rifat, *Kurtuluş Savaşında Adalet Bakanı Ahmet Rıfat Çalıka'nın Anıları* (Memoirs of Ahmet Rifat Çalıka, Justice Minister During the Liberation Struggle), ed. Hurşit Çalıka, Istanbul 1992

Çalışlar, İzzettin, *Atatürk'le İkibuçuk Yıl* (Two and a Half Years with Atatürk), Yapı Kredi, Istanbul 1993

Çelebi, Mevlüt, *Heyet-i Nasîha* (Commission of Admonition), Akademi, İzmir 1992

Çetiner, Yılmaz, *Son Padişah Vahdettin* (Vahdettin, the Last Sultan), Milliyet, Istanbul 1993

Çetinkaya, Hikmet, *Kubilay Olayı ve Tarikat Kampları* (The Kubilay Incident and Religious Brotherhood Camps), Çağdaş, Istanbul 1995

Dâver, Bülent, *Türkiye Cumhuriyetinde Lâyiklik* (Secularism in the Turkish Republic), Siyasal Bilgiler Fakültesi (SBF), Ankara 1995

Demirel, Ahmet, *Birinci Meclis'te Muhalefet: İkinci Grup* (Opposition in the First Assembly: The Second Group), İletişim, Istanbul 1994

Derin, Haldun, *Çankaya Özel Kalemini Anımsarken (1933–1951)* (Remembering the Çankaya Private Office (1933–1951)), Tarih Vakfı, Istanbul 1995

Dyer, Gwynne, 'The Origins of the "Nationalist" Group of Officers in Turkey 1908–18' in *Journal of Contemporary History*, VIII, 4, 1973

——'The Turkish Armistice of 1918' in *Middle Eastern Studies*, VIII, 2 and 3, 1972 (references are to this work, unless otherwise specified)

Edib [Edip], Halide, *The Turkish Ordeal*, John Murray, London 1926

Egeli, Münir Hayri, *Atatürk'ten Bilinmeyen Hatıralar* (Unknown Reminiscences of Atatürk), Yaşaroğlu, Istanbul 1959

Ellison, Grace, *Turkey Today*, Hutchinson, London 1928

Elman, Ahmet Şevket, *Dr Reşit Galip*, Yeni Matbaa, Ankara 1955

Emre, Ahmet Cevat, *İki Neslin Tarihi* (The History of Two Generations), Hilmi, Istanbul 1960

Ergil, Doğu, *Milli Mücadelenin Sosyal Tarihi* (Social History of the National Struggle), Turhan, Ankara 1981

Erikan, Celâl, *Komutan Atatürk* (Atatürk as a Commander), T. İş Bankası, Ankara 1972

Ertürk, Hüsamettin, *İki Devrin Perde Arkası* (Behind the Curtains in Two Eras), ed. Samih Nafiz Tansu, Ararat, Istanbul 1969

Ethem, Çerkes, *Çerkes Ethem'in Hatıraları* (The Memoirs of Çerkes Ethem), Dünya, Istanbul 1962

——*Çerkez Ethem Dosyası* (The Çerkez Ethem File), ed. Cemal Kutay, 5th edn, Boğaziçi, Istanbul 1990

Evans, Stephen F., *The Slow Rapprochement: Britain and Turkey in the Age of Kemal Atatürk 1919–38*, Eothen, Walkington 1982

Eyice, Semavi, *Atatürk ve Pietro Canonica* (Atatürk and Pietro Canonica), Eren, Istanbul 1986

Garnett, Lucy, *The Women of Turkey*, I–II, David Nutt, London 1890–1.

Georges-Gaulis, Berthe, *La Nouvelle Turquie*, Armand Colin, Paris 1924

Gilbert, Martin, *Sir Harold Rumbold – Portrait of a Diplomat*, Heinemann, London 1973

Gilmour, David, *Curzon*, John Murray, London 1994

Giritli, İsmet, *Kemalist Devrim ve İdeolojisi* (The Kemalist Reform/Revolution and its Ideology), Fakülteler Matbaası, Istanbul 1980

Gologlu, Mahmut, I, *Erzurum Kongresi* (The Congress of Erzurum), Kalite Matbaası, Ankara 1968; II, *Sivas Kongresi* (The Congress of Sivas), 1969; III, *Üçüncü Meşrutiyet* (The Third Constitution[al Period]), 1970; IV, *Cumhuriyete Doğru* (Towards the Republic), 1971; V, *Türkiye Cumhuriyeti* (The Turkish Republic), 1971; VI, *Devrimler ve Tepkileri* (The Reforms and Reactions to Them), 1972; VII, *Tek Partili Cumhuriyet* (Single-Party Republic), 1974; VIII, *Milli Şef Dönemi* (The Era of the National Leader), 1974

——*Trabzon Tarihi* (History of Trabzon), Kalite Matbaası, Ankara 1975

Gökbilgin, M. Tayyib, *Millî Mücadele Başlarken – Mondros Mütarekesinden Sivas Kongresine* (As the National Struggle Began – from the Armistice of Mudros to the Congress of Sivas), TTK, Ankara 1959

Gökçen, Sabiha, *Atatürk'le Bir Ömür* (A Lifetime with Atatürk), ed. Oktay Verel, Altın Kitaplar, Istanbul 1984

Göksel, Burhan, *Atatürk'ün Soykütüğü* (Atatürk's Genealogy), Kültür Bakanlığı, Ankara 1987

Göldaş, İsmail, *Takrir-i Sükûn Görüşmeleri* (The Debate on the Maintenance of Order [Law]), Belge, Istanbul 1997

Gövsa, İbrahim Alâettin, *Türk Meşhurları Ansiklopedisi* (Encyclopaedia of Famous Turks), Yedigün, Istanbul n.d.

Granda, Cemal, *Atatürk'ün Uşağı idim* (I Was Atatürk's Servant), Hürriyet Yayınları, Istanbul 1973

Grew, Joseph C., *Turbulent Era: A Diplomatic Record of Forty Years (1904–1945)*, I–II, Books for Libraries Press, Freeport NY 1952

Grothusen, Klaus-Detlev, 'Kemal Atatürk'e Sığınanlar' (They Sheltered with Kemal Atatürk), in *Alman Gözüyle Atatürk* (Atatürk through German Eyes), Deutsche Welle, Cologne 1988

Güneş, İhsan, *Birinci Türkiye Büyük Millet Meclisi'nin Düşünsel Yapısı* (Ideological Structure of the First Turkish Grand National Assembly), Anadolu Üniversitesi, Eskişehir 1985

Gürün, Kâmuran, *Ermeni Dosyası* (The Armenian File), TTK, Ankara 1983 (English translation: *The Armenian File: The Myth of Innocence Exposed*, Rustem, Nicosia and Weidenfeld & Nicolson, London 1985)

Hale, William, *The Political and Economic Development of Modern Turkey*, Croom Helm, London 1981 (references are to this work, unless otherwise specified)

——*Turkish Politics and the Military*, Routledge, London 1994

Harp Mecmuası (War Review), Nos. 1–27, magazine published in Istanbul from November 1331 AH (1915) to June 1334 (1918)

Heper, Metin, *İsmet İnönü: The Making of a Turkish Statesman*, Brill, Leiden 1998

Hopkirk, Peter, *On Secret Service East of Constantinople*, John Murray, London 1994

Housepian, Marjorie, *Smyrna 1922: The Destruction of a City*, Faber, London 1972

Hovannisian, Richard G., *The Republic of Armenia*, I–IV, University of California, 1996

İnal, İbnülemin Mahmud Kemal, *Osmanlı Devrinde Son Sadrıazamlar* (The Last Grand Viziers of the Ottoman Era), MEB [Ministry of Education], Istanbul 1965–9

İnan, Ali Midhat (ed.) (see under Atatürk)

İnönü, Erdal, *Anılar ve Düşünceler* (Memories and Thoughts), Idea, Istanbul, I, 1996; II, 1998

İnönü, İsmet, *Hatıralar* (Memoirs), ed. Sabahattin Selek, Bilgi, Istanbul, I, 1985; II, 1987 (references are to this work, unless otherwise specified)

——*İnönü Atatürk'ü Anlatıyor* (İnönü on Atatürk), ed. Abdi İpekçi, Cem, Istanbul 1968

Kandemir, Feridun, *İzmir Suîkastinin İçyüzü* (The Inside Story of the İzmir Assassination Attempt), I–II, Sel, Istanbul 1955

Kansu, Mazhar Müfit, *Erzurum'dan Ölümüne Kadar Atatürk'le Beraber* (With Atatürk from Erzurum until his Death [in fact only until 1923]), I–II, TTK, Ankara 1988

Karabekir, Kâzım, *İstiklâl Harbimiz* (Our War of Independence), 2nd edn, Türkiye Yayınevi, Istanbul 1969

——*İstiklâl Harbinin Esasları* (The Foundations of the War of Independence), Sinan, Istanbul 1951 (reprint of seized 1933 edition)

——*Paşaların Kavgası: Atatürk–Karabekir* (The Quarrel of the Pashas: Atatürk–Karabekir), ed. İsmet Bozdağ, Emre, Istanbul 1991

——*Kâzım Karabekir Anlatıyor* (Kâzım Karabekir Tells His Story), ed. Uğur Mumcu, Tekin, Istanbul 1990

Karaosmanoğlu, Yakup Kadri, *Butun Eserleri* (Collected Works): VI, *Vatan Yolunda* (On the Road of the Fatherland); VIII, *Atatürk*; X, *Ankara*, Birikim, Istanbul 1978–81

Kazancıgil, Ali and Özbudun, Ergun (eds.), *Atatürk, Founder of a Modern State*, Hurst, London 1981

Kılıç Ali, *Atatürk'ün Hususiyetleri* (Atatürk's Characteristics), Sel, Istanbul 1955

——*Kılıç Ali Hatıralarını Anlatıyor* (Kılıç Ali Relates His Reminiscences), Sel, Istanbul 1955

——*İstiklâl Mahkemesi Hatıraları* (Reminiscences of Independence Tribunals), Sel, Istanbul 1955

Kırzıoğlu, Fahrettin, *Erzurum Kongresi* (The Erzurum Congress), Kültür Ofset, Ankara 1993

Kocabaşoğlu, Uygur and Berge, Metin, *Bolşevik İhtilâli ve Osmanlılar* (The Bolshevik Revolution and the Ottomans), Kebikeç, Ankara 1994

Koçak, Cemil, *Türk-Alman İlişkileri* (Turkish-German Relations), TTK, Ankara 1991

Koçer, Kemal, *Kurtuluş Savaşlarımızda İstanbul* (Istanbul during our Liberation Struggles), Vakit, Istanbul 1946

Kongar, Emre, *Devrim Tarihi ve Toplumbilim Açısından Atatürk* (Atatürk from the Viewpoint of the History of Reforms and of Sociology), 2nd edn, Remzi, Istanbul 1994

——*Atatürk Üzerine* (Concerning Atatürk), Hil, Istanbul 1983

——'Turkey's Cultural Transformation' in Günsel Renda and C. Max Kortepeter, *The Transformation of Turkish Culture: The Atatürk Legacy*, Kingston Press, Princeton NJ 1986

Kubalı, Hüseyin Nail, *Atatürk Devrimi ve Gerçeklerimiz* (Atatürk's Reforms and Our Realities), Istanbul 1968

Kurt, Yılmaz, *Pontus Meselesi* (The Pontus Question), Türkiye Büyük Millet Meclisi (TBBM), Ankara 1995

Kushner, David, *The Rise of Turkish Nationalism 1876–1908*, Frank Cass, London 1977

Kutay, Cemal, *Prens Sabahattin Bey, Sultan II. Abdülhamit, İttihad ve Terakki* (Prince Sabahattin, Sultan Abdülhamit II and [the Committee of] Union and Progress), Tarih Yayınları, Istanbul 1964

——(see also under Çerkes Ethem, Fethi Okyar and Rauf Orbay)

Kürkçüoğlu, Ömer, *Türk-İngiliz İlişkileri (1919–1926)* (Turkish-British Relations (1919–1926)), SBF, Ankara 1978

Landau, Jacob (ed.), *Atatürk and the Modernization of Turkey*, Westview, Boulder Colorado 1984

Lewis, Bernard, *The Emergence of Modern Turkey*, OUP 1961

Liddle, Peter, *Men of Gallipoli*, Allen Lane, London 1976

Llewellyn Smith, Michael, *Ionian Vision: Greece in Asia Minor 1919–1922*, Allen Lane, London 1973

Loğoğlu, Faruk, *İsmet İnönü and the Making of Modern Turkey*, İnönü Foundation, Ankara 1997

Mamboury, Ernest, *Ankara: Guide Touristique*, Interior Ministry, Ankara 1933

Mazıcı, Nurşen, *Atatürk Döneminde Muhalefet* (Opposition at the Time of Atatürk), Dilmen, Istanbul 1984

McCarthy, Justin, *Muslims and Minorities*, NY University Press 1983 (references are to this work, unless otherwise specified)

——*Death and Exile: The Ethnic Cleansing of Ottoman Muslims, 1821–1922*, Darwin, Princeton NJ 1995

Menteşe, Halil, *Halil Menteşe'nin Anıları* (The Memoirs of Halil Menteşe), Hürriyet, Istanbul 1988

Millman, Brock, 'Turkish Foreign and Strategic Policy 1934–1942' in *Middle Eastern Studies*, XXXI, 3, 1995

Mumcu, Uğur, *Gazi Paşa'ya Suikast* (The Attempt on the Gazi's Life), Tekin, Istanbul 1994

——*Kürt-İslam Ayaklanması 1919–1925* (The Kurdish-Islamic Rebellion 1919–1925), Tekin, Istanbul 1994

——(see also under Karabekir)

Nadi, Yunus, *Kurtuluş Savaşı Anıları* (Reminiscences of the Liberation Struggle),

Cumhuriyet (?), Istanbul 1978 (references are to this work, unless otherwise specified)

——*Ankara'nın İlk Günleri* (The First Days of Ankara), Sel, Istanbul 1995

Nesimi, Abidin, *Yılların İçinden* (Across the Years), Gözlem, Istanbul 1977

Noel, E.M., *Diary of Major E.M. Noel: On Special Duty in Kurdistan from 14 June to 21 September, 1919,* Basra 1919

Nur, Rıza, *Hayat ve Hatıratım* (My Life and Memoirs), I–III, İşaret, Istanbul 1992

——*Dr Rıza Nur Üzerine* (Concerning Dr Rıza Nur), ed. Cavit Orhan Tütengil, Güven, Ankara 1965

Okday, Şefik, *Büyükbabam Son Sadrazam Ahmet Tevfik Paşa* (My Grandfather, the Last Grand Vizier Ahmet Tevfik Paşa), Istanbul 1986

Okyar, Fethi, *Üç Devirde Bir Adam* (A Man in Three Eras), ed. Cemal Kutay, Tercüman, Istanbul 1980

——*Serbest Cumhuriyet Fırkası Nasıl Doğdu, Nasıl Feshedildi?* (How the Free Republican Party Was Born, and How It Was Dissolved), Istanbul 1987 (references are to this work, unless otherwise specified)

——*Fethi Okyar'ın Anıları: Atatürk, Okyar ve Çok Partili Türkiye* (Fethi Okyar's Reminiscences: Atatürk, Okyar and Multi-party Turkey), T. İş Bankası, Ankara 1997

Okyar, Osman, *Atatürk ve Cumhuriyet Dönemi Türkiyesi* (Atatürk and Turkey in the Republican Era), Türkiye Ticaret Odaları, Ankara 1981

——*Milli Mücadele Dönemi Türkiye-Sovyet İlişkilerinde Mustafa Kemal (1920–1921)* (Mustafa Kemal and Turkish-Soviet Relations During the National Struggle (1920–1921)), T. İş Bankası, Ankara 1998

Olson, Robert, *The Emergence of Kurdish Nationalism and the Sheikh Said Rebellion, 1880–1925,* University of Texas, Austin 1989

Onar, Mustafa (ed.) (see under Atatürk)

Oran, Baskın, *Atatürk Milliyetçiliği* (The Nationalism of Atatürk), 3rd edn, Bilgi, Ankara 1993

Orbay, Rauf, *Cehennem Değirmeni* (The Mill of Hell), I–II, Emre, Istanbul 1993

——*Osmanlıdan Cumhuriyete: Yüzyılımızda Bir İnsanımız* (From the Ottomans to the Republic: Our Man in Our Century), ed. Cemal Kutay, I–V, Kazancı, Istanbul 1992

Önder, Mehmet, *Atatürk'ün Almanya ve Avusturya Gezileri* (Atatürk's Travels to Germany and Austria), T. İş Bankası, Ankara 1993

Özakman, Turgut, *Vahidettin, Mustafa Kemal ve Milli Mücadele* (Vahidettin, Mustafa Kemal and the National Struggle), Bilgi Yayınevi, Istanbul 1997

Özalp, Kâzım and Teoman, *Atatürk'ten Anılar* (Reminiscences of Atatürk), 2nd edn, T. İş Bankası, Ankara 1994

Özerdim, Sami N., *Atatürk Devrimi Kronolojisi* (A Chronology of Atatürk's Reforms), Çankaya Belediyesi, Ankara 1996

Özverim, Melda, *Mustafa Kemal ve Corinne Lütfü: Bir Dostluğun Öyküsü* (Atatürk and Corinne Lütfü: The Story of a Friendship), Milliyet Yayınları, Istanbul 1998

Paparrigopoulos, K., *Istoria tou Ellinikou Ethnous* (History of the Greek Nation), Eleftheroudakis, Athens 1932

Pavlova, Nina, *Au pays du Ghazi,* Revue Mondiale, Paris 1930

Perinçek, Doğu, *Komintern Belgelerinde Türkiye* (Turkey in Comintern Documents), I–II, Kaynak, Istanbul 1993–4

——(see also under Atatürk and Türk Ocağı)

Price, G. Ward, *Extra-Special Correspondent,* Harrap, London 1957

Puaux, René, *La Mort de Smyrne,* privately printed, Paris 1922

Rawlinson, A., *Adventures in the Near East,* Andrew Melrose, London 1923

Ryan, Sir Andrew, *The Last of the Dragomans,* Geoffrey Bles, London 1951

Sabis, Ali İhsan, *Harb Hatıralarım* (My War Memoirs), I–III (volume III erroneously numbered V), İnkılâp, Istanbul 1943–51

Sanders, Liman von, *Türkiye'de Beş Sene* (Five Years in Turkey), translated into Turkish and annotated by Ottoman General Staff, Matbaa-yı Askeriye, Istanbul 1337 AH (1923)

Satloff, Robert B., 'Prelude to Conflict: Communal Interdependence in the Sanjak of Alexandretta 1920–1936' in *Middle Eastern Studies*, XXII, 1986

Selek, Sabahattin, *Anadolu İhtilâli* (The Anatolian Revolution), privately printed, Istanbul 1963

Sertel, Sabiha, *Roman Gibi* (Like a Novel), Ant, Istanbul 1969

Sforza, Count Carlo, *Makers of Modern Europe*, Elkin Matthews & Marrot, London 1930

——*European Dictatorships*, Allen & Unwin, London 1932

Shaw, Stanford, *The History of the Ottoman Empire and Modern Turkey*, I, CUP 1976; II (with Ezel Shaw), CUP 1977

Sındırgılı, Süreyya, *Demirci Mehmed*, Sel, Istanbul 1955

Simavi, Lütfi, *Osmanlı Sarayının Son Günleri* (The Last Days of the Ottoman Palace), Hürriyet, Istanbul n.d.

Sinanoğlu, Suat, *Türk Humanizmi* (Turkish Humanism), TTK, Ankara 1988

Sonyel, Salahi, *Turkish Diplomacy 1918–1923*, Sage, London 1975

——(see also under Biographies)

Soyak, Hasan Rıza, *Atatürk'ten Hatıralar* (Reminiscences of Atatürk), Yapı Kredi, I–II, Istanbul 1973

Soysal, İlhami, *150'likler* (The 150 [Exiles]), Gür, Istanbul 1985

——*İşbirlikçiler* (The Collaborationists), Gür, Istanbul 1985

Soysal, İsmail, *Türkiye'nin Siyasal Andlaşmaları* (Turkey's Diplomatic Treaties), I (1920–1945), TTK, Ankara 1983 (references to Soysal are to this work, unless otherwise specified)

Sönmez, Pakize, *Atatürk'e İzmir Suikastinin İçyüzü* (Inside Story of the Attempt on Atatürk's Life in İzmir), Detay, Istanbul 1994

Sözer, Vural (ed.), *Atatürklü Günler* (Days with Atatürk), Barajans, Istanbul 1998

Steinhaus, Kurt, *Atatürk Devrimi Sosyolojisi* (Sociology of Atatürk's Reforms), trans. M. Akkaş, Sarmal, Istanbul 1995

Stoddard, Philip, *Teşkilât-ı Mahsusa* (The Special Organization) (unpublished PhD thesis), trans. Tansel Demirel, Arba, Istanbul 1993

Şahingiray, Özel (ed.), *Atatürk'ün Nöbet Defteri* (Atatürk's Guardroom Journal 1931–8), TTK, Ankara 1955 (sometimes referred to as Logbook)

Şıvgın, Hale, *Trablusgarp Savaşı ve 1911–1912 Türk-İtalyan İlişkileri* (The Tripolitanian War and Turkish-Italian Relations, 1911–1912), AKDTYK, Ankara 1989

Talât Paşa, *Talât Paşa'nın Hatıraları* (The Memoirs of Talat Paşa), ed. H. Cahit Yalçın, Güven, Istanbul 1946

Tansel, Selahettin, *Mondros'tan Mudanya'ya Kadar* (From Mudros to Mudanya), I–IV, MEB, Istanbul 1991

Tekeli, İlhan and İlkin, Selim, *Ege'deki Sivil Direnişten Kurtuluş Savaşına Geçerken Uşak Heyet-i Merkeziyesi ve İbrahim (Tahtakılıç) Bey* (The Uşak Central Committee and İbrahim (Tahtakılıç) in the Period Between Civil Resistance and the Liberation Struggle in Aegean Turkey), TTK, Ankara 1989 (references are to this work, unless otherwise specified)

——*1929 Dünya Buhranında Türkiye'nin İktisadi Politika Arayışları* (Turkey's Search for an Economic Policy in the 1929 World Crisis), ODTÜ, Ankara 1987

Tengirşenk, Yusuf Kemal, *Vatan Hizmetinde* (In the Service of the Fatherland), Kültür Bakanlığı, Ankara 1981

Terzioğlu, Said Arif, *Atatürk'ün Ahmet Çavuşu* (Atatürk's Sergeant Ahmet), Emel, Istanbul 1973

Tevetoğlu, Fethî, *Atatürk'le Samsun'a Çıkanlar* (Atatürk's Companions in Samsun), Ayyıldız, Ankara 1971

Timur, Taner, *Türk Devrimi ve Sonrası* (The Turkish Reforms and Their Aftermath), İmge, Ankara 1994

Topçuoğlu, Orhan (ed.), *Atatürk'ün Günlüğü* (Atatürk Day by Day), I–XI (1928–31), Garanti Bankası, Ankara n.d.

Toros, Taha, *Atatürk'ün Adana Seyahatleri* (Atatürk's Travels to Adana), 2nd edn, Çukurova Gazeteciler Cemiyeti, Adana 1981

Tunaya, Tarık Zafer, *Türkiye'de Siyasi Partiler 1859–1952* (Political Parties in Turkey, 1859–1952), facsimile edition, Arba, Istanbul 1952

Tunçay, Mete, *T.C.'inde Tek-Parti Yönetiminin Kurulması (1923–1931)* (The Establishment of Single-Party Rule in the Turkish Republic (1923–1931)), 3rd edn, Cem, Istanbul 1992

Tüfekçi, Gürbüz D., *Atatürk'ün Düşünce Yapısı* (The Structure of Atatürk's Thought), Turhan, Ankara 1986

——*Ataturk'ün Okuduğu Kitaplar* (Books Read by Atatürk), I (books in Turkish), II (books in foreign languages), T. İş Bankası, Ankara 1983–5

Türk Ocağı Türk Tarihi Heyeti (Turkish History Committee of the Turkish Hearths), *Türk Tarihinin Ana Hatları* (Outline of Turkish History), Devlet Matbaası, Istanbul 1930 (reprinted with introduction by Doğu Perinçek, Kaynak, Istanbul 1996)

Türkgeldi, Ali Fuad, *Görüp İşittiklerim* (What I Saw and Heard), 2nd edn, TTK, Ankara 1951

Türkiye Büyük Millet Meclisi (TBMM) [Turkish Grand National Assembly], *Gizli Celse Zabıtları* (Minutes of Secret Sessions), 24 April 1920–25 October 1934, I–IV, T. İş Bankası, Ankara 1985

Tütengil, Cavit Orhan (ed.) (see under Nur)

US Congress, *Conditions in the Near East. Report of the American Military Mission to Armenia*, 66th Cong., 2nd sess., Senate Document 266, Washington DC 1920

Us, Asım, *1930–1950 Hatıra Notları* (Notebooks 1930–1950), Vakit, Istanbul 1966

Uşaklıgil, Halid Ziya, *Saray ve Ötesi* (The Palace and Beyond), İnkılâp, Istanbul 1965

Ülkütaşır, M. Şakir, *Atatürk ve Harf Devrimi* (Atatürk and the Alphabet Reform), Cumhuriyet, Istanbul 1998

Ünaydın, Ruşen Eşref, *Atatürk: Tarih ve Dil Kurumları: Hâtıralar* (Atatürk: Historical and Language Societies: Reminiscences), TTK, Ankara 1954

Ünüvar, Veysel, *Kurtuluş Savaşında Bolşeviklerle Sekiz Ay 1920–1921* (Eight Months with the Bolsheviks during the Liberation Struggle, 1920–1921), Göçebe, Istanbul 1997

Velidedeoğlu, Hıfzı Veldet, *Bir Lise Öğrencisinin Millî Mücadele Anıları* (A Lycée Student's Reminiscences of the National Struggle), Varlık, Istanbul 1971

Walder, David, *The Chanak Affair*, Hutchinson, London 1969

Walker, Christopher J., *Armenia: The Survival of a Nation*, Croom Helm, London 1980

Waterfield, Gordon, *Professional Diplomat: Sir Percy Loraine*, John Murray, London 1973

Waugh, Sir Alexander Telford, *Turkey Yesterday, To-day and To-morrow*, Chapman & Hall, London 1930

Yalçın, Hüseyin Cahit, *Siyasal Anılar* (Political Memoirs), ed. Rauf Mutluay, T. İş Bankası, Istanbul 1976

Yalman, Ahmed (Ahmet) Emin, *Turkey in My Time*, University of Oklahoma 1956

Yılmaz, Veli, *1nci Dünya Harbinde Türk-Alman İttifakı ve Askeri Yardımlar* (The Turkish-German Alliance and Military Aid in the First World War), Ege Seramik, Istanbul 1993

Yüksel, Murat, *Ali Şükrü Bey ve Topal Osman Ağa* (Ali Şükrü and Lame Osman), Yunus Dergisi, Trabzon 1993

Zürcher, Erik Jan, *The Unionist Factor*, Brill, Leiden 1984 (references are to this work, unless otherwise specified)
——*Opposition in the Early Turkish Republic: The Progressive Republican Party 1924–1925*, Brill, Leiden 1991
——*Turkey: A Modern History*, I.B. Tauris, London 1993

ENCYCLOPAEDIAS

AnaBritannica (Turkish edition of *Encyclopaedia Britannica*), 1st edn, Ana Yayıncılık, Istanbul 1986–90
Encyclopaedia of Islam, 2nd edn (*EI²*), I–III, Luzac, London; IV–, Brill, Leiden 1954–

Index

Mustafa Kemal Atatürk's name is abbreviated to MKA. Letters with diacritical marks are treated as separate letters.